T0322056

Research Anthology on Agile Software, Software Development, and Testing

Information Resources Management Association
USA

Volume I

Published in the United States of America by
    IGI Global
    Engineering Science Reference (an imprint of IGI Global)
    701 E. Chocolate Avenue
    Hershey PA, USA 17033
    Tel: 717-533-8845
    Fax: 717-533-8661
    E-mail: cust@igi-global.com
    Web site: http://www.igi-global.com

Library of Congress Cataloging-in-Publication Data

Names: Information Resources Management Association, editor.
Title: Research anthology on agile software, software development, and
  testing / Information Resources Management Association, editor.
Description: Hershey, PA : Engineering Science Reference, [2022] | Includes
  bibliographical references and index. | Summary: "This reference book
  covers emerging trends of software development and testing, discussing
  the newest developments in agile software and its usage spanning
  multiple industries, covering topics such as global software
  engineering, knowledge management, and product development"-- Provided
  by publisher.
Identifiers: LCCN 2021040441 (print) | LCCN 2021040442 (ebook) | ISBN
  9781668437025 (h/c) | ISBN 9781668437032 (eISBN)
Subjects: LCSH: Agile software development. | Computer programs--Testing.
Classification: LCC QA76.76.D47 R468 2022 (print) | LCC QA76.76.D47
  (ebook) | DDC 005.1/112--dc23/eng/20211021
LC record available at https://lccn.loc.gov/2021040441
LC ebook record available at https://lccn.loc.gov/2021040442

British Cataloguing in Publication Data
A Cataloguing in Publication record for this book is available from the British Library.

The views expressed in this book are those of the authors, but not necessarily of the publisher.

For electronic access to this publication, please contact: eresources@igi-global.com.

List of Contributors

Table of Contents

Volume I

Section 1
Fundamental Concepts and Theories

Section 2
Development and Design Methodologies

Volume II

Section 3
Tools and Technologies

Volume III

Section 4
Utilization and Applications

Volume IV

Section 5
Organizational and Social Implications

Section 6
Managerial Impact

Preface

As organizations grow to require new and innovative software programs to improve processes, there is a need for the science of software development to constantly evolve. Agile practices have shown great benefits for improving the effectiveness of software development and its maintenance due to their ability to adapt to change. It is essential for organizations to stay current with the developments in agile software and software testing to witness how it can improve business operations.

Staying informed of the most up-to-date research trends and findings is of the utmost importance. That is why IGI Global is pleased to offer this four-volume reference collection of reprinted IGI Global book chapters and journal articles that have been handpicked by senior editorial staff. This collection will shed light on critical issues related to the trends, techniques, and uses of various applications by providing both broad and detailed perspectives on cutting-edge theories and developments. This collection is designed to act as a single reference source on conceptual, methodological, technical, and managerial issues, as well as to provide insight into emerging trends and future opportunities within the field.

The *Research Anthology on Agile Software, Software Development, and Testing* is organized into seven distinct sections that provide comprehensive coverage of important topics. The sections are:

1. Fundamental Concepts and Theories;
2. Development and Design Methodologies;
3. Tools and Technologies;
4. Utilization and Applications;
5. Organizational and Social Implications;
6. Managerial Impact; and
7. Critical Issues and Challenges.

The following paragraphs provide a summary of what to expect from this invaluable reference tool.

Section 1, "Fundamental Concepts and Theories," serves as a foundation for this extensive reference tool by addressing crucial theories essential to understanding the concepts and uses of agile software, software development, and testing in multidisciplinary settings. The first chapter of this section, "Challenges and Trends of Agile," by Prof. Jorge Marx Gómez of Carl von Ossietzky Universität Oldenburg, Germany and Prof. Fayez Salma of Carl von Ossietzky Universität Oldenburg, Germany, studies agile methodologies and different challenges with suggested solutions generated from agile philosophy itself. The last chapter of this section, "A Historical and Bibliometric Analysis of the Development of Agile," by Profs. Sathiadev Mahesh, Kenneth R. Walsh, and Cherie C. Trumbach of University of New Orleans, USA, summarizes the traditional approaches and presents the conditions that led to agile approaches such as product complexity, shortened life cycle of the market, and eventually to the widespread acceptance of Scrum.

Section 2, "Development and Design Methodologies," presents in-depth coverage of the design and development of agile software for their use in different applications. The first chapter of this section, "Software Effort Estimation for Successful Software Application Development," by Prof. Syed Mohsin Saif of Islamic University of Science and Technology, India, explains different types of software applications, software estimation models, the importance of software effort estimation, and challenges faced in software effort estimation. The last chapter of this section, "A Simulation Model for Application Development in Data Warehouses," by Prof. Nayem Rahman of Portland State University, Portland, USA, presents a simulation model of a data warehouse to evaluate the feasibility of different software development controls and measures to better manage a software development lifecycle and improve the performance of the launched software.

Section 3, "Tools and Technologies," explores the various tools and technologies used in the implementation, development, and testing of agile software for various uses. The first chapter of this section, "Use of Qualitative Research to Generate a Function for Finding the Unit Cost of Software Test Cases," by Prof. Mark L. Gillenson of University of Memphis, Memphis, USA; Prof. Thomas F. Stafford of Louisiana Tech University, Ruston, USA; Prof. Yao Shi of University of Memphis, Memphis, USA; and Prof. Xihui "Paul" Zhang of University of North Alabama, Florence, USA, demonstrates a novel use of case research to generate an empirical function through qualitative generalization. This innovative technique applies interpretive case analysis to the problem of defining and generalizing an empirical cost function for test cases through qualitative interaction with an industry cohort of subject matter experts involved in software testing at leading technology companies. The last chapter of this section, "Metastructuring for Standards: How Organizations Respond to the Multiplicity of Standards," by Prof. Ronny Gey of Friedrich Schiller University Jena, Germany and Prof. Andrea Fried of Linköping University, Sweden, focusses on the appearance and implementation of process standards in software development organizations.

Section 4, "Utilization and Applications," describes how agile software is used and applied in diverse industries for various technologies and applications. The first chapter of this section, "Social Capital and Knowledge Networks of Software Developers: A Case Study," by Prof. VenuGopal Balijepally of Oakland University, Rochester, USA and Prof. Sridhar Nerur of University of Texas at Arlington, Arlington, USA, examines the structural and relational dimensions of developers' knowledge networks, identifies the specific actionable knowledge resources accessed from these networks, and explores how entry-level and more experienced developers differ along these dimensions. The findings from the qualitative analysis, backed by limited quantitative analysis of the case study data, underpin the discussion, implications for practice, and future research directions. The last chapter of this section, "A Game Theoretic Approach for Quality Assurance in Software Systems Using Antifragility-Based Learning Hooks," by Profs. Vimaladevi M. and Zayaraz G. of Pondicherry Engineering College, India, proposes an innovative approach which uses a fault injection methodology to perform the task of quality assurance.

Section 5, "Organizational and Social Implications," includes chapters discussing the impact of agile software on society and shows the ways in which software is developed in different industries and how this impacts business. The first chapter of this section, "Media Richness, Knowledge Sharing, and Computer Programming by Virtual Software Teams," by Profs. Idongesit Williams and Albert Gyamfi of Aalborg University, Denmark, concludes, based on the case being investigated, that rich media does not fit the task characteristics of a software programmer. It further concludes that media richness does affect knowledge sharing in these virtual teams. This is because the current lean media actually enables knowledge sharing as it fits the core characteristics of the software programming process. The last chapter of this section, "On the Rim Between Business Processes and Software Systems," by Profs. Ricardo J. Machado and Maribel Yasmina Santos of Universidade do Minho, Portugal and Prof. Maria Estrela Ferreira da Cruz of Polytechnic Institute of Viana do Castelo, Portugal, uses the information existing in business process models to derive software models specially focused in generating a data model.

Section 6, "Managerial Impact," presents the impact of agile software within an organizational setting. The first chapter of this section, "Boosting the Competitiveness of Organizations With the Use of Software Engineering," by Prof. Mirna Muñoz of CIMAT, A. C. Unidad Zacatecas, Mexico, provides a research work path focused on helping software development organizations to change to a continuous software improvement culture impacting both their software development process highlighting the human factor training needs. Results show that the implementation of best practices could be easily implemented if adequate support is provided. The last chapter of this section, "Measuring Developers' Software Security Skills, Usage, and Training Needs," by Prof. Daniela Soares Cruzes of SINTEF Digital, Norway; Prof. Tosin Daniel Oyetoyan of Western Norway University of Applied Sciences, Norway; and Prof. Martin Gilje Gilje Jaatun of SINTEF Digital, Norway, presents a survey instrument that can be used to investigate software security usage, competence, and training needs in agile organizations.

Section 7, "Critical Issues and Challenges," presents coverage of academic and research perspectives on challenges to using agile software in different methods, technologies, and techniques in varied industry applications. The first chapter of this section, "Towards a Security Competence of Software Developers: A Literature Review," by Prof. Nana Assyne of University of Jyväskylä, Finland, utilises a literature review to identify the security competences of software developers. Thirteen security competences of software developers were identified and mapped to the common body of knowledge for information security professional framework. The last chapter of this section, "Open Source Software Development Challenges: A Systematic Literature Review on GitHub," by Prof. Abdulkadir Seker of Sivas Cumhuriyet University, Turkey; Prof. Banu Diri of Yıldız Technical University, Turkey; Prof. Halil Arslan of Sivas Cumhuriyet University, Turkey; and Prof. Mehmet Fatih Amasyalı of Yıldız Technical University, Turkey, reviews the selected 172 studies according to some criteria that used the dataset as a data source.

Although the primary organization of the contents in this multi-volume work is based on its seven sections, offering a progression of coverage of the important concepts, methodologies, technologies, applications, social issues, and emerging trends, the reader can also identify specific contents by utilizing the extensive indexing system listed at the end of each volume. As a comprehensive collection of research on the latest findings related to agile software, the *Research Anthology on Agile Software, Software Development, and Testing* provides software developers, software engineers, computer engineers, IT directors, students, managers, faculty, researchers, and academicians with a complete understanding of the applications and impacts of agile software and its development and testing. Given the vast number of issues concerning usage, failure, success, strategies, and applications of agile software in modern technologies and processes, the *Research Anthology on Agile Software, Software Development, and Testing* encompasses the most pertinent research on the applications, impacts, uses, and development of agile software.

Section 1
Fundamental Concepts and Theories

Chapter 1
Challenges and Trends of Agile

Fayez Salma
Carl von Ossietzky Universität Oldenburg, Germany

Jorge Marx Gómez
Carl von Ossietzky Universität Oldenburg, Germany

ABSTRACT

Rapidly increasing of requirements of business pushed researchers to define new approaches and methodologies to meet marketing needs. Agile methodology has been created and replaced the traditional-driven development methods that focus on soliciting, documenting a complete set of requirements, and take a long time comparing to market change. On the other hand, customers need to be closer to the development process and collaborate with team development. Despite agile advantages, introducing new tools, coordination, and collaboration concepts, some challenges still need to be discussed and improved. These challenges relate to achieve balanced IT service development process in the organization. As a result, new trends have been created to facilitate new changes in software development. This chapter will study agile methodologies and different challenges with suggested solutions generated from agile philosophy itself.

INTRODUCTION

The software development process was developed over several decades, offering many methodologies and aspects according to competitiveness and market, but in general, customer satisfaction and developing a product that meets the basic requirements are foundations. These requirements have direct bearing on the trend of software development methodology, as long as they require more time and various changes during the used development process, thus using more resources to finish the projects (Williams & Cockburn, 2003a). Agile has provided an appropriate solution to rapidly change of marketing and customer requirements; it is based on the iterative enhancement, each iteration represents a small scale and self-contained Software Development Life Cycle (SDLC) by itself (Al-Zewairi et al., 2017; Williams, 2010). In other hand, customers need to be closer to the development process and collaborate with team development to produce high quality software and increasing competitive advantage (Kumar & Bhatia,

DOI: 10.4018/978-1-6684-3702-5.ch001

2012). These kind of relation causes increasing the authority and sharing making decisions including those pertaining to business, process, and systems requirements (Williams & Cockburn, 2003a).

Agile birth was announced as kind of transformation from the old approach when this approach declared its inability to continue; The idea took shape when manifesto was written for agile software development in 2001 (Fowler & Highsmith, 2001; Lous et al., 2018), which is a list of four values and twelve principles that describe the philosophy behind the methodology (Lous et al., 2018). Meanwhile, agile methods such as Scrum, Kanban, Scrumban and Extreme Programming (XP) are widely used in development management in order to add the agility and flexibility to projects.

Despite their advantages which included a new approach, respond to changes quickly, new tools, coordination and collaboration concepts, some challenges emerged, making it necessary to address them in order to find appropriate solutions. These challenges vary according to the nature of each organization and each project.

Basically, applying the appropriate way of agile supposes good understanding the agile methodology in depth. Any lack or gap in any step of agile causes kind of poor management, which affects the product quality. In parallel, understanding project and environment can prevent and overcome challenges when there is lack of documentation and more informal communications which considered as huge amount of information (Altameem, 2015). However, challenges and difficulties relate to achieving a balanced process for developing IT services in the organization by doing many activities. Theoretically, communication is one of the most important factors in agile, thus applying balanced process needs effective communications between the team and the manager to understand the team's dynamics and efficient agile practice. Agile communication should be applied optimally between team members themselves as well in order to share knowledge, passing difficulties and improve product industry. In some cases, good communications cannot prevent failures if management approach conflict with agile methods, this matter imposes some updates on agile characteristics. But failure in team management or to achieve a high-quality product that can be due to the presence of many stakeholders and lack of corporation between them. This limitation requires some updates on agile and make kind of balancing between team development process and stakeholders' preo-pipeline. Externally, agile has been created to react to marketing growth and development techniques changes, but these changes happened frequently so agile should keep up and naturally define new methods and tools.

Challenges always need solutions to evolve agile and its concepts, so new trends will emerge and new technologies in development will now be reflected in Agile. This chapter will highlight two main topics related to agile conceptually:

- As long as agile is in place to contain changes in marketing and business, do they also need adjustments to adapt to changes in the structural domain?
- How is the ability of agile to adapt the challenges?

We aim to demonstrate its ability to overcome challenges and what trends emerged as a result of these challenges. This research will list some challenges based on changes in teams, large organizations and multi-site operations. In parallel, it will review some agile challenges to understand more about how agile can embrace itself for application in organizations and to define other challenges which still open and not covered. Finally, we will review some agile trends to understand better the changes and updated on agile which helped it to keep running and attracted more organizations to use it.

BACKGROUND

Generally, software developments methodologies are mainly classified into two main types: Traditional Methodology (Heavyweight) or Agile Methodology (Awad, 2005). Traditional Methodologies (Heavyweight) follow series of phases which start from gathering requirements and end with deployment, during these phases, documentations play guiding role in creating product features, based on agreement and requirements. Many traditional methodologies were created, some of them were declined while other strongly imposed itself, taking advantage of its characteristics and features such as Waterfall Model, Spiral Model and Unified Process (Awad, 2005).

Waterfall model converts product industry into sequential phases by defining these requirements as an initial step followed by analysis, design, testing and deploying. It can provide an easy way to developed complex systems by defining requirements and designing the implementation afterward into production (Szalvay, 2004). It requires extensive customer interactions in order to understand the functional and non-functional requirements and to determine the features of the required product that creates a lot of documentation. The iterative model uses the waterfall in an iterative fashion by creating a partial implementation of a holistic system, then slowly adding increasing functionality (Alshamrani & Bahattab, 2015). Spiral Model extends waterfall model by defining more phases to each cycle and dividing the life cycle of software development process into four phases: Planning, Risk Analysis, Development/Engineering and Evaluation Phase (Boehm et al., 1998). Waterfall and other models with all their huge advantages and solutions to build systems and products started to be an old fashion as a result of quick changes in world of business. These changes in business increased ascending and development process became unable to deliver output as same tempo. These feature spotted light on lot of disadvantages, most of them relate to requirements changes, these changes could happen in the middle of development as a result of changing in business process or uncertainty of requirements in the beginning of the project (Cohen et al., 2004).

Beginning in the mid-1990s, many companies found this initial requirements documentation step frustrating and, perhaps, impossible (Williams & Cockburn, 2003a). Developers decided to find another model or methodology can break them away from traditional structured, segmented, bureaucratic approaches to software development and moved towards more flexible one (McCormick, 2012). In real world, changes happen in quick frequency, the development process should be done in flexible and efficient way (Cohen et al., 2004). Actually, markets are changing quickly and pushing more new requirements which are required from customers and business competition with high quality conditions, all of this was accompanied by technological development that seemed to accelerate unpredictably and the need to find new technologies can solve the limitations in current tools and systems (Cockburn & Highsmith, 2001; Dzamashvili Fogelström et al., 2010; Williams & Cockburn, 2003b).

Companies started to find alternative methodologies in order to continuity and competitiveness, many methodologies appeared. The efforts were to define new methodology replace the traditional one with new aspects and style. Historically, the famous meeting happened on February 11–13, 2001, at The Lodge at Snowbird ski resort in the Wasatch mountains of Utah, 17 people met to talk, ski, relax and try to find common ground. It was clear for all participations the necessity to better cope with changing requirements, focusing and starting from people and it should be more flexible (Cohen et al., 2004; Highsmith & Cockburn, 2001). Finally, they defined a new methodology called Agile Methodology (Fowler & Highsmith, 2001).

They analyzed their work habits to make them more lightness which provide more relevant output with customer satisfaction (Williams & Cockburn, 2003a). as a result, they wrote Manifesto for Agile Software Development which focuses on (Fowler & Highsmith, 2001; Turk et al., 2014; Williams & Cockburn, 2003a):

- Individuals and interactions over processes and tools.
- Working software over comprehensive documentation.
- Customer collaboration over contract negotiation.
- Responding to change over following a plan.

Another 12 principle are generated and emphasis on many goals such as customer satisfaction, continuous delivery, value, and early deliveries. adaptability, competitiveness, and customer benefit. Collaboration...etc. (Highsmith & Cockburn, 2001; Laanti et al., 2013).

Agile is a result of traditional methodologies shortcomings which makes it known plan-driven methodology (Cohen et al., 2004), it focuses on people and effective communications between them, customer participate during development stage to improve opportunities and product quality (Cristal et al., 2008). Enormous efforts of software development adaptions hide behind Agile in order to meet the increasing of business requirements.

AGILE METHODS

Agile as framework defines many methods which translate agile principles and provide practical rules to be applied. Describing agile methods reflect their features, but in general it tends to be lightweight comparing to old ones which described as rigorous, disciplined, bureaucratic, heavyweight, and industrial strength (Paulk, 2002). Agile methods like Agile itself promise shorter market time, plus greater flexibility to include changes in requirements that are created from clients and the market (Dzamashvili Fogelström et al., 2010; Williams & Cockburn, 2003b). As mentioned before, there is one of the most restrictive restrictions on waterfall methodology and other traditional methodologies behind changes after the analysis phase, during the design, implementation, or production stage. These changes increased in ascending order. Thus, traditional models should be more flexible to deal with when they arise. Agile methods have brought a new perspective to software development. It can easily adapt to different requirements or environment, to provide value to customers (Janes & Succi, 2012), While more organizations seek to get more competitions in shorter time with keeping developer far away from pressure to produce new or enhanced implementations quickly (Turk et al., 2014).

A number of software development methods have been created such as extreme programming (XP), feature-driven development, crystal clear method, scrum, dynamic systems development, and adaptive software development, fall into this category (Nerur et al., 2005).

AGILE CHALLENGES

As any change in software development, several challenges appeared after using agile in organizations, that prompted researchers to classify them or study specific cases in order to understand and provide solutions to these challenges.

The deliverable of each study is considered as an attempt to develop agile methodology itself and find the best way to merging it in organization. Significantly, reviewing and focusing on group of these challenges in addition to define other challenges are main idea in this section which enable us to aware their features. Organization type is considered the main factor to determine the best way to apply agile. weather agile can be applied smoothly or need update. Nowadays, organizations begin to be larger and larger in parallel with the strong movement of agility, which has proven its strength to respond to rapid changes in the market, and thus adaptation it in companies has become an urgent need and this has created many challenges related to their ability to adapt to the large size of companies.

These challenges were not the only ones, in addition, there are others related to the team itself and what are the frameworks of maneuver the team owns

Team Level

The change in team level can be found in any kind of organization according to several criteria that ranged from team knowledge, skills, organization, management, and ability to change ... etc. For that, focusing on modern team level challenges requires understanding fundamental changes in the work team, regardless of the nature of the organization, so we can move on to know the necessary requirements for the team in large organizations.

Agile method in the organization requires improving team skills to counter this change. Ideally, the team should be able to deal with the new approach and get its advantages without any problems, but this change does not happen smoothly, and the team must be practiced and prepared. Initially, team must understand agile culture to make the organizational environment accept the agile method (Tolfo et al., 2011). The organization should pave the way for the development of specifically designed recruitment practices, use team recruiting to find the right person or hire newly appointed graduates into fast-moving projects (Conboy et al., 2011).

In other hand, team members should aware of business knowledge which means provide small training modules, recruit staff and graduates with a combination of IT and business knowledge and customer company runs training sessions. In addition, team should understand principles of agile and its philosophy by ensuring multiple members get agile training, agile coaching and championing and cross-team observation/validation of agile practices. Furthermore, transferring to agile requires increasing of team motivation to keep high quality work performance and increase productivity. Meanwhile, agile assumes more focusing on decision-making which is achieved by building a sharing and learning environment, implement a democratic voting system and requires that project manager plays the role of facilitator. At the end, there is a challenge about compliant performance evaluation which means more challenges and more need to adapt breadth of skills much higher weighting for mentoring (Conboy et al., 2011).

Skills of team members are not the only challenges a team faces, as by expanding the scope of the vision, it allows us to monitor how the work environment can affect the teams and reduce the quality of production. Therefore, organizations and the team provide the right environment for agility and preparation, and they have found that a lack of understanding of the work environment is an important factor in limiting flexible advantages (Buchan et al., 2019) which cause limitation in communication and coordination between teams.

However, environment of work leads us to think about how team management will be changed and what are the challenges which related to this domain? Beginning of agile concepts, we can realize a lot of changes on management roles and way of management. Some management roles have been changed in agile comparing to traditional methods such as product owner who has difference in responsivity and tasks. Product owner should be available to all team and active in clearing definition of requirements in backlog (Nuottila et al., 2016). Agile assumes that customer and team member should work together with strong communication, thus self-management approach has emerged further as one of the twelve principles behind Agile Manifesto (Fowler & Highsmith, 2001) to display high levels of autonomy (Hoda & Murugesan, 2016; Stray et al., 2018). So as normal result, team needs to be aware how to apply self-management and what are the accompanied difficulties behind it. Self-management requires harmony with the rest of the team and some of the skills in management, especially that some methodologies such as scrum that allow members to choose tasks flexibly from the backlog. Team member should handle some other difficulties like cross-functional (Hoda & Murugesan, 2016) which means working across various technologies and domains in order to achieve organizational tasks (Pinto & Pinto, 1990). Thus team member should share knowledge between each other to learn new things which help achieve cross-functionality to a great extent (Hoda & Murugesan, 2016). Self-management assume any member can measure the required effort to finish tasks in order to organize sprint and work between team members. For that, agile introduced planning meetings with all members to share their views on the estimations and understanding the tasks (Hoda & Murugesan, 2016).

One of the challenges that began to spread as a natural result of the organization' inflation is the increase of the remote dispersed teams, which has become a reality in many companies, and this constituted a clear contradiction with the principles of agile procedure, which pushed towards finding ways and means to overcome them. So many studies emerged that presented ideas and visions centered mostly on how to overcome problems such as communication while confidence in agile practices was an important matter that prompted the necessity of sharing knowledge (Lautert et al., 2019). While there are other keys which are important such as agile servant leader, agile team, trust, virtual work environment, inspect & adapt, and reduce waste (Lous et al., 2018). Because of its apparent inconsistency with the basic principles of agile, and the need for it constantly increasing, it becomes clear that this topic is gripping to further research and realization of the required amendments on agile.

Organization Level

Agile is characterized by many challenges at the enterprise level, and these challenges vary according to the type of organization, for example, its business activity, size or time of rapid approval.

Business can vary between public and non-public organizations, but the challenges are the same in some specific cases. However, in any agile accreditation process, there are common challenges based on the following factors. (Nuottila et al., 2016): Conflict between agile nature and organization process to reduce documentation; Education, experience and commitment; Stakeholder communication and involvement; Roles in agile set-up; Location of the agile teams and Other challenges relate to legislation and permission of information sharing while other focus on the complexity of developed systems.

These challenges have become part of other challenges that have arisen with the expansion of organizations and their large size and their tendency to take advantage of the agile procedure to implement it.

Large-scale agile appeared to refer to the generated changes when agile adoption in large organizations, these changes pushed organizations to rethink their goals and reconfigure their human, managerial, and technology components. it includes many aspects range from using agile methods in large organizations to large projects and how can agile deal with these large projects, also it means using agile in large team to large multi-team projects to making use of principles of agile development in a whole organization (Dingsøyr & Moe, 2014; Fuchs & Hess, 2018). What is mentioned above means focusing more on management, organizational, people, process, and technological issues in adopting agile methodologies (Nerur et al., 2005).

In general, we can distinguish two categories of these challenges, the first, when a large organization decides to shift to agile and replaces the old approach with agile style while the second, examines the challenges of agility after organizations become larger.

Challenges of Large-Scale Agile Adoption

A lot of challenges are studied and analyzed during large-scale agile transformations, the goal was to define main points relate to transformation process and introduce solutions. Some of these challenges fall in following points (Dikert et al., 2016; Paasivaara et al., 2018):

- Change resistance
  People are not willing to change, so any change means time to learn to understand and kind of ambiguity. That applied on management which could be not willing to change as well
- Lack of investment
  Includes lack of training and coaching, too high workload, old commitments kept and rearranging physical spaces
- Agile difficult to implement
  This challenge considered very important to apply agile in organizations as it and not follow old approach with some agile concepts. That means team should not misunderstanding agile concepts or depends on guidance from literature which hard to learn agile. In some cases, Agile customized poorly which means skipping practices, that led to problems. Difficult and challenge of implementation push people revert to the old way of working but at meantime, people should not become too evangelic, in order to avoid making people reluctance of agile development and give up transformation process.
- Coordination challenges in multi-team environment
  Coordinating the work of several agile teams introduced new challenges to organizations, if surrounding organization was not responsive enough. However, another aspect in this point relate to autonomous team model challenging and focusing on own goal instead of striking a balance between team goals and general goals of the organization. Anyway, more coordination problems were appeared when teams are distributed over many geographical locations or when using different scripts in one case which leads to problems in synchronizing and consistency of software interfaces between teams.
- Different approaches emerge in a multi-team environment
  Because of interpretation of agile differs between teams, using old and new methods side by side, management in waterfall mode even after adopting agile
- Hierarchical management and organizational boundaries

- Requirements engineering challenges
  Agile methods like Scrum and XP don not have a quite structured approach to requirements which are required in large development projects in addition estimation time for these requirements are so difficult to Product managers and business analysts while teams need to break them down into small sizes which are able to be estimated.
- Quality assurance challenges
  In some cases, agile methods lack non-functional, continuous integration and automated testing, so applying these kinds of tests is considered as an important challenge to produce high quality product.
- Integrating non-development functions
- Defining team roles
- Challenges in defining the Product Owner role

Another interesting study has been done by (Uludag et al., 2018) and identified 11 categories of challenges as following Communication & Coordination, Software-Architecture, Geographical Distribution, Knowledge Management, Culture & Mindset, Methodology, Requirements Engineering, Enterprise Architecture, Quality Assurance, Tooling and Project Management.

Challenges of Expanding the Organization to Become Larger

Second kind of challenges in large organizations based on expanding small organizations to become larger, which means limitation agile methods to adapt this expanding. Conceptually, Agile assume software projects should be small and include small teams. It effected on organizations and business style by reducing size of software projects and focusing on microservices with its advantages epically in reducing complexity and risks(Dingsøyr et al., 2019; Ebert, 2018; Flyvbjerg et al., 2003).

Many extensions and trends in this domain appeared to coordinate working between customers, teams, departments and other participations in agile. Several of these extensions have been suggested e.g., the Scaled Agile Framework (SAFe), Large-Scale Scrum (LeSS), and Disciplined Agile Delivery (DAD) (Paasivaara et al., 2018).

AGILE TRENDS

Scrum of Scrums

Scrum is used and applied in small teams, while application in large teams is difficult and does not meet the purpose assigned to them. Therefore, large teams need to expand Scrum to meet its characteristics, and from here the trend appeared to offer an expansion of Scrum. Scrum of Scrums (SOS) is a framework for large organizations where many teams work together and coordinate to complete a product. We can say that SOS focus more on structural level. It divides a large team into multiple teams communicate with each other's and work on different sides of the same project (AlMutairi & Qureshi, 2015). These team make daily or weekly meeting by one representative from each team, and these meeting could be after daily stand-up meetings to update other SOS participants, after Release Planning meeting and after the Sprint Planning meeting (Mundra et al., 2013). In general, SOS meetings aim to address team coordination (Paasivaara et al., 2012). SOS team contains product owner attends all meeting related to his product and we have scrum mater in each team who will participate in SOS meeting.

The question remains as to what nature of companies or teams SOS can be applied to. In fact, as long as SOS is to apply the same concepts of Scrum, but on another level of the teams, this means that the teams must be homogeneous and work within the same project and product (Keller et al., 2019). This is evident in the challenges facing the meetings that SOS contains when the meeting period is for a long period or contains a large number of participants or the nature of the meeting itself and therefore it cannot be described as unsuccessful (Keller et al., 2019) but needs controls and conditions that restrict the progress and direction of the nature of the meetings. This gives an indication of the work and development you need to achieve the required adjustment process.

Scaled Agile Framework (SAFe)

Scaled Agile Framework (SAFe) uses agile and lean principles to scale whole organization. It depends and works together with agile methods and other current model such as Scrum, XP, Lean, and Product Development Flow. SAFe consists of three levels: team, program, and portfolio levels in addition to the optional value stream level (Alqudah & Razali, 2016; Turetken et al., 2017; Uludağ et al., 2017):

- The team level basically consists of agile teams, which define, build, and test software in fixed-length iteration and releases. SAFe uses in team level agile project management practices (Scrum) and agile technical practices (XP), it imports concepts from them depending on each stage.
- The program level organizes the agile team, so all roles should be defined, these roles are distributed into System Team, Product Manager, System Architect, Release Train Engineer (RTE), UX and Shared Resources and Release Management Team. Product manager prioritizes the program backlog and works with product owners at the team level to optimize Feature delivery. In this level, the agile release train is the major concept, thus this agile release train produces releases which are releases are planned during a 2-days release planning event with all relevant stakeholders.
- The value stream is long-lived series of system definition, development, and deployment steps, which means insuring that multiple large teams remain aligned.
- Program Portfolio Management team consists of people with fully understand to business strategy, used technology, and financial aspects such as business managers and executives. In this level, the strategy is established and identified, then new features are created and boken down to program level.

SAFe is a solution to large organizations that need to scale agile development by scaling up 'some' of the agile practices and introducing new practices and concepts (such as release train, business, and architecture epics, portfolio backlog). There some criticism for being too prescriptive and team are not much flexible in process decisions. Even these criticisms feel that this framework is not agile because of many upfront planning and some top-down processes which implies lack of flexibility. But in general, it accelerates time-to-market, increases productivity and quality, and reduces risks and project costs. At the same time, SAFe has some weakness during the scaling process relate to project size and need to structural approaches and methodological guidelines for scaling agile in large settings, in particular for SAFe (Turetken et al., 2017).

Disciplined Agile Delivery (DAD)

Disciplined Agile Delivery (DAD), developed by Scott Ambler and Mark Lines. DAD is a framework to adapt the scrum to the organization, when this organization decides to move to agile methodology. Scrum itself does not have the full requirements; it is only part of what is required to provide complex solutions to stakeholders. The team will start using another process to fill in this gap which leads to a lot of confusion and mystery. So DAD is a hybrid approach that provides a coherent approach to delivering a graceful solution that works as a guiding and decision-making including scrum, Agile Modeling (AM), Extreme Programming (XP), Unified Process (UP), Kanban, Lean Software Development, SAFe and LeSS and many other ways.

DAD considers that agile methods focus only on one phase which is "Construction", while large projects need more. For that, it added other two phases (Inceptions and Transitions), while inception phase located before construction, transition phase focus in the stage after construction to prepare for delivery. These phases are achieved during short iterations (Alqudah & Razali, 2016).

Large Scale Scrum (LeSS)

It is an agile framework for scaling Scrum to more than one team in large organizations. So scrum is applied with some extensions like different sprint planning activity which include two members from each team plus the one overall Product Owner to decide which chunk of Product Backlog items to work on (Alqudah & Razali, 2016). In general, It is classified into two types, first one called LeSS framework-1which covers up to ten Scrum teams and another, called LeSS framework-2, has more than ten (Vaidya, 2014).

More practices were established like: Inter-team coordination meeting, a Joint Light Produce Backlog Refinement and Joint Retrospective meeting (Alqudah & Razali, 2016). These practices are mainly applied to LeSS framework-1, while in LeSS framework-2 a new Pre-Sprint Product Team Meeting is introduced in addition to overall Sprint Review meeting and Overall Sprint Retrospective meeting at the product level (Vaidya, 2014).

AGILE FUTURE TRENDS

Software systems change rapidly every day and new trends appear frequently according to many factors include market and requirements. Mobile applications, big data, social and communication media and other top topics pushed software development to find alternatives and extension to old approaches and during this development agile methodology proofed itself as flexible approach can be trusted to keep up business run.

Efforts started to study effect of rapid changes in requirements on agile, and the questions was what agile need to update. One of the essential topics focuses on manifesto and its future whether it should be developed or not, as a result of the discussion, some ideas prompt stop focusing on the future trends of the agile manifest while other supported the distribution of the agile mindset into new fields of application. In parallel, there is discussion about the future of agile methodology and if scrum should be replaced or not. The results found agile train keeps moving and Scrum is not the end of the road, in addition, maintain flexibility, stop doing stupid stuff and focus on delivering value more quickly and be professional (Hohl et al., 2018).

Agile tends to make team more self-organizing and autonomous which was one of the agile challenges as we mentioned before, this direction more important where team should make decision, estimate tasks and ensure the continuity of the organization's system. Studying barriers of autonomous agile team generated some ideas like not having clear and common goals, lack of trust, too many dependencies to others, lack of coaching and organizational support and diversity in norms (Stray et al., 2018), so the effort was to identify these barriers and attempt to understand their related factors. Main domains and related topics were leadership, coordination, organizational context, design of autonomous agile teams and team processes which suggested group of questions in order to draw borders and clear way to make team self-organized (Stray et al., 2018).

On other hands, Teams and organizations started to be bigger and bigger, thus new aspects and techniques should be followed which means update on agile and its methods. Distributed teams are located in different geographical places, taking advantage of technological development to communicate and reduce the costs. But agile has been created to handle small teams, so as we mentioned before, agile has been continuously evolved according to team natural and organization expanding, therefore agile has ability to keep going in this evolution process and this kind of work. Organizations use agile in their distributed teams by making changes on the organizational design, decision making, collaboration and coordination and in agile culture. These changes include splitting teams into specialized groups and replacing face-to-face meeting with other types using the modern communications tools while agile should be learned and understood between team members to solve challenges quickly. In other hand, the adaptions should be applied on agile itself, therefore we can notice multi-team backlog, multiple meetings, scaling the infrastructure and organizational agility (Papadopoulos, 2015).

Agile methodology defined a new extension to support new trends like Business Intelligent (BI). Uncontrolled growth of data generated new domains of manipulating, understating and analyzing data such as Big Data and BI; these domains convert data into information to be used by software systems. BI and analytics provide decisions-making information in supply chain, sales, finance, and marketing, so this necessity met the characteristics that characterize agile and this has led to extend agile to Agile Data Warehousing, Extreme Scoping which focused on the data integration aspect of BI projects (Muntean & Surcel, 2013).

This success of agile adoption encourages asking questions about the future changes and ability of agile to be applied in modern trends such as fulfil the demand of the IoT and AI or if agile can improve data analytics and data sciences. Agile should handle security and support the development of safety critical systems like autonomous vehicles and robotics which are very important in current and futures markets (Hoda et al., 2018).

CONCLUSION

During this research we can identify how agile was able to adapt to the changes that occurred on the structural structure, as it has always found solutions to most challenges at the organizational level and the level of teams. Its development and how it began to extend to departments that are not IT departments, pushes the business to develop and grow, and this is what appears in the development of concepts such as self-management and work in geographically distributed places. It also shows us through the research how the flexibility that it enjoys has always allowed in the first place the organization and the teams and researchers to find solutions to develop software and respond to market and work changes.

Agile succeeded in keeping abreast of developments in the market and business, which are directly reflected in the companies 'performance, as evidenced by the great trend of companies of various kinds towards adopting agility. Agile as others, needs many expansions and activities to be adapted and used in the procedure approved in the organization.

Education, training, and procedural understanding are essential aspects of successful organizations and projects, meanwhile, the communication between the team members, face to face, increases the effectiveness of the performance to achieve high-quality products which meet customer's satisfaction. After reviewing natural and reasons of challenges of agile, we can notice that agile should be applied as it, by understanding its basics and any update or extension should be created based on these principles.

Rapid changes prompted agile to define new trends which are suitable to large organizations or distributed teams. These changes raised questions about future of agile. This discussion about future of agile still open, but in general agile proofed its advantages to adapt new changes in business and market. Agile extensions provide the required techniques to the organization to facilitate work between teams. In the same way, modern phenomenon integrated with agile in some domains, while many questions still open about agile and some aspects relate to the vision and future of agile.

ACKNOWLEDGMENT

We thank the co-editors and IGI for the opportunity to collaborate on this book.

REFERENCES

Al-Zewairi, M., Biltawi, M., Etaiwi, W., & Shaout, A. (2017). Agile software development methodologies: Survey of surveys. *Journal of Computer and Communications*, 5(05), 74–97. doi:10.4236/jcc.2017.55007

AlMutairi, A. M., & Qureshi, M. R. J. (2015). The proposal of scaling the roles in scrum of scrums for distributed large projects. *International Journal of Information Technology and Computer Science*, 7(8), 68–74. doi:10.5815/ijitcs.2015.08.10

Alqudah, M., & Razali, R. (2016). A review of scaling agile methods in large software development. International Journal on Advanced Science. *Engineering and Information Technology*, 6(6), 828–837.

Alshamrani, A., & Bahattab, A. (2015). A comparison between three SDLC models waterfall model, spiral model, and Incremental/Iterative model. *International Journal of Computer Science Issues*, 12(1), 106.

Altameem, E. A. (2015). Impact of Agile methodology on software development. *Computer and Information Science*, 8(2), 9. doi:10.5539/cis.v8n2p9

Awad, M. A. (2005). A comparison between agile and traditional software development methodologies. University of Western Australia.

Boehm, B., Egyed, A., Kwan, J., Port, D., Shah, A., & Madachy, R. (1998). Using the WinWin spiral model: A case study. *Computer*, 31(7), 33–44. doi:10.1109/2.689675

Buchan, J., MacDonell, S. G., & Yang, J. (2019). Effective team onboarding in Agile software development: Techniques and goals. *2019 ACM/IEEE International Symposium on Empirical Software Engineering and Measurement (ESEM)*, 1–11. 10.1109/ESEM.2019.8870189

Cockburn, A., & Highsmith, J. (2001). Agile software development: The people factor. *Computer, 11*(11), 131–133. doi:10.1109/2.963450

Cohen, D., Lindvall, M., & Costa, P. (2004). An introduction to agile methods. *Advances in Computers, 62*(03), 1–66.

Conboy, K., Coyle, S., Wang, X., & Pikkarainen, M. (2011). *People over process: Key people challenges in agile development*. Academic Press.

Cristal, M., Wildt, D., & Prikladnicki, R. (2008). Usage of Scrum practices within a global company. *2008 IEEE International Conference on Global Software Engineering*, 222–226. 10.1109/ICGSE.2008.34

Dikert, K., Paasivaara, M., & Lassenius, C. (2016). Challenges and success factors for large-scale agile transformations: A systematic literature review. *Journal of Systems and Software, 119*, 87–108. doi:10.1016/j.jss.2016.06.013

Dingsøyr, T., Falessi, D., & Power, K. (2019). Agile Development at Scale: The Next Frontier. *IEEE Software, 36*(2), 30–38. doi:10.1109/MS.2018.2884884

Dingsøyr, T., & Moe, N. B. (2014). Towards principles of large-scale agile development. *International Conference on Agile Software Development*, 1–8.

Dzamashvili Fogelström, N., Gorschek, T., Svahnberg, M., & Olsson, P. (2010). The impact of agile principles on market-driven software product development. *Journal of Software Maintenance and Evolution: Research and Practice, 22*(1), 53–80. doi:10.1002pip.420

Ebert, C. (2018). 50 Years of Software Engineering: Progress and Perils. *IEEE Software, 35*(5), 94–101. doi:10.1109/MS.2018.3571228

Flyvbjerg, B., Bruzelius, N., & Rothengatter, W. (2003). *Megaprojects and risk: An anatomy of ambition*. Cambridge University Press. doi:10.1017/CBO9781107050891

Fowler, M., & Highsmith, J. (2001). The agile manifesto. *Software Development, 9*(8), 28–35.

Fuchs, C., & Hess, T. (2018). *Becoming agile in the digital transformation: The process of a large-scale agile transformation*. Academic Press.

Highsmith, J., & Cockburn, A. (2001). Agile software development: The business of innovation. *Computer, 34*(9), 120–127. doi:10.1109/2.947100

Hoda, R., & Murugesan, L. K. (2016). Multi-level agile project management challenges: A self-organizing team perspective. *Journal of Systems and Software, 117*, 245–257. doi:10.1016/j.jss.2016.02.049

Hoda, R., Salleh, N., & Grundy, J. (2018). The rise and evolution of agile software development. *IEEE Software, 35*(5), 58–63. doi:10.1109/MS.2018.290111318

Hohl, P., Klünder, J., van Bennekum, A., Lockard, R., Gifford, J., Münch, J., Stupperich, M., & Schneider, K. (2018). Back to the future: Origins and directions of the "Agile Manifesto"–views of the originators. *Journal of Software Engineering Research and Development*, 6(1), 15. doi:10.118640411-018-0059-z

Janes, A. A., & Succi, G. (2012). The dark side of agile software development. *Proceedings of the ACM International Symposium on New Ideas, New Paradigms, and Reflections on Programming and Software*, 215–228. 10.1145/2384592.2384612

Keller, A., Rössle, A., Sheik, R., Thell, H., & Westmark, F. (2019). *Issues with Scrum-of-Scrums*. Academic Press.

Kumar, G., & Bhatia, P. K. (2012). Impact of agile methodology on software development process. *International Journal of Computer Technology and Electronics Engineering*, 2(4), 46–50.

Laanti, M., Similä, J., & Abrahamsson, P. (2013). Definitions of agile software development and agility. *European Conference on Software Process Improvement*, 247–258. 10.1007/978-3-642-39179-8_22

Lautert, T., Neto, A. G. S. S., & Kozievitch, N. P. (2019). A survey on agile practices and challenges of a global software development team. *Brazilian Workshop on Agile Methods*, 128–143. 10.1007/978-3-030-36701-5_11

Lous, P., Tell, P., Michelsen, C. B., Dittrich, Y., & Ebdrup, A. (2018). From Scrum to Agile: A journey to tackle the challenges of distributed development in an Agile team. *Proceedings of the 2018 International Conference on Software and System Process*, 11–20. 10.1145/3202710.3203149

McCormick, M. (2012). *Waterfall vs. Agile methodology*. MPCS.

Mundra, A., Misra, S., & Dhawale, C. A. (2013). Practical scrum-scrum team: Way to produce successful and quality software. *2013 13th International Conference on Computational Science and Its Applications*, 119–123.

Muntean, M., & Surcel, T. (2013). Agile BI-The Future of BI. *Informatica Economica, 17*(3).

Nerur, S., Mahapatra, R., & Mangalaraj, G. (2005). Challenges of migrating to agile methodologies. *Communications of the ACM, 48*(5), 72–78. doi:10.1145/1060710.1060712

Nuottila, J., Aaltonen, K., & Kujala, J. (2016). Challenges of adopting agile methods in a public organization. *International Journal of Information Systems and Project Management, 4*(3), 65–85.

Paasivaara, M., Behm, B., Lassenius, C., & Hallikainen, M. (2018). Large-scale agile transformation at Ericsson: A case study. *Empirical Software Engineering, 23*(5), 2550–2596. doi:10.100710664-017-9555-8

Paasivaara, M., Lassenius, C., & Heikkilä, V. T. (2012). Inter-team coordination in large-scale globally distributed scrum: Do scrum-of-scrums really work? *Proceedings of the ACM-IEEE International Symposium on Empirical Software Engineering and Measurement*, 235–238. 10.1145/2372251.2372294

Papadopoulos, G. (2015). Moving from traditional to agile software development methodologies also on large, distributed projects. *Procedia: Social and Behavioral Sciences, 175*, 455–463. doi:10.1016/j.sbspro.2015.01.1223

Paulk, M. C. (2002). Agile methodologies and process discipline. *Institute for Software Research, 3*, 15–18.

Pinto, M. B., & Pinto, J. K. (1990). Project team communication and cross-functional cooperation in new program development. *Journal of Product Innovation Management, 7*(3), 200–212. doi:10.1111/1540-5885.730200

Stray, V., Moe, N. B., & Hoda, R. (2018). Autonomous agile teams: Challenges and future directions for research. *Proceedings of the 19th International Conference on Agile Software Development: Companion,* 16. 10.1145/3234152.3234182

Szalvay, V. (2004). *An introduction to agile software development.* Danube Technologies.

Tolfo, C., Wazlawick, R. S., Ferreira, M. G. G., & Forcellini, F. A. (2011). Agile methods and organizational culture: Reflections about cultural levels. *Journal of Software Maintenance and Evolution: Research and Practice, 23*(6), 423–441. doi:10.1002mr.483

Turetken, O., Stojanov, I., & Trienekens, J. J. (2017). Assessing the adoption level of scaled agile development: A maturity model for Scaled Agile Framework. *Journal of Software: Evolution and Process, 29*(6), e1796.

Turk, D., France, R., & Rumpe, B. (2014). *Limitations of agile software processes.* ArXiv Preprint ArXiv:1409.6600

Uludag, Ö., Kleehaus, M., Caprano, C., & Matthes, F. (2018). Identifying and structuring challenges in large-scale agile development based on a structured literature review. *2018 IEEE 22nd International Enterprise Distributed Object Computing Conference (EDOC),* 191–197.

Uludağ, Ö., Kleehaus, M., Xu, X., & Matthes, F. (2017). Investigating the role of architects in scaling agile frameworks. *2017 IEEE 21st International Enterprise Distributed Object Computing Conference (EDOC),* 123–132.

Vaidya, A. (2014). Does dad know best, is it better to do less or just be safe? Adapting scaling agile practices into the enterprise. *PNSQC. ORG,* 1–18.

Williams, L. (2010). Agile software development methodologies and practices. *Advances in Computers, 80,* 1–44. doi:10.1016/S0065-2458(10)80001-4

Williams, L., & Cockburn, A. (2003). Agile software development: It's about feedback and change. *IEEE Computer, 36*(6), 39–43. doi:10.1109/MC.2003.1204373

KEY TERMS AND DEFINITIONS

Agile: A software development approach to convey rapid changes in the market and customer requirements on high-quality terms.

Agile Manifesto: An alternative to documentation-driven and heavyweight software development processes.

Kanban: A method in software development which considered as a system for visualizing work and converting it into flow to reduce waste time and maximizing customer value.

Scrum: An iterative and incremental software development to handle drawbacks of traditional development methodologies. It produces many releases in short times based on customer requirements, time pressure, competition, product quality and available resources.

Scrumban: A combination of the benefits of Scrum and Kanban to improve transparency in a short time to release.

Software Development Methodology: A process or series of processes used in software development.

XP: An engineering methodology consisting of code-focused practices to ensure high quality of development.

This research was previously published in Balancing Agile and Disciplined Engineering and Management Approaches for IT Services and Software Products; pages 189-204, copyright year 2021 by Engineering Science Reference (an imprint of IGI Global).

Chapter 2
Software Architecture:
Developing Knowledge, Skills, and Experiences

Perla Velasco-Elizondo

Universidad Autónoma de Zacatecas (UAZ), México

ABSTRACT

What is software architecture? A clear and simple definition is that software architecture is about making important design decisions that you want to get right early in the development of a software system because, in the future, they are costly to change. Being a good software architect is not easy. It requires not only a deep technical competency from practicing software architecture design in industry, but also an excellent understanding of the theoretical foundations of software architecture are gained from doing software architecture research. This chapter describes some significant research, development, and education activities that the author has performed during her professional trajectory path to develop knowledge, skills, and experiences around this topic.

INTRODUCTION

What is software architecture? To say it simple: software architecture is about making the design decisions that you want to get right early in the development of a software system, because future changes are costly. Today, software architecture development is necessary as never before; no organization begins a complex software system without a suitable software architecture.

Within the context of the software life cycle (Sommerville, 2011), software architecture is an artifact produced during the design phase. A software architect, or the software architecture design team, is responsible for defining software architecture. Being a good software architect is not an easy matter (Rehman et al., 2018), (Shahbazian, Lee & Medvidovic, 2018). The author considers that, it not only requires deep technical competency which comes from practicing software architecture design in industry; but also a very good understanding of the theoretical foundations of software architecture gained from doing software architecture research.

DOI: 10.4018/978-1-6684-3702-5.ch002

Dr. Velasco-Elizondo finds the topic of software architecture fascinating. This chapter describes some of the significant research, education and, coaching activities she has undertaken during her professional trajectory path to develop knowledge, skills and experiences on this topic. She hopes that this material helps to encourage readers and, particularly, other women to get involved in science, technology and engineering.

This chapter will cover the following sections:

- **Getting it right: software architecture foundations**. This section describes how software architecture foundations are conceived and an example of why preserving them in practice is not always straightforward. It will discuss how to tackle this shortcoming with the proposal of exogenous connectors.
- **Practicing it right: software architecture methods**. In this section, the notion of software architecture lifecycle is introduced. Relevant methods for software architecture development are then briefly discussed within the context of this lifecycle, as well as some limitations related to the difficulty of adopting these methods in practice. Finally, an explanation of why and how technology has to be considered as a first-class design concept in order to tackle one of these limitations will be given.
- **Automating technology selection**. This section presents a software tool, recently developed, which uses information retrieval, natural language processing and sematic web techniques to address the problem of automating NoSQL database technologies search.
- **Software architecture education**. This section describes two educational projects Dr. Velasco-Elizondo has led to promote knowledge and practical experiences on software architecture design and development.
- **Hands on.** Dr. Velasco-Elizondo has had the opportunity to work, as a coach, with practicing software architects and developers helping them to deploy software architecture practices and methods. In this section some of these works will be described.

GETTING IT RIGHT: SOFTWARE ARCHITECTURE FOUNDATIONS

Software architecture has always existed as part of the discipline of Software Engineering. This section describes how software architecture foundations are conceived and gives an example of why preserving them in practice is not always straightforward. The proposed use of exogenous connectors to tackle this shortcoming is also included.

Foundations in Theory

Back when systems were relatively "less complex and small", abstract diagrams were drawn to give stakeholders a better understanding of software designs when describing them. Later, systems went beyond simple algorithms and data structures becoming more complex and larger in size. Therefore, similar in practice to other branches of engineering, more structured diagrams were essential to describe software system designs and communicate regarding aspects such as their main parts and responsibilities, their communication and data model, etc.

Software architecture foundations were built from a high-level model that consists of elements, form, and rationale (Perry, & Wolf, 1992). Elements are first-class constructs representing either computation, data, or connectors. Form is defined in terms of the properties of, and the relationships among, the elements. The rationale provides the underlying basis for the architecture in terms of architectural significant requirements, a.k.a. architectural drivers (Bass, Clements, & Kazman, 2012). In alignment with these foundations, in their seminal book Bass, Clements and Kazman defined software architecture as the set of structures needed for reasoning about the system, which comprises software elements (i.e. computation and data), relations among them (i.e. connectors), and the properties of both (Bass, Clements, & Kazman, 2012). In software architecture design, reasoning is vital as it supports designers in making justifiable decisions (Tang et al., 2008). Thus, all these authors agree that effective reasoning about architectural constructs and their relationships requires a high degree of understanding of these foundations.

Thus, components and connectors have become the basis of many software architecture development approaches. For example, Architecture Description Languages (ADLs) have always defined architectures of software systems in terms of components and connectors connecting them (Shaw & Garlan, 1996). Also, the current version of the Unified Modeling Language (UML) uses connectors to compose components into architectures of software systems.

Foundations in Practice

Despite software architecture foundations and well-specified software architecture design, this nonetheless, tends to erode over time (de Silva & Balasubramaniam, 2012). A number of reasons for design erosion have been identified. One reason relates to the manner in which software architecture is implemented in practice. Software architecture foundations define a component as the principal unit of computation (or data storage) in a system, while connector is the communication mechanism to allow components to interact. However, in existing system implementation approaches, communication originates in components, and connectors are only channels for passing on the control flow to other components. Connectors are mechanism for message passing, which allows components to invoke one another's functionality by method calls (or remote procedure calls), either directly or indirectly, via these channels. Thus components in these approaches mix computation with communication, since in performing their computation they also initiate method calls and manage their returns, via connectors. Consequently, in terms of communication, components implementations are not loosely coupled.

Having components containing very specific communication information hinders their reuse. Software reuse has been defined as "the systematic use of existing software assets to construct new or modified assets" (Mohagheghi & Conradi, 2007). Software reuse is an important topic in Software Engineering as it is widely accepted that it is a means of increasing productivity, saving time, and reducing the cost of software development. Separating computation from communication means that system specific composition details are not in components and therefore components can be reused many times for constructing different systems.

With these shortcomings in mind, this work proposes exogenous connectors to support component composition (Lau & Wang, 2007).

Exogenous Connectors

Exogenous connectors are first-class architectural constructs, which as their name suggests, encapsulate *loci* of communication outside components. By analyzing the control flow required in software systems, a set of useful communication schemes—here defined as specific connector types—has been identified and a catalogue of connectors proposed (Velasco-Elizondo, 2010). The communication schemes are analogous to either control-flow structures that can be found in most programming languages or to behavioral patterns. Behavioral patterns are design solutions that describe common communication schemes among objects. Table 1 contains the connectors in this catalogue and their corresponding descriptions.

Table 1. A catalogue of exogenous connectors

Name	Description
Sequencer	Provides a composition scheme where the computation in the composed components is executed sequentially one after another.
Pipe	Provides a composition scheme where the computation in the composed components is executed sequentially one after another and the output of an execution is the input of the next one and so forth.
Selector	Provides a composition scheme where the computation in only one of the composed components is executed based on the evaluation of a Boolean expression
Observer	Provides a composition mechanism where once the computation in the ''publisher'' component has been performed; the computation in a set of "subscribers" components is executed sequentially.
Chain of responsibility	Provides a composition mechanism where more than one component in a set can handle a request for computation.
Exclusive choice sequencer	Provides a composition mechanism where once the computation in a ''predecessor'' component has been performed, the computation of only one component in a set of ''successor'' components is executed.
Exclusive choice pipe	A version of the exclusive choice sequencer with internal data communication among the ''predecessor'' and in a set of ''successor'' components.
Simple merge sequencer	Provides a composition mechanism where once the computation in only one component in a set of ''predecessor'' components has been performed, the computation in a set of ''successor'' component is executed.
Simple merge pipe	A version of the simple merge sequencer with internal data communication between the ''predecessor'' and the ''successor'' component.

Figure 1 shows an example of a system architecture with exogenous connectors. It consists of a hierarchy of connectors K1-K5 representing the system's communication, sitting on top of components that provide the computation performed by the system. A connector works as a composition operator that promotes compositionality. That is, when applied to components it yields another component, which is called *composite component*. A composite component can in turn be a subject of further composition. This is illustrated in Figure 1 by the inner dotted boxes.

The control flow in the resulting system is fixed and encapsulated by the corresponding connector structure. A system with exogenous connectors has a set of possible execution paths, but when the system is executed, only one execution path is carried out. The dotted line in Figure 1 shows one possible control flow path for the system represented by the architecture. The execution of the system starts with the connector at the highest level. Thus, the connector K5 invokes the computation in the composite component (containing C1 and C2 components) by calling its top-level connector K4. After that, the connector K5 calls the composite component (containing two composite components: C3 and C4-C6 components). Internally, its top-level connector K3 calls both inner composite components. After this sequence of executions is completed, the control flow is returned back through the hierarchy until reaching the top-level connector K5 that delivers the result of the executions.

Figure 1. An example of a system architecture with exogenous connectors

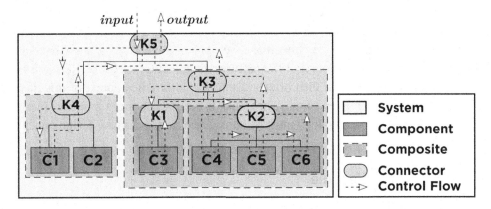

As it can be implied, exogenous connectors support an algebraic approach to component composition, namely, an approach inspired by algebra where the functionality in components is hierarchically composed into a new one of the same type. The resulting function can be further composed with other functions, yielding a more complex one. More formally, for an arbitrary number of levels (L), the connector type hierarchy can be defined in terms of dependent types and polymorphism as follows:

$L1 \equiv \text{Component} \rightarrow \text{Result};$

$L2 \equiv L1 \times \ldots \times L1 \rightarrow \text{Result};$

For $2 < i \leq n$, $Li \equiv L(j_1) \times \ldots \times L(j_m) \rightarrow \text{Result}$, for some m;

where $j_k \in \{1, \ldots, (i-1)\}$ for $1 \leq k \leq m$,

$\{ L1, i = 1$

and $L(i) = \ldots$

$L1, i = n.$

Exogenous Connectors in Practice

Since they were proposed, exogenous connectors have been utilized in a variety of systems designs and implementations. Recent examples include IoT end-user smart homes (Arellanes & Lau, 2019) and vehicle control systems (Di Cola et al., 2015). These implementation exercises have all demonstrated the elimination of design erosion caused by not preserving components and connectors as first-class constructs at implementation time. Additionally, the use of exogenous connectors lead to a bottom-up, architecture centered development from reusable constructs. These reusable constructs include both, components and connectors.

Still under investigation is the fact that the use exogenous connectors to design and code system architectures inevitably leads to big hierarchies of connectors. Refactoring techniques for connectors can provide just such a facility.

PRACTICING IT RIGHT: SOFTWARE ARCHITECTURE DEVELOPMENT METHODS

If an important process is difficult, a common approach in many disciplines, including Software Engineering, is to try to systematize that process to ensure predictability, repeatability, and high-quality outcomes. To achieve that, a number of architecture development methods have appeared during the last decade. This section introduces the notion of the software architecture lifecycle. Relevant methods for software architecture development are then briefly discussed within the context of this lifecycle. Also discussed are some limitations related to why these are difficult to adopt in practice. Finally, there is an explanation of why and how technology must be considered as a first-class design concept to tackle one of these limitations.

Software Architecture Lifecycle

Ideally, software architecture development should be carried out within the context of a software architecture lifecycle, which provides a set of stages to follow, with its corresponding activities, to developing it (Cervantes, Velasco-Elizondo, & Kazman, 2013). In general, this lifecycle comprises the following stages, which are depicted in Figure 2:

1. **Requirements,** which focuses on identifying and prioritizing architectural requirements.
2. **Design,** which focuses on identifying and selecting the different constructs that compose the architecture and satisfy architectural requirements.
3. **Documentation**, which focuses on creating the documents that describe the different constructs that compose the architecture, in order to communicate it to different system stakeholders.
4. **Evaluation,** which focuses on assessing the software architecture design to determine whether it satisfies the architectural requirements.

METHODS TO SOFTWARE ARCHITECTURE DEVELOPMENT

For the purpose of this work, a *method* is assumed to be a series of detailed steps—with the corresponding instructions for implementation—to accomplish an end. Table 2 lists a set of well-known methods in software architecture development. It is generally considered that most of them exhibit limitations to effectively adopting them in practice, namely: (i) they do not cover all the stages of the architecture lifecycle, (ii) combining them is not always practical and efficient and (iii) they say very little about technology. Next, these limitations are further explained.

Figure 2. Software architecture life cycle

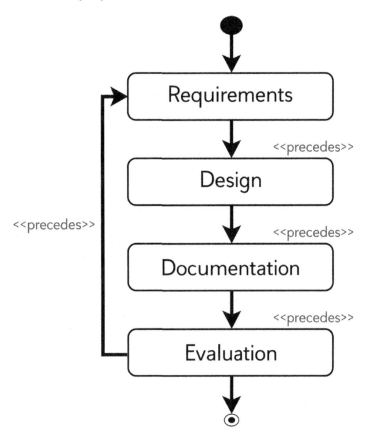

As Table 2 shows, most of the methods, apart from ACDM and RUP, do not cover all the stages of the architecture lifecycle. RUP covers them. However, RUP is a general approach to software development and the guidance that it provides with respect to each of the stages in the architecture lifecycle is very general.

The fact that architecture methods generally focus on a particular stage of the lifecycle requires, when doing software architecture development, selecting more than one method. However, the existence of more than one method to choose from for a particular stage of the lifecycle can complicate the selection. Besides, choosing an appropriate combination of the methods is not all that is required. One must also identify how the selected methods should be, practically and efficiently, used together. This is not trivial because different authors have defined these methods "in isolation". They are defined in terms of different activities, artifacts, and terminology. Thus, once an appropriate combination of methods is chosen, the architect must often modify them to avoid mismatches, omissions and/or repetitions.

Finally, architectural design is about applying a set of design decisions to satisfy architectural requirements and design decisions often involve the use of design concepts. *Design concepts* refer to a body of generally accepted architectural design solutions that can be used to create high quality architectural designs. There is a common agreement that design concepts include *reference architectures, deployment patterns, architectural patterns,* and *tactics.* Design concepts are abstract, and differ from the concepts that software architects use in their day-to-day work, which mostly come from technologies. Software architecture design methods say very little about technology, despite the fact that it is very critical to the success of and architecture design (Hofmeister et al., 2007).

Next section will describes a proposal to tackle this third limitation.

Table 2. Well-known methods for software architecture development

	Name	Software architecture lifecycle staged covered	Description
1	Quality Attribute Workshop (QAW) (Barbacci et al., 2003)	Requirements	It is a facilitated scenario-based method for defining the architectural *quality attributes* involving the stakeholders in a workshop. No other requirements types are considered.
2	Attribute Driven Design (ADD) (Cervantes & Kazman, 2016)	Design	It is an iterative method for designing software architectures in which, the designer decomposes the architecture into greater detail, considering *architectural requirements*.
3	The 4+1 view model (Kruchten, 1995)	Documentation	It is a model used for documenting software architectures, considering multiple, concurrent views from the viewpoint of different stakeholders. The four views of the model are *logical, development, process and physical*. The *use case* view serves as the 'plus one' view.
4	Views and Beyond (V&B) (Clements et al., 2010)	Documentation	It is a method and a collection of techniques for documenting software architectures, considering the following view types giving a different perspective of the structure of the system. The considered view types are: *module, component-and-connector* and the *allocation*.
7	The Software Architecture Analysis Method (SAAM) (Kazman et al., 1996)	Requirements, Evaluation.	It is a method for evaluating software architecture designs to point out the places where it fails to meet its *quality attribute requirements* and show obvious alternative designs that would work better. No other requirements types are considered.
8	Architecture Tradeoff Analysis Method (ATAM) (Clements, Kazman, & Klein, 2002)	Requirements, Evaluation	It is a method for evaluating software architecture designs relative to *quality attribute requirements* in order to expose architectural risks that potentially inhibit the achievement of an organization's business goals. No other requirements types are considered.
9	ARID (Clements et al., 2008)	Evaluation	It is a lightweight method for evaluating partial software architecture designs in its early stages. It combines aspects from ATAM and SAAM in a more tactical level.
9	Architecture Centric Design Method (ACDM) (Lattanze, 2009).	Requirements, Design, Documentation, Evaluation.	It is an iterative approach to software development; its feature is an emphasis on architecture. It say very little about technology.
10	RUP (Kroll, Kruchten, & Booch, 2003)	Requirements, Design, Documentation, Evaluation.	It is an iterative approach to software development. It say very little about technology.

Technology as a First-Class Design Concept and its use in Architectural Design Methods

In (Cervantes, Velasco-Elizondo, & Kazman, 2013) the idea of considering technologies as a first-class design concept was explicitly stated for the first time. A demonstration of how to use in ADD, a well-known method to architecture design, was also presented. Next, a recent case to demonstrate it is used.

Consider the development of an online system to apply for a place at a primary school. Via this system parents/tutors will be able to perform function such as creating an account, finding a school, filling out an application, and submitting an application. According to the software architecture lifecycle depicted in Figure 2, before starting architecture design the development team should have the architectural requirements identified. Architectural requirements include: (*i*) user requirements, which are the functions the users can perform via the software system; (*ii*) quality attributes, which are properties of software systems that are of interest in terms of it being developed or operated, e.g. maintainability, testability, performance, security; and (*iii*) constraints, which are already taken (design) decisions, i.e. mandated technologies, laws and standards that must be complied with.

These architectural requirements are outlined, in general terms, in Table 3.

Table 3. Architectural requirements for a system to apply for a place at a primary school

Architecture Requirements	Description
User requirements	UR1 - Find a school UR2 - Fill out application
Quality attributes	QA1 - Performance. A user performs a school search during peak load; the system processes the query in under 10 seconds. QA2 - Availability. A random event causes a failure to the system during normal operation; the system must be providing services again within 30 seconds of the failure. QA3 - Security. An unknown user from a remote location attempts to access the system during normal operation; the system blocks the access to this user the 99.99% of the times.
Constraints	C1- The system must run in Internet Explorer n+, Firefox 3+, Chrome 6+, and Safari 5+. C2- The system must use information stored in a MariaDB 10+ database.

Architectural patterns are proven good architecture design structures, which can be reused, e.g. layers, pipes and filters, MVC. Tactics are a proven good means to achieve a single quality attribute requirement, e.g. replication, concurrency, authentication. Considering the former, let's suppose that the architect used the ADD method, which defines the below steps, and also used architectural patterns, tactics and technologies.

1. Confirm that information about requirements is sufficient.
2. Choose a system element to decompose.
3. Identify candidate architectural drivers.
4. Choose a design concept that satisfies the drivers.
5. Instantiate architectural elements and allocate responsibilities.
6. Define interfaces for the instantiated elements.
7. Verify and refine requirements and make them constraints for instantiated elements.

8.   Repeat these steps for the next element.

Table 4 shows three design iterations of how the design process can be performed when technologies are first-class design concepts in ADD.

Table 4. Three design iterations using technologies as first-class design concepts in ADD

	Drivers (ADD step 3)	Element to decompose (ADD step 2)	Design decisions (ADD step 4)
1	User requirements Constraints	The system as a whole	Layers pattern
2	QA1 - Performance QA3 – Security	Presentation layer Business logic layer	Increase resource efficiency performance tactic – Cloudfare Detect intrusion security tactic – Cloudfare Detect service denial security tactic - Cloudfare
3	QA2 - Availability		Monitor availability tactic - Zabbix Ping/Eco availability tactic - Zabbix

The first iteration was intended to decompose the entire system (ADD step 2) and the primary concern was to define the overall system structure and allocate responsibilities to elements that the development team could develop independently. The architect decided to create a layered system using the Layers Architecture Pattern; which is a n-tiered pattern where the components are organized in horizontal layers (Clements et al., 2011). Although the layered architecture pattern does not specify the number and types of layers that must exist in the pattern, most layered architectures consist of four standard layers: presentation, business, persistence, and database.

In iteration 2, the architect decided to use several design concepts—say tactics and technologies—to address performance and security quality attributes. The *increase resource efficiency* tactic suggests looking at the ways algorithms use a resource to process an event and optimizing them to reduce their processing time. The *detect intrusion* tactic suggests monitoring traffic coming into a system against known patterns of attacks. The *detect service denial* is a tactic for detecting a special type of attack in which the system become overwhelmed with a flood of unauthorized access attempts and cannot do anything else (Sangwan, 2014). Cloudfare[1] is a technology that implements all these tactics.

With regard to performance, Cloudfare can automatically determine which resources are static, such as HTML pages, javascript files, stylesheets, images, and videos, and help cache this content at the network edge, which improves website performance. In terms of security, Cloudfare can stop attacks directed at a website by providing security from malicious activity, including denial-of-service attacks, malicious bots, and other nefarious intrusions.

In iteration 3, the architect decided to use the following tactics and technologies to address the availability quality attribute. Zabbix[2] is a monitoring software tool for diverse IT components, including networks, servers, virtual machines, and cloud services. Zabbix provides monitoring metrics, among others network utilization, CPU load and disk space consumption. Zabbix implements the ping/echo and monitor security tactics. The *monitor* tactic uses a process that continuously monitors the status of different elements of the system (Sangwan, 2014). This tactic often uses the ping/echo tactic to periodically ping an element for its status and can receive an echo indicating it was operating normally (Sangwan, 2014).

In this example, design continues along other iterations, making design decisions ranging from selecting architecture patterns and tactics to implementation options provided by technologies.

Important Considerations

As reported (Cervantes, Velasco-Elizondo, & Kazman, 2013) this approach has been applied successfully to several projects at a large company in Mexico City that develops software for government and private customers. More recently, it has been applied for refactoring existing systems and developing new ones at the Secretary of Education of Zacatecas state. For example, the online system to apply for a place at a primary school, described above, was unable to consistently handle 12,000 users at once –which is the expected load in peak time, and exhibited security breaches last time that it was in production. Using this approach the architecture of the system was redesigned and its implementation ran without incidents in 2020.

The proposed approach has been observed to be more realistic in the sense that design activities produce architectures that can be executed—and therefore tested—before they are implemented. However, it is important to consider that technology selection cannot be arbitrary, as it depends on factors such as: the development team's level of knowledge of each technology, the technology type (i.e. commercial or open source), the technology's maturity and level of support from its community, etc.

AUTOMATING TECNOLOGY SELECTION

When software architects design software architectures, they make the decision to promote a set of architectural requirements and aim for an optimal choice in the necessary trade-offs for a particular context. Assuming that software architecture can be specified in a formal manner, and its design can be done systematically via realistic design methods, a basic research question arises: could it be possible to automate software architecture development at least to some degree? The automation of software architecture design would be beneficial not only for increasing the productivity of a software architect, but also in improving the quality of the resulting architectures.

This section presents a recent tool developed, which uses natural language processing and semantic web techniques to the problem of automating technology searches (Esparza, 2019).

WHAT TECHNOLOGY SELECTION REALLY INVOLVES

The process of developing an architecture design starts by considering architectural requirements. Architectural requirements include (Cervantes et al., 2016): (*i*) user requirements, (*ii*) quality and (*iii*) constraints. Among these requirements, quality attributes and constraints are those that shape the architecture the most significantly (Cervantes et al., 2016). The process of creating an architecture design then continues by linking architecturally significant requirements to design decisions; this involves the use of design concepts that satisfy requirements. An example might be using the broker architectural pattern as a design concept to satisfy a scalability quality attribute. Next, these design decisions should be systematically linked to the implementation alternatives through the use of specific technologies, for example, selecting RabbitMQ[3] to implement the broker architectural pattern.

Technology selection involves five main factors to consider: (*i*) deciding which technologies are available to realize the decisions made; (*ii*) determining whether the available tools to support this technology choice (e.g. IDEs, simulators, testing tools, and so on) are adequate for development to proceed; (*iii*) determining the extent of internal familiarity and external support available for the technology (e.g. courses, tutorials, examples and so on); (*iv*) determining the side effects of choosing a technology, such as a required coordination model or constrained resources; and (v) determining whether a new technology is compatible with the existing stack (Cervantes et al., 2013).

As a result, technology selection is a multicriteria decision-making problem. Furthermore, given the steadily growing number of technologies, deciding which options are available to implement the selected design decisions requires being aware of the range of existing. This can be particularly challenging for inexperienced software architects.

The problem of selecting a software technology can be defined in terms of two sub-problems as follows:

1. **Technology Search**: Finding technologies that allow the implementation of specific design decisions.
2. **Technology Selection**: Selecting a technology to use from among those available.

The following section elaborates on aspects of the first sub-problem: technology search.

EXISTING SUPPORT FOR TECHNOLOGY SEARCH

Table 5 compares a set of well-known tools to support technology search. This comparison is next briefly explained.

The "Repository" section describes the way in which the tools structure and maintain information about technology products in a repository. "Frequent Update" refers to the frequency of content updates. "Automatic filling" refers to whether the information for each technology is added manually or automatically. "Multiple sources" indicates whether the technology information is obtained from more than one source.

The "Query" section groups aspects related to the facility of formulating a query considering factors such as "Type of License", "Operating System Platform", "Name of the (Technology) Product", "Category", and "Compatible Technologies".

The "Results" section is about the aspects related to the query's results. The aspects are grouped into four categories. The first one, "Basic description" includes general information about the technology. The second category, "Third party links" refers to general information elements from third parties that complement the basic description. The third section, "Technical details", contains technical information elements. Finally, the "Quality attributes" section includes the quality attributes of the technology.

Three letters are used in Table 5 to describe the level of support for information in the sections previously described, namely S = supported; P = partially supported; - = non supported. It is therefore possible to state the following findings.

The support for formulating queries is limited. Most tools support queries based on the name of the technology and the category to which it belongs. The remainder of the factors are not well supported in the reviewed tools.

Table 5. Well-known tools to support technology search

Category	Attribute	Softonic	Softpedia	Wolfram Alpha	AlternativeTo	StackShare	G2 Crowd	StackOverflow	DBEngine
Quality Attributes	Security	-	-	-	-	-	S	-	-
Quality Attributes	Scalability	-	-	-	-	-	S	-	-
Quality Attributes	Availability	-	-	-	-	-	S	-	-
Quality Attributes	Usability	S	-	-	-	-	-	-	-
Quality Attributes	Performance	-	-	-	-	-	-	-	-
Results — Technical details	Features and design	-	-	-	-	-	-	S	S
Results — Technical details	APIs	-	-	-	-	-	-	S	S
Results — Technical details	Compatible technologies	-	-	-	-	-	-	S	S
Results — Technical details	Implementation languages	-	-	S	-	-	-	S	S
Results — Technical details	Platform	S	S	-	S	-	-	S	S
Results — Technical details	Size	S	S	-	-	-	-	-	-
Results — Technical details	Product's popularity charts	-	-	-	-	-	-	-	S
Results — Technical details	Score	S	S	-	S	S	S	S	S
Results — Technical details	Information's statistics	-	S	S	S	-	-	S	-
Results — Technical details	Code examples	-	-	-	-	-	-	P	-
Results — Technical details	GUI images	S	S	-	S	-	S	-	-
Results — Third party links	Integration with other platforms	-	-	-	-	S	-	-	-
Results — Third party links	User's comments	S	-	-	S	S	S	-	-
Results — Third party links	Recommendations of other products	S	S	-	S	S	S	S	-
Results — Third party links	Links to other resources	-	-	-	-	-	-	S	P
Results — Third party links	Use cases	-	-	-	-	-	-	P	P
Results — Basic description	Companies using the products	-	-	-	-	S	-	-	-
Results — Basic description	Version	S	S	-	-	-	-	S	S
Results — Basic description	Developer / Official page	S	S	S	S	S	S	S	S
Results — Basic description	License type / Price	S	S	S	S	-	S	S	S
Results — Basic description	Description	S	S	S	S	S	S	S	S
Query	Compatible technologies	-	-	-	-	-	-	-	-
Query	Categories / Subcategories	S	S	-	S	S	S	-	S
Query	Product's name	S	S	S	S	S	S	S	S
Query	Operative System Platform	S	S	S	S	-	-	-	-
Query	License type	S	S	S	-	-	-	-	-
Repository	Multiple sources	S	S	-	-	S	S	-	S
Repository	Automatic filling	S	-	P	-	P	-	-	-
Repository	Frequent updates	S	S	S	S	S	S	S	S

S = supported; P = partially supported; - = non supported;

29

Figure 3. A screenshot of the result of a query in NoSQLFinder

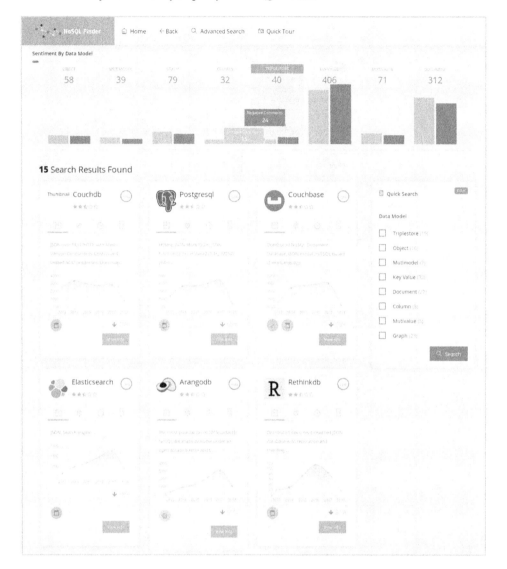

The resulting information is incomplete. Most of the tools cover all the requirements in the "Basic description" section. However, the necessary elements of the "Links to third parties" section are included in very few tools. With regards to the "Technical details" section, only two of the tools support most of the elements. Finally, information about quality attributes is limited.

NOSQLFINDER

NoSQLFinder is a functional prototype tool that helps architects to perform technology searches. NoSQLFinder uses information from various information sources, such as AlternativeTo, StackOverflow, DBpedia. Due to scope, in this prototype the focus was on supporting the search of NoSQL databases while taking into account many of the aspects described in Table 5. The design and implementation of NoSQLFinder involves the use of data extraction, linked data, semantic Web and sentiment analysis techniques. NoSQLFinder is reachable via http://dataalchemy.xyz

Figure 3 shows a screenshot of the result of a query in NoSQLFinder. Each technology is shown as a card containing the following information sections: general popularity, supported programming languages, feedback from other users about its performance, and popularity among sites frequently visited by developers like StackOverflow and Github, see Figure 4 a, b, c, and d respectively.

Figure 4. A screenshot of a database card in NoSQLFinder

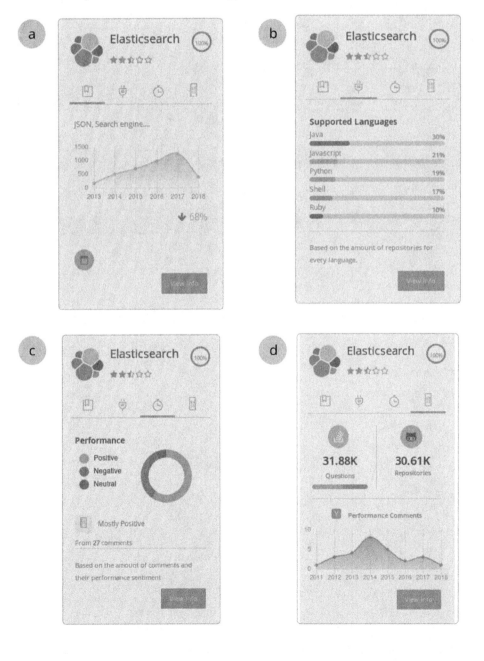

When a user selects a specific card, all the information about the corresponding database is displayed on a dashboard. The dashboard is organized into four sections that represent the categories of information elements in Table 5, namely "Basic description", "Third party links", "Technical details", "Quality attributes". Figure 5 shows a screenshot of part of this dashboard.

Figure 5. A screenshot of part of the dashboard with information for a database in NoSQLFinder

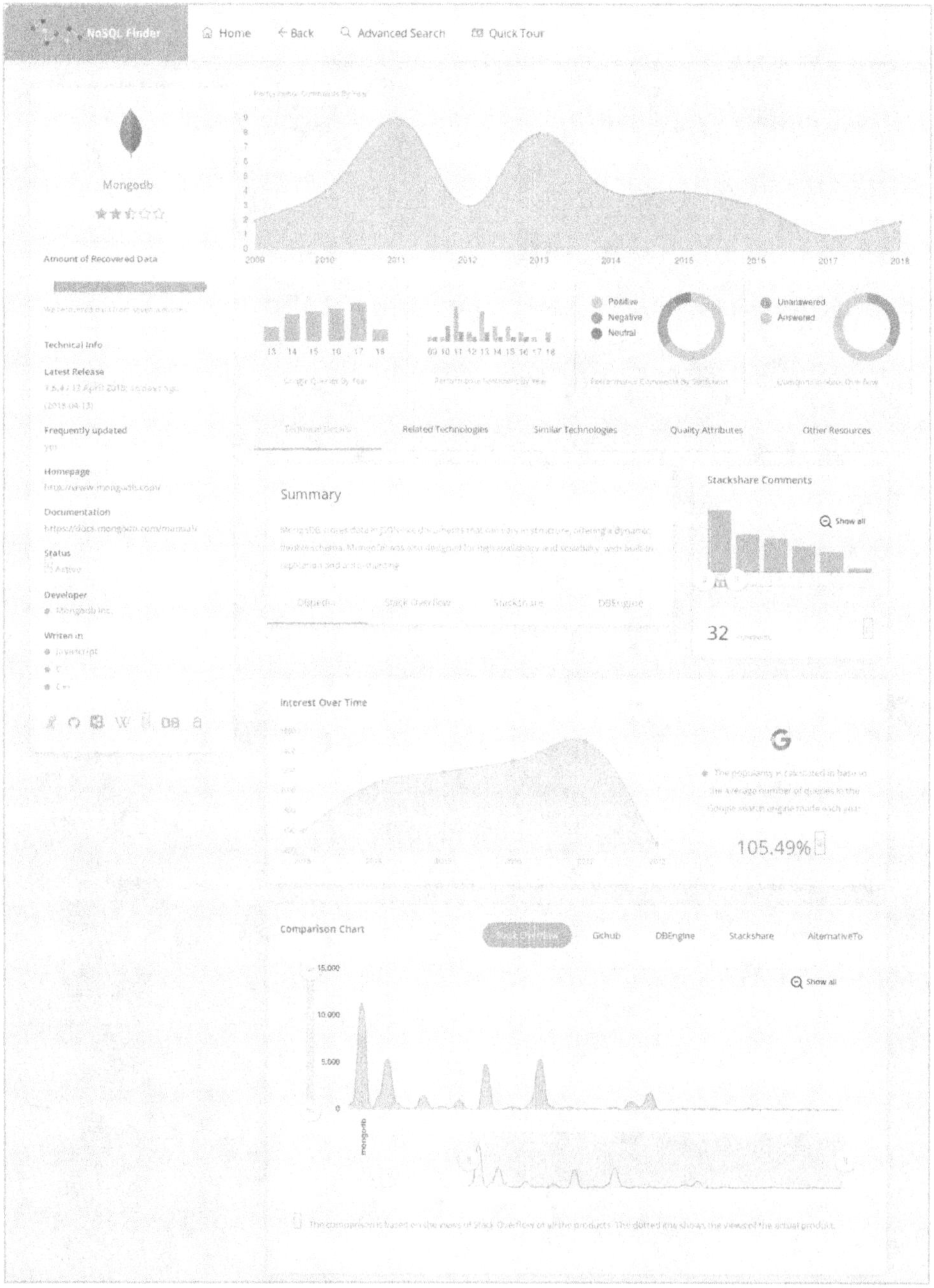

FUTURE WORK

The design and implementation of NoSQLFinder has been a great learning experience. Firstly, it was an opportunity to learn various semantic Web techniques for collecting and integrating data. Secondly, various sentiment analysis techniques in order to determine and measure the degree of user satisfaction with respect to a quality attribute from text in natural language, were learned.

We plan to generate a more robust version of the tool for searching technologies. To this end, it was planned to explore the following lines of future work: support for more quality attributes, the use of machine-learning techniques to better evaluate what people say about technologies' quality attribute, and the inclusion of other types of technologies besides NoSQL databases.

SOFTWARE ARCHITECTURE EDUCATION

Software architecture development requires not only deep technical experience, but also understanding of the body of knowledge concerning software architecture, as expressed in terms of design concepts and software architecture development methods. Mastering software architecture development requires combining both experience and knowledge to ensure high quality outcomes when developing architecture.

This section describes two educational projects created to promote software architecture knowledge and experiences.

Summer School on Software Engineering

Dr. Velasco-Elizondo is an experienced teacher. Since 2012, the she has taught software architecture to students in under- and post-graduate programs in Software Engineering and has contributed to the definition of software architecture courses in these academic programs. Dr. Velasco-Elizondo put this experience to further use in 2012, when she founded one of the few Summer Schools on Software Engineering in Mexico, which she still run each summer. In each edition of the Summer School the topic of software architecture has been present in some form.

In the Summer Schools on Software Engineering, participating students represent private and public institutions located in various states of Mexico. Attendees have lauded the School as "an excellent forum to learn exciting topics that are related to way software systems are designed and implemented". They also welcomed the opportunity to "meet with colleagues and share experiences".

In the 2019 edition of the School three courses were offered: An introduction to NOSQL databases, Agile Techniques for Risks Management and Colored Backlogs with Scrum. Scrum is an agile project management framework that can be used for software development projects with the goal of incrementally delivering a software product by supplying working requirements every 2-4 weeks. In Scrum, a backlog is a list of tasks and/or requirements that need to be completed. In the third course it was learned and practiced a technique for ensuring that architectural requirements get addressed and prioritized applying the concept of color in a Scrum backlog as follows:

- Green – functional user requirements.
- Yellow – Architectural infrastructure to support the quality requirements.
- Red – Defects that are identified and need to be addressed.

- Black – Technical debt that builds up as the product is built and key decisions are deferred or poor work done. Technical debt is a term in software development that reflects the implied cost of additional rework caused by choosing a fast and dirty solution instead of using a better approach that would take longer.

Colored Backlogs is a technique proposed by Dr. Philippe Kruchten.

Software Architecture Book

Within the context of Software Engineering, the development of software architecture deals with structuring a software system to satisfy architectural requirements, namely, user functional requirements, quality attributes and constraints. This technological moment requires people to interact with many software systems that increasingly have more complex quality attribute requirements such as performance and availability. This increasing complexity is why software architecture development is an important topic.

Taking into account their experience as specialized teachers of Software Engineering, as well as the years of collaboration and consulting with the software development industry, Dr. Velasco-Elizondo and their colleagues identified the lack of an introductory book of software architecture in Spanish. They therefore decided to write this book, which is titled "Software Arquitectura: Conceptos y Ciclo de Desarrollo", published in 2015 (Cervantes, Velasco-Elizondo & Castro, 2016).

The book places an important emphasis on software architecture foundations but also provides practical examples that allow these foundations to be related to real practice. Practitioners, and master and undergraduate students interested in design and development of software systems are the main prospective readers of this book. The book has seven chapters, covering the following topics.

Chapter 1 presents the introduction to the topic of software architecture by introducing the basic concepts and the notion of a software architecture development lifecycle defining these stages: requirements, design, documentation, and evaluation.

Chapter 2 discusses the requirements stage. To provide an initial context, the term "requirement" as used in the field of Software Engineering is described. Then the focus is on the specific aspects of the requirements stage, including fundamental concepts, activities, and a review of well-known methods to systematically perform the activities necessary to this stage.

Chapter 3 is about the design stage. This chapter begins by describing the concept and levels of design in general and then lays out the architecture design process. Next is a discussion of the design principles and concepts that are used as part of the architecture design process. A review of some well-known methods to design architectures is then presented.

Chapter 4 explores the documentation stage, initially establishing the importance of documenting software architectures. There is a particular focus on how to create documentation to effectively communicate a software architecture design to different stakeholders. Initially, the meaning of sufficient documentation is discussed in a general way, followed by an exploration of what this concept means in software architecture and why documentation is important. Relevant concepts, notations, as well as methods that can be used to support activities at this stage are also included. The chapter concludes with a list of useful recommendations for generating good quality architectural documentation.

Chapter 5 is about the evaluation stage. Once a software architecture is designed and documented, it is possible to start constructing the system. However, before doing so, it is vital to ensure that the software architecture is correct and satisfies the architectural requirements. Evaluating software architectures enables the detection of breaches and risks, which can otherwise cause of delays or serious problems when implementing software architectures. This chapter begins by discussing the concept of evaluation in general terms, and then the moves to what this means for software architectures. The chapter also includes the description of some relevant methods used to evaluate software architectures.

Chapter 6 discusses the influence of software architecture in the implementation of a software system. The work of the architect is often considered to be finished when an architecture design has been defined, evaluated, and satisfactorily meets the architectural requirements. However, the lack of follow-up during the implementation of the system is often the cause when the architecture's design is not properly implemented.

Chapter 7 describes how to perform the stages of the software architecture development lifecycle in projects that use agile methods. Within the context of Software Engineering, agile methods are a set of widely used lightweight methods currently used to support systems development relying on self-organizing, interdisciplinary, and highly flexible teams. In this chapter the content is described around Scrum, a very popular agile method today.

Importantly, the topics in each chapter are explained via a case study, which is included in full as an appendix of the book. Furthermore, the book provides a set of questions and as well as references to other information sources so that readers can reinforce and build on their knowledge of the material presented in this book.

Hands on

Since 2008 Dr. Velasco-Elizondo has had the chance to work, as a coach, with practicing software architects and developers helping them to deploy software architecture practices and methods. Dr. Velasco-Elizondo strongly believes in lean and agile principles and she had also being able to apply them within the context of software architecture design.

In this section some of these experiences are described.

SmartFlow MVP

Internet of Things (IoT) is the technology enabling the communication of a variety of devices via the Internet in order to exchange data. IoT is composed of network of sensors, actuators, and devices that allow the development of new systems and services to monitor and control process or services. Dr. Velasco-Elizondo had the opportunity to contribute to the design and implementation of a minimum viable product (MVP) of a system of this kind for the mining industry domain. Specifically, she served as the Scrum Master of the Scrum Team developing the SmartFlow MVP. A minimum viable product (MVP) is a version of a product with just enough features to satisfy early customers and provide feedback for future product development.

SmartFlow MVP was a system that used RFID tags to support real-time exchange of data with a series of RFID readers through radio waves. RFID tags are a type of tracking devices that use smart barcodes in order to identify items. RFID is short for radio frequency identification. Any entity of interest circulating in a mine tunnel, i.e. miner, vehicle, had a RFID tag attached. An RFID transmitted its location and other relevant data to RFID readers. RFID readers sent the received data to a software system that processed and displayed it for different applications, i.e. access control, collision control, and evacuation control.

The use of Scrum for the development of the SmartFlow MVP was favored. Considering the agile nature of Scrum, it was considered that the Scrum Team were much more likely to get the MVP shipped on time and on budget. In this project Dr. Velasco-Elizondo and the team had the opportunity to deploy a set of practices to make agile architecting feasible. The following practices were integrated in a customized version of Scrum for this project: (1) visualizing requirements using the colored backlog technique (2) developing an architectural spike in a Sprint 0 (3) visualizing technical debt using the colored backlog techniques and (4) keeping the architecture documentation updated. An architecture spike is an experiment to reduce risk and to improve the technical understanding of the system to build and the technology choices to build it.

Visualizing architectural requirements using a colored backlog allowed the Scrum Team to better plan its releases and be aware of architectural requirements. Developing an architectural spike helped the Scrum Team to early determine whether the defined architecture was proper to support the architectural requirements; particularly quality attributes. Visualizing technical debt using a colored backlog helped the Scrum Team not only to be aware of it, but also to prioritize it in sprint planning just like normal requirements. Finally, as Simon Brown advises the focus was given to describing in the architecture documentation only the aspects that Scrum Team could not get from the code (Brown, 2014).

Refactoring an School Enrollment System

Working as a Principal Technical Assistant at the Secretary of Education of Zacatecas state, has giving Dr. Velasco-Elizondo the chance to contribute in the refactoring work a development team performed to pay technical debt of a school enrollment system. Parents and tutors to apply for a place at a primary school in Zacatecas state using this system.

In short, refactoring is a technical term in Software Engineering to refer of the activity of modifying the internal structure of code of a system without changing its behavior. Refactoring is important to maintain the long-term quality of a system code. If there is technical debt and developers do not perform some refactoring on a regular basis, technical debt will creep into the system. In this project it was made sure to have good reasons for doing it. In this case id was necessary to improve performance, scalability, security and test coverage. These quality requirements were understood as architectural and therefore, it leads to the process to select design concepts to realize them; and then select technologies to implement them.

Besides following a systematic and quality attribute driven approach to refactoring and learning new technologies, another good thing this project generated was the design and delivering of a course that helped the development team "to link theory to practice". That is, to better understand the undelaying design decisions and design concepts and the technology choices to implement them.

CONCLUSION

It is common to hear discussions of academic–practitioner relationships that focus on the gap between academics and practitioners, between rigor and applicability, between theory and practice or similar terms. The gap between academics and practitioners has been of concern for decades. For these reasons Dr. Velasco-Elizondo is very satisfied with the opportunities a have taken to develop what she wants to become: a software architecture academic-practitioner. Thus, in this chapter the author has described some significant research, education and coaching activities the author has performed during her professional career to develop knowledge, skills and experiences related to this desire.

Often researchers tend think that they already have enough to do with our research. In her experience, "working outside an office" helps not only to develop business awareness but also to strengthen soft skills, networking, self-awareness, and practical ways to apply research and demonstrate its potential impact. The connected world of today means that software is everywhere; thus, software architecture design is everywhere too. How can a software architect come up with the simplest possible design to make sure a software system fits into the long-term goals? Well, it demands a potent blend of thoughtful design with constant experimentation. This is exactly how people learn to tackle complexity and therefore, everything else in life.

Dr. Velasco-Elizondo hopes the material communicated in this chapter will inspire readers, specifically female readers. Do you know that women did very first jobs in Software Engineering history? Ada Lovelace was the first computer programmer in history. Grace Hopper developed the first computer compiler and made programming easier for all of us. Margaret Hamilton developed the on-board flight software for the lunar lander of the Apollo 11 mission. How, then, did was developed the myth that girls do not belong in Software Engineering? Although the effort to involve women in these fields has been rising in recent years, stereotypes still exist and are preventing women to have equal opportunities to access to education and work in STEM. These stereotypes are flat wrong. It does not make sense to think that talent, ideas, efforts should be wasted simply because they come from a woman, rather than a man. In most software development projects, different decisions are taken. (Bhat et al., 2020) provides a getting-started guide for prospective researchers who are entering the investigation phase of research on architectural decision-making.

Keep always an unfulfilled desire that is waiting to be fulfilled, when one is not hungry enough, one never will find the motivation to do anything. Never be satisfied, be curious to learn more and more. Be willing to keep trying the things people say cannot be done. In other words, and as many important people have said, Dr. Velasco-Elizondo encourages you to "stay hungry, stay foolish".

REFERENCES

Arellanes, D., & Lau, K. K. (2019). Workflow Variability for Autonomic IoT Systems. In *Proceedings of the International Conference on Autonomic Computing*, (pp. 24-30). Umea, Sweden: IEEE.

Barbacci, M., Ellison, R. J., Lattanze, A. J., Stafford, J. A., Weinstock, C. B., & Wood, W. G. (2003). *Quality Attribute Workshops (QAWs), Third Edition.* Technical Report CMU/SEI-2003-TR-016, Software Engineering Institute, Carnegie Mellon University.

Bass, L., Clements, P. C., & Kazman, R. (2012). *Software Architecture in Practice.* Addison-Wesley Professional.

Bhat, M., Shumaiev, K., Hohenstein, U., Biesdorf, A., & Matthes, F. (2020). The Evolution of Architectural Decision Making as a Key Focus Area of Software Architecture Research: A Semi-Systematic Literature Study. In *Proceedings of the IEEE International Conference on Software Architecture*, (pp. 69-80). IEEE.

Brown, S. (2014). *Software Architecture for Developers - Technical leadership by coding, coaching, collaboration, architecture sketching and just enough up front design*. Leanpub.

Buschmann, F., Meunier, R., Rohnert, H., Sommerlad, P., & Stal, M. (1996). *Pattern-Oriented Software Architecture Volume 1: A System of Patterns*. Wiley Publishing.

Cervantes, H., & Kazman, R. (2016). *Designing Software Architectures: A Practical Approach*. Addison-Wesley Professional.

Cervantes, H., Velasco-Elizondo, P., & Castro, L. (2016). *Arquitectura de software: conceptos y ciclo de desarrollo*. Cengage Learning.

Cervantes, H., Velasco-Elizondo, P., & Kazman, R. (2013). A Principled Way to Use Frameworks in Architecture Design. *IEEE Software, 30*(2), 46–53. doi:10.1109/MS.2012.175

Clements, P., Bachmann, F., Bass, L., Garlan, D., Ivers, J., Reed, L., & Nord, R. (2011). *Documenting Software Architectures: Views and Beyond*. Addison-Wesley Professional.

Clements, P., Kazman, R., & Klein, M. (2002). *Evaluating Software Architectures: Methods and Case Studies*. Addison-Wesley Professional.

Clements, P., Kazman, R., & Klein, M. (2008). *Evaluating Software Architectures Methods and Case Studies*. Addison-Wesley.

de Silva, L., & Balasubramaniam, D. (2012). Controlling software architecture erosion: A survey. *Journal of Systems and Software, 85*(1), 132–151. doi:10.1016/j.jss.2011.07.036

Di Cola, S., Lau, K.-K., Tran, C., & Qian, C. (2015). An MDE tool for defining software product families with explicit variation points. In *Proceedings of the International Conference on Software Product Line*, (pp. 355–360). New York, NY: Association for Computing Machinery. 10.1145/2791060.2791090

Esparza, M. (2019). *NoSQLFinder: un buscador de bases de datos NoSQL basado en técnicas de web semántica y análisis de sentimientos* (BSc Thesis).

Hofmeister, C., Kruchten, P. B., Nord, R., Obbink, H., Ran, A., & America, P. (2007). A general model of software architecture design derived from five industrial approaches. *Journal of Systems and Software, 80*(1), 106–126. doi:10.1016/j.jss.2006.05.024

Kazman, R., Abowd, G., Bass, L., & Clements, P. (1996). Scenario-Based Analysis of Software Architecture. *IEEE Software, 13*(6), 47–55. doi:10.1109/52.542294

Kroll, P., Kruchten, P. B., & Booch, G. (2003). The rational unified process made easy. Addison-Wesley Professional.

Kruchten, P. B. (1995). The 4+1 View Model of Architecture. *IEEE Software, 6*(12), 42–50. doi:10.1109/52.469759

Lattanze, A. J. (2009). *Architecting Software Intensive Systems: A practitioners guide*. CRC Press.

Lau, K., & Wang, Z. (2007). Software Component Models. *IEEE Transactions on Software Engineering, 33*(10), 709–724. doi:10.1109/TSE.2007.70726

Mohagheghi, P., & Conradi, R. (2007). Quality, productivity and economic benefits of software reuse: A review of industrial studies. *Empirical Software Engineering*, *12*(5), 471–516. doi:10.100710664-007-9040-x

Perry, D. E., & Wolf, A. L. (1992). Foundations for the study of software architecture. *SIGSOFT Software Engineering Notes*, *17*(4), 40–52. doi:10.1145/141874.141884

Rajkumar, R., Lee, I., Sha, L., & Stankovic, J. (2010). Cyber-physical systems: the next computing revolution. In *Proceedings of the design automation conference*, (pp 731–736). IEEE.

Rehman, I., Mirakhorli, M., Nagappan, M., Uulu, A. A., & Thornton, M. (2018). Roles and impacts of hands-on software architects in five industrial case studies. In *Proceedings of International Conference on Software Engineering*, (pp 117–127). Association for Computing Machinery. 10.1145/3180155.3180234

Sangwan, R. S. (2014). *Software and Systems Architecture in Action*. Auerbach Publications. doi:10.1201/b17575

Shahbazian, A., Lee, Y. K., Brun, Y., & Medvidovic, N. (2018). Making well-informed software design decisions. In *Proceedings of the 40th International Conference on Software Engineering*, (pp. 262–263). Association for Computing Machinery. 10.1145/3183440.3194961

Shaw, M., & Garlan, D. (1996). *Software Architecture: Perspectives on an Emerging Discipline*. Prentice Hall.

Sobrevilla, G., Hernández, J., Velasco-Elizondo, P., & Soriano, S. (2017). Aplicando Scrum y Prácticas de Ingeniería de Software para la Mejora Continua del Desarrollo de un Sistema Ciber-Físico. *ReCIBE*, *6*(1), 1–15.

Sommerville, I. (2011). *Software engineering*. Pearson.

Tang, A., Tran, M. H., Han, J., & Vliet, H. V. (2008). Design Reasoning Improves Software Design Quality. In S. Becker, F. Plasil, & R. Reussner (Eds.), Lecture Notes in Computer Science: Vol. 5281. *Quality of Software Architectures, Models and Architectures* (pp. 28–42). Springer. doi:10.1007/978-3-540-87879-7_2

Velasco-Elizondo, P., & Lau, K. (2010). A catalogue of component connectors to support development with reuse. *Journal of Systems and Software*, *83*(7), 1165–1178. doi:10.1016/j.jss.2010.01.008

ENDNOTES

[1] See https://www.cloudflare.com/
[2] See https://www.zabbix.com/
[3] See https://www.rabbitmq.com/

This research was previously published in Latin American Women and Research Contributions to the IT Field; pages 217-239, copyright year 2021 by Engineering Science Reference (an imprint of IGI Global).

Chapter 3
Disciplined Teams vs. Agile Teams:
Differences and Similarities in Software Development

Antonio Alexandre Moura Costa
Federal Institute of Paraiba, Brazil

Felipe Barbosa Araújo Ramos
 https://orcid.org/0000-0002-0937-811X
Federal Institute of Paraiba, Brazil

Dalton Cézane Gomes Valadares
*Federal University of Campina Grande, Brazil &
Federal Institute of Pernambuco, Brazil*

Danyllo Wagner Albuquerque
Federal University of Campina Grande, Brazil

Emanuel Dantas Filho
Federal University of Campina Grande, Brazil

Alexandre Braga Gomes
Federal University of Campina Grande, Brazil

Mirko Barbosa Perkusich
VIRTUS, Brazil

Hyggo Oliveira de Almeida
Federal University of Campina Grande, Brazil

ABSTRACT

Software development has been considered a socio-technical activity over the past decades. Particularly, in the case of software engineering, the necessity to communicate effectively with stakeholders and team members has been progressively emphasized. Human resources play a critical role in the success of software projects. Many techniques, methods, tools, models, and methodologies have been proposed, applied, and improved in order to help and ease the management of the software development process. Regardless of the software development methodology adopted, delivering a quality product in a predictable, efficient, and responsive manner is the objective for every team. Disciplined and Agile teams have different characteristics, but also share common aspects when working to accomplish their goals. The main motivation of this chapter is to present the differences and similarities of both teams in the context of software development.

DOI: 10.4018/978-1-6684-3702-5.ch003

INTRODUCTION

Delivering high-quality products in time and without budget overrun is still a significant struggle for most software organizations. Among the most common reasons are inaccurate estimates of needed resources, unmanaged risks, sloppy development practices, poor project management, commercial pressures, among others (Charette, 2005; Macnab & Doctolero, 2019). Software projects failures have a major negative impact on the organizations and can deeply compromise its future.

Projects continue to proliferate in society today, in both the public and private sectors of the economy. Investments in projects number in the trillions of dollars annually. Just as ubiquitous as these projects, unfortunately, are their significant failure rates. The CHAOS reports have identified the current state of project success rates across organizations, noting that in spite of much higher visibility and importance placed on project performance, failure rates have remained high and relatively stable across over a decade of research. (Serrador & Pinto, 2015)

When a software project fails, it jeopardizes an organization's prospects. If the failure is large enough, it can steal the company's entire future. In one stellar meltdown, a poorly implemented resource planning system led FoxMeyer Drug Co., a $5 billion wholesale drug distribution company in Carrollton, Texas, to plummet into bankruptcy in 1996. (Charette, 2005)

For a long time, Disciplined approaches had been used to increase project success. These approaches, also known as plan-driven or heavyweight methodologies, are conducted in a linear way, whereas process activities of specification, development, validation, and evolution must be performed in sequential order, which means that an activity must be completed before the next one begins. Due to the heavy aspect of the Disciplined approaches, several consultants have developed methodologies and practices with more emphasis on people, collaboration, customer interaction, and working software, rather than on processes, tools, documentation, and plans. These approaches, known as Agile methods, have been gained popularity over the past years, especially after the advent of the Agile Manifesto in 2001 (Fowler & Highsmith, 2001). Unlike Discipline approaches such as the Waterfall model, the Agile ones promote continuous iteration of development and testing throughout the software development lifecycle.

Agile methods are based on adaptive software development, while Disciplined approaches are derived from the predictive approach. Disciplined teams work with a detailed plan and have a complete list of requirements that must be implemented in the next months or in the entire lifecycle of the product. Predictive approaches entirely depend on the requirement analysis and detailed planning at the beginning of the cycle. Any change must go through a rigorous change control management and prioritization. In adaptive methods, there is no extensive planning and only clear tasks are related to the features that must be developed. Agile teams are more adaptable to dynamic changes in product requirements. Communication and minimal documentation represent ordinary characteristics of agile software development. Also, customer interaction is another strong suit for these approaches. While Agile methods are indicated for small and medium projects, disciplined approaches are more suitable to the large ones.

Once Disciplined and Agile approaches are highlighted by different aspects, their teams also have different characteristics regarding size, roles, planning, executions, and others. For instance, Disciplined teams are composed of dozens of professionals, not necessarily co-located, usually divided into teams of specialists. For example, the project may have a programmer team, a quality assurance team, and a design team. Each of them focusing on specific phases and goals. As mention before, these kinds of projects are focused on processes and tools, thus their teams are document-driven and less flexible to change. In contrast, Agile teams are smaller, usually three to nine people, and preferably co-located. Agile projects prioritize communication over documentation; therefore, teams are more collaborative and work together on features to delivering value to the customer. Agile teams are cross-functional which means that the team must have all competencies required to fulfill the work without depending on others not part of the team. Despite the differences, these Disciplined and Agile teams present similarities under several points. Both teams work to deliver a quality product in a predictable, efficient, and responsive manner.

Human resources represent a fundamental asset in the software development cycle. They are directly involved in all process activities and can contribute to both success or failure of the company and its projects. Human resource allocation in software development is a unique challenge due to the specific characteristics of software projects and their teams. Therefore, the desired team profiles may vary depending on the development methodology adopted in the software project.

Many investigations recognize that human resources play a critical role in software project success or failure. However, people continue to be the least formalized factor in process modeling, which tends to focus more on the technical side. Defective people assignment and problems among project team members have been identified as two of the main human factor-related issues affecting software project success. (André et al., 2011)

This chapter addresses the topic of software development teams in the context of Disciplined and Agile approaches. The main idea is to present the differences and similarities of both teams in the software development lifecycle.

Background

In this section, the authors describe the basic principles of Disciplined and Agile approaches, including common practices and methods of both software development methodologies.

Discipline is the foundation for any successful endeavor. Athletes train, musicians practice, craftsmen perfect techniques, and engineers apply processes. Without these basic skills, there may be an occasional success using natural talent, but professional consistency and long term prospects are limited. The strength and comfort which come from discipline support the endeavor when things are difficult, when the body or mind is under the weather, or when something new or unexpected arises and a response is required. Discipline creates well-organized memories, history, and experience. (Boehm & Turner, 2004)

Traditional software development comprises Disciplined approaches such as the Waterfall model (Petersen et al, 2009), V-Model (Mathur & Malik, 2010), and Rational Unified Process (RUP) (Kruchten, 2004). They demand the definition and documentation of a set of requirements at the initial stage of a project. According to Sommerville (2015), there are four phases that belong to traditional software development.

- Software specification: the objective is to capture and understand a complete description of how the system is expected to perform.

- Software design and implementation: this phase represents the process of transforming a system specification into an executable system.
- Software validation: the objective is to show that the system follows its specification and that it meets the desires of the customer.
- Software evolution: this phase includes the initial development of the system and its maintenance and updates.

Disciplined approaches depend on a set of pre-established processes and documentation which is written as the work evolves and guides further development. In Disciplined projects, success relies on knowing all the requirements before the development begins. Consequently, this also means that implementing changes during the development lifecycle can be quite problematic. On the other hand, it is easier to estimate the costs of the project, set a schedule, and allocate resources accordingly (Leau et al., 2012).

The Waterfall is one of the most popular methods of traditional software development. It has been used worldwide since the 1950s when it was presented by Herbert D. Benington at the Symposium on Advanced Programming Methods for Digital Computers. During the years of its use, the model became the golden standard of this industry. This approach is based on three main principles: low customer involvement, strong documentation, and sequential structure of projects. One of the main advantages of the Waterfall model is that it does not allow overlapping phases. The phases are linear which means that the next phase only starts after the previous one is completed. This reduces the chance of having model application failures during the project. It is worthy to mention that, all phases are equally important. If at least one of them is not correctly followed, the whole structure can be compromised. Each phase is well defined and makes it clear to understand what needs to be done to get through it.

Regarding the disadvantages of this model, some practitioners argue that it is very inflexible, the Waterfall leaves almost no room for unexpected changes or revisions. Moreover, no working software is produced until late during the development lifecycle, i.e. the customer only accesses the features when the phases are already well advanced, almost at the end of the project. There is no mandatory feedback between phases, and it is not possible simply to go back to correct possible mistakes. Once an application is in the testing phase, it is very difficult to go back and change something that was not well defined in the design phase. Another disadvantage is that when the model is executed by a team, not all members may keep pace. In this case, it is necessary to wait for everyone to align their progress and then advance.

Agile methods emerged as a reaction to traditional software development, with the goal of reducing the overhead inherent in disciplined approaches and trying to meet market demand for more productivity, flexibility, and shorter deadlines (Tam et al., 2020; Dhir et al., 2019; Girma et al., 2019).

In Agile approach to software development, work is carried out in small phases, based on collaboration, adaptive planning, early delivery, continuous improvement, regular customer feedback, frequent redesign resulting into development of software increments being delivered in successive iterations in response to the everchanging customer requirements. Agile methodologies are increasingly being adopted by companies worldwide to meet increased software complexity and evolving user demands. (Matharu et al., 2015)

Agile software development is a simpler and more efficient way to build software that seeks to maximize customer satisfaction, focusing on the results and collaboration of all stakeholders. This process gained notoriety in 2001 based on the precepts of the Agile Manifesto, which was developed by several experienced professionals of the software industry, according to the following values:

- Individuals and interactions more than processes and tools;
- Working software more than comprehensive documentation;
- Collaboration with the customer rather than contract negotiation;
- Responses to change more than following a plan.

Among the most common Agile approaches are Kanban (Ahmad et al., 2018), Extreme Programming (XP) (Hameed, 2016), and Scrum (Permana, 2015). The latter is a framework created by Ken Schwaber and Jeff Sutherland (Schwaber & Sutherland, 2017) in the early 1990s to maintain and develop complex products. Scrum is used to potentialize the teamwork and to control product evolution effectively, always keeping in mind quality and deadlines. It encompasses a set of values, principles, and practices that provide the basis for an iterative and incremental process for project management and agile development. Also, this framework is an alternative to optimizing and organizing the development team. By structuring the demands and stages of the project, allow us to improve performance and deliver better results quickly and in an organized manner.

Scrum includes scheduled activity cycles, the Sprints, task planning and specific start, and end dates. The duration of each sprint can vary, but they are often short, which explains the agile denomination. During the sprint, there is a daily meeting called the daily scrum to ensure that everyone involved in the project is aware of the previous day's activities. This meeting aims to identify impediments and problems that team members may be suffering. Unlike the Waterfall model, Scrum's process is flexible and can be very adaptable to work with other approaches. Having a good Scrum team is crucial in determining how to implement the business strategy, which directly contributes to the success or failure of the initiative.

Scrum includes several artifacts, usually textual or graphic elements, which are used to provide transparency and opportunities for inspection and adaptation. The main artifacts are Product Backlog, Sprint Backlog, and Increment. The Product Backlog is an ordered list of the requirements to be developed in order to satisfy customer needs. The Sprint Backlog represents a set of Backlog items that must be delivered in the final of a Sprint. During Sprint Planning these items are broken down into technical tasks to be implemented during the Sprint. The Increment represents the sum of all Backlog Items developed in a specific Sprint. It is worthy to mention that there are other artifacts that are commonly used by Scrum teams such as Burndown Chart, Task Board, and User Stories.

Scrum is an agile team-centered methodology in which its members work collaboratively to achieve a common goal. The framework promotes effective interaction between team members, allowing them to focus on delivering business value. The Scrum Team is comprised of three key roles:

- The Product Owner (PO) is the person responsible for bridging the gap between the business area and the Development Team. The PO is a key part of an agile project, as it is responsible for designing, managing, and maintaining the Product Backlog, i.e. he decides which features will be implemented and in which order they should be done.
- The Development Team which is responsible for turning Backlog Items into potentially usable software increment. According to the Scrum Guide, the Development Team should consist of 3 to 9 members, regardless of the PO and Scrum Master.

- The Scrum Master acts as a facilitator and enhancer of teamwork. He is responsible for ensuring that the team respects and follows Scrum's values and practices. In addition, it is his job to remove any and all impediments that may interfere with the team's goal.

Disciplined and Agile approaches have aspects that help their followers to achieved specifics objectives. Table 1 summarizes the mains characteristics of each approach.

Table 1. Comparison of the characteristics of Disciplined and Agile approaches

Characteristic	Disciplined approaches	Agile approaches
Customer involvement	Requirement and delivery phases	Throughout project
Documentation	Extensive	Minimal
Focus	Process	People
Project Scale	Large	Small and medium
Requirements	Defined at the beginning of the project	Interactive input
Structure	Linear	Iterative
Testing	Completed at the end of the development cycle	Throughout the project

HUMAN RESOURCES IN SOFTWARE DEVELOPMENT

The main assets of any organization are its human resources (intellectual capital) (Hilorme et al., 2019; Macke & Genari, 2019). Therefore, organizations need to understand that cultivate people means building a successful path, since these resources are the ones responsible for conducting all the operations of the company. A successful business depends on the individual and collective triumph of its employees, which is a concrete representation of the return on investment that is made in hiring. The corporate environment requires companies and their employees to being in constant improvement. Nowadays, the reality of the market demands a high degree of dynamism, which increases the need for transformation and adaptation.

Software development has been considered a socio-technical endeavor for some time. Particularly in the case of software engineering, the need to communicate effectively with users and team members has been increasingly emphasized. Software is a by-product of human activities, such as problem-solving capabilities, cognitive aspects, and social interaction. Human beings, however, are more complicated and less predictable than computers. Therefore, the complexity of human personality gives rise to intricate dynamics in software development, ones that cannot be ignored but which have often been overlooked. (Ahmed et al., 2015)

Given the above, it is clear that software development is a human-centered activity and the people factor has a great impact on the process and its performance. In order to meet the requirements of the globalized market, companies seek to optimize their processes by balancing cost, time, and quality. To achieve this goal effectively and efficiently, the project managers need to understand the constituent elements of their processes, which are identified as procedures, technologies, and people.

Project managers can assist their organizations to improve the way the projects are implemented by reducing risks. However, this requires much more than just recognizing organizational priorities. It is necessary to have a deeper understanding of how each software development methodology can create the greatest positive impact, and at the same time, how each of these methodologies can make it unlikely that the project will be successful in the organization. Consequently, choosing the proper software development methodology, according to the project needs is the first step to success. Thereafter, it is necessary to choose the most appropriate team which must be composed of members who possess characteristics that match the software development methodology adopted.

Differences Between Disciplined and Agile Teams

In this subsection the authors present the differences between Disciplined and Agile Approaches, focusing on three main characteristics: team sizes and the roles played by their member; the customer involvement during the project execution, and how the teams participate in the planning and execution of the project.

Team Sizes and Roles

Different software development methodologies have different structures of teams. Some of these teams are quite large, others are small. Furthermore, the typical roles of their members also differ. Disciplined teams are usually composed of dozens of professionals performing several roles such as analysts, designers, testers, developers, managers, and others. For instance, the structure of Waterfall teams includes four roles: a developer, a tester, a business analyst, and a project manager. Each member is responsible for a specific part of the work and some of them act only at particular phases of the project. The overall amount of work is subdivided between the members at the beginning of the phase. After the conclusion of the design phase, every Waterfall team member knows exactly what he or she should do at the next stages of project execution. Unlike Agile teams, the Disciplined ones do not comprise the customers or their representatives, and their members are not interchangeable. Moreover, a project manager is one true leader, i.e. he or she is the principal person, responsible for the success of the project.

Agile teams are significatively smaller than the disciplined ones. They are generally composed of less than ten people, however, there is no consensus on the optimal Agile team size. Agile experts argue that smaller teams tend to be more focused, organized, transparent, and productive. For instance, communication skills are very important in Agile teams. If a team is composed of five people, there will be ten different combinations of team members interacting with another team member. Agile teams need to have strong relationships between each of the team members to achieve high performance. Therefore, each new member adds some individual level of productivity to the team. On the other hand, each new person also raises the communication overhead. Therefore, as the team size grows, the communication costs to manage those relationships increases.

Regarding the roles, Agile teams are cross-functional which means that their members are individuals with different functional and domain expertise. Each developer is a tester and an analyst at the same time. Additionally, there are no formal leaders, because they are self-organized. Potential project issues are figured out through communication between team members.

Customer Involvement

In disciplined approaches such as Waterfall, the customers negotiate the requirements of the product before any development activity starts, i.e., they do not participate in the project execution. There are two meetings the customers take part in: the initial stage of the project, in which occurs the definition and documentation of the requirements, and the product delivering, in which the product is ready to be used. In this case, it is not rare to have to low customer acceptance of the software products, since it is very difficult to have requirement changes.

Requirement changes are one of the major drawbacks of the disciplined approaches. Constant changes demand close collaboration between the customer and the development team. According to the Agile Manifesto, the customer must collaborate throughout the whole development process, making it easier for the development team to meet the needs of the customer. This increases the chances of having customer satisfaction in the early deliverables and continual feedback the later ones. In Agile approaches, the customer is represented by the Product Owner, which is part of the team, attending all meetings, and ensuring the product satisfies the business expectations.

Planning and Execution

Traditional software development is based on pre-defined phases and each of them has specific deliverables and extensive documentation that are submitted to the review process. The participation of the team is usually only focused on the execution of the project, leaving the planning to project managers and other stakeholders. For instance, the tasks that must be developed to build features of the product, are assigned without the team. The group of people responsible for the planning decides which tasks and when they need to be done, i.e. the team is simply there to produce the outcomes when necessary. Therefore, the participation of the team is very restricted during the planning stage.

In Agile approaches, the execution is quite different. The development lifecycle is done through iterations and there is no detailed plan from the beginning to the end of the project. The planning is performed throughout the development process and the team is directly involved in both planning and execution. For instance, each team member decides which tasks he or she will implement and when to complete. To facilitate this process, the tasks are selected from a prioritized list, which is limited to a specific number of tasks, but the final choice is always up to the team.

Similarities Between Disciplined and Agile Teams

In this Section, we present similarities that can be found in both types of teams, Disciplined and Agile, focusing on the commitment of the team to provide quality in every developed task, the necessity of continuous self-improvement to be up to date with market demands, and problem-solving skills which are an intrinsic characteristic of the software development.

Commitment to Quality

The concept of quality is present directly or indirectly in any product or service available at the market. When customers buy some products or hire some services, often they will be judging the product or service by its quality. In general, quality can be defined as the conformance level regarding the product or service requirements/specification. It is intrinsically related to customer's satisfaction: how good or bad a product or service is according to customer's needs and expectations. When a product or service meets or surpasses the customer's expectation, its quality is considered good, since it reaches the customer satisfaction.

Regardless of the sector's productivity, every production line has or should have a quality control program, to verify the quality of its products, keeping an acceptable level of quality for the customers. Even a company that works with services, instead of products, should care about their quality. Since software can be considered and negotiated as a product or service, every software engineering team should care about software quality during the development process, checking the compliance of the produced artifacts according to specified functional and non-functional requirements. Besides, software quality can also consider features like usability, efficiency, reliability, flexibility, and portability.

Despite more than 30 years of effort to improve its quality, software is still released with many errors. Many major products are known to have thousands of bugs. It is not for lack of trying; all major software developers have a software quality assurance effort and attempt to remove bugs before release. The problem is the complexity of the code. It is very easy to review code but fail to notice significant errors. (Parnas & Lawford, 2003)

To manage software quality, regardless of the adopted model is the Disciplined/Traditional or the Agile, it is necessary to establish a process responsible for controlling and assuring the conformance of software artifacts regarding their specifications, whatever if the specifications are well documented in a Waterfall model artifact (e.g. requirements document) or are just well described in the sprint's user stories. This way, the Software Quality Management deals with processes and practices to ensure the required quality levels in software products and services, defining and establishing quality standards and making these standards applied.

Software Quality Management (Yahaya, 2020; Stepanova, 2019; Nistal et al., 2019) can be composed of two sub-processes: Quality Assurance (QA) and Quality Control (QC). The Quality Assurance process is directly related to quality process execution, assuring that the performance of the process and the development of the software are following the planned quality requirements/standards. The Quality Control process is responsible to inspect the quality of the final products, analyzing the outcomes. While Quality Assurance aims in avoiding defects in the software during its development process, the Quality Control aims in identifying and analyzing possible defects when the software is finished, ready to be delivered. To summarize, the focus of Quality Assurance is the software quality during the development process, being a process more proactive and preventive, while the focus of Quality Control is the quality of the developed software, being a process more reactive and corrective.

Thus, even considering the differences between the two models, Disciplined and Agile, every team that concerns the success of its developed software must introduce some Software Quality Management process in its development methodology. Producing high-quality software is an essential objective in the Software Engineering field, which offers methods, techniques, and tools to accomplish this objective. Both Disciplined and Agile teams must demonstrate a commitment to improving the software quality following the steps of their respective approaches. This will increase the possibilities of delivering software with better quality, reducing the number of software defects, maximizing the probabilities of good customer satisfaction, and thus increasing the chances of success in the overall process.

Common Practices and Continuous Self-Improvement

In general, both Disciplined and Agile models have the same goal, which is related to deliver software with quality, satisfying the needs of the customers/users. This way, common operations such as planning, activities/tasks definition, coding, testing, verification, and validation, etc. are all considered by teams working with any of the models. For instance, planning the work (activity, task, use case, user story, or some other term according to the adopted model nomenclature) before it starts is a highly recommended good practice for every software engineering team. Good planning will always increase the chances of success in any project and it should always consider budget available, scope delimitation, time estimation, possible risks and mitigations (or avoidances), and quality assurance/control. This process commonly includes requirements prioritization, risk assessment, deliverables definition along the time, among other operations.

Another good practice recommended in both models is the requirements elicitation and analysis, which is directly related to the scope delimitation of the software project. The requirements are responsible to guide the software development process. Besides, based on the requirements is that the testing analysts elaborate on the different kinds of tests (functional, performance, and usability, for instance) and organize the execution of the tests plan. Furthermore, if the requirements are well documented, the verification and validation of them in the Quality Assurance Quality Control processes will tend to be easier and smoother.

The following technical workflow can be also considered when summarizing the project execution in both models:

1. Analyze the requirements and architect the solution;
2. Implement the functionalities accordingly and verify them through testing execution;
3. Validate the requirements conformance, checking software quality;
4. Deploy the software artifacts.

Once the software project is planned and its development starts, the test/quality teams have also similarities as they are always interested in finding and reporting possible problems regarding the established requirements. No matter what kind of test or process is being executed and adopted, the focus of the team will be the same: avoiding the deployment and delivery of software out of specified quality standards.

This way, although both Disciplined and Agile models differ regarding how their processes are executed, when abstractly analyzing both regarding their processes' aims, some similarities can be found, mainly because both have the same objective that is the successful software delivery, achieving the quality levels specified by the quality standards.

Regardless of the approach chosen to carry out software development, team members play roles for which they are naturally suited for. For instance, some professionals are better at focusing on team goals and delegating work, while others are more effective at checking for errors in the final work. The continuous growth of the team allows each member to develop and focus on what he or she is best and permit each member to find his/her niche so that they can contribute better as an individual while still working together.

Since each model has specific approaches to conduct the execution of the software development process, the teams can be divided according to the specific tasks in each development phase/cycle and established roles (e.g. developer, tester, analyst, project manager, etc.). Once every software development team member has a specific role, it becomes easier to improve his/her skills by focusing on what is more relevant for performing better his/her work.

Problem-Solving Skills

Software development is a problem-solving profession in which the customer highlights an issue in the current mode of operations and the software developer aims at providing a computer-oriented solution. Analytical and problem-solving skills means that one has the ability to view and look into a situation from a very logical, systematic perspective and come up with a solution fitted to the scenario. In the process of software development each role, to a certain extent, has to make decisions which directly and indirectly have impact on the overall software cost, quality, and productivity. While he or she is making decisions some choices are challenging and take careful thought and consideration. (Ahmed et al., 2015)

Many people when face a problem tend to procrastinate or avoid it completely. However, avoiding problems is a short-term solution. Having the skills and the tools to solve problems effectively and efficiently helps to accomplish the objectives of the project in faster and more viable way. Generally, software development teams from both approaches (Disciplined and Agile) have two distinct types of mental skills, analytical and creative, which are directly related to problem solving. Analytical thinking provides a logical framework for problem solving and assist to select the best option from those available by narrowing down the range of possibilities. Creativity is simply being able to find a unique solution. This means not responding to problems with a knee-jerk reaction, or some safe solution that will likely bring unsatisfactory results. These problem-solving skills provides the pathway through the problem, so the teams can develop effective solutions to resolve their issues.

FUTURE TRENDS

Over the past few decades, Agile methods have been gaining more and more space in the industry over Disciplined ones. Thereafter, there was a frequent discussion in the agile community about which is the best agile method. Scrum stands out as the most widely used agile approach However, being the most popular is different from being the best one. Many organizations choose to begin their software development journey with Scrum, but teams tend to look for other methods to complement software development and be able to deliver a higher quality product closer to customer requirements. However, by using other methods, conflicts with the terminology, team roles, and goals come to light. To mitigate these challenges, Scott Ambler, the former head of Information Technology methodology at IBM Rational, proposed in 2009 the Disciplined Agile Delivery (DAD) (Ambler et al, 2012; Lines & Ambler, 2015).

DAD uses practices and strategies from a variety of methods, including traditional software methodologies, with a focus on delivering a subset of the product life cycle, which is comprised of the following phases:

- **Inception:** It includes initiation activities. Most teams do some initial survey work at the beginning of a project that takes about a month. Therefore, at this early stage of DAD, some very light vision activities are done to frame the product correctly.
- **Construction:** In this phase, a DAD team will implement a potentially consumable solution on an incremental basis. The team can do this through a set of iterations or through a lean and continu-

ous flow approach. In addition, members can utilize hybrid approaches with Scrum, XP, Agile Modeling, Agile Data practices, and other methods to provide the solution.

- **Transition:** DAD recognizes that for agile projects in large organizations, deploying the solution to stakeholders is often not a trivial task. This explains why it is important for teams to try to simplify their deployment processes so that over time this phase lasts less and less time until it ideally disappears.

In DAD, the member roles are suggested according to team size, from teams that have up to 10 people to teams of 50 or more. It is worthy to mention that the roles are not unchangeable, anyone can perform one or more roles over the project duration. In addition, any role can have zero or many people for certain periods. Basically, the roles are divided into primary roles, which are present in all teams regardless of the project scale, and secondary roles that exist in large scale projects and only for a specific period. They are primary roles:

- Team Lead is the person responsible for facilitating team ceremonies, removing impediments, promoting collaboration, and ensuring that the process is correctly followed. This role is similar to the Scrum Master.
- Product Owner represents the interests of the Customer. This is the only person on a team who is responsible for the list of prioritized work items, for making timely decisions, and for providing product information.
- Team Member is the person responsible for developing the deliverable increment and performs activities such as modeling, programming, testing, and release activities.
- Architecture Owner is the Architect Decision Maker. This role differs from that of a traditional architect, as it is not solely responsible for defining the direction of architecture, but rather facilitating its creation and evolution.
- Stakeholders represent the people who affect or are affected by the success of the system.

They are secondary roles:

- Specialist is the person who has one or more technical skills that can directly impact the team's work. The specialist should have at least a more general knowledge of software development and the business domain. In addition, one of its most important characteristics is proactivity, as the expert must actively pursue new skills, including in other areas.
- Independent Tester is the one responsible for conducting tests that validate teamwork throughout the process lifecycle. It is an optional role, usually adopted only in large scale projects.
- Domain-expert is a person who knows in detail information that is often not known to the end user or stakeholders.
- Technical Expert is the one with specialized knowledge who works temporarily to help the team with complex problems. During his or her participation in team time, he or she transfers his skills to one or more team members.
- Integrator is the person responsible for the integration of complex systems and/or subsystems.

Previous activities performed by project managers or business analysts on traditional projects exist and tend to be increasingly done by people in agile roles as companies adopt a new way to speed up software delivery or improve their ability to change their capabilities. priorities. Moving to agile requires a paradigm shift, and part of that change is the acceptance that people's roles have changed for the better.

CONCLUSION

In corporate environments, there is a high probability of having project failures. Even minor errors can directly interfere with adherence to deadlines or even make execution costs excessively high. Additionally, the inability to assess the proper way to conduct processes can impair the productivity of professionals, generating a series of bottlenecks. All these factors contribute to the choice of the methodology being a key factor in optimizing the manager's ability to deliver what was promised in the planning stages.

There is no magic formula to define whether one methodology is better suited for one organization than another. Prior to its adoption, some details should be analyzed, such as the profile of the project to be developed, the team's capacity, and the client's availability for joint goal setting. Both methodologies can be used when the company understands which one is most productive for its projects. For this, qualified professionals are essential in identifying and directing the enterprises, according to the appropriate method.

The agile methodology adds the most present values in contemporary ways of work, focusing on innovation, creativity, and collaboration. Although some stakeholders avoid using the disciplined one, it can be very well applied in specific cases where the rules are stricter, and the client company structure does not fit the agile practice. This will greatly depend on the type of project and company culture. The company itself may prefer the traditional methodology, even more so if the project stakeholders are not used to working with an agile methodology, even if it applies to that project. The traditional methodology is suitable for more specific cases, such as something that needs to be planned and decided from the start. If the project is unlikely to change and is at low risk, it is best to have a more detailed project plan before you start.

Remember that the choice of methodology is important not only to be successful in the process, but especially in the delivery of the product. Both methodologies have advantages and can be used even together, coexisting perfectly well, even because the focus of both is on project optimization. The choice between traditional and agile methodology need not be a conflict. One must respect the premises of both methodologies and know what each can add to the objectives of each project.

ACKNOWLEDGMENT

This research was financed in part by the Coordenação de Aperfeiçoamento de Pessoal de Nível Superior – Brasil (CAPES) – Finance Code 001.

REFERENCES

Ahmad, M. O., Dennehy, D., Conboy, K., & Oivo, M. (2018). Kanban in software engineering: A systematic mapping study. *Journal of Systems and Software*, *137*, 96–113. doi:10.1016/j.jss.2017.11.045

Ahmed, F., Capretz, L. F., Bouktif, S., & Campbell, P. (2015). *Soft skills and software development: A reflection from the software industry.* arXiv preprint arXiv:1507.06873

Ambler, S. W., & Lines, M. (2012). *Disciplined agile delivery: A practitioner's guide to agile software delivery in the enterprise.* IBM Press.

André, M., Baldoquín, M. G., & Acuña, S. T. (2011). Formal model for assigning human resources to teams in software projects. *Information and Software Technology, 53*(3), 259–275. doi:10.1016/j.infsof.2010.11.011

Boehm, B., & Turner, R. (2004). Balancing agility and discipline: Evaluating and integrating agile and plan-driven methods. In *Proceedings. 26th International Conference on Software Engineering* (pp. 718-719). IEEE.

Charette, R. N. (2005). Why software fails. *IEEE Spectrum, 42*(9), 42–49. doi:10.1109/MSPEC.2005.1502528

Dhir, S., Kumar, D., & Singh, V. B. (2019). Success and failure factors that impact on project implementation using agile software development methodology. In *Software Engineering* (pp. 647–654). Springer. doi:10.1007/978-981-10-8848-3_62

Fowler, M., & Highsmith, J. (2001). The agile manifesto. *Software Development, 9*(8), 28–35.

Girma, M., Garcia, N. M., & Kifle, M. (2019, May). Agile Scrum Scaling Practices for Large Scale Software Development. In *2019 4th International Conference on Information Systems Engineering (ICISE)* (pp. 34-38). IEEE. 10.1109/ICISE.2019.00014

González-Cruz, T. F., Botella-Carrubi, D., & Martínez-Fuentes, C. M. (2020). The effect of firm complexity and founding team size on agile internal communication in startups. *The International Entrepreneurship and Management Journal*, 1–21. doi:10.100711365-019-00633-1

Hameed, A. (2016). Software Development Lifecycle for Extreme Programming. *International Journal of Information Technology and Electrical Engineering, 5*(1).

Hilorme, T., Perevozova, I., Shpak, L., Mokhnenko, A., & Korovchuk, Y. (2019). *Human capital cost accounting in the company management system.* Academy of Accounting and Financial Studies Journal.

Kruchten, P. (2004). *The rational unified process: an introduction.* Addison-Wesley Professional.

Leau, Y. B., Loo, W. K., Tham, W. Y., & Tan, S. F. (2012). Software development life cycle AGILE vs traditional approaches. In *International Conference on Information and Network Technology (Vol. 37,* No. 1, pp. 162-167). Academic Press.

Lines, M., & Ambler, S. W. (2015). *Introduction to Disciplined Agile Delivery: A Small Agile Team's Journey from Scrum to Continuous Delivery.* CreateSpace Independent Publishing Platform.

Macke, J., & Genari, D. (2019). Systematic literature review on sustainable human resource management. *Journal of Cleaner Production, 208*, 806–815. doi:10.1016/j.jclepro.2018.10.091

Macnab, C. J. B., & Doctolero, S. (2019, May). The role of unconscious bias in software project failures. In *International Conference on Software Engineering Research, Management and Applications* (pp. 91-116). Springer.

Matharu, G. S., Mishra, A., Singh, H., & Upadhyay, P. (2015). Empirical study of agile software development methodologies: A comparative analysis. *Software Engineering Notes*, *40*(1), 1–6. doi:10.1145/2693208.2693233

Mathur, S., & Malik, S. (2010). Advancements in the V-Model. *International Journal of Computers and Applications*, *1*(12), 29–34.

Nistala, P., Nori, K. V., & Reddy, R. (2019, May). Software quality models: A systematic mapping study. In *2019 IEEE/ACM International Conference on Software and System Processes (ICSSP)* (pp. 125-134). IEEE. 10.1109/ICSSP.2019.00025

Parnas, D. L., & Lawford, M. (2003). The role of inspection in software quality assurance. *IEEE Transactions on Software Engineering*, *29*(8), 674–676. doi:10.1109/TSE.2003.1223642

Permana, P. A. G. (2015). Scrum method implementation in a software development project management. *International Journal of Advanced Computer Science and Applications*, *6*(9), 198–204.

Petersen, K., Wohlin, C., & Baca, D. (2009, June). The waterfall model in large-scale development. In *International Conference on Product-Focused Software Process Improvement* (pp. 386-400). Springer. 10.1007/978-3-642-02152-7_29

Schwaber, K., & Sutherland, J. (2017). *The Scrum Guide - The Definitive Guide to Scrum: The Rules of the Game, 2017.* Academic Press.

Serrador, P., & Pinto, J. K. (2015). Does Agile work?— A quantitative analysis of agile project success. *International Journal of Project Management*, *33*(5), 1040–1051. doi:10.1016/j.ijproman.2015.01.006

Sommerville, I. (2015). *Software Engineering* (10th ed.). Academic Press.

Stepanova, V. (2019). Quality Control Approach in Developing Software Projects. *International Journal of Computer Science and Software Engineering*, *8*(1), 1–5.

Stoica, M., Mircea, M., & Ghilic-Micu, B. (2013). Software Development: Agile vs. Traditional. *Informatica Economica, 17*(4).

Tam, C., da Costa Moura, E. J., Oliveira, T., & Varajão, J. (2020). The factors influencing the success of on-going agile software development projects. *International Journal of Project Management*, *38*(3), 165–176. doi:10.1016/j.ijproman.2020.02.001

Yahaya, J. H. (2020). Software quality and certification: Perception and practices in Malaysia. *Journal of Information and Communication Technology, 5*, 63–82.

KEY TERMS AND DEFINITIONS

Agile Software Development: Is an umbrella term for a set of frameworks and practices based on the values and principles expressed in the Manifesto for Agile Software Development and the 12 Principles behind it.

Plan-Driven: Are processes where all of the process activities are planned in advance and progress is measured against this plan.

Project Manager: A project manager is a professional responsible for leading a project from its inception to execution, which includes planning, execution and managing the people, resources, and scope of the project.

Software Developers: The person who is responsible for creating the technical specification and write the software.

Software Development Methodology: Is the process of dividing software development work into distinct phases to improve design, product management, and project management.

Software Engineering: The application of a systematic, disciplined, quantifiable approach to the development, operation, and maintenance of software, and the study of these approaches.

Software Organization: Is a company whose primary products are various forms of software, software technology, distribution, and software product development.

Software Product: Is a product, software, which is usually made to be sold to users, and users pay for license which allows them to use it.

This research was previously published in Balancing Agile and Disciplined Engineering and Management Approaches for IT Services and Software Products; pages 151-166, copyright year 2021 by Engineering Science Reference (an imprint of IGI Global).

Chapter 4
Risk Management Metrics

Rimsy Dua
Chandigarh University, India

Samiksha Sharma
Chandigarh University, India

Rohit Kumar
Chandigarh University, India

ABSTRACT

This chapter describes how risk management deals with the detection, the evaluation and the precedence of the risks in the process of project management. There is always an uncertainty factor related to the decisions of an investment while managing a project. Risk management is a proactive approach to deal with such future events that can lead to slow performance of the software project management. For successful risk management; there are different metrics that have been used in the past and are being getting used in the present for inspecting the progress of a project at specific points in a timeline that help in reducing the amount of risk. For the adoption of effective metrics for risk management, data is required. All of the metrics can be applied to the different domains of project, process and product. The chapter also covers strategies to advance, distinguish, estimate, and forecast the risk management process. A review of the key point indicators (KPIs) are also integrated along with the project metrics to signify the future and the present renderings.

INTRODUCTION

Risk is a state that involves disclosure to threat. In normal day to day life people face enormous kind of risks that can happen from their personal actions or financial activities. Despite of all the other categories that belong to risk; this chapter covers the marketable and the industry risks that organizations face while executing project management. In today's era organizations suffer from broad collection of risks that can lead to negative outcomes or bogus results. Different categories of risks an organization can face are control risk, opportunity risks and hazard risks (Hopkin, 2017). Hazard risks are those than can hinder an organization from achieving particular set of objectives, developing that objective is op-

DOI: 10.4018/978-1-6684-3702-5.ch004

portunity risk and creating a fiction of unpredictability in outcomes is control risk. Risk management deals with supervising, managing and estimating such risks. Risk management is adopted in private as well as public sectors in order to have a proactive approach towards the threats that can occur. While designing software, an organization may suffer from enormous number of risks such that personal risks, technical risks, financial risks and management risks (Westfall, 2004). Personnel risks arise due to lack of preparation and skill of the working employees whereas technical risks can happen because of wrong followed procedures and standards. For financial risks; cash runs, capital and return on savings are the main cause. At last, the management itself sometimes responsible for the project risks because of communication gap, lack of planning, proper training, authority and experience among employees.

Risk management process starts with first recognizing the risks. After identifying the risk, investigation is done on various types of identified risks (Boehm, 1991). When an investigation is performed risks are prioritized according to the extent of threat they can confer to the software. A risk management plan is prepared after prioritizing various risks, that plan will involve actions to be taken against risks. A risk management plan can reduce the probability of risk occurrence to a greater extent. After the completion of plan, a set of pre-defined actions is applied to the project and a constant monitoring or tracing is performed that signifies the degree of risk at each stage of project development (Rasmussen, 1997). Tracing of project at various stages gives insight about diverse count of new risks and old plans can be updated according to the newly identified risks after tracing the development of project at different timestamps. Figure 1 given below exemplifies the risk management process.

Figure 1. Risk Management Process

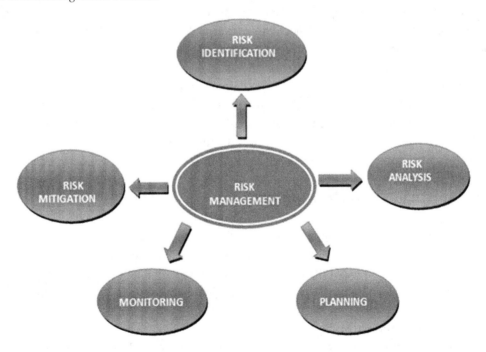

- **Risk Identification:** Risk identification deals with recognizing diverse risks that a project can come across during development process. Risk identification is the pre-process as it gives insight about risks that can lead to system failure. The process of identification involves key set of activities like communication between the team members and documentation. In the documentation, risk occurrences are defined along with their relationships.
- **Risk Assessment:** After identifying all the risks, assessment is performed where risk analysis is carried out. An evaluation process is executed that signifies how much threat it can confer to the project. So briefly risk assessment deals with analysis of the identified risks and evaluating them on the source of degree of threat that can possess. Risk assessment also helps in prioritizing different identified risks, which helps in reducing their impact.
- **Risk Control:** Subsequent to analysis and risk evaluation, control programs are being developed that holds different set of risk control activities. Controlling a risk is required as it reduces the impact of risk to a greater extent. After prioritizing the risks, control programs are applied that gives an organization a vision of how to diminish the degree of threat.
- **Monitoring:** Monitoring deals with tracing of project development process at various check points. The major advantage an organization can get is identification of new risks at various levels of project progress. Organizations keep on updating their project plans in accordance with the tracing reports and builds up new strategies to cope with the new identified project risks.

RISK MANAGEMENT IMPACT ON PROMISING MARKET DECISIONS

Enterprise risk management deals with identifying, evaluating, controlling and tracing the risks that an organization can face in terms of capital and investments or savings. In Enterprise risk management a wide range of risks including operational, accidental and financial are covered. Enterprise risk management encloses set of actions that involves inception of content, performing risk identification, evaluating and analyzing risk, giving a priority to the identified risk and reducing the impact of risks. So, enterprise risk management can be stated as a controlled and regimented approach for handling risks.

Also, ERM supports plans, technologies, method, processes and information used by the working organization to enhance its work skill to manage uncertain occurring risks. ERM thus enhances the overall performance and value of an organization by reducing the barriers of risks. Figure 2 given below demonstrates the enterprise risk management process.

Risk Assessment and Risk Management

Risk Assessment deals with performing evaluation of the existing security system in which the current security strategies adopted by the organization are estimated whereas risk management is an application used by an organization that consists of set of rules and methods that an organization can apply while evaluating the risk (O. salvi, 2006). Detecting and analyzing the risk are the major operations to be performed under risk assessment but the procedures to be followed for the risk assessment are recited in the risk management process. So both risk management and risk assessment play an important role in identifying and mitigating the discovered risks. Figure 1 represented the risk management process while figure 2 will give the insight to the different states to be followed in the risk assessment process. Let's have a brief look at the various stages of risk assessment taking an example of medical subject.

Figure 2. Enterprise Risk Management

- **Identification of Threat:** The first step towards risk assessment is identifying the threat; if an example of medical problem is taken then the identification case will comprise of finding the health issues caused due to pollutant.
- **Response Assessment:** After identifying the threat, diverse range of responses is checked for illustration let's have a quick view of the same medical case in which one will examine the health problems that can arise at different stages of exposures.
- **Exposure Assessment:** Evaluation of the degree of exposure where according the recited medical case above the total number of pollutant will be viewed that affected the population of people and the total count of the individuals being exposed to the pollutants in a specific phase of time.
- **Exemplifying Risk:** Risk characterization gives insight about the possibilities of threats that can occur from the discovered risks. With respect to the recited medical case risk characterizing will signify the other health problems that can develop from the exposed population.

All the above-mentioned steps are considered while performing the risk assessment that contributes towards the stable security system making it less prone to errors. So, the existing security system is refined by continuous evaluation using risk assessment process and the chances of failure are reduced to much lower extent.

Above mentioned steps in figure 2 contribute to risk assessment; starting with the identification phase then the response assessment and the exposure assessment. At last, characterizing risk deals with further exposure due to the discovered risk. At last in brief preface to the above explained approach, Risk management covers all the procedures and standards to mitigate the risk whereas risk assessment is to evaluate the existing security structure to make sure that the system at last suffers from fewer errors and could be made highly efficient.

Figure 3. Risk Assessment

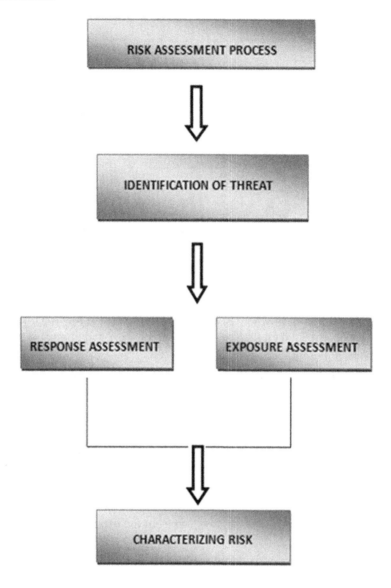

WHAT ARE THE DIFFERENT CATEGORIES OF SOFTWARE RISKS A PROJECT CAN SUFFER FROM?

Software project risk is basically a prospective event that can cause a loss in the development of software project. Most of the software projects are beset with potential risk. Software risk identification is the preeminent task in the effective risk management of the software project management. Constant and efficient software project monitoring is mandatory for the effective recognition of the potential risks in the software project. Different software project managers may be confronted with different category of risks. There can be variegation in software project risk depending on the cost, schedule and realization of software development goals. Risk assessment is an activity of evaluating the risks that can cause an expected loss in the software development project. It involves risk analysis and risk evaluation. Software project risk assessment will result in efficacious result if it is accomplished from multiple dimensions. Risk identification may involve several approaches varying from ad hoc approach to formal approach. Risk assessment in ad hoc approach depends on some program that appears at the time of software project development. Informal approach of risk identification involves discussion with all the team members who are directly or indirectly associated with the software project. It also necessitates the documentation of risks for the future use. If repetitive procedures are followed for the identification and specification of the risk then that approach is the periodic approach. Formal approach is followed when there is comprehensive assessment of the risk.

Different software projects may confront different types of risks:

- **Schedule Risk:** Individual software projects have an inimitable nature which is one of the problematic issues for the correct schedule of the software project. Continuous monitoring of the project is a prerequisite for the development of the project as per schedule.
- **Budget Risk:** Wrong cost estimation of the software project may lead to budget risks. Expanding the scope of the software project may result in budget risk. It is advisable to use more than one estimation method for the correct cost estimation of the software project. Having a good insight into the challenges of the software project is the main factor that will lead to realistic cost estimation of the software project.
- **Operational Risk:** These types of risks are associated with the day to day operational activities of the software project (Rekha, 2015). Silo approach followed by different software teams may lead to conflicts thereby affecting the operational activities of the software project. Effective team communication can reduce operational risks.
- **Technical Risk:** Sometimes companies have to reduce the functionality of the software keeping in view the budget overruns and schedule overruns. This may result in technical risk. Incessant change in requirements of the software project is one of the major causes of technical risk. Sometimes the software project is complex to implement and there is a difficulty in integrating the modules of the software project. These issues might enhance the technical risks of the software project.
- **Programmatic Risk:** These risks are beyond the operational limits and are outside the control of the program. These types of risk generally involve environmental impacts. These are fundamentally uncertain risks that may be caused due to disruptions in communication or any natural calamity.
- **Resource Risk:** Delays in software project development can occur if the employees are not skilled in designing because in most of the software projects, Employees must be skilled in HTML/CSS so that the frontend development can be completed without any delay. Project development team must not change during the development of the software project otherwise its quite difficult to maintain the same tread with the new employees.
- **Requirement Risk:** Continually changing the requirements of the software project may lead to requirement risks. Sometimes, requirements that are mandatory to be included for the software project development are incorrectly specified or are not cleared to the developer. All the requirements must be correctly specified and understood by the developer.

Risk Management Metrics

Risk is one of the critical factor due to which the development of the software project is affected. Basically, Risk identification, Risk impact analysis and Risk mitigation (Miguel.2015) are the three main stages of risk management. A decisive role is played by risk identification in the successful development of the project. If the risk is identified at a later stage of software project development then it can lead to a variance in the cost, time and budget of the software project. Basically, a Quality Assurance team is responsible for the effective risk identification. If the risk identification is good then its mitigation can be done within time. Risk management metric is basically responsible for the risk analysis, risk monitoring, risk response planning, risk control etc. Metrics can be of two categories: Base and Derived. Base metric is defined in terms of single one attribute is base metric and this is independent of all the other metrics. In view of this, Derived metric is the one that is a function of two or more values of base metric.

Risk Management Process

One of the most important things as a system analyst or project manager is that there can be a management of risk on daily basis. If a systematic risk management process is incorporated, and the core 5 risk management process steps are put into action, then it will result in a smooth working of the project.

Risk involves uncertainty, an event whose consequences on project goals can be positive or negative. An important concept is potential for a risk to have a positive or negative effect. Why? It is inappropriate if we say that risks have inherently negative effects. Your project can be developed streamlined, smarter and more profitable If you are also open to those risks that create positive opportunities, you can make your project smarter, streamlined and more profitable. Project risk may assist in creating better opportunities for the project as there is an adage that "Accept the inevitable and turn it to your advantage."

Uncertainty is at the heart of risk. It is not sure that if an event is likely to occur or not. Also, there is an uncertainty about its consequences if it did occur. Likelihood and consequence are the two components that characterize the extent of the risk. Where likelihood is the probability of an event occurring and consequence is an impact or outcome of an event.

Similar steps are followed by risk management processes, although sometimes different jargon is used to describe these steps. Simple and effective risk management process involves these five risk management process steps.

Risk Finding Techniques

To Identify Risk

- **Brainstorming:** When the participants came to know the objectives then a brainstorming conference is conducted where all the participants can give their suggestions about the various occurring risks. All are divided into teams, from which each member will recite the idea of risk probability. So, brainstorming is a group task.
- **Interviews:** For interviews, a set of questions are prepared by the expert of the field, which is then shared by the team members. Every member has to answer the cited set of questions. In this way a generalized viewpoint of every team member is collected through interviews.

- **Workshops:** After all the information is gathered regarding the risk, workshops can be facilitated in order to have more detailed conclusion about the gathered data with respect to risk threats.
- **SWOT Analysis:** SWOT stands for strength-weakness-opportunities-threats, from these four strength and weakness reside inside the organization that mainly depends upon certain factors such as structure, human source, economy and traditions of the organization; all these factors are essentials of an organization as they hold a strong impact on the success of the organization. The other two factors named as opportunities and threats are external to an organization that can be unpredictable for their occurrence. SWOT analysis deals with the precalculating the threats that can damage the working system as well as monitoring the continuous strengths and weaknesses through which organization can be made to grow successfully.
- **Maintaining Risk Surveys and Questionnaire:** An organization should keep on conducting iteratively the survey for risk identification and keeps on maintaining the questionnaire to have response of each individual regarding the threats that can occur in future.
- **Analyzing the Risk Scenario:** In this analysis is carried out based on certain situations. More emphasis is carried on the "what-if" question rather than the scenario. The consequences are noted down first and are considered for determining the future risk threats. Set of pre-defined questions are prepared for the review of the current risk situation.

Risk Ranking Techniques

A risk matrix is a type of risk assessment tool that helps in identifying the extent of the risk. Risk matrix helps in giving the insight idea about the risks occurrences and enhance the decision-making process. Risk can have variety of risk levels that depends upon the probability product with the risk sternness. So, through a risk matrix an estimate is made about the risk probability and the extent or level of the risk, not the accuracy.

Identify Risk Matrix

A risk matrix is developed while analyzing the threats and during the risk audits. Once a matrix is created, a tolerance or threshold must be maintained that will signify the acceptance level of the risk, also it will reveal about the efficacy of the measures used to mitigate the risk.

Consequence and Likelihood Ranges

A risk matrix is a four by four lattice. On the Y alignment (axis) is the "probability/likelihood" depiction range whereas the X alignment(axis) denoted the "consequence" scale. Given below figure 4 demonstrate the risk matrix with the penalty and probability scale.

Insignificant risks are less rigorous and thus acquire the lowest rank. Inversely, catastrophic risks are ranked first among all the other severe risks. The given below table 1 exhibits the rank related with the different categories of risks along with their consequences which are classified as Negligible, Marginal, Critical and Catastrophic. Let's get into the brief preface of above described categories.

Figure 4. Consequences and Likelihood Ranges

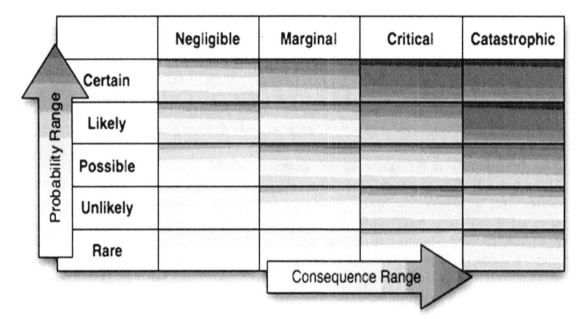

Table 1. Sample Consequence Ranking

S.NO	Risk Consequences	Rank (Numerical Vale)	Impacts
1	Negligible	1	Little or minimal damage
2	Marginal	2	Mitigatable damage where restoration activities can be done
3	Critical	3	Results in partial permanent disability
4	Catastrophic	4	Results in death or permanent disability

Risk Treatment Approaches

- **Treatment of Risk:** For the Different risk levels, various treatment plans need to be prepared. The risks that are rated high in ranking needs a treatment plan to be preplanned for curing from the large extent of threat, whereas the risks that are ranked as low need less attention and refinement based on the partners review at later stages.
    ○ Specify what kind of treatment plan will be followed.
    ○ Documenting the accepted treatment plan.
    ○ Allocating an owner to treatment plan, that will keep on monitoring the progress.
    ○ Deciding a declaration date for the target.
- **Anticipate Risk Analysis:** Anticipation involves performing the risk assessment after the treatment plans are designed. Changes in the forecast report can exist if the treatment plans or controls are not adequate for resolving the risk threats and their probability.
    ○ Checking the Probability of the identified risk.
    ○ The extent of the identified risk on the work environment.

- ○ To define the overall ranking related to different risks.
- **Implementing and Monitoring the Risk:** The owner of treatment plan will be responsible for the monitoring and implementation of treatment plan within an organization. The owner will not implement the plans directly but will ensure that all the treatment plans are completed within a given time span. Below mentioned events corresponds to the implementation of risk treatment plan.
  - ○ Whether Structure of Organization is supportive or not to the treatment plan.
  - ○ Economic condition of company to access the plan, availability of resource.
  - ○ Communication, monitoring and continuous evaluation of status of plan.

CONCLUSION

For an organization to achieve specific set of objectives, it's necessary to have risk management as risk is one of the unpredictable events that can occur within the software development process. So, organizations have diverse range of techniques through which they can identify risk and manage it before they make an actual damage to the business. Risk management helps in identifying risk at various development stages of the software product so that necessary action can be taken to protect the product development from any kind of future failures. This chapter introduced the concept of risk management implying the importance of risk, how to identify risk and why risk management is required. Different types of risk are roofed with a brief insight of their effect on the product development. At the end different approaches to treat the risk are covered that have description of how risk can be avoided during the beginning phase. Risk management thus plays an important role in the overall development of the organization as it helps in maintaining the objectives of company by identifying the threats to the future developments which results in strong business decisions without any failures in the present market. An organization can be more financially strong if it suffers from fewer risks.

REFERENCES

Aven, T. (2016). Risk assessment and risk management: Review of recent advances on their foundation. *European Journal of Operational Research*.

Boehm, B. W. (1991). Software risk management: Principles and practices. *IEEE Software*, 8(1), 32–41. doi:10.1109/52.62930

Hopkin, P. (2017). *Fundamentals of risk management: understanding, evaluating and implementing effective risk management*. Kogan Page Publishers.

Rasmussen, J. (1997). Risk management in a dynamic society: A modelling problem. *Safety Science*, 27(2), 183–213. doi:10.1016/S0925-7535(97)00052-0

Rekha, J. H., & Parvathi, R. (2015). Survey on Software Project Risks and Big Data Analytics. *Procedia Computer Science*, 50, 295–300. doi:10.1016/j.procs.2015.04.045

Salvi, O., & Debray, B. (2006). A global view on ARAMIS, a risk assessment methodology for industries in the framework of the SEVESO II directive. *Journal of Hazardous Materials*, *130*(3), 187–199. doi:10.1016/j.jhazmat.2005.07.034 PMID:16236437

Sarigiannidis, L., & Chatzoglou, P. D. (2011). Software Development Project Risk Management: A New Conceptual Framework. *Journal of Software Engineering and Applications*, *4*(05), 293–305. doi:10.4236/jsea.2011.45032

Sundararajan, S., Bhasi, M., & Pramod, K. V. (2013). An Empirical Study of Industry Practice in Software Development Risk Management. *International Journal of Scientific and Research Publications, 3*(6).

Wanderleya, M., Menezes, J. Jr, Gusmão, C., & Lima, F. (2015). Proposal of risk management metrics for multiple project software development. *Procedia Computer Science*, *64*, 1001–1009. doi:10.1016/j.procs.2015.08.619

Westfall, L. (2000, January). Software risk management. In *ASQ World Conference on Quality and Improvement Proceedings* (p. 32). American Society for Quality.

This research was previously published in Analyzing the Role of Risk Mitigation and Monitoring in Software Development; pages 21-33, copyright year 2018 by Engineering Science Reference (an imprint of IGI Global).

Chapter 5
A Glossary of Business Sustainability Concepts

Arunasalam Sambhanthan
Curtin University, Australia

ABSTRACT

This chapter presents a glossary of business sustainability concepts. The business sustainability definitions have been subjected to an abstractive decomposition. The phrases and terms derived from the abstractive decomposition has been categorized into three types, and each answers the questions of why sustainability, how it could be achieved, and where it will lead the businesses. Concepts categorized under each of these questions are defined individually and described with contextual relevance and examples from literature or industry. The glossary has been presented with a logical order to supplement the table of phrases and concepts. This work is an extension of the work reported on defining business sustainability through an abstractive decomposition.

1. INTRODUCTION

Sustainability is a well-used and popular term, but its use lacks in clarity. There are a number of terms, such as sustainable development and triple bottom line, which are interchangeably used with the term 'sustainability' (McKenzie, 2004). At the business level, sustainability is often equated with eco-efficiency (Dyllick & Hockerts, 2002). Documented research exists on the review of sustainability terms and their definitions (Glavič & Lukman, 2007). These authors give prominence to terms like cleaner production, pollution prevention, pollution control, minimization of resource usage, eco-design and other similar terms. However, there is a considerable gap in the research literature in terms of defining business sustainability with a holistic view. Being a branch of the Sustainability discipline, business sustainability has quite a number of perspectives and angles that have been researched. Investigations of the business sustainability concept include consumer behavior, climate change, stakeholder management, innovation and strategy. In the context of consumer behavior and sustainability, there are studies on measuring the gaps between customers' expectations and their perceptions on green products (Tseng & Hung, 2013);

DOI: 10.4018/978-1-6684-3702-5.ch005

investigation of factors influencing the sustainable consumption behaviors of rural residents (Wang, Liu, & Qi, 2014); the role of moral leadership for sustainable production and consumption (Vinkhuyzen & Karlsson-Vinkhuyzen, 2014); survey and analysis of consumer behavior on waste mobile phone recycling (Yin, Gao, & Xu, 2014) and the empirical investigation of green purchase behavior among the younger generation (Kanchanapibul, Lacka, Wang, & Chan, 2014). Definition of climate strategies for business (Pesonen & Horn, 2014) and the influence of stakeholders' power and corporate characteristics and social and environmental disclosure (Lu & Abeysekera, 2014) are studies that document the relation of climate change and sustainability. The climate change related studies take more of an environmental sustainability angle when looking at sustainability. In terms of innovation, the link between eco-innovation and business performance (Cheng, Yang, & Sheu, 2014) and sustainability oriented innovation in small and medium enterprises (Klewitz & Hansen, 2014) are some notable studies that have been recently published. These studies look at the economic dimension of sustainability in the context of small and medium businesses. From a management perspective, there are studies on, for example, keeping track of corporate social responsibility as a business and management discipline with particular reference to Pakistan (Memon, Wei, Robson, & Khattak, 2014); a study related to the strategic niche management of cleaner vehicle technologies from prototype to series production (Sushandoyo & Magnusson, 2014); and the critical importance of strategic competencies for sustainable development (Mulder, 2014). The management related studies have been primarily focused on the strategic and sustainable development angles of the subject. However, there is still a lack of research in terms of integrating these disciplinary perspectives in sustainability related research.

Business sustainability definitions are manifold in the published literature. Due to the complexity involved in terms of semantics and conceptualizations, it is quite challenging to find meanings for some of the terms pertaining to sustainability even in dictionaries (Glavič & Lukman, 2007). Forty-one selected terms from environmental engineering domain including cleaner production, pollution prevention, pollution control, minimization of resource usage and eco design have received prominence in the aforementioned review article. By the mid-1990s there were over hundred definitions of sustainability that have been constructed by different organizations for theorizing and measuring sustainability in their context (Marshall & Toffel, 2005). The main reason for this variability relies on the incompatibility of the sustainability definition crafted by the World Commission on Environment and Development to a variety of organizational settings. In fact, this definition has practical limitations pertaining to operationalization and implementation in organizational settings. Therefore, the practice of contextualizing sustainability definitions according the organizational requirements has been a longstanding dilemma. On the other hand, there is an observable vacuum in the current academic literature with regard to a holistic definition of business sustainability concept. Aiming to address the above vacuum, a recent documented research conceptualizes business sustainability using abstractive decomposition (Sambhanthan, Potdar, & Chang, 2017). The authors have constructed a new definition of business sustainability through analyzing and restructuring a number of existing definitions of business sustainability from the documented literature. Yet, the process level detailed view of all the building blocks of the new definition of business sustainability could be a possible extension to the aforementioned research. For example, the definition crafted by the authors includes the term stakeholder which has around a number of different classifications ranging from involvement based classification (i.e. direct, indirect) to environment based classification (i.e. internal, external). Thus, it is confusing to the readers as to what the actual term stakeholder means for the sustainability of businesses. In fact, grasping the underlying infrastructure is essential for the comprehension of the core definition in any domain. Thus, this chapter aims at clearly outlining the conceptual boundaries of business sustainability terminologies outlined in the business sustainability conceptualization documented by (Sambhanthan, Potdar, & Chang, 2017).

Software development industry is experiencing an exponential growth in the recent times with the increase of software exports to developed nations. Yet, sustainability related investigations related to software development industry are limited in the published literature except few works documented in the recent years (Sambhanthan & Potdar, 2016c); (Sambhanthan & Potdar, 2015); (Sambhanthan & Potdar, 2016b); (Sambhanthan & Potdar, 2017); (Sambhanthan et al., 2017); (Sambhanthan & Potdar, 2016a). This entails the need for an effort towards more contextualized research focused on software domain.

The next section briefly reviews and summarizes the contemporary issues related to business sustainability theorization and application.

2. THEORETICAL UNDERPINNINGS

Sustainability conceptualizations date back to 1980s when the first definition of sustainability has been propounded by the World Commission on Environment and Development (WCED) (Costanza & Patten, 1995). This definition has been crafted from a system perspective considering the economic, societal and ecological systems to remain in balance. There has been over hundred definitions of business sustainability out there in the published literature by mid 1990s according to some documented sources (Marshall & Toffel, 2005). The latest of this kind is the holistic conceptualization of business sustainability covering all four bottom lines (Sambhanthan et al., 2017). Besides this exponential growth in the definitional paradox of business sustainability research, a recent study alarms that the concept of sustainability is heavily influenced by the time factor. For example, short-termism has been highlighted to be one of the most recent trends in business sustainability research by the authors of this claim (Bansal & DesJardine, 2014).

By logic, a straightforward definition of business sustainability could be derived from the definition proposed by the WCED. This definition could likely to be as "the ability of firms to respond to their shot-term financial needs without compromising their ability to meet their future needs" (Bansal & DesJardine, 2014). However, it is questionable whether this definition covers a holistic picture of business sustainability. It is inevitable for a definition of this kind to serve the purpose of theorizing business sustainability with a multi-industry viewpoint. Hence, the following definition has been documented with a holistic perspective covering all four bottom lines of sustainability.

Business Sustainability could be achieved through efforts that are concentrated on;

1. Core competencies,
2. Effective production,
3. Embracing opportunities,
4. Exploring suitable and sustainable revenue models,
5. Focusing on economic performance,
6. Managing risks,
7. Pursuing right customer groups,
8. Supporting ecological viability in the existing infrastructure processes and systems,
9. Resource conservation using technology,
10. Growth in business,

11. Improved health and safety,
12. Reduction of environmental impact,
13. Increased production value,
14. Rewarding employees for their performance, and
15. Maintaining long-term support for organizational performance. (Sambhanthan et al., 2017)

The key issues associated with the successful usage and application of this definition relies on the clarity and comprehensibility of the definitional elements. For example, embracing opportunities is a critical part of sustainability according to the new definition. The opportunities has been highlighted as an essential part of sustainability conceptualization in a past documented research (Pojasek, 2007). A clear description and context to the conceptual element 'opportunities' could benefit the understanding and comprehensibility of business sustainability concept. Likewise, there are a variety of conceptual elements which are directly or indirectly associated with the business sustainability definition presented by (Sambhanthan et al., 2017) has been described in this research (see Table 1).

The concept clustering adapted in this article follows the work reported by (Costanza & Patten, 1995). The above research asks questions such as what? when? And how long to assess the persistency of a sustainable system. Similarly, this article asks the questions as to why? how? and where? to cluster the sustainability concepts stuffed inside the definition crafted and documented by (Sambhanthan et al., 2017). In fact, the above definition aims to be a holistic definition encompassing the maximum possible conceptual and theoretical elements of business sustainability. Anchored on the approach documented by (Costanza & Patten, 1995) the typical questions asked on classifying the sustainability concepts includes key questions such as why business sustainability is essential?, how business sustainability could be achieved? and where it will lead the businesses?. The reason for adapting this approach for classification includes that the constructs of sustainability definitions could be better represented through this kind of a classification. In fact, the clear representation and categorization of concept themes is essential to position any new concept in the context.

Anecdotal evidences suggest that there is no universally accepted definition for business sustainability exists in the published literature (Montiel & Delgado-Ceballos, 2014); (Sambhanthan & Potdar, 2016b). A survey conducted among senior managers asking them to define business sustainability highlights a substantial part of responses including all three bottom lines of sustainability (i.e. economic, social and environmental) while a few definitions emphasized exclusively the planet dimension of sustainability. The results also highlighted that only a tiny fraction of respondents mentioning about the long-term component of Corporate Sustainability (Montiel & Delgado-Ceballos, 2014). Indeed, a concurrent documented study suggests that short-termism is an essential part of corporate sustainability (Bansal & DesJardine, 2014). Hence, the standardize-ability of business sustainability definitions to differing practical contexts is a definite challenge for theoretical sustainability researchers.

In overall, sustainability conceptualizations are varying in the practice based literature. While substantially sharing major characteristics with the original definition drawn by WCED, many definitions are quite more specific to the context of certain organizations. Yet, there is an observable vacuum in terms of sustainability definitions focusing on industries and clusters. Thus, this article re-specifies the holistic definition crafted by the authors for assessing and benchmarking sustainability in organizations. This article clearly outlines the conceptual elements of business sustainability from a practical point of view.

3. SOFT SYSTEMS METHODOLOGY (SSM)

An abstractive decomposition of business sustainability definitions has been the primary method used in this article. Abstractive decomposition is an approach in systems thinking literature that has been propounded by management scientist Peter Checkland for modelling complex human activity systems and being used even after more than four decades of application and development (Checkland, 2000). Primarily, soft systems methodology has been well used in differing domains for modelling complex human activity systems (Lester, n.d.); (Richardson, 2016); (Mingers, 2000); (Holwell, 2000). The method of abstractive decomposition has been applied for analyzing the literature definitions on business sustainability (Sambhanthan et al., 2017). The definitions abstracted from the literature on the above perspectives were subjected to text analysis and phrase level categorization of concept themes from the derived pool of concept pieces. The above iterative process of categorization and re-categorization has yielded a new definition of business sustainability covering three main thematic classifications of business sustainability namely efforts, utilization and outcome. These three main thematic classifications are then tweaked into questions asking why business sustainability is important in organizations? how business sustainability could be achieved in organizations? and where the efforts directed on business sustainability will lead the businesses? These questions were asked to categorize the concept themes that are focused on areas which are relevant to these questions. The concept themes were encapsulated and clustered into these thematic concepts which are then transferred into three questions as depicted in table 1. This presentation has been done to ease the comprehensibility of the concept themes and to highlight the synergetic nature of the idea of business sustainability when approached through an abstractive decomposition.

The rationale and justifications for asking these questions as part of the categorization process is listed below.

1. **Why Business Sustainability?:** The reason for the criticality of having businesses sustained. This question answers the need of business sustainability in organization and include concepts which are focusing on the reasons for sustainable business practices in the organizations.
2. **How Business Sustainability Could Be Achieved?:** The know how or the process through which the sustainability of the businesses could be achieved. This question answers the ways in which business sustainability could be achieved including the processes and methods used for ensuring organizational sustainability.
3. **Where It Will Lead Businesses?:** The destination where businesses will be heading through implementing sustainability measures. This question answers the ultimate outcome of sustainability measures taken in the organizations.

4. GLOSSARY

This section covers the glossary of terms. The Table 1 depicts the three questions and the initial concept themes derived from the abstractive decomposition of definition. This section covers the most substantive concepts from Table 1 that are categorized under three questions that includes; why business sustainability? (Covering the reasons for the need for sustainability initiatives in organizations), how business sustainability could be achieved? (The know-how of achieving sustainability in organizations), Where sustainability will lead the businesses? (The outcome of sustainability initiatives in businesses). Each category of these questions is covered with the contextual description of relevant terms, examples from past research or industry and reasoning.

Table 1. Questions and initial concept themes derived from abstractive decomposition

Why Business Sustainability?	How Business Sustainability Could be Achieved?	Where it will lead the Businesses?
Results from => **Responsibilities** **Responsibilities can be** (i.e. Economic, Environmental, Social) (Pojasek, 2007) **To meet** => **Needs** **Needs of** (Customers, Firms, Stakeholders*) **Needs can be** (i.e. Present, Past, Future) (Laine, 2014) ***Stakeholders can be** (Direct, Indirect, Past, Present, Future, Internal, External) (Dyllick & Hockerts, 2002)	**Architectural Strategy** **Business Approach** (Galbreath, 2009) **Concentrate on Core-Competencies** **Co-ordination of** (Product Design, Manufacturing, Delivery, Distribution, Disposal) (Hong, Kwon, & Jungbae Roh, 2009) **Decision Making** (Cagnin, Loveridge, & Butler, 2013) **Design Appropriate Products** **Effort on** => (Demand, Supply) (Hong et al., 2009); (H. Breitner, 2005) **Embrace Opportunities** (Pojasek, 2007) **Find Suitable Revenue Models** (H. Breitner, 2005) **Focus Economic Performance** (Benn & Dunphy, 2014) **Focus on Infrastructure** **Focus on Production** (Hong et al., 2009) **Methodology** **Manage Risks** (i.e. Economic, Environmental, Social) (Galbreath, 2009) **Production of** (Goods, Services) (H. Breitner, 2005) **Pursue Right Target Groups** **Support Ecological Viability of** (Planet, Species) (Benn & Dunphy, 2014) **Technological Factors** **Usage of** => {Processes (i.e. operational), Systems} (Cagnin et al., 2013)	**Conservation of** => (Energy, Natural Resources) (Laine, 2014) **Development of** => (Social, Cultural, Business) (Cagnin, Loveridge, & Butler, 1999) **Ecological Viability of** (Planet, Species) (Benn & Dunphy, 2014) **Economic Viability** (Benn & Dunphy, 2014) **Equitable Democratic Practices** **Health & Safety** (Community, Consumer, Worker) (Benn & Dunphy, 2014) **Impact Reduction of** => (Earth Life, Ecosystem) (Benn & Dunphy, 2014) **Institutional-Political** **Rewarding** for Working People (Socially, Creatively) (Benn & Dunphy, 2014) **Social Justice** (Benn & Dunphy, 2014) **Spatial** (Cagnin et al., 2013) **Value** to Stakeholders (**Added, Increased**) * **Value** can be (Short term, Long term, Social, Environmental) (Galbreath, 2009)

4.1 Why Business Sustainability?

This section covers the purpose of business sustainability. Concepts related to the relevance and criticality of sustainability in businesses has been defined in this section. The key concepts that are defined under this section includes concepts such as responsibilities, needs and stakeholders.

Responsibilities

Responsibilities is defined as the obligations (both legal and moral) and commitment of the organization towards its economic growth, the environment in which it exists and the society in which it operates in both tangible and intangible forms. (i.e.: it is a responsibility of an IT organization to have a proper training program to manage the growth of their employees within their organization). Organizational attitudes and provision for training has a positive relationship with employee satisfaction and eventually results on employee retention (Acton & Golden, 2003). These responsibilities could be economic, environmental or social in nature. All sorts of tangible and intangible activities and resources which involve a monetary value in the business could be considered as *economic* responsibilities. For example, the core revenue generating projects in a software business. All sorts of activities and entities which could have an effect on the tangible and intangible space in which the business exist could be considered as *environmental* responsibilities. For example, emission rate in a factory and the scarp materials of an engine are two forms of aspects which could cause an effect on the environment. Anything related to the society in which the business exists could be considered as *social* responsibilities. For example, pressure groups in the society which could cause considerable challenge to the management in terms of environmental friendliness of the business operations.

Needs

Needs is defined as the emerging psychological drive of the consumers related to the core business specialization of the organization. A need for more updated version of a subscription based software product could be a possible need of the clients of a software company. There is a shift in software building practices being driven by supply side issues to demand side issues (Bennett et al., 2000). {Note: The client need has been noted to be of paramount concern when building the software product}

Stakeholders

Anyone who is interested in the business directly or indirectly would be defined as stakeholder. For example, customers who are interested on the product quality of the company, shareholders who are interested on the dividends of the company. Stakeholders have been categorized to be in different types: *direct* stakeholders {a term which denotes the outcomes generated straightway from something. i.e.: direct outcome of changes in policy regulations}, *indirect* stakeholders {a term which is used to denote the non-straight impacts on something. i.e.: any non-straight impact}, *internal* stakeholders {a term which is used to denote something inside the organization. i.e.: staff working in the company is internal stakeholders of the organization}, *external* stakeholders {a term which is used to denote something outside the organization. i.e.: customers of the company are external stakeholders}.

4.2 How Business Sustainability Could Be Achieved?

This section covers the know-how of business sustainability. Concepts related to the methods of achieving sustainability in businesses has been defined in this section. The key concepts that are defined under this section includes concepts such as architectural strategy, business approach, core competencies, coordination of production functions, decision making, efforts on sustainability, embracing opportunities, find suitable revenue models, economic performance, focus on infrastructure, production methodology, materials production, pursue target groups, supporting ecological viability, technological factors, usage of processes and systems.

Architectural Strategy

Architectural Strategy is defined as the core strategy applied by the organization in architecting / producing the core product / service offering in a more cost effective and lean manner that could contribute towards the total quality management and sustainable practices of the organization at large. For example, the strategy employed for developing software architectures needs to be reconsidered and evolved over the time. The architectural strategy of complex engineered systems evolves over the time. Therefore, architectural strategy could have a major impact on ensuring the sustainability of the software businesses (Woodard Charles Jason, 2006).

Business Approach

Business Approach is defined as the approach implied by the organization in enhancing the business value and marketability of its product / service offerings. Examples include internationalization of software firms, push / pull marketing strategies, growth strategies and competitive strategies. The internationalization of software firms using network relationships would have an impact on the foreign market selection and mode of entry as well as product development and market diversification activities (Coviello & Munro, 1997).

Core-Competencies

Core-competencies is defined as the total accumulation of skills, methods, know-how and capabilities a company possess in order to produce its intended products or services. Examples include Skill level of the software engineers in a software business. An investigation about identifying technical competencies of software engineers based on a case study from Spanish software development companies has documented a pyramid model which comprises of skills and competencies of software professionals from junior programmer to IT director (Colomo-Palacios, 2012).

Co-Ordination of Production Functions

The activities related to the overall organization, arrangement and direction of business activities within a specified scope boundary and responsibility level. Examples include Organization of project resource requirements for a short-term software development project. A research by (Faraj & Sproull, 2000) investigated about coordinating expertise in software development teams. The findings report a strong relationship between the expertise coordination and team performance that remains significant over and above team input characteristics, presence of expertise, and administrative coordination. The activities that are reported as production functions includes product design, manufacturing, delivery, distribution and disposal. *Product design* is the process through which the core product is built could be defined as product design. For example, internal process mechanism of a company in building its software product. *Manufacturing* is the process through which the product is manufactured could be defined as manufacturing. For example, process adapted for building, assembly and fitting of components in a car manufacturing company. *Delivery* is the completion and handing over phase of any project based organization could be defined as delivery. For example, completion, deployment and user training of the final software product. *Distribution* is the process of handing over the finished goods to the end customer. For example, the process involved in handing over a software product to the client company such as dispatching, contacting and sign off. *Disposal* is the process of destroying the scrap product at the end of its lifecycle. For example, the disposal of a used car into steel, rubber and other related materials which could be made easily recyclable or degradable.

Decision Making

The process of evaluating the options, establishing alternatives and selecting the best possible option against a certain set of standards and procedures which governs the scope boundaries of the functioning of a project / organization. Examples include Selecting the best possible vendor for outsourcing the accounting function of a multinational software company. A study by (Hersh, 1999) reports that the decision support systems are playing a major role in facilitating sustainable decision making.

Efforts on Sustainability

The activities which are undertaken by the organizations in order to initiate, expedite and successfully conclude the sustainability related endeavors which could result in favorable outcomes to the organization. Examples include making a code green policy in a software company and making the e-wastes of the company sustainable ("Virtusa Environment Day," 2010). For example, designing with current technology in mind and greening the software development as well as virtualization and consolidation are identified as two measures the companies could take in terms of ensuring the software sustainability (Hanselman & Pegah, 2007). The efforts on sustainability includes maintaining a balance between demand and supply. *Demand* is the emerging requirement for a certain product from the customer end which could also be considered as the opening through which the products could be made available to the end users. For example, the demand for higher education courses in business discipline. *Supply* is the availability of certain product / service to address the demand which could also be considered as the capability of the provider to address the demands of the customer for a certain product / service. For example, Availability of degree programs with an Information Systems major to address the emerging need for information systems business consulting professionals in software industry.

Embracing Opportunities

The activity which aims at tapping any possible opportunity in terms of being and becoming a sustainable business. For example, utilizing the opportunity created by a legislative change to better promote off the shelves software. Another example would be to leverage the upcoming technological pervasiveness to forge e-opportunities arising in the market (Fenny, 2001). The *opportunities* are defined as the avenues through which the business could develop its horizons could be considered as opportunities. For example, an IT organization could possibly utilize the opportunities opened by a positive legislative change in the country in which operate in terms of hiring foreign nationals for job. Another example would be the grabbing of a market boom created by the macro environmental political changes in the global market for software products (i.e. the market for developing cloud applications for security problems generated by the increasing data recovery issues).

Find Suitable Revenue Models

The structure and approach through which the return on investments could be leveraged. For example, advertising revenue model for a social media based business initiative.

Economic Performance

The metrics used to assess the degree of greatness between the driver and outcome of a production / service creation process. For example, measurement of overall project team between the projects initiations to delivery. For example, (Paul & Anantharaman, 2004) documented a comprehensive study on the influence of HRM practices on Organizational commitment based on a study conducted among software professionals in India. The study further suggests that HRD practitioners and researchers should further develop commitment-oriented organization policies.

Focus on Infrastructure

The overall mechanism through which the production related activities are managed, overseen and controlled. For example, IT infrastructure for managing the software development process of a company.

Production Methodology

The know-how of producing the core business outcomes (products / services) compliance with global standards on aspects such as quality, accessibility and sustainability. For example, ISO 9001 standards on product quality, W3C Accessibility Standards on design quality, Global Reporting Initiative compliance for accounting excellence. Another example would be the agile software development methods which are used in developing software products by ICT organizations. A research by (Highsmith & Cockburn, 2001) highlights that the agile development combines creative teamwork with an intense focus on effectiveness and maneuverability. Tropos is another example for Agent-Oriented Software development methods which is used in the industry (Bresciani, Perini, Giorgini, Giunchiglia, & Mylopoulos, 2004). The goods and services delivered by the organizations are processed through this production methodology. Goods are defined as the end products or things which are supplied to the customers. For example, a piece of software and the associated goods such as the user manual, implementation guide and the operation instructions which are packaged together for a software deliver could be considered as goods of a software development business. Services are defined as the services which are provided to the end users as the outcome of the business activity. For example, Software as a Service provided to the stock brokerage firms.

Pursue Target Groups

Target groups are defined as the actual beneficiaries of a certain business activity which is intended to deliver value for end users. For example, the target group for stock rating engine software could be stock brokerage firms which provide consultancy services to its clients on stock market fluctuation behaviors.

Materials Production

The process of creating the core business outcome using the methods, technologies and infrastructure present in the company, e.g. Software development in a software business. The spiral model of software development and enhancement which covers a number of process steps involved in software development such as progress through steps, evaluate alternatives, develop and verify next level product, planning for the next phase and determining objectives, alternatives and constraints (Boehm, 1988).

Supporting Ecological Viability

The total possibility of the reduction of business's impact on the environment on which it exists. For example, utilizing e-waste for further recycling to reduce environmental impact caused through the used CRT monitors. Four conceptual elements which look at corporate ecological sustainability are total quality environmental management, ecologically sustainable competitive strategies, technology transfer thorough technology-for nature- swaps and reducing the impact of populations on ecosystem (Shrivastava, 1995). These conceptual elements highlight the importance of looking at the businesses' impact on earth. In fact, all these four conceptual elements have a link to the ecological element of the business.

Technological Factors

The factors pertaining to the technological resources, infrastructure and waste. Example: e-waste. The Greening of IT including the infrastructure and e-waste is of importance to make sure the technological waste is optimized in an IT organization (Murugesan, 2008).

Usage of Processes and Systems

The utilization of processes and systems is defined as the overall utilization of all sorts of available, resources, infrastructure and facilities of the company to achieve its optimum value. Example could include the usage of unutilized solar power for producing more energy in a software firm. *Processes* are the step by step activities which direct the overall know how of the entire business happenings from strategic directions to day to day activities. For example, Recruitment process in an ICT company. *Systems* are the overall interrelationship between people, processes and business entities which make the whole of a business. For example, student management system in a university.

4.3 Where These Measures Will Lead the Businesses?

This section covers the outcome of business sustainability endeavors of the organizations. Concepts related to the outcome of sustainability related efforts in businesses has been defined in this section. The key concepts that are defined under this section includes concepts such as conservation of resources, social-cultural and business development, equitable democratic practices, health and safety, social justice and value.

Conservation of Resources

The retention and long-life usage of energy and other scarce resources to achieve the maximum outcome of energy resources. For example, utilization of low latency energy consumers in production process in a factory environment. Energy is defined as the core power generating source in any business which could be derived or transformed from any natural, man-made or alternative sources such as electricity and gas. For example, electricity could be an energy which could be created from natural sources like water, solar power or any other man-made settings like atomic energy generation practices. Natural Resources are defined to be the resources which could be harnessed from the nature itself. For example, oil and gas.

Socio-Cultural and Business Development

The development of the total accumulation of values, norms, practices and morals of a society in a more organized and targeted manner. For example, organizing cultural events to contribute towards the cultural richness of the country in which the company operates. The development of business is defined to be the total accumulation of deeds, activities, revenues, resources, infrastructures and people which are used in the creation of new goods and services to deliver value to the customers with a personalized focus. For example, software company delivering software products to its client companies.

Equitable Democratic Practices

The practices of the company which are in compliance with the equality and considerable contribution of company's wealth for the society in which operates in the form of co-operate social responsibility. For example, a software business could sponsor the cost of establishing a computer laboratory in a rural village closer to which the company is located in.

Health and Safety

The physical and mental wellbeing of the employees working for the company and any other measures taken by the organization to make the employees feel safe and comfortable to work in an environment. Examples include, ergonomically designed work environment and chair arrangements in a software company, better HR practices to govern harassment free work place in an IT company, Secure IT practices to make the journalists work independently in a publishing house. The health and safety of community, consumer and worker are mentioned here. A *community* is defined as the collective gathering of people with shared interests, norms, values and beliefs. A typical example could be a virtual community which functions as a meeting place for software developers and other software related professionals to discuss about the technical and professional issues about their respective areas of specialization. These communities are facilitated by the professional bodies such as the IEEE / ACM as well as could be open communities where anyone could create a free account to share information and knowledge about these issues. The *consumer* is defined as the people who use a certain product to satisfy a sort of need they have. For example, soap users. A *worker* is defined as the person who perform a certain sort of activity to produce a certain outcome as part of his duty. For example, software engineer.

Social Justice

The consciousness about the society and its betterment in all sorts of actions taken by the organization in regards to fulfilling its day to day operations. For example, being social responsible and committed through contributing to the social wellbeing projects which could result in better social recognition for the organization.

Value

Value is defined to be the transferable qualities added to a product or service during the process of creation or delivery. Value could be added or increased with short term or long-term focus. *Addition* is the injection of something which could be quantified in monetary terms. *Increase* is the act of scaling up in something which could be quantified in monetary terms. *Short term* is a period which is relatively smaller that could have an impact on the sustainability of the organization. For example, short term accounting reporting practices of the organization. *Long term* is a period which is relatively larger that could have an impact on the sustainability of the organizations. For example, the strategic manpower sourcing practices of the organization.

5. SUMMARY

This article covers the key terms and concepts in business sustainability according to the definition derived through abstractive decomposition. The three main categories of concepts that are defined in this article includes the questions such as why business sustainability? How to achieve business sustainability? Where it will lead the businesses? Each concept has been defined, described and related to examples from the published literature or industry to give context to the concepts. The main concentration of the article has been focused on individually defining the glossaries associated with sustainability and contextualizing those concepts to the context of software development businesses.

REFERENCES

Acton, T., & Golden, W. (2003). Training the knowledge worker: a descriptive study of training practices in Irish software companies. *Journal of European Industrial Training, 27*(2/3/4), 137–146. doi:10.1108/03090590310468958

Bansal, P., & DesJardine, M. R. (2014). Business sustainability: It is about time. *Strategic Organization, 12*(1), 70–78. doi:10.1177/1476127013520265

Benn, S., & Dunphy, D. (2014). *Can democracy handle corporate sustainability? Constructing a path forward*. Retrieved from http://www.tandfonline.com/doi/abs/10.5172/impp.2004.6.2.141#.VT8jsiGqqko

Bennett, K., Layzell, P., Budgen, D., Brereton, P., Macaulay, L., & Munro, M. (2000). Service-based software: the future for flexible software. In *Proceedings Seventh Asia-Pacific Software Engeering Conference. APSEC 2000* (pp. 214–221). IEEE Comput. Soc. 10.1109/APSEC.2000.896702

Boehm, B. W. (1988). A spiral model of software development and enhancement. *Computer, 21*(5), 61–72. doi:10.1109/2.59

Breitner, H. G. H. (2005). E-Learning (M. H. Breitner & G. Hoppe, Eds.). Heidelberg, Germany: Physica-Verlag HD. doi:10.1007/3-7908-1655-8

Bresciani, P., Perini, A., Giorgini, P., Giunchiglia, F., & Mylopoulos, J. (2004). Tropos: An Agent-Oriented Software Development Methodology. *Autonomous Agents and Multi-Agent Systems, 8*(3), 203–236. doi:10.1023/B:AGNT.0000018806.20944.ef

Cagnin, C. H., Loveridge, D., & Butler, J. (1999). *An Information Architecture to Enable Business Sustainability*. Academic Press.

Cagnin, C. H., Loveridge, D., & Butler, J. (2013). Business Sustainability Maturity Model. *Computer Communication Review*, 1–15.

Checkland, P. (2000). Soft systems methodology: A thirty year retrospective. *Systems Research and Behavioral Science*, 17.

Cheng, C. C. J., Yang, C., & Sheu, C. (2014). The link between eco-innovation and business performance: A Taiwanese industry context. *Journal of Cleaner Production, 64*, 81–90. doi:10.1016/j.jclepro.2013.09.050

Colomo-Palacios, R. (2012). *Professional Advancements and Management Trends in the IT Sector*. IGI Global. Retrieved from https://books.google.com/books?hl=en&lr=&id=8qSeBQAAQBAJ&pgis=1

Costanza, R., & Patten, B. C. (1995). Defining and predicting sustainability. *Ecological Economics, 15*(3), 193–196. doi:10.1016/0921-8009(95)00048-8

Coviello, N., & Munro, H. (1997). Network relationships and the internationalisation process of small software firms. *International Business Review, 6*(4), 361–386. doi:10.1016/S0969-5931(97)00010-3

Dyllick, T., & Hockerts, K. (2002). Beyond the business case for corporate sustainability. *Business Strategy and the Environment, 11*(2), 130–141. doi:10.1002/bse.323

Faraj, S., & Sproull, L. (2000). Coordinating Expertise in Software Development Teams. *Management Science*. Retrieved from http://pubsonline.informs.org/doi/abs/10.1287/mnsc.46.12.1554.12072

Fenny, D. (2001). *Making Business Sense of the E-Opportunity*. Retrieved April 28, 2015, from http://sloanreview.mit.edu/article/making-business-sense-of-the-eopportunity/

Galbreath, J. (2009). Addressing sustainability: A strategy development framework. *Int. J. of Sustainable Strategic Management, 1*(3), 303–319. doi:10.1504/IJSSM.2009.026284

Glavič, P., & Lukman, R. (2007). Review of sustainability terms and their definitions. *Journal of Cleaner Production, 15*(18), 1875–1885. doi:10.1016/j.jclepro.2006.12.006

Hanselman, S. E., & Pegah, M. (2007). The wild wild waste. In *Proceedings of the 35th annual ACM SIGUCCS conference on User services - SIGUCCS '07* (pp. 157–162). New York: ACM Press. 10.1145/1294046.1294083

Hersh, M. A. (1999). Sustainable decision making: The role of decision support systems. *IEEE Transactions on Systems, Man and Cybernetics. Part C, Applications and Reviews, 29*(3), 395–408. doi:10.1109/5326.777075

Highsmith, J., & Cockburn, A. (2001). Agile software development: The business of innovation. *Computer, 34*(9), 120–127. doi:10.1109/2.947100

Holwell, S. (2000). Soft Systems Methodology: Other Voices. *Systemic Practice and Action Research*, *13*(6), 773–797. doi:10.1023/A:1026479529130

Hong, P., Kwon, H., & Jungbae Roh, J. (2009). Implementation of strategic green orientation in supply chain. *European Journal of Innovation Management*, *12*(4), 512–532. doi:10.1108/14601060910996945

Kanchanapibul, M., Lacka, E., Wang, X., & Chan, H. K. (2014). An empirical investigation of green purchase behaviour among the young generation. *Journal of Cleaner Production*, *66*, 528–536. doi:10.1016/j.jclepro.2013.10.062

Klewitz, J., & Hansen, E. G. (2014). Sustainability-oriented innovation of SMEs: A systematic review. *Journal of Cleaner Production*, *65*, 57–75. doi:10.1016/j.jclepro.2013.07.017

Laine, M. (2014). Defining and Measuring Corporate Sustainability: Are We There Yet? *Social and Environmental Accountability Journal*, *34*(3), 187–188. doi:10.1080/0969160X.2014.967956

Lester, S. (n.d.). *Soft systems methodology*. Retrieved from https://www.umsl.edu/~sauterv/analysis/F2015/Soft Systems Methodology.html.htm

Lu, Y., & Abeysekera, I. (2014). Stakeholders' power, corporate characteristics, and social and environmental disclosure: Evidence from China. *Journal of Cleaner Production*, *64*, 426–436. doi:10.1016/j.jclepro.2013.10.005

Marshall, J. D., & Toffel, M. W. (2005). Framing the elusive concept of sustainability: A sustainability hierarchy. *Environmental Science & Technology*, *39*(3), 673–682. doi:10.1021/es040394k PMID:15757326

McKenzie, S. (2004). *Social Sustainability - Towards Some Definitions*. Retrieved April 28, 2015, from https://atn.edu.au/Documents/EASS/HRI/working-papers/wp27.pdf

Memon, Z. A., Wei, Y.-M., Robson, M. G., & Khattak, M. A. O. (2014). Keeping track of "corporate social responsibility" as a business and management discipline: Case of Pakistan. *Journal of Cleaner Production*, *74*, 27–34. doi:10.1016/j.jclepro.2014.03.057

Mingers, J. (2000). An Idea Ahead of Its Time: The History and Development of Soft Systems Methodology. *Systemic Practice and Action Research*, *13*(6), 733–755. doi:10.1023/A:1026475428221

Montiel, I., & Delgado-Ceballos, J. (2014). Defining and Measuring Corporate Sustainability: Are We There Yet? *Organization & Environment*, *27*(2), 113–139. doi:10.1177/1086026614526413

Mulder, K. (2014). Strategic competencies, critically important for Sustainable Development. *Journal of Cleaner Production*, *78*, 243–248. doi:10.1016/j.jclepro.2014.03.098

Murugesan, S. (2008). Harnessing Green IT: Principles and Practices. *IT Professional*, *10*(1), 24–33. doi:10.1109/MITP.2008.10

Paul, A. K., & Anantharaman, R. N. (2004). Influence of HRM practices on organizational commitment: A study among software professionals in India. *Human Resource Development Quarterly*, *15*(1), 77–88. doi:10.1002/hrdq.1088

Pesonen, H.-L., & Horn, S. (2014). Evaluating the climate SWOT as a tool for defining climate strategies for business. *Journal of Cleaner Production*, *64*, 562–571. doi:10.1016/j.jclepro.2013.10.013

Pojasek, R. B. (2007). A framework for business sustainability. *Environmental Quality Management, 17*(2), 81–88. doi:10.1002/tqem.20168

Richardson, N. (2016). Review of Soft Systems Methodology in Action. *Philosophy of Management, 15*(3), 1–4. doi:10.100740926-015-0023-5

Sambhanthan, A., & Potdar, V. (2015). Green Business Practices for Software Development Companies. *International Journal of Enterprise Information Systems, 11*(3), 13–26. doi:10.4018/IJEIS.2015070102

Sambhanthan, A., & Potdar, V. (2016a). Business sustainability frameworks a survey. In *2016 IEEE/ACIS 14th International Conference on Software Engineering Research, Management and Applications, SERA 2016* (pp. 171–177). IEEE. 10.1109/SERA.2016.7516143

Sambhanthan, A., & Potdar, V. (2016b). Organisations' Responsibilities towards Corporate Sustainability. *International Journal of Strategic Information Technology and Applications, 7*(2), 44–58. doi:10.4018/IJSITA.2016040104

Sambhanthan, A., & Potdar, V. (2016c). Waste management strategies for Software Development companies: An explorative text analysis of business sustainability reports. In *2016 IEEE 14th International Conference on Software Engineering Research, Management and Applications (SERA)* (pp. 179–184). IEEE. 10.1109/SERA.2016.7516144

Sambhanthan, A., & Potdar, V. (2017). A Study of the Parameters Impacting Sustainability in Information Technology Organizations. *International Journal of Knowledge Based Organizations.* Retrieved from https://www.igi-global.com/article/a-study-of-the-parameters-impacting-sustainability-in-information-technology-organizations/182275

Sambhanthan, A., Potdar, V., & Chang, E. (2017). *Business Sustainability Conceptualization.* Springer International Publishing; doi:10.1007/978-3-319-51472-7_1

Shrivastava, P. (1995). The role of corporations in achieving ecological sustainability. *Academy of Management Review, 20*(4), 936–960. doi:10.5465/AMR.1995.9512280026

Sushandoyo, D., & Magnusson, T. (2014). Strategic niche management from a business perspective: Taking cleaner vehicle technologies from prototype to series production. *Journal of Cleaner Production, 74*, 17–26. doi:10.1016/j.jclepro.2014.02.059

Tseng, S.-C., & Hung, S.-W. (2013). A framework identifying the gaps between customers' expectations and their perceptions in green products. *Journal of Cleaner Production, 59*, 174–184. doi:10.1016/j.jclepro.2013.06.050

Vinkhuyzen, O. M., & Karlsson-Vinkhuyzen, S. I. (2014). The role of moral leadership for sustainable production and consumption. *Journal of Cleaner Production, 63*, 102–113. doi:10.1016/j.jclepro.2013.06.045

Virtusa Environment Day. (2010). Retrieved May 18, 2015, from http://www.csrwire.com/press_releases/29830--2010-Virtusa-Environment-Day

Wang, P., Liu, Q., & Qi, Y. (2014). Factors influencing sustainable consumption behaviors: A survey of the rural residents in China. *Journal of Cleaner Production, 63*, 152–165. doi:10.1016/j.jclepro.2013.05.007

Woodard Charles Jason. (2006). *Architectural Strategy and Design Evolution in Complex Engineered Systems*. Retrieved from http://citeseerx.ist.psu.edu/viewdoc/download?doi=10.1.1.109.3608&rep=rep1&type=pdf

Yin, J., Gao, Y., & Xu, H. (2014). Survey and analysis of consumers' behaviour of waste mobile phone recycling in China. *Journal of Cleaner Production*, *65*, 517–525. doi:10.1016/j.jclepro.2013.10.006

Chapter 6
A Systematic Review of Attributes and Techniques for Open Source Software Evolution Analysis

Munish Saini

https://orcid.org/0000-0003-4129-2591
Guru Nanak Dev University, India

Kuljit Kaur Chahal
Guru Nanak Dev University, India

ABSTRACT

Many studies have been conducted to understand the evolution process of Open Source Software (OSS). The researchers have used various techniques for understanding the OSS evolution process from different perspectives. This chapter reports a meta-data analysis of the systematic literature review on the topic in order to understand its current state and to identify opportunities for the future. This research identified 190 studies, selected against a set of questions, for discussion. It categorizes the research studies into nine categories. Based on the results obtained from the systematic review, there is evidence of a shift in the metrics and methods for OSS evolution analysis over the period of time. The results suggest that there is a lack of a uniform approach to analyzing and interpreting the results. There is need of more empirical work using a standard set of techniques and attributes to verify the phenomenon governing the OSS projects. This will help to advance the field and establish a theory of software evolution.

1. INTRODUCTION

Due to the rising dominance of Open Source Software (OSS) in the software industry; not only are practitioners, but researchers as well as academicians also keen to understand the OSS development and evolution process. OSS development involves various stakeholders ranging from contributing volunteers

DOI: 10.4018/978-1-6684-3702-5.ch006

to commercial software vendors. There is need to understand the OSS development model in general and OSS evolution in particular so that the evolution process can be improved, if need be, for the future systems.

OSS evolution has attracted a lot of attention in the last decade. Easy and free availability of data on open source projects has resulted in a splurge of studies in this domain. As a result, the number of empirical studies related to OSS is much more in number in comparison to other topics in the field (Stol and Babar, 2009). Various methods have been employed in the past for analysis and prediction of OSS evolution. It is necessary to systematically summarise the empirical evidence obtained on these methods from the existing literature so that it is easy to comprehend the research work in this area, and reveal gaps in the existing work. As per the existing work in this direction, a few studies focusing on the survey of literature in the domain have been published. Fernandez- Ramil et al. (2008) discuss, in an informal way, a small sample (seven in numbers) of OSS evolution studies. Breivold et al. (2010) carry out a systematic literature review of OSS evolution studies (41 in numbers) focusing only on the evolvability characteristic of OSS systems. Syeed et al. (2013) follows a systematic literature review protocol to analyze studies on OSS Evolution. They present review of 101 research papers but their focus is on a limited set of categories of studies. Stol and Babar (2009) reviewed empirical studies reported in four International OSS conferences to assess quality of the papers from the perspective of the way they report the empirical research in OSS. Unlike the present study, their target is not review of studies on OSS evolution but assessment of quality of empirical research papers involving OSS systems. This chapter presents a systematic literature review of an extensive list of research papers published on the subject between the period of 1997 and 2016.

A number of research publications on OSS evolution have explored the phenomenon from different dimensions using different approaches. Broadly two dimensions are taken: Evolution in OSS structure, and Evolution in OSS community. Software structure exploration includes source code analysis, version history analysis, and repository information analysis. Community structure exploration includes social network analysis. Both the dimensions cannot be isolated from each other. They are useful when put together, and complement each other in answering questions regarding the OSS development and evolution process. Analyzing the links between the software structure and the developer community helps in improving software evaluation and quality.

In this chapter, we report a meta-data analysis on comprehensive review on OSS evolution published in the time period of 1997 to 2016 along with discussion on the project attributes and techniques used for analyzing software evolution (Chahal and Saini, 2016a; 2016b).

The rest of the paper is organized as follows: Section 2 presents the research questions that are addressed in this systematic review and the research criteria followed in this study for selection of primary studies. Section 3 presents the answers to the research questions identified in this work. Section 4 gives conclusions and future directions obtained from this systematic review.

2. RESEARCH METHODOLOGY

The review process follows a systematic review protocol (Kitchenham, 2007) so as to reduce the research bias. The review process included the following steps: 1) Defining the research questions, 2) Choosing a search strategy and study selection criteria, and 3) Data Extraction and Synthesis.

To begin with, research questions set the motivation for collection of relevant research studies. An objective quality assessment criterion helps in deciding the selection of studies as per their focus on research questions and quality of presentation as well. OSS evolution studies are categorized under various heads to put the related work at one place for easy understanding. The chapter summarizes the techniques and the empirical evidence available in the reviewed papers. A set of 9 different categories (see Table 1), with further subcategories, are identified for understanding the variety of techniques and methods for OSS evolution.

For detailed review methodology refer to our previous publications (Chahal and Saini, 2016a; 2016b).

Table 1. Research questions

Sr. No.	Research Question
1.	Which attributes and techniques have been used for OSS evolution analysis?
2.	Which attributes and techniques have been used for OSS evolution prediction?
3.	Is there any evidence of difference in the evolution of OSS v/s CSS?
4.	How do artifacts, other than source code, evolve in OSS systems?
5.	How has the choice of programming languages changed over the period of time in OSS evolution?
6.	What is the state of software development paradigms such as software reuse in the OSS evolution?
7.	How has the community contribution evolved?
8.	What part of the software evolution process has been automated?
9.	What is the state of the theory of OSS evolution?

3. RESULTS AND DISCUSSION

This section presents the details of the studies focusing on evolution of OSS systems. After a thorough analysis, 190 studies are selected for discussion here. All these studies address different aspects of the OSS evolution. First, we describe the meta-analysis of the research studies discussing their publication sources, and publication year. Then the results for each research question are discussed in the subsequent sections.

3.1. The Meta-Data Analysis

This section presents the meta-data analysis of the research studies identified for discussion in this chapter.

3.1.1. Publication Sources

Table 2 summarizes the details of the publications in top journals, conferences, workshops, and symposium along with the number indicating the count for studies (the table shows only the publications with count more than 3). Majority of the publications are in the International Conference on Software Maintenance (ICSM),IEEE Transactions on Software Engineering, International Conference on Software Engineering, International Workshop on Principles of Software Evolution, and Journal of Software

Maintenance and Evolution: Research and Practice. A significant portion of the studies is published as conference papers with the ICSM attracting most of the work in this domain. Interestingly, International Conference on Open Source Systems lags way behind ICSM for giving space to studies on OSS evolution, despite its focus on the core domain. It has been observed that researchers prefer to publish their work in conferences as compared to journals (Hermenegildo, 2012). Perhaps the reason is that journal papers are long and take more time to get the work published, whereas conferences let a researcher present, and publish work quickly. Conferences also provide opportunities for social/professional networking with other researchers in the field. Unfortunately, in some countries publishing work in conference proceedings is not encouraged. The University Grants Commission, India in its latest guidelines for promotion of university/college teachers does not assign any API (Application Performance Indicators) score for research publications in conferences. Only the paper presenter can claim the score, not the co-authors.

Figure 1 indicates that the journals have the second highest count in the total number of publication sources. Moreover, the research in this domain is not limited to journals or conferences; there are symposiums, workshops, book chapters, technical reports, and other forms of publication as well.

We further explored and found that majority of the publications (Journals/proceedings) are in IEEE (see Figure 2). Next is the ACM for sponsoring conferences alone or with IEEE (ACM/IEEE). In others category, there are publishers like Academia, IGI global, SECC, SERSC, Pearson, Science Direct etc., where publications related to software evolution can be found.

Table 2. A summary of top publications

Publication Name	Type	Number
International Conference on Software Maintenance	Conference	18
IEEE Transactions on Software Engineering	Journal	8
International Conference on Software Engineering	Conference	7
International Workshop on Principles of Software Evolution	Workshop	7
Journal of Software Maintenance and Evolution: Research And Practice	Journal	6
Journal of Systems and Software	Journal	4
Journal of Empirical Software Engineering	Journal	4
Working Conference on Reverse Engineering	Conference	4
International Conference on Open Source Systems	Conference	4
International Workshop on Mining Software Repositories	Conference	4
Journal of Software: Evolution and Process	Journal	4
Journal of Information and Software Technology	Journal	3
Conference on Software Maintenance and Reengineering	Conference	3
International Workshop on Emerging Trends in Software Metrics	Workshop	3
International Software Metrics Symposium	Symposium	3
IEEE Software	Journal	3

Figure 1. Type of Publication

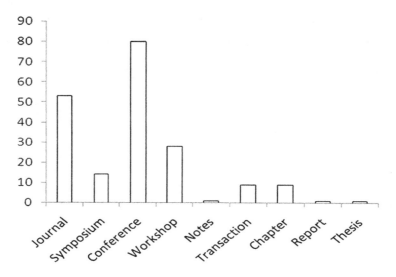

Figure 2. Top Publishers for OSS evolution Studies

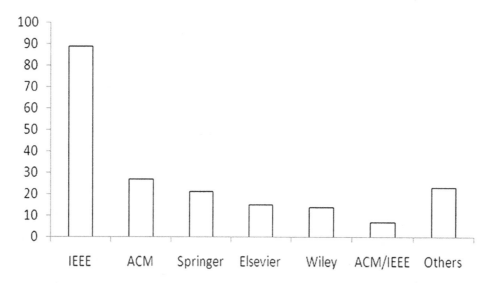

3.1.2. Year Wise Distribution

Figure 3 indicates that in almost all the years (from 1997-2016), there is a study on the software evolution. Therefore, it has been consistently a topic of active interest for the research community. Figure 3 shows that number of research studies increased continuously until 2009. After that the number dropped. It may be attributed to the shift in focus from evolution of single systems (reviewed in this chapter) to evolution of OSS eco systems (out of scope of this study (see section 2 Table 1). The significant drop in the year 2016 may be due to the fact that data for the complete year is not recorded in the study (as it may not be available online at the time of data collection).

Figure 3. Year wise distribution of studies

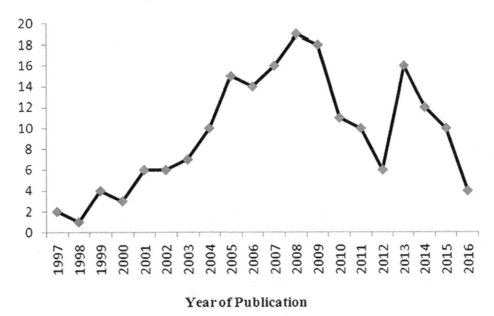

Year of Publication

3.1.3. Perspectives of OSS Evolution

In this study, our main focus is on measuring and analyzing the evolution of OSS projects. In addition to it, various tools, methods, and techniques that were used to measure the evolution of OSS projects. As indicated in Table 1, in this study 9 different categories, with further subcategories, are identified for understanding the variety of techniques and methods for OSS evolution.

Figure 4 shows that software evolution category has the highest peak in the graph. It is obvious due to the focus of this study on the topic. Other main areas on which this study have explored and given the details about evolution techniques and tools are of: software development, software maintenance, code analysis, visualization, and change analysis. This study also pointed that software evolution can be analyzed from the point of view of programming languages, co-evolution, software growth, prediction, software quality, and software communities etc.

3.2. OSS Evolution Analysis: Techniques and Empirical Results

Taking research questions as the points of reference, this section presents the various studies selected in this SLR to analyze their contribution in advancing the state of the art. It summarizes the techniques and the empirical evidence available in the reviewed papers. For a detailed discussion, please refer to these papers (Chahal and Saini, 2016a; 2016b).

Figure 4. Various perspectives of OSS evolution

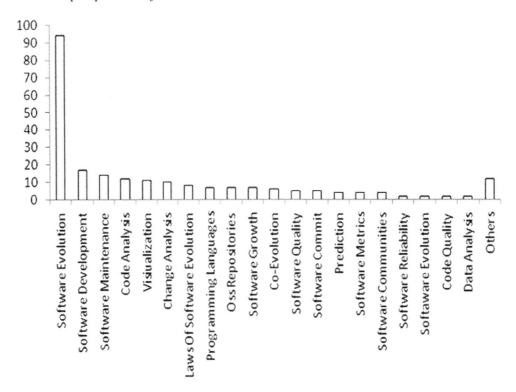

3.2.1. RQ 1: Which Attributes and Techniques Have Been Used for OSS Evolution Analysis?

Based on the studies, we identified the following categories to understand the attributes and techniques the researchers used to analyze OSS evolution.

Broadly, the data is extracted from the following sources, and researchers employ various techniques for analyzing the data:

- **Source Code Analysis:** Measuring different aspects of code has been of interest of researchers as well as practitioners in the software engineering field since long time back, when software measurement was looked up to as a tool to make software development a scientific process. The idea was to make progress in the software development measurable, so that it can be monitored and controlled. Moreover, code quality was thought of as a basis to ensure quality of a software product. Therefore, source code measurement attracted a lot of attention. Among the traditional set of source code metrics, we can include size, complexity, coupling and cohesion metrics. As the paradigms change, more metrics are added to measure the new features such as inheritance in Object Oriented Systems. After extracting the source code, it is analyzed from various perspectives. We noticed the following techniques for analyzing the software evolution in the review papers:
  - Using Metrics
    - Growth Analysis (Godfrey and Tu, 2000; Lehman et al., 2001; Robles et al., 2005; Koch, 2007)

- Complexity Analysis (Tahvildari et al., 1999; Stewart et al., 2006; Darcy et al., 2010; Girba et al.,2005b)
- Modularity Analysis (Milev et al., 2009; Capiluppi, 2009; Alenezi and Zarour, 2015; Olszak et al., 2015)
- Architectural Analysis (Capiluppi, 2004a; LaMantia et al., 2008; Wermilinger et al., 2011; Le et al., 2015; Alenezi and Khellah, 2015)
  - ○ Topic Models Based Approach (Hassan et al., 2005a; Thomas et al., 2014, Hu et al., 2015)
  - ○ Complex Systems Theory (Wu et al., 2007; Herraiz et al., 2008; Gorshenev and Pismak, 2003)
  - ○ Graph/Network Analysis Based Approach (Jenkins and Kirk,2007; Murgia et al., 2009; Wang et al., 2009; Ferreira et al., 2011; Pan et al., 2011; Chaikalis et al., 2015; Kpodjedo et al., 2013)
  - ○ Information Theory Based Approach (Abd-El-Hafiz, 2004; Arbuckle, 2009; Arbuckle, 2011)
  - ○ Qualitative Reasoning Based Approach (Smith et al., 2005)
- **Source Code Management System or Repository:** OSS development is a complex activity involving volunteers. There is need to analyze an OSS system from a wider perspective, i.e. beyond its source code files, to understand and improve the software development process (Robles et al., 2006a). An OSS project management team uses several types of repositories to track the activities of a software project as it progresses (Hassan et al., 2005b). Examples of such repositories are – Code repositories, historical repositories, and run-time repositories. Several techniques and attributes have been explored in the research literature to analyze the change management information available in a code repository.
  - ○ Change analysis (Gefen and Schneberger, 1996; Kemerer and Slaughter, 1997; Schach et al.,2003; Barry et al., 2003; Gupta et al., 2008; Ali and Maqbool, 2009; Hindle et al., 2009a; Meqdadi et al., 2013; Saini and Kaur, 2014a; Ahmed et al., 2015)
  - ○ Change request analysis (Herraiz et al., 2007a; Goulão et al., 2012)
  - ○ Commit analysis (Hattori and Lanza, 2008; Hindle et al., 2009a; Alali et al., 2008; Agrawal et al., 2015; Santos et al., 2016)

3.2.2. RQ2: Which Attributes and Techniques Have Been Used for OSS Evolution Prediction?

Prediction or forecast states the way things are going to occur in future. Time series analysis is the most commonly used tool (Yuen, 1985; 1987; 1988) to predict future attributes, e.g. size, defects of software systems.The software evolution metrics (based on project/process attributes) undertaken for prediction include

- Monthly number of changes (Herraiz, 2007a; Kemerer and S. Slaughter, 1999),
- Change requests (Goulão et al.,2012; Kenmei et al.,2008),
- Size & complexity (Caprio et al., 2001; Fuentetaja et al. 2002),
- Defects (Kläs et al., 2010; Raja et al., 2009),
- Clones (Antoniol et al., 2001), and
- Maintenance effort (Yu, 2006).

Various techniques used for software evolution prediction include. The review studies explore the following models for OSS evolution prediction:

- ARIMA (Caprio et al., 2001; Kenmei et al., 2008)),
- ARMA models (Zhongmin et al., 2010),
- Hybrid models such as ARIMA and SVN (Kemerer and Slaughter,1999; Goulão et al., 2012),
- Data mining techniques (Ratzinger et al., 2007; Siy et al., 2007),
- Signal processing techniques (Dalle et al., 2006),
- Linear regression models (Zimmermann et al.,2007),
- Simulation tools (Smith et al., 2006; Lin, 2013).

A perusal of the existing research in this area shows ARIMA modelling as the most frequently used prediction procedure. However, OSS development is a wobbly process. Unlike the traditional development in which the environment is controlled, OSS development is based on contributions from volunteers who could not be forced to work even if something is of high priority for the project (Godfrey et al., 2000). Along with this unplanned activity, there is a lack of planned documentation related to requirements, and detailed design (Herraiz et al., 2007c). Classical time series techniques are inappropriate for analysis and forecasting of the data which involve random variables (Herraiz et al., 2007b; Kemerer et al., 1999). Fuzzy time series can work for domains which involve uncertainty. Saini and Kaur (2014b) propose to use a computation method of forecasting based on fuzzy time series (Singh, 2008) to predict the number of commits in OSS projects. Fuzzy time series can work for domains which involve uncertainty. Open source projects, sans any tight organizational support, face many uncertainties. Uncertainty lies in uncontrolled development environment such as availability of contributors at any point of time. Due to uncertainty, there is a large fluctuation in consecutive values. Analysis of monthly commits of three OSS projects, Eclipse, PostgreSQL, and Wildfly, indicates that the computation method outperforms the naive random walk model. When the study was expanded to seven OSS projects, the computation method did even better than the ARIMA models (Saini and kaur, 2016).

3.2.3. RQ 3: Is There Any Evidence of Difference in the Evolution of OSS v/s CSS?

Proprietary systems or Closed Source Systems (CSS) are developed following a strict organizational control. With OSS systems getting popular, a comparison of the CSS development process model with the new bazaar style development approach is but natural.

Based on the review, some studies have focused on the comparison of characteristics of OSS with CSS from their evolutionary behavior point of view. They pointed that the evolution of OSS and CSS may or may not vary in terms of

- Growth rate (Paulson et al., 2004); Robles et al., 2003; Capiluppi et al., 2004b; Xie et al., 2009; Neamtiu et al., 2013; Ferreira et al., 2011).
- System features (Mockus et al., 2002)
- Quality of code (Stamelos et al., 2002)
- Creativity (Paulson et al., 2004)
- Changing rate (Paulson et al., 2004)
- Modularity (Paulson et al., 2004)

- Effort estimation models (Fernandez- Ramil et al., 2008)
- Bug-fixing process and release frequency (Rossi et al., 2009)

Unlike CSS systems, OSS systems do not have a constrained growth due to increasing complexity as they evolve. However, software evolution is a discontinuous phenomenon in both the cases.

3.2.4. RQ 4: How Do Artifacts, Other Than Source Code, Evolve in OSS Systems?

Several software artifacts co-evolve with source code. The researchers have studied the evolution of source code with various artifacts, such as

- Build systems (Robles et al., 2006b; Adams et al., 2008; McIntosh et al., 2012)
- Comments (Fluri et al., 2009)
- Test-code (Marsavina et al., 2014)
- Changes related to database schema (Qiu et al., 2013)
- Database related activities (Goeminne et al., 2014)

There are a few studies in which artifacts other than source code are studied together

- Test-code and production code (Zaidman et al., 2011)
- Infrastructure as Code (IaC) files along with three other types of files – source code, test, and build files (Jiang and Adams, 2015)

3.2.5. RQ 5: How Has the Choice of Programming Languages Changed Over the Period of Time in the OSS Evolution?

The development of OSS has initiated a revolution in the development process of software, as most of the software systems nowadays are developed with the support for multiple programming languages (Delorey et al., 2007). However, the choice of programming languages has changed over the period of time.

- Trend in the popularity of different set of programming languages (Karus and Gall, 2011; Bhattacharya et al., 2011)
  - Scripting and Interpreter based (platform independent) languages are more popular (Robles et al., 2006b)
- Choice of language viz-a-viz developer productivity, and defect density (Phipps, 1999; Myrtveit et al., 2008)
- Choice of language and gender of the developers (Dattero and Galup, 2004)

3.2.6. RQ 6: What Is the State of Software Development Paradigms Such as Software Reuse in the OSS Evolution?

Software reuse is a means for overcoming software crisis (Pressman, 2010). McIlroy (1968) pointed towards the reuse of code to build large reliable software systems in a controlled and cost effective way.

It has been observed that OSS projects make extensive use of (third party) reusable software components (Zaimi et al., 2015). A few other papers that studied software reuse aspects in OSS projects are as follows:

- Developers' choice of evolutionary reuse for cost efficiency (Capra, 2006).
- Differences in the nature of evolution of libraries v/s applications (Vaucher and Sahraoui, 2007).
- The effect of reuse based development style on the evolution of software systems (Gupta et al., 2008).
- The evolutionary aspects of reusable software components (Kaur, 2013).

3.2.7. RQ 7: How Has the Community Contribution Evolved?

The development of OSS is not a well-planned activity (Goulão et al., 2012). A few people start an OSS project, users of the OSS system contribute to make changes to satisfy their own requirements, and the system starts evolving. Users and developers of an OSS project are called the OSS community. Community drives the evolution of OSS (Girba et al., 2005a). Research studies discussed the OSS community from different points of view:

- To identify reasonable community size to sustain an OSS project (Mockus et al., 2002; Capiluppi, 2003).
- The community dynamics (Nakakoji et al., 2002).
- Stability of the Community support (Robles et al., 2005).
- Developer productivity (Capiluppi et al., 2004b).
- Inequality in work distribution in OSS projects (Koch et al., 2007; Mockus et al., 2002)
- Team profile and structure in large vs small OSS projects (Xu et al., 2005)
- The deadline effect (Lin et al., 2013).
- Predicting next release date on the basis of community activity (Weicheng et al., 2013).

3.2.8. RQ 8: What Part of the Software Evolution Process Has Been Automated?

Automated support for a software engineering task is always appreciated as it can not only help to handle large volumes of data but also makes the task easily repeatable. Several tools have been created to handle comparison of successive versions of OSS systems, and to answer software evolution related questions. Some of these tools are

- Beagle (Tu and Godfrey, 2002)
- Kenyon (Bevan et al., 2005)
- Ferret (Rainer et al., 2008).
- Churrasco (D'Ambros and Lanza, 2010)
- CodeVizard (Zazworka and Ackermann, 2010).
- Replay (Hattori et al., 2013)

3.2.9. RQ 9: What Is the State of Theory of OSS Evolution?

In software evolution, Lehman's laws (1974, 1978, 1996) can be the best (and the only) example of a theory, though many empirical studies have refuted these laws in the context of OSS evolution. Several studies checked the applicability of Lehman's laws:

- Anomaly in the applicability of the laws (Godfrey and Tu, 2000, Robles et al., 2005).
- Confirmed the two laws related to continuous change (1st law), and continuous growth (6th law) (Godfrey and Tu, 2000, 2001; Bauer and Pizka, 2003; Wu and Holt, 2004; Robles et al., 2005; Herraiz et al., 2006; Koch, 2005, 2007; Mens et al., 2008; Israeli and Feitelson, 2010; Vasa, 2010; and Neamtiu et al., 2013).
- The fourth law confirmed only in (Israeli and Feitelson, 2010).
- The fifth law confirmed only in (Vasa, 2010).
- Only Bauer and Pizka (2003) confirm all the eight laws.
- Lehman's laws for small v/s large systems (Roy and Cordy, 2006; Koch, 2007).

All these studies lack a uniform approach to analyze and interpret the results. There are multiple interpretations of the statements defining the laws. The metrics for measuring the constructs to validate the laws are defined differently in different studies.

With the availability of tools and data resources in the public domain, researchers can now repeat experiments and build empirical evidence to confirm/refute the laws. However, collecting empirical evidence is only the first stage for theory building. It has to be followed by hypothesis formulation, testing, and then optimization (Godfrey and German, 2008). In the new context, laws should be reformulated to suit the changing software development paradigms as they have not been since 1996.

4. CONCLUSION AND FUTURE GUIDELINES

Open Source Software has been able to get a lot of attention of the research community as it is easy not only to prove a new concept, but also to repeat the experiments on OSS data sets available in the public domain. The meta-data analysis depicts valuable facts such as:

- Most of the contributors prefer to publish their work in conferences as compared to journals.
- The evolution of OSS is measured by using different methods, tools and techniques.
- IEEE and ACM are among the publishers who published research related to OSS evolution.

Some of the other major revelations of the review results are as follows:

- Software size has been the most common attribute to analyze evolution of OSS projects. Several types of metrics have been employed to measure software size. These metrics range from coarse grained level metrics such as number of files, modules, and functions, to fine grained level metrics such as number of LOC, methods, and classes. Several approaches, other than source code analysis using metrics, to analyze OSS evolution have also been employed in the research literature.

- Lately, metrics related to change activity have also been included to understand OSS evolution. These metrics measure changes in source code such as number of program elements (functions/ classes/methods) changed in consecutive versions. Change activity as recorded in SCM systems is also used in a few cases. Most of the work deals with finding change size, change effort distributions. A few studies do change profile analysis as OSS systems evolve. But that is restricted to a few of the change categories e.g. adaptive v/s non-adaptive changes, or corrective v/s non-corrective changes. A fine-grained view of the changes can help to answer amount of progressive/ regressive work performed in a software system as it evolves. It can also be used to validate Lehman's 2nd law as Gonzalez-Barahona (2014) points to the lack of information available in this regard in their study of the glibc system.
- Herraiz et al. (2007c) observed that there are no long term correlations in the time series representing OSS activity. There is need to explore other alternative methods for time series analysis (rather than ARIMA) to deal with the uncertain evolutionary behavior of OSS systems.
- A shift in the programming languages, from procedural to object oriented, has been noticed as OSS systems, as subject systems in the corresponding studies, evolved over the period of time.
- Techniques and tools have been devised to tackle large amounts of data generated in software evolution analysis and prediction. Software evolution automation offers to collect volumes of data in a consistent manner. Software evolution visualization helps in understanding the transitions in complex and large systems in an easy way. Big data analytics can also help to analyze large sets of data generated during software evolution. Data analytics can be used to manage and understand the complex web of software evolution as it happens in source code and other related repositories.

REFERENCES

Abd-El-Hafiz, S. (2004). *An Information Theory Approach to Studying Software Evolution. Alexandria Engineering Journal, 43*(2), 275–284.

Adams, B., De Schutter, K., Tromp, H., & De Meuter, W. (2008). The evolution of the Linux build system. *Electronic Communications of the EASST, 8.*

Agrawal, K., Amreen, S., & Mockus, A. (2015). Commit quality in five high performance computing projects. In *International Workshop on Software Engineering for High Performance Computing in Science* (pp. 24-29). IEEE Press. 10.1109/SE4HPCS.2015.11

Ahmed, I., Mannan, U., Gopinath, R., & Jensen, C. (2015). An Empirical Study of Design Degradation: How Software Projects Get Worse over Time. *Proceedings of the 2015 ACM/IEEE International Symposium on Empirical Software Engineering and Measurement*, 1 – 10. 10.1109/ESEM.2015.7321186

Alali, A., Kagdi, H., & Maletic, J. (2008). What's a Typical Commit? A Characterization of Open Source Software Repositories. In *Proceedings of the 16th International Conference on Program Comprehension* (pp. 182-191). IEEE. 10.1109/ICPC.2008.24

Alenezi, M., & Khellah, F. (2015). Architectural Stability Evolution in Open-Source Systems. In *Proceedings of the International Conference on Engineering & MIS 2015 (ICEMIS '15)*. ACM. 10.1145/2832987.2833014

Alenezi, M., & Zarour, M. (2015). Modularity Measurement and Evolution in Object-Oriented Open-Source Projects. In *Proceedings of the International Conference on Engineering & MIS (ICEMIS '15)*. doi:10.1145/2832987.2833013

Ali, S., & Maqbool, O. (2009). Monitoring Software Evolution Using Multiple Types of Changes. In *Proceedings of the 2009 International Conference on Emerging Technologies* (pp. 410-415). IEEE. 10.1109/ICET.2009.5353135

Antoniol, G., Casazza, G., Penta, M., & Merlo, E. (2001). Modeling Clones Evolution through Time Series. In *Proceedings of the IEEE International Conference on Software Maintenance* (pp. 273-280). IEEE.

Arbuckle, T. (2009). Measure Software and its Evolution-using Information Content. In *Proceedings of the joint international and annual ERCIM workshops on Principles of Software Evolution (IWPSE) and Software Evolution (Evol) Workshops* (pp. 129-134). ACM. doi:10.1145/1595808.1595831

Arbuckle, T. (2011). Studying Software Evolution using Artifacts Shared Information Content. *Science of Computer Programming*, 76(12), 1078–1097. doi:10.1016/j.scico.2010.11.005

Barry, E., Kemerer, C., & Slaughter, S. (2003). On the Uniformity of Software Evolution Patterns. *Proceedings of the 25th International Conference on Software Engineering*, 106-113. 10.1109/ICSE.2003.1201192

Bauer, A., & Pizka, M. (2003). The Contribution of Free Software to Software Evolution. In *Proceedings of the Sixth International Workshop on Principles of Software Evolution* (pp. 170-179). IEEE. 10.1109/IWPSE.2003.1231224

Bevan, J., Whitehead, E. Jr, Kim, S., & Godfrey, M. (2005). Facilitating Software Evolution Research with Kenyon. *Software Engineering Notes*, 30(5), 177–186. doi:10.1145/1095430.1081736

Bhattacharya, P., & Neamtiu, I. (2011). Assessing Programming Language Impact on Development and Maintenance: A Study on C and C++. In *Proceedings of the 33rd International Conference on Software Engineering (ICSE)* (pp. 171-180). IEEE. 10.1145/1985793.1985817

Breivold, H., Chauhan, M., & Babar, M. (2010) A Systematic Review of Studies of Open Source Software Evolution. *Proceedings of the 17th Asia Pacific Software Engineering Conference (APSEC)*, 356-365. 10.1109/APSEC.2010.48

Capiluppi, A. (2003). Models for the Evolution of OS Projects. In *Proceedings of International Conference on Software Maintenance (ICSM)*. IEEE. 10.1109/ICSM.2003.1235407

Capiluppi, A. (2009). Domain Drivers in the Modularization of FLOSS Systems. Open Source EcoSystems: Diverse Communities Interacting. In C. Boldyreff, K. Crownston, B. Lundell et al. (Eds.), *Proceedings of the 5th IFIP WG 2.13 International Conference on Open Source Systems OSS '09*. Skovde, Sweden: Springer. 10.1007/978-3-642-02032-2_3

Capiluppi, A., Morisio, M., & Ramil, J. (2004a). The Evolution of Source folder structure in actively evolved Open Source Systems. In *Proceedings of the 10th International Symposium on Software metrics (METRICS '04)* (pp. 2-13). IEEE Computer Society, 10.1109/METRIC.2004.1357886

Capiluppi, A., Morisio, M., & Ramil, J. (2004b). Structural Evolution of an Open Source System: A case study. *Proceedings of the International Workshop on Program Comprehension.* 10.1109/WPC.2004.1311059

Capra, E. (2006). Mining Open Source web repositories to measure the cost of Evolutionary reuse. In *Proceedings of the 1st International Conference on Digital Information Management* (pp. 496-503). IEEE.

Caprio, F., Casazza, G., Penta, M., & Villano, U. (2001). Measuring and predicting the Linux kernel Evolution. *Proceedings of the Seventh Workshop on Empirical Studies of Software Maintenance*, 77.

Chahal, K. K., & Saini, M. (2016a). Open Source Software Evolution: A Systematic Literature Review (Part 1). *International Journal of Open Source Software and Processes*, 7(1), 1–27. doi:10.4018/IJOSSP.2016010101

Chahal, K. K., & Saini, M. (2016b). Open Source Software Evolution: A Systematic Literature Review (Part 2). *International Journal of Open Source Software and Processes*, 7(1), 28–48. doi:10.4018/IJOSSP.2016010102

Chaikalis, T., & Chatzigeorgiou, A. (2015). Forecasting Java Software Evolution Trends Employing Network Models. *IEEE Transactions on Software Engineering*, 41(6), 582–602. doi:10.1109/TSE.2014.2381249

D'Ambros, M., & Lanza, M. (2010). Distributed and Collaborative Software Evolution Analysis with Churrasco. *Science of Computer Programming*, 75.

Dalle, J. M., Daudet, L., & den Besten, M. (2006). Mining CVS signals. *Proceedings of the Workshop on Public Data about Software Development*, 12-21.

Darcy, P., Daniel, L., & Stewart, K. (2010). Exploring Complexity in Open Source Software: Evolutionary Patterns, Antecedents, and Outcomes. In *Proceedings of the 2010 43rd Hawaii International Conference on System Sciences (HICSS)*. IEEE Press. 10.1109/HICSS.2010.198

Dattero, R., & Galup, S. (2004). Programming languages and Gender. *Communications of the ACM*, 47(1), 99–102. doi:10.1145/962081.962087

Delorey, D., Knutson, C., & Giraud-Carrier, C. (2007). Programming language trends in Open Source development: An evaluation using data from all production phase Sourceforge Projects. *Proceedings of the Second International Workshop on Public Data about Software Development (WoPDaSD'07)*.

Fernandez-Ramil, J., Lozano, A., Wermilinger, M., & Capiluppi, A. (2008). Empirical Studies of Open Source Evolution. In T. Mens & S. Demeyer (Eds.), *Software Evolution* (pp. 263–288). Berlin: Springer. doi:10.1007/978-3-540-76440-3_11

Ferreira, K., Bigonha, A., Bigonha, S., & Gomes, M. (2011). Software Evolution Characterization-a Complex Network Approach. *Proceedings of the X Brazilian Symposium on Software Quality-SBQS*, 41-55.

Fluri, B., Würsch, M., Giger, E., & Gall, H. (2009). Analyzing the Co-Evolution of Comments and Source code. *Software Quality Journal, 17*(4), 367–394. doi:10.100711219-009-9075-x

Fuentetaja, E., & Bagert, D. (2002). Software Evolution from a Time-series Perspective. In *Proceedings International Conference on Software Maintenance* (pp. 226-229). IEEE. 10.1109/ICSM.2002.1167769

Gefen, D., & Schneberger, S. (1996). The Non-homogeneous Maintenance Periods: a Case Study of Software Modifications. In *Proceedings International Conference on Software Maintenance* (pp. 134-141). IEEE. 10.1109/ICSM.1996.564998

Girba, T., Kuhn, A., Seeberger, M., & Ducasse, S. (2005a). How Developers Drive Software Evolution. In *Proceedings of the Eighth International Workshop on Principles of Software Evolution* (pp. 113-122). IEEE. 10.1109/IWPSE.2005.21

Girba, T., Lanza, M., & Ducasse, S. (2005b). Characterizing the Evolution of Class Hierarchies. In *Proceedings of the Ninth European Conference on Software Maintenance and Reengineering (CSMR)* (pp. 2-11). IEEE. 10.1109/CSMR.2005.15

Godfrey, M., & German, D. (2008). Frontiers of software maintenance track. In *International Conference on Software Engineering* (pp. 129-138). IEEE.

Godfrey, M., & Tu, Q. (2000). Evolution in Open Source Software: A case study. In *Proceedings of the International Conference on Software Maintenance* (pp. 131–142). IEEE. 10.1109/ICSM.2000.883030

Godfrey, M., & Tu, Q. (2001). Growth, Evolution, and Structural Change in Open Source Software. In *Proc. of the 2001 Intl. Workshop on Principles of Software Evolution (IWPSE-01)* (pp. 103-106). IEEE.

Goeminne, M., Decan, A., & Mens, T. (2014). Co-evolving Code-related and Database-related Changes in a Data-intensive Software System. *Proceedings of the IEEE Conference on Software Maintenance, Reengineering and Reverse Engineering (CSMR-WCRE)*, 353–357. 10.1109/CSMR-WCRE.2014.6747193

Gonzalez-Barahona, J. M., Robles, G., Herraiz, I., & Ortega, F. (2014). Studying the laws of software evolution in a long-lived FLOSS project. *Journal of Software: Evolution and Process, 26*(7), 589–612. PMID:25893093

Gorshenev, A., & Pismak, M. (2003). Punctuated Equilibrium in Software Evolution. *Physical Review E: Statistical, Nonlinear, and Soft Matter Physics, 70*(6). PMID:15697556

Goulão, M., Fonte, N., Wermelinger, M., & Abreu, F. (2012). Software Evolution Prediction Using Seasonal Time Analysis: A Comparative Study. *Proceedings of 16th European Conference Software Maintenance and Reengineering (CSMR)*, 213-222. 10.1109/CSMR.2012.30

Gupta, A., Cruzes, D., Shull, F., Conradi, R., Rønneberg, H., & Landre, E. (2008). An examination of Change Profiles in reusable and non-reusable Software Systems. *Journal of Software Maintenance and Evolution: Research and Practice, 22*(5), 359–380.

Hassan, A., Mockus, A., Holt, R., & Johnson, P. (2005b). Special issue on Mining Software Repositories. *IEEE Transactions on Software Engineering, 31*(6), 426–428. doi:10.1109/TSE.2005.70

Hassan, A., Wu, J., & Holt, R. (2005a). Visualizing Historical Data Using Spectrographs. In *Proceedings of the 11th IEEE International Software Metrics Symposium (METRICS '05)*. IEEE Computer Society. 10.1109/METRICS.2005.54

Hattori, L., D'Ambros, M., Lanza, M., & Lungu, M. (2013). Answering Software Evolution Questions: An Empirical Evaluation. *Information and Software Technology, 55*(4), 755–775. doi:10.1016/j.infsof.2012.09.001

Hattori, L., & Lanza, M. (2008). On the Nature of Commits. In *Proceedings of the 23rd IEEE/ACM International Conference on Automated Software Engineering-Workshops* (pp. 63-71). IEEE.

Hermenegildo, M. V. (2012). *Conferences vs. journals in CS, what to do? Evolutionary ways forward and the ICLP/TPLP model*. Leibniz-ZentrumfürInformatik.

Herraiz, I., Gonzalez-Barahona, J., & Robles, G. (2007a). Forecasting the Number of Changes in Eclipse using Time Series Analysis. In *Proceedings of the 2007 Fourth International Workshop on Mining Software Repositories MSR'07* (pp. 32-32). IEEE. 10.1109/MSR.2007.10

Herraiz, I., Gonzalez-Barahona, J., & Robles, G. (2007b). Towards a Theoretical Model for Software Growth. In *Proceedings of the Fourth International Workshop on Mining Software Repositories* (p. 21). IEEE Computer Society. 10.1109/MSR.2007.31

Herraiz, I., Gonzalez-Barahona, J., Robles, G., & German, D. (2007c).On the prediction of the Evolution of libre Software Projects. In *Proceedings of the 2007 IEEE International Conference on Software Maintenance (ICSM '07)* (pp. 405-414). IEEE. 10.1109/ICSM.2007.4362653

Herraiz, I., Gonzlez-Barahona, J., & Robles, G. (2008). Determinism and Evolution. In A. Hassan, M. Lanza, & M. Godfrey (Eds.), *Mining Software Repositories*. ACM. doi:10.1145/1370750.1370752

Herraiz, I., Robles, G., González-Barahona, J., Capiluppi, A., & Ramil, J. (2006). Comparison between SLOCs and Number of files as Size Metrics for Software Evolution analysis. In *Proceedings of the 10th European Conference on Software Maintenance and Reengineering (CSMR '06)* (p. 8). IEEE. 10.1109/CSMR.2006.17

Hindle, A., German, D., Godfrey, M., & Holt, R. (2009a). Automatic Classification of Large Changes into Maintenance Categories. In *Proceedings of the 17th International Conference on Program Comprehension ICPC'09* (pp. 30-39). IEEE.

Hu, J., Sun, X., Lo, D., & Bin, L. (2015). Modeling the Evolution of Development Topics using Dynamic Topic Models. *Proceedings of the 2015 IEEE 22nd International Conference on Software Analysis, Evolution and Reengineering, 3-12.* 10.1109/SANER.2015.7081810

Israeli, A., & Feitelson, D. (2010). The Linux Kernel as a Case Study in Software Evolution. *Journal of Systems and Software, 83*(3), 485–501. doi:10.1016/j.jss.2009.09.042

Izurieta, C., & Bieman, J. (2006). The Evolution of FreeBSD and Linux. In *Proceedings of the 2006 ACM/IEEE international symposium on Empirical Software engineering* (pp. 204-211). ACM. 10.1145/1159733.1159765

Jenkins, S., & Kirk, S. (2007). Software Architecture Graphs as Complex Networks: A Novel Partitioning Scheme to Measure Stability and Evolution. *Information Sciences, 177*(12), 2587–2601. doi:10.1016/j.ins.2007.01.021

Jiang, Y., & Adams, B. (2015). Co-Evolution of Infrastructure and Source Code: An Empirical Study. In *Proceedings of the 12th Working Conference on Mining Software Repositories (MSR '15)* (pp. 45-55). Piscataway, NJ: IEEE Press. 10.1109/MSR.2015.12

Karus, S., & Gall, H. (2011). A Study of Language Usage Evolution in Open Source Software. In *Proceedings of the 8th Working Conference on Mining Software Repositories* (pp. 13-22). ACM. 10.1145/1985441.1985447

Kaur, K. (2013). Analyzing Growth Trends of Reusable Software Components. In H. Singh & K. Kaur (Eds.), *Designing, Engineering, and Analyzing Reliable and Efficient Software*. Hershey, PA: IGI Global; doi:10.4018/978-1-4666-2958-5.ch003

Kemerer, C., & Slaughter, S. (1997). A Longitudinal Analysis of Software Maintenance Patterns. In *Proceedings of the eighteenth international conference on Information Systems* (pp. 476-477). Association for Information Systems.

Kemerer, C., & Slaughter, S. (1999). An Empirical Approach to Studying Software Evolution. *IEEE Transactions on Software Engineering, 25*(4), 493–509. doi:10.1109/32.799945

Kenmei, B., Antoniol, G., & Penta, M. (2008). Trend Analysis and Issue Prediction in Large-scale Open Source Systems. In *Proceedings of the 12th European Conference on Software Maintenance and Reengineering (CSMR'08)* (pp. 73-82). IEEE. 10.1109/CSMR.2008.4493302

Kitchenham, B. (2007). *Guidelines for Performing Systematic Literature Review in Software Engineering*. Technical report EBSE-2007-001.

Kläs, M., Elberzhager, F., Münch, J., Hartjes, K., & Von Graevemeyer, O. (2010). Transparent Combination of Expert and Measurement Data for Defect Prediction: an Industrial Case Study. In *Proceedings of the 32nd ACM/IEEE International Conference on Software Engineering* (Vol. 2, pp. 119-128). ACM. 10.1145/1810295.1810313

Koch, S. (2005). Evolution of Open Source System Software Systems - a Large Scale Investigation. *Proceedings of the First International Conference on Open Source Systems*.

Koch, S. (2007). Software Evolution in Open Source Projects—a Large-scale Investigation. *Journal of Software Maintenance and Evolution: Research and Practice, 19*(6), 361–382. doi:10.1002mr.348

Kpodjedo, S., Ricca, F., Galinier, P., & Antoniol, G. (2013). Studying Software Evolution of Large Object Oriented Software Systems using an etgm Algorithm. *Journal of Software: Evolution and Process, 25*(2), 139–163.

LaMantia, M., Cai, Y., MacCormack, A., & Rusnak, J. (2008). Analyzing the Evolution of large-scale Software Systems using Design Structure Matrices and Design Rule Theory: Two Exploratory Cases. In *Proceedings of theSeventh Working IEEE/IFIP Conference on Software Architecture (WICSA '08)* (pp. 83-92). IEEE. doi:10.1109/WICSA.2008.49

Le, D., Behnamghader, P., Garcia, J., Link, D., Shahbazian, A., & Medvidovic, N. (2015). An Empirical Study of Architectural Change in Open-Source Software Systems. In *Proceedings of the 12th Working Conference on Mining Software Repositories (MSR '15)* (pp. 235-245). IEEE. 10.1109/MSR.2015.29

Lehman, M. (1996). Laws of Software Evolution Revisited. In *Proceedings of the European Workshop on Software Process Technology* (pp. 108-124). Springer-Verlag. 10.1007/BFb0017737

Lehman, M., Ramil, J., & Sandler, U. (2001). An Approach to Modeling Long-term Growth Trends in Software Systems. In *Proceedings of the International Conference on Software Maintenance* (pp. 219–228). IEEE.

Lin, S., Ma, Y., & Chen, J. (2013). Empirical Evidence on Developer's Commit Activity for Open-Source Software Projects. *Proceedings of the 25th International Conference on Software Engineering and Knowledge Engineering*, 455-460.

Marsavina, C., Romano, D., & Zaidman, A. (2014). Studying Fine-Grained Co-Evolution Patterns of Production and Test Code. *Proceedings of the 2014 IEEE 14th International Working Conference on Source Code Analysis and Manipulation (SCAM)*, 195-204. 10.1109/SCAM.2014.28

McIntosh, S., Adams, B., & Hassan, A. (2012). The Evolution of Java build Systems. *Empirical Software Engineering*, *17*(4), 578–608. doi:10.100710664-011-9169-5

McIlroy, M. (1968). *Mass Produced Software Components*. Keynote address in NATO Software Engineering Conference.

Mens, T., Fernández-Ramil, J., & Degrandsart, S. (2008). The Evolution of Eclipse. In *Proceedings of the 2008 IEEE International Conference on Software Maintenance (ICSM)* (pp. 386-395). IEEE. 10.1109/ICSM.2008.4658087

Meqdadi, O., Alhindawi, N., Collard, M., & Maletic, J. (2013). Towards Understanding Large-scale Adaptive Changes from Version Histories. In *Proceedings of the 2013 IEEE International Conference on Software Maintenance* (pp. 416-419). IEEE. 10.1109/ICSM.2013.61

Milev, R., Muegge, S., & Weiss, M. (2009). Design Evolution of an Open Source Project using an Improved Modularity Metric. In *Proceedings of the 5th IFIP WG 2.13 International Conference on Open Source Systems OSS '09*. Skovde, Sweden: Springer. 10.1007/978-3-642-02032-2_4

Mockus, A., Fielding, R., & Herbsleb, J. (2002). Two case studies of Open Source Software development: Apache and Mozilla. *ACM Transactions on Software Engineering and Methodology*, *11*(3), 309–346. doi:10.1145/567793.567795

Murgia, A., Concas, G., Marchesi, M., Tonelli, R., & Turnu, I. (2009). Empirical study of Software Quality Evolution in Open Source Projects using Agile Practices. *Proceedings of the International symposium on Emerging Trends in Software Metrics (ETSM)*.

Myrtveit, I., & Stensrud, E. (2008). *An Empirical Study of Software development Productivity in C and C++*. Presented at NIK-2008 conference. Retrieved from www.nik.no

Nakakoji, K., Yamamoto, Y., Nishinaka, Y., Kishida, K., & Ye, Y. (2002). Evolution Patterns of Open-Source Software Systems and Communities. In *Proceedings of the international workshop on Principles of Software Evolution* (pp. 76-85). ACM. 10.1145/512035.512055

Neamtiu, I., Xie, G., & Chen, J. (2013). Towards a Better Understanding of Software Evolution: An Empirical Study on Open-Source Software. *Journal of Software: Evolution and Process, 25*(3), 193–218.

Olszak, A., Lazarova-Molnar, S., & Jørgensen, B. (2015). Evolution of Feature-Oriented Software: How to Stay on Course and Avoid the Cliffs of Modularity Drift. In *Proceedings of the 9th International Joint Conference Software Technologies, CCIS* (Vol. 555, pp. 183-201). Springer.

Pan, W., Li, B., Ma, Y., & Liu, J. (2011). Multi-Granularity Evolution Analysis of Software. *Journal of Systems Science and Complexity, 24*(6), 1068–1082. doi:10.100711424-011-0319-z

Paulson, J., Succi, G., & Eberlein, A. (2004). An Empirical Study of Open-Source and Closed-Source Software products. *IEEE Transactions on Software Engineering, 30*(4), 246–256. doi:10.1109/TSE.2004.1274044

Phipps, G. (1999). Comparing Observed Bug and Productivity Rates for Java and C++. *Software, Practice & Experience, 29*(4), 345–358. doi:10.1002/(SICI)1097-024X(19990410)29:4<345::AID-SPE238>3.0.CO;2-C

Pressman, R. (2010). *Software Engineering – A Practitioner's Approach* (7th ed.). McGraw Hill Education.

Qiu, D., Li, B., & Su, Z. (2013). An Empirical Analysis of the Co-Evolution of Schema and Code in Database Applications. In Meeting on Foundations of Software Engineering, ser. ESEC/FSE 2013 (pp. 125–135). ACM. doi:10.1145/2491411.2491431

Rainer, A., Lane, P., Malcolm, J., & Scholz, S. (2008). Using N-grams to Rapidly Characterise the Evolution of Software code. In *Proceedings of the 23rd IEEE/ACM International Conference on Automated Software Engineering Workshops* (pp. 43-52). IEEE. 10.1109/ASEW.2008.4686320

Raja, U., Hale, D., & Hale, J. (2009). Modeling Software Evolution Defects: A Time Series Approach. *Journal of Software Maintenance and Evolution: Research and Practice, 21*(1), 49–71. doi:10.1002mr.398

Ratzinger, J., Gall, H., & Pinzger, M. (2007). Quality Assessment Based on Attribute Series of Software Evolution. In *Proceedings of the 14th Working Conference on Reverse Engineering WCRE '07* (pp. 80-89). IEEE. 10.1109/WCRE.2007.39

Robles, G., Amor, J., Gonzalez-Barahona, J., & Herraiz, I. (2005). Evolution and Growth in Large Libre Software Projects. In *Proceedings of the International Workshop on Principles in Software Evolution* (pp. 165-174). IEEE. 10.1109/IWPSE.2005.17

Robles, G., Gonzalez-Barahona, J., & Merelo, J. (2006a). Beyond Source Code: The Importance of other Artifacts in Software Development. *Journal of Systems and Software, 79*(9), 1233–1248. doi:10.1016/j.jss.2006.02.048

Robles, G., Gonzalez-Barahona, J., Michlmayr, M., & Amor, J. (2006b). Mining Large Software Compilations over Time: Another Perspective of Software Evolution. In *Proceedings of the 2006 international workshop on Mining Software repositories (MSR'06)* (pp. 3-9). ACM 10.1145/1137983.1137986

Robles-Martinez, G., Gonzlez-Barahona, J., Centeno-Gonzalez, J., Matellan-Olivera, V., & Rodero-Merino, L. (2003). Studying the Evolution of Libre Software Projects using Publicly Available Data. *Proceedings of the 3rd Workshop on Open Source Software Engineering.*

Rossi, B., Russo, B., & Succi, G. (2009) Analysis of Open Source Software Development Iterations by Means of Burst Detection Techniques, In Open Source EcoSystems: Diverse Communities Interacting. In *Proceedings 5th IFIP WG 2.13 International Conference on Open Source Systems* (pp. 83-93). Springer.

Roy, C., & Cordy, J. (2006). *Evaluating the Evolution of Small Scale Open Source Software Systems.* Academic Press.

Saini, M., & Kaur, K. (2014a). Analyzing the Change Profiles of Software Systems using their Change Logs. International Journal of Software Engineering, 7(2), 39-66.

Saini, M., & Kaur, K. (2014b). Software Evolution Prediction using Fuzzy Analysis. In *Proceedings of International Conference on Emerging Applications of Information Technology, organized by Computer Society of India at Indian Institute of Science.* Kolkata, India: IEEE Computer Society Press.

Saini, M., & Kaur, K. (2016). Fuzzy analysis and prediction of commit activity in open source software projects. *IET Software, 10*(5), 136–146. doi:10.1049/iet-sen.2015.0087

Santos, E. A., & Hindle, A. (2016). Judging a commit by its cover; or can a commit message predict build failure?. *PeerJ PrePrints, 4,* e1771v1.

Schach, S., Jin, B., Yu, L., Heller, G., & Offutt, J. (2003). Determining the Distribution of Maintenance Categories: Survey versus Measurement. *Empirical Software Engineering, 8*(4), 351–365. doi:10.1023/A:1025368318006

Singh, S. (2008). A Computational Method of Forecasting Based on Fuzzy Time Series. *Journal of Mathematics and Computers in Simulation, 79*(3), 539–554. doi:10.1016/j.matcom.2008.02.026

Siy, H., Chundi, P., Rosenkrant, D., & Subramaniam, M. (2007). Discovering Dynamic Developer Relationships from Software Version Histories by Time Series Segmentation. In *Proceedings of the 2007 IEEE International Conference on Software Maintenance* (pp. 415-424). IEEE. 10.1109/ICSM.2007.4362654

Smith, N., Capiluppi, A., & Fernandez-Ramil, J. (2006). Agent-based Simulation of Open Source Software Evolution. *Software Process Improvement and Practice, 11*(4), 423–434. doi:10.1002pip.280

Smith, N., Capiluppi, A., & Ramil, J. (2005). A Study of Open Source Software Evolution Data using Qualitative Simulation. *Software Process Improvement and Practice, 10*(3), 287–300. doi:10.1002pip.230

Stamelos, I., Angelis, L., Oikonomou, A., & Bleris, G. L. (2002). Code quality analysis in open source software development. *Information Systems Journal, 12*(1), 43–60. doi:10.1046/j.1365-2575.2002.00117.x

Stewart, K., Darcy, D., & Daniel, S. (2006). Opportunities and Challenges Applying Functional Data Analysis to the Study of Open Source Software Evolution. *Statistical Science, 21*(2), 167–178. doi:10.1214/088342306000000141

Stol, K., & Babar, M. (2009). Reporting Empirical Research in Open Source Software: the State of Practice. In *Proceedings 5th IFIP WG 2.13 International Conference on Open Source Systems OSS '09*. Skovde, Sweden: Springer. 10.1007/978-3-642-02032-2_15

Syeed, M., Hammouda, I., & Systa, T. (2013). Evolution of Open Source Software Projects: A Systematic Literature Review. *Journal of Software, 8*(11).

Tahvildari, L., Gregory, R., & Kontogiannis, K. (1999). An Approach for Measuring Software Evolution using Source Code Features. In *Proceedings of the Sixth Asia Pacific Software Engineering Conference (APSEC '99)* (pp. 10-17). IEEE. 10.1109/APSEC.1999.809579

Thomas, S., Adams, B., Hassan, A., & Blostein, D. (2014). Studying Software Evolution using Topic Models. *Science of Computer Programming, 80*, 457–479. doi:10.1016/j.scico.2012.08.003

Tu, Q., & Godfrey, M. (2002). An Integrated Approach for Studying Architectural Evolution. In *Proceedings of the 10th International Workshop on Program Comprehension* (pp. 127-136). IEEE.

Turski, W. (1996). Reference Model for Smooth Growth of Software Systems. *IEEE Transactions on Software Engineering, 22*(8), 599–600.

Vasa, R. (2010). *Growth and Change Dynamics in Open Source Software Systems* (Ph.D. thesis). Swinburne University of Technology, Melbourne, Australia.

Vaucher, S., & Sahraoui, H. (2007). Do Software Libraries Evolve Differently than Applications?: An Empirical Investigation. In *Proceedings of the 2007 Symposium on Library-Centric Software Design* (pp. 88-96). ACM. 10.1145/1512762.1512771

Wang, L., Wang, Z., Yang, C., Zhang, L., & Ye, Q. (2009). Linux Kernels as Complex Networks: A Novel Method to Study Evolution. In *Proceedings of the 25th International Conference on Software Maintenance* (pp. 41-51). IEEE. 10.1109/ICSM.2009.5306348

Weicheng, Y., Beijun, S., & Ben, X. (2013). Mining GitHub: Why Commit Stops -- Exploring the Relationship between Developer's Commit Pattern and File Version Evolution. *Proceedings of the 20th Asia-Pacific Software Engineering Conference, 2*, 165–169. 10.1109/APSEC.2013.133

Wermilinger, M., & Ferreira, H. (2011). Quality Evolution track at QUATIC 2010. *Software Engineering Notes, 36*(1), 28–29. doi:10.1145/1921532.1960273

Wu, J., & Holt, R. (2004). Linker Based Program Extraction and its use in Software Evolution. *Proceedings of the International Workshop on Unanticipated Software Evolution*, 1-15.

Wu, J., Holt, R., & Hassan, A. (2007). Empirical Evidence for SOC Dynamics in Software Evolution. In *Proceedings of the International Conference on Software Maintenance* (pp. 244-254). IEEE. 10.1109/ICSM.2007.4362637

Xie, G., Chen, J., & Neamtiu, I. (2009). Towards a Better Understanding of Software Evolution: An Empirical Study on Open Source Software. In *Proceedings of the International Conference on Software Maintenance* (pp. 51-60). IEEE. 10.1109/ICSM.2009.5306356

Xu, J., Gao, Y., Christley, S., & Madey, G. (2005). A Topological Analysis of the Open Source Software Development Community. In *Proceedings of the 38th Annual Hawaii International Conference on System Sciences (HICSS'05)*. IEEE.

Yu, L. (2006). Indirectly Predicting the Maintenance Effort of Open-Source Software. *Journal of Software Maintenance and Evolution: Research and Practice, 18*(5), 311–332. doi:10.1002mr.335

Yuen, C. (1985). An empirical approach to the study of errors in large software under maintenance. *Proc. IEEE Int. Conf. on Software Maintenance*, 96–105.

Yuen, C. (1987). A statistical rationale for evolution dynamics concepts. *Proc IEEE Int. Conf. on Software Maintenance*, 156–164.

Yuen, C. (1988). On analyzing maintenance process data at the global and detailed levels. *Proc. IEEE Int. Conf. on Software Maintenance*, 248–255.

Zaidman, A., Rompaey, B., Deursen, A., & Demeyer, S. (2011). Studying the Co-Evolution of Production and Test Code in Open Source and Industrial Developer Test Processes through Repository Mining. *Empirical Software Engineering, 16*(3), 325–364. doi:10.100710664-010-9143-7

Zaimi, A., Ampatzoglou, A., Triantafyllidou, N., Chatzigeorgiou, A., Mavridis, A., & Chaikalis, T. (2015). An Empirical Study on the Reuse of Third-Party Libraries in Open-Source Software Development. In *Proceedings of the 7th Balkan Conference on Informatics Conference* (pp. 4). ACM. 10.1145/2801081.2801087

Zazworka, N., & Ackermann, C. (2010). CodeVizard: a Tool to Aid the Analysis of Software Evolution. In *Proceedings of the 2010 ACM-IEEE International Symposium on Empirical Software Engineering and Measurement (ESEM '10)*. ACM 10.1145/1852786.1852865

Zhongmin, C., & Yeqing, W. (2010,). The application of theory and method of time series in the modeling of software reliability. In *Proceedings of the 2010 Second International Conference on Information Technology and Computer Science (ITCS)* (pp. 340-343). IEEE. 10.1109/ITCS.2010.89

Zimmermann, T., Premraj, R., & Zeller, A. (2007). Predicting Defects for Eclipse. *Proceedings of the Third International Workshop on Predictor Models in Software Engineering (Promise '07)*. 10.1109/PROMISE.2007.10

This research was previously published in Optimizing Contemporary Application and Processes in Open Source Software; pages 1-23, copyright year 2018 by Engineering Science Reference (an imprint of IGI Global).

Chapter 7
A Historical and Bibliometric Analysis of the Development of Agile

Cherie C. Trumbach
University of New Orleans, USA

Kenneth R. Walsh
University of New Orleans, USA

Sathiadev Mahesh
University of New Orleans, USA

ABSTRACT

This chapter starts with a brief history of software development from a summary of traditional approaches and presents the conditions that led to agile approaches such as product complexity, shortened life cycle of the market and eventually to the widespread acceptance of Scrum. The authors then compare the narrative to the bibliometric analysis of abstract records that can be found in the Web of Science database. They parse the terms from the abstract records to identify research trends over time and map the underlying structure of agile research. Finally, they consider the future of Agile-Scrum in light of the current pandemic.

INTRODUCTION

"Project management" can be defined as a series of activities and processes performed as part of a project by a defined set of people, from same or different areas with the aim of generating new or improved organizational products, services, and/or processes (Jrad and Sundaram, 2015). In this chapter, we discuss agile project management. This is a method of project management focused on collaboration and frequent communication. Project management techniques should help the chances of project success. In the early years of software development, project failure was too common, resulting in the development

DOI: 10.4018/978-1-6684-3702-5.ch007

of structured approaches that sought to ensure successes. Traditional structured approaches to software project management, sometimes referred to as the systems development life cycle or the waterfall method, became accepted practice. As these structured methods became standard practice, software project failure remained high and experts recognized that such a dynamic environment may require rethinking software development management. Agile methods then took the assumption that all requirements cannot be known at project initiation and that the dynamic business and technology environments will cause change during the project.

Agile software development was formalized as a methodology in 2001 with the creation of the Agile Manifesto. It refers to a set of computer programming methodologies that emphasize flexibility, collaboration, efficiency, simplicity, and most of all, delivering working products to end users within short timeframes (Codington-Lacerte, 2018). However, as time has passed, agile principles have spread into additional industries including general project management. According to Hayat (2019) almost every software company uses agile development, particularly Scrum, and these companies have experienced many positive results from its use.

This chapter starts with a brief history of Software Development from a summary of traditional approaches and presents the arguments made for agile approaches and the eventual widespread acceptance of Scrum. We then compare the narrative to the bibliometric analysis of abstract records that can be found in the Web of Science database. Finally, we consider the future of Agile-Scrum in light of the current pandemic.

BACKGROUND

From Traditional Software Development to Scrum

Early software development was done by developers who had both responsibility for analysis and coding. Such a two-step process was thought to be adequate for small scale development, but led to numerous problems for large software systems (Royce, 1970). A simple solution may have been to introduce a more sophisticated methodology with increased documentation and decomposition to allow more people to work in concert. However, such an approach is risky because errors found will inevitably lead to rework of previous steps (Royce, 1970). As an answer to this, a more sophisticated development timeline including iteration, documentation, and testing was proposed (Royce, 1970). The result of this line of thinking was an iterative and adaptive model of the phases of large-scale software development (Royce, 1970). Boehm (1983) reiterated the importance of a planned and phased approach. Boehm (1983 also emphasized the importance of documenting and completing phases before moving on to subsequent phases, although he also discussed using prototyping, incremental development, and scaffolding as ways to not necessarily defer coding until specifications were complete. This process was formalized into the familiar "analysis-design-implementation-test" steps. As the process became more formalized, particularly in the 1980s, the opportunity to automate parts of the process became more evident. However, with formalization by a wide range of practitioners, the structure of the phases may have been refined and the expense of the concepts of iteration and adaptation.

In the early stages of agile software development, prototypes followed by incremental steps were utilized. These were the first steps toward agile processes. However, these increments and prototypes were limited. They may have been applied in just one cycle where a prototype was refined to produce a finished product. Small iterations only occurred where earlier results needed to be corrected. The mindset was that iterations indicated the existence of a problem with the initial design. At this point in time, the technology to support agile development was non-existent and the development process was considered linear. The linear approach was customer friendly in that the final result of the project was clearer. As software development became more sophisticated, quality, productivity, and scalability became the focus of improving the process. More tools were developed to support the process and the models expanded to cover more aspects of the overall process. (Kneuper, 2017)). The early formal methodologies offered a solid, consistent project structure with clear management procedures and homogenous project teams. (Jovanovic and Beric, 2018). The methodologies were plan-driven with upfront requirements, documentation and detailed plans. Two examples are the waterfall and the spiral model (Li and Armin, 2009). The traditional methods do an excellent job utilizing graphical tools to support communication as well as support reports and review meetings. However, the tools used to support these methodologies such as Work Breakdown Structures, Gantt charts, and cost schedules all assume a linear process (Rodrigues and Bowers, 1996).

A traditional project has well-defined boundaries aligned with corporate goals, clear roles and responsibilities, and clear objectives. The techniques are more aligned with the operational aspects of projects. However, many fields have more complex projects with increasing uncertainty concerning project parameters. In these circumstances, traditional methodologies are insufficient for the web of risks. These projects need a broader more strategic view of project management (Jrad and Sundaram, 2015; Rodrigues and Bowers, 1996). As projects have become more complex, project failure has become more common. There are more cost overruns, schedule delays, and cancelled projects. (Rodrigues and Bowers, 1996) There are both internal and external reasons for project failures. The failures generally fall in one of three categories: political/social environment, legal agreements, and human factors. Traditional project management techniques are not designed to address these areas.

Additionally, since the traditional method is linear and structured in approach, it is difficult to change directions or make changes to the project plan. Additionally, since client and stakeholder input are focused into the earliest stages of the linear process, therefore there is minimal input from clients and stakeholders when changes are needed or to ensure that requirements are actually being met along the way (Jovanovic and Beric, 2018).

Given the limitations of traditional approaches, new approaches were needed to address the rigidity of traditional approaches and lack of methods to address the human elements of projects. As time-to-market became increasingly more important and digital markets enabled by the World Wide Web expanded, iterative approaches began to infiltrate certain aspects of the software development process. The first model to explicitly include iterations in the process beyond coding and testing was Boehm's spiral model in 1988. A few years later, rapid application development was published (J. Martin, Rapid Application Development, MacMillan, 1991). Object-Oriented development also changed the direction of software development (Kneuper, 2017).

The agile concept can be traced back to the manufacturing industry in 1991 through lean manufacturing. M. A. Youssef coined the term "agile manufacturing" in a paper in 1992 (Li and Armin, 2009; Youssef, 1992). The rise of knowledge workers and the knowledge economy along with the move toward lean production also drove the push toward new ways of thinking about project management and the introduction of Scrum as a method (Takeuchi and Nonaka) and "many new development methodologies were introduced, such as Scrum, Extreme Programming, Dynamic Systems Development Method, the Crystal family of methods, and Feature Driven Development". Together these methods added the concepts of intensive communications between the customer and the project team, fast feedback, and self-organizing teams. In comparison to traditional methodologies, agile methodologies allow for a more flexible project structure. Additionally, the process makes provision for working with the customer to change directions or alter requirements. Additionally, each software release is fully functional within a short time between each release allowing for more opportunities to get feedback and make changes. A key component of agile manufacturing is a strong relationship with clients (Jovanovic and Beric, 2018). Customer involvement is a key element in the agile methodology.

According to Ionel (2009), the two main differences between traditional and agile methodologies are based on two assumptions. Traditional methodologies assume that customers need guidance from the developers regarding the requirements. The biggest assumption is that developers actually know and understand not only what customers' need at the start of the project, but also what customers will need in the future. Since the design process is all done in one shot and the result is a completed product, the developers end up overdesigning the system, incorporating functionality that the customer often does not need. There is also a delay as a system that meets not only current requirements, but future requirements anticipated by developers, is built. Agile does not assume that the developer knows more than the customer about their needs. Neither does it assume that the customer knows their future needs. It assumes that neither the customers nor the developers fully know what the requirements should be. A simpler product is completed quickly, and additional functionality is added with each succeeding version. Such an approach accommodates future requirement changes. The flexibility build into agile methodologies can handle changes in cost, scope, and quality of software based on customer needs, even as those needs change or are revealed (Hayat et al, 2019).

In 2001, the Agile Manifesto was developed establishing agile as a formal category for methodologies. As software projects and the nature of information system changes became more complex and more unpredictable, agile methodologies were widely accepted. The mantra "faster, cheaper, quicker" continues to rule software development projects (Jrad and Sundaram, 2015).

Scrum

"Scrum is the framework of Agile Methodology" (Hayat et al, 2019). Scrum has three iterative stages: Product backlog development, main sprint, and daily sprints. The model is iterative throughout the product development process (Sommer et al, 2013). Almost every company uses Agile /Scrum and it has a positive impact on software project management. 95% of users state that Scrum has a positive impact on cost and provides an easy way to manage changes in both time and cost. When using Scrum, work is divided in small chunks and sprints are defined, developers develop their chunks on time and within budget (Hayat et al, 2019).

Over time, agile principles have spread into other areas outside of the software project management. In particular, agile principles have been of interest in the realm of product development for industrial manufacturers. The stage-gate model for product development projects has been criticized as being too simplistic. Spiral models and circular models have proven difficult to implement. However, even though Agile is beneficial, agile methodologies must be modified for these projects for successful implementation. Industrial Manufacturers integrate customer-focused agile process models like Scrum into their existing Product Development models as a hybrid model. The benefits of a hybrid model that integrates the traditional stage-gate approach applied to physical products are a faster and more adaptive response to changing customer needs, better integration of voice-of-the-customer, better team communication, improved development productivity and faster time to market.

Scrum has shown positive results in product development performance. Sommer et al (2013) presents three cases with different levels of incorporating Scrum in a hybrid manner. In all three cases, product development performance was improved. However, what is unclear, is the contribution of specific elements of Agile to improved performance.

BIBLIOMETRIC ANALYSIS

This study uses the Web of Science database. Web of Science is an electronic database which abstracts and indexes publications from 8600 journals across multiple disciplines. Our data is based on the search string "(agile or scrum) and (project or software or methodology)". This search string was selected to capture as many relevant records while excluding noise, or irrelevant records. A total of 2,826 articles fit within our topic. The abstracts were downloaded and imported into VantagePoint text mining software. VantagePoint is a text mining software specifically designed to import, parse the fields and analyze a corpus of technology abstract records, particularly abstracts from technology-focused databases. The full abstract records are parsed by field (title, keywords, author(s), author affiliation, country, year, abstract, publication) and the free text fields are parsed by words and phrases. As a result, the analysis contains information about authors, organizations, publications, countries, and topics over a timeline. These lists created from individual fields were cleaned to identify spelling variations which refer to the same underlying concept. In the next step, various groups were created to conduct further analysis. The results are captured below.

Figure 1 depicts the number of records published using the search string each year. The data for 2020 contains only those articles that were indexed in Web of Science through February 2020. There is also some delay between publication and record indexing. The number of articles per year provides an indication of the level of interest in a topic. Two pieces of data worth noting are the first time that a term appears in the literature and the trends from year to year, more so than the exact number of records. For example, as seen in our earlier discussion of the history of agile methodologies, "Agile Manufacturing" was a term coined in 1992. This indicates when discussion of the topic first appears in the public sphere. For our search term, there was a steady, but small, increase in research interest until 2001. Then, in 2001, the year of the Agile Manifesto, there was an upward turn in Agile interest that continued to increase through 2005. In 2006, there started to be a decline in the occurrence of research publication records related to agile methodologies. However, in 2008 there was a turnaround in interest that steadily continued to rise with the exception of the year 2013. This small dip in 2013 is likely to be a statistical aberration Interestingly, 2008 is also the year that the term "scrum methodology" first appeared in the abstract records, though other variations of the term "scrum" appeared earlier. Scrum added clarification for implementation and gave more specific direction to the body of agile methodologies. Abrahamsson et al (2008) describe a study in which agile methodologies including Scrum were evaluated for the impact on communication practices of software development teams. Agile practices were found to positively impact communication, but other approaches were also needed to achieve the desired overall results. There is a rapid increase in the number of records through 2019. Note that 2020 data was only collected for a couple of months.

Figure 1. Number of Articles Published for Each Year

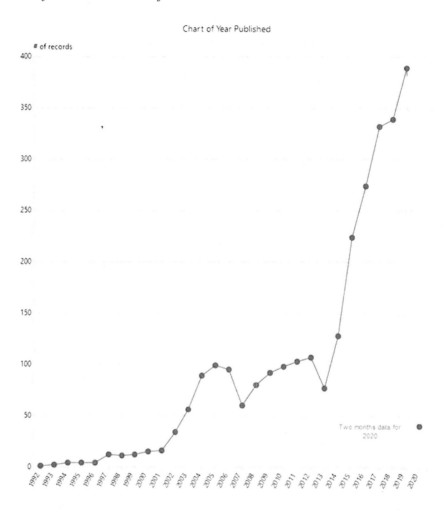

Continuing the analysis required the parsing of the abstract into terms. However, these terms must be cleaned in order to combine terms with slightly different representations but are actually the same concept. For example, the terms "agile project methodology" and "agile methodology" represent the same concept. The terms from the Abstract phrases and keywords were combined and cleaned into topic areas to demonstrate the main topics covered in the research and how those topics developed over time. The decision as to which terms to combine is somewhat subjective but should generally be done at the same level of specificity. For this first analysis, a broad generalization was used to combine terms that represent a wider topic area. The final list used for analysis contained 58 terms/topic areas. Table 1 shows the top 20 topic areas and the number of records where the topic was identified. The most common topic area is "agile teams". Some terms were basic terms that are expected from our search string, such as "project management" and "scrum methodologies" while other terms are more pertinent to research in general, such as "future research". Some notable observations are the prevalence of terms such as "supply chain", "quality requirements", "engineering education" and "risk management".

Table 1. List of Top 20 Topics

	# Records	Topic List
1	1213	Agile Teams
2	247	Supply Chain
3	216	Project Management
4	209	Manufacturing Organizations
5	195	Practical Experience
6	182	Business Environment
7	166	Information Systems
8	159	Research Limitations/Implications
9	138	Requirements Management
10	127	Extreme Programming (XP)
11	125	End-users
12	114	Process Management
13	111	Decision-making Process
14	101	Knowledge Base
15	87	Quality Requirements
16	84	Future Research
17	70	Competitive Environment
18	68	Engineering Education
19	64	Scrum Methodology
20	52	Risk Management

Another level is analysis is to review the terms as they appear by year. When did various terms first start to occur in the public sphere? When did certain terminology become more popular? How did the conversation about the topic change over time? One way to visualize the development in the conversation over time is with a Bubble Chart as shown in Figure 2. Conceptually important terms primarily from Table 2 were used as the input into the Bubble Chart. Each bubble represents the years in which those topics appear in the literature and the size of the bubble indicates the relative number of records containing that topic.

The number of references associated with all of the topics in the topic list show a growth trend of "agile" as a research topic. One very interesting finding is that while the Agile Manifesto did not occur until 2001, the discussion of agile ideas with these topics were occurring long before then. The Manufacturing industry was talking about agile ideas in 1994, the earliest of all of these major topic areas. This occurrence makes sense considering that lean manufacturing began discussing agile topics in 1991. Some topics have steadily grown over time. Others have sputtered along. While manufacturing was the first area with an interest in agile ideas, it has seen very little growth over time. Another term, "traditional methodologies" had a small steady stream of overlap in Agile records but in 2019, there has been a resurgence of discussion about traditional methods with Agile. As agile methodologies are applied in areas outside of traditional software project methods and into areas that have been dominated by traditional project management techniques, we should expect that those methods would be studied more frequently in comparison to Agile. In addition, our literature review indicated that there has been a growing interest in combining Scrum with traditional stage-gate methodologies in the realm of new product development in the industrial manufacturing industry. Hence, more references to those traditional methodologies. The most significant increases in interest have been in the areas of the competitive environment, risk management, data analysis, and quality requirements. Also, in 2014, the increase in interest in Agile in engineering education was substantial. Two noteworthy topics that are among the newest additions but have made a quick impact are "success factors" and "systematic review". A scan of titles with these two terms indicates the progression of research in Agile toward a review of research in Agile particularly with the goal of identifying the factors that make agile project management successful. Interestingly, one area that has seen interest wane in the last 8 years is agile in the virtual enterprise. Given the current state of the world, the interest in Agile or Scrum in the context of the virtual enterprise may increase.

Figure 2. Topics by Year

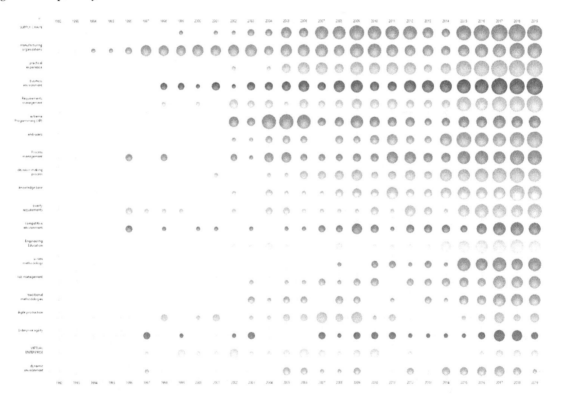

Table 3 depicts the top journals in which our search terms were found for each year considered. Again, here we see that interest in agile topics are first found lightly scattered through production related journals, indicating the interest in agile manufacturing. While research continues in these journals, just a few years after the Agile Manifesto is released, agile topics are quickly spread out to a variety of software engineering, computer science and technology journals. Notice that in 2008, IEEE Latin American Transactions began to publish Agile and Scrum related topics, indicating a rising interest in Latin America in these topics.

Table 3. Journals by Year

# Recs	Publication Name	1994	1995	1996	1997	1998	1999	2000	2001	2002	2003	2004	2005	2006	2007	2008	2009	2010	2011	2012	2013	2014	2015	2016	2017	2018	2019	2020
110	Information And Software Technology											1	1	1	2	3	3	3	9	7	5	11	20	12	8	13	9	2
107	Journal Of Systems And Software												3	2		6	3	6	2	11	6	7	9	15	17	13	7	
68	Extreme Programming And Agile Processes In Software Engineering, Proceedings											24	27	17														
60	Journal Of Software-Evolution And Process																			5	2	10	2	4	11	12	11	
53	Ieee Software					1		1		2	3	2	6	2	3	1	7	7		1	1	1	1	4		3	6	1
43	International Journal Of Advanced Computer Science And Applications																						6	5	12	10	10	
35	Empirical Software Engineering											1	1	3	1	2	1	4		2		3	7	2	3	4	1	
30	Supply Chain Management-An International Journal												1	1		1	1	3	2	1	2	4	4	1	3	1	5	
27	Benchmarking-An International Journal																						2	7	5	10	3	
26	International Journal Of Production Research				1	1	2	2	1	2				1		3		2	3	2		1	1			1		
25	International Journal Of Operations & Production Management	1				1		1	2			1	2	1	6		1		1	2	1	1	2	1		1		
24	Ieee Access																						1		2	8	12	1
24	International Journal Of Software Engineering And Knowledge Engineering													1	1	1	1	1		2	2	4	1	4	1	1	4	
23	Project Management Journal																	3	1	1		2	2	2	5	6		
21	Extreme Programming And Agile Methods - Xp/ Agile Universe 2004, Proceedings											21																
19	Ieee Latin America Transactions																1	1	2				4	7	1	1	1	
17	International Journal Of Production Economics						1				1					3	3	2	2		1							
17	Journal Of Manufacturing Technology Management																						3	4	2	5	2	1
16	Iet Software														1	1		2	1	2					2		7	

Now, let's take a look at the underlying topic structure in Agile-Scrum literature. Figure 3 shows a Factor Map created using the cleaned list of Combined Keywords and Abstract Phrases that occur in at least 10 Records. The analysis ends up including 313 terms. A process is used using PCA analysis to create clusters of terms based on the co-occurrence of terms with one another. Though all of the terms are included in the analysis, not all of the terms are included in the final cluster sets. The resulting 13 clusters which indicate the underlying topic-structure and relationships in the literature are described in the following table (Table 4).

Table 4. Cluster Descriptions

Cluster Defining Terms	Cluster description
Agile teams, software development teams, team members, software teams, team performance	All of the terms in this cluster are related to the team aspect of Agile. Teamwork, team collaboration, and effective team management are critical to the success of agile projects.
Product quality, software quality	A main driver in implementing agile methodologies is to improve the quality of the final product. These articles discuss the impact of Agile on quality.
Extreme programming	Extreme programming is a type of agile software development framework.
Global software development, systematic literature review	As an innovative idea progresses, researchers conduct systematic literature reviews. In this cluster, those reviews are related to the use of Agile in global software development.
Agile transformation, agile adoption	In any organization, Agile implementation must take preparation to adopt the practices. It will also transform the organization. These articles address those considerations.
Software Engineering Education, capstone course, effort estimation	This cluster primarily consists of articles addressing the introduction of Agile/Scrum into university curriculum, particularly in software engineering programs.
Agile capabilities, organizational agility, enterprise agility, agile strategies, agile organizations, critical factors, large organizations	Agile is not just a methodology. It will impact the organization. The organization itself must be agile in order to successfully utilize agile methodologies.
Agility evaluation, mass customization, manufacturing organization, fuzzy logic, agility assessment	When utilizing agile practices in manufacturing, measuring manufacturing agility allows the ability to quantify results.
Research limitations, practical implications, supply chain management, supply chain strategy	This is a cluster addressing practical implications of Agile, particularly as it relates the Supply chain.
Business performance, agile manufacturing, information-technology, virtual enterprise, operational performance, structural equation modeling	This cluster contains a wide variety of topics related to the business operations.
Product development, new products	These records address the specific area of Agile product development
Process planning, changing markets, concurrent engineering	This cluster topics are related to agile manufacturing and the need for Agile in the context of concurrent engineering due to the changing markets.

Figure 3. Key Terms Factor Map

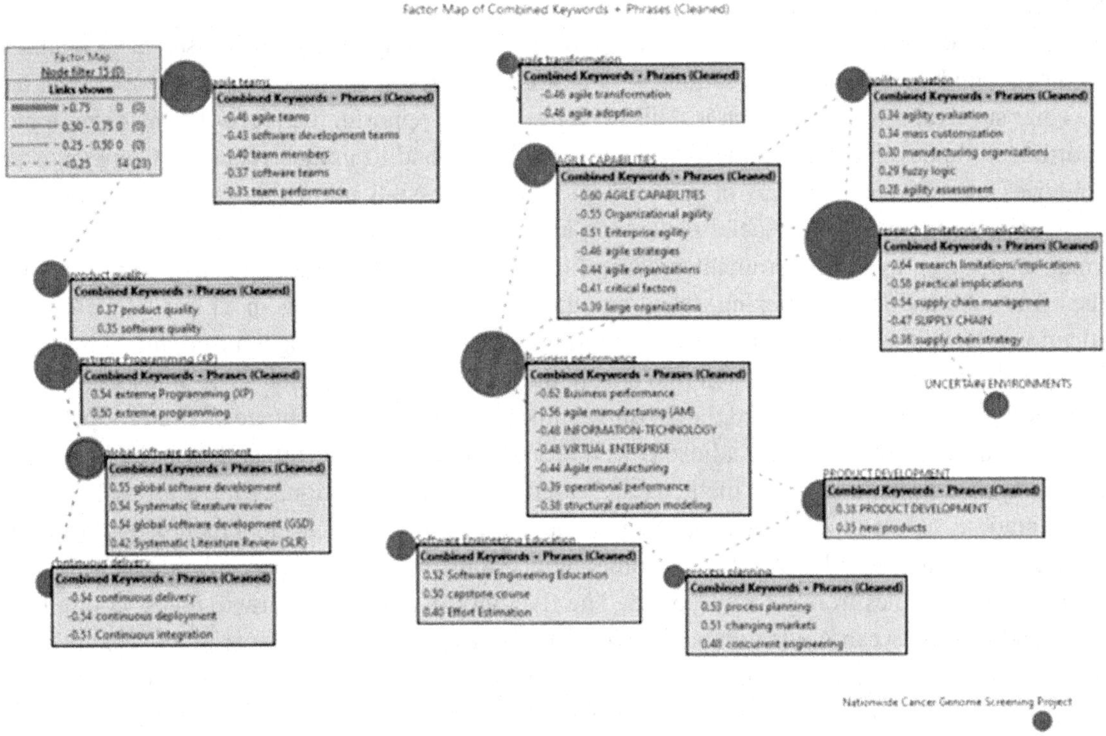

Factor Map of Combined Keywords + Phrases (Cleaned)

SCRUM, THE PANDEMIC, AND THE FUTURE

As with many areas, Covid-19 has forced many changes to organizations and most will never go back to pre-Covid times. Some organizations have had to adapt quickly to handle the variety of challenges that have occurred as a result of the pandemic. The most obvious changes are that the pandemic has forced people to work from home and use new technologies to do so. Digital adoption has increased at a phenomenal rate. A survey conducted by McKinsey and Company found that across a range of industries, there has been a 19% to over 100% increase in digital adoption due to Covid-19. The percentage of individuals working full time from home has seen an even far greater increase. For example, the percent of individuals working at home in the Media and Technology sector grew from 9% to 84%, in Professional and Business Services 5% to 74% and in Financial Activities from 5% to 70%. When asked if they expected to continue working remotely after the pandemic, 75% of those now working remotely expect to continue (Baig, et al, 2020). This is a fundamental shift in the structure of the work environment. Along with this change in the work environment, comes many challenges. The most fundamental challenge is that of physical distance from co-workers. This physical distance is an impediment to the typical ways in which employees interact not just for meetings but in the ability to chat with a co-worker in their office or engage in spontaneous break room conversations. However, the physical distance is compounded by additional challenges related to home responsibilities as parents may also be home with children who are now homeschooling or unable to attend daycare. There may not be sufficient space at home for private workspace or parents may have to assist with homeschooling. Such rapid transformational changes also require an agile approach to change management. Yet, the usual approach to agile methodologies like Scrum are based on colocation.

In addition to the rapid change in the structure of the workday, many businesses have required a short turn around on software applications with new capabilities to support a remotely operating business. Their survival might depend on it. This need has created opportunities for software development, who utilize agile development methods and can quickly respond to unique requests. Companies and/or countries are asking for an array of applications that will possibly allow them to continue to operate in their physical space such as social distancing apps for retail store reservations and check-ins, and thermal monitoring apps. Government organizations may need applications to help slow the spread of the virus such as location tracking, facial recognition, quarantine management or risk management applications. Hospitals may also need smart routing applications to manage and monitor the flow of patients and supplies around the hospital to ensure the safety of all the patients (Preimesberger, 2020). Organizations that have incorporated the Scrum methodology have the advantage of already operating as an agile organization but also must adjust as well because the basis of Scrum and other agile processes rests on physical proximity. Agile methods are based on team collocation. Almost all agile software implementations have collocated teams, often in one (small) room. This arrangement is almost impossible due to the pandemic. However, with some digital adjustments, these organizations have a strong foundation of principles from which to build. The five Scrum values of courage, focus, commitment, respect, and openness can guide companies through a transition to remote operations. The organization has to maintain a focus on scrum principles and goals and adjust the processes accordingly. It will be interesting to see how these forced changes will change the trajectory of the Scrum Methodology. These companies and the methodology must grow from its strength in being accustomed to change and flexibility. However, even beyond strength and flexibility, agile principles are conducive to the change to remote work. Rigid prioritization, small cross-functional autonomous teams, regular meetings, and agile leadership all translate well to remote operations. Organizations need to focus on core elements of iteration and collaboration while finding new ways to connect remotely.

In order to guide a team through these changes, there are some questions to consider. How agile is the project team? What does a project leader need to do to keep a project progressing? Rehburg, et. al. (2020) from Boston Consulting Group maintains that it is imperative for leadership to ensure that teams stay focused on the organization's purpose, strategy, and priorities. It is imperative that leaders also communicate intent to aid team members in efforts to stay focused. The online workday must include elements that maintain the structure for agile development. Rehburg advocates for daily 15-30-minute meetings and a weekly meeting lasting 60-90 minutes. He also stresses the importance of being available on instant messaging and making calendar availability visible. Finally, virtual tools can greatly aid in collaboration. Conferencing tools that allow for always-on connection opportunities can facilitate informal connections. However, constant online visibility may be difficult given the exceptional challenges of working from home. These challenges are not insurmountable but should not be ignored. Another level of flexibility is needed within the Scrum framework. For example, one organization allowed parents to block out periods of time on the team calendar to attend to family matters. Another organization doubled their lunch break. This flexibility allows workers to take care of home matters more easily when needed and focus on work otherwise. Organizations have also focused on ensuring that these additional meetings are working sessions that produce tangible results and not time wasters. Using a different strategy, some organizations have decided to schedule meeting-free time blocks (Agile Actors, 2020). Companies are trying different approaches to overcome these obstacles. Currently, these examples are anecdotes by consultants who have seen positive results. More research is needed to determine the impact on productivity by these various approaches.

The overall goal is to set up virtual spaces that mirror the effectiveness of physical spaces. According to Comella-Dorda, et. al. (2019) from McKinsey and Company, remote work results in inefficiency and reduced cohesion, but the causal problems can be addressed. McKinsey and Company lays out recommendations for continuing to use agile approaches with remote teams that are more detailed than Rehburg's suggestions. Table 5 shows these recommendations along with an example as to how the recommendation can be implemented remotely. The authors also reiterate that teams that were functioning cohesively prior to being thrust into remote operations will function better afterwards. Perhaps the team has ground rules about how individuals would have their turn to speak or how feedback on suggestions are provided. These same ground rules still apply in the virtual environment but altered to take advantage of the capabilities in the technology. Some of these changes may require additional training or revisions to the specific rule. Documentation is more important in remote operations, but how do you encourage the team to document more? Meetings can be recorded with transcriptions, but what meetings should be recorded and how will they be organized for efficient retrieval by others?

Table 5. Remote Agile Recommendations

Recommendations	Example
Revisit the norms and ground rules for interaction	Consider ground rules for virtual tools like whiteboards and video conferencing
Cultivate bonding and morale	Virtual team building and assume best intentions
Adapt coaching and development	Reinvent face-to-face activities but more frequently
Recalibrating remote agile processes	Start with outcomes and work backward, particularly for ceremonies
Establish a single source of truth	Documentation is more important
Adjust to synchronous collaboration	Use it but don't over rely on them
Keep teams engaged during long ceremonies	Short exercise breaks as an example
Adapting leadership approach	Be deliberate with engagement

CONCLUSION

As projects have become more complicated and there is a drive for a faster turnover of product improvements along with higher expectations in quality, agile methodologies like Scrum have become increasingly popular. Interest in agile methods has moved from Manufacturing to software development using Scrum to just about every industry. While the idea of the agile organization has been gaining in popularity, Covid-19 has thrust many organizations into new territories that would highly benefit from agile approaches, like Scrum. However, a team already operating using agile principles is in a better position to make adjustments to operating remotely than teams that are not accustomed to change. The challenge for agile teams is that the current models and tools are built upon collocation. While any change is a challenge, there are many software tools already on the market that support the same objectives in a remote situation.

REFERENCES

Abrahamsson, P., Pikkarainen, M., Salo, O., Haikara, J., & Still, J. (2008). The impact of agile practices on communication in software development. *Empirical Software Engineering.*

Agile Actors. (2020). *Solutions to common remote work issues during COVID.* Downloaded August 24, 2020, from https://www.scruminc.com/solutions-to-common-remote-work-issues-during-covid/

Baig, A., Hall, B., Jenkins, P., Lamarre, E., & McCarthy, B. (2020). *The covid-19 recovery will be digital: A plan for the first 90 days.* Retrieved August 24, 2020, from https://www.mckinsey.com/business-functions/mckinsey-digital/our-insights/the-covid-19-recovery-will-be-digital-a-plan-for-the-first-90-days

Boehm, B. W. (1983). Seven basic principles of software engineering. *Journal of Systems and Software, 3*(1), 3–24. doi:10.1016/0164-1212(83)90003-1

Codington-Lacerte, C. (2018). *Agile software development.* Salem Press Encyclopedia.

Comella-Dorda, S., Garg, L., Thareja, S., & Vasquez-McCall, B. (2019). *Revisiting agile teams after an abrupt shift to remote.* Retrieved August 23, 2020 from https://wwww.mckinsey.com/business-functions/organization/our-insights/revisiting-agile-teams-after-an-abrupt-shift-to-remote#

Cooper, R. G., & Sommer, A. F. (2016). From experience: The agile-stage-gate hybrid model: A promising new approach and a new research opportunity. *Journal of Product Innovation Management, 33*(5).

Hayat, F., Rehman, A. U., Arif, K. S., Wahab, K., & Abbas, M. (2019). *The influence of agile methodology (Scrum) on software project management.* IEEE Computer Society.

Ionel, N. (2009). Agile software development methodologies: An overview of the current state of research. *Annals of Faculty of Economics, 4*(1).

Jiang, L., & Eberlein, A. (2009). An analysis of the history of classical software development and agile development. *IEEE International Conference on Systems, Man, and Cybernetics.* 10.1109/ICSMC.2009.5346888

Jovanovic, P., & Beric, I. (2018). Analysis of the available project management methodologies," management. *Journal of Sustainable Business and Management Solutions in Emerging Economies, 23*(3), 1. doi:10.7595/management.fon.2018.0027

Jrad, R. B. N., & Sundaram, D. (2015). Challenges of inter-organizational information and middleware system projects: Agility, complexity, success, and failure. *6th International Conference on Information, Intelligence, Systems and Applications (IISA).* 10.1109/IISA.2015.7387960

Kneuper, R. (2017). *Sixty years of software development life cycle models. IEEE Annals of the History of Computing.*

Lynch, W. (2019). *The brief history of Scrum.* Retrieved August 21, 2020, from https://medium.com/@warren2lynch/the-brief-of-history-of-scrum-15efb73b4701#:~:text=Jeff%20Sutherland%20originated%20the%20first,a%20formal%20process%20in%201995

Preimesberger, C. (2020). *Startup vantiq comes to rescue in covid-19 use cases.* Retrieved August 21, 2020, from https://www.eweek.com/innovation/startup-vantiq-comes-to-rescue-in-covid-19-use-cases

Rehburg, B., Danoesastro, M., Kaul, S., & Stutts, L. (2019). *How to remain remotely agile through covid-19.* Retrieved August 22, 2020, from https://www.bcg.com/en-us/publications/2020/remaining-agile-and-remote-through-covid.aspx

Rising, L., & Janoff, N. (2000). The Scrum software development process for small teams. *IEEE Software, 17*(4), 26–32. doi:10.1109/52.854065

Rodrigues, A., & Bowers, J. (1996). Systems dynamics in project management: A comparative analysis with traditional methods. *System Dynamics Review, 12*(2), 121–139. doi:10.1002/(SICI)1099-1727(199622)12:2<121::AID-SDR99>3.0.CO;2-X

Royce, W. W. (1970). Managing the development of large software systems. *Proceedings of IEEE WESCON,* 1-9.

Singh, R., Kumar, D., & Sagar, B. B. (2019). Analytical study of agile methodology in information technology sector. *4th International Conference on Information Systems and Computer Networks (ISCON).* 10.1109/ISCON47742.2019.9036280

Sommer, A. F., Slavensky, A., Nguyen, V. T., Steger-Jenson, K., & Dukovska-Popovska, I. (2013). Scrum integration in stage-gate models for collaborative product development – A case study of three industrial manufacturers. *IEEE International Conference on Industrial Engineering and Engineering Management (IEEM).* 10.1109/IEEM.2013.6962616

Youssef, M. A. (1992). Agile manufacturing: A necessary condition for competing in global markets. *Industrial Engineering, 18*(20).

Section 2
Development and Design Methodologies

Chapter 8
Software Effort Estimation for Successful Software Application Development

Syed Mohsin Saif
https://orcid.org/0000-0001-7237-8828
Islamic University of Science and Technology, India

ABSTRACT

The recent advancements in information and communication technology (ICT) have inspired all the operational domains of both public and private sector enterprise to endorse this technology. Software development plays a crucial role in supporting ICT. Software effort estimation serves as a critical factor in software application development, and it helps application development teams to complete the development process on time and within budget. Many developmental approaches have been used for software effort estimation, but most of them were conventional software methods and therefore failed to produce accurate results when it came to web or mobile effort estimation. This chapter explains different types of software applications, software estimation models, the importance of software effort estimation, and challenges faced in software effort estimation.

INTRODUCTION

The current age is the era of information and communication technology (ICT). The diverse ICT enabled modalities has inspired almost all the operational domains of both public and private sector enterprise to endorse this technology. All these advancements made in the field of Information and Communication Technology is deployable when there is an appropriate underlying software framework to make it functional. In real essence, it is this software component that has revolutionized the modern age and has also facilitated humankind with its sophisticated serviceability at every corridor of humanity.

The Merriam-Webster dictionary defines software as a set of programs, procedures and related documentation associated with a system known as a computer program (Merriam-Webster). The most critical and challenging aspect is to design a mechanism to develop these computer programs. The design

DOI: 10.4018/978-1-6684-3702-5.ch008

and development of these computer programs remain a challenging aspect in the software development industry. Identification, selection, and implementation of a particular development strategy have a direct relationship with quality and successful development and deployment of these computer programs more broadly the software application. The identification and selection of a particular development process solely depend on the overall experience and understandability of the developer in specific and software project management in general.

Diverse people in the development industry have different opinions related to various models available to develop software applications, and some were optimal; some were contradictory; some were localized, and some were lacking specific parameters. To streamline this development process and to design a benchmark standard with universal acceptability, a collaborative deliberation among various individuals related to software development was he, and the outcome was an approach that can guarantee to deliver versatile, scalable and quality products. This improvised software development approach is now a systematic sequence of various processes known as software engineering (Mills H. D., 2010). Fritz Bauer defines software engineering as; "A systematic design and development of software products and the management of the processes (Fritz, 1968). The main objective of Software Engineering is to meet the specifications & demonstrate accurateness in completing the development process of a software system on time and within budget". The main practice of various fundamentals prescribed through software engineering as a discipline was to development conventional or traditional standalone software applications. With the advent of time, the cost of hardware technology drastically came down and subsequently, the usage of soft systems increased. The conventional software applications also saw evolutionary changes in both nature and scope. Therefore, in addition to traditional software applications, web-based and mobile based software applications came into existence. The introduction of these soft variants has almost redefined both horizontal and vertical dimensions of software engineering practices and principles.

The fundamental approach defined by software engineering to develop software based applications is known as "software development life cycle (SDLC)". SDLC describes the more lucid and systematic procedure to guide successful software development on time and within resources. With time the popularity of these soft variants increased and therefore, the use also shown exponential trends. This popularity resulted in increasing demand for software applications in general and application features & functions in particular. This rapid demand for both application and the features/functionality has made the software development process more and more complex. This growing complexity and to manage the successful development became challenging for software project management as many times project management failed to deliver the project on time or sometimes failed to develop within the allotted budgets or even were unable to understand and management development positively and progressively.

TYPES OF SOFTWARE APPLICATIONS

Software-based applications are broadly categorized into three types: traditional or conventional software applications, web-based applications, and mobile based application. All these application variants do share certain similarities, but holistically are different from one another in their nature, scope, and dimensionality. The brief description of these types in mentioned as under.

Figure 1. Different types of software applications

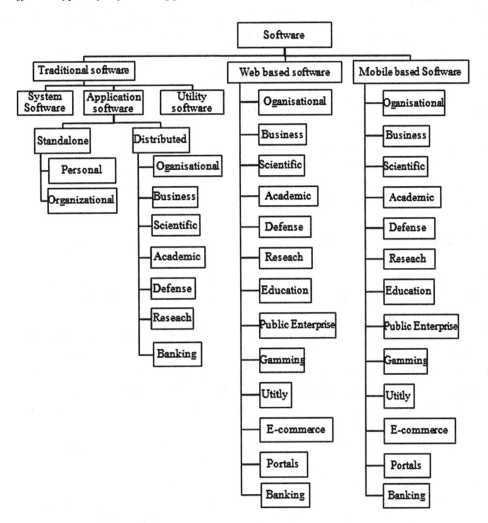

- **Traditional or Conventional Software Application:** They are generally known as software applications; they are designed, developed and deployed as standalone software systems to deliver services and operations related to a particular group or organization. This works within the boundary of that working domain only outside access is restricted, and also its scope is geographically localized and developed by more professional developers only, e.g. Banking software, UMS, etc.
- **Web-Based Applications:** Web application is any hypertext rich program with both technical and non-technical features, developed to serve some purpose accessed inside a web browser by specifying a particular URL over the network using HTTP. Web application services a vehicle to fulfill the client request by acquiring information(say internet or WWW), structures it, build a packed presentation and delivers it to serve the purpose(Web engineering, 2014).

In a broader perspective, one can say web application is a software system based on the technologies and standards of World Wide Web Consortium (W3C) that provides Web-specific resources such as content and services through a user interface, the Web browser.

- **Mobile-Based Applications:** These applications are similar to that of web applications. However, they are different in some aspects. These are specially designed to run on a small display with almost no geographic restriction meant for diverse people. Similar to web applications, a user downloads a client program to run these mobile applications and also can browse through mobile browsers to request for content on the internet. Nowadays, the trend for acquiring mobile applications is heavy increasing, and most of the services and practices that were delivered through conventional or web applications are now available as mobile applications.

EFFORT ESTIMATION

Effort estimation has been a pivotal domain for software project management that irregularities of which may lead to developmental or delivery failures. Effort estimation helps the project management team to draw budgetary estimates required to carry out successful software development on time and within budget. It is this effort estimation that generates insights about the cost of development. The inaccurate effort estimation process can result in inaccurate effort estimates or inaccurate resource identification and elicitation, which always lead to failure. This failure can sometimes completely abandon the development industry from software development market. Therefore, it is very much essential to design an efficient, effective and productive mechanism to perform effort estimation before the actual software application development is conceived.

Software effort estimation is defined as a systematic and structured approach to approximate the amount of human efforts required to perform software application development successfully on time and within budget. This development can be the development of any software application falling under traditional, web or mobile application domains. The Effort estimation processes have a direct relationship with the size of software development, and subsequently, the cost of the development is approximated. The more accuracy and perfection in size always guides to get more accurate effort estimates and therefore, the cost (Jørgensen, M., 2007). However, the approximation of the overall cost is obtained after integrating the efforts, overhead cost and profit margins with the estimated efforts (Boehm, B. 1981), inaccuracy in effort estimates can cause overestimation or underestimation which will result in miss management of projects. Accurate effort estimation not only helps the development industry to leverage its client base but also edges the development industries benchmark ahead of other similarly situated developers in the market. Positive and perfect effort estimates help the software development team to draw a clear view of all the fundamental requirements that are required to perform successful software development on time and within budget. That means effort estimation prescribes profitable budgetary schedulers for all related and relevant constructs that are subjected to be consulted or used by the development team during the software development process. The size of software development depends on various functional and non-functional requirements that are expected to be delivered by the software application when deployed in the candidate system. Therefore, it is essential and equally a crucial step in effort estimation to identify all the requirements and then map them into their respective functional or non-functional size measure to arrive at the approximate size and subsequently the cost (Briand, L., 1998).

ACTUAL AND ESTIMATED EFFORTS

To perform successful effort estimation, different techniques or models have been introduced by many researchers to be used by practitioners for successful software development and delivery. The amount of efforts that are obtained during the effort estimation process is called as estimated efforts. The amount of efforts that are actually spent on the development of software application is called as actual efforts. Actual efforts can be either same as that of estimated efforts or sometimes it can be either more or less. This difference in the value of actual and estimated efforts is called as deviation or estimation gap and can be defined as the difference between the value of actual efforts and estimated efforts. The deviation of estimated efforts from their corresponding actual efforts may cause either overestimation or underestimation. The deviation can be defined as the difference between the actual efforts and estimated efforts. Overestimation is the situation in effort estimation when the amount of estimated efforts is found to be more than the amount of actual efforts incurred in the development. While as underestimation is the situation when the observed amount of estimated efforts is found to be out less in comparison to actual efforts spent on software development. Both underestimation and overestimation are not considered as good signs for successful project management.

IMPORTANCE OF EFFORT ESTIMATION IN SOFTWARE DEVELOPMENT

The growing demand and increasing complexity in different types of software applications have resulted in several issues for software project management to perform successful software development on time and within budget. Effort estimation plays an important role to ensure adequate software development and to carry out different developmental assignments on time and within a budget Effectiveness in effort estimation always helps development industry to establish new benchmarks of success and quality product delivery. Both cases of deviation that is either overestimation or underestimation have always proved disastrous for the development industry like the development industry may fail to retain its reputation, competition and market space resulting in less profitable outcome, unsuccessful delivery, erroneous development, less user acceptance, delayed delivery and budget overruns, etc. Selection of a proper effort estimation approach and accuracy in efforts obtained before the actual development is made have greater chances of success in comparison to vague estimation and software development. Therefore, this has always been a critical task for software project management to indentify the best possible effort estimation approach to predict the efforts required to perform successful software development on time and by utilizing the allocated resources efficiently. The importance of effort estimation can be understood by drawing a simple analogy of prediction the fuel (gasoline) needed by an airplane for successful departure and arrival. If the aero-engineers failed to guess the amount of fuel there are chances that the airplane may either fail to reach the destination or may have to make emergency landing somewhere between source and destination. The accurate estimates of fuel have higher chances of successful arrival. Therefore, the technique on the basis of which the fuel consumption is predicted is very much critical.

To ensure that the effort estimation process will deliver better outcomes, it is very much preliminary for project manager to identify an experienced team to perform effort estimation. The experienced team of estimators has probably greater dynamism and wider understandability of problem domain, requirements identification and analysis thereby leading to have arrived at accurate estimates for efforts. The ill understanding of problem domain by inexperienced project management has greater chances of failure. In conclusion it can be said that the successful software development is possible only when the effort estimation team equipped with both experience and knowledge to understand the problem domain thereby designing estimation approach or select best suitable in-line with problem context. The decision making that is involved at every single stage of effort estimation process is very critical and challenging to manage when requirements are not clear, or analysis is not done scientifically.

EFFORT ESTIMATION PROCESS

As effort estimation is a systematic process, it consists of many interrelated and interdependent steps to arrive at the final estimated value for efforts required to perform successful software development. Every step in effort estimation process is meant to deliver a specific functionality needed to approximate the overall amount of efforts needed by project management. Effort estimation begins with the requirements specification, followed by the identification of functional and non-function measures. The size of the software application development depends on various functional and non-functional measures; the detailed discussion on functional and non-functional measures is provided in the subsequent parts of this chapter. Software development size has a direct relationship with the amount of efforts that may be required to accomplish a successful software development. Therefore, the accuracy of effort estimation lies on the accuracy of size approximation. Software project management always needs to contemplate on the perfection and effectiveness of the effort estimation process holistically. The group of individuals who are assigned the job of performing effort estimation needs to have much diverse knowledge and experience of the nature and scope of the development domain. The experienced team always has the potential to identify various functional and non-functional requirements attributed to a particular development to arrive at much accurate size approximation and subsequently the efforts. The demand for software applications has increased with much-unprecedented pace. Most of the organizations have endorsed software applications for delivering their diverse functions. The growing use and demand for features embedded in these software applications have made software application development much complex, and subsequently, the effort estimation processes have also become difficult for management to deal with. The abstract view of the effort estimation process is described in figure 2 below and figure 3 represents a generic effort, estimation model.

There is an array of techniques that can be selected and used to perform software effort estimation. However, each effort estimation method has got different background mechanism to deal with particular type of software effort estimation using distinguished estimation approach. The selection of a particular technique does also impact the accuracy of both size and efforts. Various effort estimation techniques used across literature are discussed under section effort estimation models later in this chapter. The best effort estimation approach helps project management to minimize the gap between actual and estimated efforts.

EFFORT ESTIMATION METRICS

Software application development in general and web or mobile application development, in particular, is an integrated activity of different processes. The nature, scope, and complexity of various software-based application developments depend upon several functional and non-functional requirements. These requirements have a direct relationship with software development size, and more requirements mean more software size. To quantify software application size, different functional and non-functional measures were identified, and based on these measures, the aggregate size could be approximated. Therefore, software development metrics are used to measure and then quantify application size in a standard metrics unit or sizing unit. Metrics can be product metrics, process metrics, complexity metrics, effort metrics, etc. which helps project managers to measure, monitor and control web development or software development (S. M. Saif, 2017) These metrics are inputs to the system where approximated efforts are obtained as output. More precisely the activity of measuring these developmental parameters is called as software metrics or and are calculated by establishing empirical relationships between functional, non-functional and complexity measures like LOC, No. of web pages, No. of new web pages, No. of media objects, etc. Web application development metrics can be broadly seen as size metrics and effort metrics.

Functional Size Measures: These are those measuring constructs that directly specify the functional aspect of the development. They depend on the services and functionality of the application. Like in case of function point analysis, these functional measures can be related to external input, external output, logical interface, internal logic files or external queries.

- **Non-Functional Measures:** These are those measuring constructs that directly do not contribute towards size but have an indirect influence on the development. These include the parameters that actually impact the development environment, the technical aspect of the development. Their presence or absence may either increase developmental efforts or may even decrease. E.g., Knowledge of development, the experience of the development team, code reusability, reliability, Difficult Programming Language, project methodology, testability, etc.

Figure 2. Abstract view of effort estimation model

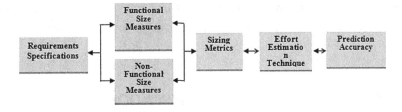

Figure 3. Components of generic effort estimation model

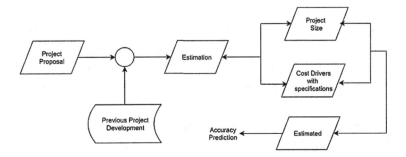

EFFORT ESTIMATION STAKEHOLDERS

As mentioned above, effort estimation is a systematic process involving diverse activities to reach out at final estimates. In order to accomplish these diverse activities related to effort estimation at different levels of project management, many individuals are directly or indirectly involved. These individuals are called as effort estimation stakeholders. Below are few prominent stockholders that are a party with effort estimation process.

- **Estimation Process Owner (EPO):** responsible identification, introduction, and maintenance of activities required in the estimation process like methods, process, models, functional and non-functional entities and the data are emanating in whole management. EPO is usually an experienced person in management who has got sufficient knowledge related to effort estimation and this position within an organization is usually a sustentative position.
- **Estimator:** An individual in project management who implements various available effort estimation models to perform effort estimation for software developments.
- **Domain Expert:** They are the experienced people in the project manager who can train or model different modalities to perform the effort estimation when sample data is limited, or there is skewness or outliers in data. By virtue of their knowledge, they guide project management to find and identify various factors that have a potential influence on effort estimation process. They have a significant role when it comes to expert-based or judgment based effort estimation.
- **Decision Marker**: A stockholder with a unique role as decision maker have indirect control or influence on effort estimation process. Whenever the estimation team arrives with the estimates that are to be provided to complete the development, in some cases, the estimated budget and the budget that the project owner (Sponsor) is willing to provide contradicts than the role of decision maker comes into practice to decide whether to accept the value from sponsor or to reject his proposal. The decision maker can also guide the estimators to revise or modify specific estimation criteria to minimize some budget to please the project owner so that the development work can be retained.

CHALLENGES TO SOFTWARE EFFORT ESTIMATION

The growing demand and increasing complexity in various types of software applications (like web or mobile applications) have raised several issues in software project management for the successful development of software application on time and within budget. These issues have resulted into developmental failures, less user acceptance, delayed delivery, and budget overruns. Effort estimation plays an important role in effective software development and helps project managers to perform development within budget and delivery on time by predicting or guessing the extent of resources of various types required for the successful and on time completion of software development. There has been several effort estimation approaches used by practitioners to perform software effort estimation however, the implementation and various methods could not be as significant as it would have been. Therefore, the failures still continued to be there in software development, delivery and deployment. The use of various effort estimation approaches across these application types to perform effort estimation has failed to deliver much-required results acceptable to both project sponsor and developer and subsequently caused many challenges in development and management of software projects.

The overall success and accuracy of software development rely on how good and perfect the efforts were estimated. As mentioned earlier effort estimation is a systematic process and to perform it, there are various approaches designed by several researchers to ensure more accuracy and perform in the said process. The identification and selection of a particular approach are very much difficult, critical and challenging for project management. The ill selection of approach definitely will lead to unsuccessful development. There is no unanimous agreement among researchers that which particular model performs effort estimation perfectly in all situations (Boehm B., Abts C. and Chulani S., 2000).

The importance of software effort estimation has been justified by many researchers in the literature. A report by Cutter Consortium in 2000 (Emilia M., 2000)shows some alarming statistics which was derived from a large database of effort estimation related to software projects in general and web-based projects in particular and is given below:

- 79% of the studied projects presented schedule delays;
- 63% of the studied projects exceeded budgets;
- 84% of the studied projects did not meet requirements;
- 53% of the studied projects did not provide the required function; and
- 52% of the studied projects had a poor quality of deliverables.

According to the study performed by the International Society of Parametric Analysis (ISPA) (Eck D., Brundick B. and Fettig ., 2009) and the Standish Group International(Lynch J., 2009), two-thirds of software projects fail to be delivered on time and within budget. And according to them the two main reasons that cause these failures are: (1) improper estimation in terms of project size, cost, and staff needed and (2) uncertainty of software and system requirements.

As there exits different types of software applications (conventional software application, web application, mobile application) and these applications are different from one another in several aspects: nature, scope, functionality, development, deployment, usage spectrum, etc. Therefore, each of these applications needs a tailor-made approach to perform effort estimation. The use of model developed for one type may be useful in some cases but cannot be a holistically successful approach. Theref0re, the deployment of ad-hoc methods will only increase the chances of failure and not a success.

It is an inevitable requirement to understand the differences between various types of software applications so that a proper type of approach can be either identified or developed to ensure accuracy in effort prediction. The project management not only needs to differentiate the type of development then has to identify and select if available a proper approach to pursue effort estimation and land in a good result. The whole success of the development industry relies on its best estimation policy and reliable estimation team. The sensitivity and seriousness of this domain make it challenging, important and critical. The literature review performed in (S. M. Saif, 2017b) describes in length the various approaches developed and used for effort estimation. These models continue to be revisited and modified to cater to more desirous demands of estimates to achieve more effectiveness and accuracy in the estimation process. Therefore, it is pretty crucial for a project manager to perform efficient effort/cost estimation in early stages of software development. As the perfection in estimation will help the development industry to perform better over bidding process, since overestimation will lead to bidding loss and underestimation will cause the company to lose money.

EFFORT ESTIMATION MODELS

Measurement and accuracy in effort estimation process is a very important and critical activity for software project management to ensure that their development is successful and effective. The identification and selection of an efficient and reliable estimation process always help the development team to obtain accurate size estimation and consequently, the cost of application development. Therefore, it is inevitable for project management to select a best suitable and reliable method to perform effort estimation at early stages of software development to draw realistic budgetary for required to accomplish a successful software development (Jacky K. and Ross J., 2008). In order to approximate software efforts estimation, several approaches or methods were introduced. Most of these approaches were developed to perform effort estimation for conventional software applications. However, they were also used to perform effort estimation for mobile and web applications, and the results obtained were not as good and promising as were obtained for conventional software's. The main reason behind this failure is purely on the nature and type of the applications, as we know, all these types of applications are different from one another. Therefore, the approaches developed for one type cannot prove out to be successful for other as well. Therefore, there is need to have tailor-made and specific effort estimation approaches specific to the particular type of application development then only successful development and accurate estimates are possible.

Different researchers have put effort estimation methods were put into several categories like Trendowicz and Jeffery (Back, T., Hammel U. and Schwefel H, 1997),(Burgess, Colin J., and Martin L., 2007) and Shepherd C. et al. (Shepherd M, and Kadoda M., 2001).However, effort estimation methods can be broadly categorized as Expert based, Algorithmic and Machine learning based models or Algorithmic and non-algorithmic models. Figure 4 represents various effort estimation methods and their corresponding sub-category. The models or approaches mentioned below have been developed for either conventional applications or mobile applications or web application.

Figure 4. Classifications of effort estimation methods

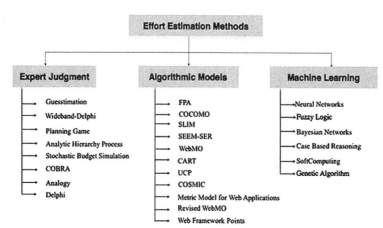

ALGORITHMIC MODELS

Algorithmic models also called as parametric models as they use mathematical equations between dependent and independent variables or empirical models to estimate efforts required for software in general and web or mobile application development in particular. These are the most popular and commonly used effort estimation approaches as they are easier and simpler to use (R D Banker, 1994). However, to make them more effective, they need calibration or adjustment with most circumstances. Algorithmic model is purely based on the state and degree of various variables required in the development process; LOC, function points, web objects, no. of web pages, no. of links, no. of multimedia files, etc. In addition to these direct parameters, there are other factors that also have an impact on the efforts and are called as cost drivers. These cost drivers correspond to all those factors that are associated with an environment where the web application is developed, and the technical resources are required to fulfill the pragmatic development process. These factors are typically called as Environmental Factors and Technical Factors. This relationship between parameters cost drivers is formalized by framing a mathematical equation between them. Equation 1 below structures such relation.

$$Estimated\ Effort = a\ Size\ of\ New\ Proj \times EAF \tag{1}$$

where, a and b are parameters chosen based on certain criteria like; type of project being developed, EAF is Effort Adjustment Factor. The relationship between effort and size can either linear or non-linear; such representation can be expressed by equation no 2 and 3 respectively obtained after applying regression analysis on past project data. Equation 2 issues the relationship as linear and equation 3 as non-linear (E. Mendes, N. Mosley and S. Counsell, 2006)

$$Estimated\ Effort = C + a_0 Estimated\ Size\ of\ New\ Proj + a_1 CD_1 + ... + a_n CD_n \tag{2}$$

$$Estimate\ Effort = C \times EstimatedSizeofNewProj^{a0} CD_1^{a1} + ... + CD_n^{an} \tag{3}$$

where, C is constant denoting initial estimated effort (assuming the size and Cost drivers to be Zero) derived from past project data (Putnam, L. H., 1978) and $a_0...a_n$ denote parameters derived from past project data.

The most popular algorithmic models used to perform effort estimation for conventional/ web/mobile applications are briefly discussed below:

Putnam's Model/ Software Life Cycle Model

The Putnam's model, developed by Larry Putnam in the 1970s, is also called as Software Life Cycle Model (SLIM) (Fenton N.E. and Pfleeger, S.L., 1997). This model was used for estimating the efforts for projects exceeding 70,000 lines of code (LOC). Putnam's model describes the time and efforts required to complete a software project development of certain size and complexity. The time-effort curve required to accomplish development is performed by using the Rayleigh Curve function or Rayleigh distribution. Putnam Suggests that staffing rises smoothly during the project and then drops sharply during the acceptance testing. The SLIM method is expressed by two variants equations: Software equation and Manpower-Buildup equation. Software equation is expressed by equation 4, states that effort is proportional to the cube of the size and inversely proportional to the fourth power of time (Albrecht A. J., 1979) and Manpower-Buildup equation represented by equation 5, states that effort is proportional to the cube of the development time.

$$Size = E \times Effort^{\frac{1}{3}} \left(t_d \right)^{4/3} \tag{4}$$

where, E is Environment or technical factor; t_d is software delivery time in years. Efforts are total project efforts in person-years. Size is an effective source lines of code (SLOC).

$$D = E/t^3 \tag{5}$$

where, D is constantly called as manpower accelerator, E is total project effort in years and 't' is a delivery time in years.

The total efforts required to develop software projects are represented by equation 6 below.

$$E = \left(\frac{\left(CE^{1/3} \right) t^{4/3}}{C} \right)^{9/7} \left(\frac{E}{t^3} \right)^{4/7} \tag{6}$$

SLIM is applied to almost all types and sizes of software projects. It computes schedules, efforts, cost, staffing for all software development phases and reliability for the main development phase.

SLIM takes SLOC, Function Points and other valid measures of functions to be created as its primary input metrics to generate efforts. Putnam's model can be used to plot software development effort as a function of time, as shown in figure 4.

Figure 5. Software development effort as a function of time in Putnam model
Source: Fenton N.E. and Pfleeger S.L., 1997

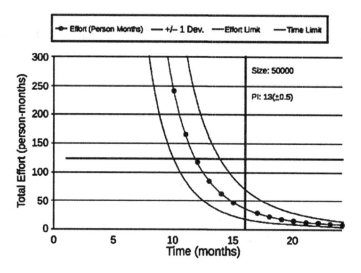

FUNCTION POINT ANALYSIS

Function point analysis (FPA) an effort estimation model developed by Allan Albrecht of IBM in 1979 (Boehm B. W., 1981). In FPA, the project management implements basic operational units known as function points to represent individual function to be delivered through a software application. In more precisely, these function points indicate different functional user requirement desired by the client from the application. Therefore, FPA approximates the overall functional complexity of application by identifying all functional size measures corresponding to each function. In FPA, five types of functional components were identified to obtain functional size measurement: external input file, external output file, external inquiry, internal logic file, external interface file. In addition to functional components, 14 value adjustment factors (VAF) or general system characteristics (GSC) are used to normalize the size. These factors are also called as cost drivers. Functional components can be either data functions or transactional functions.

The functional complexity of the web application development is directly proportional to the number of functional user requirements and there corresponding basic functional units such as record element type (RET), data element type (DET) and file type referenced (FTR). International Function Point Users Group (IFPUG), an independent organization have developed a universal standard for proper elicitation, identification, and counting of function points present in any software application development.

Once the identification of the function points is done, they are classified into simple, average and complex categories. These categories have their specific weighting factor associated to it is shown in table 1. The behavior of these function types are described in figure 6,

Figure 6. Function point model: a high-end view

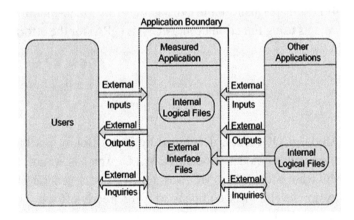

The overall function points are calculated by obtaining by multiplying function count by an adjustment factor that is defined by considering 14 technical attributes called as General system characteristics (GSC) given in table 2. The aggregate impact of these GSC is calculated as Summation of all the individual parameters, as shown by equation 7 and total function points by equation 8.

Table 1. Overview of function point analysis

Parameter description	Count		Weight Factor			Count
			Simple	Average	Complex	
Number of Inputs		×	3	4	6	
Number of Output		×	4	5	7	
Number of Inquiries		×	3	4	6	
Number of Internal Files		×	7	10	15	
Number of External Interfaces		×	5	7	10	
Function Count (Unadjusted)						

$$VAF = \left(TDI \times 0.01\right) + \sum_{i=1}^{14} F_i \tag{7}$$

where TDI is the total degree of influence and has the lowest value, 0.65 and highest value as 70. F is particular VAF

$$FP = Function_{count} \times \left[0.065 + 0.01 \times \sum_{i=1}^{14} F_i \right] \tag{8}$$

These calculated Function points are used to predict the efforts required for the development of any software application in general and web applications in particular.

Table 3 shows the effort estimate (man-month), the actual effort (man-month), and percentage MRE data of the 15 software projects using Function Point Analysis (FPA) for the effort estimation performed by (Kemerer C.F., 1987).

COCOMO

The Constructive Cost Model (COCOMO), developed by Barry Bohm in 1980s, is one of the most popular algorithmic cost estimation model (Boehm B. W., C. Abts, A.W. and Brown S., 2000). This is also called a COCOMO 81 model. COCOMO was aimed to be a generic effort estimation model to be applied by any software development company to predict early efforts. The development of this algorithmic technique was based on the study of 63 software development projects at TRW Aerospace during the 1970s. COCOMO uses simple regression formula where parameters have been derived from a past project and are adjusted based on current developmental characteristics. The most fundamental calculation in the COCOMO model is the use of effort equation to estimate the number of person-months required for project development. The effort equation is represented by equation 9 and 10.

Effort = A ×(Est Pro Size)B (9)

Table 2. Functional complexity parameter

S No	Description of Parameter	Value Range	Lowest values	Highest Values
1	Data Communication	0-5	0	5
2	Distributed data communication	0-5	0	5
3	Performance	0-5	0	5
4	Heavily used configuration	0-5	0	5
5	Transaction rate	0-5	0	5
6	Online data entry	0-5	0	5
7	End user efficiency	0-5	0	5
8	Online update	0-5	0	5
9	Complex Processing	0-5	0	5
10	Reusability	0-5	0	5
11	Installation ease	0-5	0	5
12	Operation ease	0-5	0	5
13	Multiple sites	0-5	0	5
14	Facilitate changes	0-5	0	5
	Total degree of influence -TDI		0	70
	VAF=(TDI*0.01) + 0.65		0.65	1.35

Table 3. Details of the software projects from Kemerer

Project	Estimated Effort (man –month)	Actual effort (man –month)	MRE (%)
1	344.30	287.00	19.97
2	92.13	82.50	11.67
3	731.43	1,107.30	33.94
4	192.03	86.90	120.98
5	387.11	336.30	15.11
6	61.58	84.00	26.69
7	52.60	23.20	326.73
8	264.68	130.30	103.13
9	477.81	116.00	311.91
10	2.83	72.00	103.93
11	484.24	258.70	87.18
12	192.21	230.70	16.68
13	157.36	157.00	0.23
14	390.63	246.90	58.21
15	282.91	69.90	304.74
		MMRE (%)	**102.74**

where, A is proportionality constant, B represents economy or dis-economy of scale, B depends on development mode or class (Organic, Semidetached, and Embedded). Project size is in source lines of code (SLOC)

$$Effort = a(Est\ Pro\ Size)^b EAF \tag{10}$$

where, *Effort* is estimated project effort, and *EstProSize* is the size of an application measure in thousand of delivered source instructions (KDSI), a and b are constants that determine the class of the projects to be developed(Organic, Semidetached, and Embedded), EAF is an effort adjustment factor, calculated from cost drivers.

- The organic model incorporates small and less complicated projects, and projects are familiar, stable. The project developed is similar to previously developed ones. They are developed by highly experienced teams with similar past development experience.
- Semi- Detached model incorporates projects that have intermediate characteristics (either too small or too easy). The development team has a mixed experience. This is also known as Basic COCOMO.
- Embedded Model, development is characterized by tight, inflexible constraints and interface requirements. This mode requires a great deal of innovation.

COCOMO can be applied at different stages of development to estimate the effort or cost of development at early stages of development where requirement elicitation is not clear or when detailed requirements have been specified or at later stages when application design has been finalized. These three different stages or approaches are called as Basic COCOMO, Intermediate COCOMO and Advanced COCOMO models(Nassif, A. B., Ho, D. & Capretz, L. F. (2011), RD Banker, H. Chang, C. Kemerer, 1994).

COCOMO-II

It is an enhanced variant of basic COCOMO in which new cost drivers were introduced to achieve better estimation accuracy. It uses LOC and Function Points as sizing metrics to calculate project size. COCOMO-II has three sub-models, Application composition, Early Design and Post-Architecture(R D Banker, H. Chang, C. Kemerer, 1994).The COCOMO II effort estimation model is summarized in equation 11:

$$Effort = A \times \left(size\right)^E \prod_{i=1}^{17} EM_i \tag{11}$$

where, Effort is expressed in person-months (PM). 'A' is a calibration factor, approximates productivity constant in (PM/KSLOC), it is 2.94 for COCOMO II 2000. Size is measured in KSLOC and unadjusted function points (UFP), converted to SLOC or UFP divided by one thousand. EM is effort multiplier (Table 2.3) with complexity classified into categorized into six ranking orders: very low, low, nominal, high, very high and extra high with their respective weighting factor. Exponent 'E' is an aggregation of five scale factors(SF) that accounts for the relative economics, and diseconomies of scale countered for software development of different sizes(Barry W. Bohm, 2000, Karner, G. (1993).

- if E<1.0, then project exhibits economy of scale
- if E=1.0, then project have both economy and diseconomy of scale in balance and
- if E>1.0, then project exhibits diseconomy of scale.

Kemerer C.F.,1987, analyzed many COCOMO models. COCOMO Intermediate showed the least Mean Magnitude of Relative Error (MMRE). The effort estimate (person month), the actual effort (person month), and percentage MRE of the 15 software projects are shown in Table 4.

Table 4. Details of the software projects from Kemerer

No.	Estimated Effort (person month)	Actual Effort (person month)	MRE (%)
1	917.56	287.00	219.71
2	151.66	82.50	83.83
3	6,182.65	1,107.30	458.35
4	558.98	86.90	543.25
5	1,344.20	336.30	299.70
6	313.36	84.00	273.05
7	234.78	23.20	911.98
8	1,165.70	130.30	794.63
9	4,248.73	116.00	3,562.70
10	180.29	72.00	150.40
11	1,520.04	258.70	487.57
12	558.12	230.70	141.82
13	1,073.47	157.00	583.74
14	629.22	246.90	154.85
15	133.94	69.90	91.62
		MMRE	**583.82**

Source: (Kemerer C.F.,1987)

TOP-DOWN ESTIMATION

This can be considered as specialization approach where total efforts/cost required for the software development is obtained by fine-graining the main problem into its constituent components that collectively attribute to overall efforts. Top-down Estimation is more beneficial in the early stages of software development because detailed information is not available during this stage (Kusuma B. M., 2014) (Leung H and Fan Z, 2001). Putnam's Model is an example of this technique.

BOTTOM-UP ESTIMATION

Bottom-up estimation is opposite of Top-down estimation method. This can be treated as a generalization approach wherein all the attributes that are expected to play role in effort estimation are indentified and later converged into a single collective variable. These attributes are also called as cost drivers and the cost of each software component (drivers) is combined to achieve the overall cost of the software. Goal is to derive system estimate from the accumulated estimate of the small component (Leung H and Fan H., 2001).

USE CASE POINT ESTIMATION

Objective oriented software development has now become a development strategy of choice. In objective oriented programming paradigm, use-case diagrams are considered as basic information units modeled through unified modeling language (UML) and are usually prepared at preliminary stages of software development. The behavior of use case diagrams portrays the functional strength of the application development. The interaction between user and system in use case modeling is described through use case points in general and by using actors and use cases in particular. Each use-case is represented by the use case scenario diagram. The use case scenario is mainly composed of a success scenario and an alternative scenario.

Use Case Point (UCP) model for software effort estimation based on the use case diagrams was first developed by (Karner G., 1993) to establish an estimation framework to perform early and accurate effort estimation. In the UCP model, the software size is calculated according to the number of actors and use cases in a use case diagram and every number multiplied by their corresponding complexity factor. The complexity of the use-case is determined by the strength of the transactions incurred therein to complete a specific function.

ACTORS

The actors in the use-case point model are categorized as simple, average or complex depending on the complexity of the use-case. A weight is assigned to each actor category as specified in table 5. An actor can be defined as 'simple' if interaction with the system through application programming interfaces (API). An actor can be defined as 'average' if it interacts through protocols (like TCP/IP). The actor is defined as 'Complex' if an interaction is through a Graphical User Interface (GUI). The weight assigned to them is 1, 2 and 3, respectively, and the same is given in table 5.

Table 5. Actor complexity and their respective weighting factor

Actor Complexity	Categorization criteria	Weight
Simple	through an API	1
Average	through TCP/IP protocol	2
Complex	through Graphical User interface (GUI)	3

The total unadjusted actor weight (UAW) is calculated by totaling the number of actors in each category and multiplying by its specified weight factor. All the products are added to get unadjusted actor weight. The equation for calculating unadjusted actor weight (UAW) is given as:

$$UAW = \Sigma(No.\ of\ factors \times their\ respective\ weight\ factor) \tag{12}$$

USE CASES

The use-cases are categorized as simple, average and complex, categories depending on the number of transactions including the transactions in alternative flow within a use-case. Use-case is categorized as 'simple' if the number of transactions is less than 3, a use-case is categorized as 'average' if the number of transactions is between 4-7 and use-case is categorized as 'complex' if the number of transactions is more than 7 within a use-case. The corresponding weight assigned to simple, average, complex categories are 5, 10 and 15, respectively, and the same is given in table 6.

Table 6. Use case complexity and their respective weighting factor

Use Case Complexity	Number of Transactions	Weight
Simple	<=3	5
Average	4 to 7	10
Complex	>7	15

Unadjusted use case weight (UUCW) is calculated from the number of use-cases in all the three categories simple, average and complex. The number of use-cases in the corresponding category is multiplied by its corresponding weight factor, and at the end, all values are summed to calculate unadjusted use case weight. The equation for calculating UUCW gives as:

$$UUCW = \Sigma(No.\ of\ use\ cases \times their\ respective\ weight\ factor) \tag{13}$$

Different researchers have observed that both use cases and actors have their discrete behavior and accordingly contribute to the nature of transactions. In the UCP method of software effort estimation, the following three steps are carried out to calculate efforts required for a software project:

- Calculate the number of Unadjusted Use Case Points (UUCP).
- Calculate the total number of adjusted Use Case Points (UCP).
- Calculate the overall effort based on the total man-hours needed for the development of the project.

In order to calculate UUCP, the values for UAW and UUCW are required. Both the UAW and UUCW values are used to calculate UUCP, and the equation for the calculation is given as.

$$UUCP = UUCW + UAW \tag{14}$$

where UUCP is unadjusted use case points, UUCW is unadjusted use case weight, and UAW is un-adjusted actor weight. After calculating UUCP, the UCP (use case point) value needs to be calculated using the following equation.

$$UCP = UUCP \times TCF \times ECF \tag{15}$$

where TCF is technical complexity factor, ECF is environmental complexity factor

TECHNICAL COMPLEXITY FACTORS

These are non-functional parameters that impact the development, implementation, and maintenance of web application development. These factors influence the technical characteristics associated with software application development like architecture, internal processing, interoperability, scalability, user training, etc. The technical complexity factor (TCF) is used to adjust the UCP estimate based on the perceived technical complexities of the project to be developed. TCF corresponds of thirteen (13) different parameters which are rated using a scale from 0 to 5 where value '0' implies that the parameter is 'irrelevant' and the assigned value will increase with the increase in significance and value '5' implies significance of the corresponding parameters is treated as 'essential'. The details of all the 13 technical complexity parameters with their relative weight are given in table 7. For each technical complexity factors, the influence estimate is multiplied by the corresponding weight factor, and the summation of all the calculated value is the Technical Complexity Factors (TCF) value.

Table 7. Technical factor and weight

Factor	Description	Weight (W_i)
T1	Distributed system	2
T2	Response or throughput performance objectives	1
T3	End-user efficiency (online)	1
T4	Complex internal processing	1
T5	Code must be reusable	1
T6	Easy to install	0.5
T7	Easy to use	0.5
T8	Portable	2
T9	Easy to change	1
T10	Concurrent	1
T11	Includes special security features	1
T12	Provides direct access for third parties	1
T13	Special user training facilities are required	1

The value of the TCF is calculated using the following equation.

$$TCF = 0.6 + 0.01 \sum_{i=1}^{13} Ws_i \times S_i \qquad (16)$$

ENVIRONMENTAL COMPLEXITY FACTOR

These factors are related to various characteristics associated with the development team like developers experience, skills, knowledge of technology, etc. To what extent a person possesses these attributes makes its influence proportionally on web development in general and effort estimation in particular.

Environmental complexity factor is directly dependent on software development team experience in the software project to be developed. More experienced teams will have a greater impact on the UCP computation in comparison with less experienced software teams. The software development team determines the impact of each factor on the project with respect to different parameters of ECF. The influence of eight (8) environmental complexity factor parameters on the software development effort is estimated using a scale from 0 to 5 where '0' means 'irrelevant and '5' is for 'essential'. All the eight environmental complexity factor parameter with their corresponding weights are given in table 8.

Table 8. Environmental factor and weight

Factor (E_i)	Description	Weight (W_i)
E1	Familiarity with the project	1.5
E2	Application Experience	0.5
E3	OO Programming Experience	1
E4	Lead Analyst Capability	0.5
E5	Motivation	1
E6	Stable requirements	2
E7	Part Time Staff	-1
E8	Difficult Programming Language	-1

The weight assigned based on the software project to be developed for different parameters of environmental complexity factor is multiplied with the corresponding weight of the parameter. All the eight (8) values calculated after multiplying corresponding weight are summed together to get the value of EF, which is used to calculate ECF. The environmental complexity factor (EF) can be calculated as:

$$ECF = 1.4 + 0.03 \sum_{i=1}^{8} Ws_i \times S_i \qquad (17)$$

After calculating the value of UUCP (unadjusted use case points), ECF (Environmental Complexity Factors) and TCF (Technical Complexity Factors) the values for UCP use case points is calculated using the following equation:

$UCP = UUCP \times TCF \times ECF$

In order to estimate the effort in person-hours the UCP value is multiplied by 20, as was suggested by (Karner G., 1993) to calculate efforts:

$Effort = UCP \times 20$ person-hours (18)

As use-cases based effort estimation are based on the object-oriented methodology where unified modeling language (UML) has emerged as the dominant technique for structuring requirements (Alves R., Valente P. and Numes N. J., 2013) The UCP became very popular due to its relative simplicity and applicability at early stages of software development process. The use case point method of software effort estimation has gained wide popularity due to its easy-to-use characteristic and use-case. The present state of software development is mostly using object-oriented approaches for software development, which make the availability of use-case diagrams a necessity. The use case diagrams are prepared by developers at the early stages of development, which further make the UCP effort estimation method as a suitable approach keeping in mind the present state of the software industry.

Table 9 shows the effort estimate (man-hour), the actual effort (man-hour), and percentage MRE data of the 15 projects obtained by Frohnhoft and Engels (S. Frohnhoff, and G. Engels, 2008) in thiere study.

Table 9. Details of the 15 software projects from frohnhoft and engels

Project	Industry	Effort estimates (Man-Hour)	Actual Effort (Man- month)	MRE (%)
1	Apparel industry	1,205	728	65.52
2	Automotive	11,667	15,500	24.73
3	Automotive	114,023	136,320	16.36
4	Finance	1,002	2,992	66.51
5	Finance	3,301	3,680	10.30
6	Insurance	2,115	4,800	55.94
7	Logistics	1,406	944	48.94
8	Logistics	1,751	2,567	31.79
9	Logistics	8,840	7,250	21.93
10	Logistics	52,219	61,172	14.64
11	Public	39,030	46,900	16.78
12	Public	19,442	13,200	47.29
13	Telco	3,588	2,456	46.09
14	Telco	3,186	2,432	31.00
15	Telco	1,518	1,056	43.75
			MMRE	**36.10**

Source: Frohnhoff S and Engels G., 2008

Web Objects Model

Web Objects developed by Donald J. Reifer in 2000 used for sizing a web application, Web Objects are considered as the first metric specially developed for a web application. The size of the web application is measured as a total number of web objects, a particular web application exhibits. It is an extension to function points in the sense that four more web related components were added to it (Reifer J. D., 2000). These added four components make it sizing method for a web application. web objects consist of nine component: i) external input, ii) external output, iii) external interface, iv) internal logic file, v) external quires, vi) multimedia files, vii) web building blocks, viii) scripts and ix) links.

Web Objects computes the size by considering each and every possible element of the web application by using Holsters equation (equation 19) for volume, the measurements obtained in a language independent and related to the vocabulary used to describe it in terms of operands and operators.

$$V^* = Nlog_2(n) = \left(N_1^* + N_2^*\right)log_2\left(n_1^* + n_2^*\right) \tag{19}$$

where,

N : number of total occurrences of operands and operators

n : number of distinct *operands* and *operators*

N_1^*: total occurrences of *operand* estimator

N_1^*: total occurrences of *operator* estimator

n_1^*: number of unique *operand* estimator

n_2^*: number of unique *operand* estimator

V^* : volume of work involved represented as Web Object

In order to estimate the overall size of the web application, Reifer developed "Web Object Calculation Worksheet(WOCW)". WOCW consists of all the predictors with their corresponding weighting factor assigned to low, Average or High complexity level. The worksheet and size measurement metrics became the first step in developing a model, this model is called as WebMo or Web Model that accurately estimates the size and simultaneously the cost and optimal schedule required for the development of web application.

The mathematical foundation of WebMO depends on the parameters of COCOMO II and SoftCost-OO software cost estimating models (Donald J. R., 1993). The mathematical representation of WebMo is given in equation 20 and 21 below.

$$Effort = A\prod_{i=1}^{9}cd_i\left(size\right)^{P1} \tag{20}$$

$$Duration = B(Effort)^{P2} \tag{21}$$

where

An effort is expressed in person-months and duration in calendar months

A and B are constants

P1 and P2 are power laws

cd_i are cost drives, *Size* is the number of Web Objects,

The duration was calculated based on a square-root relationship with effort based upon built-in scaling rules. The validity of this estimation equation was performed on web applications like e-commerce, financial applications, business-to-business application, and web-based information utilities.

Table 10 shows the effort estimation results obtained by Ruhe (Ruhe M., Jeffery R and Wieczorek I., 2004) for web application development using Function Points and Web Object Counts with OLS regression based effort prediction models.

Table 10. Results of effort estimation of web application development using FP, WO and Allette's expert method

Estimation Method	Min MRE	Max MRE	Mean MRE	Pred
OLS regression(FP)	0.02	0.84	0.33	0.42
OLS regression(WO)	0.00	0.60	0.24	0.67
Allette's Expert Opinion	0.12	0.68	0.37	0.25

Source: M. Ruhe, R. Jeffery, I. Wieczorek, 2003

COSMIC-FFP

COSMIC-FFP (COSMIC stands for Common Software Metrics Consortium, while FFP stands for Full Function Points) is a widely adopted effort estimation approach used for sizing software applications. It came into existence to address the challenges faced by measurement experts while using existing functional sizing methods. It was later approved as an International Standard (ISO/IEC 19761:2003 and now revised as ISO/IEC 19761:2011)(ISO/IEC 19761:2011). Data movements or transactions that correspond to any software application are fundamental identifiers for this sizing method. The basic idea underlying this approach is that, for usual software development, the biggest programming efforts are being devoted to handling data movements, and thus the number of these data movements can provide a meaningful insight of the development size (De Marco L., Ferrucci F and Gravino C., 2013). These data movements can be "to and from" persistent memory or between different users. The presence of these data movements in any application, whether core software application or web application has a direct contribution towards the size and complexity of the application. COSMIC standardize the mechanism to identify different data movements and other characteristic aspects related to them(Costagliola G., Di Martino S., Ferrucci F and Vitiello G., 2006).

COSMIC -FFP measures the functionality of the web application in terms of cosmic functional size units (CFSU). These CFSU are identified after applying a set rules, and procedures to Functional User Requirements to obtain a numerical value of CFSU's, which represents the functional size of the software. COSMIC-FFP model consists of two models: the context model and the software model(Costagliola G., Di Martino S., Ferrucci F and Vitiello G., 2006).

Figure 7. Generic flow of data attributes from functional perspectives (a) and generic software model for measuring software functional size(b)
Source: Bruegge B., Dutoit A. H., 2003

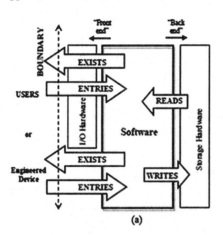 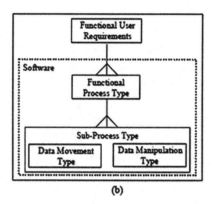

Context model establishes the boundary that separates software application from its host operating environment. It illustrates the generic functional flow of data attributes from a functional perspective. This data flow is characterized by two directions, front-end, and back-end, representing four different data movements (see Figure 6.a) entries and exits, read and write, respectively. Entries and exists allow data exchanges with the user and read and writes, which allow the exchange of data with the persistent storage hardware.

Software model assumes that software to be mapped and measure either takes input or produces useful output to users. It can also manipulate pieces of information designated as data groups, which consist of data attributes.

Software model allows us to consider that these functional user requirements are implemented by a set of functional processes, each of which represents a unique set of sub-processes performing either a data movement or a data manipulation (see Figure 6b). Four different sub-processes can be executed: entry, exit, read, write.

- Entry moves a data from user across the boundary into the functional process
- Exit moves data from the functional process across the boundary to a user
- Read moves a data from persistent storage to the functional process and
- Write moves data from the functional process to persistent storage.

The implementation of COSMIC functional measurement method takes three important aspects into consideration: measurement strategy phase, mapping phase, and measurement phase. After these phases are rendered, it becomes possible to determine the functional size that is a total number of CFP's of software application and is represented by equation 22.

$$Size(FP_i) = \sum Size(Entries_i) + \sum Size(Exits_i) + \sum Size(Reads_i) + \sum Size(Writes_i) \qquad (22)$$

Similarly, the size of software in terms of COSMIC is then the sum of the sizes of all functional processes that occur in the measured software application and is expressed in equation 23.

$$Size(software) = \Sigma Size(FP_i) \tag{23}$$

The application of COSMIC in web application sizing was first adopted by Rollo after he faced difficulties in sizing Internet Bank System with FPA method (Rollo T., 2000). The application of the COSMIC method to size Web applications was further analyzed by(Costagliola G., Di Martino S., Ferrucci F and Vitiello G., 2006) (Mendes E., Counsell S., and Mosley N., 2002)(Rollo T., 2000). The COSMIC method was found to be a suitable method for sizing web applications (Costagliola G., Di Martino S., Ferrucci F and Vitiello G., 2006).

Anda B. and Dreiem H., 2001, performed effort estimation using COSMIC-FFP and the details of estimated efforts (11,859.88 man-hour), the actual effort (6,308 man-hour), and percentage MRE (88.01%) data of the case study and the results obtained are shown in table 11 below.

Table 11. Details of the software projects from

Case	Estimated Effort (Man-Hour)	Actual effort (Man-Hour)	MRE (%)
1	3,670	2,550	30.52
2	2,860	3,320	16.08
3	2,740	2,080	24.09
		MMRE	27.30

Source: Anda B. and Dreiem H., 2001

EXPERT JUDGMENT

The estimation approach to predict the effort required for software application development by means of subjective expertise of an expert on similar development projects. The estimation of the new project involves that the expert must possess the developmental experience and knowledge of similarly situated project development. Later on, the estimates are drafted by these experts accordingly on the basis of their similarity with exiting projects. The expert estimation methods can be a single expert estimates, or it can be more than one experts consulting before forwarding the final estimates. The accuracy of this method is directly proportional to the experience, competence, skill set, environmental and technical knowledge of the expert or experts (Melanie R., Ross J., and Isabella W., 2003). There is no doubt that these methods are widely used in software and web development industry (Emilia M., Mosley N., and Steve C., 2006), and 70-80% of the industrial estimates made by experts are being performed without using any formal estimation models. The effectiveness of this approach is reduced because of bias, inter expert conflicts, political pressure, and expert centric approach. The simplest instance of this method is also known as guesstimation approach as a single expert provides final estimates. Expert-based estimation is adaptable at certain stages of software development and in situations where the development team lacks quantified and empirical data from the previously computed projects (Kirmani, M.M. and Wahid, A., 2015). Expert estimation method has a limitation in quantifying and determining the factors that have been used to derive an estimate so that this can be used as a pattern of further estimation prediction. Expert estimation can produce much more efficient and accurate estimates when used in combination with other algorithmic models (Gray R., MacDonell S.G., Shepperd M.J., 1999)(Myrtveit I. and Stensrud E., 1999). Despite of its usefulness expert judgment have some drawbacks (Leung H. and Fan, Z., 2002) (Heemstra J. F., 1992)

- Depends highly on expert opinion.
- Very difficult to reproduce and use the knowledge and experience of an expert
- The estimation is not repeatable and means of deriving an estimate are not implicit.

Delphi Technique

Delphi was originally developed for the purpose of making future predictions about some issues by guiding the individuals involved in decision making to propose better prediction after carrying out an assessment on each individual opinion. This constitutes the preliminary stage in the Delphi technique. This assessment is performed by the coordinator to generate a tabular report. In the next stage, this tabular report is distributed among the participants to revisit and reassess the various interpretations mentioned in the report. The feedback from the participants is collected and further analyzed by the coordinator to project better estimation outcome. In original Delphi, there is no group consultation or deliberation on the assessment of issues, but in more open type of Delphi, Wideband Delphi accommodates group discussions between the participants in different assessment rounds(Boehm B., 1981) (Jørgensen M., 2007). The Wideband of Delphi technique can be used for software effort estimation in the following manner;

1. A coordinator begins by providing every expert a project's specification chart and a response sheet.
2. The experts will anonymously respond to various fields mentioned in the response sheet to nullify any bias.
3. The coordinator collects responses and summarizes them to prepare projections for effort estimation.
4. In case the skewness among responses is very high or unusual, the coordinator invites experts for further discussion to get a more aligned opinion.

This methodology is relatively easier to implement, less-expensive, and accurate in comparison to other techniques only when the experts have good expertise in the problem domain for which efforts are being estimated. The main disadvantage of this method is the lack of sensitivity analysis, dependency on experienced estimators; human error and pessimistic approach or unfamiliarity with key aspects of the project (Boehm B., 1981)(Jørgensen M., 2007).

Work-Breakdown Structure Approach

In this approach, software development is divided into modules or sub-processes therefore, and this is also known as the divide-and-conquer approach. To further fine-grain the work-breakdown structure, these sub-processes are further divided into smaller units. The efforts required to develop these sub-processes are estimated by experts on the bases of the previously completed similar software projects. This estimation of this sub-process is fewer errors prone in comparison to estimating the efforts for the whole project at once. The overall effort is estimated by aggregating the efforts corresponding to these sub-processes. A WBS actually consists of two hierarchies, one representing the software product itself, and the other representing the activities needed to build that product (Boehm B., 1981).

COBRA

COBRA (Cost estimation, Benchmarking and Risk Assessment), a hybrid cost modeling technique introduced by Briand in late 1990s (Briand L., El Emam K. and Bomarius F., 1998) to overcome the limitations floating from existing cost estimation methods. COBRA is based on both expert knowledge and quantitative project data. This particular technique frees measurement experts by allowing the usability of any functional size measure and data model to estimate cost. COBRA is actually a framework of activates that are required for the development of the COBRA model.

The fundamental objective of this method is to develop a productivity estimation model by clubbing overhead cost estimates with the productivity model. Productivity model estimates productivity from cost overheads. In other words, the COBRA model has two core components. The first component is a casual model that produces overhead cost estimates and the second component uses data from past completed projects o the basis of similarity in characteristics (Melanie R., Ross J., and Isabella W., 2003).

- **Causal Model**: to calculate the overhead cost estimate, the causal model considers local cost factors or drivers that have a direct relationship with the cost overhead of the project. This particular relationship can be either direct or interaction between any two cost drivers (Briand L., El Emam K. and Bomarius F., 1998) and shown in figure 8. All those factors need to be identified that have an additive effect on the cost of the project. This particular activity of estimating overhead is carried out by expert knowledge acquisition.
- **Estimation Cost Overhead**: The estimation of cost overhead begins with the identification of most relevant cost drivers among the available drivers in the literature that have a direct role in the cost of the project. The list of identified 39 and 12 was retained to have a greater impact on overhead cost estimation. Cost drivers were grouped into four categories: Product, Process, Project and Personnel (Syed M. S. and Abdul W., 2017a). The qualitative causal model was developed to further investigate the impact of individual cost factor on cost estimation and their relative complexity. The implementation of the causal model is followed by a reliable questionnaire to measure and validate the impact of cost factors on the cost estimation. Frequency scale, Evaluation scale, and Agreement scale were used to collect responses regarding cost factors (Syed M. S. and Abdul W, 2017b). After the acquisition of this conceptual, qualitative model, the experts were asked to "quantify" the effect of each of these cost factors on the development cost, by expressing in the percentage of overhead above an "optimal" application that each factor may induce, called as overhead multipliers. The next step ahead is to express the relationship and the estimates of multipliers and project questionnaire variables in the form of equations. The relationship between these variables can be direct, two way or three-way interaction and are expressed in (Briand L., El Emam K. and Bomarius F., 1998). These are then translated into parameters of triangular distribution (minimum, most likely or maximum). Monte Carlo simulation is used to obtain an overhead cost estimate by considering a sample from each triangular distribution. The same is shown in figure 9. This procedure is repeated 1000 times to obtain the distribution of cost overhead of the

project. During these multipliers from all the experts are combined. The mean of this distribution can be randomly selected as the estimated value of cost overhead for the project.

Figure 8. Causal model example

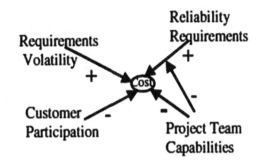

Figure 9. Overview of the productivity estimation model

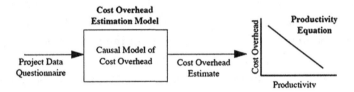

WEB-COBRA

The combinative nature of COBRA: expert opinion and formal modeling, increases its scope to perform effort estimation of web application development. The adoption of COBRA for estimating efforts was performed by Ruhe by developing a web-specific version of COBRA, the Web-COBRA (Melanie R., Ross J., and Isabella W., 2003). Web-COBRA has been modified in several aspects to make it suitable for estimating efforts for web applications. The working framework of Web-COBRA was obtained after conducting personal interviews with the experts of Allete Systems using open questions (Ruhe M., 2002) (Jacky K. and Ross J., 2008). In contrast to COBRA, the quality causal model developed had only direct relationships of cost factors with a cost. Further in Web-COBRA interactions were avoided by deriving a minimum set of independent cost factors. Quantification of relationships within the causal model was refined by conducting personal interviews with Allete System experts to obtain multipliers, in addition to this experts were in command to discuss and understand the cost factors and the multipliers together to improve and validate the quantitative causal model. To aggregate the multiple responses from experts for cost overhead a measure of "central tendency" was used and no weighting was done as Allete System experts were very similar in experience (Banker R D, Chang H. and Kemerer C., 1994).

Machine Learning

These are the most recent methods developed to estimate the efforts for software applications in general and web and mobile applications in particular. Machine learning models are based on computational intelligence extended from human problem-solving characteristics. These models were developed to overcome the challenges faced using expert and other algorithmic models. The irony is that there is yet no "silver bullet" method for estimating the efforts. Machine learning based methods do have both strengths and limitations as well. They largely depend on their context where they are applied. Machine learning methods have the characteristic feature to get trained, and then it automatically recognizes the complex pattern of variables to predict estimates by adopting intelligent decision making. There are different machine learning estimation methods like; Genetic algorithm (Back, T., Hammel U. and Schwefel H.,1997)(Burgess, Colin J., and Martin L., 2007), fuzzy logic(Kumar S., Krishna B. A. and Satsangi P. S., 1994), regression trees(Schofield C., 1998), neural networks (Shepperd M. J., Schofield C. and Kitchenham B., 1996)and case-based reasoning(CBR) (Shepperd M. J., and Kadoda G., 2001). The brief discussion on few popular machine learning based effort estimation methods is given under;

Neural Network

Neural network based model for estimating software efforts has been conceived from the work behavior of the human nervous system. The human nervous system acquires or perceives certain input from the environment through its distinguished perceptions and later activates desired actuators to deliver by responding through proper action. As processing/responding power of the nervous system is instant and fast, based on the same logic, an effort estimation algorithm is designed to perform fast, accurate and instant effort estimation. A simple neuron model is provided in figure 10. The neural network has become the most common and popular software effort estimation model-building technique and is a computer-assisted learning process that inherits the working principles of the human brain. Neural networks are massively parallel and complex and have the capability to solve complex problems with much speed and accuracy. Neural network based effort estimation model works by feeding neural network with historical data of previously completed software projects or web application to get it trained to learn the future course of data on the similar patterns to generate corresponding output. The trained neural network automatically configures or adjusts algorithmic parameters and corresponding weights in order to generate more significant and optimal solution(here in this case estimates)

The actual design of the neural network model begins with the development of an appropriate layout, intermediate levels and links between neural nodes. These neural nodes compute the weighted sum of their corresponding input to generate output. If the sum of the weights exceeds a certain threshold, then this output can be either excitatory or inhibitory input to neuron or nodes of intermediate levels. This passing of input from one node to another in intermediate level continues till the final output is generated (Mair C., Gada K. and Martin L., 2000). The applicability of neural networks for estimating software efforts was extensively studied by Mair and Aggarwal (Gray A. and MacDonell S., 1996)(Aggarwal K.K., Singh Y.and Chandra P., 2005). The performance of the neural network is pretty sensitive to the training date set the feed to it.

Analogy Based Effort Estimation

Estimation by analogy is a systematic method where the estimation of efforts primarily involves characterization of features for the software project for which estimates are required. On the basis of these identified features, similar or analogous projects from already completed past projects are extracted. This characterization, identification of analogous projects forms the basic framework for analogy based

Figure 10. A neural network estimation model

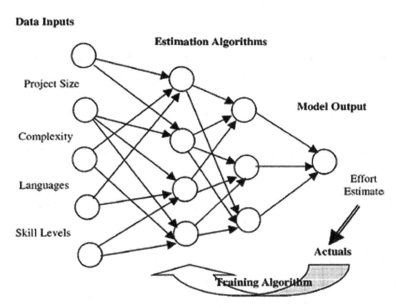

effort estimation (ABE) method. The efforts of these completed projects are used to construct estimates for new but similar projects. This method of estimation is also called a systematic form of expert judgment since both involve the identification of similar projects to obtain estimates (Martin, 1996). Analogy Based Effort Estimation method has been widely used for developing software effort estimation models based upon retrieval by similarity among the projects effectively (Azzeh M., Neagu D. and Cowling P., 2010). The main challenging issue that needs further elaboration is "how to find similar projects ?", identification and prioritization of features.

The data driven ABE method involves four primary steps (Shepperd M and Schofield C., 1997) (1) select k nearest analogies using Euclidean distance or Manhattan distance. (2) Reuse efforts from the set of nearest analogies to find out the effort of the new project. (3) Adjust the retrieved efforts to bring them closer to the new project. Finally, (4) retain the estimated project in the repository for future prediction.

To find analogous projects and to perform effort estimation, an automated tool like ANGEL is used. It automatically finds the best combination of attributes used to find a similar score.

The main disadvantage of analogy method is that it requires considerable amount of computation to reveal similarity done previous projects like using Euclidian distance, etc. Walkerden and Jeffery (Walkerden F. and Jeffery R., 1999)," have compared few techniques for analogy-based software effort estimation with each other furthermore with a linear regression model. The outcomes demonstrated that human brains work superior than tools at selecting analogies for the considered dataset.

Case Based Reasoning

It is another variant of analogy based effort estimation approach, wherein estimates for the new project is initiated by adapting efforts of the most similar and relevant projects from the project pool of successfully completed projects. The process of Case-Based Reasoning (CBR) begins with the detection of most relevant characteristics of the project, called as cost drivers. These cost drivers give a real sense of project size. The similarity between the two projects is found by using Euclidean Distance to obtain distance metrics.

CBR is actually based on the principle that "new problems are often similar to previously dealt problems". Similarly, the estimates obtained for previously developed projects can be a solution to a new project to develop. CBR can be accomplished in four steps (Trendowiz A. and Joffery R., 2014):

1. Retrieve those projects that are similar to new projects to be estimated form projects completed already (historical data).
2. The solution of the identified projects in step 1 above means the efforts and attributes are reused to generate a solution for the current estimation problem.
3. The results obtained for new project estimates can be revisited against the actual estimate.
4. After successfully evaluating the estimates, that is to find the deviation either positive or negative between the actual and estimated efforts and the results are retained for future reference.

The estimation process in CBR is more or less similar to that of analogy based effort estimation. The implementation of CBR in order to obtain effort estimates for software applications in general and web application, in particular, is performed after taking following decisions in order (Shepherd M, and Kadoda M., 2001):

*   Selecting attributes
*   Scaling attributes
*   Identifying analogies
*   selecting analogies and
*   Adapting analogies

Bayesian Belief Networks

Bayesian belief network (BBN) or simply Bayesian network is a directed acyclic graph in which nodes represent random variables, these variables can either be discrete or continuous. The edges of the graph express the probabilistic dependency among the connected nodes with different variables. Therefore, each of these nodes is associated with a conditional probability table(CPT) that quantifies its probability distribution. Relationship between two nodes is represented by an arrowhead stating from influencing variable and terminating on an influenced variable that is the direction from a child node to a parent node.

Figure 11. Bayesian belief network

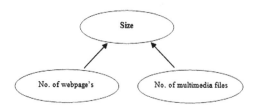

Figure 11 represents the believed causal dependencies between size and selected web application sizing metrics that is "no. of pages" and "no. of multimedia files". In this case, root node "size" has two child nodes: "no. of pages" and "no. of multimedia files". These kinds of topologies represent the belief that the size of the web application is influenced by "no. of pages" and "no. of multimedia files". BBN actually represents a model that supports reasoning with uncertainty and is mainly used in the situation where the knowledge of unknown events is obtained from the knowledge of observed events and are updated accordingly (Emilia M., 2012)(Jensen F.V, 1996). BBN can have broadly two events, Hypothesis and Evidence. Hypothesis(H) are those events which are yet to be explored, and Evidences(E) are those events that have been observed. The interpretation of these events is performed by probability calculus and Bayes theorem, and it continues across the belief to explore the entire hypothesis and update them to evidences, the observed events. To build BBN for estimating the efforts for software applications in general and web applications in particular, the number of issues surface (Emilia M, 2012)

- As BBN in context of the web application is concerned, the datasets used to build belief network needs to be large enough to capture all the possible relationships and the respective states of nodes so that probabilities can be easily mapped.
- Identification of variables that represents all the factors within a specific domain.
- Different structure and probability learning algorithms lead to different prediction accuracy (Mendes E., and Mosley N., 2008).To differentiate between the models is time-consuming.
- Implementation of hybrid BBN model the structure of these models needs to be jointly elicited by more than one domain expert to generalize its diverse applicability.
- The probabilities used by data-driven and hybrid models need to be investigated by at least one domain expert. this may sound like to check the probability of all the nodes of BBN, which is almost not feasible.
- The choice of variable discretization, structure learning algorithms, parameter estimation algorithms, and a number of categories used in the discretization all affect the accuracy of the results, and there is no proper guideline to make the best choice.

Regression Based Estimation Techniques

Regression analysis is a statistical method to investigate the relationship between two variables. One variable is regarded as independent or response/outcome and the second one regarded as dependent or predictive/explanatory. This technique is used to predict the relationship that exists between these variables. It is an important tool for modeling and analyzing data. The main advantages of using regressions analysis are: it indicates the significant relationships between the dependent and independent variable, it also indicates the behavior, impact of multiple independent variables on the dependent variable. In the case of estimating efforts, efforts are a dependent variable, and it depends on various independent variables that collectively make the size of particular software or web application.

Regression analysis can be pursued in different ways, depending on the number and behavior of its predictors or independent variables, few popular regression-based techniques implemented to predict effort estimates are mentioned and described briefly

Linear Regression

It is one of the most widely known modeling techniques. In this technique, the dependent variable is continuous, the independent variable(s) can be, and the nature of the regression line is linear.

Linear Regression establishes a relationship between the dependent variable (Y) and one or more independent variables (X) using a best fit straight line (also known as a regression line).

It is represented by an equation 24

$$Y = a + b*X + e, \tag{24}$$

where a is intercept, b is the slope of the line and e is error term. This equation can be used to predict the value of the target variable based on a given predictor variable(s).

MULTIPLE LINEAR REGRESSIONS

The relationship between dependent variable (Y) and independent variables (Xi) in multiple linear regression (MLR) is expressed by equation 25

$$Y = \beta 0 + \beta 1 X 1 + \beta 1 X 1 + ... + \beta n X n + \varepsilon \tag{25}$$

where, X1, X2, ..., Xn are repressors or predictors; $\beta 0$ is the intercept parameter; $\beta 1$, $\beta 2$, ..., βn are the regression coefficients; and ε is the error component.

MLR technique is usually employed when: (i) the number of cases is significantly higher than the number of parameters to be estimated; (ii) the data has a stable behaviour; (iii) there is a small number of missing data; (iv) a small number of independent variables are sufficient (after transformations if necessary) to linearly predict output variables (also transformed if necessary), so as to enable an interpretable representation (Gray A. R. and MacDonell S. G., 1997). Application of the MLR method requires verification of the associated assumptions. The major assumptions to be considered are (Freund R. J. and Wilson W. J., 1998)(Ott R. L. and Longnecker M., 2010):

- **Linearity:** The relationship between each Xi and Y is linear. Thus the model adequately describes the behavior of data;
- The error component is an independent and normally distributed variable with constant variance and means value zero.

The difference between simple linear regression and multiple linear regression is that multiple linear regression has (>1) independent variables, whereas simple linear regression has only 1 independent variable. Now, the question is "How do we obtain the best fit line?"

Stepwise Regression

This form of regression is used when we deal with multiple independent variables. In this technique, the selection of independent variables is done with the help of an automatic process, which involves no human intervention.

This feat is achieved by observing statistical values like R-square, t-stats and AIC metric to discern significant variables. Stepwise regression basically fits the regression model by adding/dropping covariates one at a time based on a specified criterion. Some of the most commonly used Stepwise regression methods are listed below:

- Standard stepwise regression does two things. It adds and removes predictors as needed for each step.
- Forward selection starts with the most significant predictor in the model and adds variable for each step.
- Backward elimination starts with all predictors in the model and removes the least significant variable for each step.

The main approach of implementing regression-based modeling is to find the set of independent variables that best explains the variation in the dependent variable. The goal of regression is to find the function $f(x)$ that best models the data. In linear regression, this is done by finding the line that minimizes the sum squares error on the data.

Evaluation Criteria

To investigate the effectiveness and accuracy of various effort estimation approaches that are being used by practitioners to perform software effort estimation, various evaluation criteria are used. Evaluation of effort estimation models is carried out by using data sets of past projects developed by the various organizations in the past. Using these datasets on these various models gives the idea about the effectiveness and accuracy in effort estimation by just looking on the deviation obtained(Actual efforts-estimated efforts using different models) The evaluation criteria statistically analyse the results using various mathematical or statistical/ probability distributions like Magnitude of Relative Error(MRE),Mean Magnitude of Relative error(MMRE), Median Magnitude of Relative Error(MdMRE), Mean Absolute error (MAE), Median Absolute Error(MdAE), Standard Deviation, PRED(x), Skewness, Significance tests(Z-test, t-test, chi-square test etc)(Syed M. S., Abdul W., 2017a).

LIMITATIONS OF EFFORT ESTIMATION MODELS

Different effort estimation approaches that have been introduced from time to time by several researchers to perform effective effort estimation have got both advantages and disadvantages with them. The most common limitations and advantages of few popular effort estimation models is provided in table 12 below:

Table 12. Advantages and disadvantages of effort estimation models

Type	Approach	Advantages	Disadvantages
Algorithmic Method	LOC	Very easy in implementation to Estimate the size of software	Prediction of line is tough in early stages, not good for very large project and language dependent
Algorithmic Method	Putnam's Model	Time, Size and Effort are easily collected for past projects	It does not consider the other phases of SDLC
Algorithmic Method	FPA	Tools, methods and language are independent to achieve the fast result	Time, Quality and manual work are not considered
Algorithmic Method	SEER-SEM	Used in very large projects	50 input parameters are required which increased the complexity and uncertainty
Algorithmic Method	COCOMO	Estimating the cost is simple and gets the clear result	Details of past project are required
Algorithmic Method	COCOMO II	It provides more support for modern software development processes and an updated project database. Provide support to mainframe, code reusability and batch processing.	It cannot estimate the effort at all the different phase of SDLC. Its prediction is .68 which is quite good.
Algorithmic Method	Detailed COCOMO	Phase sensitive effort multipliers are each to determine the amount of effort required to complete each phase.	Lots of parameters involved in estimation time complexity is high. Its prediction is .70 which is good.
Non-Algorithmic Method	Analogy based Estimation	Experience and knowledge are used for actual projects	Attributes are required
Non-Algorithmic Method	Expert Judgment	New technology, domain and architecture are the basis to estimate the cost	Experience of similar projects
Non-Algorithmic Method	Top-Down	It requires very less detail about the project, moreover it is faster, simple and easier to use. Unlike other approaches it focuses on activities like integration, management etc	Low level problems are difficult to Identify
Non-Algorithmic Method	Bottom-Up	This technique is more stable and error estimation is also performed	Time and system level activities are not considered
Machine learning Methods	Linear Regression	statistical models	Relationships between dependent and independent variables
Machine learning Methods	Support Vector Machine	Flexibility, Robustness, Unique solutions	computation is expensive, binary classifier
Machine learning Methods	Neural Network	Powerful method, mathematical formula, eases to use. Consistent with unlike databases, power of reasoning	Large complexity of network structure. There is no guideline for designing, the performance depends on large training data
Machine learning Methods	K-Means	Fast Result, Easy to implement	Difficult to predict K-value, Global clusters
Machine learning Methods	Hierarchical cluster	Easy to decide the clusters	Time complexity, Not possible to undo the previous step
Machine learning Methods	Fuzzy	Training is not required, flexibility	Hard to use, maintaining the degree of meaningfulness is difficult
Machine learning Methods	Artificial neural network based estimation	Artificial Neural Network based estimation methods are consistent with unlike databases and they provide power of reasoning in estimation process	Large amount of training data is required No guidelines or instructions are provided for designing.

Source: Rajeswari K. and Beena.R., 2018; Tailor O., Saini J. and Rijwani P. 2014

CONCLUSION

Importance and usability of software applications are continuously increasing. Therefore, it is inevitable for project management to ensure security, reliability, and effectiveness in various software projects. Overriding the benefits of soft systems, most of the organizations are using software-based applications as an interface to access or deliver a multitude of services. To manage growing complexity and demand for quality of services, there is much-required need to have good software application development approach. Better development methodology helps project managers to develop software applications on time and within budget to meet user requirements effectively. Effort estimation plays a major role in effective web application development by predicting the efforts required for web development and subsequently, the cost of development. Accuracy in effort estimation helps project management to draw efficient budgetary estimates so that web development can be monitored and carried out in a systematic manner.

Many developmental approaches have been used for software effort estimation but, most of them were conventional software methods and therefore, failed to produce accurate results when it comes to web or mobile effort estimation. Several web specific effort estimation methods were also developed by researchers from the past few years, but, their results are still questionable. Due to their inaccuracy, the tradition of using conventional approaches is still continuing to remain effort estimation approaches for web or mobile effort estimation.

The existing literature highlights that the existing software effort estimation strategies are not adequate to produce accurate and effective estimates, therefore, advocates the need to develop a more customized and tailor-made model for effort estimation inline within changing development technology to ensure accurate and effective effort estimation at early stages of software development.

REFERENCES

Aggarwal, K. K., Singh, Y., Chandra, P., & Puri, M. (2005). Bayesian regularization in a neural network model to estimate lines of code using function points. *Journal of Computational Science, 1*(4), 505–509. doi:10.3844/jcssp.2005.505.509

Albrecht, A. J. (1979). Measuring application development productivity. In *Proceedings of the joint SHARE, GUIDE and IBM application development symposium.* IBM Corporation.

Alves, R., Valente, P., & Numes, N. J. (2013). Improving Software Effort Estimation with Human-Centric Models: a comparison of UCP and iUCP accuracy. *Proceedings of the 5th ACM SIGCHI symposium on Engineering interactive computing systems, 287*-296. 10.1145/2494603.2480300

Anda, B., & Dreiem, H. (2001). Estimating software development effort based on use cases-experiences from industry. *Fourth International Conference on the UML, 487*–502. 10.1007/3-540-45441-1_35

Azzeh, M., Neagu, D., & Cowling, P. (2010). Fuzzy grey relational analysis for software effort estimation. *Empirical Software Engineering, 15*(1), 60–90. doi:10.100710664-009-9113-0

Back, T., Hammel, U., & Schwefel, H. (1997). Evolutionary Computation: Comments on the History and Current State. *IEEE Transactions on Evolutionary Computation, 1*(1), 3–17. doi:10.1109/4235.585888

Banker, R. D., Chang, H., & Kemerer, C. (1994). Evidence on Economies of Scale in Software Development. *Information and Software Technology, 1994*(5), 275–282. doi:10.1016/0950-5849(94)90083-3

Bauer, F. (1968). Software engineering: A report on conference sponsored. NATO Science Committee.

Boehm, B. (1981). Software Development Cost Estimation Approaches-A Surey. *Annals of Software Engineering, 10*, 177-205.

Boehm, B., Abts, C., & Chulani, S. (2000). Software development cost estimation approaches: A survey. *Annals of Software Engineering, 10*(1), 177–205. doi:10.1023/A:1018991717352

Boehm, B. W. (1981). *Software engineering economics* (Vol. 197). Englewood Cliffs, NJ: Prentice-Hall.

Boehm, B. W., Abts, C., Brown, A. W., Chulani, S., Clark, B. K., Horowitz, W., ... Steece, B. (2000). *Software Cost Estimation with COCOMO 11*. Prenctice Hall.

Briand, L., & Emam, K. (1998). COBRA: A Hybrid Method for Software Cost Estimation, Benchmarking, and Risk Assessment. *Proc. of the Intern. Conference on Software Engineering (ICSE'98)*, 390-399. 10.1109/ICSE.1998.671392

Briand, L. C., & Wieczorek, I. (2002). *Resource Estimation in Software Engineering. In Encyclopedia of Software Engineering* (Vol. 2, pp. 1160–1196). John Wiley & Sons.

Bruegge, B., & Dutoit, A. H. (2003). *Object-Oriented Software Engineering: Using UML, Patterns and Java* (2nd ed.). Prentice-Hall.

Burgess, C. J., & Martin, L. (2007). Can genetic programming improve software effort estimation? A comparative evaluation. *Information and Software Technology, 43*(14), 863–867. doi:10.1016/S0950-5849(01)00192-6

Burgess, C. J., & Martin, L. (2007). Can genetic programming improve software effort estimation? A comparative evaluation. *Information and Software Technology, 43*(14), 863–867. doi:10.1016/S0950-5849(01)00192-6

Costagliola, G., Di Martino, S., Ferrucci, F., Gravino, C., Tortora, G., & Vitiello, G. (2006). A COSMIC-FFP approach to predict web application development effort. *Journal of Web Engineering, 5*(2), 93–120.

Costagliola, G., Di Martino, S., Ferrucci, F., & Vitiello, G. (2006). A COSMIC-FFP approach to predict web application development effort. *Journal of Web Engineering, 5*(2), 93–120.

De Marco, L., Ferrucci, F., & Gravino, C. (2013). Approximate COSMIC size to early estimate Web application development effort. *Presented at the Software Engineering and Advanced Applications, 2013. SEAA 2013. 39th EUROMICRO Conference*, 349– 356.

Donald, J. R. (1993). *SoftCost-OO Reference Manual*. Torrance, CA: Reifer Consultants, Inc.

Donald, R. J. (2000). Web Development estimating quick-to-market software. *Software IEEE, 17*(6), 57–64. doi:10.1109/52.895169

Eck, D., Brundick, B., & Fettig, T. (2009). Parametric estimating handbook. The International Society of Parametric Analysis (ISPA).

Emilia, M. (2012). Using Knowledge Elicitation to Improve Web Effort Estimation: Lessons from Six Industrial Case Studies. In *34th International Conference on Software Engineering (ICSE)*. IEEE.

Emilia, M., Mosley, N., & Steve, C. (2006). Web Effort Estimation. In Web Engineering. Springer.

Emilia, M., & Steve, C. (2000). Web Development Effort Estimation using Analogy. *Software Engineering Conference, 2000, Proceedings*.

Fenton, N. E., & Pfleeger, S. L. (1997). *Software Metrics: A Rigorous and Practical Approach*. International Thomson Computer Press.

Freund, R. J., & Wilson, W. J. (1998). *Regression Analysis: Statistical Modeling of a Response Variable*. San Diego, CA: Academic Press.

Frohnhoff, S., & Engels, G. (2008). Revised Use Case Point Method - Effort Estimation in Development Projects for Business. In *Proceedings of the CONQUEST 2008 - 11th International Conference on Quality Engineering in Software Technology*. Potsdam: Dpunkt Verlag.

Gray, A., & MacDonell, S. (1996). A Comparison of Techniques for Developing Predictive Models of Software Metrics. *Information and Software Technology*, *39*, 1997.

Gray, A. R., & MacDonell, S. G. (1997). A comparison of techniques for developing predictive models of software metrics. *Information and Software Technology*, *39*(6), 425–437. doi:10.1016/S0950-5849(96)00006-7

Gray, R., MacDonell, S. G., & Shepperd, M. J. (1999). Factors Systematically associated with errors in subjective estimates of software development effort: the stability of expert judgment. *Proceedings of the 6th IEEE Metrics Symposium*. 10.1109/METRIC.1999.809743

Heemstra, F. J. (1992). Software cost estimation. *Information and Software Technology*, *34*(10), 627–639. doi:10.1016/0950-5849(92)90068-Z

ISO/IEC 19761:2011, *Software engineering -- COSMIC: a functional size measurement method*. International Organization for Standardization.

Jacky, K., & Ross, J. (2008). Automated Support for Software Cost Estimation using Web-CoBRA. In *15th Asia Pacific Software Engineering Conference*. IEEE Computer Society.

Jensen, F. V. (1996). *An introduction to Bayesian networks*. London: UCL Press.

Jørgensen, M. (2007). Forecasting of software development work effort: Evidence on expert judgement and formal models. *International Journal of Forecasting*, *23*(3), 449–462. doi:10.1016/j.ijforecast.2007.05.008

Karner, G. (1993). Metrics for objector. University of Linköping.

Kemerer, C. F. (1987). An empirical validation of software cost estimation models. *Communications of the ACM*, *30*(5), 416–429. doi:10.1145/22899.22906

Kirmani, M. M., & Wahid, A. (2015). Revised Use Case Point (Re-UCP) Model for Software Effort Estimation. *International Journal of Advanced Computer Science and Applications*, *6*(3), 65–71.

Kumar, S., Krishna, B. A., & Satsangi, P. S. (1994). Fuzzy systems and neural networks in software engineering project management. *Journal of Applied Intelligence, 4*(1), 31–52. doi:10.1007/BF00872054

Kusuma, B. M. (2014). Software Cost Estimation Techniques. *International Journal of Engineering Research in Management and Technology, 3*(4).

Leung, H., & Fan, Z. (2001). *Software Cost Estimation.* Academic Press.

Leung, H., & Fan, Z. (2002). Software Cost Estimation. In Handbook of Software Engineering and Knowledge Engineering. Hong Kong Polytechnic University. doi:10.1142/9789812389701_0014

Lynch, J. (2009). *Chaos manifesto.* The Standish Group. Retrieved from http://www.standishgroup.com/newsroom/chaos_2009.php

Mair, C., Gada, K., & And Martin, L. (2000). An investigation of machine learning based prediction. *Journal of Systems and Software, 53*(1), 23–29. doi:10.1016/S0164-1212(00)00005-4

Martin. (1996). Effort Estimation Using Analogy. *Proceedings of ICSE-18*, 170-178.

Melanie, R., Ross, J., & Isabella, W. (2003). Cost Estimation for Web Applications. *Proceedings of the 25th International Conference on Software Engineering (ICSE'03).*

Mendes, E., Counsell, S., & Mosley, N. (2002). Comparison of web size measures for predicting web design and authoring effort. *IEE Proceedings. Software, 149*(3), 86–92. doi:10.1049/ip-sen:20020337

Mendes, E., & Mosley, N. (2008). Bayesian Network Models for Web Effort Prediction: A Comparative Study. *Transactions on Software Engineering, 34*(6), 723–737. doi:10.1109/TSE.2008.64

Software. (n.d.). In *Merriam-Webster.* Retrieved from https://www.merriam-webster.com/dictionary/software

Mills, H. D. (2010). The management of software engineering, part 1: Concepts of software engineering. *IBM Systems Journal, 19*(4), 414–420. doi:10.1147j.194.0414

Myrtveit, I., & Stensrud, E. (1999). A Controlled Experiment to Assess the Benefits of Estimating with Analogy and Regression Models. *IEEE Transactions on Software Engineering, 25*(4), 510–525.

Nassif, A. B., Ho, D., & Capretz, L. F. (2011). Regression model for software effort estimation based on the use case point method. *International Conference on Computer and Software Modelling, 14*, 106-110.

Ott, R. L., & Longnecker, M. (2010). *An Introduction to Statistical Methods and Data Analysis.* Belmont: Cengage Learning Inc.

Putnam, L. H. (1978). A General Empirical Solution to the Macro Software Sizing and Estimating Problem. *IEEE Transactions on Software Engineering, 4*(4), 345–361. doi:10.1109/TSE.1978.231521

Rajeswari, K., & Beena, R. (2018). A Critique On Software Cost Estimation. *International Journal of Pure and Applied Mathematics, 118*(20), 3851–3862.

Rollo, T. (2000). Sizing E-Commerce. *Proceedings of Australian Conference on Software Measurement.*

Ruhe, M. (2002). *The early and accurate effort estimation of web applications.* Kaiserslautern, Germany: University of Kaiserslautern.

Ruhe, M., Jeffery, R., & Wieczorek, I. (2003). Using web objects for estimation software development effort for web applications. Presented at *Ninth International Software Metrics Symposium (METRICS '03)*, Sydney, Australia. 10.1109/METRIC.2003.1232453

Schofield, C. (1998). *An empirical investigation into software estimation by analogy* (Unpublished doctoral dissertation). Department of Computing, Bournemouth University, Bournemouth, UK.

Shepherd, M., & Kadoda, M. (2001). Comparing Software prediction Techniques using Simulation. *IEEE Transactions on Software Engineering, 23*(11), 1014–1022. doi:10.1109/32.965341

Shepperd, M., & Schofield, C. (1997). Estimating software project effort using analogies. *IEEE Transactions on Software Engineering, 23*(11), 736–743. doi:10.1109/32.637387

Shepperd, M. J., & Kadoda, G. (2001). Using simulation to evaluate prediction technique. In *Proceedings of the IEEE 7th International Software Metrics Symposium* (pp. 349-358). IEEE.

Shepperd, M. J., Schofield, C., & Kitchenham, B. (1996). Effort estimation using analogy. *Proceedings of, ICSE-18*, 170–178.

Syed, M. S., & Abdul, W. (2017). Web Effort Estimation Using FP and WO: A Critical Study. *Proceedings of the 2nd International Conference on Computing Methodologies and Communication (ICCMC 2018)*.

Syed, M. S., & Abdul, W. (2017a). Web Complexity Factors: A Novel Approach for Predicting Size Measures for Web Application Development. *Proceedings of the International Conference on Inventive Computing and Informatics(ICICI 2017)*.

Syed, M. S., & Abdul, W. (2017b). Effort Estimation Techniques for Web Application Development: A Review. *International Journal of Advanced Research in Computer Science, 8*(9), 125-131.

Tailor, O., Saini, J., & Rijwani, P. (2014). Comparative Analysis of Software Cost and Effort Estimation Methods: A Review. *International Journal of Computer Science and Mobile Computing, 3*(4), 1364-1374.

Trendowiz, A., & Joffery, R. (2014). Case Based Reasoning. In *Software Project Effort Estimation*. Springer International Publishing.

Walkerden, F., & Jeffery, R. (1999). An empirical study of analogy-based software effort Estimation. *Empirical Software Engineering, 4*(2), 135-158.

KEY TERMS AND DEFINITIONS

Actual Effort: The actual extent of resources that are utilized to perform successful software development.

Effort Estimation: Process of calculating the budget required to develop a software application.

Effort Estimation Models: Different models that practitioners use to perform effort estimation for different software developments.

Estimated Effort: The approximate prediction of efforts projected by estimator to perform application development on time and within the budget.

Mobile Application: Similar to that of web application in certain parameters developed to run on handheld devices with understandable interface.

Software Application: Conventional or traditional software application developed to deliver a specific kind of functionality meant to be used within the boundary of a particular organization.

Software Development: Systematic approach followed in development industry to develop software products

Web Application: Type of software application developed to be accessed via web browser and meant to address the requirements or diverse people with non-geographical access restriction.

This research was previously published in Tools and Techniques for Software Development in Large Organizations; pages 45-97, copyright year 2020 by Engineering Science Reference (an imprint of IGI Global).

Chapter 9
Analysis and Comparison of Neural Network Models for Software Development Effort Estimation

Kamlesh Dutta

Department of CSE, National Institute of Technology, Hamirpur, India

Varun Gupta

Amity School of Engineering and Technology, Amity University, Noida, India

Vachik S. Dave

Department of CSE, National Institute of Technology, Hamirpur, India

ABSTRACT

Prediction of software development is the key task for the effective management of any software industry. The accuracy and reliability of the prediction mechanisms used for the estimation of software development effort is also important. A series of experiments are conducted to gradually progress towards the improved accurate estimation of the software development effort. However, while conducting these experiments, it was found that the size of the training set was not sufficient to train a large and complex artificial neural network (ANN). To overcome the problem of the size of the available training data set, a novel multilayered architecture based on a neural network model is proposed. The accuracy of the proposed multi-layered model is assessed using different criteria, which proves the pre-eminence of the proposed model.

DOI: 10.4018/978-1-6684-3702-5.ch009

1. INTRODUCTION

An accurate estimation is the key objective of any prediction model. Software development effort estimation is one of the important research domains for software organizations. However, there are several problems associated with making an accurate estimation. Stutzke (1996) a) attributed ambiguity about the meaning of estimation; b) Confliction of project goal; c) Lack of requirement information; d) Inclusion of Reusable code; e) New development procedures and tools; and f) Relation of inputs to output. Software development effort prediction depends on several factors such as software size, people involved in software development, use of technology, software complexity, and many more. Further, these factors are correlated to each other and influence the software development process directly or indirectly. The effort estimate can be derived from the size of software products, if it is estimated reliably. Defining software development lifecycle and development process that is followed to specify, design, develop, and test the software is necessary for the estimation of the software development effort from software size. Developing new software is not just a task of coding the software functionalities. Rather, coding the software is just a single part of the whole software development process and its effort. Designing the software or deliverables, implementation of the prototypes, writing & reviewing documentation, and reviewing & testing the code take up the larger portion of overall project effort. The project effort estimate requires identifying and estimate, and then sum up all the activities, one must perform to build a product of the estimated size.

The main objective of this paper is to develop neural network based software effort estimation model. A series of experiments are conducted to explore the suitable model and reported in the subsequent sections. The paper is organized as follows. In Section 2 we have enlighten the portion related to the neural networks based estimations of software development effort as reported in the literature. Section 3 gives an overview of various criteria's used for assessing the suitable prediction model for software development estimation. Section 4 presents a series of experiments conducted to analyze the performance of various models. Most of the researchers emphasized the benefit or dominance of the ANN model over other traditional models. Here, the experimental studies are conducted to find out the best suitable ANN model for software effort estimation. Based on the analysis, a multilayered ANN model for the software effort estimation task is proposed in section 5. The model makes use of three categories for input parameters. The categories are based on the impact factor of the inputs. The suitability of the proposed model is further tested and verified through a series of simulation. Section 6 summarizes the results and concludes with the future scope of work in improving the accuracy of software development effort estimation.

2. RELATED WORK

Various approaches have been adopted in literature to make an accurate estimation of software effort. In recent years, application of machine learning approaches has been attempted. This has been possible due to the availability of data sets of a large number of completed projects. Among various machine learning techniques, neural networks based models are newly emerging models. Though several researchers (Venkatachalam, 1993; Finnie et al., 1997; Samson et al, 1997; Lee et al.,1998; Heiat, 2002; Ideri et al, 2002; Idri et al, 2004; Tadayon, 2005; Idri et al, 2006; Kanmani et al, 2007; Tronto et al., 2007; Park and Beak, 2008; Tronto et al, 2008; Iwata et al, 2009; Reddy and Raju, 2009; Ajitha et. al, 2010; Kaur et al,

2010; Bhatnagar et al, 2010; Balich and Martin, 2010; Reddy et al, 2010; Pendharkar, 2010; Attarzadeh and Ow, 2010; Dave and Dutta, 2011a, 2011b, 2011c; Shepperd and MacDonell, 2012; López-Martín, 2014) have worked on Neural Networks based models. However, there is still a need for more research work and attempts to find out the most suitable model for software effort prediction in term of accuracy, configurability and reasoning associated with the suitability of model. The detailed review of 21 articles related to the effort/cost estimation of software using neural networks is presented in Dave and Dutta (2014). The paper also suggests to research on neural networks based models for more accuracy.

Malhotra et. al. (2011) have used dataset of 499 projects for comparing the regression model with Machine learning methods and concluded that machine learning methods are giving satisfactory results. Mahajan et. al. (2011) have derived a model from neural networks and shown its dominance over CO-COMO II model. Kaur et al. (2010) have shown that a neural network is better than Halstead model, Walston-Felix model, Bailey-Basili model and Doty model, same as Vahib Khatibi et al. (2011) have investigated 15 research articles and compared it with neural networks and concluded that neural networks outperforms most algorithmic methods.

Bhatnagar et al. (2010), and Barcelos Tronto et al. (2008) have also proved that neural network models are better than Regression analysis model. Kaur et. al.(2012) conducted a study for the comparison of neural network with other traditional methods and concluded the same that neuron based model is better than other methods.

3. EVALUATION CRITERIA FOR ACCURACY ANALYSIS

As a software development effort estimation is an important task in the software development project, the accurate effort estimation is still a great challenge for the software management team as well as customer. Various techniques and models are applied for software development effort estimation, but accuracy of the software effort prediction is inadequate for all the traditional methods. The main challenge of the software effort estimation can be explained by the cone of uncertainty (Boehm, 1981).

3.1. Cone of Uncertainty

In the early stages of a software project, precise details of the software functional requirement, specification about the nature of the software product to be built, details of the functional solution, software project plan, project staff, and other project variables are blurred and undecided. The uncertainties in these effecting factors add inconsistency in software project effort estimates. Since the inaccurate estimation is attributed to the inconsistent and imprecise phenomenon, the inherent variable behavior of this phenomenon should be taken into consideration while making estimations. If we are able to understand and quantify this variability, the variability on the project can also be quantified and actual nature of the project can be understood. This phenomenon is known as the "Cone of Uncertainty".

Cone of uncertainty describes the preciseness of the effort estimation that can be achieved in different stages and it shows that there is a decrease in the error rate as we progress from one stage to another and eventually, only at the final stage we are able to uncover the exact effort value. The goal of the paper is to find out a suitable software effort estimation technique, which would improve this accuracy at the early stages. Which is the best or most suitable model for the software development effort estimation?

To answer this question each model should be evaluated using certain evaluation criteria. Performance of competitive models is evaluated using MMRE, SD, RSD and Pred(25).

3.2. Mean Magnitude Relative Error (MMRE)

For assessing the performance of a prediction model the most widely used criterion is a Mean Magnitude Relative Error (MMRE). The fundamental metric of the MMRE criterion is Magnitude Relative Error (MRE) (Foss, et. al, 2002), which is a relative residual error. The MRE can be calculated using equation (1):

$$MRE = \frac{\left| Y - \widehat{Y} \right|}{Y}$$

(1)

where:

Y = Actual Value

$\hat{Y}$ = Predicted Value

The formula used to compute MRE contains the absolute difference between estimation and actual values (absolute error) in the numerator and as the denominator the actual value is used without changes in it. This means, for the same error, the MRE value can fluctuate as per the actual value. This signifies that MRE is not independent of the estimated parameter value. The detailed study about this type relation is carried out by Stensrud et al.(2003). Equation (2) is used to find out MMRE:

$$MMRE = \frac{1}{n} \sum_{i-1}^{n} MRE_i$$

(2)

Though, widely used for the assessment of the prediction model, MMRE is not actually an accuracy measure of a prediction model and is normally used for comparing two prediction models only as shown by various researchers (Port and Korte, 2008; Dave and Dutta 2011b). MMRE provides a measure of spread (i.e. Standard deviation) (Kitchenham et. al, 2001) only. Foss et al. (2003) also showed that MMRE is not a reliable comparison criterion for preferring selection between prediction models. They suggested the use of Standard Deviation (SD) and Relative Standard Deviation (RSD).

3.3. Standard Deviation (SD)

Standard deviation (SD) is the measure of the divergence between original (actual) value and estimated or calculated value. This is a regular measure used for finding the prediction model accuracy, which shows the difference of the estimated value from its actual value. The formula to calculate SD is shown in equation (3):

$$SD = \sqrt{\frac{\sum\left(Y - \widehat{Y}\right)^2}{n-1}}$$ (3)

where:

    Y = Actual Value

    $\hat{Y}$ = Predicted Value

    n = the number of test cases

3.4. Relative Standard Deviation (RSD)

RSD is the absolute value of the coefficient of variation, which is a normalized measure of dispersion of a probability distribution. Equation (4) is used to compute the RSD value:

$$SD = \sqrt{\frac{\sum\left(\frac{Y - \widehat{Y}}{X}\right)^2}{n-1}}$$ (4)

where:

    Y = Actual Value

    $\hat{Y}$ = Predicted Value

    X = Input Value

    n = the number of test cases

3.5. Pred (N)

Pred(N) specifies the consistency in accuracy of the prediction model. This criterion indicates that, how much percentage of estimation results are within N% of the actual values. To find out the Pred(N), the pseudo code is described here:

```
Count =0 ;
for(i=1;i<=T;i++)
{
        If(MRE_i  =<  (N/100))
{       Count++;}
}
Pred(N) = Count *100 / T.
```

4. SOFTWARE EFFORT ESTIMATION MODELS

Different estimation models are used for software development effort estimation task (Jorgensen and Shepperd, 2007). Regression model is the most frequently used models. Few other models based on this method such as COCOMO (Boehm, 1981; Boehm et. al., 2000), Halstead model (Halstead, 1977), Doty model (Herd et. al., 1977), Bailey-Basili model (Bailey and Basili, 1983), Walston and Felix (1977) etc. are popularly used for the purpose of software effort estimation. All these models are based on some fixed mathematical formula with input variables to predict the software development effort. The reason, these models are not adequate, is all the models are derived from limited size of the database. There are several independent parameters involved in estimating effort which these models cannot accommodate, resulting in an inaccurate estimation model. To handle all possible influencing factors, models are required to adopt the changes occurring in environment as independent variables. The Neural Network model is preferred over other models because of the following reasons:

- Non-linearity:
  - Interconnection of linear and/or non linear neuron;
  - Very important for real world problems;
- Learning Ability:
  - Learning with teacher (supervised learning);
  - Learning without teacher (unsupervised learning);
- Adaptivity:
  - Adapting the environmental changes via free parameters (synapses);
- Evidential Response:
  - Efficient for pattern matching and classification;
- Fault tolerance:
  - Doesn't result in catastrophic failure;
  - Graceful degradation.

A series of experiments are conducted to understand the behavior of various models employed for the purpose of prediction of software effort estimation. The parameters used in the experiments are taken from the COCOMO model.

The superiority of Neural Network over regression analysis is shown by many other authors in their research paper (Heiat, 2002; Tronto et. al, 2007; Bhatnagar, et .al. 2010). Dave and Dutta (2011) have also shown the promising results shown by Neural Network models. In order to understand, what really makes neural network models a better choice over other models such as regression model, a series of experiments are conducted as follows:

Experiment 1: Regression versus Neural Network based technique.
Experiment 2: Comparison of Feed-forward Neural Network (FFNN) and Radial Basis Neural Network (RBNN) based models:
    a.   Source Line Of Code (SLOC):
        i.   (Parameters of experiment a i.e. SLOC), Complexity of the software (CPLX), Analyst Capabilities (ACAP), Programmer Capabilities (PCAP);

ii. (Parameters of experiment b), Experience in similar application (AEXP), Software tool (TOOL), Software reliability requirement (RELY), Virtual machine volatility (VIRT);

b. Source Line Of Code (SLOC) is used as an input with all 15 effort multipliers of the COCOMO'81 model().

4.1. Experiment 1

Experiment 1 is conducted to compare neural network models with the regression model. The study is conducted to verify previous work carried out by various researchers (Heiat, 2002; Tronto et. al, 2007; Bhatnagar, et .al. 2010). For this experiment, database available in article (Kaur et. al. 2010) is used.

Regression model can be trained from historical data and able to adopt the changes in environment as per different organizations. Regression analysis is used as a prediction mode in almost every field. Logically, it finds best fit real value of a dependent variable from given one or more independent variable(s). This method basically helps to understand how the value of dependent variable changes as values of independent variables is changed. The basic equation for regression is shown in equation (5):

$$Y_{est} = f(x) \tag{5}$$

The simplest form of regression is a linear regression model. The formula is shown in equation (6):

$$Y_{Est} = \beta_0 + \beta_1 X_1 + \beta_2 X_2 + \ldots \ldots \beta_n X_n \tag{6}$$

The function f in $f(x)$, shown in equation (5), can be any function such as linear function, exponential function, logarithmic function, etc. For software development effort estimation, the relation between input (independent variables) and output (effort value) is neither linear nor exponential. Most suitable functions for software effort estimation is logarithmic function, which can be calculated using equation (7):

$$Y_{Est} = \beta_0 + \beta_1 x \ln\left(X_1\right) + \beta_2 x \ln\left(X_2\right) + \ldots \ldots \beta_n x \ln\left(X_n\right) \tag{7}$$

For our experiment, linear as well as logarithmic equation based regression models are used.

For the training of Feed Forward Neural Network (FFNN) prediction model, first 13 data projects of the Dataset are used. Remaining data of 5 projects are used for testing the model. The FFNN model is trained using standard back-propagation training algorithm. Since the amount of data available for learning is very small, high learning rate of 0.85 with 1500 learning iteration is chosen for the experiment. Using this model, estimation effort value for test data set is calculated. Coefficients for linear and Logarithmic regression equations are also calculated using a same training dataset. Using these equations, effort value for testing dataset is calculated.

The result of estimated values for the test dataset for all three models is shown in Table 1. Table 1 demonstrates that, for linear regression, estimated values are always higher than the original, for example, test case with 5 person months is estimated as 6.33 person months, and for the test case with 98.7 person months, the value obtained is 111.13 person months., In the case of logarithmic regression, the estimated values are fluctuating for example test case with 98.7 person months estimation goes up as 107.86 person months and for 23.9 person months the estimation is 20.01 person months. FFNN estimated values are also fluctuating near original values, but with less displacement, such as, for test case with 5 person months the estimation is 5.02 person months and for 98.7 person months the estimated value is 99.97.

Table 1. Results of Experiment1

Test Cases (in Person Month)	Estimated Effort (in Person Month)		
	Linear Regression	Logarithmic Regression	Feed-Forward NN
5	6.327	3.906772	5.023160037
8.4	10.3	8.64812	8.344414857
98.7	111.132	107.8629	99.97681567
15.6	16.739	15.86895	14.35436601
23.9	20.575	20.01865	17.75815711

The experiment is evaluated using four different criteria, MMRE, RSD, SD and Pred(10), mentioned in section 3. The evaluation results are shown in Table 2. The obtained values show that the lowest value of MMRE is 7.22 and it is obtained for the FFNN model. The highest value of 16.59 is obtained for linear regression model. In Table 2 for RSD and SD, FFNN gives lower value of 0.25 and 3.197 respectively, while for linear regression, RSD is 0.4 and SD value is 6.56.

Table 2. Evaluation of Experiment1

Evaluation Criteria	Linear Regression	Logarithmic Regression	Feed-Forward NN
MMRE (%)	16.59	10.41	7.22
RSD	0.41	0.31	0.25
SD	6.56	5.01	3.20
Pred (10)	0.2	0.6	0.8

4.2. Experiment 2.a

The experiment demonstrated the suitability of using neural network models for software effort estimation. Hence, for further research, we compare the subsequent most commonly used neural network models: Feed-forward Neural Network (FFNN) and Radial Basis Neural Network (RBNN) based models.

In order to compare the performance of these models, the experiment is conducted on cocomonasa_v1 dataset containing 60 projects. In this dataset, 60 NASA projects were collected from the different NASA centers. These projects were developed during 1980's and 1990's. This database contains the size in term of source lines of code (SLOC). The database contains KSLOC value, which means thousand SLOC. It also contains effort in person months and 15 other effort multipliers as described in COCOMO model.

In this experiment, only the size of the software in terms of KSLOC as an input parameter to the software effort prediction model is used. Experiment 2a is conducted to compare regression model (using logarithmic regression) and Neural Network models (Feed-Forward Neural Network -FFNN and Radial Basis Neural Network- RBNN).

In the experiment, for training and testing of prediction models, dataset is divided into two parts. Training set contains 53 projects of the dataset. Remaining 7 projects are used for testing the models. Coefficient of regression equation using training data is calculated to find out effort estimation for test data. FFNN is trained using standard back propagation learning algorithm with the learning rate 0.9 with 1500 training iteration. Using this training configuration FFNN is trained estimated values for the test dataset using the trained network is calculated. RBNN is trained using a Resilient Propagation algorithm with 1000 training iterations. Using this configuration RBNN is trained and effort values for test dataset are calculated.

For neural network based models five readings (results) are taken. The results are shown in Table 3, 4 and 5. In Table 3, the FFNN estimated values show high deviation up to 900 person months, more than the original, for test case with 973 person months and test cases with values 1368 and 571.4 in person months, resulting in higher displacement. Though, in the case of RBNN, the results in Table 4 show slightly better accuracy, as compared to FFNN, the test case with 973 person months values estimated are falling between 1596.6 and 1901.33 person months.

Table 3. Results of FFNN (Experiment 2a)

Test Cases (in Person Month)	Estimated Effort Using FFNN (in Person Month)				
	Reading 1	Reading 2	Reading 3	Reading 4	Reading 5
2300	2593.39	2510.78	2528.47	2526.76	2521.67
400	313.73	253.16	278.24	272.51	273.87
973	1961.3	1834.98	1924.74	1849.04	1908.68
1368	1941.51	1814.32	1904.46	1828.50	1888.20
571.4	309.68	250.14	274.94	269.26	270.61
98.8	134.26	122.58	133.86	129.70	131.52
155	147.32	132.03	144.43	140.17	141.98

Table 4. Results of RBNN (Experiment 2a)

Test Cases (in Person Month)	Estimated Effort Using RBNN (in Person Month)				
	Reading 1	Reading 2	Reading 3	Reading 4	Reading 5
2300	3242	1307.59	2331.51	2387.00	2365.66
400	405.71	450.54	224.33	361.58	272.745
973	1596.60	1666.74	1794.66	1901.34	1813.09
1368	1552.52	1614.25	1785.90	1871.53	1797.90
571.4	401.76	443.99	219.65	357.36	267.81
98.8	37.942	62.07	108.96	60.48	106.51
155	94.74	100.66	103.47	97.20	108.07

As depicted in Table 5, for regression analysis, almost every result shows higher error value, compare to FFNN and RBNN. For example, for the test case with 2300 person months, the average displacement of estimated values for FFNN is 235 person months, and for RBNN, the average displacement is 425 person months approximately, while regression model shows displacement more than 1000 person months.

Table 5. Result of regression analysis (Experiment 2a)

Test Cases (in Person Month)	Estimated Effort (in Person Month)
2300	1289.36
400	690.71
973	1148.096
1368	1144.82
571.4	686.16
98.8	0.04
155	187.88

The experimental results are evaluated using four criteria: MMRE, RSD, SD, Pred(25). The evaluated results are shown in the Table 6 for FFNN and RBNN and in Table 7 for regression analysis. The evaluation in Table 6 shows that, the RSD values for FFNN are continuously nearer to 2.55, while this fluctuation is high in the case of RBNN. In Table 6, value for Pred(25) is 28.57 for almost both models. The MMRE values for RBNN vary between 34.23 and 37.91, while for FFNN this variation is very low. The lowest SD value for FFNN is 430.6, while in the case of RBNN it's providing value 409.37. For regression analysis, SD is 449.14 as shown in Table 7.

Table 6. Evaluation of FFNN and RBNN (Experiment 2a)

Reading No.	MMRE(%)		RSD		SD		Pred(25)	
	FFNN	RBNN	FFNN	RBNN	FFNN	RBNN	FFNN	RBNN
1	37.78	35.73	2.55	2.977	494.82	508.24	42.86	28.57
2	37.46	34.23	2.52	2.37	474.32	473.72	42.86	42.86
3	38.80	37.91	2.64	2.70	465.99	442.53	28.57	28.57
4	37.02	37.02	2.52	2.64	435.82	409.90	28.57	28.57
5	38.50	34.81	2.60	2.42	430.60	409.37	28.57	28.57

Table 7. Evaluation of regression analysis (Experiment 2a)

MMRE (%)	41.74
RSD	4.09
SD	449.14
Pred(25)	57.143

For the purpose of comparison with regression analysis model, the poor results of the neural network based models are taken. The values of MMRE and RSD confirm that ANN models are more accurate. The SD values are not in agreement with that for particular poor case, but 60% of SD values from RBNN and FFNN are better than regression model. The Pred(25) by regression analysis is high, which shows that MRE is lower in several test cases. The MMRE value of regression analysis is also very high, which proves that regression is extremely disappointing for other results.

The comparison of two neural network models is also conducted in the experiment. The evaluation of the experimental using MMRE and SD show that RBNN is more accurate and suitable prediction model for software effort prediction, while RSD gives very fluctuating values and contradictory results. The Pred(25) comparison of RBNN and FFNN proves that FFNN gives inconsistent result and hence is not a very reliable model.

4.3. Experiment 2b

Experiment 2b is conducted to assess the impact of various factors in the software effort estimation. In this experiment same cocomonasa_v1 dataset containing 60 projects is used. For the experiment, three effort effecting input parameters of COCOMO with the size of the software in terms of KSLOC are chosen. The chosen parameters are:

- Complexity of the software;
- Analyst capability;
- Programmer capability as input parameter with KSLOC, which are CPLX, ACAP and PCAP effort multipliers in our database (COCOMO model).

In this experiment only neural network based models are compared:

- Feed-Forward Neural Network (FFNN)
- Radial Basis Neural Network (RBNN)

For this experiment, again the same training set of 53 and testing datasets of 7, as described in section 4.2 is used. FFNN is trained using standard back propagation learning algorithm. In this algorithm, learning rate of 0.9 is assumed. The training iterations used is 2000. Using this training configuration, FFNN is trained and estimated values for the test dataset using the trained network are calculated.

RBNN is trained using a Resilient Propagation algorithm. In this training, 1500 training iterations are used. Using this configuration RBNN is trained and the effort values for test dataset are calculated.

For this experiment, five readings are taken. The results for FFNN are shown in Table 8. The results for FFNN estimation proves higher displacement for large scale projects with 600 or more person months, such as test case with 973 person months is estimated very high values around 1750 person months. Test cases with 1368 and 571.4 person months, the displacement is approximately 300 person months.

In Table 9, the results from RBNN are shown, which is varying close to original effort. The results of RBNN show that for large scale project with very high effort value cannot be estimated accurately, such as, for a test case with 2300 person months the only first reading is adequate. Other readings show very high displacement. The RBNN shows very good accuracy for reading 3 with a very small displacement with almost every test case except test case with large effort of 2300 person months.

Table 8. Results of FFNN (Experiment 2b)

Test Cases (in Person Month)	Estimated Effort Using FFNN (in Person Month)				
	Reading 1	Reading 2	Reading 3	Reading 4	Reading 5
2300	2797.55	2788.58	2830.54	2818.39	2773.06
400	364.19	347.84	389.32	384.68	363.97
973	1701.80	1724.99	1781.90	1742.67	1774.21
1368	1682.57	1706.77	1760.72	1723.22	1755.21
571.4	357.18	357.18	382.07	377.30	357.57
98.8	121.67	115.07	121.18	103.05	107.79
155	133.76	126.63	135.75	117.84	123.35

Table 9. Results of RBNN (Experiment 2b)

Test Cases (in Person Month)	Estimated Effort Using RBNN (in Person Month)				
	Reading 1	Reading 2	Reading 3	Reading 4	Reading 5
2300	2286.60	1530.64	1103.78	1564.19	1421.71
400	473.76	299.88	578.54	497.33	372.73
973	892.94	1451.19	987.82	1166.69	1204.71
1368	891.33	1444.86	1029.74	1158.23	1196.99
571.4	467.31	296.01	571.16	485.65	362.56
98.8	35.14	148.11	156.21	52.88	175.17
155	76.09	156.19	193.61	69.32	159.13

The experimental results are evaluated using the four criteria mention in section 3. The evaluation values are shown in Table 10. For MMRE criterion the values are varying approximately from 27 to 30 for both models. If we consider RSD, FFNN is always provides 1.9 with small displacement, while for RBNN smallest value is 2.55. The highest value of SD for RBNN is 513.52 and smallest is 208.3, while for FFNN this value is approximately 400 for each result.

Table 10. Evaluation of FFNN and RBNN (Experiment 2b)

Reading No.	MMRE(%)		RSD		SD		Pred(25)	
	FFNN	RBNN	FFNN	RBNN	FFNN	RBNN	FFNN	RBNN
1	28.97	27.95	1.92	2.99	392.81	208.31	71.43	57.14
2	29.80	30.30	1.91	2.55	401.80	390.47	71.43	28.57
3	29.40	29.42	1.93	2.71	433.37	513.53	57.14	57.14
4	27.67	29.76	1.85	2.67	413.64	328.94	57.14	57.14
5	29.60	28.26	1.92	3.10	421.06	388.27	57.14	57.14

This experiment is conducted to find out, whether the increase in the input by additional effort effecting parameters impact on the effort estimation accuracy? The answer, we can easily conclude from MMRE, SD and Pred(25) values of this and previous experiment is yes, it does impact considerably on effort estimation.

The other thing that comes out of the experiment is comparison between FFNN and RBNN. The values of RSD and Pred(25) criteria, shows that FFNN is more accurate in software effort estimation.

4.4. Experiment 2c

For this experiment, again cocomonasa_v1 dataset containing 60 projects as experiment 2 and 3 is used. In the previous experiment (section 4.3), it is concluded that with the increase in the number of effort effecting parameters, the effort accuracy improves for both the neural network based models. Hence, in this experiment we have used 7 effort effecting parameters from our database with the size of the software (KSLOC). Here, three input parameters are same as previous experiment (CPLX, ACAP, PCAP). The other included parameters are: experience in similar applications, the impact of software tool, virtual machine volatility and software reliability required by customer. The added parameters are available in the database as effort multiplier. This experiment continues testing on FFNN and RBNN models.

For this experiment, again we have used the same training set of 53 and testing datasets of 7, as described in section 4.2. The training configuration is the same as previous experiment for FFNN. The training iterations used for RBNN is increased to 2000 for this experiment, whereas other configurations remains same as previous experiment, described in section 3.2. The five results taken for FFNN and RBNN, are depicted in Table 11 and 12. In the Table 11, for test case with 973 person months, the estimated effort value is 1645 person months or above. In Table 11, for test cases with 1368 and 571.4 person months are presenting approximate displacement of 200 person months compare to the actual effort value.

Table 11. Results of FFNN (Experiment 2c)

Test Cases (in Person Month)	Estimated Effort Using FFNN (in Person Month)				
	Reading 1	Reading 2	Reading 3	Reading 4	Reading 5
2300	2429.40	2297.53	2334.80	2197.23	2333.41
400	377.06	379.45	411.65	327.72	402.84
973	1645.08	1656.90	1664.27	1565.74	1694.69
1368	1629.66	1647.20	1651.33	1553.67	1682.42
571.4	371.97	373.32	405.87	322.61	397.06
98.8	133.41	119.62	130.39	103.27	134.72
155	151.64	136.27	151.48	118.30	154.07

As shown in Table 12, the estimated value for RBNN is highly displaced from the original value for almost every test case. Only for the test cases with 2300 and 98.8 person months, the approximate displacement is varying from 50 to 150 person months, compared to its original effort respectively.

Table 12. Results of RBNN (Experiment 2c)

Test Cases (in Person Month)	Estimated Effort Using RBNN (in Person Month)				
	Reading 1	Reading 2	Reading 3	Reading 4	Reading 5
2300	2398.07	1550.72	2336.76	2191.76	2586.73
400	184.92	312.04	235.88	229.85	346.67
973	461.23	567.27	376.23	394.24	243.57
1368	454.00	557.68	349.69	383.79	216.06
571.4	182.24	307.32	231.99	226.85	345.56
98.8	78.41	61.80	85.47	112.41	116.60
155	83.37	76.10	110.55	116.24	122.02

In this experiment the evaluation is carried out using the MMRE, RSD, SD, Pred(25) criteria explained in section 3. The calculated evaluation values are shown in Table 13. The minimum value of MMRE is 37.68 for RBNN, while for FFNN MMRE values are lying between 22 and 25 approximated. In Table 13, maximum RSD for FFNN is 1.9 and lowest RSD for RBNN is 2.5. The SD for FFNN is almost 200 units, down compared to RBNN.

Table 13. Evaluation of FFNN and RBNN (Experiment 2c)

Reading No.	MMRE(%)		RSD		SD		Pred(25)	
	FFNN	RBNN	FFNN	RBNN	FFNN	RBNN	FFNN	RBNN
1	24.52	44.62	1.93	3.24	310.49	467.29	57.14	28.57
2	23.40	41.44	1.71	2.98	312.55	494.59	71.43	14.29
3	22.77	39.99	1.79	2.81	313.02	506.41	57.14	28.57
4	24.11	39.68	1.81	2.77	278.35	494.08	71.43	28.57
5	23.83	37.68	1.94	2.51	329.78	576.85	57.14	57.14

From this experiment more accurate results with very less value of error were expected. But the results are contradictory with the RBNN case, while for FFNN, the results are supportive to some extent.

From this experiment, it is concluded that, with the increase in the number of effort effecting parameter as input to neural network model, the accuracy of software effort estimation may not improve. Several experiments were conducted to figure out the reason for this unexpected behavior of RBNN. The answer lies in the basic architecture of the RBNN and Cover's theorem (1965). The statement of the theorem is:

A complex pattern-classification problem, cast in a high-dimensional space nonlinearly, is more likely to be linearly separable than in a low-dimensional space, provided that the space is not densely populated. (Cover, 1965)

The theorem suggests that, as the number of input increases, neuron present in radial basis layer also required to increase. During RBNN training, changes are done for radial basis function centers and free parameter of the neural network i.e. synaptic weights. To train high dimensional radial basis layer, a large training set is required. Here, we have used the same training set as previous experiments containing 53 project values, which leads to degradation of the RBNN results.

4.5. Experiment 2d

This experimentation is motivated by the results of the previous experiment, which concluded that, every time increase in the effort effecting parameters as input doesn't increase the prediction accuracy for RBNN. Here for this experiment, every effort multipliers of the COCOMO II model is used as an input from the cocomonasa_v1 dataset with the KSLOC value.

In this experiment, results from FFNN are obtained and compared with the previous experimental results of FFNN to verify, whether FFNN faces the same problem as RBNN with high number of inputs. 15 effort multipliers (COCOMO) with KSLOC are used for experiment. The training and testing sets remain same as section 4.2 for this experiment also. The training algorithm is same back-propagation used with 2500 and 3000 number of training iterations and 0.9 learning rate. For this experiment also, five results are taken for FFNN, which are shown in Table 14. Table 14 shows that, for almost every test case, estimated results have small displacement from original effort value. For the test case with 973 person months effort, every result is estimated 100 to 150 person months more than the original, while for the test case with 571.4 person months the estimated values are 150 to 200 person months lesser always. For other test cases, the displacement is fluctuating more and less, as compared to the actual effort value of respective test cases.

The evaluation results (Table 17) of the experiment shows, MMRE value fluctuates between 22.17 and 24.88, while for RSD minimum value achieved is 2.1 units. For SD, rise and fall of values are high ranging from 143.3 to 208.67. For almost every test case, the value obtained for Pred(25) is 71.43.

This experiment is performed to validate that, the problem of a limited size of training dataset is also affecting the FFNN when we use a large number of inputs. The results and evaluation of the experiment are shown in Table 14 and 15. The values of MMRE and Pred(25) criteria concludes that, both results are competitive. The values of RSD and SD criteria results in contradictory conclusion about the experiment. The SD criterion proves that, the increase in the inputs makes the estimation more accurate for FFNN and RSD shows that, the increase in the inputs significantly decreases the accuracy in the case of FFNN also.

Table 14. Results of FFNN (Experiment 2d)

Test Cases (in Person Month)	Estimated Effort Using FFNN (in Person Month)				
	Reading 1	**Reading 2**	**Reading 3**	**Reading 4**	**Reading 5**
2300	2129.96	2328.51	2387.81	2242.34	2298.79
400	233.16	357.44	262.62	356.88	297.25
973	1104.61	1222.31	1330.05	1174.82	1202.33
1368	1086.80	1206.00	1307.88	1160.01	1186.48
571.4	244.24	394.65	249.11	400.10	330.33
98.8	113.26	158.34	119.74	160.56	144.37
155	125.38	181.63	131.52	184.69	161.73

Table 15. Evaluation of FFNN and RBNN (Experiment 2d)

Reading No.	MMRE(%)	RSD	SD	Pred(25)
1	24.88	2.14	208.67	71.43
2	22.53	2.44	145.21	57.14
3	24.57	2.11	209.18	57.14
4	22.98	2.51	143.30	71.43
5	22.18	2.18	161.42	57.14

5. PROPOSED NEURAL NETWORK MODEL ARCHITECTURE

The proposed Neural Network architecture is primarily an outcome of the search for the best neural network model for software effort estimation. The number of parameters influencing the software development effort is really high. In the section 4, the conducted experiments show that, neural network faces a particular problem in getting trained for such a high number of input parameters with comparatively very small database.

The fundamental problem with software development effort estimation is that for any software organization, the historical projects are not enough to develop large database or training set. The particular case of prediction of software effort estimation, the main challenge is to handle too many independent variables for a single prediction. The general neural network architecture needs to be modified, as the independent variables increases, the number of hidden layers and hidden neurons need to be increased. The increase in hidden layers and hidden neurons exponentially (not strict exponential), increases the number of connections (synapses), which are free parameter in the neural network architecture. The neural network model adapts to the environmental changes through these free parameters. The training of the neural network is carried out by adjusting these synaptic weights. During the training session, the free parameters are adjusted and adopt the environmental situations. For the training of neural network, the historical data of the particular association or organization is used.

Now, the problem is clear that, as a number of independent variable increases, the neural network model needs more historical data to train a large number of synaptic weights. For the software development effort estimation this is the basic problem, that size of historical data is not sufficient to properly train more complex neural network, which accommodates the big number of input parameters also.

There are only two straightforward possible solutions available:

1. Increase the size of the historical database;
2. Decrease the input parameters.

The first solution of the problem is impossible for practical world software organizations. This solution may work like, one can prepare large artificial database using small available genuine database. This task can also be done by ANN or some other techniques.

The second solution is not actually impossible to implement, but decreasing the number of input parameter will actually affect the accuracy of the prediction model. In the section 4, it is clearly shown that the increase in the input parameters actually leads to high accuracy by the prediction models. Hence, decreasing the independent variable is not convenient option to solve this problem.

Hence, as explained above, none of the common solution is practically acceptable to use for solving the problem with software development effort estimation. There should be some different approach applied to solve this problem. Here we have proposed novel multilayered neural network architecture for solving the problem. The block diagram of the proposed architecture is shown in the Figure 1.

Figure 1. Block diagram of the proposed solution

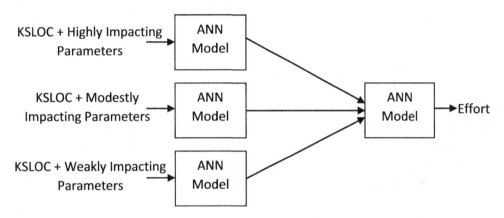

Figure 1 portrays that, there are three different ANN models in layer one and one ANN model in Layer two. The inputs to first layer ANN models are highly impacting parameters, modestly impacting parameters and weakly impacting parameters, all with KSLOC. The grouping of parameters can be implemented through a principle component analysis approach as well. The second layer ANN model gets input from the layer one ANN models and hence second layer ANN model receive three inputs and result in an estimated value of effort. This architecture is more suitable to the software effort estimation problem, because it solves the basic problem explained above that, the single ANN model is unable to handle more input parameters, if the training set is not large enough. Using this architecture, there are five, four and nine inputs to first layer ANN models, which is quite easy to handle and train, using a comparatively small database. The one more advantage of the architecture is that, the second layer ANN model adjusts the weightage of three inputs and results in one more accurate estimated value. This ANN model is basically adjusting the influence factor of all three models, which improves the accuracy of the whole architecture.

5.1. Categorization of Parameters

Different input parameters, 15 in number, from cocomonasa_v1 dataset are used as effort multipliers of the COCOMO model (Boehm, 1981). An insight into the behavior of parameter show that, some parameters are more important than other ones. For proposed model, these parameters are categorized into three types depending on the influence of the parameter on the software development effort value:

- Highly Impacting Parameters;
- Modestly Impacting Parameters;
- Weakly Impacting Parameters.

A series of experiments conducted in section 4, is helpful in categorizing these parameters. The categorization shall be helpful in selecting appropriate models based on input parameters.

5.2. Highly Impacting Parameters

The Highly Impacting Parameters are, in sequence, Complexity of the Software (CPLX in COCOMO), Capabilities of Analysis Team (ACAP in COCOMO), Software Reliability Requirements (RELY in COCOMO) and Experience of the development team in the Software Application domain (AEXP in COCOMO).

5.2.1. Software Product Complexity (CPLX)

This parameter is used to find out the complexity level of the software product. To find out the related rating of the CPLX parameter five different sections need to be considered. These five operational sections are Control Operations, Computational Operations, Device dependent Operations, Data Management Operations, and User-Interface Management Operations. This is one of the important parameters used to predict software development effort. The software product or component is rated between Very Low to Extra High complex depending on the five operational sections.

5.2.2. Analyst Capability (ACAP)

The software development processes during initial stage or basic level contain requirement analysis, and designing of the product from the analysis. This is done by the analyst team assigned for the software project. The considerable features of an analyst team are: The ability of the team for analysis and designing, the diligence and efficiency of the team, and the skill of communication and co-operation. These are a few important characteristics of an analyst team, depending on which the ACAP parameter is rated between a Very Low to Very High. This is one of the significant parameters influencing the software effort value.

5.2.3. Required Software Reliability (RELY)

This parameter specifies that, up to which extent the software continues performing its intended functionality in adverse operating conditions. If the failures of the system or software results in just a little inconvenience then RELY value goes down. On the other hand, if the failure results in a risk of human life or more, than RELY value goes to very high. As the RELY value goes up, the effort require to develop the software also increases, because it needs more time and manpower in the testing phase of the software process. When this parameter contains value very high or very low, its influence to the software development effort is significant.

5.2.4. Application Experience (AEXP)

This parameter describes the level of experience in the similar type or same application by the software development team. The AEXP parameter is rated using the experience of the development team in the same project or equivalent type of software project in terms of time. If the project development team has experience in related type of application is less than 2 months, the AEXP parameter is rated Very Low. If the team is having experience more than 6 years, then this parameter is rated as Very High.

5.3. Modestly Impacting Parameters

Modestly Impacting Parameters are Ability of the Coding team (PCAP in COCOMO), Abilities of software tools (TOOL in COCOMO) and Virtual Machine Volatility (VIRT in COCOMO).

5.3.1. Programmer Capability (PCAP)

After analysis and designing the next step of the software development process is the coding phase. In this phase the software programming is done by the coding team. The considerable features of a coding team are the ability of the team in programming, the diligence and efficiency of the team, and the skill of communication and co-operation. Again in this parameter the characteristics of the team is considered instead of personal attributes. The experience of the team or individual is not considered in this parameter rating.

5.3.2. Use of Software Tool (TOOL)

There are many different tools are available for assisting the software development processes. The capability, maturity and integration of the tool going to be used by the software development team for the software project is discovered by the value of this parameter. If the basic, simple editing, coding or debugging tool is used than the TOOL is rated as Very Low, and if matured and practical lifecycle tool with high integration with functionalities, methods and reusability is used than TOOL is rated as Very High.

5.3.3. Virtual Machine Volatility (VIRT)

The virtual machine consists of the hardware and the software that a given software system uses to perform its functionalities. The VIRT rating depends on the changing frequency of the virtual machine.

5.4. Weakly Impacting Parameters

Weakly Impacting Parameters are Experience in Programming Language and the Virtual Machine (LEXP and VEXP in COCOMO), Testing Database Size (DATA in COCOMO), Execution Time constraint (TIME in COCOMO), Main Memory Constraint (STOR in COCOMO), Computer Turnaround Time (TURN in COCOMO), Modern Programming Practice (MODP in COCOMO) and the changes in the development Schedule (SCED in COCOMO).

5.4.1. Programming Language Experience (LEXP)

This parameter describes the experience level of the software development team in the programming language in which the software product is going to be developed. The LEXP parameter is rated using the experience of the development team in the exact same language or similar type of programming language in terms of time. If the project development team has experience is less than 2 months, the LEXP parameter is rated Very Low. If the team is having experience more than 6 years, then this parameter is rated as Very High.

5.4.2. Database Size (DATA)

This parameter is used to identify the effect of the size of the testing database on project development effort. The measure of this parameter is calculated using the ratio between bytes in testing database and SLOC of the software product. This ratio is called D/P, and depending on D/P value the DATA parameter varying from Low to Very High range. The significance of the parameter is to generate the testing data and test the software using them need some special effort for development or testing team.

5.4.3. Execution Time Constraint (TIME)

This parameter is used to measure constraints on the execution time of the software product. The TIME parameter value is determined by comparing the actual execution time and the available or expected execution time in terms of the percentage. That is, how much percentage of time is used by software product to execute from expected execution time?

5.4.4. Main Storage Constraint (STOR)

This parameter is used to identify the constraint imposed on the software product for usage of main storage. This isn't much important effecting parameter for predicting software development effort.

5.4.5. Computer Turnaround Time (TURN)

This is the machine dependent parameter, it specifies the machine response time. The rating of the TURN is expressed in terms of the level of the computer response time available.

5.4.6. Virtual Machine Experience (VEXP)

The virtual machine consists of the hardware and the software that a given software system uses to perform its functionalities. VEXP is used to indicate the experience with the specific virtual machine in terms of the time period.

5.4.7. Modern Programming Practices (MODP)

This parameter is used to identify the level of the modern programming language and platform used for development.

5.4.8. Required Development Schedule (SCED)

The compression or expansion of the software development schedule is a considerable effort effecting parameter, which is illustrated using the SCED parameter. The value of SCED increases effort value when a project developed on an accelerated schedule compare to a project developed on its optimum schedule. Mostly, when the schedule is expanded the effort value remains constant by an increase in staff of the project.

5.5. Simulation Study

Simulations are carried out to demonstrate that the proposed multilayered architecture described in section 5.2, is better than the single layered or regular ANN models. To verify this, the experiment is conducted to compare the proposed architecture based model containing all FFNN with regular FFNN with all 16 inputs described in section 4.5, which demonstrated better results as compared to all other models tested.

5.5.1. Parameter Normalization

The experiment is conducted using the cocomonasa_v1 dataset, which contains all parameters explained in the section 5.3. The parameters are normally rated in six different levels: Very Low, Low, Nominal, High, Very High, and Extra High. Some parameters are never rated with very low, very high or/and extra high.

To use these parameters with neural network model, parameters need to be converted into a numeric form and also within the range of 0 to 1. All high values are put in the upper range of 0.5, very high being assigned at 0.7 and extra high equals to 0.95. For lower values, the rated value is assigned as 0.099 for low and 0.01 for very low values. For the values having nominal rating, 0.3 is assigned. This normalization process is done for the experiment using fixed value assignment for certain levels of the parameter as shown in Table 16.

Table 16. Assignments for parameter rated level

Ratting Level	Assigned Value
Very Low	0.01
Low	0.10
Nominal	0.3
High	0.5
Very High	0.7
Extra High	0.95

The other main input parameter is, the size of the software, which is measured in term of SLOC. In the database, the size is given as a count in term of KSLOC. The target parameter, which is effort value, is given as a count of person months. These values are also required to be normalized within the range 0 to 1, for which min-max normalization method is used.

5.5.2. Experiment

This experiment is conducted to assess the improvement of the proposed model over regular FFNN. For this experiment, we have used only FFNN as ANN model in the proposed architecture depicted in

Figure 1. The training set includes 53 project data and the testing set contains 7 project data. As in the experiment only FFNN is used, the traditional back-propagation training algorithm is used. The training iterations for every FFNN model 2500 training iterations are used, except for one FFNN, which reflects weakly impacting factor with KSLOC as input parameters. For this FFNN model, 3000 training iterations are used. The learning rate is constant throughout the complete model, which is 0.9. For the comparison with the previous experimental (section 4.5) results, five experiments were conducted to show the variation in the results due to a randomized pattern of training. The actual effort value associated with the test cases under study is shown in column 1 of Table 17 and the result of the experiment is shown in the subsequent column as readings.

Table 17. Results of proposed model

Test Cases (in Person Month)	Estimated Effort (in Person Month)				
	Reading 1	**Reading 2**	**Reading 3**	**Reading 4**	**Reading 5**
2300	2360.14	2330.05	2303.10	2356.27	2291.06
400	394.54	391.97	405.51	387.89	392.92
973	1181.73	1149.83	1191.71	1179.05	1149.94
1368	1156.55	1127.21	1170.32	1154.46	1120.01
571.4	397.48	398.17	413.33	389.93	398.24
98.8	95.03	87.36	94.61	92.22	89.11
155	129.21	118.98	130.12	125.94	119.73

In Table 17, the estimated values of the test case with actual effort of 973 person months and the test case with actual effort of 1368 person months, shows the fluctuation of 100 person months approximately as compared to original effort. For the test case with 571.4 person month, displacement goes up to 150 person months. The evaluation criteria (section 3): MMRE, RSD, SD, Pred(25) for the results (Table 18) obtained from the experiment conducted in section 5.5.2. The evaluation of the proposed Gupta-Dave-Dutta model is shown in Table 18, which gives values of SD around 143 unites. The MMRE values vary from 12.34 to 14.47. The Pred (25) is constant at 85.71.

Table 18. Evaluation of proposed Gupta-Dave-Dutta model

Reading No.	MMRE(%)	RSD	SD	Pred(25)
1	13.11	1.15	143.09	85.71
2	14.89	1.33	142.39	85.71
3	12.343	1.08	136.98	85.71
4	14.20	1.24	144.45	85.71
5	14.48	1.30	143.91	85.71

To demonstrate that, the proposed work is better than any of previous work on neural network models, the best results of the previously conducted experiments as per related criterion are taken for experiment. As explained in the previous section, FFNN of experiment 2d in section 4.5, demonstrates the most accurate result as per MMRE, SD and Pred(25) criteria. Hence, the MMRE, SD and Pred(25) evaluation of current experimental results with evaluation results in section 5.5, which are depicted in Figure 2, 4 and 5. The FFNN from experiment 2c in section 4.4 gives better results as per RSD criterion, so the RSD evaluation of the current experiment is compared to RSD of FFNN in section 5.5 shown in Figure 3.

Figure 2. MMRE comparison for proposed model

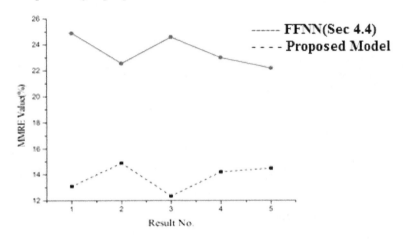

Figure 3. RSD comparison of proposed model

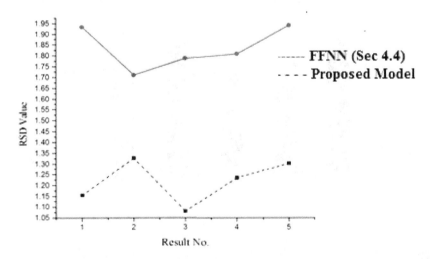

The simulation of the proposed model is conducted and the results are assessed using four different criteria. The evolution of the proposed model positively supports the superiority of the model over all previous experimental work done. The MMRE, RSD and Pred(25) shows improvement in terms of accuracy of the estimation by the proposed model. The Pred(25) also shows the consistency of the estimation accuracy. In the case of SD, two results are competitive, but none of the results are more accurate than the proposed model. All the results of the proposed model show better accuracy in the obtained results from any of the other experimented results.

Figure 4. SD based comparison proposed model

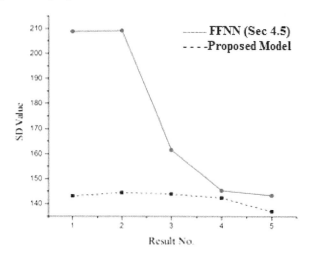

Figure 5. Pred(25) comparison for proposed model

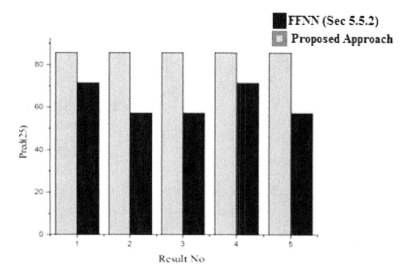

6. CONCLUSION

In the last decade the neural network model is getting more popularity, especially since last 5 to 6 years. The reason for this is attributed to the characteristics of the neural network in solving complex and non-linear relation problems. The neural network model is more suitable for software development effort estimation problem than other traditional linear regression or algorithmic techniques. In this paper, five experiments are conducted to explore the most suitable model for software effort estimation. The first and second experiments were conducted to validate that neural network based models are better than the traditional regression analysis based models. After this, the third experiment (experiment 2b) was performed to verify that if we increase the number of effort effecting parameters as input, the estimation accuracy increases. The results of the third experiments were affirmative.

On account of the positive results of third experiments, experiments were conducted to find out the more suitable and accurate model for software development effort estimation from FFNN and RBNN. But, the results of the fourth experiment (Experiment 2c) were disappointing for RBNN, while FFNN gave expected results. The reason for the inadequate results of RBNN is that, the size of training dataset is not large enough to train such a complex RBNN with high dimensional input layer.

The final experiment (Experiment 2d) was encouraged by the reason of the inaccuracy of RBNN, whether the same problem occurs for FFNN with large number of inputs. The two evaluation criteria showed that, even though input parameters were doubled, no major enhancement in the estimation accuracy took place. The other criterion RSD and SD gave conflicting results. SD is contradicting the assumption that, for FFNN also, high dimension of the input layer estimation accuracy decreases. But the three criteria were notified that, for FFNN also the very high dimensional input layer produces inaccurate estimation results or fluctuation in accuracy of estimation.

With many input parameters and limited historical data, radial basis neural network (RBNN) doesn't provide agreeable results. The other option for software development effort estimation is to use Feed-Forward Neural Network (FFNN). The Majority of researchers have found FFNN to be more suitable model for this task. The accuracy of the effort estimation is the primary objective for every research in recent time (Heiat, 2002; Kaur et. al., 2010; Balich, and Martin, 2010).

The software development effort cannot be predicted up to an adequate level of accuracy, even though the neural network based model is producing more accurate results than other traditional models. Authors observed and realized that further research is needed in the field of neural network itself. There are many different architectures and models available in neural network, but finding the most appropriate model for the software effort estimation problem is still a research issue (Balich, and Martin, 2010). A series of experiments were conducted to gradually progress towards the accurate estimation of the software effort. However, while conducting these experiments it was found that the size of training set was not sufficient to train large and complex neural network. Since, the problem of size could not be solved; the only option was to change the estimation model architecture.

A multilayer architecture containing more than one neural network model is proposed which is more suitable and also solves the problem of training size. In this paper, a novel multilayered architecture based on neural network model is proposed for solving the software development effort estimation problem. For the simulation studies, FFNN as the neural network model is used in the proposed architecture. The simulations conducted, produced the projected results, i.e., it provided the most accurate estimation of software effort value than all other previously experimented models. The accuracy of the proposed model is assessed using different criteria, which proves the pre-eminence of the proposed model.

In the future, the proposed architecture can also be used with other different neural network models. The other more suitable models for some group of parameters can be used as the first layer. The other possible research field is the classification of the input parameters which can be done at the fine grain level and thereby increase the number of neural network models in the first layer itself.

REFERENCES

Ajitha, S., Suresh, T. V., Geetha, D. E., & Rajani, K. (2010). Neural network model for software size estimation using use case point approach. In *5th IEEE International Conference on Industrial and Information Systems* (pp. 372-376). IEEE. 10.1109/ICIINFS.2010.5578675

Attarzadeh, I., & Ow, S. H. (2010). Proposing a New Software Cost Estimation Model Based on Artificial Neural Networks. In *2nd International Conference on Computer Engineering and Technology (ICCET1)* (Vol. 3, pp. 487-491). IEEE.

Bailey, J. W., & Basili, V. R. (1983). A meta-model for software development and resource expenditures. In *Proceedings of the 5th International Conference on Software Engineering*. New York: Institute of Electrical and Electronic Engineers.

Balich, I. K., & Martin, C. L. (2010). Applying a feed-forward neural network for predicting software development effort of short-scale projects. In *Eighth ACIS International Conference on Software Engineering Research, Management and Applications* (pp. 269-275). IEEE Computer Society. 10.1109/SERA.2010.41

Bhatnagar, R., Bhattacharjee, V., & Ghose, M. K. (2010). Software development effort estimation –neural network vs. regression modeling approach. *International Journal of Engineering Science and Technology*, *2*(7), 2950–2956.

Boehm, B. W. (1981). *Software Engineering Economics*. Englewood Cliffs, NJ: Prentice-Hall.

Boehm, B. W., Abts, C., Brown, A. W., Chulani, S., Clark, B. K., Horowitz, E., ... Steece, B. (2000). *Software Cost Estimation with Cocomo II*. Prentice Hall PTR.

Cover, T. M. (1965). Geometrical and statistical properties of systems of linear inequalities with applications in pattern recognition. IEEE Transactions on Electronic Computers, 14(3), 326-334. doi:10.1109/PGEC.1965.264137

Dave, V. S., & Dutta, K. (2011a). Application of Feed-Forward Neural Network in Estimation of Software Effort. In *IJCA Proceedings on International Symposium on Devices MEMS, Intelligent Systems & Communication (ISDMISC)* (pp. 5-9). New York: Foundation of Computer Science.

Dave, V. S., & Dutta, K. (2011b). Neural Network based Software Effort Estimation and Evaluation Criterion MMRE. In *IEEE International Conference on Computer and Communication Technology ICCCT-2011*, Allahabad.

Dave, V. S., & Dutta, K. (2011c). Comparison of regression model, feed-forward neural network and radial basis neural network for software development effort estimation. *Software Engineering Notes*, *6*(5), 1–5. doi:10.1145/2020976.2020982

Dave, V. S., & Dutta, K. (2014). Neural network based models for software effort estimation: A review, Artificial Intelligence Review. *International Review*, *42*(2), 295–307.

Finnie, G. R., Wittig, G. E., & Desharnais, J. M. (1997). A comparison of software effort estimation techniques: using function points with neural networks, case-based reasoning and regression models. *Journal of Systems and Software, 39*(3), 281–289. doi:10.1016/S0164-1212(97)00055-1

Foss, T., Myrtveit, I., & Stensrud, E. (2002). MRE and heteroscedasticity: an empirical validation of the assumption of homoscedasticity of the magnitude of relative error. In *Eighth IEEE International Symposium on Software Metrics*. IEEE.

Foss, T., Stensrud, E., Kitchenham, B., & Myrtveit, I. (2003). A Simulation Study of the Model Evaluation Criterion MMRE. *IEEE Transactions on Software Engineering, 29*(11), 985–995. doi:10.1109/TSE.2003.1245300

Halstead, M. H. (1977). *Elements of Software Science (Operating and programming systems series)*. New York: Elsevier Science Inc.

Heiat, A. (2002). Comparison of artificial neural network and regression models for estimating software development effort. *Information and Software Technology, 44*(15), 911–922. doi:10.1016/S0950-5849(02)00128-3

Herd, J. R., Postak, J. N., Russell, W. E., & Steward, K. R. (1977). *Software cost estimation study: Study results (Final Technical Report, RADC-TR77- 220)*. Rockville, MD: Doty Associates, Inc.

Ideri, A., Abran, A., & Mbarki, S. (2004). *Validating and Understanding Software Cost Estimation Models based on Neural Networks. In Information and Communication Technologies from Theory to Applications* (pp. 433–434). IEEE.

Ideri, A., Abran, A., & Mbarki, S. (2006). An Experiment on the Design of Radial Basis Function Neural Networks for Software Cost Estimation. In Information and Communication Technologies, ICTTA (pp. 1612 -1617). IEEE.

Ideri, A., Khosgoftaar, T. M., & Abran, A. (2002). Can Neural Network be easily interpreted in software cost estimation? In *World Congress on Computational Intelligence*, Honolulu, HI (pp. 1162-1167). 10.1109/FUZZ.2002.1006668

Iwata, K., Anan, Y., Nakashima, T., & Ishii, N. (2009). Using an artificial neural network for predicting embedded software development effort. In *International Conference on Software Engineering, Artificial Intelligences, Networking and Parallel/Distributed Computing* (pp. 275-280). IEEE Computer Society. 10.1109/SNPD.2009.49

Jorgensen, M., & Shepperd, M. (2007). A systematic review of software development cost estimation studies. *IEEE Transactions on Software Engineering, 33*(1), 33–53.

Kanmani, S., Kathiravan, J., Kumar, S. S., & Shanmugam, M. (2007). Neural network based effort estimation using class points for OO systems. In *Proceedings of the International Conference on Computing: Theory and Applications (ICCTA'07)*. IEEE Computer Society. 10.1109/ICCTA.2007.89

Kaur, M., & Verma, M. (2012, March). Computing MMRE and RMSSE of software efforts using neural network based approaches and comparing with traditional models of estimation. *International Journal of Computer Science and Technology, 3*(1), 316–318.

Kaur, S., Singh, S., Kahlon, K. S., & Bassi, P. (2010). Neural network-a novel technique for software effort estimation. *International Journal of Computer Theory and Engineering, 2*(1), 17–19. doi:10.7763/IJCTE.2010.V2.109

Kitchenham, B. A., Pickard, L. M., MacDonell, S. G., & Shepperd, M. J. (2001). What accuracy statistics really measure. *IEE Proceedings. Software, 148*(3), 81–85. doi:10.1049/ip-sen:20010506

Lee, A., Cheng, C. H., & Balakrishnan, J. (1998). Software development cost estimation: Integrating neural network with cluster analysis. *Information & Management, 34*(1), 1–9. doi:10.1016/S0378-7206(98)00041-X

López-Martín, C. (2014). (2014) Predictive accuracy comparison between neural networks and statistical regression for development effort of software projects. *Applied Soft Computing.* doi:10.1016/j.asoc.2014.10.033

Mahajan, J., and Devanand. (2011, September). Reusability in Software effort estimation model based on artificial neural network for predicting effort in software development, research cell. *International Journal of Engineering Science, 4*, 544–554.

Malhotra, R., & Jain, A. (2011, January). Software effort prediction using statistical and machine learning methods. *International Journal of Advanced Computer Science and Application, 2*(1), 146–152. doi:10.14569/IJACSA.2011.020122

Park, H., & Baek, S. (2008). An empirical validation of a neural network model for software effort estimation. *Expert Systems with Applications, 35*(3), 929–937. doi:10.1016/j.eswa.2007.08.001

Pendharkar, P. C. (2010). Probabilistic estimation of software size and effort. *Expert Systems with Applications, 37*(6), 4435–4440. doi:10.1016/j.eswa.2009.11.085

Port, D., & Korte, M. (2008). Comparative Studies of the Model Evaluation Criterions MMRE and PRED in Software Cost Estimation Research. In *Proceedings of the Second ACM-IEEE international symposium on Empirical software engineering and measurement* (pp. 51-60). ACM.

Reddy, C. S., & Raju, K. V. S. V. N. (2009). A Concise Neural Network Model for Estimating Software Effort. *International Journal of Recent Trends in Engineering, 1*(1), 188–193.

Samson, B., Ellison, D., & Dugard, P. (1997). Software cost estimation using an Albus perceptron (CMAC). *Information and Software Technology, 39*(1), 55–60. doi:10.1016/0950-5849(96)01124-X

Shepperd, M. J., & MacDonell, S. G. (2012). Evaluating prediction systems in software project estimation. *Information and Software Technology, 54*(8), 820–827. doi:10.1016/j.infsof.2011.12.008

Prasad Reddy, P.V.G.D., Sudha, K.R., Rama, P. & Ramesh S.N.S.V.S.C. (2010). Software effort estimation using radial basis and generalized regression neural networks. *Journal of Computers, 2*(5), 87–92.

Stensrud, E., Kitchenham, B., & Myrtveit, I. (2003). A Further Empirical Investigation of the Relationship between MRE and Project Size. *Empirical Software Engineering, 8*(2), 139–161. doi:10.1023/A:1023010612345

Stutzke, R. D. (1996). Software Estimating Technology: A Survey. *Crosstalk, 9*(5).

Tadayon, N. (2005). Neural Network Approach for Software Cost Estimation. In *Proceedings of the International Conference on Information Technology: Coding and Computing (ITCC'05)*.

Tronto, I. F. B., Silva, J. D. S., & Sant'Anna, N. (2007). Comparison of Artificial Neural Network and Regression Models in Software Effort Estimation. In *Proceedings of International Joint Conference on Neural Networks*, Orlando, FL. 10.1109/IJCNN.2007.4371055

Tronto, I. F. B., Silva, J. D. S., & Sant'Anna, N. (2008). An investigation of artificial neural networks based prediction systems in software project management. *Journal of Systems and Software*, *81*(3), 356–367. doi:10.1016/j.jss.2007.05.011

Vahid, K. B., Jawawi, D. N. A., Hashim, S. Z. M., & Khatibi, E. (2011, November). Neural networks for accurate estimation of software metrics. *International Journal of Advancements in Computing Technology*, *3*(10), 54–66. doi:10.4156/ijact.vol3.issue10.8

Venkatachalam, A. R. (1993). Software cost estimation using artificial neural networks. In *Proceedings of International Joint Conference on Neural Networks*. 10.1109/IJCNN.1993.714077

Walston, C. E., & Felix, C. P. (1977). A method of Programming Measurement and Estimation. *IBM Systems Journal*, *16*(1), 54–73. doi:10.1147j.161.0054

This research was previously published in the Journal of Cases on Information Technology (JCIT), 21(2); pages 88-112, copyright year 2019 by IGI Publishing (an imprint of IGI Global).

Chapter 10
Markov Decision Theory–Based Crowdsourcing Software Process Model

Kamalendu Pal

ⓘ https://orcid.org/0000-0001-7158-6481

City, University of London, UK

ABSTRACT

The word crowdsourcing, a compound contraction of crowd and outsourcing, was introduced by Jeff Howe in order to define outsourcing to the crowd. It is a sourcing model in which individuals or organizations obtain goods and services. These services include ideas and development of software or hardware, or any other business-task from a large, relatively open and often rapidly-evolving group of internet users; it divides work between participants to achieve a cumulative result. It has been used for completing various human intelligence tasks in the past, and this is an emerging form of outsourcing software development as it has the potential to significantly reduce the implementation cost. This chapter analyses the process of software development at a crowdsourced platform. The work analyses and identifies the phase wise deliverables in a competitive software development problem. It also proposes the use of Markov decision theory to model the dynamics of the development processes of a software by using a simulated example.

INTRODUCTION

Crowdsourcing is the Information Technology (IT) mediated engagement of crowds for the purposes of problem-solving, task completion, idea generation and production (Howe, 2006; Howe, 2008; Brabham, 2008). The latest breakthroughs in Information and Communication Technologies (ICT) have ushered a new dawn for researchers to design innovative crowdsourcing systems that can harness Human Intelligence Tasks (HITs) of online communities. The prime aim of crowdsourcing is to facilitate the *wisdom of crowds*. The theory suggests that the average response of many people, even amateurs, to a question is frequently more accurate than the view of a few experts. In this respect, a community of individuals with common interests and facing the same tasks can deliver better products and solutions than experts alone

DOI: 10.4018/978-1-6684-3702-5.ch010

in the field. Information systems scholars Jean-Fabrice Lebraty and Katia Lobre-Lebraty confirmed that the "*diversity and impudence of the members of a crowd*" is a value addition to crowdsourcing operations (Lebraty & Lobre-Lebraty, 2013).

Therefore, the advantages of crowdsourcing lie mainly in the innovative ideas and problem-solving capacity that the diverse contributors – which may consist of experts and interested amateurs – can provide. The crowd can provide expert and faster solution to an existing problem. Depending on the challenge at hand, the solution provided may also prove innovative. In this way, crowdsourcing has emerged as a new labour pool for a variety of tasks, ranging from micro-tasks on Amazon Mechanical Turk (mTurk) to big innovation contests conducted by Netflix and Innocentive. Amazon mTurk today dominates the market for crowdsourcing small task that would be too repetitive and too tedious for an individual to accomplish. Amazon mTurk established a marketplace where requesters can post tasks and workers complete them for relatively small amount of money. Image tagging, document labeling, characterizing data, transcribing spoken languages, or creating data visualizations, are all tasks that are now routinely being completed online using the Amazon mTurk marketplace, providing higher speed of completion and lower price than in-house solutions.

Competitive crowdsourcing is reward based and has been used for variety of tasks from design of T-Shirts to research and development of pharmaceuticals and very recently for developing software (Howe, 2008; Lakhani & Lonstein, 2011; Stol & Fitzgerald, 2014).The mTurk is one of the best-known crowdsourcing platforms where HITs or microtasks are performed by thousands of workers (Ipeirotis, 2009).

There are different types of crowdsourcing platforms, such as virtual labour markets (VLMs), tournament crowdsourcing (TC) and open collaboration (OC), which each have different roles and characteristics (Estelles-Arolas & Gonzalez-Ladron-de-Guevara, 2012; Prpic, Taeihagh & Melton, 2014). Along with the growth of crowdsourcing, crowdsourcing platforms are very important to mediate the transactions. At the same time, IT-mediated platforms improve efficiency and decrease transaction costs and information asymmetry. However, these platforms are domain specific.

Crowdsourced Software Engineering derives from crowdsourcing. Using an open call, it recruits global online labour to work on different types of software engineering works, such as requirement elicitation, design, coding and testing. This emerging model has been claimed to reduce time-to-market by increasing parallelism (Lakhani et al., 2010; LaToza et al., 2013; Stol & Fitzgerald, 2014), and to lower costs and defect rates with flexible development capability (Lakhani et al., 2010). Crowdsourced Software Engineering is implemented by many successful crowdsourcing platforms, such as TopCoder, AppStori, uTest, Mob4Hire and TestFlight. Crowdsourced Software Engineering has also rapidly gained increasing interest in both industrial and academic communities.

In this chapter only, software development related crowdsourcing business activities and relevant platforms are considered. Software development is creative and ever evolving. Organizations use various software development process models and methodologies for developing software. A software process model (SPM) specifies the stages in which a project should be divided, order of execution of these stages, and other constraints and conditions on the execution of these stage (Sommerville, 2017). However, the software development methodology (also known as SDM) framework did not emerge until the 1960s. The system development life cycle (SDLC) is the oldest formalized framework for building information systems. The main idea of the SDLC has been "to pursue the development of information systems in a very deliberate, structured and methodical way, requiring each stage of the life cycle – from inception of the idea to delivery of the final system – to be carried out rigidly and sequentially (Elliott, 2004) within the context of the framework being applied. The main objective of this framework in the 1960s was to develop large scale functional business systems in an age of large-scale business conglomerates, whose information systems activities revolved around heavy data processing and number crunching routines.

It is worth to explore strategies for successful use of software engineering and look at the history that forms the basic understanding of good software design and development practices. The history is important because the basics seem to have been ignored in many 1990s commercial enterprises seeking to develop large and complex software systems. In October 1968, a NATO conference on software engineering was held in Garmisch, Germany (Nauer & Randell, 1969). The conference organizers coined the phrase '*software engineering*' as a provocative term to "imply the need for software manufacture to be based on theoretical foundations and practical disciplines traditional to engineering". The highlights of the conference were discussions related to process: how to produce quality software efficiently, how to provide customer-oriented service, and how to protect a business investment in software. Good software engineering was equated with good project management.

As a matter of fact, software engineers aim to use software development models for building software that meets user requirements and is delivered within the specified time limit and budget. The objective of software crowdsourcing is to produce high quality and low-cost software products by harnessing the power of crowd. To meet this objective, the crowd workers who agree to work on the task are given some financial or social incentives (Hoffmann, 2009). The tasks could be executed in a collaborative or competitive manner based on the organization style. Wikipedia and Linux are viewed as well-known collaborative crowdsourcing examples (Howe, 2008; Doan, 2011). Developing a software through crowdsourcing blurs the distinction between a user and developer and follows a cocreation principle (Tsai, Wu, & Huhns, 2014).

With the increasing interest in crowdsourcing software development, it is significant to analyze the development process methodology used by crowdsourcing platforms. This chapter analyzes the process of software development at a crowdsourced platform. The work identifies various artifacts needed at each development phase and the order of events that occur along with the deliverables of each phase. The development process is modeled using a Markov Decision Process (MDP) that provides a mathematical framework for modelling decision making in situations where outcomes are partly random and partly under the control of the decision-maker. The reminder of this chapter is organized as follows. Section 2 introduces the background information of crowdsourcing. Section 3 presents a literature review. Section 4 describes the application development process of a crowdsourced platform. Section 5 explains the basis of modelling the process. Section 6 depicts the Markov Decision Process representation; and finally, Section 7 provides concluding remarks and future direction this research.

BACKGROUND OF CROWDSOURCING

The term 'crowdsourcing' was coined by Jeff Howe in 2006 through an article in the wired magazine as "the act of a company or institution taking a function once performed by employees and outsourcing it to an undefined (and generally large) network of people in the form of an open call" (Howe, 2006). The activities are executed by people who do not necessarily known each other, and interact with the company, the 'requester', via virtual tools and an internet connection. They become 'the workers': they can access tasks, execute them, upload the results and receive various forms of payment using any web browser. This is a labour market open 24/7, with a diverse workforce available to perform tasks quickly and cheaply.

Figure 1. Schematic diagram of Amazon's Mechanical Turk system

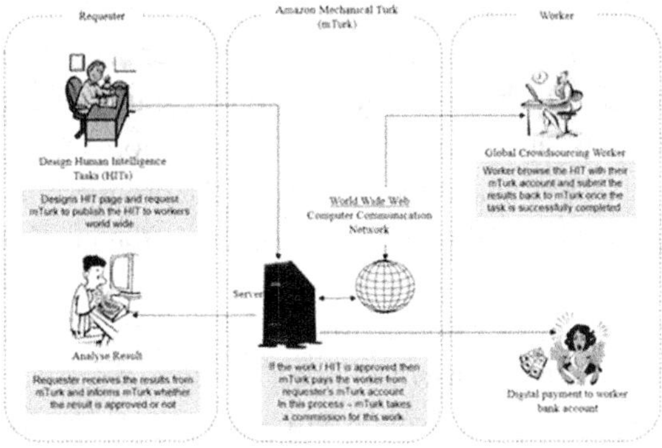

A diagrammatic representation of well-established crowdsourcing platform Amazon's Mechanical Turk (mTurk) - (www.mturk.com) is shown in Figure 1. In this diagram, the "requesters" both design and post tasks for the Crowd to work on. In mTurk, tasks given to the "workers" are called Human Intelligence Tasks" (HITs). Requesters can test workers before allowing them to accept task and establish a baseline performance level of prospective workers. Requesters can also accept, or reject, the results submitted by the workers, and this decision impacts on the worker's reputation within the mTurk system. Payments for completed tasks can be redeemed as 'Amazon.com' gift certificates or alternatively transferred to a worker's bank account. Details of the mTurk interface design, how an API is used to creates and post HITs and a description of the workers' characteristics are beyond the scope of this chapter. With each result submitted by a worker the requester receives an answer that including various information about how the task was processed. One element of this data is a unique "workerID" allowing the requester to distinguish between individual workers. Using this "workerID" it is possible to analyse how many different HITs each worker completed.

A definitive classification of Crowdsourcing tasks has not yet been established, however Corney and colleagues (Corney et al., 2010) suggest three possible categorizations based upon: nature of the task (creation, evaluation and organization tasks), nature of the crowd ('expert', 'most people' and 'vast majority') and nature of the payment (voluntary contribution, rewarded at a flat rate and rewarded with a prize). Similarly, Crowdsourcing practitioners, such as Chaordix (from the Cambrian House (www.cambrianhouse.com)) describes Crowdsourcing models as a Contest (i.e. individual submit ideas and the winner is selected by the company, 'the requester'), a Collaboration (i.e. individuals submit their ideas or results, the crowd evolves the ideas and picks a winner), and Moderated (i.e. individuals submit their ideas, the crowd evolves those ideas, a panel – set by 'the requesters' select the finalists and the crowd votes on a winner). In recent decades academics across many different disciplines have started reporting the use of Internet Crowdsourcing to support a range of research projects, e.g. social network motivators (Brabham, 2008), relevance of evaluations and queries (Alonso & Mizzaro, 2009; Kostakos, 2009), accuracy in judgment and evaluations (Kittur et al., 2008). Some of relevant research issues are described in the next section.

REVIEW OF LITERATURE

Since the coining of the term crowdsourcing, studies have been carried out on different aspects of crowdsourcing. Researchers have analyzed the economics of crowdsourcing contests, proposed models for pricing strategies and done analysis on earning reward and reputation, in general. Huberman (Huberman, 2009) analyzed data set from YouTube and demonstrate that the productivity exhibited in crowdsourcing exhibits a strong positive dependence on attention, measured by the number of downloads (Huberman, Romero, & Wu, 2008).

The purpose of this literature review section is two-fold: (i) Firstly, to provide a comprehensive survey of the current research progress on using crowdsourcing to support software engineering activities. (ii) Secondly, to summarize the challenges for Crowdsourced Software Engineering and to reveal to what extent these challenges were addressed by existing work. Since this field is an emerging, fast-expanding area in software engineering yet to achieve full maturity. The including literature may directly crowdsource software engineering tasks to the general public, indirectly reuse existing crowdsourced knowledge, or propose a framework to enable the realization or improvement of Crowdsourced Software Engineering.

In simplistic sense, the term 'Crowdsourced Software Engineering' to denote the application of crowdsourcing techniques to support software development. It emphasizes any software engineering activity included, thereby encompassing activities that do not necessarily yield software in themselves. For example, activities include project management, requirement elicitation, security augmentation and software test case generation and refinement. The studies specifying the use of crowdsourcing for developing software are few in literature. In his work Vukoic M (Vukoic, 2009) presented a sample crowdsourcing scenario in software development domain to derive the requirements for delivering a general-purpose crowdsourcing service in the Cloud (Vukovic, 2009). LaToza and colleagues (LaToza et al., 2014) developed an approach to decompose programming work into micro tasks for crowdsourced software development (Latoza, Towne, & Adriano, 2014). In their work Stol and Fitzgerald (2014) presented an industry case study of crowdsourcing software development at a multinational corporation and highlighted the challenges faced (Stol & Fitzgerald, 2014). Zhenghui H. and Wu W. (2014) applied the famous game theory to model the 2-player algorithm challenges on TopCoder (Hu & Wu, 2014).

Crowdsourced Software Engineering has several potential advantages compared to traditional software development methods. Crowdsourcing may help software development organizations integrate elastic, external human resources to reduce cost from internal employment, and exploit the distributed production model to speed up the development process.

For example, compared to conventional software development, the practice of TopCoder's crowdsourced software development was claimed to exhibit the ability to deliver customer requested software assets with a lower defect rate at lower cost in less time (Lakhni et al., 2010). TopCoder claimed that their crowdsourced development could reduce cost by 30% - 80% when compared with in-house development or outsourcing (Lydon, 2012). Furthermore, in the TopCoder American Online case study (Lakhani et al., 2010), the defect rate was reported to be 5 to 8 time lower compared with traditional software development practices.

In another study published in Nature Biotechnology (Lakhani et al., 2013), Harvard Medical School adopted Crowdsourced Software Engineering to improve DNA sequence gapped alignment search algorithms. With a development period of two weeks, the best crowd solution was able to achieve higher accuracy and three orders of magnitude performance improvement in speed, compared to the US National Institutes of Health's MegaBLAST.

The work on competitive crowdsourcing for developing software is in its infancy and our work analyses the development process model and build a Markov Decision Process (MDP) representation of the system. MDP has been widely used for representing sequential decision making and applied to wide range of problems for obtaining optimal solutions. Researchers in the past have used MDP to find optimal scheduling policy for a software project (Padberg, 2004); and for the assessment of the quality of the developed software (Korkmaz, Akman, & Ostrovska, 2014).

CROWDSOURCED PROCESS MODEL

Different crowdsourcing platforms are available for the development of software applications. Business enterprises like RentACoder, oDesk, Elance, Topcoder, uTest adopt different approaches for crowdsourcing (Hu & Wu, 2014). This chapter focuses on the development methodology used by TopCoder. This section presents that how software is developed through crowdsourcing, and the different phases of development along with the deliverables of each phase and the sequence of activities followed.

Software Application Development Methodology

TopCoder founded by Jack Hughes is one of the largest competition-based software development-portal that posts software developed tasks as contests (TopCoder, 2018) (Hu & Wu, 2014). With over 700,000 members it is one of the world's largest competitive crowdsourcing community (TopCoder, 2018). It has online community of digital creators who compete to develop and refine technology, web asserts, extreme value analytics, and mobile applications for customers (Begel, Bosh, & Storey, 2013). Contests on the TopCoder platform are conducted under three categories: Algorithm Contests, Client Software Development Contests and Design Contests (Lakhani & Lonstein, 2011). The algorithm contests are conducted through single round matches that are posted fortnightly and attract many contestants. This study concerns the client software development contests that are conducted on this platform. Development of real-world complex systems is broken into a variety of competitions and the development proceeds through distinct phases of these competitions. TopCoder provides mechanisms and infrastructure to manage and facilitate the creation of problem statements and their solutions. A platform manager is assigned to each project who closely works with the client to formulate the problem and host it onto the platform in the form of competitions. The software application development methodology at the TopCoder platform is shown in the Figure 2.

Phase Specific Deliverables

The application development process progresses in phases. Each phase is executed through a competition or a series of competitions and the winning entry serves as an input to the subsequent phases. The client of a crowdsourced platform may use an existing component from the platform catalogue or request for creation of a new component. There are six broad phases namely – Conceptualization, Specification, Architecture, Component Design and Development, Testing and Assembly.

Conceptualization

The competitions under Conceptualization phase are conducted to identify and document the needs and ideas of the project stakeholders. These competitions can commence by either running a series of Studio competitions to create graphical conceptualization artifacts like Storyboards, Wireframes and Prototypes, or a series of Conceptualization contests to create a Business Requirement Document and High-Level Use Cases.

After the component design competition is completed, the detailed component design specifications act an input into Component development competition. During this competition the component is implemented.

Figure 2. Software application development methodology

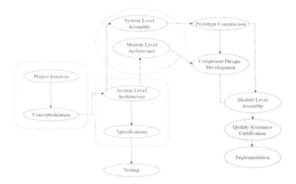

Specification

During the Specification competitions, the application requirements are formulated in as much detail as necessary in order to accomplish the goals for this application module. The high-level use cases that are identified during Conceptualization contests are assigned to modules during System Architecture phase, and during the Specification phase all the individual scenarios that make up those use cases are broken up in text and graphical form using UML Activity Diagrams.

Architecture

The System Level Architecture competition takes the business requirements and prototype defined in conceptualization phase as input to define the overall technical approach that will be employed to meet those requirements. Module-Level Architecture Phase defines the lower-level technical design of an independent module of a larger application. This phase is responsible for defining the components and their interactions that will implement the requirements for the module.

Design and Development

During the component design competition, competitors get an opportunity to clarify any unclear requirements and define technical details for implementation. Component design competitions take the component requirements developed during the architecture phase as input and produce a detailed component design specification.

Table 1. Phase Wise Deliverables

Software Development Phase	Input	Source	Related Artifacts as input	Related artifacts towards output	Deliverables
Conceptualization (CC)	Conceptualization Questionnaire	C	Wireframes / Storyboards	UCD	BRD Prototype
System Level Architecture (SL-AC)	BRD Activity Diagrams Technical Questionnaire	CC SC C	Storyboards / Wireframes / Prototype Technical Questionnaire	Sequence Diagram Interface Diagram	SDS Integration Plan
Specification (SC)	Conceptualization Documents High level Use Cases Specification Template	CC	Wireframes / Storyboards / Prototypes	Activity Diagram	ARS
Testing (TC)	BRD SDS	CC SL-AC	Activity Diagrams / Use Cases / Prototypes	Test Scripts	QA Plan Application test suite
Module Level Architecture (ML-AC)	BRD Storyboards / Wireframes / Protype Activity Diagram Technical Questionnaire	CC G-CC SC C	Wireframes / Storyboards / Prototypes	Module Sequence Diagrams / Module Interface Diagrams	Module Design Specifications / Component Requirement Specifications
System Level Assembly (SL-AYC)	BRD System Level Architecture	SC SL-AC	Prototype	Deployment Document	Assembly Source
Protype Assembly (P-AYC)	Application Specification Documents	C	Prototype	Deployment Document	Assembly Code
Component Design / Development (CDDC)	Component Specification	SL-AC ML-AC	Component Design Requirements	Unit Tests	Component Design CGC Component Documentation
Module Level Assembly (ML-AYC)	BRD UCD Activity Diagram QA Plan Application Design Specification Component Sequence and Deployment Diagram	CC SC TC ML-AC	Custom and Generic Components	Deployment Document	Assembly Source
Certification	Completed Assembly Requirement Documents	ML-AYS SC	Test Cases	JIRA Issues	Bug Fixes

C: Client; UCD: Use Case Diagram; BRD: Business Requirement Document; CC: Conceptualization Competition; SC: Specification Competition; SDS: System Design Specification; ARS: Application Requirement Specification; SL_AC: System Level Architecture Competition; G-CC: Graphical Conceptualization Competition; ML-AC: Module Level Architecture Competition; TC: Testing Competition; ML-AYC: Module Level Assembly Competition

After the component design competition is completed, the detailed component design specifications act an input into Component development competition. During this competition the component is implemented.

Testing

Testing competitions provide the mechanism for verifying that the requirements identified during the initial phases of the project were properly implemented and that the system performs as expected. The test scenarios developed through these competitions ensures that the requirements are met end-to-end.

Assembly

The System Assembly competition creates the foundation for the application. This includes creating the build scripts that will be used throughout the application as well as incorporating all identified components into the shell that implements the application's cross-cutting corners. The Prototype Assembly competition focuses on the logic and functionality required as part of the front end and converts a prototype into the presentation-layer shell of the application. This competition is run after the protype has been approved by the client. Since this competition does not focus on back-end functionality or architecture, it can be run before or during the architecture phase.

Module Assembly competition integrates components developed during the component production process into the shell application built during System Assembly. The core functionality of the application is put in place and a fully-functional application is an output of this phase. After the application is assembled, certification verifies that the application functions correctly. Using the test cases produced by Testing Competitions, as well as Bug Hunt Competitions, the application is compared to the requirements for the purpose of Validation. Table 1 shows the major deliverables from the various phases of the development process.

Activity Sequence

The platform also provides a service called 'TopCoderDirect', which is more like a self-service mode in which there is no intervention of the employees of TopCoder. In this service, a platform manager acts as a Co-pilot to educate the client on the working of the platform and the hosting of the competitions is done directly by the client. A Co-pilot or a Platform Manager who is assigned to a project has the responsibility of hosting the competitions of each phase and each phase of the development process follows the sequence of activities as listed in Figure 3.

The setup activity is undertaken before the competition is posted and on an average is of 02 days duration. Once the competition is posted, the registration time duration of around two days is given to the competitors to register for the competition. The competitors after registering for the event work on developing their solution for around one to five days. The competitors may ask queries or discuss their

Figure 3. Activity sequence

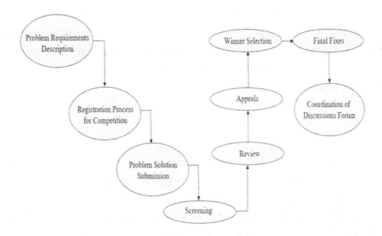

problems in the forum, before submitting the solution. After the submission phase closes, quick screening of the submitted solutions is done as per the minimum quality standards set by the platform to decide eligible entries to the review phase. A panel of three members then reviews each solution that has passed the screening on a scorecard. The process takes around a day and after its completion, the competitors get an opportunity to appeal for anything they believe to be an error in scoring. The time duration for making an appeal is around a day. After the appeal process is completed, the final score of each submission is calculated and a winner is declared based on the highest score submission. The winner then may address any issues that were identified during the review process and after the final fixes and review the winning contestant is required to support a contest by answering forum questions for that contest.

Advantages

The competition-based development model used by TopCoder has successfully created software for the use of individuals and organizations. Some of the benefits of the competition-based development model to a project in an organization are as listed below:

- The time and cost needed to hire, train and fire people are lowered.
- The cost of networking, communication and infrastructure is reduced.
- The participants possess diverse skills and experience there by creating innovative solutions.
- The individual's interest and choice of working on a problem increases the chances of submitting solutions as per the deadline.
- The solutions to the problems are not depend on individuals.
- The intensive review process ensures the selection of the best and quality work as a winning solution.
- Winning solution is rewarded with a fixed pre-decided amount only if the solution meets the specifications and is delivered on time there by reducing cost of development.

There are numerous benefits that crowd workers realize to be active participants in the competition-based development model. Individuals are keen to participate a competitor either to spend quality time on the internet for fun or to earn extra income. The social and financial incentives gained by competitors are often a driving factor for continuous participation in the competitions at a crowdsourced platform. The flexibility of working as per their convenience and having no requirement of reporting to their bosses is an attraction for many.

System Modelling

It is important to model the behavior of the system to demonstrate progression and evaluate performance. Markov Decision Process (MDP) is a useful technique to abstract the model of dynamics of the development process (16). This section formalizes the software development process as an MDP which represents a way of modelling a system, through states and transition. An MDP is a discrete time stochastic control process, formally presented by a tuple of four objects (S, A, Pa_i, Ra_i) (19). S is the state space; $s \in S$ is the current state of the system. A is the action space, where $a_i \in A$ is the action taken based on the current state. $P_{a_i}(s, s')$ is the probability that action a_i in state s at time t will lead to state s' at time t + 1. Ra_i is the immediate reward obtained on performance action a_i.

Software development process occurs in phases and a phase ends when the deliverables of that phase have been produced and this characteristic of the phase allows us to use a discrete-time, MDP as a mathematical model. This chapter presents the software development process that has been adopted as a sequential decision problem in which the set of actions, rewards, cost, and transition probabilities depend only on the current state of the system and the current action being performed. In a crowdsourced software development methodology, a platform manager works with the client to formulate a project road map for building the software. The development then progresses in phases from conceptualization contests in order to finalize BRD, to conducting a series of specification contests to finalize ARS and developing application's wireframes and storyboards, to conducting architecture contests for final SDS and for creation of new components through design and development competitions towards assembly competitions, generation of QA plan through testing competitions and eventually deployment. In this chapter the development process is built in a way that different states and an action results in the transition from one state to another.

States

The state of a system is a parameter, that describes the system. The state of software project changes at the end of each phase. The state consists of four parts:

1. A status vector (V)
2. An accomplishment vector (V_a)
3. A progress vector (P)
4. A countdown variable (C)

The status vector has an entity for each component that defines the status of the component. As the development progresses the project moves from initialization towards completion. There are many artifacts, intermediate deliverables and components that are developed as the project progresses. The status of these components can have any of the following values:

- ND; Not Developed
- TD: To be Developed
- UQ: Under Qualification
- AD: Almost Developed
- SD: Successfully Developed
- CD: Cancelled Development

The set of all possible status values would be {ND, TD, UD, UQ, AD, SD, CD}. The ND state is the initial state of the component. The TD state is a state when the development has not yet started but is in pipeline/ The UD state is the state in which the component is being developed. The UQ is the under-qualification state of the component where qualification is termed as the criteria for deciding the component to qualify for the acceptance. The AD state is a state when the development is almost completed but needs final fixes before completion. The SD state is termed as the completion of the component. CD state represent a cancelled development status of the component.

The status vector of a project defines the status of project components:

$$V = (v_1, v_2, v_3, \ldots v_z, \ldots v_N)$$

where v_z represents the status of the zth project component at the end of the current phase and N is the total number of project components. For example, the vector (TD, UQ, SD) can be considered a valid status vector for a project having three components.

The accomplishment vector V_a is the contestant ID who is a wining contestant and has successfully accomplished the task of developing a component. It has a value of 0 if no contestant is a winning contestant for successful development of the component so far. For example, the vector (1, 3, 0) can be considered a valid assignment vector for a project having three components. The progress vector P defines the time that has been spent working on a component in a phase. If the work is completed on the component and it has been successfully developed the value of P would be infinity. If the competition has been set up and no submissions have been received, then the value would be 0.

Every project has a deadline and the platform manager in consultation with the client establishes an estimated development time for a project. The countdown variable c is the time left for the completion of the project as per the predetermined development time.

Actions

An action defines what is done with the project deliverable at a given development phase. Actions may depend on the current state and phase of development. On performing a particular action, the state is changed to a new state. The new state of the component depends on what action is performed. The possible actions that can be performed based on the activity sequence as discussed in previous section are as stated below:

1. Reuse existing component (a_1)

2. Setting-up Competition
   a. Reviewing Requirements to setup (a_2)
   b. Establishing Project Goals (a_3)
   c. Identifying Important Processes (a_4)
   d. Contest Posting (a_5)
   e. Cancelling Contest (a_6)
3. Registration and Submission
   a. Member registration for Competition (a_7)
   b. Forum Discussion (a_8)
   c. Submission of solution by registered competitors (a_9)
   d. Submission Closed (a_{10})
   e. Screening of the submission (a_{11})
   f. Cancelling Contest (a_6)
4. Reviewing
   a. Reviewing of screened submissions (a_{12})
   b. Evaluating scorecard (a_{13})
   c. Addressing appeals (a_{14})
   d. Selecting Winner (a_{15})
   e. Final Fixes and Reviews (a_{16})
   f. Winning Contestant Support (a_{17})
   g. Cancelling Contest (a_6)

$A = \{a_1, a_2, a_3, \ldots a_{17}\}$

Transition Probabilities

The transition probability, P_{ai} (s, s') represents the probability of a system to move from one state, s to another s' under a stated action a_i. The next state is not determined alone by the stochastic nature of selected dynamics, it occurs with some probability. We have assumed the transition probability from a Not Developed (ND) state to Successfully Developed (SD) state directly, on choosing to reuse a component from the existing catalogue of the platform and not entering the development phases. We have assumed the probabilities based on the statistical data as published in the literature. According to the case study (7), 60 percent of the times a reusable component is selected from the existing catalogue. It is assumed that the remaining 40 percent of the times the development progress through competitions, 90 percent of the times the progression is smooth and 10 percent of the times, the progression encounter issues to cancel and roll back competitions.

Immediate Reward

Moving from one state to another on taking a particular action a_i, results in getting an immediate reward Ra_i. The reward can be positive or negative number from a set of real numbers R. In the present model, it has been assumed that moving from one state to another represents progression and an immediate stationary reward of positive 5 units is attained uniformly for all states when progression is towards completion. Any cancelling action undertaken during the development of a component at any state, results in a negative reward of 5 units, as it depicts cost incurred and penalty. Since development is a time-based process, it is to be noted that the impact of cancelling contest during a latest stage of development results in more loss as compared to the early states.

MDP REPRESENTATION AND RESULTS

An MDP model is given in Figure 3. The circle represents the state of the component at a given time t in the system. The edges represent the chosen action that causes the state to be changed and depicts admissible transition. The probability of a system to move to new resultant state (s') at time (t + 1) after a stated action is taken is depicted along with the edges. The representation of various states is as follows: State 0: ND; State 1: TD; State 2: UD; State 3: CD; State 4: UQ; State 5: AD; State 6: SD. The Transition probability Maximum and the Immediate Reward Matrix are given at Table 2 and Table 3 respectively.

Table 2. Transition probability matrix

To From	State 0	State 1	State 2	State 3	State 4	State 5	State 6
State 0	0.0	0.4	0.0	0.0	0.0	0.0	0.6
State 1	0.0	0.0	0.9	0.1	0.0	0.0	0.0
State 2	0.0	0.0	0.0	0.1	0.9	0.0	0.0
State 3	0.0	0.0	0.0	0.0	0.0	0.0	0.0
State 4	0.0	0.0	0.0	0.1	0.0	0.9	0.0
State 5	0.0	0.0	0.0	0.0	0.0	0.0	1.0
State 6	0.0	0.0	0.0	0.0	0.0	0.0	0.0

Table 3. Transition probability matrix

To From	State 0	State 1	State 2	State 3	State 4	State 5	State 6
State 0		5					
State 1			5	-5			
State 2				-10	5		
State 3							
State 4				-15		5	
State 5							5
State 6							

CONCLUSION AND FUTURE WORK

IT enterprises these days are keen on crowdsourcing the tasks to their internal employees for optimal utilization of their resources. In times to come we may see a total change in the way software is being developed. Rather than hiring people for specific tasks and creating a workforce, or crowdsourcing to their own employees, organizations might switch to this peer production mode of getting software developed through genera crowd. There being limited studies on the development process models for developing software, the presented work provides an insight into the various phase, deliverables and integration strategies resulting into a final product. This chapter modeled the development process as a Markov Decision Process and present different states a component can be in, probably actions and their resulting states.

Figure 4. MDP representation of the model

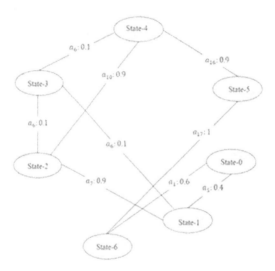

In the long term, the methods presented here could also be used for building up databases of 'solutions and decisions' that machine intelligence requires. In other words, an Internet crowd could be used for the generation "cases", by exposing them to decision-making situations the system will encounter. Once analyzed and amalgamated, these could be stored and embedded into the system's knowledge bases, from which they can be pulled and put into action when necessary. In this way the crowd, a "knowledge network", becomes the solution provider. The proposed model would enable to depict and monitor the progress of development of software through a crowdsourced platform. The extension of the work would be a stochastic simulation of the proposed model is to estimate the optimal scheduling strategies for developing software through a crowdsourced platform.

REFERENCES

Alonso, O., & Mizzaro, S. (2009). Relevance criteria for e-commerce: a Crowdsourcing-based experimental analysis. *Proceedings of the 32nd International ACM SIGIR Conference on Research and Development in Information Retrieval*, 760-761. 10.1145/1571941.1572115

Begel, A., Bosh, J., & Storey, M. A. (2013). Social Networking Meets Software Development: Perspectives from GitHub. *Software*, *30*(1), 52–66. doi:10.1109/MS.2013.13

Brabham, D. C. (2008). Crowdsourcing as a model for problem solving an introduction and cases. *Convergence*, *14*(1), 75–90. doi:10.1177/1354856507084420

Brabham, D. C. (2008a). Moving the crowd at iStockphoto: The composition of the crowd and motivations for participation in a Crowdsourcing application. *First Monday*, *13*(6). doi:10.5210/fm.v13i6.2159

Corney, J. R., Torres-Sanchez, C., Jagadeesan, A., Prasanna, R., & William, C. (2010). Outsourcing labour to the cloud. *International Journal of Innovation and Sustainable Development*, *4*(4), 294–313. doi:10.1504/IJISD.2009.033083

Doan, A., Ramakrishnan, R., & Halevy, A. Y. (2011). Crowdsourcing systems on the World-Wide Web. *Communications of the ACM*, *54*(4), 86. doi:10.1145/1924421.1924442

Elliott, G. (2004). *Global Business Information Technology: an integrated system approach*. Person Education Limited.

Estelles-Arolas, E., & Gonzalez-Lodron-De-Guevara, F. (2012). Towards an integrated crowdsourcing definition. *Journal of Information Science*, *38*(2), 189–200. doi:10.1177/0165551512437638

Hoffmann, L. (2009). Crowd Control. *Communications of the ACM*, *52*(3), 16–17. doi:10.1145/1467247.1467254

Howe, J. (2006). *The rise of crowdsourcing. Wired Magazine*.

Hu, Z., & Wu, W. (2014). A Game Theoretic Model of Software Crowdsourcing. In *Proceedings of Service Oriented System Engineering* (pp. 446–453). SOSE. doi:10.1109/SOSE.2014.79

Huberman, B. A., Romero, D. M., & Wu, F. (2009). Crowdsourcing – Attention and Productivity. *Information Science*, *35*(6), 758–765. doi:10.1177/0165551509346786

Ipeirotis, P. G. (2009). *Analyzing the Amazon Mechanical Turk Marketplace*. ACM XRDS.

Kitur, A., Chi, E. H., & Suh, B. (2008). Crowdsourcing user studies with mechanical turk. In *Proceeding of the Twenty-sixth Annual SIGCHI Conference on Human Factors in Computer Systems*. ACM. 10.1145/1357054.1357127

Korkmaz, O., Akman, I., & Ostrovska, S. (2014). Assessing Software Quality Using the Markov Decision Processes. *Human Factors and Ergonomics in Manufacturing & Service Industries*, *24*(1), 86–104. doi:10.1002/hfm.20355

Kostakos, V. (2009). Is the crowd's wisdom biased? A quantitative analysis of three online communities. *International Symposium on Social Intelligence and Networking (SIN09)*, Vancouver, Canada. 10.1109/CSE.2009.491

Lakhani, K. R., Boudreau, K. J., Loh, P. R., Backstrom, L., Baldwin, C., Lonstein, E., ... Guinan, E. C. (2013). Prize-based contests can provide solutions to computational biology problems. *Nature Biotechnology*, *31*(2), 108–111. doi:10.1038/nbt.2495 PMID:23392504

Lakhani, K. R., Garvin, D. A., & Lonstein, E. (2010). *TopCoder(A): Developing software through crowdsourcing*. Harvard Business School Case.

Lakhani, K. R. & Lonstein, E. (2011). *TopCoder(A): Developing Software through Crowdsourcing (TN)*. Harvard Business Teaching note, 611-671, March 2011.

Latoza, T. D., Ben Towne, W., Adriano, C. M., & Van Der Hock, A. (2014). Microtask Programming: Building Software with a Crowd. *User Interface Software and Technology Symposium*, 43-54. 10.1145/2642918.2647349

Lebraty, J., & Lobre-Lebraty, K. (2013). *Crowdsourcing: one Step Beyond*. London: John Wiley & Sons. doi:10.1002/9781118760765

Lydon, M. (2012). *Topcoder overview*. Retrieved from http://www.nasa.gov/pdf/ 651447main.TopCder_Mike_D1_830am.pdf

Nauer, P., & Randell, B. (1969). *Conference on Software Engineering*. NATO Scientific Affairs Division.

Padberg, F. (2004). Linking software process modelling with Markov decision theory. *Proceedings of the 28th Annual International Computer Software and Application Conference, COMPSAC 2004*, *2*, 152-155.

Prpic, J., Taeihagh, A., & Melton, J. (2014). Experiments on Crowdsourcing, Policy Assessment. In *Proceeding of IPP 2014*. Oxford Internet Institute.

Puterman, M. L. (1994). Markov Decision Processes: Discrete Stochastic Dynamic Programming. Academic Press.

Sommerville, I. (2017). *Software Engineering*. Person Education Limited.

Stol, K., & Fitzgerald, B. (2014). Two's Company, Three's a Crowd: A Case Study of Crowdsourcing Software Development. *Proceedings of ICSE*, *2014*, 187–198.

Stol, K., & Fitzgerald, B. (2014). Researching Crowdsourcing Software Development: Perspectives and Concerns. *Proceedings of CSI-SE*, 7-10. 10.1145/2593728.2593731

TopCoder. (2018). Available: http://www.topcder.com

Tsai, W. T., Wu, W., & Huhns, M. N. (2014). Cloud-Based Software Crowdsourcing. *Internet Computing*, *18*(3), 78–83. doi:10.1109/MIC.2014.46

Vukovic, M. (2009). Crowdsourcing for Enterprises Maja Vukovi. Proceedings of Congess on Services-I, 686-692.

KEY TERMS AND DEFINITIONS-

Crowdsourcing: Crowdsourcing is the Information Technology mediated engagement of crowds for the purposes of problem-solving, task completion, idea generation, and production.

Crowdsourcing Software Engineering: Crowdsourcing software engineering derives from crowdsourcing. Using an open call, it recruits global online labour to work on different types of software engineering works, such as requirement elicitation, design, coding and testing.

Human Intelligence Tasks: In crowdsourcing business model, employers post jobs known as Human Intelligence Tasks (HITs), such as identifying specific content in an image or video.

Markov Decision Theory: In practice, decision is often made without a precise knowledge of their impact on future behaviour of systems under consideration. The field of Markov Decision Theory has developed a versatile approach to study and optimize the behaviour of random processes by taking appropriate actions that influence future evolution.

Software Process Model: In software engineering, a software process model is the mechanism of dividing software development work into distinct phases to improve design, product management, and project management. It is also known as a software development life cycle. The methodology may include the pre-definition of specific *deliverables* and *artifacts* that are created and completed by a project team to develop or maintain an application.

Chapter 11
Requirements to Products and Processes for Software of Safety Important NPP I&C Systems

Vladimir Sklyar
National Aerospace University KhAI, Ukraine

Andriy Volkoviy
Mellanox Technologies Ltd., Kyiv R&D Center, Ukraine

Oleksandr Gordieiev
Banking University, Ukraine

Vyacheslav Duzhyi
National Aerospace University KhAI, Ukraine

ABSTRACT

Features of software as a component of instrumentation and control (I&C) systems are analyzed. Attention is paid to the importance of functions performed by software and hazards of such software. Requirements for characteristics of software as a component of I&C systems are analyzed. Different regulatory documents are considered in order to disclose common approaches to the use of dedicated software and off-the-shelf software components. Classification of software, as well as classification of requirements, is described. Criteria of selection and structuring of requirements, as well as criteria for software verification, are defined. As long as the characteristics of software components directly depend on the quality of the processes of software development and verification, requirements for software life cycle processes are considered.

DOI: 10.4018/978-1-6684-3702-5.ch011

INTRODUCTION

Regardless of the purpose and application area any modern digital systems has software as integral part of the system. Instrumentation and control systems are not exceptions and may include software in many various forms: firmware and embedded software (written for particular hardware and usually executed without an operating system), system software (e.g. operating systems and platforms), middleware and device drivers, application software (typically written to be run under operating systems and usually interact with users), configuration for FPGA devices, etc. Software of different forms and types has specific properties. Moreover functions that are performed by software impose constraints on both software as a product and software lifecycle as a processes. For example, use of operating systems and application software has a very limited scope in safety important systems.

In the context of safety important I&C systems, increase in portion of software-produced or software-supported functions requires more attention to software. In this chapter software (SW) for nuclear power plant's (NPP) instrumentation and control (I&C) systems is concerned. That means that references to specific regulations for nuclear power engineering are given, particular terminology and classifications are used.

BACKGROUND

The increase of the number of nuclear power plant I&C software executed functions causes an increase of the "weight" of software device defects and its possible sources of failures. Based on different estimates such defects cause up to 70% of the failures of computer systems of critical application complexes, of the total number of those attributed to nuclear power plant I&C systems (Everett, 1998) (Lyu, 1996). Given this, the present trend is having an increasing dynamic role over time.

In the 1960s software defects caused up to 15% of the failures, and in the 1970s it was 15-30%, and by the year 2000 they were the cause of up to 70% of computer system failures. This trend shows up even more in space rocket technology (Aizenberg, 2002). Analysis of the cause of accidents and catastrophes of space rocket systems, where on board and ground computer systems have already been in use for several decades, allows one to determine that in the past 40 years each fifth accident is related to failure of a digital control system. Six of seven failures of these systems were caused by the occurrence of software defects. One such defect of computer software of the Ariane-5 navigational system in 1997 led to an accident which cost nearly one half billion dollars (Adziev, 1998). In nuclear power generation programmable I&C systems have had a shorter history, however, here also there have been accidents due to software defects.

The reliability of software, as for the I&C system as a whole, depends on the design quality at stages that directly precede development of the software:

- Development of requirements for I&C system.
- Mathematical modeling.
- Software implemented functioning algorithms.

Errors committed at these stages become sources of complex defects in software. In this sense, software, on the one hand, accumulates the deficiencies of the preceding stages, and on the other hand, is the "field," in which they can show up and be eliminated. However, the efforts that must be made to do this, increase by an order of magnitude.

Consequently, software is becoming an even more important factor determining the safety of nuclear power plant I&C system. This explains the fact that software of nuclear power plant I&C system, in accordance with national and international normative documents, is a separate and very important object of safety standardization.

SOFTWARE OF NUCLEAR POWER PLANT I&C AS AN OBJECT OF SAFETY REQUIREMENT ESTABLISHMENT

Aspects of Software in Establishing Safety Requirements

Software has a number of important features that should be taken into account in establishing requirements for it. The main of these features are listed below.

1. On the one hand, software is a component of I&C system and shall comply with general requirements for the system, and on the other hand it is an independent and specific object for establishment of requirements, which is confirmed by a large number of international and national standards and methodological normative documents completely devoted to software.

2. Defects that are committed during the development and are not revealed during software verification, can be actuated under certain conditions in the I&C system operating process and lead to their failure. This failure cannot be compensated even if redundant channels are available. If that channels use identical software versions, software defects are in all channels and reveal themselves simultaneously leading to the same kind of distortion of information at the outputs. Therefore, software defects are potential and quite likely source of common cause failure. For this reason, on the one hand software requirements include both requirements for its characteristics (structure, functions and properties) and software lifecycle processes; on the other hand there is a requirement for whole I&C system related to adherence of diversity principle, that is addressed primarily to software, because the use of several program copies increases the likelihood of failures and faults, caused by their hidden defects.

3. At different stages of the software lifecycle (primarily design, coding, integration and testing) different tools are widely used. These tools are also software products, which are intended to reduce the number of defects and increase the reliability of I&C software. However, defects can also be introduced into the I&C software through the software tools. It is the common approach when control systems are based on programmable logic controllers (PLC) for which specialized computer-aided design (CAD) tools are used, and in view of the complexity of such CAD tools both intrinsic defects of a tool and improper use of a tool can be the source of I&C software defects. Therefore, requirements for software must include requirements for software tools used in development and verification.

4. Because documentation is an integral part of software, the requirements for I&C software also include requirements for documentation that is used at all stages of the lifecycle.

5. Software must be examined not only as an independent object of safety standardization, but as a necessary means that will ensure conformity of the I&C system to requirements established for it with regard to redundancy, maintainability, technical diagnostics and so forth.

6. Software requirements are not permanent. The experience with creation and use of I&C system as well as improvement of the information technologies lead to the necessity to improve the requirements. Therefore, requirements must reflect basic and most stable situations considering this experience and prospects of software development technologies.

7. Nuclear power plant I&C systems are complex systems which can consist of several subsystems, each produced with the use of one or several platforms. Consequently, software of I&C system is a set of various software components (computer programs), which differ in functional purpose, developer companies, programming languages and technologies used, etc. This causes asymmetry of requirements for different software components.

8. Quantitative requirements for reliability are difficult to establish for software, in contrast to I&C system hardware items. There are several factors causing the absence of common and standard methods of quantitative evaluation of software reliability. These factors include: uniqueness of software as an object of evaluation, in spite of actively continuing industrialization of development processes and introduction of numerous standards for techniques of developing software; insufficient development of theoretical aspects of this evaluation and lack of a mutual opinion about its expediency; complexity of representing objective and complete information on defects that are discovered at different stages of the software lifecycle, and others.

Classification of I&C Software

Specification of requirements for different kinds of software depends on and usually based on I&C software classification. The following classification features are recommended to use (see Figure 1):

-   Affiliation of the software with various I&C system and subsystems.
-   Functional purpose.
-   Level of approval.
-   Effect on safety.

The selection of these classification features is made on the basis of analyzing modern international standards for I&C software, which are important for nuclear power plant safety, in particular (IAEA, 2000), (IEC, 2006, a) and (IEC, 2008).

Based on these features software has a multidimensional (parallel) classification, in which individual groups of its types are relatively independent. The arrows between components of individual facets indicated the most preferred combinations of software types, which are classified according to different features. It should be noted that some facets can be more detailed and presented in the form of hierarchical classifications.

By affiliation software can be a part of: I&C system, I&C platform, some automation devices or equipment.

Based on purpose software is classified into: general (or system) software; application (or functional) software; instrumentation (or toolkit) software, which is used in development, testing and verification.

Figure 1. Classification of I&C software

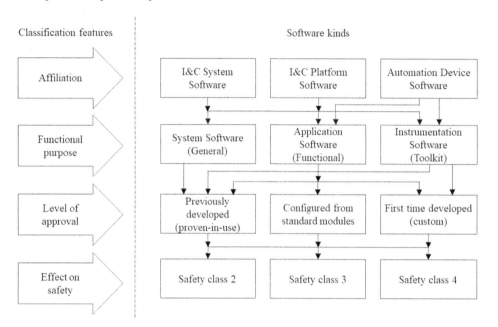

The examples of instrumentation software include different tools, which are intended for processes of design, translation, configuration control, debugging, and verification.

Level of approval is an important classification feature according to which there are:

- Previously developed (proven-in-use) software, also known as off-the-shelf (OTS) software. This kind of software can include commercially accessible software, developed and supplied by other companies, and also standard application software, which is created and approved in similar or different projects.
- Software configured from standard (previously developed) software modules (library blocks). The configuration tools for such software usually is proven-in-use software.
- First time developed (custom) software. Such software is created especially for the given system and has no operational experience in other applications.

Previously developed (OTS) software further be classified by other features, such as source code availability (openness), possibility of changes, amount of operating experience, etc.

Influence on safety is determined by I&C system safety class in which this software is used. According to the Ukrainian legislation any I&C system must be assigned to one of three safety classes, denoted by numbers 2, 3 and 4. Moreover for functions performed by I&C system are assigned to the category denoted by letters A, B or C. Therefore I&C system can be:

- Safety class 2(A), if at least one function of that system has category A.
- Safety class 3(B), if system does not perform category A functions and at least one function of that system has category B.

- Safety class 3(C), if system does not perform category A and B functions and at least one function of that system has category C.
- Safety class 4, if none of its functions are classified by category (such systems are consider as non-safety).

It is important, that affiliation of software does not affect I&C software requirement directly. Purpose of software affect on the requirement, because special set of requirements is established for tools that are used for development and verification. Level of approval strongly influences the software requirements, e.g. required methods and scope of verification can be very different for proven-in-use and for custom software. But, of course, the greatest dependence is between software requirements and influence on safety, expressed by Safety Class. Moreover, safety class defined for I&C system imposes requirements for software of all components, platforms and even related automation devices.

The Criteria of Selection and Structuring of Requirements

Selection and any activities aimed at meeting requirements are impossible without establishing a clear classification features, determining factors and selection criteria. The main factors and criteria are considered below.

1. General criteria for selection of requirements or, in other words, "requirements for requirements." Among such criteria for nuclear power plant I&C software the most important are the criteria of necessity, completeness, adequacy, correctness, verifiability, and openness. These criteria are related to the criteria that were developed and are used for evaluating the execution of requirements for software during expert analyses (Vilkomir, 1999), (Vilkomir, 2000). For example, in accordance with the criterion of completeness during generation of many requirements for software elements must be separated and taken into account that reflect "covering" by requirements of these components such as: completeness of conformity to specifications; completeness of consideration of software lifecycle stages; completeness of the diagnostics, and so forth.
2. Classification and content of I&C system requirements as a whole. The full set of these requirements includes:
    a. Requirements for the composition of the functions.
    b. Requirements for quality of the execution of these functions.
    c. Requirements for reliability of function execution.
    d. Requirements for stability of function execution against external influences.
    e. Requirements for lack of influence on other systems.
    f. Requirements for procedures and processes that support meeting requirements for functions, quality, reliability and stability.

This set should be designed for the full set of software requirements and should be correspondingly supplemented and specified. In particular, the subsets of requirements for processes of software development and verification, which play a priority role from the standpoint of assurance of reliability and safety, should be expanded and worked out in maximum degree.

3. Particular features of software as an object of safety standardization. The following set of the software features have a direct effect on the selection of classification features and generation of subsets of requirements:

   a. Software is both a component of the system for which regulatory requirements have been established and a means that assures fulfillment of the regulatory requirements for I&C system. Consideration of this feature is most important in defining requirements for monitoring and diagnosis, reliability and stability. In doing so different external disturbing influences for software should be examined.

   b. Software is a possible source of common cause failure. Nature of software makes it necessary to have requirements for protection from common cause failures due to improvement of software development and verification processes and use of the diversity principle, which in turn determines the necessity of classification features for methods and means of diversity implementation.

   c. Software is a multi-component system. During the statement and classification of requirements the purpose, level of approval and safety class of different software components have to be considered.

   d. Software is a product and a process. This feature of software is one of the critical ones in selecting classification features of requirements and generation of their complete sets, which considers the certain influence of development and verification processes on software characteristics.

4. The existing regulations, which include standards determining software requirements. On the basis of these standards requirements for I&C software can be selected as the socalled normative profile for software. In the general case normative profile is a subset and/or combinations of the positions of basic standards for a specific subject area, which are required for implementation of the required functions in the system. In this case, we mean the normative profile of requirements for I&C software that is important for nuclear power plant safety. The said standards form the profile-forming base for producing the normative profile of software requirements (for example, software lifecycle models, structure of requirements for software, set of metrics and methods of evaluation, requirements for tools, etc.).

5. Possible variants of requirement structuring. This factor is conceptual in nature, because it determines the general approaches, priority and interconnection between different requirements for I&C software. Several variants of software requirements structuring are possible:

   a. Product-oriented: requirements that determine characteristics for software as a component of I&C system. It does not take into account the fact that software characteristics are built in and implemented at different stages of the software lifecycle.

   b. Process-oriented: requirements correspond to software lifecycle processes and define features of process and intermediate product of each stage in the form of "stage-tasks-requirements" statements. This approach is widely used and allows clear process management and quality assurance, but complicates the definition of software product features and for complex software can lead to difficulties with integration.

   c. Mixed process-product-oriented: requirement are divided in two groups and describe both features of development processes and features of final product. In this case the advantages of the first two approaches are used.

General and Functional Requirements

The classification of software requirements can be performed in two stages: in the first stage, which corresponds to the upper level of the hierarchy, we determine the place of normative requirements among the full set of requirements for software (classification of kinds of requirements for software); in the second stage, which corresponds to the lower level of the hierarchy, we carry out the classification of general requirements for software, based on the process-product approach.

The set of requirements for software corresponds to the set of requirements for I&C system, because it contains both requirements and functions, and for their quality (properties), and to reliability, stability, and processes (both development and verification). The particular features of this full set for software consist of:

1. Requirements for software as an element of I&C system are determined based on requirements for the I&C system as a whole.
2. Requirements for the structure in software elements precede requirements for functions. In this case we are speaking of general requirements for software functions that are important for safety, and not about functions that are determined by its purpose.
3. Full set of quality characteristics we have separated out one, which is most important from the standpoint of safety standardization, which determines the requirements for monitoring and diagnostics.
4. Requirements for processes are determining to a great extent, because they are expanded and worked out in detail with consideration of safety assurance.

In order to conduct classification for requirements we shall distinguish three features: source of requirements; type of requirements; object of requirements assignment (Figure 2).

For the first of them we can distinguish requirements of the regulatory (normative) documents and requirements that are contained in the requirement specifications for development of I&C system and development of software.

Figure 2. Classification of software requirements

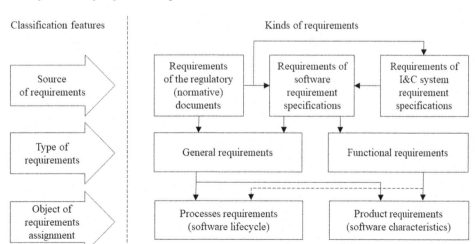

In the development of specifications for software or I&C system (as a whole) requirements of the regulatory documents must be taken into account. Requirements of the specifications of the software are developed with consideration of the specifications for I&C system.

According to the type of requirement software requirements are divided into general and functional. General requirements do not depend directly on what the functions are implemented in I&C software, but are determined only by the safety class, level of approval and its purpose. Functional requirements depend completely on the purpose of the I&C and tasks which are solved by the software. The functional category normally includes requirements for productivity, synchronization, information protection, required service lives, portability and so forth.

Depending on the object of assignment one can distinguish requirements for software lifecycle processes (development and verification) and product requirements (software characteristics). In the regulatory documents general requirements are normally given as those pertain to processes and products. Functional requirements as a rule pertain to software and to the product, although they can determine some of the requirements for the process of software creation with consideration of specific features of the design, the tools used and so forth.

The classification of the general requirements is considered below.

Results of the classification of general requirements for software characteristics (software as a product) and processes of its creation are given in Figures 3 and 4 respectively. In the classification of requirements for software characteristics two groups of requirements are delineated: for structure and for properties. The first group includes requirements for features of the construction and functioning of software. The second of these groups brings together requirements for software properties such as requirements for its sufficiency and adequacy for functions execution, monitoring and diagnosis, reliability and stability, protection against cyber threats.

Figure 3. Classification of requirements for products (software characteristics)

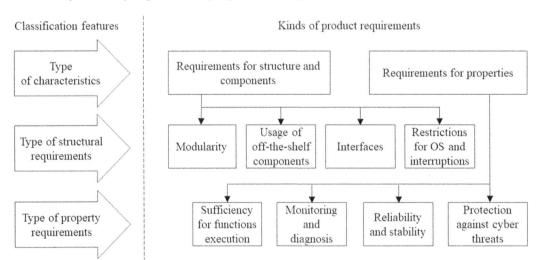

Requirements for Software Characteristics

Requirements for structure and components includes the following requirements:

1. Requirements to modularity.
2. Requirements to use of off-the-shelf components (pre-developed software).
3. Requirements to interfaces.
4. Restrictions for use of the operating system and interrupts.

The first subgroup of the requirements is due to the need to present software in the form of a modular structure. In doing so the source code of one module must contain a limited number of operators, and the modules must have a clear structure, be easily modifiable and tested.

The second subgroup determines the preference of the use of previously developed software. Using OTS software components one must: evaluate its conformity to the functions and characteristics of I&C system, where the use of OTS components is preferred for which one should determine the functions and characteristics of the OTS components and correlate them with specifications for I&C software; analyze the results of OTS components operation from the standpoint of its conformity to the adopted criteria, norms and rules of safety; develop, if necessary, a list of the required modifications for adaptation of the OTS components to conditions of its use in I&C system; execute such adaptation and perform testing; develop and implement the plan for verification of the changes made. The amount and extent of evaluation of conformity of OTS software components to these criteria are determined by the safety class (I&C safety class). The importance of requirements for the use of OTS components (both developed as special purpose and COTS-components) for safety of the I&C systems as a whole should be emphasized. According to existing estimates (Kersken, 2001), the amount of OST components in software of mature systems can reach 80-85% of the total amount of software.

The third of the listed subgroups of requirements determines the need for complete and clear description of the interfaces between the software being examined and the operator (also known as human-machine interface), hardware platform and peripheral hardware (sensors, drives and so forth) of a given I&C system, and also other I&C devices, systems and subsystems. This description determines the limits of the software being analyzed.

Restrictions for use of the operating system and interrupts are included in requirements for I&C software of safety class 2. If the use of the operating system is deemed necessary, it should execute only the simplest functions. The use of interrupts in the course of executing the most critical functions should be prohibited. One should note that in order to fulfill this requirement more precise criteria should be developed, after providing a detailed explanation of the functions for which the use of the operating system must be limited.

Requirements for monitoring and diagnostics can be divided into four groups with consideration of the kinds of processes and objects, for evaluation of the state of which software is used:

1. Requirements to monitoring I&C system by programming means.
2. Requirements to diagnosis (search for malfunctions) of I&C system by software means.
3. Requirements to self-monitoring of software.
4. Requirements to self-diagnostics of software.

Figure 4. Classification for requirements for processes (software lifecycle)

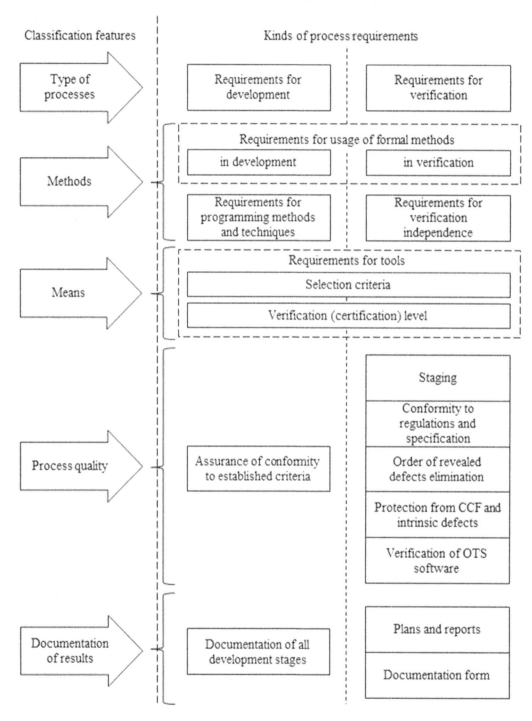

In other words the main requirements for monitoring and diagnosis are:

1. Software should perform (a) continuous automatic monitoring of operating condition and (b) periodic function checks of the I&C system.
2. Software should provide diagnostics of I&C system at the level required by specification.
3. Software should provide self-monitoring and self-diagnosis.

For this purpose, the following should be used: monitoring of intermediate and the final results of the execution of programs and their allowable duration; repeated counting and comparison of the results; discovery of prohibited situations; monitoring data in memory and so forth. For monitoring of I&C software of safety class 2 different types of diversity can be used.

It is necessary that in the process of monitoring and diagnosis: all functions are checked that are important for I&C system safety; during periodic testing it is mandatory to check devices which are not built-in or permanently connected monitoring devices; all degradations of characteristics of safety functions are discovered on a timely basis; if any failure is discovered timely automatic actions that correspond to the situation are generated.

Moreover, an important part of requirements for monitoring and diagnosis are the requirements related to execution of mandatory limitations and procedures during their implementation: implementation of monitoring and diagnostic programs (self-monitoring and self-diagnostics) should not affect fulfillment of programs of the main information and control functions and/or lead to unacceptable degradation of a characteristic; one should make an analysis of the situations and procedure, which allow to avoid false errors; the software should provide automatic recording, storage and display of data on results of monitoring and diagnostics (self-monitoring and self-diagnostics).

Requirements for reliability and stability: By reliability of software we mean its property of preserving serviceability and converting raw data to the result being sought under the given conditions in the assigned time. By stability of software we mean its ability to execute its functions in anomalous situations (during breakdowns and failures of hardware devices, operator errors and errors in the raw data).

Requirements for software related to assurance of reliability and stability can be classified according to a scheme, whose basic elements are: sources of failures and influences on software and I&C system; kind of failures and influences; methods of protection from them.

Sources of failures can be: internal sources with respect to I&C system (both software and hardware); external sources with respect to the I&C system (other I&C systems; operating personnel; repair personnel).

By kind of failures, which should be compensated by means of programming devices, we can distinguish: failures (breakdowns) of hardware devices; failures (breakdowns) caused by the appearance of software defects, which are introduced at the design stage and are not detected during testing and verification.

In turn, software anomalies that can be the cause of I&C system failure are classified into:

1. Defects that appear under certain conditions of the system, its individual components and sets of input signals.
2. Defects that appear during non-standard functioning of hardware of the I&C system.
3. Defects caused by incorrect or incomplete specifications of the software.
4. Defects introduced in development of the software (at all stages of the lifecycle).

5. Defects related to the use of tools and that depend on other software and interfaces between parts of the software or other systems.

The main kinds of influences, resistance to which should be assured by software are the following: unintentional or intentional errors of personnel; unauthorized actions or unauthorized access to programs, data, operating systems; malicious software, including viruses, spyware and trojans, which are sets of instructions that execute actions not stipulated by the specifications and that represent a threat to safety; distortions of incoming information that arise from measurement devices (sensors) and along communication channels from other systems.

Thus, requirements for software related to reliability and stability consist in that the software must implement protection from all of the listed kinds of failures and actions. In this case protection should be assured from failures by general factors, which are due to the appearance of intrinsic defects of the software, by failures and breakdowns of hardware devices of the I&C system.

The following methods are used to protect from the listed kinds of failures and influences on software.

1. Technical diagnostics (monitoring and determination of the cause of a failure or breakdown), reconfiguration of the structure and restoration of the computational process or control process. This method is universal and by appropriate loading of its constituents can assure protection from a broad class of failures. In the I&C system it should be used for protection from hardware failures.
2. Software, functional or other kinds of diversity. The use of diversity is a systems requirement, which is aimed at protection from common cause failures and is related to the use of different kinds of redundancy in the process of creation (development and verification) of software and in the final product, i.e. the software itself. Software diversity (usage different software versions) is achieved by using different algorithms, languages, libraries, programming approaches, operating systems and so forth. Functional diversity is assured by using more than one criterion for identification of each situation that requires the initiation of control actions.

It should be emphasized that for software of safety control systems, which execute emergency protection functions, the emergency situations must be discovered by several methods based on different physically interconnected production parameters, while the analysis of data on the values of these parameters should be performed by different software modules.

For I&C software of safety class 2, in addition, when using software, functional or other kinds of diversity, one must: evaluate the degree of correlation of different versions (analyze the actual level of diversity), their capability for joint compensation of software defects; analyze the substantiation and influence on safety for additionally introduced components – different software or hardware versions. Software diversity should not create a danger of non-fulfillment of functional requirements.

3. Establishment of access categories, application of different password systems, digital signature procedures, use of special encoding algorithms and others. These methods assure protection from errors of personnel and unauthorized actions.
4. Monitoring reliability and protection of incoming information from distortions. In this case one should check: incoming signals being present in zones of access, established in accordance with the specification; logical non-contradictory nature of values of input variables and so forth.

Note that during the use of all protection methods software is an object of protection and a means of assuring reliability and safety. In this case, there must be the introduction of additional software components, which in turn can be sources of failures and therefore they must be carefully analyzed. Functional characteristics of the software and I&C system as a whole should not be degraded to an unacceptable value (just as during monitoring and diagnostics).

Protection against cyber threats: The software of I&C system shall be protected from undesirable and unsafe interference to work and unauthorized changes via external computer networks and the use of non-resident storage media.

To achieve such protection connection with Internet shall be excluded and any changed can be possible only after appropriate authorization. Also special methods of protection from viruses and other malware should be used.

At the same time, measures against cyber threats should not affect the execution of applications software and deteriorate performance of the functions that are implemented by software.

Requirements for Development of Software

Requirements for methods of software development are divided into two main groups:

1. Requirements to use of formal methods.
2. Requirements to programming methods and approaches.

The first group of requirements is to a certain extent recommendatory in nature and indicates the need (expediency) of using at all stages of development and verification formal methods that are based on rigorous mathematical description of formulations of problems related to different stages of software improvement and verification with use of a theoretical apparatus of algorithms, mathematical logic, graph theory and so forth, and also on proof of the correctness of solving these problems by means of standard procedures. Such methods are used in particular for:

1. Transition from verbal to formal description of general and functional requirements for software and development of its formal specifications.
2. Mathematical proof of the conformity of software to specifications or requirements of previous stages of development.
3. Development of application programs using formal procedures of synthesis.
4. Analysis of syntactic and semantic correctness and carrying out test verifications of execution of functional requirements for software.
5. Improvement of the verifiability of software and formalization of the evaluation of results during independent verification and validation.

The best developed and best known methods of formalized checks of software are methods based on formal procedures of logical output, proof of the correctness of algorithms and programs (Anderson, 1979), and also FTA- and FME(C)Aanalysis methods that are widely used to analyze hardware (IEC, 2006, c) and (IEC, 2006, b). The first of them is based on constructing fault tree and events analyses. The second is based on analysis of the fault modes and effects criticality analyses.

The second group of requirements is determined by the preference of using standardized designations of variables in software, files of constant and predefined length, subroutines with minimal number of parameters (e.g. with one output and one input), etc. Moreover, this group of requirements is related to the need to exclude methods in programming development that complicate the software, e.g. complex branches and cycles in the programs, complex indexes in the files and so forth. Note that in the methodological normative documents, which are used in some countries, requirements are contained regarding the need of use of systems in software development that are important for nuclear power plant safety, special methods that improve its reliability, in particular the so-called method of defensive programming (Lawrence, 2002), (Ben-Ari, 2000).

Requirements for tools used to develop software reflect two aspects that are related to their usage:

1. Determination of the criteria for selecting automated development and verification tools.
2. Degree of verification of these tools.

It should be noted, that in the existing normative documents the selection criteria of tools are not given, but the need for the software developer to provide substantiation of such criteria and demonstrate proof that the devices used conform to them is postulated.

The main principle applicable for the tools is that tools used to generate code, must pass through verification with the same requirements as the I&C software itself.

Requirements for Software Verification

Software verification is an important part of I&C software lifecycle. Verification of software is defined as the process of proving the conformity of results obtained at a certain stage of software development with the requirements established in the preceding stage. As noted earlier, the majority of requirements for methods and means of development and verification are uniform. An important distinguishing feature of this group of requirements for verification is the necessity of assuring its independence, that is, carrying it out by persons who are not direct developers of the software.

Requirements for Verification Independence: The integral requirements of independence are level of independence of the experts (organizations) that conduct software verification, and the agreement of these levels with the software safety classes.

The following levels of independence are possible:

1. **Maximum Independence**: Verification is conducted by experts or organizations that administratively and/or financially are independent of the software developers. This level of independence can be broken down into two sublevels:
    a. Administrative independence.
    b. Administrative and financial independence. In this case we are speaking of conducting verification by representatives of a different organization, which specializes in solving such tasks.
2. **Partial Independence**: Verification is carried out by other experts of the same organization, and their administrative and/or financial independence from the software developers is not required. In this case there can be partial administrative and/or financial independence, if the verification is conducted by experts of a different subdivision of the organization, for example by representatives of quality control service, are subordinate directly to the director.

3. **Minimal Independence**: Verification is conducted by the developers themselves, and the review of its results is performed by other experts.

By means of the technology of independent verification and validation (IV&V) one can implement the principle of diversity with respect to the software creation process. In order to assure the highest degree of verification it is necessary that one use tools (utilities), that are different from those which the developer used.

It should be noted that conducting an independent verification can be accomplished according to different systems and with different depth, which depends on the software safety class, worthwhile tasks and existing resources.

Actually three basic scenarios of verification implementation are possible:

1. Full verification and validation of the entire project is carried out, which repeats practically all stages of verification within limits of the project, using intrinsic (diverse) tools and methodologies.
2. Independent consecutive evaluation (rechecking) of all results of the verification performed by the developer organization is carried out. In this case all checks are conducted that are stipulated by the verification and validation plans, and also checks proposed by specialists of the expert analysis organization, and tools of both the inspected and inspecting organizations are used.
3. Independent sampling evaluation (recheck) of results of the verification of the most important functions from the safety standpoint is carried out, which is made by the developer organization.

Quality of Verification: The use of independent verification and validation techniques allows one to improve the quality of this process. By software verification quality we can mean the degree of conformity of software to regulatory requirements after it is carried out and elimination of any discovered defects.

The verification quality is evaluated by analyzing fulfillment of the following requirements:

1. Requirements to staging of the process. The essence of the requirement consists in that the verification must be carried out after each software development stage (specification, design, and coding and others).
2. Requirements to verification of software conformity to requirements of normative documents (general requirements for characteristics and software development, described earlier) and specifications (functional requirements).
3. Requirements to order of elimination of any discovered defects and malfunctions. Components of this requirement are constituents of the process of elimination of defects, time periods for defect elimination, conformity of the time periods of elimination of defects to the software safety class. The process of eliminating defects, independent of the software safety class, includes that a mandatory stabilizing when discovered in the process of development, testing and verification; analysis of the causes, degree of influence on safety; introduction of the necessary changes to the software; repeated check of software with documentation of the results.
4. Requirements to protection from intrinsic defects and common cause failures. Elements of this check are discovery of potential sources of CCF, caused by defects of the software or other components; analysis of their influence on safety of the software and I&C systems as a whole; evaluation of the effectiveness of using devices to protect against these failures.
5. Verification of different kinds of software, including previously developed (OTS) software.

Requirements for Documentation: Documenting is an important part of the verification process and implies the development of two basic documents (groups of documents):

1. The software verification plan, which can consist of a general (coordination) and several particular verification plans and test methods;
2. The software verification report (reports and test protocols) for software verification.

Requirements for documenting software verification results include requirements for the presence, structure and content of a plan (plans), produced before the beginning of verification, and report (reports), which is produced based on results of verification and requirements for the form of material presentation.

All documentation related to development and verification should be set forth in an accessible form, understood by experts, who did not participate in creating the software. The given requirements imply, in particular, traceability of all actions executed in the verification process, which allows one to establish a comparison between the input and output elements at each of the software creation stages and to make a transparent check of the completeness of execution of all requirements, beginning from requirements for the I&C system, then general and functional requirements for the software and ending in reports on verification (tests) of different subsystems or software functions.

The software verification plan should determine: choice of verification strategy and sequence for conducting it; methods and devices used in the verification; sequence of documenting actions and evaluation of verification results.

EVALUATION OF SOFTWARE FOR NUCLEAR POWER PLANT I&C SYSTEM

Criteria and Principles of Evaluation

The goal of the software evaluation is to check conformity to established requirements. This evaluation is conducted by analyzing the documentation submitted by the software developers, and also by verification of software using special tools. The project documentation (for example, the design description) and documents issued by the developer particularly for the licensing purposes (for example, safety analysis report) can be examined. During the expert evaluation some additional information can be requested from developer to clarify issues of the main documentation.

The purpose of the expert work is to improve the level of quality and reliability of the software. Therefore, all comments and recommendations of the experts should be transferred to the developers for timely elimination of any discovered defects. As a result of the joint activity of developers and experts corrections can be made to the design and, thereby, reduce the number of software defects.

The basis of the software expert evaluation methodology is assessment of the meeting the requirements for software at different stages of the lifecycle. In this case it is necessary to evaluate functional and general requirements for software, and also requirements for development and verification. The indicated requirements are to be combined in the criteria, which the software must satisfy, as well as processes of development and verification.

It is suggested that the following five criteria be used (Vilkomir, 1999):

- Completeness

- Documentation
- Accessibility
- Independence
- Successfulness

Software meets the criterion of completeness if its specifications completely correspond to the specifications of the I&C system and the software meets general and functional requirements of the specification, including requirements for development and verification.

Software meets the criterion of documentation, if the composition and structure of the documents developed for all stages of design, verification and operation, correspond to requirements of standards, norms and rules. The documentation criteria and completeness are interconnected: in accordance with the completeness criterion the content aspect of software development is analyzed; in accordance with the documentation criterion the formal aspect of evaluation is evaluated.

Software meets the criterion of accessibility if the documentation for development and verification of software is presented in a form that is clear and understandable to experts, who do not participate directly in their development. Moreover, in accordance with this criterion traceability (transparency, verifiability, checkability) of step by step execution of requirements for software at different stages of the lifecycle must be assured.

Software meets the criterion of independence if the degree of independence of software checking corresponds to the safety class of the system. For systems of safety class 2 the evaluation must be performed by a group of experts (organization), which is administratively and/or materially independent of the experts (organizations) which developed the software. For systems of safety class 3 the development and verification must be carried out by different specialists, however the administrative and financial independence is not required.

Software satisfies the criterion of successfulness if the inspection was successfully completed before beginning of system usage and if by that time all discovered defects and deficiencies have been analyzed and eliminated.

The criteria are an important part of the overall system of software evaluation. Conformity of the criteria and evaluated requirements can be given in the form of a matrix, which contains particular evaluations of the meeting individual requirements and summary evaluations based on the criteria. At the outset the evaluation in accordance with each of the five previously described criteria is formed on the basis of analyzing individual requirements, and then a concluding evaluation is produced.

Along with the general principles of systems approach and expert knowledge additional principles shall be implemented in the expert evaluation of software:

1. The principle of diversity of methods, hardware, actions of experts, methods of generating expert evaluations of software. This requirement determines the internal diversity of the evaluation process, thereby supplementing external diversity, which results in the fact that the expert evaluation and independent verification assure increasing reliability of software evaluation.

2. The principle of asymmetry of efforts distribution. A particular feature of software evaluation is the fact that due to its complexity it is impossible to assure complete testing of the behavior of software for all theoretically possible sets of input data. Therefore, while carrying out expert evaluations under conditions of limited time and resources the main efforts must be concentrated in critical steps and results of software development, analysis of the completeness and reliability of tests.

Next we will propose the content of operations for software evaluation at all basic stages of the life-cycle: development of requirements for software, design and coding of software, verification (development of the verification plan, preparation of the verification report).

In the stage of software requirements development the evaluation contains three steps: evaluation of the conformity of requirements for software to the requirements for the system; evaluation of the representation and specifications of requirements for software and general requirements; transfer of findings to the developer and obtaining back the corrective and additional requirements.

At the software design stage the evaluation contains four steps: evaluation of implementation of software requirements in the design; analysis of the structure for a subject of assured protection from common cause failures due to software errors; listing of requirements and functions of software for use in subsequent stages of the evaluation; transfer of findings to the developer and obtaining from him information and corrective actions for software design and evaluation of their adequacy.

At the stage of software verification plan development the evaluation contains four steps: evaluation of the existence in the verification plan of programs and methods for software testing; evaluation of accessibility of the verification plan; evaluation of reflection in the verification plan the requirements from the detailed list, which is compiled in the preceding stage of the evaluation; evaluation of the completeness and adequacy of the number of tests included in the verification plan. If necessary these stages can be supplemented by defining recommendations for additional testing of the functions more important for safety, transmission of comments and additions to the developer and obtaining a corrected and supplemented verification plan from him.

In the stage of software verification report preparation the evaluation contains six steps: evaluation of the existence in the verification report of protocols and official statements for each program and method of testing; evaluation of the completeness of the tests carried out; evaluation of independence of the verification conducted; evaluation of the software tools used in the development and verification; evaluation of the rate of success of completion of all tests; statement of recommendations for the regulatory body on the possibility of using the software.

The stages of evaluating the plan and the report on software verification are the most important. At these stages the regulatory body has the opportunity to receive evidence of achievement of the required level of quality and reliability of the software. For this purpose the plans, programs and methods of software testing are evaluated before the beginning of the tests, and the additions and comments made are transmitted to the software developer for their consideration.

Evaluation of Software Characteristic

Tasks and approaches to evaluation: Evaluation of the software characteristics includes the following tasks.

The first task is analysis of software conformity to general requirements defined in national and international standards. These requirements do not depend directly on the functional purpose of the software, but are determined by the designation and safety classification of systems.

The second task is evaluation of the completeness and quality of implementation of functional requirements in the software, which are defined in the software requirement specification. For reusable software an evaluation of the conformity of functions implemented in the software to the requirements is determined based on the context of the intended usage.

The first of the listed tasks is universal in nature and therefore can be partially or completely formalized. To this end, general methodology should be defined. Such methodology can include: obtaining the normative profiles (requirements) of the software; development (systematization, profiling, selection) of parameters for evaluation of characteristics (properties) of software and the established requirements; analysis of the results of evaluation and determination of the level of satisfaction of the requirements established for software; procedures (algorithms) of software evaluation using different parameters.

The evaluation of software requires determination of the composition of the corresponding characteristics and parameters, and also methods of their evaluation. Software quality can be evaluated by several characteristics, among which there are functionality, reliability, usability and so forth. The significance of each of these characteristics depends on the area of software application. For software systems that are important to safety a determining characteristic is reliability.

Given the controversies regarding the understanding and use of the term "software reliability" two existing approaches to its evaluation, which conventionally are called "qualitative" and "quantitative," can be considered.

The qualitative approach is used everywhere and is oriented to a system (hierarchy) of requirements, i.e. profiles determined by standards, industry regulations and normative documents of companies, the fulfillment of which is checked during software reliability evaluation. Results of reliability evaluation in this case are formulated in the form of the conclusions "corresponds" or "does not correspond" for individual components, which directly or indirectly affect reliability.

The quantitative approach to evaluation is oriented to the development of models, that receive as input parameters characteristics of both processes (development and verification) and software itself, and gives as output the indicators that characterize reliability (Lyu, 1996).

These indicators most frequently are analogues of reliability indicators of equipment with the difference that such events as "component failures," are formulated as "manifestation of software defects." Moreover, special indicators (metrics) are also used that determine the level of residual defects, rate of their discovery during testing and so forth.

Nevertheless, the instability of the manifestation of defects in sophisticated software systems and their uniqueness do not allow one with high degree of accuracy to determine quantitative values of the characteristics of quality and reliability. To solve this problem, the special methods of analysis such as FTA (Fault Tree Analysis), RBD (Reliability Block Diagram), FME(C)A (Failure Modes, Effects (and Criticality) Analysis) and others, can be used.

Metrics, indicators and raw data for evaluation: There are different approaches to defining of metrics and their relationship to the concepts of software quality and reliability indicators (Pressman, 1997).

The first approach (in accordance with the IEEE standards (IEEE, 1990), (IEEE, 1988, a) and (Pressman, 1997)) views this relationship on the basis of the categories "absolute-relative" and is based on the following definitions.

Absolute indicators (measures) are quantitative indicators that characterize absolute values of different attributes of software and the development process (for example, the number of defects discovered in each software module, the number of lines of initial software text and so forth). In this approach the metrics, in contrast to absolute indicators, are intended especially for comparison of different software designs. For example, comparison of two software applications based on an absolute indicator such as total number of defects discovered is not informative because lack of possibility for judging the size (measured in the lines of source code or number of operators) of comparable programs, their complexity, conditions of development, testing and other characteristics. It is obvious that it is more expedient in this example to use metrics that determine the relationship of the total number of defects to the size of software, quality of programming modules, test time and so forth.

The special feature of the second approach is the fact that metrics are interpreted as dedicated indicators (supplemental with respect to known indicators), which can be given as absolute or relative evaluations of software.

It should be emphasized that the boundary between metrics and reliability indicators of software is quite difficult to draw. Reliability indicators are primarily quantitative characteristics similar to indicators used in classic reliability theory (probability of no-failure, mean time before failure and so on), while metrics are specific indicators for software, which can evaluate reliability indirectly or with respect to other products (reference standards).

Next we will discuss metrics with consideration of the more common second approach. It should be noted that metrics can also give a quantitative evaluation of any given property as well as requirements for software. In this case, by raw data, or parameters (primitives) of metrics we mean the initial quantitative values that are needed for their calculation. The raw data can be other indicators or metrics as well as different constants, coefficients and so forth.

Software developer organizations should be encouraged to use various metrics, because they allow one to evaluate the level of quality and reliability of software being developed and their design processes, and also to discover existing problems (for example, inadequate testing of software, failure to follow the standards, ineffective work of individual groups of developers and so forth) and to take the necessary measures to solve them. Moreover, the need for calculation and analysis of various metrics arises during verification and validation of software, because these processes must rely to a greater degree on accurate quantitative evaluations, and not on subjective opinion of developers or customers.

Basic standards that define metrics and sequence of their computing are:

- IEEE standard 982.1-1988 (IEEE, 1988, a), which defines the list and order of reliability metric calculations.
- IEEE standard 982.2-1988 (IEEE, 1988, b), which clarifies the sequence of using the standard IEEE 982.1-1988.
- ISO/IEC standard 25010 (ISO, 2010), which defines the software quality model.
- ISO/TEC standard 25023 (ISO, 2011), which establishes the basic nomenclature of external software quality metrics, including metrics of reliability, and defines basic principles of their selection and evaluation.
- Ukrainian standard DSTU ISO/IEC 25010:2016 (DSTU, 2016), which is harmonized national edition of international standard ISO/IEC 25010 (ISO, 2010), that began to operate in 2018.

A quality model is presented in standard (ISO, 1999), according to which software is evaluated with a set of internal, external and quality in use metrics. In this case software quality is defined as the total set of properties that determine software capability to satisfy assigned requirements in accordance with its purpose.

The application area of external quality metrics is validation and expert evaluation of the software. The group of external quality characteristics and metrics corresponding to them describe the programming product that is completed and ready for use. In order to evaluate software quality the standard (ISO, 1999) defines six groups of external and internal characteristics.

1. Functionality is a set of software properties that determines its ability to execute the established functions.
2. Reliability is the set of properties that enable the software to retain its serviceability and to convert raw data into the desired result under predetermined conditions in an established period of time.
3. Usability is the set of properties that characterizes the necessary conditions of software use by users.
4. Efficiency is the set of properties that characterizes conformity of the software resources used to quality of execution of its functions.
5. Maintainability is the set of properties that characterizes the level of efforts needed to execute the required software modifications.
6. Portability is the set of properties that characterizes the adaptability of software to work in different functional environments.

The set of metrics that pertain to each group of higher level characteristics is again divided into several sub-characteristics. For example, the software reliability, which is defined as the capability of software to maintain its level of performance under stated conditions for a stated period of time, includes the following sub-characteristics:

1. Maturity is the set of indicators that describe frequency of occurrence remaining in the software.
2. Fault tolerance is the ability of software to retain a certain functioning level during the onset of software malfunctions.
3. Recoverability is the property of software to restore its ability to work (assigned level of functioning), and also program data.
4. Reliability compliance is the degree of software conformity to normative requirements for reliability (standards), and also to customer requirements.

The basic nomenclature, calculation sequence and scale of possible values for metrics of software quality that pertain to each group of quality products with reference to the lifecycle process in which the metric is used, and composition of the necessary documentation for determining input parameters for calculation are defined in (ISO, 2000).

In addition to the listed categories the standard (IEEE, 1988, a) determines a number of functional groups that characterize different properties of reliability of the software itself (indicators, or product measures), as well as the design process (process metrics), based on which the reliability metrics are classified.

Examined standards can be used to create profiles of the evaluation and quality assurance of software. Figure 5 shows the interconnection of the standards IEEE 982.1-1988 (IEEE, 1988, a) and ISO/IEC 25010 (ISO, 2010). The standard ISO/IEC 25010 is fundamental and assures comprehensive inclusion of software quality. Evolution of software quality models in context of the standard ISO/IEC 25010 (Gordieiev Oleksandr, Kharchenko Vyacheslav, Fominykh Nataliia & Sklyar Vladimir, 2014) and features of standard ISO/IEC 25010 were represented in (Gordieiev Oleksandr, Kharchenko Vyacheslav & Fusani Mario, 2015), (Gordieiev Oleksandr, Kharchenko Vyacheslav & Vereshchak Kate, 2017), (Gordieiev Oleksandr & Kharchenko Vyacheslav, 2018). At the same time the standard IEEE 982.1-1988 allows one to assure more thorough analysis of software reliability as one of the top priority quality characteristics of software of information and control critical systems.

Figure 5. Interconnection and scopes of standards IEEE 982.1and ISO/IEC 25010

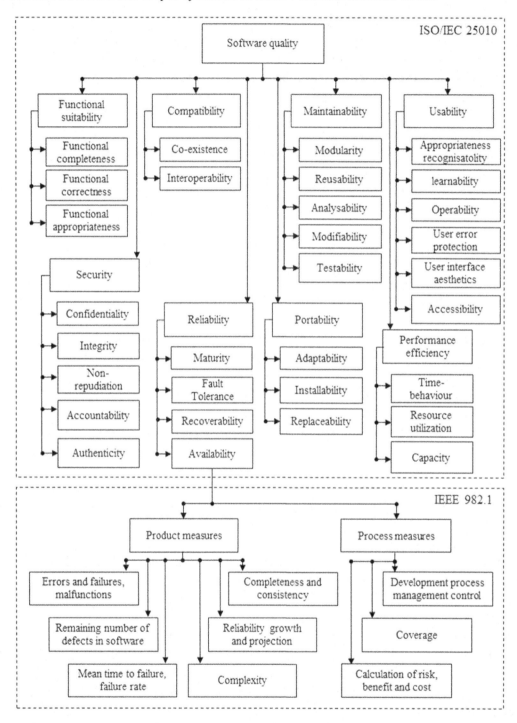

Based on an analysis of the classifications presented above for the systematic description of quality metrics and reliability a unified system of classification features is proposed (Figure 6). Development of the systemic classification of reliability metrics and software quality is a necessary condition of successful harmonization of normative documents and creation of effective methods of evaluation and assurance of quality of the software being developed.

Production and analysis of initial information for determining metrics: Analysis of the standards IEEE 981.1-1988 (IEEE, 1988, a) and IEEE 981.2-1988 (IEEE, 1988, b) allows to conclude that in order to determine input parameters for calculation of different metrics various information sources are required at the different stages of the software lifecycle. Among the main sources of information we can distinguish the following:

- General information on the software project. This includes dates of the beginning and completion of each step of the software lifecycle, description of processes of verification, number of releases (that is versions, outputs) of software and so forth. The reporting of general information on the course of execution of the software design process is executed by the manager of the software project.
- The report on results of performing software verification after completion of each step of the software lifecycle. The report should include information on the nature of defects discovered, reason for their introduction and later discovery, time lost for preparation and conducting verification, and also information. The report is compiled directly by analysts-experts, as a rule manually.
- The report on software testing results. This includes information on time of discovery, level of seriousness and nature of software defects and information on reasons and time (date or stage of the software lifecycle) of the introduction of the corresponding defects, time of their correction, and also the test kits used, number of successful runs of the program and so forth. The report is compiled directly by test engineers manually or using automated recording devices.
- Technical description of the software release that is provided for testing or verification. This should include information on the overall number of procedures and functions (modules), number of modified, supplemented and deleted modules in comparison with the preceding release, and also the modular structure of the software for the possibility of converting the software to a state graph. The technical description is compiled directly by programming engineers, manually as a rule.
- The source code and executable code, which allow one to determine objective characteristics of the software; number of lines in the source code, size of the program, number of operators and operands used, and also the total number of their occurrence on the program and so forth. The software source code can be used along with corresponding utilities to produce a state graph of software as a whole and of individual modules. The software presentation in the form of a graph is necessary for calculating individual metrics and for developing test benches and executing the testing itself.
- Technical documentation for the software, which includes requirements for the software (specification), technical description and so forth. In calculating certain metrics the production of a comprehensive result requires that the experts propose evaluations or assignments of weighting factors (significance) for different software characteristics, input parameters or intermediate results. These factors can be determined based on analysis of corresponding sections of the software technical documentation.

Thus, the executed analysis allows one to insert additional classification features for quality metrics and their parameters: source of information for the determination of input parameters to calculate quality metrics (reports on fulfillment of verification and testing processes, technical description of the software release, source code and so forth); information compiler (project manager, system analysts, programmer-managers and test engineers and so forth); degree of objectivity (reliability and completeness) of the presented information.

It should be emphasized that the process of determining numerical values of input parameters for calculation of reliability metrics manually is unfeasible because of complexity and considerable amount of initial data. Therefore, the task of developing (or selection) support tools for gathering the initial information and automatic determination of input parameters for the calculation to metrics is needed. For this reason software source code analyzers are used as objective sources of information for determining input parameters for calculation of software quality metrics.

Figure 6. Classification scheme of reliability metrics and software quality

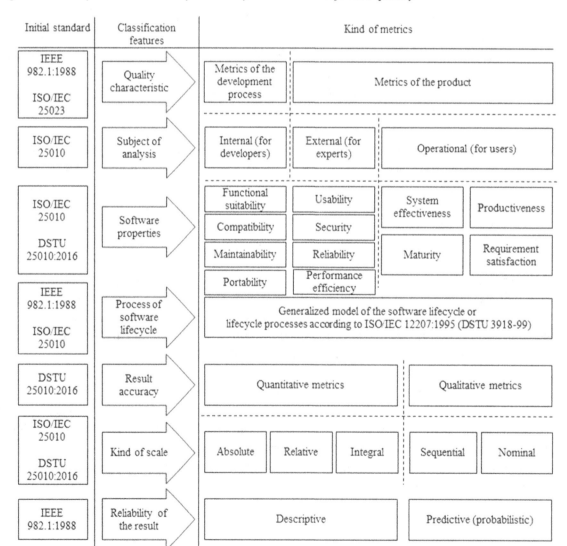

Based on the examined standards and analysis of publications (IEEE, 1988, a), (ISO, 2000) and (Pressman, 1997) a database of reliability indicators (metrics) and tools has been developed, which allows one to make a choice of indicators with consideration of the previously listed classification features, and also the stage of the lifecycle at which the reliability evaluation is made, and to produce their quantitative value. The calculation of measures is carried out by using deterministic methods of evaluation described in a standard (IEEE, 1988, b), while for calculation of predictive measures various probability reliability models can be used.

Evaluation of Software Development and Verification Processes

An evaluation of software development processes is accomplished by examination and analysis of documentation in accordance with the requirements for methods, devices and documentation of development described above (see Figure 4). In this case, one can use special metrics, and the evaluation overall can be carried out and presented by means of radial metric diagrams.

The ratio of the number of software modules (or subsystems), which have been developed using such methods, to the total number of modules (subsystems) can be used as metrics for evaluating the fulfillment of requirements for the use of formal methods.

The quality of software development, fulfillment of requirements for the number of modules, complexity of relations among them can also be evaluated by using special metrics (for example, the Halstead metric, McCabe metric and others (Pressman,1997)).

It should be emphasized that evaluation of the fulfillment of requirements for software by nature is subordinate with respect to evaluation of verification, because these requirements are overall requirements for development and verification, or are checked directly together with evaluation of software verification. This pertains, in particular, to evaluation of the development results themselves, execution of requirements for methods and tools.

Tasks and criteria of software verification evaluation: The quality of conducting verification of software is of great significance for reliability and safety of the I&C system. The tasks of software verification evaluation are: analysis of software requirements based on requirements for the system and general requirements, which are determined by normative documents; check of the conformity of task formulations for software development to these requirements; quality check of the verification plan, test methods and their completeness in accordance with the tasks assigned to the software; the quality check of verification reports and their conformity to plans and methods.

One should note that these tasks, and also the tasks of evaluating the quality of their solution from the standpoint of fulfillment of requirements for safety, are not easy to formalize. Usually the verification analysis is accomplished by traditional methods of documentation analysis, and individual results can be checked by using specially developed tools. At the same time, considering the high criticality and importance of a maximally objective and complete evaluation of software verification, one must find approaches to the development of models that describe this process and allow one to improve its quality.

The process of software verification evaluation of I&C systems that are important for nuclear power plant safety can be constructed by means of (Kharchenko, 2000): formation and structuring of the full set of requirements for software, which must be checked in the verification process at different stages of the lifecycle; development of a system of criteria for evaluating software verification; compilation of a system of verification evaluation criteria and set of requirements established for the software; formalization of the verification analysis processes and its evaluation for basic criteria; creation and use of tools for support of software safety analysis during verification, licensing and expert analysis.

Criteria for verification is similar to the criteria of software evaluation represented above and includes the criteria of completeness, independence, successfulness, documentation and accessibility.

Software verification corresponds to the completeness criteria if during the verification the conformity of software to all requirements of specifications, standards and other normative documents was tested.

Software verification corresponds to the independence criteria in accordance with the software safety class. Thus, for class 2 verification is conducted by a group of specialists (organization), which are administratively and/or financially independent of the specialists (organization), which developed the software.

Software verification corresponds to the criterion of successfulness, if the verification was finished completely prior to placing the system in use, that is by this time all defects found were analyzed and eliminated (or a well-founded decision for their subsequent elimination was made).

Software verification corresponds to the criterion of documentation if a plan and report were issued which describe in detail the course and results of verification. In this case individual parts of a verification plan and report, which have individual significance (programs, test methods, protocols and so forth) can be issued in the form of individual documents.

Software verification corresponds to the accessibility criterion if all of the documentation on software verification was set forth in a form understandable to specialists who do not participate in conducting the development and verification.

Software verification corresponds to the accessibility criterion if all of the documentation on software verification was set forth in a form understandable to specialists who do not participate in conducting the development and verification.

Evaluation of Documents Related to Software Development: During the expert evaluation of documents on software development the requirement specification and design documentation are evaluated. In the expert analysis of the requirement specification the following are established and evaluated: the extent to which software requirements are correct and not contradictory; to what extent the functional requirements for software correspond to requirements for the I&C system; how fully are general requirements for software reflected in the feasibility study (requirements, which are established independently of specific functional purpose of the I&C system).

The evaluation of software requirements is conducted with consideration of: safety class of the I&C system, which includes software is a component; level of software approval; software purpose.

During expert examination of the design documentation one will analyze: description of the composition, structure and functions of component parts of the software; information on methods and means of testing and running experiments with software.

The evaluation of verification documents: The basic verification documents for evaluation are verification plan and verification report.

The software verification plan (SVP) evaluation is conducted based on criteria of documentability, accessibility, completeness, independence.

1. In the evaluation based on documentability criterion one establishes that the SVP was issued prior to the beginning of software verification and defines: choice of verification strategy; sequence of conducting verification; methods and devices used in the verification process; sequence of documentation of verification actions; sequence of verification results evaluation.

2. In the evaluation based on accessibility criterion one establishes that the SVP is set forth in a form understandable for specialists who did not participate in the software development process.

3. Based on the completeness criterion one carries out the evaluation of the following items stipulated in the SVP:

    a. Sequence of conducting verification. In evaluating the sequence of conducting verification one must establish that the verification stipulates after each step of the software development: generation of requirements for software; design; coding.

    b. Completeness of tests. In evaluating the completeness of tests it should be established that the sets of tests that are selected for verification will assure the possibility of checking all stipulated functions and interfaces of the I&C system, and also the check of fulfillment of requirements for software.

    c. Software verification and development tools. In evaluating the tools of software verification and development it should be established that the SVP stipulates the use of automated design and testing tools and indicates the selection criteria for them. One should evaluate the conformity of the proposed criteria to the requirements of norms, rules, standards and recommendations; in particular, when using automated tools to generate code one must check that the given tools have gone through verification with the same requirements as the software itself.

    d. Particular features of the verification of different kinds of software.

4. For an evaluation based on the independence criterion it should be established that in the SVP: for software of I&C system of safety class 2 it is stipulated that verification will be carried out by a group of specialists (organization), who are administratively and/or financially independent of the specialists (organization) that developed the software; for software of I&C system of safety class 3 it is stipulated that the verification will be conducted by specialists who have not participated directly in development of the software (administrative and financial independence is not required), or by software developers on the condition that the review and evaluation of the verification results will be done by independent specialists.

Comments and recommendations made during the expert examination must be considered in the final version of the SVP, which is used in performing the software verification.

Evaluation of the software verification report (SVR) is conducted based on criteria of documentability, accessibility, completeness, independence and successfulness.

1. In the evaluation based on the criterion of accountability one should establish the fulfillment of requirements for the SVR structure, which should contain: lists of input and output signals during software tests; results of tests and their evaluations; deficiencies discovered during tests; conclusions based on results of analysis of the discovered deficiencies and measures to eliminate them, and also to evaluate the degree of detail of the documentation of all stages of the software verification process.

2. In the evaluation based on the criterion of accessibility one should establish that the SVR is set forth in a form that can be understandable for specialists who did not participate in the software verification process.

3. According to the completeness criterion one will evaluate the conformity sequence, strategy and order of conducting verification, methods, tests and software verification tools used that are stipulated in the SVP and actually used (reflected in the SVR).

4. In the evaluation based on the independence criterion one should compare the independence of the specialist (organization) that conducted the verification as stipulated in the SVP and the actual dependence from the specialist (organization) that developed the software.

5. Based on the successfulness criterion one will check correctness of the evaluation of results of each test and establish that all deficiencies discovered in the course of the software verification are recorded, analyzed, eliminated and results of subsequent evaluations are presented.

Tools to Support Evaluation

There are the following classification features for tools: functional purpose of the tool; degree of process automation; number and nomenclature of lifecycle stages and processes, supported by the tool; project components (its components or stages of development, verification or expert examination), supported by the tool; degree of intelligence; possibility of integrating a given tool with other tools.

These features allow classifying of tools as follow.

1. By functional purpose one can distinguish tools for informational, analytical, and organizational support.

2. By degree of process automation tools can be subdivided into manual (partially formalized), automated, and automatic. In determining the type of tool based on this feature one must consider the degree of automation of preparation, input, analysis, documentation and display of information.

3. By the number of supported stages tools are divided into local, compositional, and end-to-end. This feature determines the boundaries and scope of the operation of a tool.

4. By kind of project components one can distinguish tools that support evaluation of: products (requirements, specifications, design components, codes, methods, reports and so forth); processes (specification, design, coding, testing, verification and so forth).

5. By level of intelligence one can distinguish: non-intelligent tools, or traditional kind of tools (without using knowledge-based methods); intelligent tools; and combined tools.

6. According to possibility of integration tools are divided into integratable, which allow one to use a given tool together with other ones, and non-integratable.

By grouping the different (by purpose, level of intelligence and so forth) tools it is possible for carrying out various scenarios of the expert examination, which require use of analytical, information and organizational type tools, intelligent or combined tools and so forth.

Informational tools are intended for the generation, preliminary processing and analysis of information required for carrying out independent verification and expert examination of software and, as a rule, are automated, local or composite tools of non-intelligent or combined type, which support, above all, verification and expert examination of products.

Tools of this kind provide:

1. Generation of a profile-like base of national and international normative documents, which determine the software requirements and order of evaluating their execution during verification and software expert examination.

2. The generation of general and particular normative profiles of software based on an analysis of profile-like documents:

     a.   Software requirements (structure and properties; inspection and diagnostics; reliability and tolerance; development; verification).

     b.   Methods of evaluating the fulfillment of requirements.

     c.   Evaluation of the quality of the process and expert examination results.

3.   The formalized analysis of the general and functional requirements for the software that has been examined by experts based on the submitted documents.

4.   Formalized preparation of data on the expert analyzed software and processes of its development and verification based on templates (questionnaires).

5.   Databases on software expert examination that have been carried out and are being carried out, which include full systematized information on tasks, expert analysis object, course and results of the expert examination.

6.   A transition from verbal to formal description of software requirements (partially formalized verbal matrices, semantic trees, product rules, Z-notations).

7.   Databases of quality metrics and software reliability.

8.   Database of software reliability models.

Results of execution of the informational tools are databases of profile-like documents, metrics, models, expert examinations; normative profiles; standardized plans of the verification and its evaluation; completed templates (questionnaires).

The questionnaires and templates are used to run individual procedures of the expert examination and verification in accordance with chosen methods.

Analytical tools are intended for carrying out direct analysis of software and to evaluate conformity of the verified (expert analyzed) software to established requirements, reliability of verification and expert examination and are automatic local tools that are both intelligent (combined) and nonintelligent, which support primarily verification and expert examination of products.

Analytical tools support:

1.   Verification of normative profiles (completeness, correctness and consistency of the general requirements) of the software designs being developed and analyzed by experts.

2.   Statistical analysis of software.

3.   Dynamic testing of software.

4.   Selection and rating of metrics and reliability measures (quality) of software.

5.   Selection and verification of software reliability models.

6.   Analysis of the fulfillment of general and functional requirements for expert analyzed software.

7.   Analysis of the reliability and safety of software based on standardized methods.

8.   Evaluation of the completeness, reliability and other characteristics of independent verification and expert examination.

Results of running the analytical tools are technical reports on verification of normative profiles; static and dynamic testing of software; selection and rating of metrics, measures and models of software reliability; analysis of the fulfillment of requirements for expert analyzed software; evaluation of characteristics of reliability, completeness and resources for carrying out independent verification and expert examination.

Organizational support tools are intended for planning, organizing and controlling the process of independent verification and expert examination and are automated or manual, local or composite tools of the non-intelligent type, which support verification and expert examination of processes and products.

Tools of this kind use as initial information normative documents; design documentation; data and results of running information and analytical tools.

Organizational support tools provide:

1. Planning of the expert examination (tasks, schedules, resources, personnel).
2. Timely analysis of the course and results of the expert examination.
3. Management of expert analysis process.
4. Documenting the results of the expert examination (partial and summary reports).
5. Analysis and evaluation of the quality of the process for conducting independent verification and expert examination of software.

Results of running the organizational support tools are general planning documents; diagrams of work execution while conducting independent verification and expert examination of software; technical reports on the course, results of independent verification and expert analysis, evaluation of the process of carrying them out; summary reports.

It should be emphasized that at the present time tools of the analytical type have been the most popular for evaluation of software, which support the solution of statistical analysis and software dynamic testing tasks.

SOLUTIONS AND RECOMMENDATIONS

Specific features of software development and usage require proper regulation requirements towards the program components.

At the same time requirement to software should be agreed with requirements to I&C system. Categories of functions performed by I&C system have influence with software requirements, including requirements for composition of the functions, quality, reliability, stability, interaction with other components, procedures and processes.

Therefore developing of requirements for software components shall be done taking into account features of target I&C system, international and national regulatory requirement. For the solution of this issue systematic approach and methods, supported with appropriate tools, are required.

Modern model-based methods and techniques should be applied to assess NPP I&C software, in particular, model-checking (Lahtinen et al., 2010) and invariant-oriented evaluation (Kharchenko (Ed), 2012), software safety analysis techniques (Hui-Wen Huang et al., 2011) etc.

FUTURE RESEARCH DIRECTIONS

To match the latest trends and industry requests software components of I&C systems become more complex. Development of software engineering technologies also opens up new aspects and generates new issues for designing and implementation of software. Therefore possible implications of new programming technologies must be analyzed to ensure timely and adequate adaptation and clarification of regulatory frameworks.

Also attention should be paid to the fact that in large projects of I&C systems several organizations with different background and possibly from different countries can participate. Thus harmonization of requirements and ensure their adequate interpretation may be beyond the common regulatory aspect. In this scope, issues of personnel training, establishment of effective communications between the development teams and the utilities and other become important.

All these issues require systematic study and comprehensive scientific researches.

CONCLUSION

1. Software is a specific object for safety regulation. It is a component of I&C system to which requirements are applicable, and also it is a means of ensuring the satisfaction of regulatory requirements. At the same time software is the most likely sources of common cause failures. Therefore the need to minimize risks of common cause failures is reflected in the requirements to processes of software development and verification, as well as application of diversity.
2. Standardization, evaluation and assurance of software safety should be based on processand-product-approach. I.e. harmonized requirements for the program as a product and the processes related to the creation, evaluation and use of programs at various stages of the lifecycle should be used.
3. Degree of completeness, adequacy and correctness of requirements to software is the determining factor in assessing their compliance, and thus ensure the quality, reliability and safety of both software and I&C system of NPP.
4. Methods that are used for software evaluation should be standardized and cover all aspects of software development and application. If it is necessary, correct application of such methods can be evaluated by experts. From this point of view special significance is acquired by criterion of documentation.

REFERENCES

Adziev, A. V. (1998). Myths about software safety: Lessons of famous disasters. *Open Systems, 6*. Retrieved December 16, 2012, from http://www.osp.ru/os/1998/06/179592/

Aizenberg, A., & Yastrebenetsky, M. (2002). Comparison of safety management principles for control systems of carrier rockets and nuclear power plants. *Space Science and Technology, 1*, 55–60.

Anderson, R. B. (1979). *Proving Programs Correct*. New York: Wiley.

Ben-Ari, M. (2000). *Understanding programming languages*. Wiley.

DSTU-25010. (2016). *Systems and software engineering – Systems and software Quality Requirements and Evaluation - System and software quality models*. Author.

Everett, W., Keene, S., & Nikora, A. (1998). Applying Software Reliability Engineering in the 1990s. *IEEE Transactions on Reliability, 47*(3-SP), 372-378.

Gordieiev Oleksandr & Kharchenko Vyacheslav. (2018). IT-oriented software quality models and evolution of the prevailing characteristics. In *Proceedings of the 9 International Conference Dependable Systems, Services and Technologies - DESSERT'2018*, (pp. 390-395). Kyiv, Ukraine: Academic Press.

Huang, H.-W., Wang, L.-H., Liao, B.-C., Chung, H.-H., & Jiin-Ming, L. (2011). Software safety analysis application of safety-related I&C systems in installation phase. *Progress in Nuclear Energy, 6*(53), 736–741. doi:.2011.04.002 doi:10.1016/j.pnucene

IAEA (2000). IAEA NS-G-1.1. Software for computer based systems important to safety in nuclear power plants.

IEC (2006,a). IEC 60812. *Analysis technique for system reliability – Procedure for Failure Mode and Effects Analysis (FMEA)*.

IEC (2006,b). IEC 60880. *Nuclear power plants – Instrumentation and control systems important to safety – Software aspects for computer-based systems performing category A functions*.

IEC (2006,c). IEC 61025. *Fault tree analysis*.

IEC (2008). IEC 61508. *Functional Safety of Electrical/Electronic/Programmable Electronic Safetyrelated Systems*.

IEEE (1988,a). IEEE 982.1. *Standard Dictionary of Measures to Produce Reliable Software*.

IEEE (1988,b). IEEE. 982.1. *Standard Guide of Measures to Produce Reliable Software*.

IEEE (1990). IEEE 610.12. *Standard Glossary of Software Engineering Terminology*.

ISO/IEC (2010). ISO/IEC 25010. *Systems and software engineering – Systems and software Quality Requirements and Evaluation (SQuaRE) – System and software quality models*.

ISO/IEC (2011). ISO/IEC 25023. *Systems and software engineering – Systems and software Quality Requirements and Evaluation (SQuaRE) – Measurement of system and software product quality*.

Kersken, M. (2001). *Qualification of pre-developed software for safety-critical I&C application in NPP's*. Paper presented at CNRA/CSNI Workshop on Licensing and Operating Experience of Computer-Based I&C Systems, Hluboka-nad-Vltavou, Czech Republic.

Kharchenko, V. S. (Ed.). (2012). CASE-assessment of critical software systems. Quality. Reliability. Safety. Kharkiv, Ukraine: National Aerospace University KhAI.

Kharchenko, V. S., & Vilkomir, S. A. (2000). *The Formalized Models of Software Verification Assessment*. Paper presented at 5th International Conference Probabilistic Safety Assessment and Management, Osaka, Japan.

Lahtinen, J., Valkonen, J., Bjorkman, K., Frits, J., & Niemela, I. (2010). *Model checking methodology for supporting safety critical software development and verification.* Paper presented at ESREL 2010 Annual Conference, Rhodes, Greece.

Lawrence, S., Hatton, L., & Howell, C. (2002). *Solid Software.* Prentice Hall.

Lyu, M. R. (1996). *Handbook of software reliability engineering.* McGraw-Hill Company.

Oleksandr, G., Vyacheslav, K., & Kate, V. (2017). Usable Security Versus Secure Usability: an Assessment of Attributes Interaction. In *Proceedings of the 13th International Conference on ICT in Education, Research and Industrial Applications. Integration, Harmonization and Knowledge Transfer*, (pp.727-740). Kyiv, Ukraine: Academic Press.

Oleksandr, G., Vyacheslav, K., & Mario, F. (2015). Evolution of software quality models: usability, security and greenness issues. In *Proceedings of the 19-th International Conference on Computers (part of CSCC 15),* (pp. 519-523). Zakynthos Island, Greece: Academic Press.

Oleksandr, G., Vyacheslav, K., Nataliia, F., & Vladimir, S. (2014). Evolution of software Quality Models in Context of the Standard ISO 25010. In Proceedings of Dependability on Complex Systems DepCoS – RELCOMEX (DepCOS) (pp. 223-233). Brunow, Poland: Academic Press.

Pressman, R. S. (1997). *Software Engineering: A Practioner's Approach.* McGraw-Hill Company.

Vilkomir, S., & Kharchenko, V. (2000). *An "asymmetric" approach to the assessment of safety-critical software during certification and licensing.* Paper presented at ESCOM-SCOPE 2000 Conference, Munich, Germany.

Vilkomir, S. A., & Kharchenko, V. S. (1999). Methodology of the review of software for safety important systems. In G. I. Schueller, P. Kafka (Eds.), *Safety and Reliability. Proceedings of ESREL'99 - The Tenth European Conference on Safety and Reliability* (pp. 593-596). Munich-Garching, Germany: Academic Press.

KEY TERMS AND DEFINITIONS

Common-Cause Failure (CCF): Failure of two or more structures, systems, or components due to a single specific event or cause.

Common-Mode Failure (CMF): Failure of two or more structures, systems, and components in the same manner or mode due to a single event or cause.

Diversity: Presence of two or more redundant systems or components to perform an identified function, where the different systems or components have different attributes so as to reduce the possibility of common cause failure, including common mode failure.

Fault Tolerance: Is the ability of software to retain a certain functioning level during the onset of software malfunctions.

Fault Tree Analysis (FTA): Deductive technique that starts by hypothesizing and defining failure events and systematically deduces the events or combinations of events that caused the failure events to occur.

Failure Mode, Effects, and Criticality Analysis (FMECA): Is a reliability evaluation/design technique which examines the potential failure modes within a system and its equipment, in order to determine the effects on equipment and system performance.

Off-the-Shelf (OTS) Software Component: Pre-developed software components, usually developed by other organization and designed for specific solutions.

This research was previously published in Cyber Security and Safety of Nuclear Power Plant Instrumentation and Control Systems; pages 97-131, copyright year 2020 by Information Science Reference (an imprint of IGI Global).

Chapter 12
Towards a Conceptual Framework for Security Requirements Work in Agile Software Development

Inger Anne Tøndel

 https://orcid.org/0000-0001-7599-0342

Department of Computer Science, Norwegian University of Science and Technology (NTNU), Trondheim, Norway & SINTEF Digital, Trondheim, Norway

Martin Gilje Jaatun

 https://orcid.org/0000-0001-7127-6694

SINTEF Digital, Oslo, Norway

ABSTRACT

Security requirement work plays a key role in achieving cost-effective and adequate security in a software development project. Knowledge about software companies' experiences of security requirement work is important in order to bridge the observed gap between software security practices and security risks in many projects today. Particularly, such knowledge can help researchers improve on available practices and recommendations. This article uses the results of published empirical studies on security requirement work to create a conceptual framework that shows key concepts related to work context, this work itself and the effects of this work. The resulting framework points to the following research challenges: 1) Identifying and understanding factors important for the effect of security requirements work; 2) Understanding what is the importance of the chosen requirements approach itself, and; 3) Properly taking into account contextual factors, especially factors related to individuals and interactions, in planning and analysis of empirical studies on security requirements work.

DOI: 10.4018/978-1-6684-3702-5.ch012

INTRODUCTION

In today's interconnected world, we would claim that software security is an aspect to consider in most software development projects. Currently, agile development methodologies are prominent in software development. Such methods are used even for large scale development (Dikert, Paasivaara, & Lassenius, 2016) and for security critical and safety critical software (Hanssen, Stålhane, & Myklebust, 2018; Heeager & Nielsen, 2018; Oueslati, Rahman, & ben Othmane, 2015). Thus, good ways of working with security within an agile development paradigm is necessary.

There has been done a lot of work on suggesting ways to deal with software security in agile development projects, including proposals for integrating security into agile methodologies like XP (Aydal, Paige, Chivers, & Brooke, 2006) and Scrum (Pohl & Hof, 2015). In 2009 the Microsoft Security Development Lifecycle (SDL) (Howard & Lipner, 2006; Microsoft, n.d.) was released in a version specific for agile development (Agile SDL) (Microsoft, 2009), and abuser stories have for some time been a suggested way of representing security requirements within agile development (Peeters, 2005). Additionally, there exist method-agnostic approaches to software security that should be possible to integrate with agile development, such as the touchpoints for software security (McGraw, 2004, 2006), the Building Security in Maturity Model (BSIMM) (McGraw, Migues, & West, 2018) and the OWASP Software Assurance Maturity Model (SAMM) (OWASP, n.d.). There thus seems to be no lack of methods for doing software security work also within an agile paradigm. Still, many have observed that security is frequently not given proper attention in software development projects today (Tøndel, Jaatun, Cruzes, & Moe, 2017; Nicolaysen, Sassoon, Line, & Jaatun, 2010; Terpstra, Daneva, & Wang, 2017).

As is well communicated by the abovementioned software security approaches, software security should be an integrated part of development and have a role in the various software development activities, including requirements, design, coding, testing, deployment and operations. Security is not something that can be successfully added on as an afterthought, but should be built into the system from the beginning. This however means that the total number of suggested security activities can be quite overwhelming. It is possible for projects to spend a lot of effort on security, even over-spending, if not properly addressing the security needs. Thus, we consider security requirements work as foundational to achieving cost-effective security in a project.

In this article, we define software security requirements work as activities performed in relation to a software development project to: 1) decide whether and how to identify security needs, risks or requirements for a project; 2) do the requirements elicitation; 3) communicate the identified security needs, risks or requirements, and; 4) integrate these and make priorities related to them in development. By agile development we mean software development that in large part is guided by the Agile principles, as outlined in the Agile Manifesto (Beck et al., 2001), including various methods such as Scrum and XP. Compared to a waterfall development approach, requirements management in agile development is "far more temporal, interactive and just in time" (Leffingwell, 2010). Additionally, the need for requirements prioritization can be considered to be built into the approach; "[w]e admit up front that we can't implement (nor even discover) all potential requirements" (Leffingwell, 2010). Security is only one of the types of requirements a development project needs to consider. When negotiating the three variables cost, schedule and requirements (Leffingwell, 2010), requirements may be modified or dropped altogether.

There exist few empirical studies on how security requirements are handled in software development projects (Terpstra et al., 2017), thus "[h]ow practitioners in the field think about security requirements and how they devise their processes of coping with the issues these requirements pose, is hardly known"

(Terpstra et al., 2017). Empirical studies of software security practices within agile development can help us understand what makes companies and projects adopt (or not adopt) software security practices, how different practices may help, what works well and what is challenging in certain contexts, etc. Such knowledge is important in order to bridge the observed gap between software security practices and software security needs and risks in many projects today. In particular, such knowledge can help researchers improve on existing support provided to agile development projects in terms of available practices and recommendations.

In this article, we aim to improve understanding of security requirements work within an agile development approach. Our study aims to answer the following research questions:

- What factors are found in current empirical research to influence and/or characterize security requirements work in agile projects in an industry setting?
- How do these factors impact the security requirements work and its effect?

We build on published empirical studies that cover security requirements work, emphasizing results from studies performed in an industry setting. The findings from these studies are used to build a conceptual framework that shows important concepts that impact and/or characterize security requirements work, and the relations between these concepts. The conceptual framework is a step towards a comprehensive understanding of security requirements work in agile projects, and can act as a basis for further research on this topic, both in prioritizing which research studies to undertake, and as input to planning and analysis in future empirical studies within this topic.

The remainder of this article is structured as follows. It starts by giving an overview of literature reviews related to security requirements work in agile development and introducing two previously suggested conceptual framework related to this type of work. Then it moves on to explaining the method used to identify empirical sources and construct the conceptual framework. Following the method description, the article introduces the selected studies and the concepts derived from these studies before it presents the resulting conceptual framework. Then it discusses the validity of the conceptual framework and its implications for research. The article ends with a summary of the main conclusions of the article and introduces future work.

RELATED WORK

Since the publication of the Agile Manifesto in 2001 (Beck et al., 2001), many researchers and practitioners have worked on how to include security into agile software development. These discussions started quite early; Systematic Literature Reviews (SLRs) identify papers from the very beginning discussing security in relation to agile development (Saldanha & Zorzo, 2019). One example of such a paper is Beznosov's suggestions from 2003 on how to integrate security and eXtreme Programing (XP) (Beznosov, 2003). Although security in agile development has been a topic of discussion and research since then, and a substantial amount of literature is available on the subject (Bishop & Rowland, 2019), many authors point to the need for more research to better understand and solve the challenges today's software development projects are facing when it comes to security (Bishop & Rowland, 2019; Saldanha & Zorzo, 2019; Villamizar, Kalinowski, Viana & Fernández, 2018).

Lately, several literature reviews have been performed regarding agile software development and security, and even specifically on security requirements in agile development. In this section, we give an overview of these literature reviews and position this article in relation to these reviews. Additionally, this section describes conceptual frameworks that have already been developed related to security requirements in agile development.

Overview of Systematic Literature Reviews

In 2015, Oueslati et al. performed a literature review aimed at identifying "challenges of developing secure software using the agile approach" (Oueslati et al., 2015). Fourteen challenges were identified, and the challenges were categorized into five categories: "Software development life-cycle challenges" concerned security activities not being included in agile methods, and difficulty integrating security in every iteration due to short iteration times. "Incremental development challenges" were related to dealing with frequent changes. "Security assurance challenges" were related to documenting and testing the system in a manner expected for security assurance. "Awareness and collaboration challenges" included neglection of security requirements, lack of experience and security awareness, and challenges separating the developer and reviewer roles. "Security management challenges" concerned how added costs and a lack of incentives resulted in security not being prioritized.

In 2016, Khaim et al. studied what approaches are suggested for software security in agile, the role of the security expert in these approaches, and what kind of challenges emerge when integrating security and agile development (Khaim et al., 2016). They found that half of the studies consider integration of security into agile in a general way, 15% consider integration into Scrum, 23% XP and 12% FDD. In over half (54%) of the papers they studied, the security expert role was not specified, and the impression of Khaim et al. is that those papers that include the security expert role do not do this in a clear way and in a way that ensures involvement throughout development. Khaim et al. identified a long list of challenges, including separating the software developer and security expert roles, security assurance in the case of continuously changing code, documentation needs, refactoring, lack of security experience of developers, tracking security requirements in case of frequent changes, neglecting security requirements, unaware customers, etc.

In 2017, Alsaqaf et al. performed an SLR on quality requirements in large scale agile development in order to identify practices and proposed approaches to cope with quality requirements challenges in large scale distributed agile development (Alsaqaf, Daneva & Wieringa, 2007). Security was considered a type of quality requirement. They found that, despite many available approaches, none of the approaches they identified had been "tried out in real life settings" (Alsaqaf et al., 2017). Challenges were identified related to the techniques available (no widely accepted techniques; inadequacy of the existing techniques; traceability), the priorities made (functionality is prioritized; ignore some types of requirements; validated late; insufficient analysis) and related to the Product Owner (lack of knowledge; workload; availability; dependence). They pointed out that the challenges in large part relate to agile-specific practices and that "some characteristics of agile [requirements engineering] pitched as strengths in agile textbooks (e.g. the role of the product owner, the use of user stories) can be considered in fact as inhibitors to engineering of [quality requirements]" (Terpstra et al., 2017).

In 2019, Bishop and Rowland analyzed literature in order to understand "the effect of security practices on software development agility" (Bishop & Rowland, 2019). Additionally, they provided a taxonomy that can be used to organize and summarize work on software security in agile. They divided papers into two main categories: phase focused and phase independent. The requirements phase was identified as the phase that had received the most research attention. Still, they pointed to a need for more research, and especially empirical research, to extend the current body of knowledge related to software security in agile development.

Additionally, 2018 and 2019 saw the publication of three literature studies that specifically considered security requirements in agile development. Both Saldanha & Zorzo (2019) and Villamizar et al. (2018) performed systematic mapping studies to understand the approaches taken to handle security requirements in agile development projects, and to assess the coverage of current research on this topic. Villamizar et al. found that most approaches are related to Scrum, and that most approaches address specification and elicitation of security requirements. Both studies found that solutions typically involve modifying the agile method or introducing new artefacts or guidelines to handle security. Saldanha & Zorzo however also point to the importance of security training and its possibility to impact the security level of the software. Both systematic mapping studies identify a lack of empirical research, including empirical evaluations of existing approaches to security requirements engineering in agile development. Other research gaps identified include tool support and verification and validation of security requirements (Villamizar et al., 2018). Muneer et al. performed a systematic literature review to compare "modern requirements management techniques with classic techniques for managing Non-Functional require-ments (NFRs) in agile Software Methods", focusing primarily on security requirements as a type of NFR (Muneer, Nadeem & Kasi, 2019). Their review concludes that modern techniques have the potential to overcome some of the method weaknesses identified.

Objective of This Work

The work presented in this article is not an SLR, but a lighter and less comprehensive form of literature review with a goal to complement existing SLRs in this area. Previous SLRs have covered challenges related to security and agile (Oueslati et al., 2015), have identified the approaches covered in research literature (Khaim et al., 2016; Saldanha & Zorzo, 2019; Villamizar et al., 2018; Bishop & Rowland, 2019; Alsaquaf et al., 2017), the weaknesses and strengths of available approaches (Muneer et al., 2019), the effect on agility (Bishop & Rowland, 2019), and the role of the security expert (Khaim et al., 2016). Most SLRs point to the need for more empirical research (Alsaquaf et al., 2017; Bishop & Rowland, 2019; Saldanha & Zorzo, 2019; Villamizar et al., 2018). We are however not aware of any SLR that gives an overview of what we can learn from the empirical research that has already taken place on security requirements work in agile development projects. This article is an attempt to fill this gap.

As a mean to give an overview of what we can learn from existing empirical research on this topic, this article combines previous findings into a conceptual framework. A conceptual framework can be defined as "a network, or 'a plane', of interlinked concepts that together provide a comprehensive understanding of a phenomenon or phenomena" (Jabareen, 2009). It is a product of theorization (Jabareen, 2009) and has particular benefits for designing studies as it "forces you to be selective to decide which variables are most important, which relationships are likely to be most meaningful, and, as a consequence, what information should be collected and analyzed at least at the outset" (Miles & Huberman, 1994). Thus, a conceptual framework based on existing empirical research can be used to guide future empirical re-search on security requirements in agile development, a type of study that is most needed. Conceptual frameworks can be "rudimentary or elaborate, theory-driven or commonsensical, descriptive or causal" (Miles & Huberman, 1994). However, in this article we take the advice from Jabareen (2009) to take an interpretative approach, rather than a causal/analytical approach; stating "[c]onceptual frameworks aim to help us understand phenomena rather than to predict them" (Jabareen, 2009).

Existing Conceptual Frameworks Related to Security Requirements in Agile Development

We are aware of two existing attempts to create conceptual frameworks related to security requirements in agile development. These have a different foundation than the conceptual framework presented in this paper.

Conceptual Framework on Security Requirements as Viewed by Agile Practitioners

Terpstra et al. (2017) conducted a survey of practitioners' postings on social media (LinkedIn) to discover how agile practitioners reason about security requirements and how they cope with this type of requirements. The analysis resulted in the identification of 21 concepts that indicate problems regarding security requirements in agile, and 15 coping strategies. The problems identified are varied, with central themes being the business value of security, the priorities that have to be made, the tendency that security gets lost in the process, and the lack of awareness and knowledge. The analysis additionally resulted in the development of a descriptive conceptual framework from the viewpoint of the development team. This conceptual framework has been redrawn in Figure 1. The boxes in this figure represent conceptual categories defined by Terpstra et al. that map to the figure in the following way:

- **Ownership of security requirements:** Who is responsible for security requirements? Developers? Business representatives/Product owner?
- **Definition of "done" (DoD):** Does the DoD need a revision?
- **Business case:** Is the business case clear on security requirements?
- **Attitude towards security requirements:** Why people do not care? No incentives to do something about these requirements? No understanding of what the requirements mean?
- **Organizational setup:** Is the organizational context conductive to quickly finding the problem?
- **Perceptions of priority:** Are there different perceptions of priority?

The conceptual framework developed by Terpstra et al. describe important influences and challenges with security requirements work in agile. It is however only based on one study.

Conceptual Framework Showing Important Categories When Integrating Security Requirements Into Agile Development

Daneva & Wang (2018) performed a document analysis of seven "well documented agile secure development frameworks put forward by companies or non-profit industry organizations supported by companies." Based on the practices that were part of these documents, they created the conceptual framework depicted in Figure 2. The central overarching category of the framework is "Absorb security requirements", representing that "the development team absorbs the needs and the responsibility for engineering security requirements" (Daneva & Wang, 2018). What this means is represented by the other concepts in the framework:

Figure 1. Conceptual framework developed by Terpstra et al. (2017)

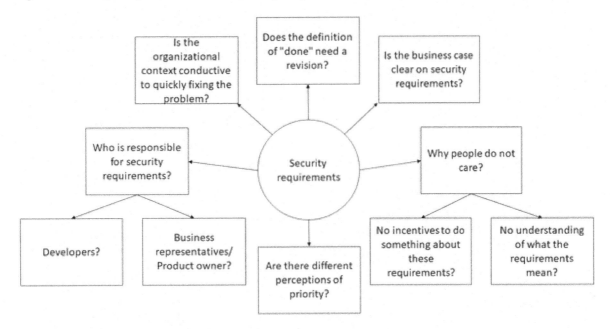

- **Activities:** Introducing security activities (organizational and/or technical);
- **Artefacts:** Examples include abuser stories and risk assessments;
- **Roles:** Organizational or technical roles that could mirror agile specific roles (such as Scrum master or product owner), or adding security expertise to the team;
- **Competencies:** Having necessary competence, e.g. on security testing and secure architecture.

This conceptual framework presents important categories for security requirements work, as documented by key players. It however only describes current practice to the extent that the documented frameworks are used as written in these documents.

RESEARCH METHOD

In order to construct a conceptual framework based on existing empirical studies, we performed a series of phases: identifying published studies to use as a basis for the framework, analyzing the published results of these studies to identify central concepts related to security requirements work, and synthesize these concepts into a conceptual framework. In the following we describe each of these phases in more detail. An overview of our approach is given Figure 3. As can be seen from this figure, our approach was cyclical. In all we did three iterations of this cycle.

Figure 2. Conceptual framework developed by Daneva and Wang (2018)

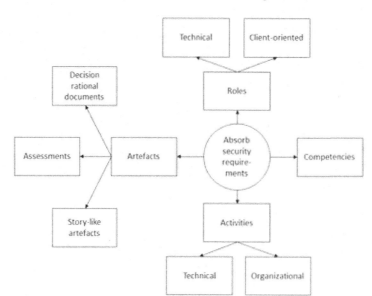

Figure 3. Method for constructing the conceptual framework

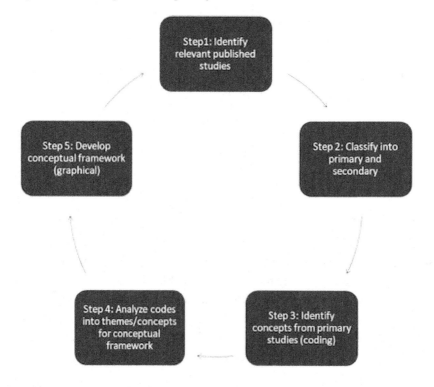

Identify Studies (Step 1)

Our goal in this step was to identify empirical studies covering aspects of security requirements work in agile development. We were primarily interested in studies performed in industry settings. We did not aim for an SLR. Instead we used the following strategy to identify relevant studies: 1) identify relevant and recent SLRs and use them to find relevant papers, and; 2) supplement references from SLRs with searches on Google Scholar for more recent studies. We did this in three rounds and over a period of three years. The first round used the SLRs of Khaim et al. (2016) and Oueslati et al. (2015), in addition to searches on Google Scholar to identify more recent studies that were not covered by the published SLRs. We deliberately searched for empirical studies covering software security in agile, and not specifically security requirements work, because we use this term in a broader sense than eliciting and documenting security requirements. The second round used the SLR of Alsaqaf et al. (2017) as well as additional searches on Google Scholar. The third round used the SLRs of Bishop and Rowland (2019), Saldanha and Zorzo (2019), Villamizar et al. (2019) and Muneer et al. (2019).

We selected this lightweight approach to identifying empirical studies for two reasons: 1) we did not believe it necessary to repeat the identification of relevant publications already performed by other researchers, and 2) we did not have the goal to collect all relevant empirical evidence, but rather sufficient evidence to create a first version of a conceptual framework that could later be extended as new evidence is published.

The searching for and screening of literature was done by one researcher, and was done based on title and abstract. For the studies that seemed to fit the inclusion criteria (empirical studies of security requirements work in agile development), we further inspected the methods and results sections to determine if they were relevant for this study. In the end, we ended up with the papers listed in Table 1.

Analyze Study Results (Step 2 and Step 3)

Our approach was inspired by Jabareen (2009), who proposed a method called conceptual framework analysis particularly suited for multidisciplinary phenomena. Jabareen's method is based on the grounded theory model, and consists of seven phases: 1) "Mapping the selected data sources", 2) "Extensive reading and categorizing of the selected data", 3) "Identifying and naming concepts", 4) "Deconstructing and categorizing the concepts", 5) "Integrating concepts, 6) "Synthesis, resynthesis, and making it all make sense" and 7) "Validating the conceptual framework" (Jabareen, 2009). We did not follow this method in detail, as we are not aiming for a multidisciplinary framework with as extensive sources as is recommended by Jabareen. Instead we used aspects of this method adjusted to our needs. In particular, we took the advice to read and reread sources, and to categorize them based on importance (Jabareen, 2009) and relevance (Maxwell, 2013). All the included studies (Table 1) were divided into two categories: primary studies and secondary studies. The first category consists of studies where security requirements work is a main part of the topic studied, the study is done in an industry setting and with adequate research method (including adequate method description). Secondary studies are studies with results that could be relevant for security requirements work, but where security requirements is only a minor part of the overall study or where the study is not adequately described, has obvious methodological limitations or is performed in a student setting. Only the primary studies were used to identify concepts, while results from the secondary studies were used where relevant to better understand and to validate/contradict the findings in the primary studies. Concepts were identified by reading the results and discussion part of the primary studies in detail, identifying any results related to security requirements work, and adding codes to these results.

Table 1. Overview of included papers and which SLRs that also include them

Identified Paper	Oueslati et al. (2015)	Khaim et al. (2016)	Alsaquaf et al. (2017)	Bishop & Rowland (2019)	Saldanha & Zorzo (2019)	Villamizar et al. (2019	Muneer et al. (2019
Adelyar & Norta (2016)				x			
Aydal et al. (2016)		x					
Baca & Carlsson (2011)				x	x		
Baca et al. (2015)		x			x		
Bartsch (, 2011)	x			x	x		x
Bellomo & Woody (2012)	x						
Fitzgerald et al. (2013)					x		
Ghani et al. (2014)				x	x	x	
Kongsli (2006)	x	x		x		x	
Nicolaysen et al. (2010)							
Pohl & Hof (2015)		x					
Poller et al. (2017)				x			
Rajba (2018)				x			
Renatus et al. (2015)							
Rindell et al. (2016)					x		x
Sachdeva & Chung (2017)				x		x	x
Savola et al. (2012)		x					
Terpstra et al. (2017)	ʼ			x	x		x
Tøndel et al. (2017)							
van der Heijden et al., 2018				x			
Williams et al. (2009)							
Williams et al. (2010)					x		

Synthesize (Step 4 and Step 5)

The method used for constructing a conceptual framework builds on the practical advice of Miles and Huberman (1994). To cite Miles and Huberman, "[s]etting out bins, naming them, and getting clearer about their interrelationships lead you to a conceptual framework." (Miles & Huberman, 1994). According to Miles and Huberman, conceptual frameworks are best done graphically, one should expect to do several iterations, and they suggest using prior theorizing and empirical research as important inputs.

Additionally, they recommend that one should avoid the non-risk framework with only global level variables and "two-directional arrows everywhere" (Miles & Huberman, 1994).

As will be seen from the following section, we made tables of concepts from the primary sources, as suggested by Jabareen. In making these tables we integrated and synthesized concepts, as suggested by Jabreen, in an iterative manner. Using Mind Manager, initial concepts identified from the primary studies were grouped into overall concepts. This was done first for the different study types identified, and then we combined concepts from the different study types into a modified and combined table of concepts that we used to create the conceptual framework. In creating the graphical conceptual framework, we looked again to the primary studies to identify what relations between the concepts were visible in those studies.

CONCEPTS FROM EMPIRICAL STUDIES

In the following, we give an overview of the identified primary studies and the concepts identified from these studies. An overview of the primary studies can be found in Table 2, while an overview of secondary studies can be found in Table 3. We start with presenting studies that cover software security in agile development in a broader sense, and then move on to studies of specific techniques relevant for software security work. The study by Terpstra et al. (2017), although it could be considered part of the first study category, is described in a separate section. This is because Terpstra et al. provide a conceptual framework based on their findings, thus concepts from this study have already been identified.

Table 2. Overview of primary studies

Reference	Study Goal	Study Method
Adelyar & Norta (2016)	Identify challenges in the customer and developer practices	Interviews, 4 teams, team manager and 2-3 developers from each team
Baca et al. (2015)	Evaluate SEAP (more security resources in the team; incremental risk analysis)	Action research, one project, four versions, 8 development teams
Bartsch (2011)	Understand challenges and mitigations in security-critical agile development	Interviews (10 interviewees from 9 companies)
Nicolaysen et al. (2010) (interview part)	Understand whether software security was a specific concern in agile development	Six interviews with software developers
Poller et al. (2017)	Impact of external audit and training	Questionnaires, observations, document studies, interviews (15); 13 months
Terpstra et al. (2017)	Discover how agile practitioners reason about security requirements and how they cope with this type of requirements	Postings on LinkedIn, two discussion threads
Tøndel et al. (2017)	Identify risk-centric practices in software security	Interviews; 23 organizations
van der Heijden et al. (2018)	Identify security challenges in large-scale agile development	Interviews (ten interviews from five teams) in a financial organization
Williams et al. (2010)	Effect of using Protection Poker (a technique for security risk estimation)	Case study (observations, survey) in one team, 3 months

Table 3. Overview of secondary studies

Secondary Study	Reason for not Including as Primary Study
Aydal et al. (2016)	Lack of information about research method
Baca & Carlsson (2011)	Security requirements is not a main focus
Bellomo & Woody (2012)	Security requirements is not a main focus; Some information on research method is lacking
Fitzgerald et al. (2013)	Limited focus on security requirements work
Ghani et al. (2014)	Lack of information about research method
Kongsli (2006)	Experience report
Nicolaysen et al. (2010) (case study part)	Case study in research project and with unclear research method
Pohl & Hof (2015)	Evaluation with students; weak research method
Rajba (2018)	Lack of information about research method
Renatus et al. (2015)	Security requirements is not a main focus; unclear research method
Rindell et al. (2016)	Security requirements is not a main focus
Savola et al. (2012)	Limited focus on security requirements work
Sachdeva & Chung (2017)	Lack of information about research method
Williams et al. (2009)	Evaluations with students

Studies That Provide an Overview of Security Requirements Work and Challenges

Six of the primary studies concern software security in agile development in a general sense, not tied to any particular security technique and not limited to security requirements work. Five of these studies use interviews as the mean of data collection. Adelyar and Norta performed interviews with 3-4 representatives from four teams, with the goal to identify security challenges in agile practices (Adelyar & Norta, 2016). Bartsch performed ten interviews with participants from nine companies, with the goal to "expand on the theoretical findings on security-critical agile development through an exploration of the challenges and their mitigations in typical agile development projects" (Bartsch, 2011). In the interviews, they focused on the following topics: "Customer involvement", "Developer security awareness and expertise", "Effects of 'agile' on security", "Security practices" and "Authorization". van der Heijden et al. performed ten interviews with varying roles in five teams, to understand challenges in large-scale agile development (van der Heijden, Broasca & Serebrenic, 2018). Nicolaysen et al. (2010) performed six interviews with software developers from different companies who were using agile methodologies. The goal of the interviews was to understand whether software security was a specific concern in agile software development. Tøndel et al. (2017) performed interviews with representatives from 23 different public organizations related to their software security practices and challenges. The goal of the study was to understand how current software organizations can work with security in a risk-centric way, and it included both people in development teams and people in information security positions in the organizations. The organizations mainly used some type of agile development practices. The study by Poller et al. is a case study using a broader set of data collection methods (Poller, Kocksch, Türpe, Epp & Kinder-Kurlanda, 2017). Poller et al. followed a product group over 13 months, starting shortly after an external security audit, and they aimed to explore how the development group's work routines were affected by this external security audit and training.

Table 4 gives an overview of the main concepts identified from these studies. In the following we introduce the main findings from these studies in more detail.

Adelyar and Norta (2016): Challenges With Agile Practices

Adelyar and Norta identified several agile practices that posed challenges to important security principles. Frequent changes in software, different developer pairs involved, and unclear and inconsistent requirements and priorities from the customer were found to pose challenges on security, because they limited the possibility for having a system-wide view of the software, a simple design and having an ongoing development attention on security. Additionally, it made it challenging to maintain limitation of privileges and separation of privileges.

Bartsch (2011): Effects of Agile Development on Security

Bartsch found that the individuals and their relationships are highly important when it comes to security, including whether and to what extent security requirements are identified. The role of customers and developers was explored. For customers, Bartsch found that security awareness among customers was heterogenous. Half of the interviewees talked about problems that stemmed from a lack of security awareness with customers. On the other hand, one interviewee explained about a project where "the customer was very security-aware and developed very specific security requirements because the developers were rather unaware" (Bartsch, 2011). The trust relationship between the customer and the development team impacts security. Often, customers can "only state unclear security requirements leading to implicit security requirements" (Bartsch, 2011) and customers may lack the necessary technical expertise to understand the basis for the security measures. Thus, customers usually assume that developers take appropriate measures to ensure adequate quality. However, a majority of the interviewees mention that "irrespective of the customer's security awareness, close customer participation improves the security requirements elicitation with their domain knowledge" (Bartsch, 2011). For developers, their individual interest in and sense of responsibility for security is important as security awareness is generally built in an informal way; security knowledge is spread as part of informal discussions and is often self-taught from news sources and blogs.

Bartsch found that the agile development approach has benefits when it comes to security, despite some well-known challenges (e.g. "neglected assurance practices from the pressure of short iterations" (Bartsch, 2011)). Agile practices can bring on a simpler software design and a more holistic development approach for the individual developer. Bartsch found that this could lead developers to feel responsible for the project, and thus increase their motivation regarding security. Compared to pre-agile development, interviewees stated that "improved communication among developers and quality assurance helped" (Bartsch, 2011) in addition to external audits and intra-company competition on quality.

In general, security requirements are refined over several iterations. Bartsch explains that in one project the authorization requirements were complicated and difficult to elicit bottom up, thus a simpler top down model was implemented that then had to be refined and adapted in production. In another project, functional changes repeatedly required security to be discussed.

Van der Heijden et al. (2018): Challenges in Large-Scale Agile Development

Of the challenges that van der Heijden et al. (2018) identified in their study, they were particularly concerned with which challenges were specific for large-scale agile development. These were "alignment of security in a distributed setting", "developing a common understanding of roles and responsibilities", and "integration of low-overhead security testing tools". In addition, the study identified challenges that had been identified previously in the study performed by Bartsch (2011), and thus was considered to be challenges also in smaller-scale agile: "implementing low-overhead security documentation", "spreading security awareness and expertise in the team", "formulating clear security requirements", and "fostering Product Owner commitment to security".

Table 4. Overview of concepts from the studies of agile software security overall

Concept	Relevant Findings
Priorities (functionality vs. security)	• Functional requirements get prioritized over software security (Nicolaysen et al., 2010; Tøndel et al., 2017)
Project constraints	• Management commits to fixed time and budget, resulting in few resources spent on security (van der Heijden et al., 2018)
Business case for security	• As security was not considered a feature, it was not part of feature requests (that is, not part of expected deliveries and current priorities) (Poller et al., 2017) • Security not seen as part of working software – it costs extra time and money without providing functionality (van der Heijden et al., 2018)
Pressure (time and other tasks)	• Short iterations lead to pressure, which can lead to problems integrating security activities (Bartsch, 2011) • Security gets lost in daily work due to time-pressure and other tasks that need to be finished (Poller et al., 2017)
Customers and customer relations	• Customers' security awareness and priorities is heterogeneous and it impacts software security in the projects (Bartsch, 2011; Nicolaysen et al., 2010) • The trust relationship with customers impacts software security, as non-technical customers have a hard time comprehending security in a technical way and often trust developers to just handle this (Bartsch, 2011) • Vendors are trusted to take care of security (Tøndel et al., 2017) • Customers (Bartsch, 2011) and Product Owners (van der Heijden et al., 2018) contribute to security with their domain knowledge, even if their security awareness is low. Close involvement of the customer/Product Owner is thus recommended. • There are "unclear privileges and responsibilities between customers and developers" (Adelyar and Norta, 2016)
Individuals and their security posture and competence	• "The overall security in a project depends on the security expertise of the individuals, either on the customer or developer side" (Bartsch, 2011) • Architects have a potentially important role, but this is dependent on their personal initiative and interest in security. In practice, few software architects seem to have security as a main interest (Tøndel et al., 2017) • Product Owners are "often not aware enough of the added business value for performing certain security actions" (van der Heijden et al., 2018). • Developers lack intrinsic motivation for security (Poller et al., 2017) • (Lack of) software security competence impacts software security (Nicolaysen et al., 2010) • Perceived threats, in particularly related to reputation (Nicolaysen et al., 2010) and concrete threats expressed in monetary terms (Bartsch, 2011), increase security awareness. However, this increased concern for security does not necessarily lead to a commitment to software security (Nicolaysen et al., 2010). • Much of developers' security expertise is self-taught and come from news and blogs. Developers are motivated to learn security due to a feeling of responsibility for the project with a holistic development approach. (Bartsch, 2011) • There are wide variations in security awareness. Training is important (van der Heijden et al., 2018). • Organizations lack a structured approach for software security training (Tøndel et al., 2017; Baca et al., 2015; Terpstra et al., 2017) • There is a high turnover in development teams, particularly due to inclusion of external consultants. These consultants do as they are asked to, thus if they are not asked to consider security they will not pay attention to it (van der Heijden et al., 2018).
Responsibility	• The responsibility for identifying and deciding on security requirements for the development projects seems fragmented - no one fights for software security (Tøndel et al., 2017) • Accountability for security actions is unclear (van der Heijden et al., 2018)
Preferred security strategy	• Other ways to secure the system (e.g. infrastructure security) reduces the perceived need for software security (Nicolaysen et al., 2010).

continues on following page

Table 4. Continued

Concept	Relevant Findings
Legislation, audit	• Legal requirements are a key driver for performing risk analysis (Tøndel et al., 2017) • Privacy legislation can make it difficult to work according to agile principles (Nicolaysen et al., 2010) • External audits can increase security motivation of developers (Bartsch, 2011; Poller et al., 2017)
Communication	• Improved communication among developers and quality assurance impacts security motivation of developers (Bartsch, 2011) • Intra-company competition can impact security motivation of developers (Bartsch, 2011) • Developers may hold incorrect assumptions about managers' security priorities when these are not made explicit (Poller et al., 2017) • Security awareness and expertise spreads between developers in informal discussions (Bartsch, 2011) • Important decisions are made in sprint meetings, and security people are not present in these meetings (Tøndel et al., 2017) • Security people are sometimes involved, but seem to be passive, either waiting to be invited or participating in the beginning and then leaving the project to fend for itself (Tøndel et al., 2017) • Silo structure - security and legal competence in the organizations does not necessarily benefit development (Tøndel et al., 2017) • There is tension between different groups, e.g. between architects and legal/security experts. Hard to make compromises. (Tøndel et al., 2017) There is a lack of understanding between information security officers and the development team; feels like "chasing different goals" (van der Heijden et al., 2018). • Lack of documentation makes communication between the team and the security officer ineffective (van der Heijden et al., 2018) • Security-related information should be easily available to the team (van der Heijden et al., 2018) • Close involvement with a Security Officer is beneficial for teams, especially since this increases acceptance of security (understand why) (van der Heijden et al., 2018)
Development approach	• A holistic development approach can lead to a more complete picture of the system for developers, and can impact developers' sense of responsibility for security. A more complete picture of the system can additionally, together with iterative and incremental development, lead to improved and simpler design (Bartsch, 2011). • Team autonomy can make it more difficult for managers to prescribe security activities (Poller et al., 2017) • Frequent changes in software requirements cause repetition of work, pressure on developers, more complex designs, illogical sequences of integration. This impacts the attention developers give to security, and make it hard to keep a system-wide view and demonstrate that the important threats have been identified and mitigated (Adelvar and Norta, 2016).
Representation of security requirements	• Security requirements can be implicit or explicit. Customers can often only state implicit and unclear security requirements (Bartsch, 2011). • Security was considered a matter of quality, and developers were expected to deal with quality matters without these being explicit and visible (Poller et al., 2017) • Developers often derive security requirements from functional requirements. Some document them as part of Definition of Done (DoD) to make the security requirements explicit (Bartsch, 2011). • Having a formal security requirements process can be considered too theoretical and bureaucratic (Poller et al., 2017) • It is unclear what it means to "properly take care of security concerns", e.g. what the documentation requirements are (van der Heijden et al., 2018) • The security requirements formulated by security management were considered too technical, but also ambiguous. From the security side there is the desire to keep the requirements generic (van der Heijden et al., 2018).
Iterative process	• Security requirements are usually refined over several discussions and iterations. Functional changes as well as the complexity of security requirements can impact the need for refinement and iterations on the security requirements (Bartsch, 2011).

Table 5. Overview of concepts from the studies of security requirements techniques

Concept	Relevant Findings
Incremental security analysis in the team	• An incremental risk analysis process improves identification and handling of risk. Security issues are solved in the team (distributed, not centralized), more detailed analysis is performed, more severe risks are identified and more risks are corrected. This leads to more cost-effective risk management. (Baca et al., 2015)
Security resources in team	• With security resources in the project it is possible to work distributed and solve issues in the team (Baca et al., 2015).
Security discussions in the team	• Using a technique for discussing security implications of functional requirements in the full team leads to improvements in software security as it results in improved spread of security knowledge and improved security skills (e.g. skills to think like an attacker), in addition to leading to identification of security needs in the project in form of security requirements, training needs and security activities (Williams et al., 2009).

Nicolaysen et al. (2010): Software Security as a Concern in Agile Development

Nicolaysen et al. found that many factors negatively impact how the need for software security is perceived and prioritized. In general functionality is given priority. About half of the customers express some security concerns, but customers' influence on security is not necessarily positive. They give an example of this; one customer "thwarted a security solution [...] because they did not like it" (Nicolaysen et al., 2010). The studied companies have a lack of security competence, few state that they have experienced any security breaches, and in general security protection is achieved through the infrastructure (e.g. firewalls). Reputation damage is something that worries the interviewees, but the worry is not enough to commit to increased security efforts. Nicolaysen et al. state that that "[n]one of the companies had found or created any fully developed technique for integrating software security into agile software development" (Nicolaysen et al., 2010).

Tøndel et al. (2017): Risk Centric Software Security Practices

Tøndel et al. found that practices in the studied organizations were not risk based, although the organizations performed some activities that could be said to be part of a risk-based approach to security. Legal requirements were found to be an important driver for software security activities and requirements.

Responsibility for software security was fragmented in many of the studied organizations. In particular it seemed unclear where the responsibilities of security people in the organization end and where the responsibility of the development organization starts when it comes to software security. Although the organizations might have security experts in-house, this expertise did not necessarily benefit the security work in the development projects, due to the silo structure of the organizations. People working on security or other non-functional requirements did not necessarily have a place at the table when important decisions on security were made in the projects. In many projects, involvement of security expertise was considered challenging because development was done by external vendors. The organizations offered limited formal training on software security. Software architects were pointed out as potential allies in the software security work, but with the challenge that few architects were considered to be particularly interested in security. As a result, it seemed arbitrary whether or not security was considered for the projects. In general, functionality was often prioritized over security.

Poller et al. (2017): Effects of External Security Audits on Organizational Change in Relation to Software Security

Poller et al. (2017) found that software security was considered a quality aspect among other quality aspects, and that in the studied company developers were thus expected to deal with security (as with other quality aspects) without this being made explicit and visible. This was considered by Poller et al. as a main reason for software security work not being established in the company. For developers, the feature requests represented expected deliveries, and as security was not considered a feature it was not on the feature request list. This resulted in security being perceived as not important by some developers. There was a perception that managers "would see security as being in a resource conflict with feature development" (Poller et al., 2017). The study however found that managers did not seem opposed to security, but rather that security "had not yet come to their specific attention" (Poller et al., 2017), and that it was considered a quality matter that developers were trusted to deal with as a technical issue. Additionally, security lacked visibility in the team and the developers in general lacked intrinsic motivation for security; their motivation was to "put something together and seeing it work" (Poller et al., 2017).

The study identified challenges with having autonomous and self-organizing teams in that managers had limited means of prescribing security activities. Instead they had to rely on less direct approaches, e.g. indicators or training. Developers, on the other hand, found that security got "lost in the daily work since we always have time-pressure, the release needs to be finished, tests need to be done" (Poller et al., 2017), thus they did not find time to really go deep on security. Additionally, lack of resources was considered one reason.

There was an attempt by security experts to establish a formal security requirements elicitation process, but this met resistance from managers and developers because it was considered theoretical and bureaucratic, and they were not convinced it would improve security.

Related Findings From Secondary Studies

Baca and Carlsson (2011) used interviews to evaluate the cost and benefit of the Microsoft SDL, the Cigital Touchpoints and Common Criteria for agile development. They found that none of these approaches were a good match with agile development because of high cost and a lack of benefits. However, the activity of writing security requirements was endorsed, as developers believed it could help identify easy gains and help guide the project. Aydal et al. (2006) demonstrated that software security can be integrated with XP practices. In their study, security requirements were introduced rather late in the process and they found that this could lead to many changes in the system. They suggested using the Planning Game to establish security requirements within iterative and incremental development.

There is some evidence in the study of Savola, Frühwirth & Pietikäinen (2012) that indicate that regulations in a domain can impact the work on security requirements. In their study on metrics they found that "the practitioners emphasized compliance (with legal and industry regulations, customers' needs and organizational policies), whereas 80% of researchers emphasized the metrics' ability to offer a high-level overview of security" (Savola et al., 2012). Rindell, Hyrynsalmi & Leppänen (2016) report on using Scrum for a regulated project with positive results. In the studied project, security was however to some extent viewed as being on the side of the project (implemented in side tracks to the main sprint cycle) and much of the extra security related work was documentation related.

Rajba (2018) presents a journey of one company in improving their security processes. Challenges identified in the beginning of this journey included complex security checklists that were considered too technical and not relevant, people being more interested in passing security reviews than making more secure applications, challenges in scoping the security work so as to not having to undertake too much at once, repetitive tasks, and a lack of documentation, security requirements and knowledge. Many of these challenges were addressed with improvements in training and security checklists, provision of templates, tool support, and improved use of an internal security review team.

Nicolaysen et al. (2010), in addition to reporting on interviews (as described above), report on a case study of a research project. Due to the domain (healthcare), security was initially given attention in the studied project. In the end, however, the resulting product had many security concerns (vulnerable to seven out of the OWASP top 10 issues), and they found that "only the functional results of the security design made it out of the backlog [...] leaving most non-functional security aspects alone in the dark" (Nicolaysen et al., 2010). Nicolaysen et al. point to some reasons for this, mainly a lack of continuity in the security experts assigned to the project, resulting in delays. Thus, the security design was not completed as planned and implementation started before security had been properly considered. Communication problems is also mentioned, although Nicolaysen et al. is not concrete on what kind of communication problems there were and how they influenced development.

Studies of Specific Techniques

Though there are several suggested techniques for identifying and working with security requirements in agile development, few of these techniques have been studied and evaluated in an industrial environment. Two of the primary studies we identified study specific techniques related to software security requirements work. Baca et al. performed an action research study at Ericsson, where they studied the effects of implementing a security-enhanced agile software development process (SEAP) (Baca, Boldt, Carlsson & Jacobsson, 2015). This process includes several software security activities (e.g. code review, penetration testing), but the study reported focused on two key aspects of SEAP: adding more security resources in the project and the development teams, and performing incremental risk analysis. The study of SEAP included one product with 88 staff members distributed among 8 development teams. Four versions of the product were considered, of which the three latest versions were developed using SEAP. Effort and identification and treatment of risk was compared between versions.

Williams et al. proposed Protection Poker (Williams, Meneely & Gegick, 2010), which is a technique for security risk estimation of requirements, as well as for security awareness building and exchange of security information in the team. The technique is particularly suited for agile teams, and Protection Poker is intended to be played in the planning meeting of every development iteration. The effects of using Protection Poker were studied in a case study including one maintenance team at Red Hat. The team had eleven participants (seven developers, three testers and one manager), and used Scrum as their development methodology. The team studied had no security expert, and the knowledge of software security varied among team members; some very knowledgeable, some relatively new to software security. The study lasted for three months with five Protection Poker sessions in total. Data collection was done using observation and a short survey.

Neither SEAP nor Protection Poker is specifically about security requirements. However, performing incremental risk analysis and doing security risk estimation could be considered part of security requirements work as defined in this paper. Table 5 gives an overview of the main concepts identified from these two studies. In addition to the findings from the studies of the techniques themselves that are used as a basis for this table, an underlying assumption is that the technique itself is a factor that impacts security requirements work. In the following we explain the results of the two studies in more detail.

Baca et al. (2015): The Effect of Added Security Resources and a Distributed and Incremental Approach to Risk Assessment in an Agile Development Project

In their study, the introduction of SEAP was found to improve identification and handling of risk, and because of this, the risk management was found to be more cost-efficient than with the approach previously used by Ericsson.

Three aspects are however important to note related to this study. First, the process for risk analysis used is not explained in detail. In the study, the risk analysis of four software versions of the same product is compared, where v1.0 was developed using the traditional Ericsson approach, and v2.0 - 4.0 were developed using SEAP. With the traditional approach, risk analysis was performed once a year (per release) and involved six to eight persons for a day. With SEAP, the frequency of risk analysis was 30-40 per year, involving three to four persons for an hour each time. The scope of risk analysis with SEAP is much smaller than with the traditional approach. Another main difference between SEAP and the traditional approach is the security resources involved in the analysis and in the project in general. Traditionally the risk analysis was led by the security manager, and this role was not directly involved in the development. With SEAP, more security resources are added to the project (the equivalent of four full time positions), and one of these roles (the security master) is assigned to two or three teams (25% per team). Available time apart from security work is spent as a regular developer. The security master leads the risk analysis work. Based on the description of the risk assessment process in SEAP we thus know that the frequency is increased, the scope for each analysis is reduced, and the approach is more distributed.

Second, the reason for the identified improvement is not discussed in detail in the paper. The authors claim that a main reason for the improvement is that security issues are dealt with in a more distributed fashion, and thus more issues are solved directly by the team. Though not discussed in the paper, it should also be expected that when security resources are added to the team, the security people are more likely to understand the product and thus their analysis is likely to improve. However, there are alternative explanations that are not discussed by the authors. One example of a factor that may have influenced the results is related to the study design and its use of comparison. The traditional approach was used for v1.0, and SEAP for later versions. The ability to identify more high risks with SEAP may be due to the method, but may also be because v2.0 and up contain more risky features. This, and other alternative explanations, are not discussed by the authors.

Third, the product developed in the study was related to online money transfer and was thus considered to be security-critical. This allowed investing in the additional security resources required by SEAP. Thus, we do not know whether or not the resources needed for SEAP can be justified for projects that are less security-critical.

Williams et al. (2010): Risk Estimation Using Protection Poker

Williams et al. found that a main effect of using Protection Poker in this case study was that software security knowledge was spread among team members, and key risks were discussed; "[d]uring Protection Poker sessions, all team members participated in the conversation - some asking questions, some sharing their software security expertise, all becoming incrementally better at thinking like an attacker with each Protection Poker session" (Williams et al., 2010). The playing of Protection Poker led to revisions of two requirements for added security, resulted in a request for education on cross-site scripting, identified the need for more security testing, etc. It was found that Protection Poker supported participation from all team members, also those with passive, quiet personalities. Note however, that we cannot say from this study whether similar results could have been achieved with another technique.

Related Findings From Secondary Studies

Protection Poker has also been studied in a trial with 50 advanced undergraduate students taking a software engineering course (Williams, Gegick & Meneely, 2009). In that study, it was found that Protection Poker resulted in more discussion and learning about software security compared to previous semesters where Protection Poker was not used. In the discussions, general lessons about security surfaced fast, e.g. discussions on input validations, common exploits, etc.

Kongsli (2006) reports on experiences with using misuse stories and automatic testing of security in the development of web applications, and points to similar benefits as Baca et al. (2015) and Williams et al. (2010) although using a different technique (misuse stories). Reported benefits include increased security awareness in the development team and team ownership of security issues. Additionally, Kongsli reports that when security is sufficiently broken down (in terms of misuse stories) it is easier to relate to and handle by developers, though with the risk of misuse story incompleteness as security concerns not directly related to a user story can be overlooked. This risk is not pointed out by Baca et al. (2015) and Williams et al. (2010). Kongsli also points out that the need for a security specialist on the team is not completely eliminated with the used security techniques.

Ghani, Azham and Jeong (2014) suggest adding the Security Backlog and the role of a Security Master to Scrum, and evaluate how this impacts agility. Results are positive, in that agility is actually found to slightly improve. This may be due to adding more security expertise and workforce.

Renatus, Teichmann and Eichler (2015) suggested a method for threat assessment in line with agile principles and a method for evaluating agility of methods, and the method itself was evaluated in one SME. Central to the method they suggested was a split between the tasks of developers without in-depth security expertise and the security curator. Security curators got the task of pre-modeling the features soon to be implemented, while the developers were tasked with figuring out how to implement the controls (Renatus et al., 2015). This is in line with SEAP and Protection Poker when it comes to an incremental approach to development but represents a slightly different approach to dealing with the need for security expertise. Renatus et al. report that it was seen as a valuable approach by the SME.

The positive effect of incremental security analysis is supported by findings from Fitzgerald, O'Sullivan & O'Brien (2013) who found that continuous compliance activities and transparency of project status facilitate risk mitigation. In particular they point to benefits of risk prioritization, as tackling the most significant risks first can improve risk mitigation. Bellomo & Woody (2012) report on an interview study among agile program managers and Accreditation Reviewers at the Department of Defense (DoD), mainly concerning high risk software where accreditation is necessary. Bellomo and Woody underline the importance to support prioritisation of security requirements and the need for security expertise being available to the team. Additionally, they advocate a risk-based incremental approach to security feature design and development, as this can mitigate the temptation to "focus on delivering the low hanging fruits first (the easy stuff) and ignore developing the more complex, high risk capabilities" (Bellomo & Woody, 2012). Bellomo and Woody additionally found that enforced use of a security impact assessment field in the backlog increases the likelihood that security risks are continuously assessed.

Sachdeva & Chung (2017) report on a case study of two software projects, one in which security and performance requirements were handled implicitly and as an afterthought, and one in which they were identified and addressed early and added to the backlog. They found clear benefits of the latter approach. Thus, though other studies point to benefits of incremental analysis, this study point to the importance of early inclusion of security.

Pohl and Hof (2015) suggested Secure Scrum; a way to integrate security into development without changing the underlying Scrum process. Their evaluation of Secure Scrum comes with its weaknesses; relying on small student projects that lasted only a week. Bearing this in mind, the results from this study are relevant as they point to effects of having a security technique. Pohl and Hof found that security was not taken care of by the student developers that did not use Secure Scrum, but that when equipped with this technique they were able to elicit security requirements and implement some of these requirements. Security techniques can thus act as the reminder that is needed by developers to include software security.

Conceptual Framework by Terpstra et al. (2017)

Terpstra et al. (2017) created a conceptual framework based on the results they got in their study of professionals' posts on LinkedIn. This conceptual framework is shown in Figure 1. In the following we explain the conceptual categories of Terpstra et al. in more detail.

The conceptual category *perceptions of priority* was used by Terpstra et al. to represent issues related to prioritization of security requirements at inter-iteration time. They found that customers and business representatives often push for functionality and do not prioritize security. However, developers' priorities may be different. This is related to the conceptual category *ownership of security requirements* that was used by Terpstra et al. to represent findings that show that no role takes or is given full responsibility for security requirements in development projects. As stated by Terpstra et al. "business representatives and product owners usually have little awareness of security requirements and rarely work towards their elaboration early on" (Terpstra et al., 2017). This is supported by identified challenges such as "[t]he product owner has often too much power and instills his attitude of treating non-functional require-ments", and "[t]he product owner is sometimes acting like a business owner or stakeholder and pushes only for features" (Terpstra et al., 2017). Additionally, they found that "developers who understand risks associated with poorly treated security requirements, may not know how to communicate the possible security issues to their product owner and convincingly present him with information on how much it would cost if not fixed and if a problem arises" (Terpstra et al., 2017).

These challenges can in part be explained by findings related to the conceptual category *business case*. Some of the challenges identified by Terpstra et al. was that "[a]gile techniques are business-value driven" and "[s]ecurity is hard to 'sell' as a business value". Additionally, "[s]ecurity requirements cost money to elaborate due to experts' involvement" and "[p]eople drop security because they perceive it a fight not worth fighting" (Terpstra et al., 2017). To add to this, the conceptual category *attitude towards security requirements* was used by Terpstra et al. to represent findings that in some cases "team members 'do not care' about security requirements just because there is no incentive to do so (...). Or, because no one really understands completely what these requirements are" (Terpstra et al., 2017). Terpstra et al. found that using security regulation to justify the security requirements was one coping strategy used by practitioners.

The conceptual category *organizational setup* was used by Terpstra et al. to represent findings that show that the organizational culture can both help and hurt the security requirements work. Terpstra et al. in particular found that the organizations' approaches to educating developers on software security could have an impact. Coping strategies identified include educating the business on security, raising awareness in the development team, adding a security expert to the team, making sure the product owner is supporting security, and having cross functional streams to help not forgetting about security. Some of the challenges identified by Terpstra further explain how the agile development approach in itself may be a challenge in having security being prioritized, e.g.: "People do care about security, but do not think about it"; "Agile techniques are vulnerable for forgetting things like security" and; "Security require-ments get often delivered in the last minute" (Terpstra et al., 2017). The conceptual category *definition of "done" (DoD)* was used by Terpstra et al. to represent the opinion of some of the professionals that the DoD should include security requirements. They found that security requirements often were poorly defined, and that coping strategies included integrating security into the DoD, estimates, acceptance criteria and user stories.

RESULTS: THE MAIN CONCEPTS AND THEIR RELATIONS

In the previous section we identified several concepts relevant to security requirements work as reported in the identified primary studies (see Table 3 and Table 4). Based on the concepts we identified, as well as those identified by Terpstra et al. (2017), we then identified what we consider the most important and prevalent concepts in the primary studies, and the relations between these concepts. We used this to create a conceptual framework with a graphical representation. In this section we describe the result of this work.

Main Concepts

Table 6 shows how the concepts from the primary papers have been grouped into a set of main concepts. The main concepts are as follows:

- **Teams' security posture and competence:** The security awareness and competence of the team and the individual team members are important in remembering security, identifying the need for security, following it up with performing security activities and in having the competence needed to adequately handling the security (Terpstra et al., 2017; Bartsch, 2011; Nicolaysen et al., 2010). Benefits have been identified that can be tied to a decentralized approach to security analysis (Baca et al., 2015), but this implies commitment and capability of the development teams in doing this work;
- **Customers' security posture and competence:** The interviews reported by Bartsch (2011) in particular, but also the interviews reported by Nicolaysen et al. (2010), show the importance the customer plays in the work on security requirements. Both these studies show that customers have the influence both to drive and hinder the work on security requirements;
- **Customer relation and involvement:** Customers have been found to provide valuable competence to the discussions on security requirements, and their competence and the trust relationship with the developers can influence how security requirements are specified (Bartsch, 2011; van der Heijden et al., 2018);
- **Business case for security:** Functionality is often prioritized over security (Nicolaysen et al., 2010; Terpstra et al., 2017). Security is in many cases not seen as part of the software or something that adds value, but rather as a cost (Terpstra et al., 2017; Poller et al., 2017; van der Heijden et al., 2018). However, legislation or audits that put requirements on security can motivate security effort (Terpstra et al., 2017; Nicolaysen et al., 2010; Bartsch, 2011);
- **Organizational culture and setup:** Several aspects with the organizational culture have been found to have an effect on security requirements work. Examples are the communication between teams and central resources on quality (Bartsch, 2011) and the organization's approach to software security training (Terpstra et al., 2017). In addition, the organization has the potential to make decisions that impact what security resources are available in a team and the formal ownership for software security in projects;

- **Process for making priorities on requirements:** In agile projects, decisions on what security work to prioritize can be made without any security experts being involved and the decision can be highly dependent on the security posture of individuals (Terpstra et al., 2017);
- **Development approach:** An agile development approach can impact the security requirements positively, e.g. it has been found that developers with a holistic view of the software they develop can feel more responsibility for security (Bartsch, 2011). However, there are also known challenges (e.g. pressure of short iterations) (Bartsch, 2011; Nicolaysen et al., 2010) and frequent changes (Adelyar & Norta, 2016);
- **Security requirements elicitation approach:** Having a defined process for security to make sure security is remembered throughout the project can make a difference. Additionally, the approach selected can impact the effect of the work. As an example, approaches such as Protection Poker where the full team discusses security can lead to certain effects that would maybe not be present in a more expert oriented approach. Security requirements work is commonly considered to be iterative (Bartsch, 2011) and this should be supported by any selected elicitation approach;
- **Security requirements representation:** Security requirements often end up being implicit (Bartsch, 2011; Adelyar & Norta, 2016). Having security requirements as part of the Definition of Done is one suggested way to make them more explicit and actionable (Bartsch, 2011; Terpstra et al., 2017).

Table 6. Main concepts

Main Concepts	Table 4 Concepts	Table 5 Concepts	Concepts Terpstra et al. (2017)
Teams' security posture and abilities	Individuals and their security posture and competence; Responsibility; Preferred security strategy	Security resources in the team	Attitude towards security
Customers' security posture and competence	Customers and customer relations; Individuals and their security posture and competence; Preferred security strategy	-	Perceptions of priority
Customer relation and involvement	Customers and customer relations	-	-
Business case for security	Priorities; Project constraints; Business case for security; Pressure; Legislation, audit	-	Business case
Organizational culture and setup	Communication; Development approach; Responsibility	Security resources in the team	Organizational setup; Ownership of security requirements
Process for making priorities on requirements	Priorities; Project constraints; Representation of security requirements	-	Perceptions of priority
Development approach	Development approach; Pressure	-	-
Security requirements elicitation approach	Iterative process,	Incremental security analysis in the team; Security discussions in the team	-
Security requirements representation	Representation of security requirements	-	Definition of "done"

Identifying Relations Between Concepts

In the introduction, security requirements work was described as comprising activities to: 1) decide whether and how to identify security needs, risks or requirements for a project; 2) do the requirements elicitation; 3) communicate the identified security needs, risks or requirements, and; 4) integrate these and make priorities related to them in development. These security requirements work activities take part in a context that highly influence this work in various ways. Figure 4 depicts the conceptual framework we ended up with based on the analysis of the selected papers. Here we have divided the identified concepts into two main categories: 1) contextual factors, i.e. factors that are outside the requirements work itself, but impact the security requirements work in some way (e.g. impact the priority the security work is given, who participates, how it is done, etc.), and; 2) concepts related to the more practical aspects of the work and how it is performed (e.g. who actually participates in an activity, how the work is actually done, etc.).

In the following we describe the relations between the concepts in more detail. Additionally, we introduce a third overall category that is largely missing from the identified papers, namely that of the effect of the security requirements work.

Figure 4. Conceptual framework based on the selected empirical studies (SR is in the figure an abbreviation of 'security requirements')

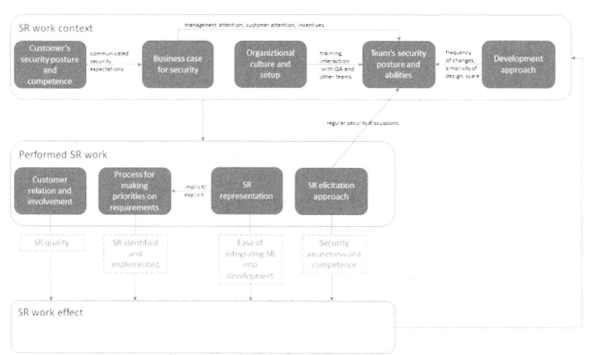

Security Requirements Work Context

The team's security posture and abilities can be influenced by a number of factors. An obvious influence is training (Bartsch, 2011; Terpstra et al., 2017), however, this training does not need to be formal. Protection Poker is an example of a technique that has been found to spread security awareness and knowledge in a team through regular security discussions. Additionally, teams can increase their security competence through communication with quality assurance functions in the company or even a sense of competition with other teams (Bartsch, 2011). Aspects of the development work can additionally have a major impact on security posture of the team. The size and scale of the project itself can impact what type of challenges a project experience in their security work (van der Heijden et al., 2018). Adelyar & Norta (2016) found that frequent changes to software under time pressure negatively impacted developers' security attention. Additionally, they found that it impacted the ability to have a simple design and made the software more complex. Bartsch (2011) found that having a holistic development approach can motivate software security and lead to simpler designs. Agile development methods can thus impact positively or negatively on the security posture and abilities of the team depending on the circumstances.

Customers' security posture and competence and the way customers are involved in the security requirements work impact software security work in many ways. It can, together with the relation between the team and customer, impact how security requirements are initially presented, especially their quality and whether they are implicit or explicit (Bartsch, 2011). Additionally, customers' security posture impacts the business case for security, e.g. by the customer making security a clear priority (Bartsch, 2011; Nicolaysen et al., 2010; Terpstra et al., 2017). The business case again influences the security posture of the individuals involved (Terpstra et al., 2017).

Performed Security Requirements Work

Several of the concepts identified fall within the category of performed security requirements work. The relations between these concepts (e.g. how the way requirements are elicited influence how they are prioritized, etc.) are however not discussed much in the papers we have studied. The main relation present is that of the impact of having implicit vs. explicit security requirements (Bartsch, 2011; Poller et al., 2017), and having security included as a feature (Poller et al., 2017).

Security Requirements Work Effect

We find that one category is largely missing from the primary and secondary studies we have identified, namely that of the effect; what makes the security requirements work useful in terms of impact. Figure 4, that shows the conceptual framework we ended up with based on the primary studies, thus includes this effect but without further concepts to help understand it. To move towards an understanding of the effect, we have however added what we understand from the sources to be potential effects of the factors included in the category 'Performed security requirements work', namely the quality of security requirements, the fact that they are identified and implemented, how easy they are to integrate into development, and the security awareness and competence that is built by doing security requirements work. Though we do not have any solid evidence to support that these are important factors characterizing the effect of security requirements work, these have support in the identified papers and can point towards factors that potentially are important for the effect of this type of work.

One effect of software security work that is somewhat available in the primary studies is that of cost. We have however not added that effect to the conceptual framework as it is not clear from the sources what the cost-benefit relationship associated with the security requirements work part is. Cost is however one likely factor of the effect of software security requirements work as well.

Figure 4 shows a possible relationship between the effect of the security requirements work and the security requirements work context. In the papers we build on, there are some pointers to the potential of security requirements work to impact the context, e.g. in form of changes in security competence and awareness among key actors, such as the Product Owner.

DISCUSSION

In the following we discuss recommendations for future research based on the conceptual framework we developed, followed by a discussion of the validity of the conceptual framework.

Implications for Research

The conceptual framework depicted in Figure 4 shows that several contextual factors influence the software security requirements work in agile development projects. This can be understood in more than one way. One possible understanding is that the contextual factors are the factors that are best understood in the underlying research, and thus future research should aim to identify and understand also factors related to the security requirements work itself and the outcome. However, another possible understanding is that contextual factors are highly important for security requirements work and thus need to be properly understood in order to have an effective approach to software security requirements work in an agile setting. This may point to the need for more research on these factors, also keeping in mind that the contextual factors included in Figure 4 are rather complex, covering characteristics of individuals, the organization, and their interactions.

In the empirical studies we identified, the role of the approach or technique used for security requirements work is not clearly understood. Though there have been studies of different techniques and approaches, there is a difference between evaluating one technique and finding out the effects of that technique vs. understanding what makes the technique behave as it does compared to other techniques. We believe there is a need for more studies evaluating various techniques and approaches, especially in industry settings and over longer periods of time.

From the conceptual framework in Figure 4 one can see that the empirical studies we used provide limited understanding of what causes security requirements work to have effect. It may be more difficult to study and understand the effect of the work than to understand factors impacting the security requirements work, since effects may be longer term and harder to pinpoint. Still, the motivation of doing security requirements work would be an adequate level of implemented security, and if a security requirements approach does not make a significant contribution towards that then it is not worth the effort.

As can be seen from Table 7, many of the concepts we identified can be said to be directly related to the values of the Agile Manifesto (Beck et al., 2001); "[i]ndividuals and interactions over processes and tools" (V1 in Table 7), "[w]orking software over comprehensive documentation" (V2), "[c]ustomer collaboration over contract negotiation" (V3), and "[r]esponding to change over following a plan" (V4) (Beck et al., 2001). This points to the conceptual framework being related to agile development in particular, and not to other types of development approaches. However, this is not necessarily the case. Kanniah & Mahrin (2016) identified a set of factors impacting successful implementation of software development practices based on an SLR. Many of the factors they identified are related to the factors we have identified for security requirements work in agile development; the institutional context, people and action, the project context and the system development process are all represented in the conceptual framework in Figure 4. The factors identified by Kanniah and Mahrin are not considered to be specific for agile development. Based on the current evidence it is thus difficult to say what impact an agile development approach has on software security work, and thus what in the conceptual framework we developed are specific to agile development, even if the conceptual framework is entirely based on studies done on projects and companies using some kind of agile development approach. Of the four agile principles, it is the value "Individuals and interactions over processes and tools" (Beck et al., 2001) that seems to be most influential on security requirements work. Of the ten factors that Kaniah and Mahrin later identified as the most influential (Kanniah & Mahrin, 2018), a majority can also be considered to be concerned with individuals and interactions.

To sum up, there is a need for a deeper understanding of software security work in agile development. Especially there is a need to understand better what factors are important for the effect of the work, and to understand the role of the particular approach in bringing about this effect. However, a conceptual framework has a role not only in directing research priorities but also to "identify potential validity threats to your conclusions" (Maxwell, 2013). It is clear that contextual factors are important and influence software security work in agile development in many ways, especially factors concerning individuals and their interactions. Thus, understanding these and taking these factors into account in future studies is essential in order to properly understand the findings. Thus, the conceptual framework can be used to guide future research priorities, but also be input to planning and analysis of future empirical studies.

Table 7. Main concepts and their relation to the principles of the Agile Manifesto (Beck et al., 2001)

Identified Main Concept	V1 Individuals	V2 Software	V3 Customer	V4 Change
Teams' security posture and abilities	x			
Customers' security posture and competence	x		x	
Customer relation and involvement	x		x	
Business case for security		x		
Organizational culture and setup	x			
Process for making priorities on requirements	x			x
Development approach	x	x		
Security requirements elicitation approach	x			x
Security requirements representation	x			

Validity of the Conceptual Framework

The conceptual framework presented in this paper is based on nine empirical studies; five interview studies addressing software security in agile (Adeyar and Norta, 2016; Bartsch, 2011; Nicolaysen et al., 2010; Tøndel et al., 2017; van der Heijden, 2018), one case study on the impact of external security audits on development (Poller et al., 2017), two evaluations of approaches or techniques relevant for security requirements work (Baca et al., 2015; Williams et al., 2010) and one analysis of professionals' postings on LinkedIn related to security requirements in agile (Terpstra et al., 2017). These nine studies together address the topic of security requirements work in agile from varying perspectives and using varying methods, something that can be considered a strength. Still, the nine primary studies we build on can be considered to be rather few, thus we have used a set of secondary studies to improve understanding of the concepts identified from the primary studies.

As previously explained, we decided not to do a comprehensive and systematic search for literature, as one would expect if doing an SLR. We made the initial assessment that given the recent SLRs on software security in agile (Khaim et al., 2016; Oueslati et al., 2015) that we could use as a basis for this work, it was not worthwhile to do a comprehensive search for literature. At later stages in the process we used even more recent SLRs (Alsaquaf et al., 2017; Bishop & Rowland, 2019; Saldanha & Zorzo, 2018; Villamizar et al., 2018) to add to the initial selection of papers. Deciding not to do a full SLR is a weakness of our approach, and it can potentially have impacted the conceptual framework we ended up with, as more identified studies could have resulted in more and/or different concepts and relations between them. However, we never intended this conceptual framework to be a complete and "'finalised" conceptual framework, but rather a work in progress that should be improved as more research becomes available (Maxwell, 2013). We would additionally like to point out that the SLRs we used to identify papers seem to vary in what papers are included (see Table 1), something that may indicate challenges in identifying all relevant papers also when doing an SLR. Several of the SLRs we have used as a basis state that the current number of published empirical studies on software security in agile development is rather low (Alsaquaf et al., 2017; Bishop & Rowland, 2019; Saldanha & Zorzo, 2018; Villamizar et al., 2018), thus identification of a high number of studies should not be expected regardless of method for identifying studies.

The conceptual framework presented in this paper is based solely on published empirical studies. Restricting ourselves to only using such studies as a basis for the conceptual framework represents a narrowing of focus, ignoring other sources of knowledge of security requirements work such as unpublished results and the general experiences of researchers and practitioners (Maxwell, 2013; Robson, 2011). Also, for this reason, this conceptual framework is to be considered work in progress, and something that will need to be refined including more sources.

Relying on published empirical studies additionally pose limitations in that we only have access to as much information about the studies as is available in the published papers. For the study category consisting of more general studies, we would generally have benefited from more information on study context as this would help us understand the results and the selected concepts in more depth. For the studies of specific techniques, the results and thus the concepts are highly related to the specifics of the techniques; if other techniques had been studies it is likely that other concepts would have emerged from the results. It is hard to know what is the effect of the studied approaches (SEAP, Protection Poker) compared to that of other techniques, i.e., which effects are due to the particular way of working in the technique, and which are due to other factors.

Although the work of creating this conceptual framework has been done in a structured way, there is always an element of creativity also in scientific work (Collins, 2019). In this work, the coding of results from the primary sources (step 3), the reorganizing of these codes into themes/concepts for the conceptual framework (step 4) and the development of the graphical representation of the conceptual framework (step 5) all represent some form of creative work, although based on a structured process and although we have aimed to preserve the link between the resulting framework and the findings in the primary sources. It is likely that other researchers would make slightly different categorizations and end up with a different graphical representation of the conceptual framework. In many cases the concepts we ended up with using, both the initial concepts identified based on the primary studies (Table 4 and Table 5) and the main concepts used in the conceptual framework (Table 6), are somewhat overlapping. To illustrate, the security discussions in the teams that are part of Protection Poker in many ways represent one form of incremental security analysis done by the team, and such a discussion influences the security resources in the team. The concepts we ended up with using represent out best effort to group key findings from the primary studies into meaningful and related concepts. The concepts and the framework we ended up with should however not be viewed as a final version, but as a starting point and something that can be improved upon as more empirical research becomes available.

Further evaluation of this conceptual framework is needed. In its current state, the conceptual framework has been primarily developed by one researcher. Future work includes discussing the conceptual framework with more colleagues and validating and improving the conceptual framework when new evidence becomes available. Note however that the concepts in the framework bear similarities to the categories of challenges identified by Oueslati et al. (2015), especially to their categories "[a]wareness and collaboration challenges" and "[s]ecurity management challenges" and to challenges identified by Khaim et al. (2016) and Alsaquaf et al. (2017). Thus, the factors we have identified have been pointed out also by other researchers aiming to understand challenges relating to software security in agile development or quality requirements in agile development. Compared to the conceptual framework developed by Daneva and Wang (2018), it integrates their key concepts of activities, competencies, roles and artefacts, although in a slightly different way. Also, note that the last iteration of the framework that included adding two more primary studies (Adelyar and Norta, 2016; van der Heijden et al., 2018) resulted in only minor updates to the final concepts and to the conceptual framework. Thus, we have reason to believe that this conceptual framework is able to cover the key findings in current empirical research on software security requirements work in agile development.

In the Research Method section, we restated the recommendation from Miles and Huberman (1994) to avoid a non-risk framework with only global level variables and two-directional arrows. The conceptual framework we have presented in this paper is not a non-risk framework, but could be said to be a low-risk framework with many high level concepts and mainly high-level relations between the concepts. This is in many ways a result of limited studies to use as a basis for the conceptual framework. Both Maxwell (2013) and Robson (2011) recommend an inclusive approach at the initial stage. However, the conceptual framework should become more focused as it is refined (Maxwell, 2013). Thus, future revisions should move towards more specific concepts, and even excluding concepts that are less important. Revisions can be made based on new data becoming available, or could utilize other sources like experience, a broader set of literature, and thought experiments (Maxwell, 2013; Robson, 2011).

CONCLUSION AND FUTURE WORK

This paper suggests a conceptual framework for software security requirements work in agile development, with the motivation to increase understanding of this type of work and guide further research. The conceptual framework is based on published empirical studies covering aspects of software security requirements work in agile in an industrial setting. The results point to a need for further empirical studies in this area, especially to improve understanding of factors important for gaining impact from the work on software security requirements in agile projects, as this is largely missing in current work. There is additionally a need for understanding to what extent the concrete approach adopted for security requirements work shape the impact of this work given varying contexts. This would help practitioners in deciding what methods to adopt for their particular case. Contextual factors seem to be highly influential on the way security requirements are treated in current software projects. Thus, these are important to take properly into account in future empirical research studies, especially in plans for data collection and in the analysis phase.

In our own work, we are in the process of using this conceptual framework as an input to planning and analysis of ongoing case studies related to software security requirements work in agile software development. Especially, we plan to use the conceptual framework to provide some structure to the analysis. Additionally, we plan to use the results of the ongoing and future case studies to improve this conceptual framework.

ACKNOWLEDGMENT

This work was supported by the SoS-Agile: Science of Security in Agile Software Development project, funded by the Research Council of Norway (grant number 247678).

REFERENCES

Adelyar, S. H., & Norta, A. (2016, September). Towards a secure agile software development process. In *Proceedings of the 2016 10th International Conference on the Quality of Information and Communications Technology (QUATIC)* (pp. 101-106). IEEE. 10.1109/QUATIC.2016.028

Alsaqaf, W., Daneva, M., & Wieringa, R. (2017). Quality requirements in large-scale distributed agile projects–a systematic literature review. In *Proceedings of the International working conference on requirements engineering: Foundation for software quality* (pp. 219–234). Academic Press. 10.1007/978-3-319-54045-0_17

Aydal, E. G., Paige, R. F., Chivers, H., & Brooke, P. J. (2006). Security planning and refactoring in extreme programming. In *Proceedings of the International conference on extreme programming and agile processes in software engineering* (pp. 154–163). Academic Press. 10.1007/11774129_16

Baca, D., Boldt, M., Carlsson, B., & Jacobsson, A. (2015). A novel security-enhanced agile software development process applied in an industrial setting. In *Proceedings of the 10th international conference on availability, reliability and security (ARES)* (pp. 11–19). Academic Press. 10.1109/ARES.2015.45

Baca, D., & Carlsson, B. (2011). Agile development with security engineering activities. In *Proceedings of the 2011 international conference on software and systems process* (pp. 149–158). Academic Press.

Bartsch, S. (2011, Aug). Practitioners' perspectives on security in agile development. In *Proceedings of the 2011 sixth international conference on Availability, reliability and security (ARES)* (p. 479-484). doi:10.1109/ARES.2011.82

Beck, K., Beedle, M., Van Bennekum, A., Cockburn, A., Cunningham, W., Fowler, M., ... others (2001). Manifesto for agile software development. Retrieved from http://www.agilemanifesto.org

Bellomo, S., & Woody, C. (2012). DoD Information Assurance and Agile: Challenges and Recommendations Gathered Through Interviews with Agile Program Managers and DoD Accreditation Reviewers. Carnegie-Melon University.

Beznosov, K. (2003, October). Extreme security engineering: On employing XP practices to achieve' good enough security'without defining it. In *Proceedings of the First ACM Workshop on Business Driven Security Engineering (BizSec)*. Academic Press.

Bishop, D., & Rowland, P. (2019). Agile and secure software development: An unfinished story. *Issues in Information Systems*, *20*(1).

Collins, H. (2019). *Forms of Life: The Method and Meaning of Sociology*. MIT Press.

Daneva, M., & Wang, C. (2018, August). Security requirements engineering in the agile era: How does it work in practice? In *Proceedings of the 2018 IEEE 1st International Workshop on Quality Requirements in Agile Projects (QuaRAP)* (pp. 10-13). IEEE.

Dikert, K., Paasivaara, M., & Lassenius, C. (2016). Challenges and success factors for large-scale agile transformations: A systematic literature review. *Journal of Systems and Software*, *119*, 87–108. doi:10.1016/j.jss.2016.06.013

Fitzgerald, B., Stol, K.-J., O'Sullivan, R., & O'Brien, D. (2013). Scaling agile methods to regulated environments: An industry case study. In *Proceedings of the 2013 international conference on software engineering* (pp. 863–872). Academic Press. 10.1109/ICSE.2013.6606635

Ghani, I., Azham, Z., & Jeong, S. R. (2014). Integrating Software Security into Agile-Scrum Method. *TIIS*, *8*(2), 646–663. doi:10.3837/tiis.2014.02.019

Hanssen, G. K., Stålhane, T., & Myklebust, T. (2018). SafescrumOR -agile development of safety-critical software. Springer.

Heeager, L. T., & Nielsen, P. A. (2018). A conceptual model of agile software development in a safety-critical context: A systematic literature review. *Information and Software Technology*, *103*, 22–39. doi:10.1016/j.infsof.2018.06.004

Howard, M., & Lipner, S. (2006). *The security development lifecycle*. Microsoft Press.

Jabareen, Y. (2009). Building a conceptual framework: Philosophy, definitions, and procedure. *International Journal of Qualitative Methods*, *8*(4), 49–62. doi:10.1177/160940690900800406

Kanniah, S. L., & Mahrin, M. N. (2016). A review on factors influencing implementation of secure software development practices. *International Journal of Computer and Systems Engineering*, *10*(8), 3032–3039.

Kanniah, S. L., & Mahrin, M. N. (2018). Secure software development practice adoption model: A delphi study. *Journal of Telecommunication, Electronic and Computer Engineering (JTEC)*, *10*(2-8), 71–75.

Khaim, R., Naz, S., Abbas, F., Iqbal, N., & Hamayun, M. (2016). A review of security integration technique in agile software development. *International Journal of Software Engineering and Its Applications*, 7(3).

Kongsli, V. (2006). Towards agile security in web applications. In *Companion to the 21st ACM SIGPLAN symposium on object-oriented programming systems, languages, and applications* (pp. 805–808). ACM.

Leffingwell, D. (2010). *Agile software requirements: lean requirements practices for teams, programs, and the enterprise*. Addison-Wesley Professional.

Maxwell, J. A. (2013). *Qualitative research design: An interactive approach* (Vol. 41). Sage publications.

McGraw, G. (2004, March). Software security. *Security & Privacy*, 2(2), 80–83. doi:10.1109/MSECP.2004.1281254

McGraw, G. (2006). *Software Security: Building Security In*. Addison-Wesley.

McGraw, G., Migues, S., & West, J. (2018). *BSIMM 9*. Synopsys, Inc.

Microsoft. (2009, June 30). Security development lifecycle for agile development, version 1.0.

Microsoft. (n.d.). Microsoft security development lifecycle (No. Accessed 2019.08.07). Retrieved from https://www.microsoft.com/en-us/SDL

Miles, M. B., & Huberman, A. M. (1994). *Qualitative data analysis: An expanded sourcebook* (2nd ed.). Sage.

Muneer, S. U., Nadeem, M., & Kasi, B. (2019). Comparison of modern techniques for analyzing NFRs in Agile: A systematic literature review. *Journal of Software Engineering Practice*, 3(3), 1–12.

Nicolaysen, T., Sassoon, R., Line, M. B., & Jaatun, M. G. (2010). Agile software development: The straight and narrow path to secure software? *International Journal of Secure Software Engineering*, 1(3), 71–85. doi:10.4018/jsse.2010070105

Oueslati, H., Rahman, M. M., & ben Othmane, L. (2015). Literature review of the challenges of developing secure software using the agile approach. In *Proceedings of the 10th international conference on availability, reliability and security (ARES)* (pp. 540–547).

OWASP. (n.d.). Software assurance maturity model - a guide to building security into software development. version 1.5 (Tech. Rep.). *Open Web Application Security Project*.

Peeters, J. (2005). Agile security requirements engineering. In *Proceedings of the Symposium on requirements engineering for information security*. Academic Press.

Pohl, C., & Hof, H.-J. (2015). Secure scrum: Development of secure software with scrum.

Poller, A., Kocksch, L., Türpe, S., Epp, F. A., & Kinder-Kurlanda, K. (2017). Can security become a routine?: a study of organizational change in an agile software development group. In *Proceedings of the 2017 ACM conference on computer supported cooperative work and social computing* (pp. 2489–2503). Academic Press. 10.1145/2998181.2998191

Rajba, P. (2018, August). Challenges and mitigation approaches for getting secured applications in an enterprise company. In *Proceedings of the 13th International Conference on Availability, Reliability and Security* (pp. 1-6). Academic Press. 10.1145/3230833.3233276

Renatus, S., Teichmann, C., & Eichler, J. (2015). Method selection and tailoring for agile threat assessment and mitigation. In *Proceedings of the 10th international conference on availability, reliability and security (ARES)* (pp. 548–555). Academic Press. 10.1109/ARES.2015.96

Rindell, K., Hyrynsalmi, S., & Leppänen, V. (2016, August). Case study of security development in an agile environment: building identity management for a government agency. In *Proceedings of the 2016 11th International Conference on Availability, Reliability and Security (ARES)* (pp. 556-563). IEEE. 10.1109/ARES.2016.45

Robson, C. (2011). *Real World Research* (3rd ed.). John Wiley & Sons.

Sachdeva, V., & Chung, L. (2017, January). Handling non-functional requirements for big data and IOT projects in Scrum. In *Proceedings of the 2017 7th International Conference on Cloud Computing, Data Science & Engineering-Confluence* (pp. 216-221). IEEE. 10.1109/CONFLUENCE.2017.7943152

Saldanha, L. R., & Zorzo, A. (2019). Security requirements in agile software development: a systematic mapping study. Pontifical Catholic University of Rio Grande Do Sul, 2019, 32p.

Savola, R. M., Frühwirth, C., & Pietikäinen, A. (2012). Risk-driven security metrics in agile software development-an industrial pilot study. *J. UCS*, *18*(12), 1679–1702.

Terpstra, E., Daneva, M., & Wang, C. (2017). Agile practitioners' understanding of security requirements: Insights from a grounded theory analysis. In *Proceedings of the 2017 IEEE 25th international requirements engineering conference workshops (REW)* (pp. 439–442). IEEE Press.

Tøndel, I. A., Jaatun, M. G., Cruzes, D. S., & Moe, N. B. (2017). Risk centric activities in secure software development in public organisations. *International Journal of Secure Software Engineering*, *8*(4), 1–30. doi:10.4018/IJSSE.2017100101

van der Heijden, A., Broasca, C., & Serebrenik, A. (2018, October). An empirical perspective on security challenges in large-scale agile software development. In *Proceedings of the 12th ACM/IEEE International Symposium on Empirical Software Engineering and Measurement* (pp. 1-4). Academic Press. 10.1145/3239235.3267426

Villamizar, H., Kalinowski, M., Viana, M., & Fernández, D. M. (2018, August). A systematic mapping study on security in agile requirements engineering. In *Proceedings of the 2018 44th Euromicro Conference on Software Engineering and Advanced Applications (SEAA)* (pp. 454-461). IEEE. 10.1109/SEAA.2018.00080

Williams, L., Gegick, M., & Meneely, A. (2009). Protection poker: Structuring software security risk assessment and knowledge transfer. In *Proceedings of the International symposium on engineering secure software and systems* (pp. 122–134). Academic Press.

Williams, L., Meneely, A., & Shipley, G. (2010). Protection poker: The new software security game. *IEEE Security and Privacy*, *8*(3), 14–20. doi:10.1109/MSP.2010.58

This research was previously published in the International Journal of Systems and Software Security and Protection (IJSSSP), 11(1); pages 33-62, copyright year 2020 by IGI Publishing (an imprint of IGI Global).

Chapter 13
Adaptation of Modern Agile Practices in Global Software Engineering

Moiz Mansoor
Institute of Business Management, Pakistan

Muhammad Waqar Khan
Institute of Business Management, Pakistan

Syed Sajjad Hussain Rizvi
Hamdard University, Pakistan

Manzoor Ahmed Hashmani
University Technology PETRONAS, Malaysia

Muhammad Zubair
IQRA University, Pakistan

ABSTRACT

Software engineering has been an active working area for many decades. It evolved in a bi-folded manner. First research and subsequently development. Since the day of its inception, the massive number of variants and methods of software engineering were proposed. Primarily, these methods are designed to cater the time-varying need of modern approach. In this connection, the Global Software Engineering (GSE) is one of the growing trends in the modern software industry. At the same time, the employment of Agile development methodologies has also gained the significant attention in the literature. This has created a rationale to explore and adopt agile development methodology in GSE. It gained rigorous attention as an alternative to traditional software development methodologies. This paper has presented a comprehensive review on the adaptation of modern agile practices in GSE. In addition, the strength and limitation of each approach have been highlighted. Finally, the open area in the said domain is submitted as one of the deliverables of this work.

DOI: 10.4018/978-1-6684-3702-5.ch013

INTRODUCTION

Agile Software Development (ASD) and GSE are two rapidly growing fields in the software development industry (Cockburn 2002). This growth has translated into a significant advancement in both industry and academia. GSE is an extensive concept incorporating software development methods across both, organizational and geographical borders (Rodríguez,et. al. (2012). While ASD emphasis on the development of close collaboration between users and developers. It focuses on delivering software within timelines considering budget constraints. This process is repetitive, adaptive, and shortly defined (Kruchten, 2013).

During the last several years the trend of globalization of business has witnessed, that brought changes in industries. Most of the companies started working on Global Software Engineering (GSE), to get results more efficient, cheaper and faster. However, these benefices are not easy to accomplish. Culture, collaboration between teams, language, time zones, economic conditions, insufficient knowledge of client's interest and many more make the tasks harder to achieve. Researchers have investigated this issue and have identifies teamwork as a significant actuating parameter to handle the issues of GSE.

During the past decade, the hybridization of Agile Software Engineering (ASE) and Global Software Engineering (GSE) concept has submitted the significant change in software industry. This includes, but not limited to, rapid application development, round the clock development, taking the most eminent professional on board irrespective of their geographical location, reduced production cost, less time to launch etc. (Kaur, et. al. 2014). In spite of the fruitful benefits of agile GSD, it is faced with some challenges. One important challenge is the effective and adequate communication in between distributed teams and customers (Jalali, et. al. 2010). Poor communication is an extensive risk to agile GSD (e.g., delivering an inaccurate, incomplete or inefficient message (Abrahamsson, et. al. 2017). Knowledge sharing and communication is the constitutional concern of distributed global agile development environments (Èmite et. al. 2011). During the recent years organizations are moving to the development of Global Software Engineering. The Projects which are been developed by separate teams have been noted as more challenging as compare to those project which are been running at one platform (Kaur, et. al. 2014). Furthermore knowledge of all possible challenges and potential mitigation strategies of GSE is essential for running a successful project. The collected challenges may further arrange into checklists. Moreover the developed checklists separated into risk management process particularly risk identification and risk mitigation planning.

In recent literature, the researchers have investigated the hybridization of ASD and GSE (Wohlin, 2014). This has evolved a trend of implementing agile development in global software projects. Moreover, the hybridization of ASD and GSE has also accumulated their strengths. This includes, but not limited to, rapid development, optimum resource utilization, integration of global experts, better communication, reduce coordination issues, increased trust, improved productivity, etc (Kaur, st. al. 2014)

In addition, the implementation of the agile method in GSE is also encouraged by the fact that agile development gained huge attentiveness from industry (Kaur, st. al. 2014). In recent literature, although there is a growing interest in becoming agile and globalized for rapid and optimal software development. However, a few works have been reported in this connection.

The main goal of agile development focuses on face-to-face communication among collocated teams compared to geographically dispersed (Global Software Development) GSD teams (Šmite, et. al. 2010). The increase in the use of agile approaches in GSD along with the literature on communication challenges has recently become of interest (Lanubile et. al. 2010). Communication challenges in agile GSD are required to be studied and the tools, methods, and strategies to address these challenges need to be developed (Dullemond, et. al. 2010).

Due to the successful agile software development and implementation, its application in GSD is gaining momentum day by day. Apparently, the scenario looks benefiting however, distributed project team encountered some inherent constraints to apply agile practices (Nguyen-Duc et. al. 2015). One of the basic reason is the need for effective communication, to overcome the logical issue it essentially requires team members to be collocated. Other major difficulties faced are usually related to communication, personnel, culture, different time zones, trust, and knowledge management (Kaur, et. al. 2014). Nonetheless, several strategies, methods, and solutions are reported in the recent literature to handle these challenges.

In the subsequent part of this paper first, a comprehensive review of the existing well knows agile practices in global software development is presented. The discussion includes the strengths, limitations, and potential barriers of each ASD in GSE.

GSE has various potential advantages, including shortening time-to-showcase cycles by utilizing time-zone contrasts and enhancing the capacity to rapidly react to customers' needs (Singh et. al. 2015). Globally distributed software engineering also allows organizations to profit by access to a bigger qualified asset pool with the guarantee of reduced development costs(Kaur, et. al. 2014). Another conceivably positive effect of globally distributed engineering is creativity, as the blend of designers with various social cultures may trigger new thoughts (Casey, 2009, July). The mutual reason behind coming together was to lessen the production value and to attain something productive at the same time. Additional reasons included consumption of time effectively, the foundation of new business openings with new accomplices, adaptability as for the quantity of in-house assets and solving issues of accessibility of local assets (Wright et. al. 2010). Following are the main advantages of GSE

Less Costly

Maybe the first and most looked for after advantage of GSE has been that of decreased cost of development. The reason for this advantage is that organizations are globalizing their product improvement exercises to use less expensive workers situated in a more economical area (Nguyen-Duc et. al. 2013). This has been made possible by the fast communication links enabling the quick exchange of the essential item within reach (Abrahamsson, et. al. 2017). The difference in salaries crosswise over locales can be huge, with a US programming specialist's wage being greater than that of a man with an equal level of expertise in Asia or South America (Ågerfalk, 2008). It is true that companies are currently searching in areas where they offer more excellent execution in terms of getting the work done branched forward with the guarantee of less expensive work.

Intercultural Workforce

A large pool of skilled labor by coordinating across distance is a major catch in this for the companies where the activity of development may contain contributions from skilled worked located in any part of the world (Conchúir et, al. 2009). The organizations possess the opportunities to enhance the scope of thie software engineering activities. This could be managed by accumulating the contributions of diversified skilled workers. This is because the geographically disperse location have diverse skill set of software development. Moreover, the intercultural competency depends upon different factors like cognitive, affective, and behavioral aspects (Holmstrom et. al. 2006). In addition, the unified foreign language skills are also necessary to communicate in an culturally diverse environment (Abrahamsson, et. al. 2017). This facilitate the environment to set a common goal, and to enhance the trust level among team members.

Time-Zone Effectiveness

Having designers situated in various time-zones can enable associations to increment the quantity of day by day working. This is primarily because it based on 'follow-the-sun' working model. This also facilities to diminish process duration (Conchúir, 2006). In this connection, the organization can attain the maximum productivity for the constraint amount of time. (Šmite, 2010). In addition the approach facilitated the to drive out from the severe pressure to improve 'time-to-market 'parameter.

Skilled Workers

It is broadly realized that talented engineers have the best effect on advancement, efficiency, and quality.. GSE can possibly encourage access to a vast majority of exceptionally gifted engineers . Therefore, it has been suggested that due to the diverse backgrounds of GSE actors can lead to increased innovation and shared best practice amongst team members (Carmel et. all. 2001). The GSE also motivated the worker to enhance their skills for the competitive advantages

Closeness Towards the Market and Customers

Another benefit is the proximity it offers to market and customers. Not only is the whereabouts of the local market easily available for the customers to get their hands on but also for the businessmen and companies, it is accessible now to learn the location of their potential customers (Cimolini et. al. 2012). Subsequently, this can create new jobs can create goodwill with local customers. Indeed, it may be a business necessity to locate closer to customers in order to expand to other markets. By branching out into the local markets or in new countries where the customers are located, a more direct interaction becomes possible.

Accountability

A formal record of communication provides increased traceability and accountability. Also, Projects process maturity can be well monitored this way and each individual will be entitled to deliver on task this way. Requirements-related communication between two different entities from distant locations is mostly done through "formal" mediums, i.e. the bi-weekly meetings when the communication is focused merely on urgent matters (Conchúir, et. al 2006). Whenever work-related issues arise that required cross-site communication, including an email, making a phone call or waiting for formal requirements meeting to take place.

Improved Task

The product architecture should determine the team structure, rather than the other way around. The idea of GSE drives groups to part their work according to element content well-defined independent modules, without "stepping on each other's toes" (Conchúir, et. al 2006). This allows decisions to be made about each component by the experts of that particular realm. Partitioning tasks can result in efficient work (Conchúir, et. al 2006).

GUIDING PRINCIPLES OF THE MODERN AGILE MOVEMENT

In the recent era of software engineering and development, the Agile-based approaches have been proposed. Primarily, these approaches rendered the concept of rapid development in software engineering. Moreover, it limits many of the traditional and classical software design and development phase for fast application development (Mohammad et. al. 2013). Likewise, with the growth of Information and Communication Technology (ICT), the concept of Global Software Development (GSD) has gained significant attention. GSD is the process of structuring the software design and development team beyond the local and geographical boundaries.

Modern Agile's first true meaning comes from its four guiding principles. They are Make People Awesome; Make Safety a Prerequisite; Experiment & Learn Rapidly, and Deliver Value Continuously (Rao et. al. 2011). Following are the details of these principles:

Designing and developing software applications with the express purpose of empowering the users of those applications is known as "Make People Awesome". The software development company is also likely to transform its processes based on this principle (Phil 2015). The design of the software system also provides the fundamental platform to the software product

Make Safety a Prerequisite increases the issues of quality and safety to a foundational ingredient for success according to the creators of Modern Agile. Fear of failure tends to smother the effectiveness of software development teams. According to this principle, attaching fault is never a focus; everyone works together to solve hitches. With this safe environment, leads to the overall advanced quality level in software delivery (Wood et. al. 2013).

Experiment and Learn Rapidly cracks the elimination of the fear of failure into a system where experimentation and learning are supported. This is expressly vital bearing in mind the rapid rate of transformation in the software industry with new digital strategies and innovations happening on a regular basis. Speediness is of the essence of research (Phil 2015). If an experiment doesn't work, the developer simply moves on to another idea.

Deliver Value Continuously is an important principle for Modern Agile, and is vastly relevant for companies with a Continuous Delivery program. The emphasis is getting the value into the customer's hands as quickly as possible (Phil 2015). The other three principles of Modern Agile combine to make this last principle possible.

Modern Agile is a comparatively new concept and opinions on it are mixed. Implementing some of the principles as part of a traditional Agile or DevOps program makes perfect sense, especially for companies already doing Continuous Delivery (Wood et. al. 2013).

AGILE TESTING METHODOLOGY

Agile testing methodology is primarily a software testing approach. This approach is based on the fundamentals of agile software development system. The close collaboration between the client and the development is essential for executing the project towards the goal. Specifically, the collaboration, is an important ingredient for agile testing (Cockburn, 2002). Moreover, the supports to align the development of the stakeholders is well needs of smooth execution.

Following are some of the advantages of Agile Testing:

1. Agile Testing saves time and money. As the matter of the fact the time and money are the two principle constraints for any business application
2. Fewer documentations to fill out and write up. This make the process documented with little efforts.
3. In Agile Testing the system contain the regular and intensive user feedback. This helps to establish a close and robust testing environment (Cockburn, 2002)
4. In this approach the daily standup meetings are the integral part of this approach. This style of meeting support rapid resolution the problems. Moreover, it limit any bottleneck into the system

AGILE METHODOLOGY PHASES

The agile methodology process also consists of its own life cycle. There are six phases in agile methodology (Kruchten et. al. 2013). Following are the six phases:

1. **Concept:** The problem statement and the rationale of solution is identified logically
2. **Inception:** Gather the need resources of the and initiation of the project as a formal start
3. **Construction:** The project team begins to work on the project's development using software implemented
4. **Quality:** To identify the quality parameters and their corresponding measures
5. **Production:** Development and optimization of the product
6. **Retirement:** Closures of product.

RECENT AGILE METHODS

The strength of agile methodologies is its ability to accommodate any change in requirement during any stage of the SDLC. This makes the system driving it to be more convenient and flexible. Agile methods are highly recommended in dynamic forceful environments where there is a frequent change appear in requirements (Wood et. al. 2013). This approach is appropriate when customer and developers work together in a highly intractable environment; many of the software houses have published their successful experience of implementing agile methods in software development environment (Wood et. al. 2013). Nevertheless, a lot of challenges are linked with the implementation process, especially in global software engineering. The set of difficulties faced includes, but not limited to: communication, personnel, culture, different time zones, trust, and knowledge management, to overcome the challenges and to get it to work efficiently extensive efforts is a growing need (Ji et. al. 2011). In the following part of this section, a brief description of the above stated ASD is presented with their working principle, strength, and limitations.

Extreme Programming

Extreme Programming (XP) was first proposed in March 1996. First, it starts with conducting require-ment gathering process. Subsequently, based on the requirements, the project is then decomposing into the small number of cycles/iteration. The cycles are set up using pair programming approach. Therefore, any change in user requirements can be accommodated during the development phase. The iteration plan shall be re-developed accordingly (Wood et. al. 2013). In the final stage the software quality assurance where the developed feature will be tested for bugs, if identified; the bugs shall be resolved in the next iteration. After completion of all acceptance testing, project tracing shall be executed in which feedback is taken from the project owner that how much job has already been done (Ji et. al. 2011). The pictorial illustration of XP is shown in Figure 1.

The following are the major advantages of XP

1. It is one of the most simplest ASD
2. XP save the time and money by limiting unnecessary documentation and other formalities
3. Close loop and constant feedback
4. XP contributes to ascend the employee satisfaction and retention
5. The entire process of XP is visible and accountable to every entity of the system

Despite the above advantages of XP following are some of the limitations of XP

1. XP relies on the code rather the design. It is a known fact that an optimum design will result in the quality product
2. XP does not guarantee the code quality assurance
3. Due to its intensive interaction with the team member, XP is not suggested for GSD

Figure 1. Extreme programming

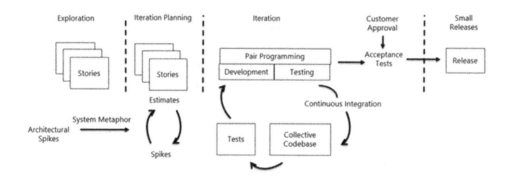

SCRUM

SCRUM founded in 1993 at the Easel Corporation, the structure of SCRUM mainly consists of sprints (Munassar et. al. 2010). In each sprint, the team finishes its tasks in a result of developing a small part of the product. The requirements initiated to go into a sprint and managed through a product backlog (Munassar et. al. 2010). Release backlog and sprint backlog is developed during sprint backlog meeting. The sprint is usually of timeframe, two to four weeks and is bound to end on time whether task achieved or not. If for somewhat reason some of the work is not completed they are shifted back to the product backlog. The complete sprint cycle is usually managed by the SCRUM master (Schwaber et. al. 2002), (Schwaber et. al. 2004).

The following are the major advantages of SCRUM

1. Up to the mark adaptively to project requirements changes within the project management cycle.
2. The product owner is constantly in coordination with the development team to sustain process transparency .
3. The testing phase takes place after each iteration, the bugs and unnecessary features are fixed quickly.
4. Execution of a roll-back plan to a previous version is quite easy.

Despite the above advantages of SCRUM following are some of the limitations of SCRUM

1. As the product requirement process is on-going and adjusted often, they are hardly documented. It means the development process can be the shift to some other dimension if the product owner is not absolutely clear of the product requirements.
2. Experienced professionals are required to monitor and control such a project management model which will act as a Scrum Master and make sure the project is moving towards right direction.
3. Initial timelines are adjusted quite frequently and delivering the expected product precisely on time is not a thing happening often.

Figure 2. SCRUM

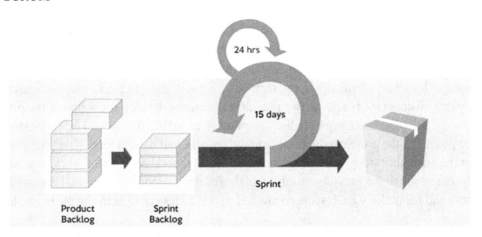

Feature Driven Development (FDD)

Feature Driven Development (FDD) emphasis on design and development phases and doesn't go through the complete development life cycle. In the Development phase, a team of software developers and domain experts are formed to design the architecture and build the overall model of the domain to establish the scope of the system (Tirumala et. al. 2016). In a list down Features phase, the cross-functional team categorizes a required list of features, subsequently, the features are combined together to form a set of features.

List of features designed are then prioritized in a plan by feature phase and then high-level project plan is developed which includes the order in which feature sets will be developed (Tirumala et. al. 2016). In the next step, the Design by Feature and Build by Feature phase the series of iterations are practiced and assign to different feature teams to execute the design. The steps shall be repeated until all features are realized (Highsmith et. al. 2001).

The following are the major advantages of FDD (Palmer et. al. 2001):

1. It usually works great for extensively large-scale products with a number of modules requiring frequent updates and constantly delivers value .
2. The requirements and other supporting papers are well-documented; making easy for developers with any experience can easily jump in and find their role to work on the project.
3. The end product is always better than the initial ones.

Despite the above advantages of FDD following are some of the limitations of FDD (Palmer et. al. 2001)

1. The model is not feasible to be used for smaller projects with strict deadlines
2. The win-win situation in this model relies mainly on having the highly-skilled and experienced project leads monitoring the process throughout the development cycles
3. Documentation is unusual if any. The product owner gets the feature, yet its exact description is outside the scope of FDD model.

Dynamic Systems Development Method

Dynamic Systems Development Method (DSDM) is a verified method of agile project management and quick product delivery (Sani et. al. 2013). It includes a well-defined process area for effective monitoring and controlling at the same time. Requirements are then classified into must have, should have, could have, and want to have for prioritization, the technique is also called Moscow rule technique. The feasibility study and business study are the two phases that actually develop the scope of the project. Both of the studies shall be conducted sequentially (Chapram et. al. 2018). The actual development is done in the last three phases of the project, which are usually iterative and incremental. The problem statement is defined in the feasibility study and costs estimation and technical review of system development and project delivery is done which provides an output in the form of feasibility report and development scope plan. Business and technology analysis is conducted by a business analyst in the business study phase.

Figure 3. FDD processes with outcomes
(Source: Palmer, SR, Felsing, JM 2002. p 57)

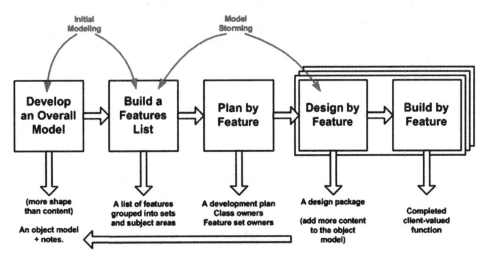

The output of this phase is designing system architecture and detailed development strategy that includes a plan for prototyping, testing, and configuration management (Sani et. al. 2013). Then it comes to the iterative phase of the development process in which analysis, coding and testing are executed which is also called 'functional model iteration' and is the first incremental and iterative phase of the process.

In Design and Build iteration, which is also called in UAT (user acceptance testing) phase, the system is handed over to the user securely to perform its testing (Chapram et. al. 2018). The objective of this phase is to resolve tweaking bugs and to cover the non-functional requirements of the user. The final step is the implementation phase in which the final product is delivered on the Live environment (Sani et. al. 2013). The pictorial representation of DSDM model is illustrated in Figure 4.

The following are the major advantages of DSDM:

1. The product owner/ Business users understand and get hands-on in the software development
2. The deliverables are quick in terms of functionality and achieving milestones.
3. Offers effective communication between end users and software developers.

Despite the above advantages of DSDM following are some of the limitations of DSDM:

1. The DSDM methodology is quietly costly as far as implementation is a concern.
2. It is not suitable for small sized organizations.

Adaptive Software Development

Adaptive Software Development is mainly focused on requirement as the creator of the method states that requirements may be fuzzy during the initiation of the project. It consists of developing objectives and mission, identifying requirements, gap analysis and Time box (Highsmith et. al. 2013). These are based on a fact of developing a set of requirements; define scope, estimates and resource allocation. The span of iteration is depending on project size and level of uncertainty. The team defines the goal and develop an objective statement for each iteration and then time box is assigned to each iteration (Calinescu et. al. 2012). The developers along with the cross-functional team assign features for each iteration. Cooperation requires teamwork which is full of trust and respect (Agovic, et. al. 2014). The team must collaborate on quick decision making, requirements, and problems. In this phase, focus groups provide feedback, formal technical reviews, and analyses (Stoica et. al. 2013). The Adaptive Software Development method replaces the traditional waterfall model and real-world testing of the model is in progress (Jalali et. al. 2012).

Figure 4. DSDM project lifecycle

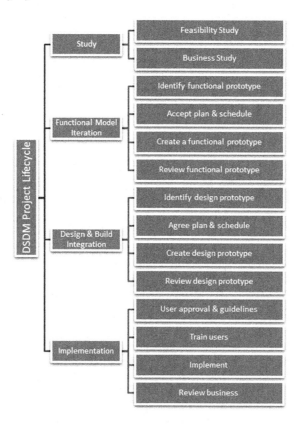

IMPLEMENTATION OF AGILE METHODS IN GSE

Over the past few years, the repaid growth of information and communication technology (ICT) has been observed. This growth has played the catalytic role in business, education, health, finance, government, economics etc. Likewise, GSE and GSD are also the beneficiaries of this growth. This subsequent part of this session, a summarized view on the scope, benefits, and limitations of the hybrid GSE and GSD are presented .

Figure 5. Adaptive software development process

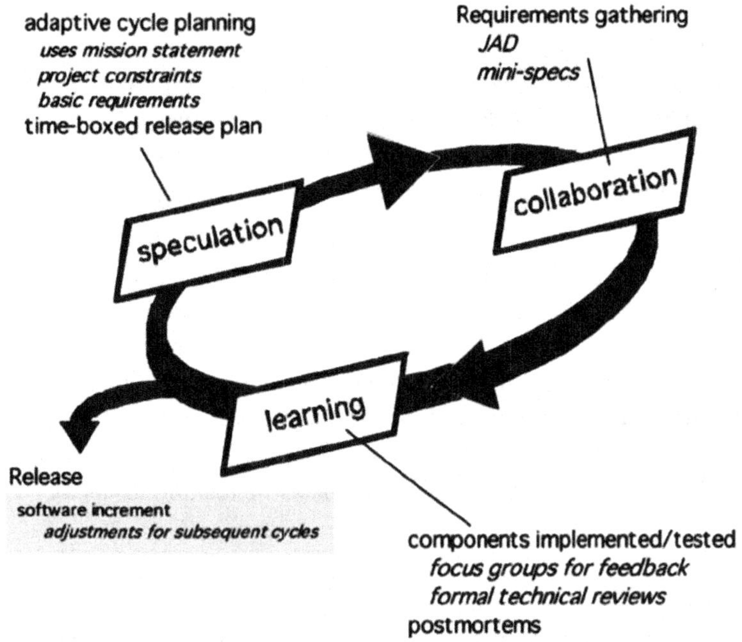

XP

1. Small releases lower the complexity results quick validation of features by the global customer
2. Small iterations shall be practiced and executed weekly, ensuring developer would have enough task in hand so as to reduce to and fro.
3. As global customers are not available on-site, story cards can be used to transfer the requirements to developers. Allowing it to communicate in pieces.
4. The development team can work into two groups. One would be responsible for reverse engineering, developing the functional specification and communicating with off-site customers. The second group will put their efforts into the forward engineering process.

SCRUM

1. Communication challenges can overcome by adjusting working hours so as to participate in daily scrums
2. To overcome face-to-face meetings difficulty due to geographical distance, teams shall use tools for synchronous communication; such as teleconference; videoconference; web-conferencing; audio/video Skype; Team Viewer with Live Meeting; and/or desktop sharing
3. Occasional visits and frequent communication by distributed team members for sprints reduces cultural misunderstandings
4. Project kick-off sprint sometimes called as print "zero" can be used to understand vision, mission, strategy, and goals.

FDD

1. FDD can be used for effective global software maintenance
2. No notable implementation of FDD found in global software engineering
3. Communication might act as a barrier in large scale global project.
4. Global project teams should be compensated properly for dedication to the completion of the project.
5. Informal communication shall be made part of the formal meetings to prevent conflicts due to lack of documentation.

DSDM

1. Beneficial to be used for small size projects and will not support complex global projects.
2. Privilege to enrich itself by composing with XP agile methodology, it inherits limitations of XP into DSDM
3. Communication barriers can be overcome using the same techniques as SCRUM and XP

ASDM

1. The chief product owner should prioritize user stories align with business representatives during requirement exploration
2. The technical product owner should play an important role in a technical liaison between the on-shore and offshore team.
3. The on-shore team should support and help offshore members to learn their culture, processes, and technology.
4. Daily scrum meeting should be conducted every day for 15 minutes during the development phase, it plays a vital role in global software development

CHALLENGES OF AGILE IN GSE

In the recent era of software engineering and development the Agile based approaches have been proposed. Primarily, these approaches rendered the concept of rapid development in software engineering. Moreover, it limit many of the traditional and classical software design and development phase for fast application development. Likewise, with the growth of Information and Communication Technology (ICT), the concept of Global Software Development (GSD) has gained the significant attention. GSD is the process of structuring the software design and development team beyond the local and geographical boundaries. In the recent literature, the researchers have proposed to employ Agile approaches in the GSD. Apparently, the scenario looks benefiting, however; it also turns into some challenges as a by-product. When there are collocation and frequent communication between the developers and the customers, agile methods are the most suitable. Incorporating agile methods in GSD requires an ample amount of effort (Jalali et. al. 2012). Following are the challenges of agile development in GSE

Communication

Communication is one of the main challenges in the agile GSD, it is considered as one of the most valuable element in Global Software Engineering especially in DS environments where the sharing of info between the members and understanding of the requirements of a customer is allowed (Jalali et. al. 2012). Communication between different developers located at different geological locations is necessary and this is a challenge . Various causes of the communication challenges are contrasting working hours, the absence of communication mediums, language barrier, insufficient face-to-face interaction, and greater communication costs .

Different Time Zones

The change in time zones increments the communication gap which is the communication in between distributed teams becomes arduous. Most common time zone difficulties occur when developers are located in countries like USA, India, Japan etc. "The difference is of 12.5 hours between USA and India, therefore communication within the distributed team members may prove difficult (Hanssen et. al. 2011)

Lack of Communication Tools

Applicable communication tools are required in agile projects between onshore and offshore development teams including the customers. The agile projects might fail if the proper communication tools are absent such as video conferencing etc. (Hanssen et. al. 2011). Therefore, it is required of distributed teams to have authorization to different communicational tools and employ them in accordance with their necessity for efficient communication.

Language Barrier

Associations among various members from various countries speaking various languages are usually hard due to their different native languages (Hanssen et. al. 2011). Members whose native language is not English often face problems when the mode of communication among members is in English making the meeting time longer than usual as it becomes harder to express the views. To increase the availability of intercultural collaboration, machine translations can be used (Dullemond et. al. 2009).

High Communication Cost

The tools used for communications are very costly, organizations are required to spend money so that they can administer better communicational facilities to their teams.

Lack of Teamwork

Collaboration among the team members in distributed agile development is of utmost importance so that high-quality products can be obtained (Dullemond et. al. 2009). It is important for each team member to know of the importance of contribution and teamwork, lack of communication may result in the fall in the morale of team members.

Cross-Cultural Diversity

A major issue in communication is Culture, an example of which is the pass of information between offshore and onshore members is only confirmed instead of critical (Dullemond et. al. 2009). Communication and collaboration between members may be affected if cultural issues are not handled properly (Dullemond et. al. 2009).

Personal Selection

The selection of personnel is highly important in agile development as requirement keeps on varying hence it becomes demanding to have cross-functional teams having developers, analysts, and testers. Usually, programmers who fail to implement plan-driven approaches and are unable to handle the dynamic requirements prove to be a liability for the team, accordingly pair programming is among agile practices which are used in development to pick a coding partner with common aims (Jalali et. al. 2010).

Feeling of Insecurity

Insecurity is often an issue faced by new team members or junior members which results in these members failing to easily communicate and put forward their concepts in team discussions. Due to this developing trust in a team becomes burdensome (Jalali et. al. 2010).

The Sense of Belonging to a Team

Poor team bonding is a result of the lack of constant face-to-face communication or any type of communication among members located at different geographical and geological locations. Another reason for lack of trust results from many socio-cultural differences and difference in languages of the distributed team members (Jalali et. al. 2010)

Temporal Distance

Admirably, face to face communication is most adequate means of communication in GSE. In GSE the project team is not only distribute geographically but it can be distribute into different adjoining time zones. Temporal distance add challenges to attain effective communication among distributed teams and shorten the communication (Paasivaara et. al. 2015).

Geographical Distance

One of the main benefit of implementing GSE is to employing from low cost developers from low wage countries (Inayat et. al. 2015). It means that software development process is not done in one platform. So it generates geographical distance. Thus face to face communication is seemed to effective communication process (Inayat et. al. 2015)

Socio-Cultural Distance

The team members which are working in GSE projects belongs to different nationalities. Cultural diversity can be develop factor in GSE. Cultural diversity in GSE projects can be develop factor. Cultural distance can be exist between two organizations, not always between two nationalities (Hoda et. al. 2017). Language difference is usually indicate as one of the challenges in communication caused by socio-culture distance (Hoda, et. al. 218). . Misconceive of message is usually happen when two communicating parties talking in foreign language. Moreover it causes mutual understanding between project members (Hoda et. al. 2017).

CONCLUSION

The current research literature on the recent trends of different agile methodologies practiced in Global Software Engineering was briefly described in this study. The implementation of agile in GSE is not yet well explored. However, it is clear that numerous challenges are associated with the process. There is not sufficient evidence found to conclude that agile was successfully implemented in large distributed global projects. In most of the studies that we reviewed, the customized agile method is explained. The main factor communication is found to play a vital role in practicing agile method in global software engineering also explained in this study. These results can be used towards proposing such a comprehensive framework for agile applicability in GSE. This study is fundamentally provides a logical platform to the researchers for further investigation in the domain of the adaptation of agile software development practices in global software engineering. The description present in this chapter strongly advocate for the adaptation of agile software development practices in global software engineering. In addition, this chapter also submit a comprehensive review on the limitations of this integration. This has created a pressing need to devise the new methods in agile development and software engineering to overcome these challenges.

REFERENCES

Abrahamsson, P., Salo, O., Ronkainen, J., & Warsta, J. (2017). *Agile software development methods: Review and analysis.* arXiv preprint arXiv:1709.08439

Ågerfalk, P. J., Fitzgerald, B., Olsson, H. H., & Conchúir, E. Ó. (2008, May). Benefits of global software development: the known and unknown. In *International Conference on Software Process* (pp. 1-9). Berlin, Germany: Springer. 10.1007/978-3-540-79588-9_1

Agovic, A., & Agovic, A. (2014). *U.S. Patent No. 8,719,781.* Washington, DC: U.S. Patent and Trademark Office.

Anwer, F., Aftab, S., Waheed, U., & Muhammad, S. S. (2017). Agile Software Development Models TDD, FDD, DSDM, and Crystal Methods: A Survey. *International Journal of Multidisciplinary Sciences and Engineering, 8*(2), 1-10.

Calinescu, R., Ghezzi, C., Kwiatkowska, M., & Mirandola, R. (2012). Self-adaptive software needs quantitative verification at runtime. *Communications of the ACM, 55*(9), 69–77. doi:10.1145/2330667.2330686

Carmel, E., & Agarwal, R. (2001). Tactical approaches for alleviating distance in global software development. *IEEE Software, 18*(2), 22–29. doi:10.1109/52.914734

Casey, V. (2009, July). Leveraging or exploiting cultural difference? In *2009 Fourth IEEE International Conference on Global Software Engineering* (pp. 8-17). Piscataway, NJ: IEEE. 10.1109/ICGSE.2009.9

Chapram, S. B. (2018). An Appraisal of Agile DSDM Approach. *International Journal of Advanced Studies in Computers. Science and Engineering, 7*(5), 1–3.

Cimolini, P., & Cannell, K. (2012). Agile Software Development. In Agile Oracle Application Express (pp. 1–13). New York, NY: Apress. doi:10.1007/978-1-4302-3760-0_1

Cockburn, A. (2002). *Agile software development.* Agile Software Development Series.

Conchúir, E. Ó., Ågerfalk, P. J., Olsson, H. H., & Fitzgerald, B. (2009). Global software development: Where are the benefits? *Communications of the ACM, 52*(8), 127–131. doi:10.1145/1536616.1536648

Conchúir, E. Ó., Holmstrom, H., Agerfalk, J., & Fitzgerald, B. (2006, October). Exploring the assumed benefits of global software development. In *2006 IEEE International Conference on Global Software Engineering (ICGSE'06)* (pp. 159-168). Piscataway, NJ: IEEE. 10.1109/ICGSE.2006.261229

Dullemond, K., van Gameren, B., & van Solingen, R. (2009, July). How technological support can enable advantages of agile software development in a GSE setting. In *2009 Fourth IEEE International Conference on Global Software Engineering* (pp. 143-152). Piscataway, NJ: IEEE. 10.1109/ICGSE.2009.22

Dullemond, K., Van Gameren, B., & Van Solingen, R. (2010, August). Virtual open conversation spaces: Towards improved awareness in a GSE setting. In *2010 5th IEEE International Conference on Global Software Engineering* (pp. 247-256). IEEE.

Èmite, D., & Wohlin, C. (2011). A whisper of evidence in global software engineering. *IEEE Software, 28*(4), 15–18. doi:10.1109/MS.2011.70

Hanssen, G. K., Šmite, D., & Moe, N. B. (2011, August). Signs of agile trends in global software engineering research: A tertiary study. In *2011 IEEE Sixth International Conference on Global Software Engineering Workshop* (pp. 17-23). Piscataway, NJ: IEEE. 10.1109/ICGSE-W.2011.12

Highsmith, J., & Cockburn, A. (2001). Agile software development: The business of innovation. *Computer, 34*(9), 20–127. doi:10.1109/2.947100

Highsmith, J. R. (2013). Adaptive software development: a collaborative approach to managing complex systems. Boston, MA: Addison-Wesley.

Hoda, R., Salleh, N., & Grundy, J. (2018). The rise and evolution of agile software development. *IEEE Software, 35*(5), 58–63. doi:10.1109/MS.2018.290111318

Hoda, R., Salleh, N., Grundy, J., & Tee, H. M. (2017). Systematic literature reviews in agile software development: A tertiary study. *Information and Software Technology, 85*, 60–70. doi:10.1016/j.infsof.2017.01.007

Holmstrom, H., Conchúir, E. Ó., Agerfalk, J., & Fitzgerald, B. (2006, October). Global software development challenges: A case study on temporal, geographical and socio-cultural distance. In *2006 IEEE International Conference on Global Software Engineering (ICGSE'06)* (pp. 3-11). Piscataway, NJ: IEEE. 10.1109/ICGSE.2006.261210

Inayat, I., Salim, S. S., Marczak, S., & et al, . (2015). A systematic literature review on agile requirements engineering practices and challenges. *Computers in Human Behavior, 51*, 915–929. doi:10.1016/j.chb.2014.10.046

Jalali, S., & Wohlin, C. (2010, August). Agile practices in global software engineering-A systematic map. In *2010 5th IEEE International Conference on Global Software Engineering* (pp. 45-54). IEEE. 10.1109/ICGSE.2010.14

Jalali, S., & Wohlin, C. (2010, August). Agile practices in global software engineering-A systematic map. In *2010 5th IEEE International Conference on Global Software Engineering* (pp. 45-54). Piscataway, NJ: IEEE. 10.1109/ICGSE.2010.14

Jalali, S., & Wohlin, C. (2012). Global software engineering and agile practices: A systematic review. *Journal of Software. Ecological Processes, 24*(6), 643–659.

Ji, F., & Sedano, T. (2011, May). Comparing extreme programming and Waterfall project results. In *2011 24th IEEE-CS Conference on Software Engineering Education and Training (CSEE&T)* (pp. 482-486). Piscataway, NJ: IEEE. 10.1109/CSEET.2011.5876129

Kaur, P., & Sharma, S. (2014). Agile software development in global software engineering. *International Journal of Computers and Applications, 97*(4).

Kruchten, P. (2013). Contextualizing agile software development. *Journal of Software: Evolution and Process, 25*(4), 351–361.

Lanubile, F., Ebert, C., Prikladnicki, R., & Vizcaíno, A. (2010). Collaboration tools for global software engineering. *IEEE Software, 27*(2), 52–55. doi:10.1109/MS.2010.39

Mohammad, A. H., & Alwada'n, T. (2013). Agile software methodologies: Strength and weakness. *International Journal of Engineering Science and Technology, 5*(3), 455.

Munassar, N. M. A., & Govardhan, A. (2010). A comparison between five models of software engineering. *International Journal of Computer Science Issues, 7*(5), 94.

Nguyen-Duc, A., & Cruzes, D. S. (2013, August). Coordination of Software Development Teams across Organizational Boundary--An Exploratory Study. In *2013 IEEE 8th International Conference on Global Software Engineering* (pp. 216-225). IEEE.

Nguyen-Duc, A., Cruzes, D. S., & Conradi, R. (2015). The impact of global dispersion on coordination, team performance and software quality–A systematic literature review. *Information and Software Technology, 57*, 277–294. doi:10.1016/j.infsof.2014.06.002

Paasivaara, M., Blincoe, K., Lassenius, C., et al. (2015, May). Learning global agile software engineering using same-site and cross-site teams. In *2015 IEEE/ACM 37th IEEE International Conference on Software Engineering* (Vol. 2, pp. 285-294). Piscataway, NJ: IEEE. 10.1109/ICSE.2015.157

Palmer, S. R., & Felsing, M. (2001). A practical guide to feature-driven development. London, UK: Pearson Education.

Phil, M. (2015). Comparative analysis of different agile methodologies. *International Journal of Computer Science and Information Technology Research, 3*(1).

Portillo-Rodríguez, J., Vizcaíno, A., Piattini, M., & Beecham, S. (2012). Tools used in Global Software Engineering: A systematic mapping review. *Information and Software Technology, 54*(7), 663–685. doi:10.1016/j.infsof.2012.02.006

Rao, K. N., Naidu, G. K., & Chakka, P. (2011). A study of the Agile software development methods, applicability and implications in industry. *International Journal of Software Engineering and Its Applications, 5*(2), 35–45.

Sani, A., Firdaus, A., Jeong, S. R., & Ghani, I. (2013). A review on software development security engineering using dynamic system method (DSDM). *International Journal of Computers and Applications, 69*(25).

Schwaber, K. (2004). *Agile project management with Scrum.* Microsoft Press.

Schwaber, K., & Beedle, M. (2002). *Agile software development with Scrum* (Vol. 1). Upper Saddle River, NJ: Prentice Hall.

Singh, A., Singh, K., & Sharma, N. (2015). Agile in global software engineering: An exploratory experience. *International Journal of Agile Systems and Management, 8*(1), 23–38. doi:10.1504/IJASM.2015.068607

Šmite, D., Moe, N. B., & Ågerfalk, P. J. (Eds.). (2010). Agility across time and space: Implementing agile methods in global software projects. Berlin, Germany: Springer Science & Business Media. doi:10.1007/978-3-642-12442-6

Šmite, D., Wohlin, C., Gorschek, T., & Feldt, R. (2010). Empirical evidence in global software engineering: A systematic review. *Empirical Software Engineering, 15*(1), 91–118. doi:10.100710664-009-9123-y

Stoica, M., Mircea, M., & Ghilic-Micu, B. (2013). Software Development: Agile vs. Traditional. *Informatica Economica, 17*(4).

Tirumala, S., Ali, S., & Babu, A. (2016). A Hybrid Agile model using SCRUM and Feature Driven Development. *International Journal of Computers and Applications, 156*(5), 1–5. doi:10.5120/ijca2016912443

Wohlin, C. (2014, May). Guidelines for snowballing in systematic literature studies and a replication in software engineering. In *Proceedings of the 18th international conference on evaluation and assessment in software engineering* (p. 38). New York, NY: ACM. 10.1145/2601248.2601268

Wood, S., Michaelides, G., & Thomson, C. (2013). Successful extreme programming: Fidelity to the methodology or good teamworking? *Information and Software Technology, 55*(4), 660–672. doi:10.1016/j.infsof.2012.10.002

Wright, H. K., Kim, M., & Perry, D. E. (2010, November). Validity concerns in software engineering research. In *Proceedings of the FSE/SDP workshop on Future of software engineering research* (pp. 411-414). New York, NY: ACM. 10.1145/1882362.1882446

This research was previously published in Human Factors in Global Software Engineering; pages 164-187, copyright year 2019 by Engineering Science Reference (an imprint of IGI Global).

Chapter 14
The Applicability of Process–Orientation to Software Development Projects:
The Applicability of Process–Orientation to Software Development Projects

Viktorija Ponomarenko
Riga Technical University, Riga, Latvia

ABSTRACT

The progress in the digital single market (DSM) has been acknowledged as one of the 10 political priorities by the European Commission since 2015. It could contribute € 415 billion per year (GDP) to the economy of the 28 EU Member States and create hundreds of thousands of new jobs. Nowadays, the ICT sector and the European Digital Agenda have declared it as one of the seven pillars of the Europe 2020 strategy. In order to speed up the development of new information technology and its commercialisation, it is necessary to increase software quality aimed at accelerating and improving technology transfer, taking into account process quality management. The aim of this article is to give an overview of a new approach to producing an additional value of the software development projects to improve the technology transfer process.

INTRODUCTION

ICT industry is rapidly developing all over the world and in Europe, and progress directly depends on a technological solution that solves the issue better by saving time, money and energy. Many software developers are struggling to find customers for their developed prototypes. In most cases, they keep a lot of prototypes in laboratories and their documents, but they don't about their position in the market, opportunities and future direction. Usually, it is difficult to check when the software complies specification and is ready to move on the market. At the same time every day many software components are

DOI: 10.4018/978-1-6684-3702-5.ch014

developed that could be used again and save developers time. In order to speed up the development of new information technology and its commercialization, it is necessary to increase the software quality aimed at accelerating and improving the technology transfer taking into account process quality management. The aim of this study is to give an overview to a new approach to producing an additional value of the software development projects to improve the technology transfer process.

For this purpose, were conducted an investigation of three information technology standards, six-sigma method, and process-oriented method.

The paper consists of 6 parts and conclusions. The first section is devoted to materials and methods. The second section represents process-oriented approach that is known as knowledge management approach to the development of software projects. Next parts describe this approach implementation, including the definition of software development processes, self-assessment systems development. The last section of the paper presents the results of the proposed approach and future work.

BACKGROUND

This paper is devoted to help the software developers set the best operation plan and make a right decision in their projects. It is applied to:

- Checking, analysing and improving existing projects;
- Set the improvement plan;
- Increase the quality of the projects.

Within the framework of this article, authors offer an evaluation of software quality with knowledge management, which combines knowledge about software development processes, asset protection, and marketing activities with the aim of creating an added value for research organization. For knowledge management is applied process-orientation method (Yin & Xiong, 2016). For process assessment and decision making was used information technology process assessment standard ISO/IEC 333020:2015 (ISO/IEC, 2015) and Capability Maturity Model (Mark et al., 1993) combined with six-sigma method (Montgomery & Woodall, 2008). For defining software development processes IEEE information technology standard 1517 – 2010 (IEEE, 2010) was chosen.

PROCESS-ORIENTED APPROACH TO DEVELOPMENT
OF SOFTWARE PROJECTS

Process orientation is known as knowledge management approach where knowledge is considered as a set of process to help managers to set the best operation plan and make right decisions. It is possible to give out six phases of process management:

Step 1: Processes have to be clearly set and documented.
Step 2: Process's performance has to be checked by using quantifiable metrics.
Step 3: Process performance has to be analysed with the help of graphical images, diagrams, causal relationship analysis or others.

Step 4: Process's stability has to be analysed and new aims and tasks have to be set, if necessary.

Step 5: Process's improvements have to be planned in coordination with new aims and tasks.

Step 6: The set process's improvements have to be implemented for fulfilling the aim.

Process approach will help to justify strong and week sides of the software development project, determine the causes for the problems and define necessary changes. The advantages and disadvantages of this approach are listed below (Table 1).

Table 1. The advantages and disadvantages of process-oriented approach

Advantages	Disadvantages
• Opportunity to check, analyze and improve existing projects • Opportunity to check, analyze and improve existing projects • Increase projects quality • Identify process improvement opportunities • Adapt processes for changes • Improve quality of the final product	• Measurement errors • Difficult to plan improvements • Time needed for implementation

The process-oriented approach allows developing an integrated system for documenting, analyzing and improving knowledge activities.

DEFINITION OF SOFTWARE DEVELOPMENT PROCESSES

Sustainable software development is initiated with actual or potential end-users needs definition, including requirements analysis, architectural design and creating documentation, and ends with the satisfaction of all identified needs. A part of the processes for software commercialization can be covered by the end-user or some mediator/ marketing department. However, the software developer must understand and evaluate the full lifecycle of software, including software protection and commercialization issues.

For defining software development processes was chosen IEEE information technology standard 1517™ –2010 (IEEE Standard for Information Technology, 2010) and Inventor's Technology Transfer Guides (IPIRA, 2017; SUOTL, 2017) that were designed to provide a broad overview of the technology transfer process. Software components that completely comply the requirements according to the criteria for reuse can offer additional gain for developers for use in several contexts as they are easily modified. It is also important for a software developer to ensure that all ramifications – including applicable protection options for software and market overview – are clearly understood. For this matter, a set of processes was designed which includes all software development processes and commercialization questions to gain profit from the developed technology (Table 2).

Table 2. Software development and the commercialization processes

Process	Activities	Value
P1. Software Implementation Process	A1.1. Evaluate the size and complexity of the project 1.1.1. Select a life-cycle process model 1.1.2. Assess and document model capabilities A1.2. Choose standards, methods, tools and programming language A1.3. Create and document project plan A1.3.1. Define resources and procedures for software development A1.3.2. Promote standards, methods, tools and programming languages for reuse of the project A1.4. Include in project: feedback and notification mechanisms	from 0 to 1
P2. Software Requirements Analysis Process	A2.1. Include software reuse requirements in the project A2.1.1. Assess the reassurance experience of re-use of similar projects A2.1.2. Assess the re-use asset defects A2.1.3. Assess the results of testing for re-used assets against system and software requirements	from 0 to 1
P3. Software Architectural Design Process	A3.1. Create a software architecture with reusable components that make up the structure and document the result A3.2 Obtain interface assets for reuse A3.3. Obtain database samples for reuse A3.3. Create user documentation for reuse A3.4. Define the initial testing requirements that can be reused A3.5. Evaluate the software architecture, interface, and database design according to the reusability criteria's and document the result	from 0 to 1
P4. Software Detailed Design Process	A4.1. Select and reuse a detailed design for each component of the software A4.2 Develop and document interface reuse assets A4.3. Select and reuse database documentation A4.4. Create and document user documentation the requirements according to the criteria for reuse A4.5. Reuse test requirements A4.6. Evaluate and document the result A4.7. Use a domain engineering feedback mechanism and a reuse asset management communication mechanism	from 0 to 1
P5. Software Construction Process	A5.1. Review the current test result documentation for reuse	from 0 to 1
P6. Software Integration Process	A6.1. Create and document an integration plan, reusing an applicable integration plan template A6.2. Document the software components and test results A6.3. Develop a set of qualification tests, test cases, and test procedures, using applicable test assets A6.4. Evaluate the integration plan, software design, code, tests and user documentation A6.5. Use a domain engineering feedback mechanism and a reuse asset management communication mechanism	from 0 to 1
P7. Software Qualification Testing Process	A7.1. Document the results of software qualification testing reusing applicable documentation assets A7.2. Evaluate the software design, code, test assets, and user documentation according to reusability criteria A7.3. Use a domain engineering feedback mechanism and a reuse asset management communication mechanism	from 0 to 1
P8. Software Protection	A8.1. Select the protection options for Software A8.1. Assess the protection options for Software A8.2. Choose more applicable protection solution for software	from 0 to 1
P9. Software Marketing/ Commercialization	A.9.1. Define potential end-users of particular software A9.2. Appropriate companies that could be interested in commercializing the particular software A9.3. Create a market overview A9.4. Identify existing business relations A9.5. Assess the sources of funding A9.6. Choose the optimal commercialization path	from 0 to 1

ASSESSMENT OF SOFTWARE DEVELOPMENT AND THE COMMERCIALIZATION PROCESSES

Information technology process assessment standard ISO/IEC 333020:2015 Process assessment. Process measurement framework for assessment of process capability (ISO/IEC, 2015) and Capability Maturity Model (Mark et al., 1993) was used as a base for process assessment. This standard allowed to make software quality assessment with to determine software profile with process levels.

Within the framework of the paper system of self-assessment was developed. It allows assessing software project quality with help of five process performance levels (PPL). Five performance levels for each task were proposed for quantifiable metrics, every condition has a set value from 0 to (Table 3). The software developer should mark process performance level and value opposite each defined process.

Table 3. Self-assessment system for software development projects

PPL	Value	Description
0	0	Process is not defined
1	0.1	Process is defined
2	0.2	Process is defined and documented, but the action is not yet started
	0.3	Process is started
3	0.4	Process is implemented
	0.5	Process is implemented and the results are documented
4	0.6	Process is assessed
	0.7	Process is assessed and results are documented
5	0.8	Process optimization requirements are defined
	0.9	Process is optimized
	1	Process is optimized and documented

Based on Capability Maturity Model and ISO/IEC 333020:2015 as widely applied this self-assessment system allows define software project profile, measure process performance on a scale and detect errors at an early stage. With this system, every software implementation process can be controlled in compliance with project requirements. This system can be used to measure effectiveness and for further performance analysis.

PROCESS PERFORMANCE ANALYSIS FOR SOFTWARE DEVELOPMENT PROJECTS

To assess whether the software development project comply with the specifications six sigma methodology was chosen. For the process control are set limitation which is considered a process undesirable event. The lowest specification limit (LSL) is defined as 0.5 when the process is implemented and the results are documented, and the upper specification limit is 1- the process is optimized and documented.

To reach quality in software development project and to comply with the specifications Cp an Cpk indicators should be equal to or larger than 1 (see Table 4).

Table 4. Quality indicators

Cp		8.33	4.167	2.778	2.083	1.167	1.389	1.19	1.042	0.926	0.833
Sigma	0	0.01	0.02	0.03	0.04	0.05	0.06	0.07	0.08	0.09	0.1
μ	Cpk										
0.5	complies	0.00	0.00	0.00	0.00	0.00	0.00	0.00	0.00	0.00	0.00
0.51	complies	0.33	0.17	0.11	0.08	0.07	0.06	0.05	0.04	0.04	0.03
0.52	complies	0.67	0.33	0.22	0.17	0.13	0.11	0.10	0.08	0.07	0.07
0.53	complies	1.00	0.50	0.33	0.25	0.20	0.17	0.14	0.13	0.11	0.10
0.54	complies	1.33	0.67	0.44	0.33	0.27	0.22	0.19	0.17	0.15	0.13
0.55	complies	1.67	0.83	0.56	0.42	0.33	0.28	0.24	0.21	0.19	0.17
0.56	complies	2.00	1.00	0.67	0.50	0.40	0.33	0.29	0.25	0.22	0.20
0.57	complies	2.33	1.17	0.78	0.58	0.47	0.39	0.33	0.29	0.26	0.23
0.58	complies	2.67	1.33	0.89	0.67	0.53	0.44	0.38	0.33	0.30	0.27
0.59	complies	3.00	1.50	1.00	0.75	0.60	0.50	0.43	0.37	0.33	0.30
0.6	complies	3.33	1.67	1.11	0.83	0.67	0.56	0.48	0.42	0.37	0.34
0.61	complies	3.67	1.83	1.22	0.92	0.73	0.61	0.52	0.46	0.41	0.37
0.62	complies	4.00	2.00	1.33	1.00	0.80	0.67	0.57	0.50	0.44	0.40
0.63	complies	4.33	2.17	1.44	1.08	0.87	0.72	0.62	0.54	0.48	0.44
0.64	complies	4.67	2.33	1.56	1.17	0.93	0.78	0.67	0.58	0.52	0.47
0.65	complies	5.00	2.50	1.67	1.25	1.00	0.83	0.71	0.62	0.56	0.50
0.66	complies	5.33	2.67	1.78	1.33	1.07	0.89	0.76	0.67	0.59	0.54
0.67	complies	5.67	2.83	1.89	1.42	1.13	0.95	0.81	0.71	0.63	0.57
0.68	complies	6.00	3.00	2.00	1.50	1.20	1.00	0.86	0.75	0.67	0.61
0.69	complies	6.33	3.17	2.11	1.58	1.27	1.06	0.90	0.79	0.70	0.64
0.7	complies	6.67	3.33	2.22	1.67	1.33	1.11	0.95	0.83	0.74	0.67
0.71	complies	7.00	3.50	2.33	1.75	1.40	1.17	1.00	0.87	0.78	0.71
0.72	complies	7.33	3.67	2.44	1.83	1.47	1.22	1.05	0.92	0.81	0.74
0.73	complies	7.67	3.83	2.56	1.92	1.53	1.28	1.09	0.96	0.85	0.77
0.74	complies	8.00	4.00	2.67	2.00	1.60	1.33	1.14	1.00	0.89	0.81
0.75	complies	8.33	4.17	2.78	2.08	1.67	1.39	1.19	1.04	0.93	0.84
0.76	complies	8.00	4.00	2.67	2.00	1.60	1.34	1.14	1.00	0.89	0.81
0.77	complies	7.67	3.83	2.56	1.92	1.53	1.28	1.10	0.96	0.85	0.77
0.78	complies	7.33	3.67	2.44	1.84	1.47	1.22	1.05	0.92	0.81	0.74
0.79	complies	7.00	3.50	2.33	1.75	1.40	1.17	1.00	0.87	0.78	0.70
0.8	complies	6.67	3.33	2.22	1.67	1.33	1.11	0.95	0.83	0.74	0.67
0.81	complies	6.33	3.17	2.11	1.59	1.27	1.06	0.90	0.79	0.70	0.64
0.82	complies	6.00	3.00	2.00	1.50	1.20	1.00	0.86	0.75	0.67	0.60
0.83	complies	5.67	2.83	1.89	1.42	1.13	0.95	0.81	0.71	0.63	0.57
0.84	complies	5.33	2.67	1.78	1.34	1.07	0.89	0.76	0.66	0.59	0.53
0.85	complies	5.00	2.50	1.67	1.25	1.00	0.83	0.71	0.62	0.56	0.50
0.86	complies	4.67	2.33	1.56	1.17	0.93	0.78	0.67	0.58	0.52	0.47
0.87	complies	4.33	2.17	1.44	1.09	0.87	0.72	0.62	0.54	0.48	0.43
0.88	complies	4.00	2.00	1.33	1.00	0.80	0.67	0.57	0.50	0.44	0.40
0.89	complies	3.67	1.83	1.22	0.92	0.73	0.61	0.52	0.46	0.41	0.36
0.9	complies	3.33	1.67	1.11	0.84	0.67	0.56	0.48	0.41	0.37	0.33
0.91	complies	3.00	1.50	1.00	0.75	0.60	0.50	0.43	0.37	0.33	0.30
0.92	complies	2.67	1.33	0.89	0.67	0.53	0.44	0.38	0.33	0.30	0.26
0.93	complies	2.33	1.17	0.78	0.59	0.47	0.39	0.33	0.29	0.26	0.23
0.94	complies	2.00	1.00	0.67	0.50	0.40	0.33	0.29	0.25	0.22	0.19
0.95	complies	1.67	0.83	0.56	0.42	0.33	0.28	0.24	0.21	0.18	0.16
0.96	complies	1.33	0.67	0.45	0.34	0.27	0.22	0.19	0.16	0.15	0.13
0.97	complies	1.00	0.50	0.33	0.25	0.20	0.17	0.14	0.12	0.11	0.09
0.98	complies	0.67	0.33	0.22	0.17	0.14	0.11	0.10	0.08	0.07	0.06
0.99	complies	0.33	0.17	0.11	0.09	0.07	0.06	0.05	0.04	0.04	0.02
1	complies	0.00	0.00	0.00	0.00	0.00	0.00	0.00	0.00	0.00	0.02

Cpk indicator is used to check how far the average value of processes is from the specification. Cp index indicates the potential capacity of the project and shows how many times 6 sigmas can be contained in a range. The higher the Cpk value, the better the process complies with the requirements. Green values mean that project fully complies with the specification, orange- process complies with the specification, but strict control is necessary, and red - the process is not capable to satisfy project requirements.

Three formulas are used for calculations (Wooluru et al.,2014):

$$Cp = (USL\text{-}LSL) / 6\sigma \tag{1}$$

$$Cpk = \min\left((USL\text{-}\mu)/3\sigma;\ (\mu\text{-}LSL)/3\sigma\right) \tag{2}$$

$$\sigma = \sqrt{\frac{\sum\left(x_i - x\right)^2}{n-1}} \tag{3}$$

where μ is average process value, but σ (sigma) is standard deviation, x_i is an individual value, x is the mean/expected value, n is the total number of values.

PROCESS IMPROVEMENTS FOR SOFTWARE DEVELOPMENT PROJECTS

During the realization of the project, its execution is controlled to determine whether the project is progressing towards the set aims. The results specify the appropriateness, suitableness, and efficiency of each process in regard to the aims. In a case when the project fully complies with specification and all commercialization issues are sold the decision maker could move developed product to the market. The result could be also achieved partly and only some reusable software components cold be sold or used by developer teams to create a new software development project. If the results are far from the aims and the process does not comply with the specification, corrective measures are implemented when the problem is transformed to a new aim. The project manager should decide what direction the project will take, what specifically the software developers must do to achieve the set aims. The aims should include the result, and actions to achieve the aim also must be indicated.

In every project process improvement should be planned in coordination with new aims and are recorded in the table or task list. Software developer team must perform the established process improvements for achieving the aim.

CONCLUSION

Within this study was given an overview to the process-oriented approach to produce an additional value of the software development projects. The process-oriented approach allowed developing an integrated system for documenting, analyzing and improving knowledge activities. For a software project control was developed continuous quality assessment methodology that is based on based on Capability Maturity Model and ISO/IEC 333020:201. Based on process performance analysis project manager can get software project profile and see the progress with its strong and weak points. This understanding offers an opportunity to completely finish and optimize software development processes for successful commercialization and gaining profit from software introduction to the market.

For defining software development processes, development processes for software of repeated use were chosen, so that they would be modular and easily modified. Existing software components that completely comply with the specification can offer additional gain for developers for use in several contexts as they are easily modified.

In the future, quality indicators with recommendations to project manager should be generated by an expert system. The expert system will use the collected knowledge about a particular project and project manager's experience and will give an advice based on the answers given by the developers during self-assessment. This system will help the decision makers and software developers learn more about the problem they are trying to solve while performing the software development project.

REFERENCES

European Commission. (2017a). *Commission and its priorities. 10 priorities.* Retrieved from https://ec.europa.eu/commission/priorities/digital-single-market_en

European Commission. (2017b). *Strategy. Digital Single Market. Europe 2020 strategy.* Retrieved, from https://ec.europa.eu/digital-single-market/en/europe-2020-strategy

IEEE Standard for Information Technology. (2010). *1517-2010 System and Software Life Cycle Processes. Reuse Processes.* USA: IEEE.

Mark, C., Curtis, B., Chrissis, M. B., & Charles, V. Weber. (1993). Capability Maturity Model for Software. Technical Report. Version 1.1. Pittsburgh, PA: Carnegie Mellon University

Montgomery, D. C., & Woodall, W. H. (2008). An Overview of Six Sigma. *International Statistical Review*, *76*(3), 329–346. doi:10.1111/j.1751-5823.2008.00061.x

Office of Intellectual Property & Industry Research Alliances (IPIRA). (2017) *An Inventor's Guide Technology Transfer at the University of California.* Retrieved September 25, 2017, from http://ipira.berkeley.edu/sites/default/files/shared/docs/InventorsGuide.pdf

Project Management Concepts. (n.d.). *Process Based Management.* Retrieved September 25, 2017, from https://www.tutorialspoint.com/management_concepts/process_based_management.htm

Standard ISO/IEC. 33020 (2015) Information technology. Process assessment. Process measurement framework for assessment of process capability (2). Switzerland: ISO/IEC.

Office of technology licensing, Stanford University (SUOTL). (2017). *Inventor's Guide.* Retrieved from https://otl.stanford.edu/documents/OTLinventorsguide.pdf

Wooluru, Y., Swamy, D. R., & Nagesh, P. (2014). The Process Capability Analysis – a Tool for Process Performance Measures and Metrics - a Case Study. *International Journal of Qualitative Research*, *8*(3), 399–416.

This research was previously published in the International Journal of Information Technology Project Management (IJITPM), 10(2); pages 1-7, copyright year 2019 by IGI Publishing (an imprint of IGI Global).

Chapter 15
Software Development for Information System – Achieving Optimum Quality with Security

Syeda Umema Hani

GSESIT, Hamdard University, Karachi, Pakistan & DHA Suffa University, Karachi, Pakistan

Abu Turab Alam

Surrey University, Guildford, UK

ABSTRACT

Information Systems acquisition, implementation, and development have been taking place in business organization to gain the competitive advantage. Rapid advancement of Technology is also popping up unethical issues involving violations of End users' data protection and privacy. This article discusses standard quality practices adhere to which a good quality software product is guaranteed while supporting the organizational strategic needs. It presents a framework that bridges Quality software development process improvement with strategic needs of an organization. Standard practices under consideration includes Capability Maturity Model for Development (CMMI-DEV) while using multi-model Process Improvement approach where an organization could use Balance Score Card technique while setting its strategic goals and monitoring their performance related to Information System development, and also link it with Information System management framework "Control Objectives for Information and Related Technology" (COBIT) - 5 released by Information Systems Audit and Control Association (ISACA), so that users could easily switch between the two standards. In last benefits are reported for using quality practices to realize attainment of competitive advantage.

INTRODUCTION

The "Information Technology" based system depends intensely on "Software Development" activities due to the rapid changing advances and also to cope up with the day to day business challenges in today's global business market (Kroenke, 2009). Therefore, a quality development of software is unavoidable

DOI: 10.4018/978-1-6684-3702-5.ch015

nowadays. Whereas highly successful software projects circumstances have shown the ability to acquire accurate estimates in the beginning, good grip on Project management and control activities and effective Quality Control (Jones, 2017).

This study discusses important aspects related to current trends of using software development practices and their changing impacts on quality software development. These current trends comprise of possible Software Process Improvement (SPI) methods and the possible metrics used for the quantification of Software development quality benefits and the organizational performance improvement in order to achieve the competitive advantage in the market.

It discusses how to cover up major gaps in between Information System development and business process that effect overall business system's quality. These gaps are related to the involvement of collaboration of Information System's related Strategic management, the performance monitoring of IT organization and finally with Software Development unit that exists in an IT setup being aware of IT Asset's protection.

LITERATURE REVIEW

Day to day business operations in an organization generates data that an Information System (IS) processes into strategic or tactical information that helps the management in effective decision making. Its biggest advantage is that Information can flow up in the MIS information pyramid faster and more effectively. There exist three levels of information management in any organization (Laudon & Laudon, 2011). The first one is "Executive level that comes on the top level of management pyramid and at this level of management long-term and unstructured decisions takes place. The Second level is a Managerial level that comes on the middle level of management pyramid and at this level of management semi-structured decisions take place covering weeks and months. The Third level is an Operational level that lies at bottom of the management pyramid where structured decisions need to be taken on daily basis.

There are mainly two broad categories of IS which are utilized at aforementioned three levels of "Information Management" in any organization. Let's take a quick look at different possible types of an IS which are used at different management levels of an organizations (Tiến, 2012).

1. **Management Support System:** It supports managerial level strategic decision making for achieving competitive advantage and business level tactical decision making. It further comprises of Management Information System (MIS) which facilitates managers with pre-specified analysis and reporting tools, Executive Information System (EIS) which facilitates executives with strategic as well as tactical information management and Decision Support System (DSS) that facilitates executives with strategic as well as tactical information management. It provides interactive support for non-routine decisions what-if analysis for End-users through text and graphs.
2. **Operation Support System:** It supports business processes and operations. It further comprises of Enterprise Communication System (ECS) that facilitates operations through team collaboration and communication, Process Control Systems (PCS) which supports operations and monitor and control industrial and manufacturing process. And Transaction Processing Systems (TCS) which supports operations, and updates operational databases.

It can be seen from the above discussion that Information Systems are mainly software-based solutions. Therefore, it is important to understand what quality practices are required for the development and maintenance of an IS.

What is Quality?

Definition of Gerald Weinberg defines quality as "Something that values to some person. The tricky part is to find out who that person should be. It is a value that makes a user's high-quality system to low quality to someone else. Therefore, it is also important to decide who is measuring quality and then find out how to assess it". Another definition by Roger Pressman defines it as "Conformance to explicitly defined functional and implicit characteristics that are expected of professionally developed software". Capers John adds into it that "the professionally developed software should be either defect free or have a tolerable level of defects". From different definitions of what is meant by the quality it can be concluded that the quality must meet two criteria i.e. it must be measurable, and it should be predictable before it occurs (Jones, 2008).

Quality Challenges to Information Systems and Its Targeted Benefits

Nowadays the challenges encountered by Information Systems include difficulty in developing them, security breaches, maintenance of huge information, employee's turnover and mistrust conditions, ethical issues such as integrity and privacy of information (Potter & Sakry, 2011). Every above challenge has further details to deal with; if business overcomes above challenges, as a result, it adds value to the customer which could be measured as tangible i.e. quantifiable benefits as well as intangible unquantifiable benefits. Through the quality development of information systems, we could achieve primarily benefits comprise of Tangible goals which are quantifiable measurable goals and include for example improved inventory control, increased production, and reduced administration cost as well as some intangible goals. And intangible goals which are usually difficult to measure for example enhanced customer service, greater customer loyalty, and enhanced public image (Kamel, 2003). These tangible and intangible goals help in to achieve benefits like enhanced competitiveness, confinement of market opportunities, improved products and services quality, increase in market share, support for the corporate strategy, enhanced productivity of staff, increased revenue, reduced costs, increased customer service, good market exposure, and market visibility etc. And to realize these benefits an organization must attain an ability to realize benefits (ISACA, 2015).

Realization from this section could be concluded as since the goal of information systems is to enable the organization to achieve its business goals therefore, it is important to build (develop and acquire) information systems while implementing effective information security along with a proper enforcement of ethics. Such that, the developing organization should target its goals related to the challenges it is facing and monitor their performance to guarantee successful completion of an information systems' build process.

Current Quality Trends for Developing IS

Organizations who are involved in developing IS are already advised to use "Total Quality Management" approach to facilitate Quality Improvements within a business using some well-known quality standard for information system like ISO 9001 or SPI framework CMMI. Adaptation of these Quality standards leads to a Continuous Process Improvement (CPI) using which we could develop and maintain quality Information Systems. There is another term Business Process Redesign (BPR) which could also be managed well through achieving CPI.

Dependency of IS on Competitive Advantage

Varying industry to industry an organization's goals and objectives are determined through its competitive strategy (Kroenke, D., 2009). Competitive strategies could be achieved by the organization targeting following type of goals:

A. Related to their products and services: To create, enhance or distinguish its products and services from other competitors across its industry or across industry segment.
B. Related to developing better business process: To catch customer via high switching costs, to lock its suppliers through facilities and discouraging them from changing to another business, collaborate with other organizations and set standards, purchase costs could be reduced to provide benefits to everyone, and by reduce costs which in turn reduces prices and increases profitability to become a cost leader across its industry or across industry segment.

Competitive strategies require a business process that offers its customers benefits and value. Value to the customer means, his willingness in investing over product, service, or resource the system is offering.

The business process comprises of set of activities related to support (i.e. HR, Admin and management, Procurement, and Technology) and primary (i.e. logistics, operations, Sales and marketing, and services) that adds margin of value to organization's products and services through applying competitive strategies.

Conclusion is that once the business process has been defined, IS then be structured which can improve operational efficiency, and customer-supplier relationship through utilizing benchmarking and industry best practices i.e. adaptation of Process Improvement activities.

Desirable Goals for IS to become a Competitive Advantage

Suggests following goals which are used to make ground for current study:

1. Understand Information System for strategic organizational success. Strategic support includes doing the things in smarter way by setting direction i.e. vision, by creating standard i.e. setting performance goals and setting strategy for reaching goals.
2. Understand need for developing an Information System's business case.
3. Understand Technological innovations to improve competitive advantage. It includes following:
    a. Organizational learning i.e. to improve organizational behavior by using acquired knowledge and insights.
    b. Using Total Quality Management (TQM) for monitoring the improving quality of operations, products and services.
    c. Automation for performing operations faster and for doing things in better way using patterns and trends.

4. In addition to all above goals understanding the implementation of Ethics, Data Integrity, and User Privacy is also very important.

Need of Quality Development and Acquisition for IS

ISACA is a body that formalizes different functions of information systems (ISACA, 2015). These functions are related to its governance, audit, security and assurance professionals worldwide. ISACA has introduced the COBIT-5 framework. It focuses over the effective usage of IT for achieving the strategic objectives and the realization of business benefits achieved but its previous versions does not formalizes the software development activity of Information Systems.

Generally, two approaches have been used for the development of IS i.e. Process oriented approach (proceeds trough GUI designing and approached towards data storage needs) and a Data oriented approach (data storage is first implemented then forms are designed to use the stored data). No matter what approach the organization use, they usually adopt different software development methodologies as model or multi-model driven approach for quality implementation of Information Systems without being known their benefits. These methodologies may include Agile, Xtreme Programming (XP), Team Software Process (TSP), CMMI with Spiral life cycle model, and RUP methodologies. These approaches have varying quality impacts which are covered in detail in last section (Jones, 2012).

At this point the Strategic Management field should get connected with Software Engineering field. Another type of Information Systems called ecosystems involve different industries working together for delivering value to the customer. For them IT also helps in establishing collaboration among participant firms and requires more advanced forms of software-based solutions. This study is about to understand standardization of Software Engineering and related practices, which could provide more value to the customers while interacting with Strategic Management field.

Enabling Ethical Culture and Implementing Information Security

In spite of following Process Improvement for Software Development it is now unavoidable to have a proper implementation of Code of Ethics and Business Conduct book following relevant COBIT 5 Enabler processes following the given important steps like defining the mission and value statement, Building trust and credibility, establishing environment of respect for the individual, creating a culture of open and honest communication, setting Tone, upholding the law (competition, proprietary information, selective disclosure, health and safety), avoidance of conflict of interest, etc. Subsequently, information security should then be aligned with Process centric view (Frisken, 2015; Chatterji, 2016).

Different Process Improvement Approaches

To achieve the challenges highlighted in previous section there is a need to understand what Process Improvement (PI) is and what different approaches and combinations could be used to develop Information System as a competitive advantage. Process Improvement could be categorized as per its usage approaches i.e. Classic Process-Centric approach and the Goal-Problem-Centric approach.

1. **Process Centric Approach:** Improvement in which is started by following processes and progress towards business goals by looking into the business problems this approach has high risk of fail-

ure because before starting PI the organization has not targeted to bring solution of any specific problems therefore common result might be confusing and make the organization lost.

2.   **Goal-Problem Centric Approach:** This approach came in as a solution to the first approach, using it we could specify our goals first for resolving the problems which our current working process is facing. In order to resolve these problems, we then define and specify PI efforts. Therefore, our improvement actions will be in turn compliant with the goal actions. COBIT framework is developed for IT governance and is beneficial for IT audits but when software development quality is concerned at process side we could use PI standards like SEI CMMI, ISO9001 etc.

Here frameworks provide tailor-able PI suggestions to the organizations where standards like ISO focuses more on documentation. There is another classification of PI approach as a Data Driven, Model Driven or Multi Model (Hefner, 2005).

1.   **Data-Driven:** In data driven approach one needs to charter team and clarify what its customer wants. Map process and specify critical to quality goals. Determine what your processes can do, apply Statistical Process Control for process performance measurement. Identify root causes of problems. Identify and prioritize improvement opportunities and implement improvement solutions. Apply causal analysis of data to control and assure mission success by identifying the customer's needs and reducing defects. Six Sigma and Lean comes under this category.

2.   **Process or Model-Driven:** Such models determine the industry's best practices as (benchmarking and models) and comparing your current practices to the model. Appraisals and staff training is performed. Improvement opportunities are identified, prioritized and institutionalized. Finally, the organizational process is optimized by going through continuous PI. CMMI framework or COBIT framework comes under this category.

3.   **Multi Model Approach:** In multi model approach data driven models could be used in process-based models to facilitate process improvement. For example, "Six Sigma Processes" or "Balanced Score Card" approach could be used for supporting CMMI based process improvements.

For Information System development a Goal Centric approach with Multi Model approach would make right combination. As goal centric could link strategic goals with PI need and multi model could help us in reaching towards something that could be stated as perfect solution. For details check solution and recommendation section.

FRAMEWORK FOR PROCESS IMPROVEMENT

This section first presents recommendations by industrial experts and then it discusses different possibilities of achieving quality development of an IS.

Recommendations by Industrial Experts

This section presents understanding of industrial experts what they think should be necessary for Quality Software Development. For example, Juan Lopez, CSM the director of software development at TRX,

Inc. presents following list of most important software development practices which are required for the quality software development:

1. An organizational commitment to excellence with a strong customer focus;
2. Data-based estimation, planning, budgeting, and program management including internal and external (e.g. ISBG) cost model comparisons; earned value management; risk management with value analysis; and dashboard monitoring;
3. Involved domain expertise in defining the concept of operation, use case scenarios, and system requirements with a strong focus on human-system integration;
4. Incremental and iterative engineering processes that are hybrids of CMM-I level 3 or above, Six Sigma, TSP/PSP, extreme programming, object-oriented methods, model-driven engineering; and employ formal change control and defect prevention practices including pre-certified components, formal specification with automated verification, joint application design, and quality function deployment;
5. Disciplined quality assurance and quality control with program and defect metrics, complexity analysis, static code analysis, coding standards, inspections, walk-through, integration and test planning, automated test coverage analysis, and test automation.
6. Data gathering and analysis is built in and makes it very easy to learn from personal mistakes, how to remove them, and how to prevent them.

Whereas, Wayne Mack the Project Manager, Avaya Government Solutions, Washington D.C considers that the majority of issues related to software quality tend to be acts of omission rather than acts of commission – issues tend to be things that the software development team did not do rather than things that they did wrong. This belief shapes into following points:

1. The development team must be actively involved in requirements gathering. The development team needs to have an inherent understanding of the issues to be addressed and this cannot be fully communicated through paper documents.
2. The development team must be given training in how to test. Although Test Driven Development (TDD) and "Do the simplest thing that could possibly work" address software that is developed from scratch, when using external components and libraries, the development team needs to understand how find inappropriate generic operation and restrict the capabilities to those needed for a particular design.
3. We need to bring back the concept of software reuse at an application or project level. The focus needs to be on having a library of simple, common operations rather than complex generic algorithms. Wrap all GUI components into business data type specific components so that the data type is handled consistently throughout the application.
4. We need to have the development team focus on design for today rather than designing for future considerations. Focus needs to be on developing solutions to well-understood issues rather than attempting to solve poorly understood potential requirements. It is often these future capabilities that dramatically increase development time and test time, and when the future issue is actually realized, the design often turns out to be a poor fit. This results in wasted future effort in trying to save a poorly thought out approach when the future necessitates a change or addition.

5.   Code refactoring needs to be embraced by management as a necessary step in ongoing software development efforts. The software structure needs to be continuously improved throughout the development and maintenance process. We need to change from believing "If it ain't broke, don't fix it" to "You probably don't know how broke it actually is." Lack of experience can lead to bad decisions; development teams need to be able to address these in the future. Schedule deadlines can lead to shortcuts; development teams need to be able to address these in the future. Refactoring needs to be explicitly recognized as a necessary step by management and not be relegated to a hidden activity by the development team. These steps lead to added responsibilities to the development team and require the development team to take on more tasks than simply programming all day. The senior level staff and team leads need to take on a broader range of skills and not be ever more focused on intricate details of specific programming languages and environments.

Whereas, the list to produce the best possible software by Cor Lageweg (Project Manager, Molina Healthcare, Irvine, California) is as follows:

1.   An organization-wide stated and active commitment to quality (allow quality to occur).
2.   Promote quality at ALL levels; requirements, development, testing, configuration, implementation, support and mature team members (technical, functional and executive).
3.   Clear, concise and transparent processes that promote and reward quality.
4.   Verification of quality; static code analysis, code audits, automated testing, manual testing, etc. and metrics of some sort (# bugs, # missed features, etc.).
5.   Positive motivation; reward systems for individuals and projects that obtain a certain level of quality.

This section concludes that the major economic value of high quality Information System is to achieve shorter development schedules, lower development costs, lower maintenance costs, lower cost of quality, and lower total cost of ownership. Just concerning with the software defects is not enough for quality to drive benefits.

Misconceptions About Process Improvement Frameworks

Before selecting any specific approach for SPI we should also knows that, there exist few misconceptions about different SPI techniques. One thing to notify here is no matter which approach is adapted, care should be taken for so that a good model combination in a Multi Model approach could be selected (Johnson & Kulpa, 2010). As far as CMMI framework is concerned, it supports all classic as well as agile methodologies of software development and it could be easily adapted for the Quality development of Information System.

Option 1: CMMI Based Framework for Developing Quality IS

These days almost every business uses strategy maps to set and tract their business goals related to four viewpoints related to Financial, Customer, Internal Business Process, Learning and Growth. Balance Score Card approach is used to keep the performance track of Key Performance Indicators (KPI). These KPI are mapped with the goals defined in strategy map.

A framework is proposed that should link its business strategy map with benefits of achieving competitive advantage through Information System development, following quality framework like CMMI. If an organization adapts process improvement practices like CMMI framework then it could link its goals with the KPI inside the balance score card tool. Through it they can keep track of overall organizational performance by tracking the performance of its KPIs. The performance measurement is facilitated in BSC as each KPI is associated with some quantifiable metric value and KPI value predictions could also being made more accurately if empirically derived equations are set in same tool instead of just using target values for performance monitoring.

Figure 1 shows details of proposed framework. In other terms we could say the performance of CMMI benefits (interpreted as KPI) could be viewed and measured in to strategic management's four perspectives.

Figure 1. Interaction of strategy map with CMMI process areas for developing IS with competitive advantage

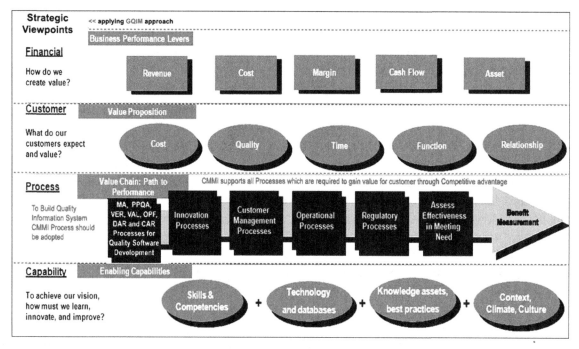

Strategy map helps to maintain link in-between Strategic level and all the way long to project level process tracking. There are mainly three steps to be followed, in Step 1 in order to align CMMI framework with BSC, there is a need to make some strategy. The strategy for CMMI should not only focus over its constellation and later on dumped over business strategy but should be derived from business requirements. In Step 2 Goal Question Indicator Metric (GQIM) could be followed and question could be asked like: what are the main problems faced in business? and what role IS development will play in it. In Step 3 the organization aligns process by answering issues. Prioritize the answers while focusing over initiatives with measurable results. Intention to finding measurable indicators should be about asking the right question.

Alignment of CMMI process areas with business goals using proper KPI provides value to organization as they make investments and improvements whereas BSC helps in checking effectiveness of adapted strategy. In an environment where one has to use multiple methods there is a need of alignment in between their relevant areas or steps. Table 1 presents different KPI considered to be used in BSC for Quality benefit measurement based on studies (Rohm & Malinoski, 2012) and (Mead & Allen, 2009).

Table 1. Possible performance goals and KPI for developing Quality IS

Business Perspectives	Mission Objective or KPI or performance measures
FINANCIAL (Business Performance Levels)	
Questions to be asked: To create value for stakeholder, what financial objectives the organization must accomplish?	Revenue or Revenue Growth
	Cost invested on Software Development
	Margin or Operating Margin
	Cash Flow
	Assets
	Economic Value Added
	Maximize Shareholder Value
	Profitability
CUSTOMERS (Value Preposition)	
Questions to be asked: What do our customers expect and value? To achieve our financial objectives, what customer needs must we serve?	Cost or Price of Service
	Quality
	Time
	Function
	Relationship/Customer Satisfaction
	Customer Loyalty
	Image
	Service
Strategic competitiveness	Sustainable Competitive Advantage
	Inside Out market position
	Increase market share
INTERNAL PROCESS (INTERNAL BUSINESS PROCESS) (Value Chain: Path to performance)	
Questions to be asked: What processes are required for customer through competitive advantage? To satisfy our customer and stakeholders, in which internal business process must we excel?	Safety
	Innovation Process / process Enhancement
	Customer Management Process
	Operational Process or Operational Efficiency
	Regulatory Processes
	Access Effectiveness in meeting needs
	Productivity
	Business Efficiency
	Cycle Time
	Cost
	Quality

continues on following page

Table 1. Continued

Business Perspectives	Mission Objective or KPI or performance measures
LEARNING AND GROWTH (Enabling capability)	
Questions to be asked: How must we learn to innovate and improve? To achieve organizational goal how must our organization learn and innovate?	Employee Satisfaction
	Skill and competitiveness or Employee personal development
	Technologies and Databases
	Knowledge assets and best practices
	Intellectual assets
	Context, Climate, Culture Or Organizational Enhancement
	Continuous Improvement
	Market Innovation

A Management cycle has been proposed which is usually being followed in organizations for the implementation of BSC (Chang, R. Y., Morgan, M. W., 2000). Table 2 shows mapping of its different steps with CMMI process areas where alignment is necessarily needed.

Table 2. Mapping CMMI Process Area alignment with the Management Cycle of performance score cards

Step Number	Management Cycle	Alignment with CMMI Process Areas
1: Collect/ Plan or Revise Plan	Collect Information	OPF SP1.2, OPF SP3.4, IPM SP1.7, and generic practice GP3.2. discover flaws in current process and IS Products
2: Create/ Do	Create the scorecard design	By gaining understanding of current process flaws from MA SG1 and OPF SG2. OPF SG2 Plans and implement required organizational process improvements through CMMI. DAR helps in decision making for selecting productive alternative as per added customer value criteria. BSC and cost benefit analysis could be performed here for evaluation purpose.
3: Cultivate	Cultivate acceptance and the measurement culture	MA (GQM) is properly applied and management is convinced by linking it with its goals and objectives.
4: Cascade	Cascade measures down through the organization	In OPM maintain BSC that sets a framework for MA SP1.1 i.e. what information do we need, and what are the measurement objectives associated with that need Then MA SP1.2 – MA SP1.4 establish the measurement infrastructure required to address that information need / measurement objectives.
5: Connect	Connects objectives and measures to employees	IPM process guarantees 1. Implementation of required organizational process improvements through OPF (Implementation of CMMI). 2. OPM SG1
6: Confirm/ Check	Confirm effectiveness through evaluation leading to ongoing improvement	OPP gathers data from projects to measure and predict quality and business critical processes performance and quality product characteristics. In next cycles it could be termed as benefit measurement of deployed process improvement through OPM. OPM maintain analyze process performance using BSC.
7: Improvement/ ACT		From QPM and OPP it detects product and process deficiencies through applying root cause analysis in CAR.

Following CMMI Process Areas (PA) needs to be implemented:

Measurement and Analysis (MA) Maturity Level 2: Measurement and Analysis PA creates measurement capability and produces quantifiable results for all areas of Engineering, Project Management and Business thus it supports Management Information. Different process areas derive data based on its principles. Figure 2 highlights its major steps of MA PA.

Figure 2. Measurement and Analysis Process Area

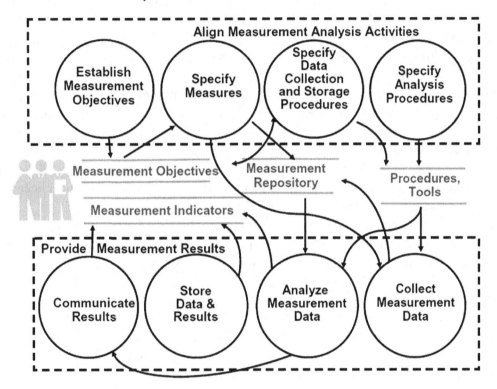

It states that for the alignment of measurement and analysis activities one has to establish measurement objectives first then specify measure and specify its related data collection and storage procedures, and the analysis procedure.

To provide measurement results one needs to collect measurement data then analyze it and finally store its results. By adapting Measurement and Analysis process area of CMMI we could proceeds towards the fine adaptation of the proposed framework.

Process and Product Quality Assurance (PPQA) Maturity Level 2: It provides an objective insight into processes and products. It objectively evaluates process and product tasks, identify non-compliance issues, provide feedback of QA to relevant staff and confirm that non-conformance issues have been taken care off.

Organizational Process Focus (OPF) Maturity Level 3: based on current organizational process strength and deficiencies it plans and implement required organizational process improvements. Interacting with integrated Product and process Planning PA it guarantees organizational commitment and availability of resources required for process group for effective deployment of improvements.

Integrated Product and Process Development (IPPD) Maturity Level 3: It gives parallel development approach and integrates product development process with related processes for which product is being developed. These integrated processes accommodate information provided by the stakeholders related to all phases of product lifecycle from both business domain and technical software development functions and they also accommodate processes for teamwork. In latest version CMMI-Dev it is replaced with OPD PA and OID is introduced at level 5 (Siemens AG, 2013).

Decision Analysis and Resolution (DAR) Maturity Level 4: It helps in decision making process. It analyzes multiple decisions and helps in identifying productive alternatives. Provides structured decision making process comparing alternatives against success criteria and selects the best. For developing IS to achieve competitive advantages, SWOT analysis method should be used for business planning, strategic planning, competitor evaluation, marketing, business and product development and research reports. SWOT stands for to evaluate the strengths, weaknesses, opportunities, and threats. It can evaluate decisions like a company value, product or brand, business idea, a strategic option of entering into new market or introducing new product or service, a method for sales or an opportunity to make acquisition, a potential partnership, changing a supplier, outsourcing a service, activity or resource or an investment opportunity.

Organizational Performance Management (OPM) Maturity Level 5: The OPM process area enables the organization to manage its organizational performance in order to meet its business objectives by iteratively analyzing aggregated project level data to identify performance gaps against the business objectives, and then selecting and deploying improvements to bridge the identified gaps. Business objectives may include improvement in all productivity related parameters. See last section for its details. This PA is an extension of OPF practices by focusing on PI based on a quantitative understanding of the It interacts with MA PA to measures impact of deployed process and technology improvement by measuring related metrics as discussed in section "Standard Metrics for measuring benefits of SPI". Need of this PA has already been discussed in previous section "Quality challenges to Information Systems and its targeted benefits". These objectives or benefits stands as KPI's in balance score card system.

Organizational Process Performance (OPP) Maturity Level 5: This PA establishes measurements and gathers data from all projects. These measures are used to quantify process performance for the prediction of, quality and business critical processes and quality product characteristics. Once all necessary measurements have been established and models are constructed then it needs Quantitative Project Management to be implemented in parallel to realize process performance.

Quantitative Project Management (QPM) Maturity Level 4: It manages process using statistical measures for process control either using SPC or six sigma approach.

Inclusion of CMMI-DEV for Security

CMMI-DEV version 1.3 which is a latest version of CMMI framework provides a framework for security activities that lead to secure products following four new process areas. Similarly, the CMMI for Services has an inclusion for security during service (Siemens AG, 2013). See Figure 3.

Figure 3. CMMI Dev- Security PA

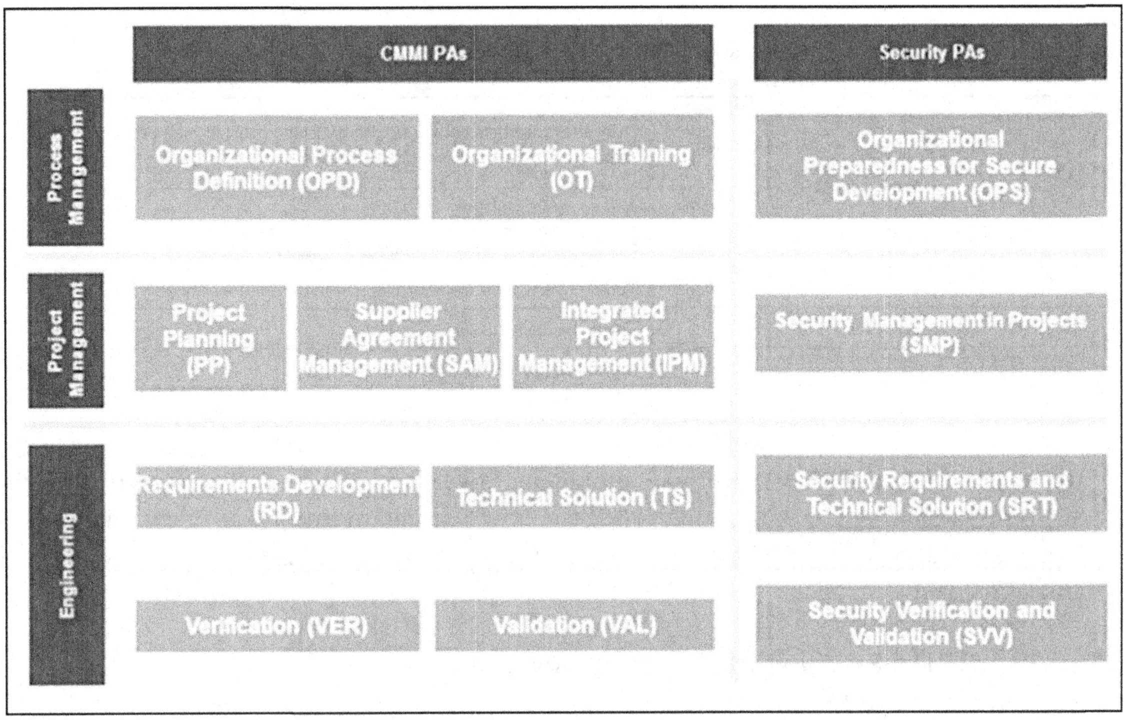

Execution of Framework for Developing a Process Improvement Plan

Following are the important steps to follow in-order to develop a Process Improvement Plan, these steps are also in compliant to the above proposed framework (Potter & Sakry, 2011).

1. Scope the Improvement:
    ◦   Identify Organizational Goals or the Business goals, achievement of which could be taken as the benefits achieved by Process Improvement activity.
    ◦   Identify problems or issues in current organizational process.
        i.   For Example if the goal is to successfully deliver product A on dated: dd/mm/yy then the associated Problem1 might be an need of proper client requirements which should be track able and changes made into them should also be tracked as code is not traceable with their requirements at the time of testing, and Problem 2 may be associated with frequent changes in product goals which causes hinder to synchronize management's directions with the product version.
    ◦   Prioritize them and select the ones which are critical for business.
2. **Develop Action Plan:** List down actions following some process framework like CMMI and organize the actions according to their goals and problems.
3. Depending on action priority perform actions, check their progress and take corrective actions. Now follow only those Process Improvement framework practices that could help you in gaining control on the identified problems which exists in your Organizational Process (see Table 3).

Table 3. Process Improvement Plan

Goals communicates the results we want to achieve	Purpose communicates why we want to achieve this goal	Actions	Priority * = compulsory
To reduce software development cycle time to some month range	To deliver earlier in order to get competitive advantage in market	Only allow changes at interface level. Enhancements will be entertained in next cycles on extra change.	1*
		Assign responsibility	2*
		Check progress and take corrective steps	
		Make Investigation for improvement in current functionality	3
		Track change requests	4
		Baseline changes	5

4. **Determine Risks and Plan to Mitigate, Implement the Plan and Check Progress:** By checking that is the organization making progress (the Goals or Our Improvement Plan or the Improvement Framework) depending on which process improvement approach we have adapted and conclude lessons learned.

Option 2: COBIT5 Framework for the Governance and Management of IT Enterprise

It defines value creation while realising the benefits utilizing optimal resource cost while optimising risk. It maps enterprise goals with IT-related goals and finally IT goals supported by critical processes. It also includes a capability model with objectives of process improvement and support in compliant to ISO/IEC 15504 Software Engineering process assessment standard.

CMMI Process Areas Support in COBIT-5

COBIT5 covers CMMI processes related to application building and acquisition processes in its Build Acquire Implement (BAI) track and some organizational and quality related processes from the Align Plan and Organize (APO) track. Table 4 shows CMMI to COBIT 5 process area mappings related to Software Development.

Measurement for Software Process Improvement

Tracy O'Rourke, CEO of Allen-Bradley - "Without the right information, you're just another person with an opinion".

Measurement is necessary to gain insight of organizational processes. If the processes are goal driven, then its measures should also be derived thorough goals. In order to help address business goals, software management functions could be fall into three categories: i.e. project management, process management, and product engineering (Florac, 1998). Each of which has its own objectives and issues.

Table 4. Mapping of CMMI Process Areas with COBIT5 Process Areas

	COBIT5 Process Areas	CMMI-Dev Process Areas
Process for Governance of Enterprise IT		
Evaluate Direct and Monitor (EDM)		Out of Scope for this study
Processes for Management of Enterprise IT		
Align Plan Organize (APO)		
	01: Manage the IT management framework	OPD, OT
	02: Manage Strategy	OPF
	03: Manage Enterprise Architecture	
	04: Manage Innovation	
	05: Manage Portfolio	
	06: Manage Budget and Costs	
	07: Manage HR	
	08: Manage Relationships	APO081-5 - IPM SG2
	09: Manage Service Agreements	
	10: Manage Suppliers	SAM
	11: Manage Quality	OPD, OPF
	12: Manage Risks	RM
	13: Manage Security	New Inclusion of CMMI-Dev V1.3
Build Acquire and Implement (BAI)		
	01: Manage Programs and Projects	OPD BAI01.9-OPM BAI01.8-PP, BAI01.11-PMC BAI01.3-IPM:
	02: Manage Requirements Definition	BAI02.01-RD, BAI02.01-DAR,
	03: Manage Solution Identification and Builds	BAI03.1- TS SG1 BAI03.2-TS SG2 BAI03.3-TS SG3 BAI03.5-PIntegration BAI03.6-PPQA perform QA BAI03.7-Validation BAI03.8-Validation BAI03.9-RM
	04: Manage Availability and Capacity	CMMI-SERVICES
	05: Manage Organizational Change Enablement	BAI05.1-7 – PMC SG3
	06: Manage Changes	CM
	07: Manage Change Acceptance and Transitioning	CM
	08: Manage Knowledge	PP and PMC, MA
	09: Manage Assts	PP and PMC, MA
	10: Manage Configuration	CM
Deliver Service and Support (DSS)		Out of scope for this study
Monitor Evaluate and Assess (MEA)		For Assessment Purpose
	01: Monitor Evaluate and Assess performance and Conformance	PPQA and VER at project level
	02: Monitor Evaluate and Assess the System of Internal Control	
	03: Monitor Evaluate and Assess the System of External Control	

Figure 4. Process Management and Measurement Perspectives

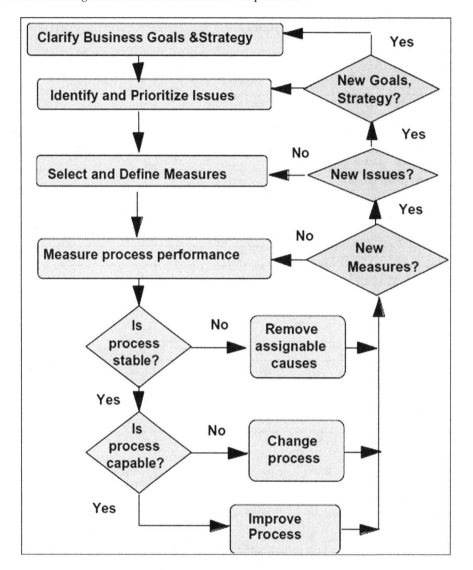

Project management is concerned with to meet planned commitments regarding cost, schedule, quality, and functionality while tracking product status. Table 5 shares sample product metrics communicating goals related to project and process issues. Process management confirms that process is showing expected behavior and is under control. In case of any abnormal behavior it makes sure that improvement have been made to ensure it meets the business goals. Figure 4 depicts five perspectives of Process Management.

How Software Quality Standards or Quality Models Helps in Metrics Selection

Quality models comprises of a set of quality characteristics which specifies non-functional quality requirements and criteria for quality assessment (Sadana, 2012). This study highlights different types of Quality Models that could be used to establish measurements for assessing quality include MacCall

Model, Boehm Model, FURPS Model, ISO 9126, Dromey Model and Quality Factor Model. For example, Barry Bohem uses Testability, Efficiency, Usability, Reliability, Human Engineering, Maintainability, Changeability, and Portability for assessing quality and exempt Correctness, Flexibility (extendibility, adaptability, and maintainability), Functionality, Integrity in terms of security, Interoperability, Process Maturity, and Reusability. If any organization follows any specific quality model for the measurement of quality practices adapted as part of its SPI program then that quality models contains some quality characteristics which should be accommodated while choosing measurement metrics.

Table 5. Mapping of Business Goals with Measurable attributes

Serial No	Business Goals	Measurable Product and Process Attributes
1	**Increase Function** Project Issue: Product Growth and stability Process Issue: Product Conformance	Number of Requirements, Product Size, Product Complexity, Rates of Change, Percent Non-Conformance
2	**Reduce Cost** Project Issue: Budgets expenditure rates Process Issue: Efficiency, Productivity, Rework	Product Size, Product Complexity Effort, Number of Changes, Requirements Stability
3	**Reduce the Time to Market** Project Issue: Schedule Progress Process Issue: Production Rate Responsiveness	Elapsed time, Normalized for product characteristics
4	**Improved Produced Quality** Project Issue: Product Performance, Product Correctness, Product Reliability Process Issue: Predictability, Problem Recognition, Root Cause Analysis	Number of Defects introduced Effectiveness of defect detection activities

Standard Metrics for Measuring Benefits of SPI

The benefit measurement classes related to Project, Product and process include Effort, Schedule, Cost, Quality, Productivity, Customer Satisfaction, and Return on Investment (ROI). A doctorial research by the author proposes common measures of SPI benefit measurement which could be adapted across multiple organizations for the measurement and prediction of Quality and performance for IS development activities (Hani, 2009; Hani, 2017). Also, a manual is available by PSM on standard metric definitions for measuring Software Process Improvement (Florac, 1998).

Impact of different Software Process Improvement Techniques on Software Quality

Many studies have been performed by different researchers and professionals for highlighting exact benefits of implementing different SPI techniques for example a research (Johnson & Kulpa, 2010, March) shows benefits of adapting CMMI PI framework in to five major PI classes such as: Costs shows 10% decrease per maturity level (Northrop Grumman), Schedules shows 50% reduction (General Motors, Boeing), Productivity shows 25-30% increase in productivity within 3 years (Lockheed Martin, Harris, Siemens), Quality shows 50% reduction of software defects (Lockheed Martin), and Customer Satisfaction has shown 55% increase in award fees (Lockheed Martin).

Raking Grain Level Software Engineering Methods Based on Benefits

A research (Jones, C., 2012, January) shares benefit results of ten software engineering methodologies and compares them in three major categories i.e. 1. Speed: Development schedules, effort, and costs. 2. Quality: Software quality in terms of delivered defects and 3. Economics: Total Cost of Ownership (TCO) and Cost of Quality (COQ).

Table 6. Software engineering methodologies comparison speed wise (Schedules, Staff, Effort, Productivity)

	Methodologies	Schedule Months	Staff	Effort Months	FP Month	Development Cost
1	Extreme (XP)	11.78	7	84	11.89	$630,860
2	Agile/scrum	11.82	7	84	11.85	$633,043
3	TSP	12.02	7	86	11.64	$644,070
4	CMMI 5/ spiral	12.45	7	83	12.05	$622,257
5	OO	12.78	8	107	9.31	$805,156
6	RUP	13.11	8	101	9.58	$756,157
7	Pair/iterative	13.15	12	155	9.21	$1,160,492
8	CMMI 3/iterative	13.34	8	107	9.37	$800,113
9	Proofs/waterfall	13.71	12	161	6.21	$1,207,500
10	CMMI 1/waterfall	15.85	10	158	6.51	$1,188,870
	Average	13.00	8.6	112.6	9.762	$844,852

For applications of 1000 function points above data shows that the XP and Agile methods are the least time-consuming methods, with TSP coming in third.

Here speed based and Quality based comparisons have been presented which could help us in concluding priority of different software engineering methodologies to bring quality in software development process. The first comparison concerns with development speeds, costs, and short-term issues. Table 6 is sorted by the speed of development. Second comparison is as per software quality, we have considered defect potentials, defect removal efficiency, delivered defects, and high-severity defects. The phrase "defect potential" refers to the sum of defects found in requirements, design, source code, documents, and "bad fixes." A bad fix is a new defect accidentally injected during an attempt to repair a previous defect (about 7% of attempts to fix bugs include new bugs). The phrase "defect removal efficiency" refers to the combined efficiency levels of inspections, static analysis, and testing (see Table 7).

When the focus of the evaluation turns to quality rather than speed, TSP, CMMI 5, and RUP are on top, followed by XP. Agile is not strong on quality so it is only on number 8 out of 10. The Agile lack of quality measures and failure to use inspections will also have an impact in the next comparison (see Table 8).

The phrase "be careful of what you wish for because you might get it" is appropriate for these methodology comparisons. Agile that focuses on speed are very quick. Methods such as TSP, RUP, and CMMI 5 that focus on quality have very few defects.

Table 7. Software Engineering Methodologies comparison Defects wise (Software Defect Potentials, Removal, and Delivery)

	Methodologies	Defect Potential	Defect Removal	Defects Delivered	High Severity Defects
1	TSP	2,700	96.79%	87	16
2	CMMI 5/ spiral	3,000	95.95%	122	22
3	Rational Unified Process (RUP)	3,900	95.07%	192	36
4	Extreme (XP)	4,500	93.36%	299	55
5	Object Oriented (OO)	4,950	93.74%	310	57
6	Pair Program /Iterative model	4,700	92.93%	332	61
7	Agile/scrum	4,800	92.30%	370	68
8	CMMI 3/ Iter.	4,500	91.18%	397	73
9	CMMI 1/ Waterfall Model.	6,000	78.76%	1,274	236
	Average	4,370	92.23%	374	69

Table 8. Best Software engineering methods

Benefit Category	Methodology
Effort	CMMI ML 5
Cost	CMMI ML 5
Men Power	Agile
Schedule	XP
Quality (Defect potentials, Defect removal efficiency, Delivered defects, High-severity defects)	TSP
Total Cost of Ownership (TCO) and Cost of Quality (COQ)	TSP

FUTURE RESEARCH DIRECTIONS

Although businesses have started using ISACA COBIT 5 framework but quantitative data over its benefit realization is still not publicized. This study intensely highlights that both the discussed options are very important and should be used in right collaborative manner in order to turn your business success through quality and secure information system development while observing proper ethical code. For upcoming research needs, organizations like individual businesses and standardization bodies like ISACA need to publicize their benefit data for option two. Whereas, more work needs to be done for defining ethical and security standards for a rapidly changing technology needs that must linked with verification and validation activities for technologies like E-Commerce, Artificial Intelligence based decision making systems, Machine Learning, and IoT.

CONCLUSION

Information Systems acquisition, implementation, and development have been taking place in business organization to gain the competitive advantage. Rapid advancement of Technology is also popping up unethical issues involving violations of End users' data protection and privacy. This study discusses standard quality practices adhere to which a good quality Software product is guaranteed while assuring implementation of ethical policies and information security. It presents a framework that connects secure and quality software development process improvement with strategic needs of an organization. Standard practices under consideration includes Capability Maturity Model for Development (CMMI-DEV version 1.3 for security) while using multi-model Process Improvement approach where an organization could use Balance Score Card technique while setting its strategic goals and monitoring their performance related to Information System development, and also link it with Information System management framework "Control Objectives for Information and Related Technology" (COBIT)-5 released by "Information Systems Audit and Control Association" (ISACA) which already supports security in Risk related process area, so that users could easily switch between the two standards. In last benefits are also reported while comparing 10 different software development methods. Agile methods are good for achieving goals quicker on smaller projects. The methods that emphasize quality such as TSP, RUP, and CMMI 5 have also achieved their goals, and deliver very few defects. No single method appears to be perfect therefore multi model approach is best.

REFERENCES

Chang, R. Y., & Morgan, M. W. (2000). *Performance scorecards*. Jossey-Bass.

Chatterji, S. (2016, June). *Improving Business with COBIT 5*. COBIT FOCUS.

Florac, A. (1998). Practical Software Measurement: Measuring for Process Management and improvement. *Paper presented at SEPG98*.

Frisken, J. (2015). Leveraging COBIT to Implement Information Security, With COBIT 5. COBIT FOCUS.

Hani, U. S. (2009, December). Impact of Process improvement on Software Development Predictions, for measuring software development project's performance benefits. In *FIT proceedings*. ACM. 10.1145/1838002.1838064

Hani, U. S. (2017). *Impact of Process Improvement on Software Development Predictions*. Unpublished doctoral dissertation, Graduate School of Engineering Science and Information Technology, Hamdard University, Pakistan.

Hefner, R. (2005, November). Achieving the Promised Benefits of CMMI. *Presented at CMMI Technology Conference & User Group*.

ISACA. (2015). *Certified Information System Auditor* (26th ed.). ISACA.

Johnson, K. A., & Kulpa, M. (2010, March). Agile CMMI: Obtaining Real Benefits from Measurement and High Maturity. *Presented at conference SEPG-2010*.

Jones, C. (2008, January). *Applied Software Measurement: Global Analysis of Productivity and Quality* (3rd ed.). Tata McGraw-Hill.

Jones, C. (2012, January). Evaluating ten Software Development Methodologies. *Software Magazine.*

Jones, C. (2017, November). *Achieving Software Excellence.* Namcook Analytics LLC.

Kamel, S. (2003). Introduction to Business Information System: Internet Marketing: Corporate and Business Unit Strategy. *Presented at the American University,* Cairo.

Kroenke, D. (2009). Information Systems for Competitive Advantage. In *Using Management Information Systems: Managing a digital firm* (2nd ed.). Prentice Hall.

Laudon, K. C., & Laudon, J. P. (2011). Information Systems, Organizations, and Strategy. In Using Management Information Systems: Managing a digital firm (Ch. 3, 12th ed.). Prentice Hall.

Mead, N. R., & Allen, J. H. (2009). *Making the Business Case for Software Assurance (Special Report).* Software Engineering Institute, Carnegie Mellon University.

Potter, N., & Sakry, M. (2011). *Making Process Improvement Work: A Concise Action Guide for Software Managers and Practitioners.*

Rohm, H., & Malinoski, M. (2012). *Strategy-based Balanced Scorecards for Technology Companies.* Balanced Scorecard Institute.

Sadana, V. (2012). *A survey based Software Quality Model.* Department of Computer Science, University of Missouri-Rolla.

Siemens, A. G. (2013). *Security by Design with CMMI for Development, Version 1.3 An Application Guide for Improving Processes for Secure Products (Special Report).* Software Engineering Institute, Carnegie Mellon University.

Tiến, L. N. (2012). *Information Systems Analyses and Design.* Retrieved 2010 from http://tienhuong. files.wordpress.com/2010/03/slides.ppt

This research was previously published in the International Journal of Information System Modeling and Design (IJISMD), 8(4); pages 1-20, copyright year 2017 by IGI Publishing (an imprint of IGI Global).

Chapter 16
Applying Software Engineering Design Principles to Agile Architecture

Chung-Yeung Pang

 https://orcid.org/0000-0002-7925-4454

Seveco AG, Switzerland

ABSTRACT

Most enterprise IT systems are very complex with a combination of COBOL and Java programs running on multiple platforms. What is needed is a solid IT architecture that supports the operation and growth of a cross-platform IT system. It must enable the iterative and incremental development of applications that are foreseen in an agile development process. The design concept of such an architecture with its infrastructure and development tool is presented in this chapter. This design concept is based on the design principles and architectural patterns of software engineering. The architecture is a combination of layered, component-based, and service-oriented architectural patterns. The agile development process is based on a model-driven approach. The architecture and development approaches were first introduced in 2004. Since then, many applications have been developed on time and within budget.

INTRODUCTION

Despite advances in software engineering, software development remains a challenge for IT professionals. Statistics have shown that most software projects run too late and too expensive. The problem becomes even more apparent when a mix of legacy and modern applications in a complex IT system comes into play. In fact, IT enterprise systems typically go through a long development phase. Over the past decades, software projects have evolved into some of the most complex software systems. For large companies, mainframe applications programmed in COBOL often form the backbone of the IT structure. New applications and components are often developed using a language such as Java on a UNIX or LINUX platform. Often, business processes require collaboration between components on different platforms.

DOI: 10.4018/978-1-6684-3702-5.ch016

Maintaining and updating an IT system that combines legacy and modern platforms is one of the toughest challenges many companies are facing today. Modern businesses have high demands on IT systems to work in highly stable yet flexible and fast environments, and to introduce new features and processes to meet their steady growth. The agile software development process, which follows the evolutionary and iterative approach of software development and focuses on adapting to change (Ambler, 2010; Larman, 2003), seems to meet the requirements. However, the process alone does not guarantee the success of a software project. There are many other factors. Attempts to use only the agile approach to software development can still fail (Harlow, 2014; Ismail, 2017). Through years of evolution in software engineering, there are design principles and techniques that can help tackling the complexity involved in application development in an enterprise IT system. They must be incorporated into the agile development process.

A cross-platform enterprise IT system requires a software architecture that supports operations and growth. The architecture must enable the iterative and incremental development of applications. The purpose of this chapter is to introduce the design and implementation concept of such an architecture. The design concept is based on design principles and architectural patterns that have emerged from decades of research in software development. It is also based on years of hands-on experience of the author with an iterative incremental process and a continuous integration approach to software development.

The materials presented in this chapter focus on four areas: what, why, how and consequences. The first section covers the historical background of software engineering and the agile development process. The following section is the "what" topic that gives an introduction to the design principles that have resulted from software development and object-oriented programming, as well as the software architecture and agile development methodology. The next section discusses the "why" and explains the motivation behind the principles of software engineering, software architecture, and the agile development process. The section "how" develops agile architecture design and its use in the agile approach to enterprise application development. In the section "consequences" the applicability as well as the experiences from the practice are presented. The chapter ends with future research directions and conclusions.

BACKGROUND

As background, the following subsections introduce the disciplines of software engineering and the agile development approach.

Software Engineering

In the early days of software history, programmers tended to develop their programs without documentation in an ad-hoc style. The programs are usually not structured and organized. With the development with many new features, the underlying software becomes unmanageable and unmanageable. One result was the software crisis of the 1960s, 1970s and 1980s (Software Crisis, 2010).

Software engineering (2010) is a discipline that offers solutions to counteract the software crisis. It defines standards, disciplines, methodologies and processes for software development. In recent decades, many new programming languages, design principles and architectural patterns, and development paradigms have been developed. Programming styles such as structural programming (Yourdon & Constantine, 1979; Jackson, 1975), object-oriented programming (Booch, et al., 2007), etc. have been introduced. In addition to programming, great emphasis was placed on analysis and design with the right documentation. The waterfall model for the development process was introduced, defining the development phases with an initial requirements analysis and specification, software design, implementation, testing and deployment, and subsequent product maintenance (Royce, 1970; Bell & Thayer, 1976).

The waterfall model for software development has long been a standard. Application development had led to the belief that a complete, detailed requirement specification had to be prepared before further development activities could be undertaken. It turns out that requirements are often a moving target and change over time. Creating a complete, detailed requirement specification for complex applications is nearly impossible. Many projects did not survive the analysis phase before the budget was used up. New development models are required.

Agile Development Approach

In 2001, a group of well-known software developers came together to define a set of principles for software development. What emerged was the Agile Manifesto (Agile Manifesto Group, 2001). It triggered a new movement in the software community with an agile development process and was widely accepted. The agile development process follows the evolutionary and iterative approach of software development (Ambler, 2010; Larman, 2003) and focuses on adapting to change. Requirements and solutions result from the collaboration of self-organizing, cross-functional teams. It promotes adaptive planning, evolutionary development, early deployment and continuous improvement, and promotes a rapid and flexible response to change.

The agile approach to software development eliminates the large documents resulting from the waterfall model and thus reduces the significant effort required for the requirements specification. The process also forces the development team to stop focusing on high-level concepts that are designed to be developed with early prototypes. The approach has numerous advantages over the conventional waterfall model.

Despite its many advantages, the agile approach also has many down sides. Rakitin (2001) criticized the agile approach as an attempt to undermine the discipline of software engineering. The concept of "working across a large document" leads to "we want to spend all our time programming, remember that real programmers do not write documentation." This leads back to ad hoc programming style. While the concept of developing program elements iteratively in small trunks and continuously integrating them into the IT system is well founded, the basic structure and mechanism of how the program elements can be developed and integrated must be well understood. Applications must be structured in such a way that they can be flexibly and easily adapted to changes. In other words, an agile software architecture is needed. There are many articles in the literature on how to use an agile approach. Most examples show that it is applied to the development of Web applications with an underlying architecture behind the http protocol. Frameworks like Wordpress, Drupal, Laravel, Node.js etc. all have their architecture. For a project that requires more than simple Web elements, proper architecture is still required.

The 2015 Standish Group CHAOS report (Hastie & Wojewoda, 2015) shows that the success rate for an agile approach is more than three times higher than for a waterfall approach. An agile approach is certainly the better choice than a traditional waterfall approach. However, the report also shows a 39% overall success rate for the agile software development approach. There is further need for improvement. One should try to consider applying the principles of software engineering that have developed after so many years of experience.

BRIEFING OF SOFTWARE ENGINEERING DESIGN PRINCIPLES, ARCHITECTURE AND AGILE METHOD

This section provides a brief description of the principles of software development, architecture, and agile methods. The focus is on the "what". The chapter is divided into three subsections. The first subsection deals with the design principles of software engineering, the second with the agile enterprise software architecture and the last with the most popular agile method Scrum.

Software Engineering Design Principles

The software design derives a solution that meets the software requirements. There is no general agreement on the design principles of software so far. The main goals of the design principles are to help developers manage the complexity of the IT landscape and provide guidelines on how to easily build and maintain software. "Divide and Conquer" and "Separation of Concern" are probably the main goals behind most design principles. This section presents a number of well-known design principles from the literature (Huang, 2010). The principles contained are listed below:

- **Rigor and Formality**: The Standish Group has suggested that the formal methodology is one of the key success factors in software development (Krigsman, 2006). The software design must be strictly formal documented to avoid ambiguity. Formal design documents, such as pseudocode or UML models, can show the basic logic of a program with sequences of steps, iterations with for and while loops, and selections with if-else statements or symbols. They improve the readability of design concept and algorithm compared to text documents. The main goal of a formal design document is to explain exactly what a program should do exactly to make it easier for developers to design. It helps both programmers and analysts to understand the programs and thus serves as documentation for the software product. In industry, the approach of documentation is essential. And here a formal design document proves to be crucial.

- **Abstraction**: A software developer cannot work on more than a few concepts and their relationships at the same time. An abstraction makes it possible to suppress unimportant details and to emphasize the important information. Abstraction is the process of identifying a set of essential features of an entity without paying attention to its details. Abstraction helps manage the intellectual complexity of software. It provides a higher-level concept that ignores certain detailed properties altogether (Colburn & Shute, 2007).

- **Modularization**: "Divide and conquer" is the main approach to dealing with complexity. The idea is to first divide or subdivide the problem into small and distinct modules. This helps to treat various individual aspects of a problem and we can focus on each part separately. Modularity in software engineering refers to the extent to which an application can be divided into smaller modules (Baldwin & Clark, 2000). Modularity is also a kind of separation of concerns. A complex problem is divided into modules so that details of each module can be handled individually and separately. In a sense, modularity is a logical subdivision of software design that allows complex software to be managed for implementation and maintenance. The logic of partitioning can be based on related functions, implementation considerations, data connections, or other criteria. The modularity offers better manageability of software development.

- **Information Hiding**: The idea of information hiding was introduced in 1972 by Parnas (Parnas, 1972). It is a principle of separation of design decisions in one module that are likely to change, protecting other modules from being changed when the design decision is changed. Parnas defined hiding information as a way to shield clients from internal program flow. To achieve hiding of information, a module may disclose a stable functional contract (e.g. an interface) that other modules can access. The internal implementation would be hidden from the outside. Therefore, changing the internal design of other modules would not be affected.

- **Cohesion**: Cohesion is a measure of the relationship between elements in a module. It is the degree to which all elements being the participants to perform a single task are included in the module. Cohesion is basically the composition of the relevant elements that hold the module together. A good software design has a high cohesion that only relevant elements for performing the module specific task are included in a module. There are different types of cohesion. Their description can be found in an article by Josika (Josika 2017).

- **Coupling**: Coupling is the measure of the degree of interdependence between the modules. Strong coupling between modules can mean that a module cannot perform its specific task without the other modules. Therefore, the module is not independent. It cannot be unit tested or used independently of each other. Sagenschneider (Sagenschneider, 2019) gave an analogy that a software system with strongly coupled modules is like a puzzle. Each module is part of the puzzle and the software system can only take on the right shape if all the pieces fit together well. If changes are made, we need to rearrange the puzzle. Parts of a puzzle do not usually fit in other puzzles. In another perspective, a software system built from strong coupling modules cannot be built using an iterative incremental approach with continuous integration. The final software product is anything but agile. A good software has a low coupling. Best of all, each module is independent and autonomous.

- **Anticipation of Change**: Each software system would undergo a number of changes and improvements throughout its life cycle. It is important to recognize elements that are likely to change in the early phase of software development. When anticipated changes are identified, special care must be taken in designing so that future changes can be easily applied. The requirement of a software system or application is often a moving target. It is nearly impossible to identify the full requirements of a software system at an early-stage with every detail. The agile development approach is widely accepted as the focus is on rapid adaptation to change. The anticipation of changes is a guideline for every software design.

- **Reusability**: The reusability of software artefacts does not normally fit into the equation of the agile software development process. However, reusing existing software artefacts can significantly speed development, especially if development iteration should only take a short time. Reusable artefacts include code, software modules, test suites, designs, and documentation. Most developers would think of reusing existing modules and code. Since the publication of the book by Gamma et al. (1995), software developers have been made aware of patterns that one is constantly using. A pattern is defined as the solution to a problem in a particular context. If one encounters a similar problem as before, one can always adapt the same solution to the problem. Patterns provide a wider dimension of software reuse. Reusability is not just a concept limited to the reuse of the existing elements. It can give software developers new thinking and discipline in designing and programming. With reusability in mind, developers can begin designing and programming a module that can solve more common problems rather than a very specific problem of an application. The design is not rigidly bound to the current requirement, making it more general, flexible, extensible, and less complex.

In addition to the design principles above, there are design principles specific to an object-oriented approach to analysis, design, and programming. The specific features of the object-oriented approach include generality, encapsulation, inheritance, and polymorphism (Booch et al., 2007). In addition to these features, Martin (2000, 2017) described the SOLID design principles. SOLID is an acronym with the following meaning:

- **S Stands for SRP (Single Responsibility Principle)**: This principle states that "a class should have only one reason to change" which means every class should be responsible to a single actor and not others.
- **O Stands for OCP (Open Closed Principle)**: Originally by Meyer (1988), this principle states that "software entities (classes, modules, functions, etc.) should be open for extension, but closed for modification". Martin (2000) reformulated it that interfaces instead of super-classes should allow for various implementations that one can replace without changing the objects that use them.
- **L Stands for LSP (Liskov Substitution Principle)**: The principle was proposed by Liskov (1988), that objects in a program should be replaced by instances of their subtypes without altering the correctness of that program.
- **I Stand for ISP (Interface Segregation Principle)**: This principle states that many custom interfaces are better than a universal interface.
- **D Stands for DIP (Dependency Inversion Principle)**: This principle states that object dependencies refer only to abstractions, not to concretions.

The SOLID principle helps to reduce tight coupling and make the code more reusable, maintainable, flexible and stable.

Agile Enterprise Software Architecture

The concept of software architecture emerged in the early 1980s in response to the increasing complexity and diversity of software systems. Architecture is defined as the governing of rules, heuristics and patterns:

- Partitioning the problem and the system that is to be built into discrete pieces.
- The techniques used to create interfaces between these pieces.
- The techniques for managing overall structure and flow.
- The techniques used to interface between the system and its environment.
- Appropriate use of development and delivery approaches, techniques and tools.

An architecture contains the methods, standards, tools, frameworks, policies, and administrative statements. Over the last 30 years, many architectural patterns have evolved from this concept. Some of the most popular are listed in the following list:

- Client/server and multi-tier
- Layered architecture

- Component-based architecture
- Event-driven architecture
- Broker architecture
- Model-view-controller (MVC)
- Pipe-filter
- Service-oriented architecture (SOA)
- Message/service bus

The list shown here only gives some of the common architectural patterns. Detailed descriptions of these patterns can be found in the book by Richards (Richards 2015). Different patterns take into account of different architectural concerns. SOA and Broker architectures are communication-related patterns, while component-based and layered architecture addresses the overall structure of the system. There are also patterns for exception handling. The design of enterprise software architecture would generally combine multiple architectural patterns to cover all requirements.

Agility is essentially about moving fast and accepting change. It is a continuous improvement. The agile software architecture provides a good solution and framework for rapid development, integration, and removal of high-quality modules.

Agile Method Scrum

There are different agile methods. The most popular is probably Scrum. Scrum is based on autonomous and self-organized teams (Drumond, 2019). It relies on an iterative (usually cyclically repeated at short intervals) and incremental (gives new functions) process. In a Scrum process (Rehkopf, 2019), product owners and business analysts would involve end users to define user stories that they would include in the product backlog. User stories are short requests or requirements written from the perspective of an end user. In an enterprise application, there are usually other stories that relate to non-functional requirements. A series of related and interdependent stories would form an epic. In other words, an epic is an extensive work that can be divided into a series of smaller tasks that are recorded in stories. A collection of epics working toward a common goal is an initiative. Themes are used for large focus areas that span the organization.

In a Scrum development process, software elements are developed in iterations called sprints. A sprint has a timeframe of not more than a month and usually two weeks. For each sprint, the project team picked up one or more user stories from the product backlog and implemented the appropriate software elements or modules. The sprint is not complete until the implementation has been fully tested. Continuous integration is generally recommended that the software elements or modules be integrated into the system with an integration test. The software system will be released to the end user once all essential features have been implemented and fully tested.

MOTIVATION BEHIND DESIGN PRINCIPLES, ARCHITECTURE, AND AGILE DEVELOPMENT PROCESS

In this section, we explore the motivation behind design principles and software architectures in an agile development process. The section is divided into three subsections. The first subsection examines the reasons for using software engineering principles and architectures. The second section, why we need design principles and architecture in an agile development process, is explained. The last subsection presents the requirements for an agile enterprise architecture.

Needs for Software Engineering Design Principles and Architecture

It is not uncommon for a large company's IT system to contain hundreds of thousands of software modules interacting in a very complex way. Maintenance and enhancements to new business needs are always a nightmare. As mentioned earlier, the software engineering design principles are based on years of experience to support the production of high quality software. These are basic guidelines for creating software that is stable, functional, flexible, easy to change, and easily adaptable to new features.

To ensure business and IT flexibility, the overall complexity of the IT system must be resolved and managed. A proper software architecture is required (Babar et al., 2014). Isotta-Riches and Randell (2014) reported that architecture was a key factor in the success of an agile approach at Aviva UK. IBM's Hopkins and Hardcombe (2014) also discussed the need for a suitable architecture for the development of complex agile systems. Netherwood states that architecture is important because it (Malan & Bredemeyer, 2010):

- Controls complexity.
- Enforces best practice.
- Gives consistency and uniformity.
- Communicates skill requirements.
- Reduces risk.
- Enables reuse.

Proper architectural design with its supporting infrastructure and tools are critical to the success of an IT project. The architecture provides an overview of how software components should be structured and developed, and how continuous integration should work. It ensures the agility of the entire system, allowing the agile development approach to run throughout the software lifecycle with little or no technical debt. It must reduce, not increase, the complexity of the IT system. Software tools and standards must simplify the development process and not make it more complicated.

The Standish Group research shows that 70% of the application code is the infrastructure (Johnson et al., 2001). There should be a clear separation between the implementation of business and technical aspects. The technical infrastructure is generally stable and the same for all applications. One can develop code segments and patterns that can be parameterized as required. Application developers should focus only on the business-related aspects and include the infrastructure code segments and patterns in their programs as needed. The application developers should not have to master the infrastructure. The overhead of writing 70% of the infrastructure-related application code can also be saved.

Design Principles and Architecture for Agile Development Process

It seems that the agile community is convinced that software design is generally not an issue. The design of a software architecture was considered by many to be a prime example of "great design in the foreground," which is in contrast to general agile practices. There are many examples that show implementations that are based only on user stories without architectural and modular design effort. These examples are typically simple Web applications that are already based on an event-driven architecture framework using the http protocol. Implementing an event triggered by clicking a button or simply sending the data of a web form to the web server does not require in-depth design work.

In many cases, especially complex IT systems, proper architecture and modularity are required. In fact, there are many examples of the huge problems caused by architectural debts. If one allows an ad hoc development style without proper architecture, it is easy to have a structure with tightly coupled modules, as shown in Figure 1. In fact, such a modular structure can be found in most large IT enterprise systems. Modules cannot be developed and tested individually. One may forget the flexibility, and changes are not easy.

Figure 1. Illustration of tightly coupled modules

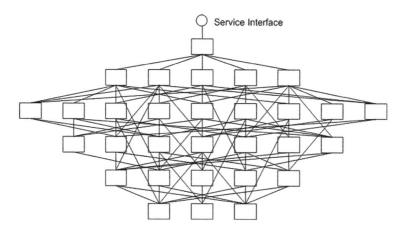

In a Scrum process, themes, initiatives, epics and stories are fundamentally different levels of abstraction of the problems to be solved by the software system. Different themes are usually handled by different teams. There is a need for high-level abstraction with the concept of hiding information for the services or interfaces provided by different themes. Initiatives and epics contain the coherent stories and their implementation. A modular structure of the software system is indispensable if small granular modules are to be implemented in a sprint every two weeks. Modules that are heavily coupled with other modules cannot be fully implemented and tested without the dependent modules. The coupling between modules must be kept to a minimum for an iterative approach of implementation.

Ideally, one wants to develop each module independently, perform unit testing, and integrate it into the system in an iteration. This requires each module to be autonomous and to have a single responsibility. Modules seldom work independently of each other. They have to work with other modules and exchange data. So we need a mechanism for indirect interaction of modules so that data can be exchanged without one module directly accessing another. All this requires a central process control that calls the individual modules under the right conditions. Because flexibility is paramount in agile development and changes can be easily customized, anticipating change is a key principle. All the points described require an agile architecture. In fact, an agile approach like Scrum cannot be used if one has a modular structure like the one shown in Figure 1. To use an agile approach to enterprise application development, software engineering principles and agile architecture are essential.

Facilities Provided by an Agile Architecture and Development Tools

The purpose of the software architecture design is to provide a structural framework of a modular system, techniques and mechanisms for the operation and collaboration of individual parts, as well as rules and standards to which the programs should conform. The agile architecture is required to provide the following facilities:

1. Allow the integration of web-based applications.
2. Enable cross-platform application integration.
3. Enable business domain partitions and divide business domains into business components (different levels of business abstractions).
4. Ensure separation of infrastructure and application code (maximize cohesion of functions and features).
5. Enable independent development of software elements or modules (minimize coupling and promote modularity).
6. Provide mechanisms for plug-and-play and continuous integration of modules.
7. Provide style and techniques for object-oriented programming to follow SOLID principles.
8. Maximize flexibility, usability, hiding information, and reusability.

In addition to an agile architecture framework, we need development tools that provide the following capabilities:

1. Rigorously formalize the design and implementation documentation.
2. Provide a way for rapid autonomous module development.
3. Facilitate the integration of autonomous modules into the system.

HOW TO DESIGN AND BUILD AN AGILE ARCHITECTURE

In the previous sections the descriptions and motivations of the design principles, the architecture and the tools were presented together with agile methods. This section explains how to design and build an agile architecture. The first section deals with the design of an agile architecture with two subsections, one about enterprise architecture and the second about plug and play framework. The second topic deals with the use of UML modeling and code generation tools as well as the implementation of applications based on the architecture framework. The topic is also divided into three subsections. The concept of using UML models and the CASE tool for code generation is briefly explained in the first subsection. The second part deals with the implementation in a legacy platform with IBM CICS and COBOL. The third part deals with the Java implementation, which contains some open source frameworks.

Enterprise Architecture

With the advances in web technology, companies must consider integrating web-based applications into their existing applications. Integration can take place via an SOA. In the SOA, messages exchanged between the service provider and the consumer are generally XML or JSON. In addition, a client application is not tied to a single server. A service consumer can use services from different platforms. One can implement an Enterprise Service Bus (ESB) to redirect service requests to the right service providers on different platforms. Messages in XML or JSON allow interoperation between applications written in different languages. SOA, together with the use of an ESB, provides architectural patterns for communication and application integration (Chappell, 2004).

In its book Simple Architectures for Complex Enterprises, Sessions (2008) suggested that partitioning is essential for managing complexity in enterprise architectures. A structural pattern, such as a component-based architecture, can be used to provide the basic structure of business domain partitions. In this pattern, related programs are combined into a single component. Each component has one or more well-defined interfaces that provide windows for interacting with other components. Internal processing (including access to the data store) is completely encapsulated in the component.

Component-based architecture can be combined with SOA. Rather than providing interfaces in Java or COBOL, a component can provide a service interface with XML or JSON. Sessions suggested that when partitioning a corporate IT system, the services provided by each partition can be defined. In the proposed architecture, the enterprise IT system is divided into business components and components that are service providers.

Architecture patterns such as component-based architecture and SOA provide comprehensive concepts for partitioning business domains and organizing programs for an enterprise IT system. There are still many detailed problems, such as security, error handling and logging, ACID transaction processing, etc., which need to be addressed. The solutions to these problems would ultimately be the designs of the basic infrastructure framework into which the applications can be integrated.

A layered structure can be integrated into the component-based service-oriented architecture. Layering is widely used in enterprise architecture. The architecture presented here has a three layer structure. The top layer is a service and mediation layer. At this level, incoming XML or JSON messages are parsed, and the data is mapped to an input data object (such as a Java JSON object). Service requests are resolved after the security check and dispatched to the correct components. The service consumer must be authenticated and authorized to access the requested service. Control is via the standard platform infrastructure. The outputs of the components are rendered into XML or JSON. An additional feature in this layer is service transaction management. Errors can occur in all business components involved in the service. Transactions across all components would either be committed or rolled back by the transaction manager at the service and mediation level.

Another set of infrastructures is implemented at a vertical layer, providing functions such as error handling and logging. All business components can access this layer for error handling and logging. Service errors are temporarily stored in the database. They are archived after a certain time. They can be obtained from the service support team member through a standard web service.

The layered structure is shown in figure 2a. The enterprise IT system is based on a layered, component-based and service-oriented architecture. As shown in figure 2b, a business component can cut across three horizontal levels. The service interface of a business component would reside in the service and mediation layer. Business components can communicate with each other in the business processing layer. The lowest level is the persistent level where components interact with their persistent tables in the database. In this layer, modules from different business components are not allowed to interact with each other. On the other hand, they can interact with the infrastructure layer for error handling and logging.

Figure 2. Illustration of the layered, component based and service oriented architecture

(a)   (b)

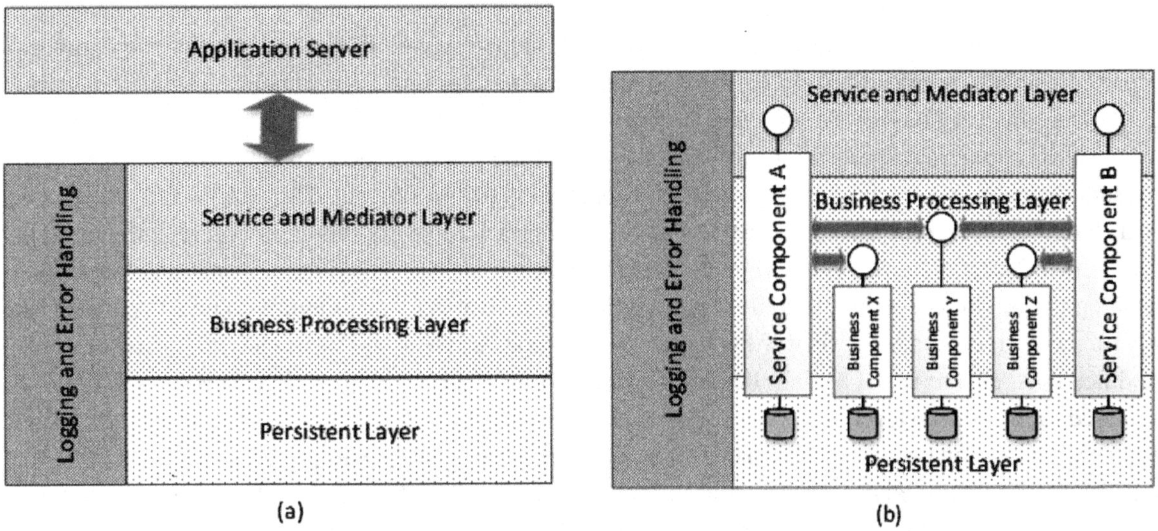

Using an Enterprise Service Bus (ESB), SOA enables cross-platform communication as seen in Figure 3. Together with the use of ESB, the enterprise architecture patterns meets the 1, 2 and 3 facilities described in the previous section.

Figure 3. Illustration of inter-platform communication with service oriented architecture

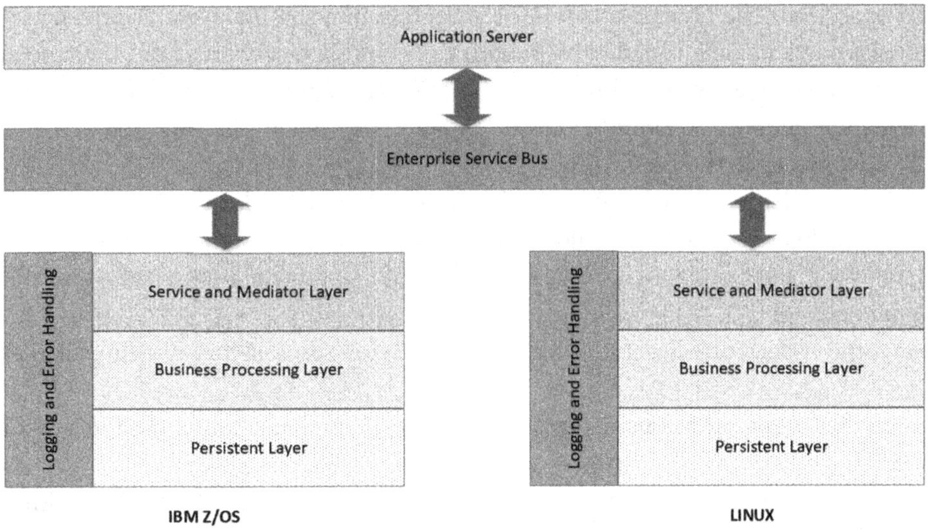

Plug and Play Architecture

The IT architecture with its infrastructure framework helps manage the complexity of the entire enterprise business. Applications are partitioned according to their business domains. The next design is architecture in every business component or service.

Business components very rarely contain only a few modules or objects. In fact, most business components themselves are complex and consist of many modules or objects. They are usually developed by different teams for the different business areas. In the stack of layers shown in Figure 2, the modules in the lower layers are activated by the modules in the upper layers. This requires a mutual dependence between the module to be activated and the module that activates it. The module to be activated would rely on the correct data being forwarded by the module that activates it. The module that activates other modules must ensure that it has all the data needed by the enabled modules. If a new module needs to be added to the bottom level of the stack, or if a module at the bottom level needs new input data, it will ripple the changes in many modules in the stack. This structure usually results from an early implementation without architectural design. The maintenance and expansion of the final software usually requires a huge effort. It also breaks the concept of iterative development of autonomous modules with single responsibility (SOLID principles) that can be unit tested.

Modules seldom work independently of each other. They need to work with other modules and share data. So one needs a mechanism for indirect interaction of modules so that data can be exchanged without one module directly accessing another. With all this archived, a central process control is still required, which calls the individual modules under the right conditions.

The event-driven architecture pattern fits in well with the central process control and provides agility to the software. In this pattern, each module is reactive. One can use the event-driven business process flow mechanism. The process controller is basically a finite state machine. Each module must deliver an event after execution. The process controller checks the state and the event and decides on the next module to invoke. Each module is called by the process controller, which operates independently. Depending on the business logic processing and the state data, the processing of the module would lead to different events. The process controller would consider the actual state and the outbound event to determine the next process to be performed.

The process controller must not be responsible for providing input data to all modules. Therefore, a service context container is used. A module retrieves the required data by providing a logical name for the context container. The output data of the module would be assigned a logical name and placed in the context container.

In summary, the architecture design for the process of a service has the following characteristics:

- Process control is centralized using a process controller implemented in the form of a finite-state machine.
- Modules are independent autonomous units with well-defined contracts to fulfil (fulfilling SOLID principles).
- Apart from invocations of external services offered by other business components, modules are not supposed to make direct calls to other modules.
- A plug-and-play architecture is in place so that a module can be plugged in at any time for continuous integration.
- All state data will be held in a context container.

- Status data (COBOL structure in COBOL and object in Java) can be stored under a specific logical name in the context container and retrieved using this logical name.
- Each module will fetch the required state data from the context container and put new or updated state data in the context container.

The process sequence of a service is given in the following list:

1. Upon receiving a service request, the service mediator would first carry out the security and access control.
2. The service mediator parses input in XML or JSON and creates the proper input data object (COBOL structure for COBOL and Java object for Java).
3. The service mediator creates the context container and puts the input data object into the context container.
4. The service mediator identifies and activates the process-controller module, as well as setting the initial state and event.
5. The process controller determines the module to be invoked, based on the current state and event.
6. The process controller invokes the module and sets up a new state.
7. The module fetches its input data from the context container.
8. The module carries out the execution of the business. Logic.
9. The module puts output data associated with logical names, into the context container.
10. Depending on the outcome, the module sets a new event.
11. It repeats Step 5 until the business process completes, unless an error has occurred.
12. In the event of an error, the module would log the error message using the error handling and logging facility.
13. The module puts the error message into the context container and sets an error event for the error case.
14. The process controller terminates the process and returns to the service mediator when the business process is completed, or when an error occurs.
15. The service mediator fetches the output data from the context container and renders the output into XML or JSON.
16. The service mediator will either commit the transaction or rollback the transaction if an error has occurred.

When data needs to be processed or retrieved by an external component, a module can interact directly with the external component. Alternatively, a wrapper can be created that retrieves the input data for the external component from the context container and calls the external component. The output data of the external component is put into a context container by the wrapper. The wrapper also sets a new event for process control.

For business components that need to work with the main service component of a service, their processing steps are very similar to the list above. However, they do not provide a service interface, only interfaces for calls. In these cases, one needs process dispatchers to perform the tasks of the service mediator. Tasks such as security and access control, XML or JSON analysis, and transaction management are not required in a process dispatcher.

Plug-and-play, along with the enterprise architecture described in the previous subsection, meets all the agile architecture requirements discussed in the previous section.

Design Model and CASE Tools

A rigorous formal approach to document design (one of the principles of software engineering) is the use of UML models. Service message interfaces can be well documented by business analysts in UML class diagrams. The process flow can be modeled in UML state diagrams. The state diagrams can be further refined and each state activity converted into a program module. The state machine is constructed with a fixed algorithm and is controlled by a state transition table. The state table can be easily created or automatically generated from the process flow model.

A CASE tool that supports UML modeling can be used. The CASE tool must support code generation so that software artifacts can be generated directly from models. Code templates and patterns can be used for code generation. They offer a high degree of reusability, which will be shown in the next two subsections.

Model and Implementation in Legacy Platform

The design of the architecture presented in this chapter is not limited to implementation in specific languages. This subsection introduces the architecture implementation and module programming in COBOL.

IBM provides an infrastructure for processing TCP / IP and HTTP protocols as well as the message queue (MQ). It also facilitates XML parsing in COBOL. This allows us to build the basic infrastructure required for SOA.

The main elements of our applications are the following:

- A service mediator.
- A context container.
- Application components and their modules.
- A process controller and process-control descriptor.
- An XML parser and data-object descriptors.

The service mediator in the first layer of our architecture contains a generic module that handles security and access control, transaction management, and resource creation including the context container, and so on. It is part of the SOA infrastructure. The service mediator module uses the IBM infrastructure to retrieve the input message from our service client. The input is in XML format with a standard SOAP (Simple Object Access Protocol). After identifying the requested service and resolving the main process control module, a module is called to parse the XML data, map the XML data into COBOL record structures (copy books), and place the record structures in the context container. The mapping is based on a data object descriptor for a particular service. This data object descriptor contains meta-information for the mapping between the native COBOL data structure to / from the XML data structure. When the business process is completed, the service mediator also calls a module to retrieve the COBOL output record structures from the context container and uses the metadata in the data object descriptors to render the output XML. To develop a service, the data object descriptors must be created along with the process control descriptors and configured to allow the service mediator to perform its functions.

As already mentioned, the service interface is modelled in the UML class diagram. UML classes are used with extended attributes properties to capture both COBOL and XML data structures and their mappings. Data object descriptors and other artefacts are generated from UML class diagrams. An illustration of the UML class model and generated software artefacts is shown in Figure 4.

Figure 4. Class model and software artifacts generation

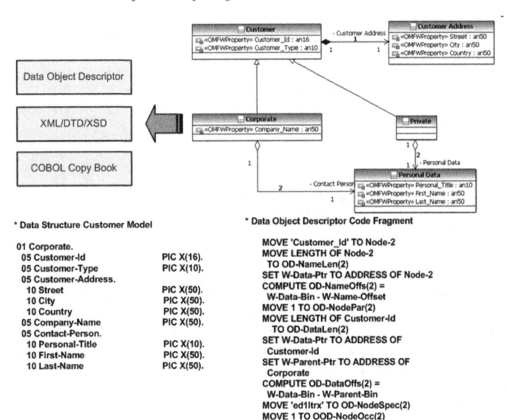

* **Data Structure Customer Model**

```
01 Corporate.
   05 Customer-Id          PIC X(16).
   05 Customer-Type        PIC X(10).
   05 Customer-Address.
      10 Street            PIC X(50).
      10 City              PIC X(50).
      10 Country           PIC X(50).
   05 Company-Name         PIC X(50).
   05 Contact-Person.
      10 Personal-Title    PIC X(10).
      10 First-Name        PIC X(50).
      10 Last-Name         PIC X(50).
```

* **Data Object Descriptor Code Fragment**

```
MOVE 'Customer_Id' TO Node-2
MOVE LENGTH OF Node-2
   TO OD-NameLen(2)
SET W-Data-Ptr TO ADDRESS OF Node-2
COMPUTE OD-NameOffs(2) =
   W-Data-Bin - W-Name-Offset
MOVE 1 TO OD-NodePar(2)
MOVE LENGTH OF Customer-Id
   TO OD-DataLen(2)
SET W-Data-Ptr TO ADDRESS OF
   Customer-Id
SET W-Parent-Ptr TO ADDRESS OF
   Corporate
COMPUTE OD-DataOffs(2) =
   W-Data-Bin - W-Parent-Bin
MOVE 'ed1ltrx' TO OD-NodeSpec(2)
MOVE 1 TO OOD-NodeOcc(2)
```

Figure 5 shows the state chart with a code segment of a process controller. In this illustration, the process is quite simple, as each activity leads to a single event. Normally, an activity can lead to a number of different events that branch out in different process flows. The technical error handling uses a standard flow pattern that does not need to be included in the process flow model. In the event of an error, an exception is thrown and the process terminates with error messages returned to the service consumer.

An activity in the state chart represents a COBOL module. Each module is programmed as a separate unit. It is activated by the process controller with the transfer of the context container. The required data is retrieved from the context container, without knowing where and how this data is made available. The output data is stored in the context container. An event is generated by the module depending on the result of its action. When modelling the process flow, it must be ensured that each module finds its required data in the context container. For early testing of the process, dummy modules can be inserted that just generate the events and updated the state data in the context container. These dummy modules can be successively replaced by real modules in the iterative process.

Figure 5. State model and code generation of a process controller

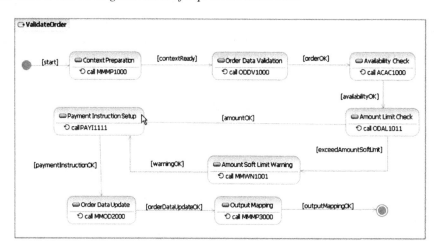

```
* Process Control Descriptor Code Segment:

MOVE "OrderOK" TO CP-Event(3)
MOVE "Order Data Validation" TO CP-State(3)
MOVE "ACAC1000" TO CP-Activity-Name(3)
MOVE "Availability Check" TO CP-Next-State(3)
```

All usages of the infrastructure can be put into a number of code patterns that can be parameterized. Therefore, developers can easily use these patterns in the model and set the parameters without worrying about the code behind the infrastructure. There are also many repeatable business patterns that can be integrated into reusable code patterns using parameters. Along with reusable code templates, reuse can be significantly increased. Reusable code segments are generally well tested. This reduced the effort for troubleshooting and testing. As mentioned above, 70% of the code usually refers to the infrastructure. The expense of writing this code portion can be significantly reduced if reusable code patterns are included in the model.

Figure 6 shows an example of the activity diagram and the generated code. The activity model has the following characteristics:

- Program rules and logic are modelled in the UML activity diagram.
- Each action in the model can contain code or a link to a code pattern with parameters.
- The code generator uses different structures for different actions with different stereotypes.
- Different code templates are also used to generate COBOL modules for different purposes.

To create a service, one must use UML class diagrams to create the data object descriptors. Process control descriptors for process control can be generated based on state charts. COBOL modules can be developed using activity diagrams.

Figure 6. Activity modeling of module logic and code generation

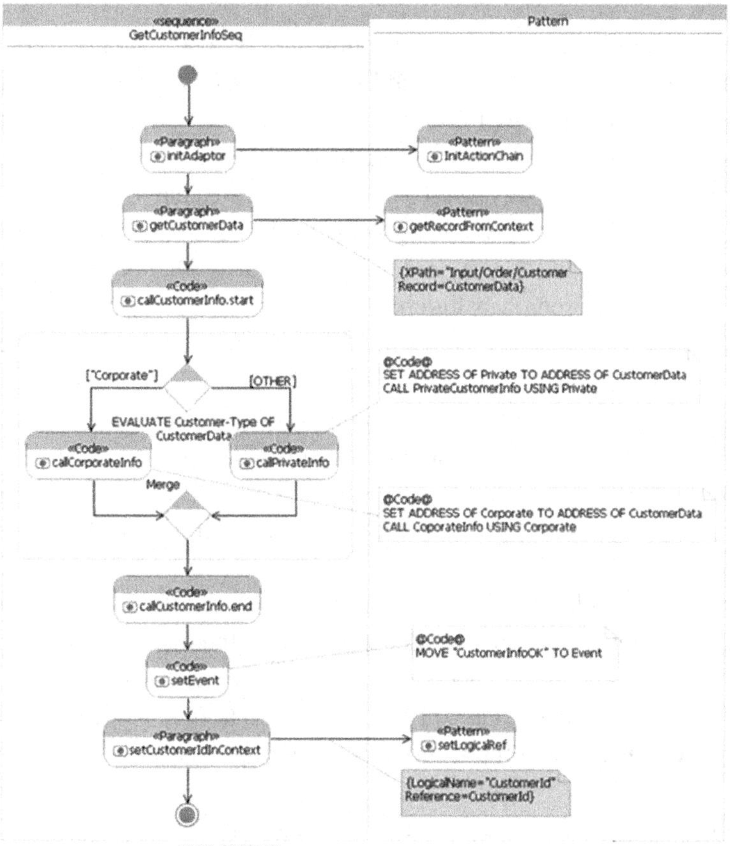

```
MAIN SECTION.
    MOVE 0 TO Status-Code
    PERFORM WITH TEST BEFORE
        UNTIL W-GetCutstomerInfoSeq-End
        OR Status-Code > 4
    EVALUATE TRUE
        WHEN W-InitAdaptor
          PERFORM initAdaptor
        WHEN W-GetCustomerData
          PERFORM getCustomerData
        WHEN W-CallCustomerInfo
          EVALUATE Customer-Type OF CustomerData
            WHEN "Corporate"
                SET ADDRESS OF Corporate TO
                    ADDRESS OF CustomerData
                CALL CorporateInfo USING Corporate
            WHEN OTHER
                SET ADDRESS OF Private TO
                    ADDRESS OF CustomerData
                CALL PrivateCustomerInfo USING Private
          END-EVALUATE
        WHEN W-SetEvent
          MOVE "CustomerInfo" TO Event
        WHEN W-SetCustomerIdInContext
          PERFORM setCustomerIdInContext
        WHEN OTHER
          SET W-GetCutstomerInfoSeq-End TO TRUE
    END-EVALUATE
    IF (Status-Code NOT = 0) THEN
      PERFORM HANDLE-TECH-ERROR
    END-IF
    ADD 1 TO W-State-GetCutstomerInfoSeq
    END-PERFORM
    GOBACK
```

Model and Implementation in Java With Frameworks

Many tools and standards for service-oriented development in Java are available. For example, standards such as Simple Object Access Protocol (SOAP) and Web Services Description Languages (WSDLs) are defined by W3C. There are many open source tools support these standards. Services can be implemented as Web-service servlets or endpoint of message-oriented middleware (MOM) using components such as ActiveMQ. Enterprise Service Buses (ESB), such as Mule ESB, can be used as a service integration platform to provide services creation and hosting, message brokering, message forwarding, data transformation, transaction management, security control, and security Database access etc.

The high-level architecture presented in this chapter combines the patterns of SOA, component-based, and layered architecture. The basic design concept of the component-based architecture is listed below:

- Business Service components should be autonomous, pluggable and application-specific objects.
- Objects of a component can be plain old Java objects (POJOs) or Enterprise Java Beans (EJBs) with a single responsibility.
- Objects and / or beans of a component are packed together in a JAR, EAR or WAR file (for web services).
- Each component has a well-defined interface and contract to fulfill independently of the other components (that is, they are completely decoupled from the other components).
- To access objects across packages, one should always use the interfaces with dependency injections provided by frameworks such as Spring framework. In this way, the coupling and dependencies of objects across different components can be reduced.

The first layer of the layer architecture pattern shown in Figure 2 is primarily a structural and logical concept. Framework like Mule ESB already provides the infrastructure needed for service dispatching, transaction management, security control, and more. Figure 7 shows how to use the Mule ESB design tool. Services and components contain objects for business processing and data persistence. Error handling and event logging components must be accessible through their interfaces for all objects and beans. Error and log messages must be easily accessible, traceable, and understandable to support teams (that is, no print stack or long log files). One may need to archive error and log messages.

In the proposed architecture, the processing of the business logic of a service is performed by a central process controller. This process control separates the detailed data processing from the process flow. It helps to free the business components from handling application-specific processes and improve their reusability. The process flow is modeled using UML state charts as shown in Figure 8. The process controller is basically a finite state machine. This finite state machine is driven by a state transition table. The state machine can be implemented on a template for generating the process controller. Therefore, the code for the process controller class can be generated with its state transition table based on the state model shown in Figure 8. For each component, a processor interface is implemented, as shown in figure 8. Action for each state in the state diagram is associated with activating the processor of the component.

The context container in the architecture uses the application context from the Spring Framework. Data beans, which mainly contain business data, are used for communication between objects and components. These beans are implementations of their interfaces. They are instantiated by Spring Framework and injected into the objects and components when they are need. Only the interfaces of the data beans are exposed to the objects and components that use them.

Figure 7. Service design using Mule ESB design tool

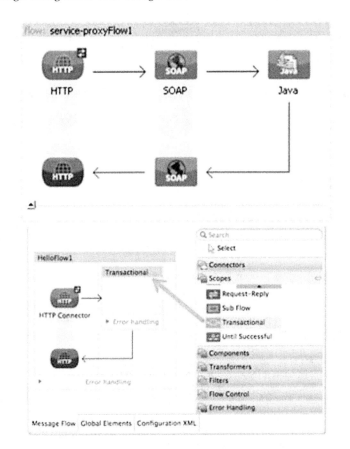

CONSEQUENCES AND APPLICABILITY

Many IT projects still fail even when the agile development approach is used. The author has observed a lot of project failure is due to the lack of proper architecture. As mentioned before, an application cannot be developed incrementally and iteratively without an architecture and mechanism that allow the development of autonomous modules. A key to success in software projects is to master complexity and have an agile IT architecture. The development of loosely coupled services, components and autonomous modules is relatively simple. With continuous, iterative system integration, it is unlikely that a project will go awry. The design and implementation approach of an architecture presented in this chapter can fulfil these purposes. It be used in any enterprise IT system. It takes accounts of software engineering design principles and help to manage IT complexity through different levels of abstractions and modularity. The proposed plug and play mechanism also demonstrate how modules can be developed independently and iteratively.

The architecture with tools has been used since 2004 in a large financial institution for application development (Pang, 2015; Pang, 2016). The infrastructure of the layered, component-based service-oriented architecture was in place. Since then, many applications using this approach have been successfully developed and delivered on time and within budget. It has been shown that the total development costs can be reduced by a factor of four. No project has failed.

Figure 8. Service design using Mule ESB design tool

```
stateTable.put(ProcessState.start, null, ProcessState.Context_Preparation, contextProcessor);
stateTable.put(ProcessState.contextReady, ProcessState.Context_Preparation,
  ProcessState.Order_Data_Validation, orderDataProcessor);
stateTable.put(ProcessState.orderOK, ProcessState.Order_Data_Validation,
  ProcessState.Availability_Check, accountProcessor);
....

while (!state.equals(ProcessState.processCompleted) && !event.equals(ProcessState.processFailed){
  currentProcessor = stateTable.getProcessor(event, state);
  newState = stateTable.getNewState(event, state);
  event = currentProcess.processTransition(newState, context);
  state = newState;
}
```

VISION FOR THE FUTURE

A code-centric approach to software development has persisted for the past 50 years. Most programmers and project managers, even in the community with agile approaches, still believe that this is the way to develop software. A vision for the future is that coding, while still needed, should not be the main task in the development of quantitative and qualitative applications. The new development of low-code and no-code software platforms has aroused great interest among IT managers. This should be the future and deserve more attention and research.

Business processes in different business areas of a large company typically have very similar patterns. For example, all payment and trade transactions in a financial institution require the retrieval of customer and account information, availability and credit checks, generation of customer position movements, debiting and / or crediting of accounts, posting the transaction in the general ledger, and so forth. The future is to develop standard model templates for the high-level abstractions of business applications and create rigorous patterns for business process models. These model patterns can be tailored to different infrastructures and business components by providing the code segments and wrappers. Programs can then be generated from these models. Thus, one can have standard models for business processes that can be used for different business areas.

CONCLUSION

In this chapter, description and motivation of software engineering design principles and architecture are presented. It is shown that the agile development approach with successive increment and iteration of modules cannot be done without a proper architecture. The chapter presents an architectural blueprint for an agile and model-driven approach to software development. The design of the architecture is based on software engineering principles.

Patterns like layered, component-based and service-oriented architecture form the basis of the architectural design. The architecture has been further refined to provide centralized process control in the form of a finite state machine, context container, and autonomous module development. Infrastructure and modelling tools have been developed to support application development through architecture. Major modelling artefacts include UML class diagrams, state charts, and activity diagrams. Codes are generated from these models for both COBOL and Java. With a centralized process control software architecture proposed in this chapter, software components or modules can be developed as autonomous units and tested for units. The architecture also provides a plug-and-play mechanism for components and modules. The software architecture forms a basis for the rapid development of individual software components and continuous integration. It makes changes and extensions rather uncomplicated tasks.

An agile approach combined with a model-driven approach enables the implementation of an iterative and incremental development process with rapid delivery of useful software. It eliminates the heavy documents, but also provides useful documentation of the models. In addition to the requirement specifications, programming can also begin at an earlier point in time. The approach was applied to many projects, all of which were successfully completed on time and on budget.

REFERENCES

Agile Manifesto Group. (2001). Manifesto for Agile Software Development. *Agile Manifesto*. Retrieved July 26, 2010, from http://agilemanifesto.org

Ambler, S. W. (2010). Agile Modeling. *Ambysoft*. Retrieved July 26, 2010, from http://www.agilemodeling.com/

Babar, M. A., Brown, A. W., & Mistrik, I. (2014). *Agile Software Architecture*. Waltham, MA: Morgan Kaufmann.

Baldwin, C. Y., & Clark, K. B. (2000). *Design Rules: The power of modularity*. Cambridge, MA: MIT Press. doi:10.7551/mitpress/2366.001.0001

Bell, T. E., & Thayer, T. A. (1976). Software Requirements: Are They Really a Problem? In *Proceedings of the 2nd International Conference on Software Engineering*, (pp. 61-68). IEEE Computer Society Press.

Booch, G., Maksimchuk, R. A., Engle, M. W., Young, B. J., Conallen, J., & Houston, K. A. (2007). *Object-Oriented Analysis and Design with Applications* (3rd ed.). Upper Saddle River, NJ: Addison-Wesley.

Chappell, D. A. (2004). *Enterprise Service Bus*. Sebastopol, CA: O'Reilly.

Colburn, T., & Shute, G. (2007). Abstraction in Computer Science. *Minds and Machines, 17*(2), 169–184. doi:10.100711023-007-9061-7

Drumond, C. (2019). What is Scrum? *Atlassian*. Retrieved July 11, 2019, from https://www.atlassian.com/agile/scrum

Fowler, M. (2006). *Patterns of Enterprise Application Architecture*. Boston, MA: Addison-Wesley.

Gamma, E., Helm, R., Johnson, R., & Vlissides, L. (1995). *Design Patterns: Elements of Reusable Object-Oriented Software*. Reading, MA: Addison-Wesley.

Harlow, M. (2014). Coconut Headphones: Why Agile Has Failed. *Code Rant*. Retrieved December 11, 2014, from http://mikehadlow.blogspot.ch/2014/03/coconut-headphones-why-agile-has-failed.html

Hastie, S., & Wojewoda, S. (2015). Standish Group 2015 Chaos Report - Q&A with Jennifer Lynch. *InfoQ*. Retrieved from May 26, 2019, from https://www.infoq.com/articles/standish-chaos-2015

Hopkins, R., & Harcombe, S. (2014). Agile Architecting: Enabling the Delivery of Complex Agile Systems Development Projects. In M. A. Babar, A. W. Brown, & I. Mistrik (Eds.), *Agile Software Architecture*. Waltham, MA: Morgan Kaufmann. doi:10.1016/B978-0-12-407772-0.00011-3

Huang, M. (2010) Software Engineering Principles. *Lecture Note from University of Arkansas*. Retrieved May 26, 2019, from http://www.csce.uark.edu/~mqhuang/courses/3513/s2010/lectures/SE_Lecture_3.pdf

Ismail, N. (2017). UK wasting 37 billion a year on failed agile IT projects. *Information Age*. Retrieved May 26, 2019, from https://www.information-age.com/uk-wasting-37-billion-year-failed-agile-it-projects-123466089/

Isotta-Riches, B., & Randell, J. (2014). Architecture as a Key Driver for Agile Success. In M. A. Babar, A. W. Brown, & I. Mistrik (Eds.), *Agile Software Architecture*. Waltham, MA: Morgan Kaufmann. doi:10.1016/B978-0-12-407772-0.00014-9

Jackson, M. A. (1975). *Principles of Program Design*. Cambridge, MA: Academic Press.

Johnson, J., Boucher, K. D., Connors, K., & Robinson, J. (2001). Collaborating on Project Success. *SOFTWAREMAG*. Retrieved July 26, 2010, from http://www.softwaremag.com/archive/2001feb/collaborativemgt.html

Josika, K. (2017) Software Engineering I Coupling and Cohesion. *GeeksForGreeks*. Retrieved June 6, 2019, from https://www.geeksforgeeks.org/software-engineering-coupling-and-cohesion/

Krigsman, M. (2006). Success Factors. *ZDNet*. Retrieved July 26, 2010, from http://www.zdnet.com/blog/projectfailures/success-factors/183

Larman, C. (2003). *Agile and Iterative Development: A Manager's Guide*. Reading, MA: Addison-Wesley.

Liskov, B. (1988). Keynote address - data abstraction and hierarchy. *ACM SIGPLAN Notices*, *23*(5), 17–34. doi:10.1145/62139.62141

Malan, R., & Bredemeyer, D. (2010). Software Architecture and Related Concerns. *Resources for Software Architects*. Retrieved July 26, 2010, from http://www.bredemeyer.com/whatis.htm

Martin, R. (2000). *Design Principles and Design Patterns*. Retrieved July 12, 2017, from https://web.archive.org/web/20150906155800/http://www.objectmentor.com/resources/articles/Principles_and_Patterns.pdf

Martin, R. (2017). *Clean Architecture: A Craftsman's Guide to Software Structure and Design*. Upper Saddle River, NJ: Prentice Hall PTR.

Meyer, B. (1988). *Object-oriented Software Construction*. Upper Saddle River, NJ: Prentice Hall PTR.

Pang, C. Y. (2015). Ten Years of Experience with Agile and Model Driven Software Development in a Legacy Platform. In A. Singh (Ed.), *Emerging Innovations in Agile Software Development*. Hershey, PA: IGI Global.

Pang, C. Y. (2016). An Agile Architecture for a Legacy Enterprise IT System. *International Journal of Organizational and Collective Intelligence*, *6*(4), 65–97. doi:10.4018/IJOCI.2016100104

Parnas, D. L. (1972). On the Criteria To Be Used in Decomposing Systems into Modules. *Communications of the ACM*, *15*(12), 1053–1058. doi:10.1145/361598.361623

Rakitin, S. R. (2001). Manifesto Elicits Cynicism: Reader's Letter to the Editor by Steven R. Rakitin. IEEE Computer, (34), 4.

Rehkopf, M. (2019). User Stories. *Atlassian Agile Guide*. Retrieved May 22, 2019, from https://www.atlassian.com/agile/project-management/user-stories

Richards, M. (2015). *Software Architecture Patterns*. Sebastopol, CA: O'Reilly.

Royce, W. (1970). Managing the Development of Large Software Systems. *Proceedings of IEEE WESON*, (28) 1-9.

Sagenschneider, D. (2019). Local Microservices: Object Orientation Behavior Coupling Problem. *DZone*. Retrieved June 6, 2019, from https://dzone.com/articles/local-microservices-object-orientation-behaviour-c

Sessions, R. (2008). *Simple Architectures for Complex Enterprises*. Redmond, WA: Microsoft Press.

Software Crisis. (2010). Software Crisis. *Wikipedia*. Retrieved July 26, 2010, from http://en.wikipedia.org/wiki/Software_crisis

Software Engineering. (2010). Software Engineering. *Wikipedia*. Retrieved July 26, 2010, from http://en.wikipedia.org/wiki/Software_engineering

Yourdon, E., & Constantine, L. L. (1979). *Structure Design: Fundamentals of a Discipline of Computer Program and System Design*. Upper Saddle River, NJ: Yourdon Press.

ADDITIONAL READING

Agile Software Development Process, & the Agile Manifesto Group. (2001). Manifesto for Agile Software Development. *Agile Manifesto*. http://agilemanifesto.org

Ambler, S. W. (2010). Agile Modeling. *Ambysoft*. Retrieved July 26, 2010, from http://www.agilemodeling.com/

Bass, L., Clements, P., & Kazman, R. (2003). *Software Architecture in Practice* (2nd ed.). Reading, MA: Addison-Wesley.

Coplien, J., & Bjornvig, G. (2010). *Lean Architecture for Agile Software Development*. West Sussex, UK: John Wiley & Son.

Erl, T. (2009). *SOA Design Patterns*. Upper Saddle River, NJ: Prentice Hall PTR.

Fowler, M. (1997). *Analysis Patterns: Reusable Object Models*. Reading, MA: Addison-Wesley.

Fowler, M. (2006). *Patterns of Enterprise Application Architecture*. Reading, MA: Addison-Wesley.

Gamma, E., Helm, R., Johnson, R., & Vlissides, L. (1995). *Design Patterns: Elements of Reusable Object-Oriented Software*. Reading, MA: Addison-Wesley.

Garland, J., & Anthony, R. (2003). *Large-Scale Software Architecture: A Practical Guide using UML*. West Sussex, UK: John Wiley & Son.

Geetha, C., Subramanian, C., & Dutt, S. (2015). *Software Engineering*. Delhi, India: Pearson Education India.

Hohpe, G., & Woolfe, B. (2004). *Enterprise Integration Patterns: Designing, Building, and Deploying Messaging Solutions*. Reading, MA: Addison-Wesley.

Hunt, J. (2006). *Agile Software Construct*. London, UK: Springer.

Larman, C. (2003). *Agile and Iterative Development: A Manager's Guide*. Reading, MA: Addison-Wesley.

Martin, R. (2017). *Clean Architecture: A Craftsman's Guide to Software Structure and Design*. Upper Saddle River, NJ: Prentice Hall PTR.

McGovern, J., Ambler, S. W., Stevens, M. E., Linn, J., Sharan, V., & Jo, E. K. (2003). *A Practical Guide To Enterprise Architecture*. Upper Saddle River, NJ: Prentice Hall PTR.

Mellor, S. J., Scott, K., Uhl, A., & Weise, D. (2004). *MDA Distilled: Principles of Model-Driven Architecture*. Reading, MA: Addison-Wesley.

Model-Driven Approach to Software Development. Arlow, J. & Neustadt, I. (2004). Enterprise Patterns and MDA: Building Better Software with Archetype Patterns and UML. Reading, MA: Addison-Wesley.

Sommerville, I. (2015). *Software Engineering* (10th ed.). Essex, UK: Pearson Education Limited.

KEY TERMS AND DEFINITIONS

Agile Software Architecture: A software architecture that lays out blueprints of the organization and structure of software components as well as well-defined mechanism on how components can be tested and integrated into the system that would sustain the agile approach throughout the software development life cycle.

Agile Software Development Process: An evolutionary and iterative approach to software development with focuses on adaptation to changes.

COBOL: The programming language designed for commercial business data processing used for applications that often form the backbone of the IT structure in many corporations since 1960.

Component-Based Architecture: A software architecture that breaks down the application design into reusable functional or logical components that expose well-defined communication interfaces.

Enterprise Service Bus (ESB): A software architecture model used for designing and implementing the interaction and communication between mutually interacting software applications in service-oriented architecture (SOA).

JSON (JavaScript Object Notation): An open-standard file format that uses human-readable text to transmit data objects consisting of attribute–value pairs and array data type.

Layered Architecture: A software architecture from which the concerns of the application are divided into stacked groups (layers). Each level would interact only with the levels above and below.

Mainframe: Mainframe computer systems like IBM z/OS.

Model-Driven Approach to Software Development: A model centric rather than a code centric approach to software development with code generated from models.

Service-Oriented Architecture (SOA): A technical software architecture that allows client applications to request services from service provider type applications in a host system.

SOAP: Simple Object Access Protocol, a standard from W3C.

Software Component: A software unit of functionality that manages a single abstraction.

Software Crisis: A term used in the early days when software projects were notoriously behind schedule and over budget and maintenance costs were exploding.

Software Engineering: The application of engineering to the development of software in a systematic method.

SOLID: An acronym for object-oriented design principles proposed by R. Martin in 2000.

Spring Framework: An application framework and inversion of control container for the Java platform.

Waterfall Model: A sequential design, used in software development processes, in which progress is seen as flowing steadily downwards (like a waterfall) through the phases of Conception, Initiation, Analysis, Design, Construction, Testing, Deployment, and Maintenance.

WSDL: Web Service Description Language, a standard from W3C.

XML (Extensible Markup Language): A markup language that defines a set of rules for encoding documents in a format that is both human-readable and machine-readable.

This research was previously published in Software Engineering for Agile Application Development; pages 82-108, copyright year 2020 by Engineering Science Reference (an imprint of IGI Global).

Chapter 17
Agility in Software Development and Project Value:
An Empirical Investigation

VenuGopal Balijepally
Oakland University, Rochester, MI, USA

Gerald DeHondt
Ball State University, Muncie, IN, USA

Vijayan Sugumaran
ⓘD https://orcid.org/0000-0003-2557-3182
*Department of Decision and Information Sciences, Oakland University, Rochester, MI, USA, &
Department of Global Service Management, Sogang University, Seoul, Korea*

Sridhar Nerur
University of Texas at Arlington, Arlington, TX, USA

ABSTRACT

Agile Development Methods, considered as an alternative to the traditional plan-based methods, have received much attention since their inception. These practices have evolved and developed over time, culminating in 2001 with the Agile Manifesto. Since that time, preferred methodologies, implementations, and best practices have continued to evolve with a focus on doing what works best for the individual company or project. However, the concept of agility in software development has remained quite nebulous, lacking in clarity particularly about its underlying dimensions. In this research the authors conceive agility in terms of four distinct dimensions. Drawing from the theoretical perspective of holographic organization, they develop a model explaining how each of these underlying dimensions of agility contributes to project value in software teams. The authors test the model using survey data collected from industry practitioners and discuss findings.

DOI: 10.4018/978-1-6684-3702-5.ch017

INTRODUCTION

From wearable devices to cars and appliances, software pervades practically every aspect of our lives. With ever increasing reliance on software, it is imperative that we evolve appropriate means to build virtually defect-free applications in a timely manner. Furthermore, the software, once designed and deployed, should meet stated requirements while blending seamlessly into the context where it is being used. Agile software development (ASD) has become increasingly popular in industry, primarily because it uses a customer-engaged, evolutionary delivery model to continually deliver high-quality software. By all accounts, ASD has replaced traditional approaches that were dictated by a waterfall process model or some form of it (Dingsøyr, Nerur, Balijepally, & Moe, 2012; Torrecilla-Salinas, Sedeno, Escalona, & Mejias, 2015). Despite the fact that ASD is the most dominant approach in industry today, there exists little empirical evidence of its efficacy, particularly in terms of delivering business value.

Agile development seeks to limit software development strictly to activities that add business value for the customer (Conboy, 2009). With the exception of a few empirical papers ([e.g., (Balijepally, Sugumaran, De Hondt, & Nerur, 2014; Bonner, Teng, & Nerur, 2010; Grenning, 2001; Manhart & Schneider, 2004; Serrador & Pinto, 2015)] and some anecdotal accounts, the efficacy of Agile Development Methodology (ADM) has hardly been subjected to empirical scrutiny. Furthermore, there has been only modest effort to substantiate the claims that practices such as iterative development, self-organizing teams, process flexibility (e.g., interchangeable roles), and test-driven development deliver stakeholder value. This is partly attributable to the difficulty involved in conceptualizing and measuring software value which is partly subjective and is inherently multi-dimensional. Considering the widespread acceptance and adoption of ADM we need theoretically-grounded research that seeks to address the value proposition of ADM. Our study aims to fill this void. Specifically, this research seeks to examine the following main research question: what aspects of agility in software development methods contribute to project value? We use the theoretical perspective of holographic organization (Morgan, 1998; Nerur & Balijepally, 2007) to explicate the value proposition of agility in software teams and to derive the main hypotheses.

The data for this research were gathered from a survey of industry practitioners, conducted by Ambysoft, Inc. (Ambler, 2013). Respondents were from companies across the world representing varied IT roles including developers, Quality Assurance professionals, business analysts and subject matter experts, and project managers. We believe that this broad group of participants—including managerial and technical professionals, dispersed geographically across multiple organizations of varying sizes—will provide a better assessment of the overall business value that accrues to organizations using ASD.

The remainder of the paper is organized as follows. We first provide a brief description of Agile Software Development and related research. This is followed by an overview of the holographic principles of organizational design, which provides the theoretical rationale for the main hypotheses of the study. Subsequently, we outline the research method, followed by a presentation of the data analysis and the results of hypothesis testing. Finally, we discuss the implications of our research findings and suggest some directions for future research.

AGILE SOFTWARE DEVELOPMENT

Ambler (Ambler, 2012) defines agile development as "an iterative and incremental (evolutionary) approach to software development which is performed in a highly collaborative manner by self-organizing teams within an effective governance framework, with 'just enough' ceremony that produces high quality solutions in a cost effective and timely manner which meets the changing needs of its stakeholders." In this research we adopt this definition which is quite consistent with the principles and values enunciated in the agile manifesto (AgileAlliance, 2001).

The increasing frustration with software failures served as a catalyst to evolve ASD, a methodology that made people a priority, allowing them to express their software development prowess without being trammeled by ironclad rules and rigid processes. Furthermore, ASD embraced a perspective that ran counter to long-standing software practices, for it: a) emphasizes expeditious delivery of valuable software while doing nothing wasteful; b) advocates the deep involvement of the customer throughout the process; and c) leverages change by explicitly recognizing that change is not an uncommon occurrence, or an event that should be anticipated and controlled through extensive planning.

Over the last fifteen years, a host of agile methods (e.g., Scrum, eXtreme Programming) have dotted the software development landscape. Consistent with the principles outlined in the Agile Manifesto (AgileAlliance, 2001), these methods are placed primary on iterative development, team empowerment and collaboration, adaptive planning, active customer engagement, continuous process improvement, and value to stakeholders (Cockburn & Highsmith, 2001; Highsmith & Cockburn, 2001). Further, they eschew unnecessary documentation and rely on self-organizing teams to respond to problematic situations that inevitably emerge during the development process.

Conboy (2009) defines agility as the "continual readiness of an ISD method to rapidly or inherently create change, proactively or reactively embrace change, and learn from change while contributing to perceived customer value (economy, quality, and simplicity), through its collective components and relationships with its environment" (p.340). Erickson et al. (2005) note that agility is often associated with such related concepts as nimbleness, suppleness, quickness, dexterity, liveliness, or alertness. At its core, agility means to strip away as much of the heaviness, commonly associated with traditional software-development methodologies, as possible to promote quick response to changing environments, changes in user requirements, accelerated project deadlines, and the like. Lee and Xia (2010) emphasize sense-and-respond, cross-functional teams, and continuous adaption as underpinning agile development. In the project management literature, where the concept of agility is gaining increasing attention, agility refers to "the project team's ability to quickly change the project plan as a response to customer or stakeholder needs, market or technology demands in order to achieve better project and product performance in an innovative and dynamic project environment" (Conforto, Amaral, da Silva, Di Felippo, & Kamikawachi, 2016). Sheffield and Lemétayer (2013) suggest organizational culture and empowerment of the project team as critical factors contributing to software development agility in successful projects.

Agile methodologies seek to imbue flexibility in software development projects, thereby enabling software development teams to perform more effectively (Maruping, Venkatesh, & Agarwal, 2009; Vlaanderen, Jansen, Brinkkemper, & Jaspers, 2011). The iterative approach to development allows for the product under development to be refined based on feedback collected at an earlier stage (Brhel, Meth, Maedche, & Werder, 2015). Any missteps during the development process can be quickly remedied, with learning integrated into further development cycles.

By all accounts, the principles and practices advocated by "agilists" have been adopted or adapted to varying degrees by companies around the world (Conboy, 2009; Dingsøyr et al., 2012; Vijayasarathy & Butler, 2015), although some difficulties have been reported when scaling agile methods to large and complex projects (Batra, VanderMeer, & Dutta, 2011; Dybå & Dingsøyr, 2008). It is reported that when Agile Principles are properly deployed, they can help produce products that yield twice the value in half the time (Johnstone, 2015) and contribute to higher levels of job satisfaction (Tripp, Riemenschneider, & Thatcher, 2016), developer productivity, and customer satisfaction (Dybå & Dingsøyr, 2008). Developers in agile teams feel empowered to influence organizational outcomes to a greater extent than their counterparts in traditional software teams (Tessem, 2014).

Several other studies have also noted the successful use of agile methods ([e.g. (Bonner et al., 2010; Grenning, 2001; Manhart & Schneider, 2004; Serrador & Pinto, 2015)]. Bonner et al. (2010) found that development process agility, a construct that subsumes evolutionary development and process flexibility, reduced perceived development complexity while enhancing developers' feeling that the methodology is compatible with their prior experience, work practices and values. Further, reduced complexity and increased compatibility were found to be positively associated with perceived benefits from ASD. Thus, process agility positively impacted perceived benefits of ASD both directly and indirectly through the two mediators—i.e., by reducing perceived complexity and enhancing feeling of compatibility. Based on a large sample survey, Serrador and Pinto (2015) report the degree of effort in agile planning to be positively impacting project efficiency (i.e., meeting project goals related to scope, cost and time) and stakeholder satisfaction. Quality of project goals (i.e., congruence of project goals with the organization's strategic goals or project portfolio) moderated this relationship, but project complexity and level of experience of agile teams did not affect this relationship.

In terms of project value expected from ASD, Alahyari, Berntsson Svensson, and Gorschek (2017) identify delivery time as the most valued outcome emphasized in software development organizations, followed by software quality (perceived/actual) and project cost. These findings resulted from an empirical study involving semi-structured interviews with participants from multiple organizations. The study also highlighted differences in the value perceptions across industries (i.e., telecom. automobile, consulting, and defense) and across participant roles (i.e., project managers vs. product owners).

It is suggested that the principles and practices underpinning ASD are not meant to be viewed as isolated ideas, but as closely interrelated and interdependent concepts (Erickson et al., 2005). However, there is some evidence (Conboy, 2009) that developers rarely adhere to specific agile methods, but use tailored variants or in-house creations based on contextual factors such as project type, project complexity, project goals, team size, technical knowledge, user availability, etc. (Campanelli & Parreiras, 2015). These custom variants demonstrate an organization's desire to tread their own path and implement what works best for their situation. Taken together, flexibility, compatibility, and simplicity are key components of ASD that led to its increasing following within the development community.

While organizations have increasingly embraced agile methods, their sustained usage is contingent on several factors related to the organization (e.g. support of top management, having a methodology champion, and having compatible organization structure), agile team (e.g., agile experience, agile mindset, etc.) and agile technical issues (e.g., effective use of specific agile practices and having related tool support) (Senapathi & Drury-Grogan, 2017). In addition to transforming software development teams, agile development offers positive externalities to the organization at large. For instance, use of agile approaches within the organizational space of action could potentially impact the overall organizational culture in positive ways (Vinekar, Slinkman, & Nerur, 2006). Agility at the individual project level could also evolve into agility at other levels in the organization (e.g., project portfolio management) through a conscious effort focused on diffusing best practices from agile teams related to routines (e.g., standup meetings, product reviews), structure (e.g., self-managing) and culture (e.g., collaborative, transparent and trusting) (Stettina & Hörz, 2015).

From the above it is evident that while prior research tried to illuminate several aspects of agile development, exploring the value proposition of ASD received scant attention. Considering that the operations of contemporary organizations are increasingly automated and computerized, they are becoming increasingly dependent on their often-complex IT systems. Huge amounts of money are invested in IT projects aiming to develop, improve, and maintain these systems (Gingnell, Franke, Lagerstrom, Ericsson, & Lillieskold, 2014). As these systems are a tremendous investment in terms of time and corporate resources, better understanding of the critical aspects of agility and those factors that will provide the greatest value are critical to helping organizations understand where to invest corporate resources. This research seeks to delineate the underlying dimensions of agility and their contribution to the project value. The next section provides a brief description of the Holographic principles of organizational design that underpin the research hypothesis.

HOLOGRAPHIC PRINCIPLES OF ORGANIZATIONAL DESIGN

A hologram is a picture created with laser-based technology where the whole is embodied in each of its parts. Thus, if there is an accidental damage, a hologram can easily be rebuilt from any of its parts (Morgan & Ramirez, 1984). Human brain is believed to be organized based on holographic principles with memory distributed across different parts of the brain. When the hologram metaphor is extended to the organizational setting, holographic principles of organizational design suggest ways social systems faced with turbulent environments could be designed for adaptability and responsiveness (Morgan & Ramirez, 1984).

The five principles underlying holographic design are: building whole into parts, requisite variety, redundancy of functions, minimal critical specification, and learning to learn [also see (Nerur & Balijepally, 2007)]. When designing a social system such as an organization or a workgroup for high responsiveness and adaptability required in dynamic environments, the holographic principle of manifesting the whole in each of its parts advocates creating holistic self-organized teams that could quickly learn and adapt to situational demands. The next holographic principle is based on Ashby's law of requisite variety (Morgan & Ramirez, 1984), which specifies that the variety and internal sophistication of a system should be consistent with the variability and complexity of its external environment.

The holographic principle of redundancy of functions highlights the need for a social system to have spare interchangeable resources at its disposal so that in case of problems in one area, these spare resources could be deployed with minimal disruptions to its working. Unlike traditional organizational designs that seek to minimize redundancies and overlaps between resources for gaining efficiencies, holographic design entails some redundancy of functions/resources so that the system has flexibility to respond quickly and effectively to sudden demands.

The holographic principle of minimal critical specification underscores the futility of trying to foresee and plan for all possible demands on an organizational system, particularly in turbulent environments, which hampers innovation and constrains system response. Instead, the system should be specified with minimal essential requirements so that it could learn and alter its response to changing demands emanating from its environment. Minimum critical specification, which is one of the principles of socio-technical systems (STS) theory, provides the rationale for effecting local autonomy of teams to facilitate self-organization. The conceptual underpinnings of STS [see (Cherns, 1987)] could potentially influence agile practices in myriad ways. The interested reader may refer to Nerur et al. (2010) for a discussion of STS principles relevant to the context of agile software development.

The last holographic principle of 'learning to learn' is highly essential to the working of a system operating in dynamic environments. This entails reflection and constant questioning of the current assumptions so that the organizational system is able to sense and learn quickly from the environment and from its own actions. Empowering the system for self-organization is essential for enhancing its responsiveness.

Drawing from these principles, Nerur and Balijepally (2007) highlight how agile software development teams could be conceived as holographic organizations. In the next section we use the holographic principles as the theoretical lens when deriving our research hypotheses.

AGILE PRACTICES AND PROJECT VALUE

Agile software development embraces the reality that complexity and change are inevitable when information systems are designed and developed in a turbulent business environment. Any efforts to control change through elaborate planning exercises would be wasteful and misguided. Hence, it is best to accept and embrace change by adapting the development processes and practices for quick learning and responsiveness. Basing on the principles outlined in the agile manifesto, agile methods specify different best practices and organizing frameworks for promoting agility in software teams. Basing on the criteria for agility in software teams articulated by Ambler (2009), we group the processes and practices of agile development into the following categories: stakeholder collaboration, continuous validation/testing, reflection & review, and self-organization/team governance. Unlike Ambler (2009), which considers creating stakeholder value through regular delivery of working software as a condition for agility, we conceptualize it as an outcome of adopting agile development processes and practices. We argue that when software teams embrace agile processes and practices covering these four dimensions, they create project value. Figure 1 showcases our research model.

Stakeholder Engagement and Project Value

An important tenet of agile development is to get stakeholders actively involved throughout the development process (Cockburn & Highsmith, 2001). Where feasible, a collocated user representative (e.g., product owner as in Scrum), who is available for populating and prioritizing the backlog and for regularly processing requirements for the current iteration, is considered highly valuable. Active stakeholder collaboration in the agile development process is consistent with the holographic principles of 'building whole into parts', 'minimum critical specification' and 'learning to learn'. When product owners or user representatives with requisite business knowledge and skills become available to the agile teams on a continuous basis, stakeholders' goals and priorities at the macro level get translated and integrated into the elemental parts of the system at the micro level. The agile teams should however be cognizant of mitigating barriers to effective knowledge sharing (Ghobadi & Mathiassen, 2016) and decision-making (Drury-Grogan, Conboy, & Acton, 2017). Thus, as the system takes shape it is more likely to satisfy stakeholder interests at multiple levels.

Figure 1. Research Model

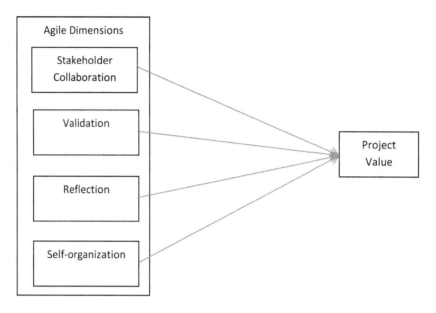

Stakeholder Engagement and Project Value

Agile methods skimp on elaborate requirements gathering and big upfront design in favor of minimum critical specification of requirements/design. Implicit in this principle is the assumption that stakeholders or their agents are available to agile teams on a regular basis so that short cycles of requirements specification/design are done for the iteration at hand. Stakeholder collaboration and engagement also fosters team learning through shorter feedback cycles and through dynamic learning processes of perspective making and perspective taking (Boland & Tenkasi, 1995). Stakeholder engagement is also likely to curb scope creep, which has been the bane of software projects undertaken with plan-driven methods. Further, stakeholder participation in evolving test cases and acceptance criteria, particularly in test-driven development, not only helps in managing the expectations of the stakeholders, but also facilitates the delivery of higher business value to them. Thus, active stakeholder collaboration throughout the software development process should contribute to higher project value for the stakeholders. Hence, we hypothesize:

Hypothesis 1: Stakeholder collaboration in agile teams is positively related to the creation of project value

Validation Processes and Project Value

Constant validation of system features and functionality with the desired system requirements throughout the developmental process is an important aspect of agile development. Validation oriented practices such as Test-Driven Development (TDD), multiple levels of system testing, and product demos to stakeholders at various stages of development/version releases are all consistent with the holographic principles of 'building whole into parts', 'requisite variety', and 'learning to learn'. Writing test cases ahead of coding, instituting a continuous testing regimen involving multiple levels of testing (e.g., unit tests, regression tests, user acceptance tests, black box vs. white box testing etc.) and doing product demos (e.g., demos of proof of concept/prototypes, demos of pre-release/final versions, etc.) throughout the development process helps validate the system from whole to the part and vice-versa. Frequent demos/reviews not only help in managing customer expectations, but also enable the developers to detect and correct errors early, thus eliminating expensive rework at a later time. The continual cycles of design-code-test-reflect enable opportunistic designs [see (Guindon, 1990)] as developers gain insights from an evolving software product that incrementally adds business value. The combined use of such varied testing and validation processes also minimizes, if not completely eliminates, the chances that the completed system has major bugs or is lacking in some essential features. In Test Driven Development, where each unit test is designed to first fail and only pass once the feature or functionality is fully implemented, the constant feedback provided by the battery of tests is a great learning tool for agile development teams. The system that finally results from such integrated testing and validation regimen could be expected to contribute to higher project value for the stakeholders. Thus, we predict:

Hypothesis 2: Validation in agile teams is positively related to the creation of project value

Reflective Improvement and Project Value

Agile methods encourage constant reflection and questioning of the current state of affairs and the underlying assumptions throughout the development process (Williams & Cockburn, 2003). Agile processes that foster team reflection and learning are quite consistent with the holographic design principles of 'building whole into parts', requisite variety, and learning to learn (Morgan & Ramirez, 1984). Agile practices such as daily standups, code analysis (both static and dynamic), team reflection sessions conducted at the end of one or more iterations and/or after major releases, post mortem reviews conducted after project completion, and reviews carried out by external auditors, all facilitate 'reflection in action' (Schön, 1983) and contribute to process improvements and project value. By providing multiple opportunities for reflection from varied sources (e.g., team members, product owners, other project stakeholders etc.), such reviews/reflection sessions provide rich opportunities for learning and course corrections to agile teams. Practices such as paired development as in eXtreme Programming (XP) (Beck, 2000), where the work of each developer gets to be constantly inspected and reviewed by the coding partner with instant feedback cycles, also helps bring in the benefits of reflective improvements to the level of an individual developer, not just at the level of the project team. It has also been argued that evolutionary delivery of software that includes practices such as self-organization and reflection workshops is conducive to the creation and integration of knowledge (Dissanayake, Dantu, & Nerur, 2013). This leads us to the next hypothesis.

Hypothesis 3: Reflection in agile teams is positively related to the creation of project value

Self-Organization and Project Value

Agile approaches place great trust in empowered self-organized teams to come up with creative solutions to the problems and issues they confront during the systems development process. For instance, team work quality in agile teams is known to positively impact team member satisfaction and learning (Lindsjørn, Sjøberg, Dingsøyr, Bergersen, & Dybå, 2016). Prior research also suggests that team coordination practices and team cohesion do matter for team performance (Dingsøyr, Fægri, Dybå, Haugset,

& Lindsjørn, 2016). Many agile practices that foster self-organization and empowerment of agile teams are consistent with several holographic design principles. The decision latitude available to agile teams through empowerment is in line with the principles of minimal critical specification and building whole into the parts. Such empowerment seeks to bring in high level strategic thinking to the level of team members and the product owner. Thus, such self-organizing teams would be able to simultaneously alternate between the strategic intent or the 'big picture' and the demands of the specific task at hand. They could learn quickly by doing complex mental simulations of the cause and effects of various decisions/ actions and thus make more informed decisions contributing to enhanced project value. Redundancy of functions is a critical aspect of self-organization, as it allows developers to assume varied roles based on the demands of the problem at hand. An approach where developers' roles are interchangeable leads to transfer of knowledge about architectural design, databases, networking, and other aspects of software development. This leads to the next hypothesis:

Hypothesis 4: Self-organization in agile teams is positively related to the creation of project value

RESEARCH METHOD

We tested the above outlined research model using a secondary data source—i.e., a survey conducted during 2013 by Ambysoft, Inc. (Ambler, 2013) that included 174 industry practitioners from across the world. Eliminating incomplete responses resulted in 97 usable responses. Respondents' IT roles ranged from developers, architects, business analysts, quality assurance professionals, to project managers and product owners. Table 1 summarizes the demographic details of respondents.

Table 1. Demographic Details of Survey Respondents

Demographic Variable	Number of Respondents	Percentage
Agile Experience		
Project teams that are agile	47	48.5
Project teams trying to become more agile	33	34.0
Currently not on an 'agile team', but have been in the past	17	17.5
Never involved with an agile team	-	-
Position		
Scrum Master/Team Lead	27	27.8
Agile Team Member	12	12.4
Architect/Architecture Owner	9	9.3
IT Manager	9	9.3
Project Manager	8	8.2
Programmer	7	7.2
Product Owner	7	7.2
Business Analyst	5	5.2

continues on following page

Table 1. Continued

Demographic Variable	Number of Respondents	Percentage
QA/Testing	3	3.1
Business Stakeholder	1	1.0
Others	9	9.3
Location		
N. America	46	47.4
Europe	30	30.9
Australia/New Zealand	7	7.2
Asia	6	6.2
South/Central America	4	4.1
Africa	4	4.1
Industry Sector		
Technology (incl. software)	38	39.2
Financial	16	16.5
IT Consulting	12	12.4
E-Commerce	10	10.3
Government	9	9.3
Manufacturing	1	1.0
Others	11	11.3
Department Size (Number of IT/System Development People)		
1 to 10	21	21.6
11 to 50	23	23.7
51 to 100	16	16.5
101 to 500	23	23.7
501 to 1000	2	2.1
1000+	12	12.4%

In this research project value is conceived as the dependent measure that captures the stakeholder value created by the project. The four independent variables in the research model represent different dimensions of agility in software development processes—stakeholder collaboration captures the extent of stakeholder engagement in the software development process; validation dimension represents the level of quality assurance processes adopted by software teams; team reflection dimension captures the extent of reflection and review practices instituted by software teams for pursuing continuous improvements; and self-organization dimension represents the extent of team empowerment and self-governing principles and practices embraced by software teams.

The main survey questionnaire items require respondents to select the agile practices that are used in their software development teams. That is, for each item subjects provided responses on a binary scale of yes or no categories. For this research we grouped relevant items from the survey to create ordinal scales for each construct in the model. For this, the authors first identified a set of 41 items from out of 53 items in the survey questionnaire that were related to the five constructs of interest here. These questionnaire items were then randomly ordered before each author independently did a Q-sort on them, matching each item with its related construct from the research model. Based on the Q-sort results, one more item that was mapping into more than one construct was dropped from further consideration. The remaining 40 items were mapped into the five constructs of interest here. The Cohen's Kappa values for the initial pair-wise agreement between the four authors ranged from 0.615 to 0.808 with the average being 0.662. The authors then discussed each item where there was a difference between author mappings and jointly identified the final set of items for each construct. For instance, for stakeholder collaboration, we identified 11 items from the survey questionnaire that capture the construct and coded subject responses on an ordinal scale of 0 to 11, based on the number of items selected by the subjects. Using a similar approach, we coded other constructs of the research model into ordinal scales as follows: Validation/Testing – 0 to 9; Reflective Reviews – 0 to 8; Self-organization – 0 to 5; Project Value - 0 to 7).

Our analysis included two control variables—respondent's Agile Experience and Position in their organization. The Agile experience elicited at 4 levels was coded as an ordinal scale as follows: 1 – Never involved with an agile team; 2 – currently not on an agile team, but have been in the past (and will discuss the most recent one); 3 – currently on a project team where we are trying to become more agile; 4 – currently on a project team where we believe we are agile. Subjects indicated their current positions by selecting from a list of 12 categories. To account for possible differences in perceptions between respondents in technical positions vs. business/management positions, we grouped respondents into two categories as follows: 1 – Technical Positions (Agile team member, Architect/Architecture owner, Operations/support, Programmer, QA/Testing, and Scrum master/Team lead); 2 – Business/Management Positions (Business Analyst, IT manager, Product owner, Project Manager, Business Stakeholder, and Other).

DATA ANALYSIS AND RESULTS

Table 2 summarizes the descriptive statistics and correlations for the various constructs of the model. The correlation matrix reveals that project value is positively correlated with all the four independent variables and one of the control variables, i.e., agile experience of respondents. This suggests that respondents with more experience with agile methods perceive higher project value than the ones with lower experience with agile methods. Incidentally, project value is negatively correlated with Position/IT role of the respondents indicating that respondents in technical positions rated project value higher compared to the ones in business/project management positions.

We used hierarchical ordinary least square (OLS) regression to test the main hypotheses of this research. We estimated the initial model (Model 1) using the first control variable—i.e., Agile experience. Then we added the second control variable (i.e., job position) when estimating Model 2. Subsequently in Model 3 we added the four independent variables to the two control variables in the previous model. The full model reads as follows:

Project Value $= \beta_0 + \beta_1 * \text{AEXP} + \beta_2 * \text{POSN} + \beta_3 * \text{STCO} + \beta_4 * \text{VALN} + \beta_5 * \text{REFL} + \beta_6 * \text{SORG}$

where β_0 is the constant term; β_1 through β_6 are the coefficients for the two control variables (AEXP = Agile Experience; POSN = Position/IT Role) and the four independent variables of interest (STCO = Stakeholder Collaboration; VALN = Validation; REFL = Reflection; SORG = Self-Organization).

Table 2. Correlations and Descriptive Statistics

No.	Variable	Mean	Std. Dev.	1	2	3	4	5	6	7
1	Project Value	3.844	1.482	1.000						
2	Stakeholder Collaboration	5.615	2.069	0.571***	1.000					-
3	Validation	4.552	1.967	0.564***	0.482***	1.000				
4	Reflection	2.865	1.658	0.432***	0.245***	0.385***	1.000			
5	Self-Organization	3.115	1.025	0.268***	0.210**	0.323***	0.257***	1.000		
6	Agile Experience	3.312	0.758	0.362***	0.158*	0.314**	0.118	0.116	1.000	
7	Position/IT Role	1.604	0.492	-0.201**	-0.234**	-0.207**	-0.041	-0.118	0.081	1.000

$n = 96$; $*p < 0.10$, $** p < 0.05$, $***p < 0.01$

Table 3. Regression Analysis Results for the Project Value Dependent Variable

		Model 1	Model 2	Model 3
Constant	Unstd. Coeft. [Std. error]	1.498** [0.638]	2.499*** [0.742]	-0.048 [0.713]
Control Variables				
Agile Experience of Respondent	AEXP	0.708*** [0.188]	0.745*** [0.184]	0.422*** [0.153]
Job Position of Respondent	POSN		-0.700** [0.283]	-0.239 [0.232]
Independent Variables				
Stakeholder Collaboration	STCO			0.253*** [0.061]
Validation	VALN			0.160** [0.071]
Reflection	REFL			0.203*** [0.072]
Self-Organization	SORG			0.048 [0.114]
R^2		0.131	0.185	0.522
F		14.210***	10.551***	16.219***
Adj-R^2		0.122	0.167	0.490
ΔR^2		0.131	0.054	0.337
ΔF		14.210***	6.118**	15.715***

$*p < 0.10$, $** p < 0.05$, $***p < 0.01$

Table 3 summarizes the results of the regression analysis. Results for Model 1 and 2 indicate that the overall models are significant (p = 0.000) and that the two control variables (i.e., Agile experience and Position) are significantly related to project value (p = 0.000 and p = 0.015 respectively). Model 3 includes the four independent variables of interest and the two control variables. The overall model is again significant, and three of the four main effects and one of the two control variables (agile experience) are significant, as is the change in R^2 relative to the base model containing only the two control variables (R^2 change = 0.49 - 0.167) (F change = 15.715; p = 0.000).

Hypothesis 1 predicted Stakeholder Collaboration in agile teams to be positively related to Project Value. Results from the regression analysis suggest that the coefficient for the main effect of Stakeholder collaboration is positively significant (β_3 = 0.253; p < 0.01) lending support to Hypothesis 1. Hypothesis 2 predicted Validation in agile teams to be positively related to Project Value. From Table 2 it can be seen that the regression coefficient for the main effect of Validation is positive and significant (β_4 = 0.160; p < 0.05). Thus, Hypothesis 2 is also supported. Hypothesis 3 predicted Reflection in agile teams to be positively related to Project Value. Results from the regression analysis (Table 3) suggest that the regression coefficient for the main effect of Reflection to be positively significant (β_5 = 0.203; p < 0.01). Therefore, Hypothesis 3 is also supported. Hypothesis 4 predicted that Self-Organization in agile teams to be positively related to project value. However, regression results from Table 3 suggest that the coefficient for the main effect of Self-organization is not significant (β_5 = 0.048; p > 0.10). Thus, Hypothesis 4 is not supported. The results of hypotheses testing are summarized in Table 4.

Table 4. Results of Hypotheses Testing

Hypothesis	Result	t statistic	p-value
Hypothesis 1: Stakeholder collaboration in agile teams is positively related to the creation of project value	Supported	4.149	0.000
Hypothesis 2: Validation in agile teams is positively related to the creation of project value	Supported	2.251	0.027
Hypothesis 3: Reflection in agile teams is positively related to the creation of project value	Supported	2.818	0.006
Hypothesis 4: Self-organization in agile teams is positively related to the creation of project value	Not Supported	0.421	0.675

DISCUSSION

Our study seeks to verify the claim that stakeholder collaboration, continuous testing and validation, team reflection, and self-organization lead to project value. As mentioned earlier, our measures were constructed using responses to a survey administered by Ambysoft, Inc. (Ambler, 2013). As evident from the results of the regression analysis, all of our hypotheses, but one, were supported.

Our results show that stakeholder collaboration is positively associated with project value. The rationale for our hypothesis was that stakeholder engagement would ensure that the evolving code would satisfy acceptance criteria, allow the stakeholders to have realistic expectations of what the software would and would not deliver, provide opportunities for the exchange of valuable domain knowledge, manage the introduction of new requirements later in the lifecycle, and ensure that high business value is delivered early and often. While it may not be realistic for stakeholders to be constantly engaged throughout the development process, increasing the opportunities for agile teams to collaborate frequently with the stakeholder can add tremendous value to a project.

Continual testing and validation positively impacts project value. Frequent testing helps in isolating errors early, has the potential to get to the root-cause of the problem, creates options (i.e., opportunistic designs), facilitates learning and exchange of knowledge, and eventually leads to fewer defect densities. Our findings affirm the value that accrues to a project because of continual validation built into the development process.

Our results provide strong support for our hypothesis that team reflection leads to higher project value. ADM affords ample opportunities to software teams to assess progress, reflect and introspect on activities to gain an understanding of what works and what doesn't, and adjust their behaviors in light of knowledge acquired during the process. Knowing the criticality of reflection to creating project value, agile teams have to institute processes for team reflection at the end of every sprint or after each release as well post mortems at the conclusion of the project for fostering learning and team adaptation.

Our hypothesis with regard to the positive impact of self-organization on project value was not supported. A plausible explanation for the lack of support is that our contrived measure of self-organization and governance did not adequately capture the richness of the construct. Interestingly, a recent study could not find team work quality (a related construct that includes dimensions such as communication, coordination, balance of member contribution, mutual support, effort and cohesion) to be impacting team performance as perceived by product owners (Lindsjørn et al., 2016). Indeed, the concept of self-organization, which is arguably the crux of ADM, has received scant attention in the literature. Prior research emphasizes the need for simultaneously balancing high levels of individual autonomy, team autonomy and organizational responsibility for fostering agile development (Dybå & Dingsøyr, 2008). Also, self-organization may entail overcoming several barriers at both the organizational (e.g., specialist culture) and team (e.g., individual commitment) levels (Moe, Dingsoyr, & Dyba, 2009). Thus, there is a need to explicate this concept, both theoretically and empirically, to understand its various dimensions and how they should fit together for optimal outcomes. Future research may examine this and also develop a robust measure of self-organization for assessing its effectiveness in delivering project value.

A major limitation of our study relates to the way we tested the model using data from a secondary source. We used data from an existing survey which was compiled for a different purpose—i.e., for understanding the current state of agile implementation in IT organizations. Accordingly, we had to map the questionnaire items to the constructs relevant to our study. As most questionnaire items were measured on a binary scale of yes or no responses, we selected items relevant to the constructs in our research model and created variables with ordinal scales. Thus, validity testing using traditional statistical means could not be done. However, we believe the items carry face validity/content validity as these items were used in multiple prior surveys by Ambysoft, Inc. using industry respondents. Also, the authors evaluated each item by conducting independent Q-sort, then discussed between them and included only the ones with face validity that are relevant to the constructs of interest here. However, we believe the research model presented here should be validated in a future large sample survey with measures constructed and validated through traditional means.

Although, we used data from a secondary source (Ambler, 2013), our research model and findings are quite different from the ones reported therein. As alluded to earlier, based on Ambler (2009), we group the processes and practices of agile development into the following categories: stakeholder collaboration, continuous validation/testing, reflection & review, and self-organization/team governance.

In addition to the above four factors, Ambler (2013), whose data underpins our study, conceives stakeholder value as the fifth factor for agility. Accordingly, Ambler (2013) reports the % of respondents that report using the various agile practices grouped under the above five factors. Unlike Ambler (2013), we conceptualize project value as an outcome of adopting agile development processes and practices related to the other four factors. Accordingly, we tested the theoretical model and related hypotheses using hierarchical regression and found stakeholder collaboration, validation and reflection in ASD to be positively related to project value.

Project value is a broad concept that could be conceptualized from multiple perspectives. One perspective is based on the question, value to who? Is it for the business users, or the sponsors who fund the system, or for the entire stakeholders of the system? Stakeholders of a system under development typically include users (direct or indirect), managers at different levels, sponsors funding the project, operations staff, portfolio/program managers, maintenance staff and even developers in other projects who need to integrate their system with the system under development (Ambler, 2002). Consistent with the agile principles, the questions used in this research explored project value from the viewpoint of stakeholders.

Another perspective is related to the question, value realized at what time? Is it during the project duration, after project completion or at a much later time? As agile principles emphasize early and continuous delivery of software after every two or three iterations, value is realized on a continuous basis throughout the development process. Certain stakeholders such as operations staff or maintenance staff could realize value from a high quality system much later than say business users or managers who start realizing value from the point a working software is delivered to them. In this study we have examined stakeholder value at the end of project completion. Future studies may consider measuring project value at multiple points—during the course of the project, at project completion, and even during system operation/support phase—for understanding how value creation in ASD is distributed temporally.

Beyond the dimensions of agility explored in this study, several other project related factors could potentially impact project value. We tried to control for two such factors, agile experience of respondents and their position in their organizations (technical vs. business/management). Incidentally, both were found to be significantly correlated to project value in the regression model. Future studies may examine or control for the effect of other factors that could impact project value such as developer abilities, familiarity with technologies involved, project complexity, etc.

CONCLUSION

Agile methodologies have been proposed and practiced by organizations that develop commercial and non-commercial software for more than a decade. While considerable progress has been made in adapting agile practices when implementing within organizations, much work remains to be done in clearly understanding which practices work best under what circumstances and empirically demonstrating which practices add the most value and contribute to project success. Practitioners and researchers are still trying to clearly delineate the parameters and practices that contribute to different levels of agility in the development process. This paper has identified several key dimensions of the agile development process and has investigated their impact on the overall project value. Several hypotheses have been developed based on relevant underlying theory and the research model has been validated using the survey data collected by Scott Ambler (Ambler, 2013), one of the leading thinkers of the ADM. The results indicate that stakeholder collaboration is essential for adding value to the project. Similarly, continuous testing and validation contributes to improving project value. Reflective improvement is also a key ingredient for ensuring project value. However, contrary to the basic belief within the agile community, self-organization was not found to have a significant impact on project value. The lack of support for this hypothesis possibly stems from the limitations of the data collection and the survey instrument design. However, this does raise the question of how best to systematically study the impact of self-organization and governance on project value. To sum up, the findings from the study have generated some useful insights for the successful execution and management of agile projects. Since the empirical data included responses from agile development practitioners, the results provide a glimpse into the state of the development practices and help identify ways to improve the overall agile development process.

Our study provides a good starting point for empirically investigating the value delivered by the many abiding principles of agile development. Specifically, future research should attempt to evolve richer and more nuanced measures of value drivers such as process flexibility and/or agility, evolutionary development, validation and continuous improvement, and self-organization. The agile literature has long considered self-organization as a defining feature of ADM. Yet, a good scale for the construct eludes our grasp. Future research may also be directed towards identifying and validating mediating and moderating factors that impinge on the value ADM purports to deliver.

REFERENCES

AgileAlliance. (2001). Manifesto for Agile Software Development. Retrieved from http://www.agile-manifesto.org

Alahyari, H., Berntsson Svensson, R., & Gorschek, T. (2017). A study of value in agile software development organizations. *Journal of Systems and Software, 125,* 271–288. doi:10.1016/j.jss.2016.12.007

Ambler, S. (2002). *Agile Modeling: Effective Practices for eXtreme Programming and the Unified Process.* Wiley.

Ambler, S. (2012). Disciplined Agile Software Development: Definition. *Agile Modeling.* Retrieved from http://www.agilemodeling.com/essays/agileSoftwareDevelopment.htm

Ambler, S. W. (2009). Criteria for a Disciplined Agile Team. Retrieved from https://www.ibm.com/developerworks/community/blogs/ambler/?entry=agile_criteria&lang=en

Ambler, S. W. (2013). How Agile Are You? 2013 Survey. Retrieved from http://www.ambysoft.com/surveys/howAgileAreYou2013.html

Balijepally, V., Sugumaran, V., De Hondt, G., & Nerur, S. (2014). Value Proposition of Agility in Software Development - An Empirical Investigation. *Paper presented at the 20th America's Conference on Information Systems,* Savannah, GA.

Batra, D., VanderMeer, D., & Dutta, K. (2011). Extending Agile Principles to Larger, Dynamic Software Projects: A Theoretical Assessment. *Journal of Database Management, 22*(4), 73–92. doi:10.4018/jdm.2011100104

Beck, K. (2000). *Extreme Programming Explained: Embrace Change.* Reading, MA: Addison Wesley.

Boland, R. J. Jr, & Tenkasi, R. V. (1995). Perspective Making and Perspective Taking in Communities of Knowing. *Organization Science, 6*(4), 350–372. doi:10.1287/orsc.6.4.350

Bonner, N., Teng, J., & Nerur, S. (2010). The Perceived Advantage of Agile Development Methodologies By Software Professionals: Testing an Innovation-Theoretic Model. *Paper presented at the 16th America's Conference on Information Systems.*

Brhel, M., Meth, H., Maedche, A., & Werder, K. (2015). Exploring Principles of User-Centered Agile Software Development: A Literature Review. *Information and Software Technology, 61,* 163–181. doi:10.1016/j.infsof.2015.01.004

Campanelli, A. S., & Parreiras, F. S. (2015). Agile methods tailoring – A systematic literature review. *Journal of Systems and Software, 110*(C), 85–100. doi:10.1016/j.jss.2015.08.035

Cherns, A. (1987). Principles of Socio-Technical Design Revisited. *Human Relations, 40*(3), 153–162. doi:10.1177/001872678704000303

Cockburn, A., & Highsmith, J. (2001). Agile Software Development 2: The People Factor. *IEEE Computer, 34*(11), 131–133. doi:10.1109/2.963450

Conboy, K. (2009). Agility from First Principles: Reconstructing the Concept of Agility in Information Systems Development. *Information Systems Research, 20*(3), 329–354. doi:10.1287/isre.1090.0236

Conforto, E. C., Amaral, D. C., da Silva, S. L., Di Felippo, A., & Kamikawachi, D. S. L. (2016). The agility construct on project management theory. *International Journal of Project Management, 34*(4), 660–674. doi:10.1016/j.ijproman.2016.01.007

Dingsøyr, T., Fægri, T. E., Dybå, T., Haugset, B., & Lindsjørn, Y. (2016). Team Performance in Software Development: Research Results versus Agile Principles. *IEEE Software, 33*(4), 106–110. doi:10.1109/MS.2016.100

Dingsøyr, T., Nerur, S., Balijepally, V., & Moe, N. B. (2012). A decade of agile methodologies: Towards explaining agile software development. *Journal of Systems and Software, 85*(6), 1213–1221. doi:10.1016/j.jss.2012.02.033

Dissanayake, I., Dantu, R., & Nerur, S. (2013). Knowledge Management in Software Development. *Paper presented at the 19th America's Conference on Information Systems*, Chicago, IL.

Drury-Grogan, M. L., Conboy, K., & Acton, T. (2017). Examining decision characteristics & challenges for agile software development. *Journal of Systems and Software, 131,* 248–265. doi:10.1016/j.jss.2017.06.003

Dybå, T., & Dingsøyr, T. (2008). Empirical studies of agile software development: A systematic review. *Information and Software Technology, 50*(9-10), 833–859. doi:10.1016/j.infsof.2008.01.006

Erickson, J., Lyytinen, K., & Siau, K. (2005). Agile Modeling, Agile Software Development, and Extreme Programming. *Journal of Database Management, 16*(4), 88–100. doi:10.4018/jdm.2005100105

Ghobadi, S., & Mathiassen, L. (2016). Perceived barriers to effective knowledge sharing in agile software teams. *Information Systems Journal, 26*(2), 95–125. doi:10.1111/isj.12053

Gingnell, L., Franke, U., Lagerstrom, R., Ericsson, E., & Lillieskold, J. (2014). Quantifying Success Factors for IT Projects - An Expert-Based Bayesian Model. *Information Systems Management, 31*(1), 21–36. doi:10.1080/10580530.2014.854033

Grenning, J. (2001). Launching Extreme Programming at a Process-Intensive Company. *IEEE Software, 18*(6), 27–33. doi:10.1109/52.965799

Guindon, R. (1990). Designing the Design Process: Exploiting Opportunistic Thoughts. *Human-Computer Interaction, 5*(2), 305–344. doi:10.120715327051hci0502&3_6

Highsmith, J., & Cockburn, A. (2001). Agile Software Development 1: The Business of Innovation. *IEEE Computer, 34*(9), 120–127. doi:10.1109/2.947100

Johnstone, J. (2015). Agile Quality. *Quality Progress, 48*(7), 63.

Lee, G., & Xia, W. (2010). Toward Agile: An Integrated Analysis of Quantitative and Qualitative Field Data an Software Development Agility. *Management Information Systems Quarterly, 34*(1), 87–114.

Lindsjørn, Y., Sjøberg, D. I. K., Dingsøyr, T., Bergersen, G. R., & Dybå, T. (2016). Teamwork quality and project success in software development: A survey of agile development teams. *Journal of Systems and Software, 122*(C), 274–286. doi:10.1016/j.jss.2016.09.028

Manhart, P., & Schneider, K. (2004). Breaking the Ice for Agile Development of Embedded Software: An Industry Experience Report. *Paper presented at the Proceedings of the 26th International Conference on Software Engineering.* 10.1109/ICSE.2004.1317460

Maruping, L. M., Venkatesh, V., & Agarwal, R. (2009). A Control Theory Perspective on Agile Methodology Use and Changing User Requirements. *Information Systems Research, 20*(3), 377–399. doi:10.1287/isre.1090.0238

Moe, N. B., Dingsoyr, T., & Dyba, T. (2009). Overcoming Barriers to Self-Management in Software Teams. *IEEE Software, 26*(6), 20–26. doi:10.1109/MS.2009.182

Morgan, G. (1998). *Images of Organization*. San-Francisco, CA: Berrett-Koehler Publishers, Inc.

Morgan, G., & Ramirez, R. (1984). Action Learning: A Holographic Metaphor for Guiding Social Change. *Human Relations, 37*(1), 1–27. doi:10.1177/001872678403700101

Nerur, S., & Balijepally, V. (2007). Theoretical Reflections on Agile Development Methodologies. *Communications of the ACM, 50*(3), 79–83. doi:10.1145/1226736.1226739

Nerur, S., Cannon, A., Balijepally, V., & Bond, P. (2010). Towards an Understanding of the Conceptual Underpinnings of Agile Development Methodologies. In T. Dingsøyr, T. Dybå, & N. B. Moe (Eds.), *Agile Software Development: Current Research and Future Directions* (pp. 15–29). Springer. doi:10.1007/978-3-642-12575-1_2

Schön, D. A. (1983). *The Reflective Practitioner: How Professionals Think in Action*. Basic Books.

Senapathi, M., & Drury-Grogan, M. L. (2017). Refining a model for sustained usage of agile methodologies. *Journal of Systems and Software, 132*(C), 298–316. doi:10.1016/j.jss.2017.07.010

Serrador, P., & Pinto, J. K. (2015). Does Agile work? — A quantitative analysis of agile project success. *International Journal of Project Management, 33*(5), 1040–1051. doi:10.1016/j.ijproman.2015.01.006

Sheffield, J., & Lemétayer, J. (2013). Factors associated with the software development agility of successful projects. *International Journal of Project Management, 31*(3), 459–472. doi:10.1016/j.ijproman.2012.09.011

Stettina, C. J., & Hörz, J. (2015). Agile portfolio management: An empirical perspective on the practice in use. *International Journal of Project Management, 33*(1), 140–152. doi:10.1016/j.ijproman.2014.03.008

Tessem, B. (2014). Individual empowerment of agile and non-agile software developers in small teams. *Information and Software Technology, 56*(8), 873–889. doi:10.1016/j.infsof.2014.02.005

Torrecilla-Salinas, C. J., Sedeno, J., Escalona, M. J., & Mejias, M. (2015). Estimating, Planning, and Managing Agile Web Development Projects Under a Value-Based Perspective. *Information and Software Technology, 51*, 124–144. doi:10.1016/j.infsof.2015.01.006

Tripp, J. F., Riemenschneider, C., & Thatcher, J. B. (2016). Job Satisfaction in Agile Development Teams: Agile Development as Work Redesign. *Journal of the Association for Information Systems, 17*(4), 267–307.

Vijayasarathy, L. R., & Butler, C. W. (2015). Choice of Software Development Methodologies: Do Project, Team and Organizational Characteristics Matter? *IEEE Software, 33*(5), 86–94. doi:10.1109/MS.2015.26

Vinekar, V., Slinkman, C. W., & Nerur, S. (2006). Can Agile and Traditional Systems Development Approaches Coexist? An Ambidextrous View. *Information Systems Management, 23*(3), 31–42. doi:10.1201/1078.10580530/46108.23.3.20060601/93705.4

Vlaanderen, K., Jansen, S., Brinkkemper, S., & Jaspers, E. (2011). The Agile Requirements Refinery: Applying SCRUM Principles to Software Product Management. *Information and Software Technology, 53*(1), 58–70. doi:10.1016/j.infsof.2010.08.004

Williams, L., & Cockburn, A. (2003). Agile Software Development: It's About Feedback and Change. *IEEE Computer, 36*(6), 39–43. doi:10.1109/MC.2003.1204373

This research was previously published in the Journal of Database Management (JDM), 28(4); pages 40-59, copyright year 2017 by IGI Publishing (an imprint of IGI Global).

APPENDIX

Survey Questionnaire Items [From Ambler (2013)]

1. Project Value

    What strategies does your team follow to provide value to your stakeholders? Please select that apply (if any)
    - We are producing working software every iteration/sprint during construction
    - We have a definition of what it means to be done
    - We actively consider usability issues in the development of the solution
    - We are producing supporting documentation, such as user manuals or operating manuals
    - We are implementing improvements to the business process
    - We are making business personnel changes as a result of this project

    What strategies does your team follow when working with your stakeholders? Please select all that apply (if any)
    - We have written requirements specification which defines what we need to deliver

2. Stakeholder Collaboration

    What strategies does your team follow to provide value to your stakeholders? Please select all that apply (if any)
    - At the start of the project we identified our key stakeholders and their goals
    - We have regular discussions with key stakeholders to understand their goals throughout the project

    What strategies does your team follow when working with your stakeholders? Please select all that apply (if any)
    - Our team has a product owner who represents the stakeholder community
    - We work with specific stakeholders, or particularly domain expert, on an as needed basis
    - We have access to stakeholders, or their representatives, on a daily basis
    - Stakeholders work with business analysts who provide requirements to our team directly
    - We did some initial requirements envisioning with our stakeholders to identify the scope and to populate our backlog at the start of the project
    - Stakeholders work with business analysts who provide requirements to our product owner
    - Throughout the project we hold modeling sessions with stakeholder groups to populate the backlog

    What strategies does your team follow to organize how they work together? Please select all that apply (if any)
    - We produce a status report at least once an iteration for senior management
    - At least once a week, a senior manager will attend our daily standup meetings to get a status update

3. Validation/Testing

    What strategies does your team follow to validate their work? Please select all that apply (if any):
    - We perform our own regression testing on a regular basis
    - We take a TDD approach at the design level (e.g., via xUnit)
    - We take a TDD approach at the requirements level (e.g., via acceptance tests or story tests)

      ○   Regression testing is performed by an independent test team in parallel to development

      ○   At the end of the project, "final" testing is performed before releasing the system by an independent test team

      ○   At the end of each iteration we demo our work to key stakeholders

      ○   We have "all hands" demo to a wide range of stakeholders every so often

      ○   We demo the solution to stakeholders every iteration/sprint during construction

      ○   We have a demo sandbox where stakeholders can work with an interim version of the system whenever they like

4.   Reflective Reviews

What strategies does your team follow to improve the way that they work together? Please select all that apply (if any)

      ○   External auditors may review what we are doing during the project to help identify potential improvements

      ○   We hold a post-mortem meeting at the end of each project to identify potential improvements for future project teams

      ○   We hold a retrospective/reflection session several times throughout the project to identify potential improvements for our team

      ○   We had a retrospective/reflection session at the end of each iteration/sprint to identify potential improvements for our team

What strategies does your team follow to validate their work? Please select all that apply (if any).

      ○   We include static code analysis in our build

      ○   We include dynamic code analysis in our build

      ○   We follow non-solo development techniques such as pair programming

      ○   We review our work with other technical people external to the team

5.   Self-Organization

What strategies does your team follow to organize how they work together? Please select all that apply (if any)

      ○   Each iteration/sprint we hold a planning meeting where the team determines who will do what that iteration

      ○   The project manager/coach/scrum master assigns tasks to team members

      ○   We hold standup meetings to coordinate our activities

      ○   Our product owner is responsible for prioritizing what our team produces

      ○   Our tools are instrumented and populate a project reporting dashboard to automatically provide status information

Chapter 18
Agent–Based Approach for Monitoring Risks in Software Development Projects

Jirapun Daengdej
Assumption University, Thailand

ABSTRACT

According to various surveys conducted, regardless of how many studies in software development projects have been done, the chance that software development projects may fail remains very high. A relatively new approach to the problem of failure is using the concept of artificial intelligence (AI) to help automate a certain part(s) of the projects in order to minimize the issue. Unfortunately, most of the works proposed to date use AI as a standalone system, which leads to limiting the degree of automation that the overall system can benefit from the technology. This chapter discusses a preliminary work on a novel risk monitoring, which utilizes a number of agent-based systems that cooperate with each other in minimizing risks for the projects. The proposed model not only leads to a high degree of automation in risk management, but this extensible model also allows additional tasks in risk monitoring to be easily added and automated if required.

INTRODUCTION

Issues of software development project failure has long been recognized long time ago. In 1994, one of the most talk about reports by Standish Group called "Chaos Report" rises the issue that only around 16% of software development projects success worldwide (Clancy, 1994). Almost a decade after that, in 2012, a research team of McKinsey Digital in collaboration with University of Oxford found that only around 50% of projects, which cost more than $15 million, completed projects within their budgets. In fact, they report that large IT projects usually spend 45% over budget, while delivering only around 56% less value than what originally planned (Bloch, et. al., 2012). Regardless of how much resources and researches have been put in area of Software Project Management, chance of software project failure

DOI: 10.4018/978-1-6684-3702-5.ch018

still remains very high. According to the latest survey by KPMG, 70% of organizations has at least one project failure in the past 12 months (Krystal, 2019).

One of the reasons of such a high rate of failure is because there are a large number of risks can occur during project lifecycle. As a result, these risks have to be closely and efficiently monitored in order to minimize issues that may occur. Risk monitoring is considered to be one of the most crucial areas in project management in general. Unfortunately, the necessity and difficult in monitoring these risks can easily be magnified when comes to software development projects. The risks are higher in software development projects than other kind of projects because software is intangible in nature. Successfulness of the projects, in many cases, cannot be easily seen and judge explicitly. Progress of the software projects is also very difficult to measure. This is the reason why agile concept, which focus on final products rather than what happen during the project, has been recently introduced and rapidly accepted and adopted by industry (Burger, 2018)(Wolpers and West, 2019).

The goal of this research is to investigate how agent-based approach proposed by Artificial Intelligence (AI) community, which has already been applied in various areas, can be used in risk monitoring of software project management. This chapter provides a preliminary discussion on how the agent-based approach can be used in performing the task and layout issues that require further investigations for those who are interested.

BACKGROUND

The following discusses three main concepts related to focus of the paper. These concepts include project management, risk management, and agent-based approach.

Software Project Management

Project management has been considered as one of the most mature fields as far as industry is concerned (Spalek, 2005). However, regardless of the success of the field in helping projects to meet their expected results, a large number of software development projects are still considered as challenges or even fails (Coronado and Jaén, 2002). According to Anantatmula and Anantatmula, M. (2008), regardless of the success and failures occurred until today, in general, software project management consist of the following steps:

1. Initiation
2. Project Planning
3. Project Execution
4. Project Monitoring and Controlling
5. Project Termination

As far as the failure or challenges is concerned, according to Arnuphaptrairong (2011), example of issues that can occur during the projects include:

- Misunderstanding of requirements
- Lack of top management commitment and support

- Lack of adequate user involvement
- Failure to gain user commitment
- Failure to manage end user expectation
- Changes to requirements
- Lack of an effective project management methodology

With regard to the steps in project management, the project monitoring and controlling is considered to be the most crucial activities in managing the projects (Rozenes, et. al., 2006)(Clayton, 2019).

Risk Management

In most cases, risks in Distributed Software Development (DSD) can include issues such as trust, communication, difference in time zone and culture (Jiménez, et. al., 2009). The issues can occur in both general software development projects, and where agile approach is used in managing the projects (Bosnić, et. al. 2019)(Nadeem and Lee, 2019).

According to result of a research done by Enfei (2015), **risk factors** in software development projects can be classified into 6 groups. Table 1 depicts some of examples of the risks.

Table 1. Six groups of risk factors

Risks	Examples
Personnel	- Lack of effective "people skills" - Insufficient responsibilities
User	- Lack of cooperation and support from users - Users resistance to change
Requirements	- Users are not clear about requirements - Continually changing requirements
Technology	- Introduction of new technology - Change of development tools
Organization/Environment	- Lack of effective development process/methodology - Lack of top management commitment to the project - Change in organizational management
Planning/Control	- No planning or inadequate planning - Inadequate estimation of required resources - Project progress not monitored closely enough

Source: (Enfei, 2015)

Similarly, from practitioner's perspective, according to an article by Cast Software Inc., Risk Management in Software Development and Software Engineering Projects includes:

1. **New, unproven technologies**. New technologies often lead to project failure due to unfamiliarity and uncertainty in applying the technologies the projects.

2. **User and functional requirements.** Similar to most of the discussions found in literature about requirements from users, in most case, requirements from users are unclear, complex, and, in many cases, lengthy, which increase the chance of failure of the projects.

3. **Application and system architecture.** Unlike most of the discussions about risk existed in software development projects, this particular article also includes the fact that ability to clearly to architecture of the system has a direct impact to the successful of software development projects.

4. **Performance.** Expectations of users and all stakeholders on performance of the system being developed is critical for the success of projects. Therefore, it is important to ensure that risk management also take into consideration on how the system can achieve the expected performance.

5. **Organizational.** Ensuring that adequate resources are acquired into a project and they are properly organized in order to meet with expectations of all stakeholders are crucial for the success of the projects.

With regard to risks that can occur with software development project in particular, according to Test Institute, a well-known certification body in the area of software testing, software risk management is specifically about risk quantification of risk, which includes:

1. Giving a precise description of risk event that can occur in the project
2. Defining risk probability that would explain what are the chances for that risk to occur
3. Defining how much loss a particular risk can cause
4. Defining the liability potential of risk

Monitoring Project Risks

According to the Project Management Institute (PMI), a worldwide institute specializes in project management, as far as risks monitoring is concerned, PMBOK 5th Edition, the document includes a process called "Control Risks" which is defined as:

The process of implementing risk response plans, tracking identified risks, monitoring residual risks, identifying new risks, and evaluating risk process effectiveness throughout the project.

However, small change has been in the 6th edition of the document. In the 6th Edition of PMBOK, the "Control Risks" process is changed to "Monitor Risks". The process is described as:

"Monitor Risks is the process of monitoring the implementation of agreed-upon risk response plans, tracking identified risks, identifying and analyzing new risks, and evaluating risk process effectiveness throughout the project." (PMBOK Guide, 2017).

Furthermore, Hall of Project Risk Coach describes that there are four steps to monitoring project risks

1. **Monitor Agreed-Upon Risk Response Plans**: Upon identifying possible risks within a project, a response must be planned in order to ensure that proper actions are taken, if the risk occurs.

2. **Track Identified Risks:** In general, a project tracking tools is used to track all identified risks of the project. In this case, triggers are defined in order to ensure that all risks are notified, if occurs.

3. **Identify and Analyze New Risks:** Regardless of how much efforts are given in planning the project, new risks can always arise. Identifying new risks and rechecking existing risks are recommended to be done periodically. The following events are suggested with regard to when to identifying new risks:
   a. Major changes to the project or its environment
   b. Key milestones reached
   c. Occurrence of a major risk
   d. Unexpected risks
   e. Changes in key team members or stakeholders
4. **Evaluate Risk Process Effectiveness**. A plan or process usually must be monitored and revised regularly. The risk management process is the same. There are seven main activities involved in the process:
   a. Plan for risk management
   b. Identify risks
   c. Perform qualitative risk analysis
   d. Perform quantitative risk analysis
   e. Plan risk responses
   f. Implement risk responses
   g. Monitor risks

Evaluation must be carried out periodically to ensure that the process can still efficiently and effectively lead to expected result.

Agent-Based Approach

Artificial Intelligence (AI) is a concept that currently has been applied in almost every area. According to one of the latest reports by PWC "2019 AI Predictions: Six AI Priorities You Can't Afford to Ignore":

Most executives know that artificial intelligence (AI) has the power to change almost everything about the way they do business—and could contribute up to $15.7 trillion to the global economy by 2030.

In addition, a number of recent articles well-known entities such as Forbes, PWC, Harvard Business Review suggests that, regardless of the size of businesses, every business must think very carefully how can they utilize the concept in their organizations before they are left behind (Marr, 2019)(Rao, et. al., 2019)(Chui, et. al.,2018). According to Marr (2019), regardless of the size of companies, examples of AI applications in organizations include:

- Developing more intelligent products
- Developing more intelligent services
- Making business processes smarter
- Automating repetitive business tasks
- Automating manufacturing processes

For small business, in particular, an AI system can be used to monitor inventory and sales recording databases and inform owners of the business that certain supplies are needed. The AI can even be programmed to place an order, if the business owner allows (Mills, 2019).

The fundamental of AI is to build a system that can mimic how human think and perform our tasks (Daugherty and Wilson, 2019)(Pesheva and Menting, 2020). In general, since the systems will work in the same way that human do things, understanding how human think and solve problems are the key to the concept. Unfortunately, one of the most difficult issues in building an intelligent system is ability acquire knowledge that cover all possible situations that the system may face in its operation.

One of the solutions to this knowledge acquisition issue is to, rather than trying to develop one very large system, develop a number of small systems that and allow them to interact with each other in solving problems. This idea of system development lead to an approach called agent-based software development (Schlesinger and Parisi, 2001). The approach is heavily influenced by the way human experts work together in solving problems (Bonabeau, 2002).

As far as the goal of development is concerned, the main focus of this agent-based approach is to get all small programs or agents to work together, learn how to deal with problems at hand, and finally make decision (DeAngelis and Diaz, 2019). In general, agents have to be designed and developed specifically for each type of problems. As a result, various architectures of agents, which are suitable for different kinds of tasks, have been proposed in literature. This includes logic-based architecture, reactive architecture, BDI architecture, hybrid architecture, cognitive architecture, and semantic architecture (Chin, et. al., 2014)(Girardi and Leite, 2013). However, despite the maturity of all the concepts proposed, note that the issues related to acquiring proper environment and information for the agents are still open-issues that require further investigations. These issues are detailed in research directions at the end of the chapter.

Agent-based approach has been applied in various areas. Ronal, Sterling, and Kirley (2007) use the approach to model pedestrian behavior. Kirer and çırpıcı (2016) discuss and compare a number of agent-based approach for complex networks, which especially focus on modeling of complex networks. With the approach ability to deal with highly dynamic situations, Carter, Levin, Barlow, and Grimm (2015) use the approach to model tiger population and territory dynamics.

Agent-Based Approach in Risk Monitoring

As mentioned earlier, agents are usually designed and developed specifically for a certain task. For monitoring risk in software development projects, each of the agents have to be quite flexible in dealing various input that can occur during the projects. As a result, the current research focuses on using Belief-Desire-Intension or BDI architecture as the blueprint for the agent development. The architecture is known to be a well suite architecture for complex task like what existed in software development projects (Chin, et. al., 2014). In fact, one of the recent works by Microsoft also utilize the BDI architecture in building their Travel Assistant Agent (TAA) (Perez, 2019). Figure 1 shows overview of the BDI architecture by Perez (2019).

According to Caillou, Gaudou, Grignard, Truong and Taillandier (2015), the followings describe details of the architecture and how each of its components help in monitoring risks in software development activities.

- **Perception**: According to Figure 1, Belief-Revision-Function (BRF) receives or perceive input from sensors. This input is can be one or a number of events that occurs in the environment. The BRF accept the input then pass it to the "Beliefs".
- **Plan and Action**: In Figure 1, plan and action are what the agents will do before they act or output back to the environment.
- **Filter**: The filter function is used to filter previously obtained desires in order to turn them to intentions.

Figure 1. BDI Agent Architecture
Source: Perez, 2019

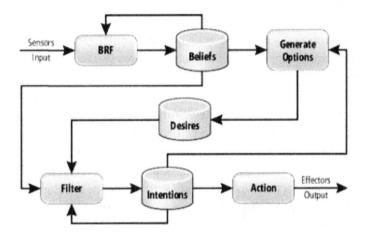

In addition, the BDI can be described as:

- **Belief:**. It is the internal knowledge existed in the agents about the world. Depending on what happened in the word surrounding the agents, which are perceived by the BRF, this belief is regularly updated according to its environment. The belief can be seen as knowledge that is responsible for "What the agents think?".
- **Desires**: It is the objectives that the agents would like to achieve. Desires are usually equipped with priority values, but, similar to what happen to beliefs, these values can be dynamically changed during agent's executions because what happen in the environment can influence these priority. In general, the desire can be seen "What the agents want?".
- **Intensions**: Intensions are what the agents choose to do according to what happen to desire that input to the filter. Output from the intensions are the plans and actions that will be carried out to the environment.
  The following model is used to develop an agent-based system for risk monitoring.
  FOR each type of the risk identified{
  agent = createAnAgent();
  agent.setGoal();
  agent.setBelief();
  agent.getCurrentStatusOfEnvironment();

```
WHILE project is still on{
agent.updateBelief();
agent.updateDesire();
agent.createPlan();
agent.createActions(plan);
agent.executeAction();
}
}
```

FUTURE RESEARCH DIRECTIONS

Despite the fact that the proposed solutions can deal with complex risk monitoring tasks, this research is only considered to be a preliminary work, a number of issues still require further researches. The two most important issues are:

- **Providing Environmental Input that are Suitable (and Sufficient) for Agent to Perceive**: While the BDI is considered by industry to be one of the most practical agent-based architectures available today, designing environmental data that can be efficiently perceived by the agents is not at all simple. The reason is because there are large amount of crucial information related to activities in software development projects that can heavily influence the chance of projects' success. In addition, in many cases, quantifying this information is a very difficult task. Example of the information include attitude of project members during the project (Edwards, 2010), strategies used by management of the projects with regard to managing project members, processes and resources (Discenza and Forman, 2007), and level of quality of works relative to expectation of stakeholders of the projects (Pawlak and Poniszewska-Marańda, 2018).
- **Setting up Values Used by BDI Agent**: The three components: beliefs, desires, and intensions, have to be able to efficiently interact with each other in order for the agents to efficiently act toward its goal. Wrongly processing and using wrong values can directly make the agents misbehave or unable to achieve the goal (Ring and Orseau, 2011). Unfortunately, computerized systems can only best process or compare quantitative values. This is the reason why issue of having proper data is one of the 3 most important issues in one of the latest reports commissioned by IBM (Aslett and Curtis, 2019). Reasoning with symbolic values and images are still a major challenge even with today technology (Matheson, 2019a)(Matheson, 2019b). In addition, misbehaving of AI systems is a major concern today for both academic and industry (Behzadan, et. al., 2018). With regard to the values of beliefs, desires, and intensions, similar to most of the systems that require setup, to our knowledge, there is no systematic approach toward the questions what values should be used and how to best represent all these values in such a way that the all agents can most benefits from them.

CONCLUSION

Issues in risk management, especially risk monitoring, within project management is considered to be one of the most difficult tasks in software project management. Keeping track of all possible risks required large amount of efforts for the project team. This chapter explains a preliminary work on using agent-based approach. With the nature of the approach that allows multiple agents, which are responsible for different tasks to run simultaneously, can result in increasing efficiency of the overall picture of monitoring process. Since the agents can also autonomously update their own knowledge and necessary information about the project and its environment, the approach requires less efforts (manual works) in doing the task.

On the other hand, while the overview picture of how the approach can be applied in risk monitor of the software development projects, regardless of the fact there are a number of agent-based tools and platforms currently available, a number of issues related to preparing input from environment and information that the agents used internally still require further investigations.

REFERENCES

A Guide to the Project Management Body of Knowledge. (2017). (6th ed.). PMBOK® Guide. Project Management Institute.

Anantatmula, V. S., & Anantatmula, M. (2008). *Use of Agile Methodology for IT Consulting Projects*. Paper presented at PMI® Research Conference: Defining the Future of Project Management, Warsaw, Poland.

Arnuphaptrairong, T. (2011). Top Ten Lists of Software Project Risks: Evidence from the Literature Survey. *Proceedings of the International Multi Conference of Engineering and Computer Scientists*.

Aslett, M. & Curtis, J. (2019). *Accelerating AI with Data Management; Accelerating Data Management with AI*. Pathfinder Report. 451 Research.

Behzadan, V., Munir, A., & Yampolskiy, R. V. (2018). A Psychopathological Approach to Safety Engineering in AI and AGI. *Proceedings of International Conference on Computer Safety, Reliability, and Security*. 10.1007/978-3-319-99229-7_46

Bloch, M., Blumberg, S., & Laartz, J. (2012). *Delivering Large-Scale IT Projects on Time, on Budget, and on Value*. Retrieved from https://www.mckinsey.com/business-functions/mckinsey-digital/our-insights/delivering-large-scale-it-projects-on-time-on-budget-and-on-value#

Bonabeau, E. (2002). Agent-Based Modeling: Methods and Techniques for Simulating Human Systems. *Proceedings of the National Academy of Sciences*.

Bosnić, I., Čavrak, I. & Žagar, M. (2019) Assessing the Impact of the Distributed Software Development Course on the Careers of Young Software Engineers. *ACM Transactions on Computing Education (TOCE)*, *19*(2).

Caillou, P., Gaudou, B., Grignard, A., Truong, C. Q., & Taillandier, P. (2015). A Simple-to-Use BDI Architecture for Agent-based Modelling and Simulation. *Proceedings of the Eleventh Conference of the European Social Simulation Association (ESSA 2015)*.

Carter, N., Levin, S., Barlow, A. & Grimm, V. (2015). *Modelling Tiger Population and Territory Dynamics Using an Agent-Based Approach*. Ecol. Model.

Chin, K. O., Gan, K. S., Alfred, R., Anthony, P. & Lukose, D. (2014). Agent Architecture: An Overview. *Transactions on Science and Technology*, *1*(1).

Chui, M., Henke, N., & Miremadi, M. (2018, July). Most of AI's Business Uses Will Be in Two Areas. *Harvard Business Review*, 20.

Clancy, T. (1994). *The Chaos Report*. The Standish Group.

Clayton, M. (2019). *7 Uncomfortable Truths for Project Managers. Project Management Update*. Retrieved from https://www.projectmanagementupdate.com/ estimate/monitoring/?open-article-id= 9629696&article-title=7-uncomfortable-truths-for-project-managers &blog-domain=projectmanager. com&blog-title=projectmanager-com

Coronado, S., & Jaén, J. A. (2002). *A Software Project Management Method: A3*. Paper presented at PMI® Research Conference 2002: Frontiers of Project Management Research and Applications, Seattle, WA.

Daugherty, P. R., & Wilson, H. J. (2019, Apr.). Using AI to Make Knowledge Workers More Effective. *Harvard Business Review*, 19.

DeAngelis, D. L. & Diaz, S. G. (2019). Decision-Making in Agent-Based Modelling: A Current Review and Future Prospectus. *Journal of Frontiers in Ecology and Evolution*, 6.

Discenza, R., & Forman, J. B. (2007). *Seven Causes of Project Failure: How to Recognize Them and How to Initiate Project Recovery*. Paper presented at PMI® Global Congress 2007.

Edwards, J. (2010). A Process View of Knowledge Management: It ain't What You Do, It's the Way That You Do It. *Proceedings of the 11th European Conference on Knowledge Management*.

Enfei, L. (2015). *Risk Factors of Software Development Projects in Chinese IT Small and Medium Sized Enterprises*. KTH Royal Institute of Technology.

Girardi, R., & Leite, A. (2013). A Survey on Software Agent Architectures. *IEEE Intelligent Informatics Bulletin, 14*(1).

Hall, H. (n.d.). *What Project Managers Should Know About Monitoring Project Risks*. Project Risk Coach. Retrieved from https://projectriskcoach.com/monitoring-project-risks/

Jiménez, M., Piattini, M. & Vizcaíno, A. (2009). Challenges and Improvements in Distributed Software Development: A Systematic Review. *Advance in Software Engineering*.

Kirer Silva Lecuna, H. (2016). A Survey of Agent-Based Approach of Complex Networks. *Ekonomik Yaklasim.*, *27*(98), 1. doi:10.5455/ey.35900

Krystal. (2019). *Top 8 Causes of Project Failure in 2020*. Retrieved from https://www.softwaresuggest.com/blog/top-causes-project-failure/

Marr, B. (2019). *Why Every Company Needs An Artificial Intelligence (AI) Strategy For 2019*. Forbes. Retrieved from https://www.forbes.com/sites/bernardmarr/2019/03/21/why-every-company-needs-an-artificial-intelligence-ai-strategy-for-2019/#18da0fd468ea

Matheson, R. (2019a, Nov. 2). *Better Autonomous "Reasoning" At Tricky Intersections: Model Alerts Driverless Cars When It's Safest to Merge into Traffic at Intersections with Obstructed Views*. MIT News.

Matheson, R. (2019b, May 22). *Bringing Human-Like Reasoning to Driverless Car Navigation: Autonomous Control System 'Learns' to Use Simple Maps and Image Data to Navigate New, Complex Routes*. MIT News.

Mills, K. (2019, June). How AI Could Help Small Businesses. *Harvard Business Review*, 3.

Nadeem, M. A. & Lee, S. U-J. (2019). Dynamic Agile Distributed Development Method. *Mathematics*, *7*(10).

Pawlak, M., & Poniszewska-Marańda, A. (2018). Software Test Management Approach for Agile Environments. *Information Systems Management*, *7*(1).

Perez, A. (2019, Jan.). Leveraging the Beliefs-Desires-Intentions Agent Architecture. *MSDN Magazine*.

Pesheva, E. & Menting, A. M. (2020, Winter). One Giant Step: Researchers are Building an Artificial Intelligence System that can Mimic Human Clinical Decision Making. *Harvard Medicine*.

Rao, A., Likens, S., Baccala, M., & Shehab, M. (2019). *AI Predictions Six AI priorities you can't afford to ignore*. PWC. Retrieved from https://www.pwc.com/us/en/services/consulting/library/artificial-intelligence-predictions-2019.html

Ring, M., & Orseau, L. (2011). Delusion, Survival, and Intelligent Agents. *Proceedings of the 4th International Conference, AGI 2011*.

Ronald, N., Sterling, L., & Kirley, M. (2007). An agent-based approach to modelling pedestrian behaviour. *Simulation*, *8*(1), 1473–8031.

Rozenes, S., Vitner, G., & Spraggett, S. (2006). Project Control: Literature Review. *Project Management Journal*, *37*(4), 5–14. doi:10.1177/875697280603700402

Schlesinger, M. & Parisi, D. (2001). The Agent-Based Approach: A New Direction for Computational Models of Development. Developmental Review. *Science Direct, 21*(1).

Spalek, S. (2005). *Critical Success Factors in Project Management: To Fail or Not to Fail, That is the Question!* Paper presented at PMI® Global Congress 2005—EMEA, Edinburgh, UK.

Test Institute. (n.d.). *What is Software Risk and Software Risk Management?* Retrieved from https://www.test-institute.org/What_Is_Software_Risk_And_Software_Risk_Management.php

This research was previously published in Transdisciplinary Perspectives on Risk Management and Cyber Intelligence; pages 91-104, copyright year 2021 by Information Science Reference (an imprint of IGI Global).

Chapter 19
Agile Scrum Issues at Large-Scale Distributed Projects:
Scrum Project Development At Large

Ayesha Khalid
University of Lahore, Lahore, Punjab, Pakistan

Shariq Aziz Butt
https://orcid.org/0000-0002-5820-4028
University of Lahore, Lahore, Punjab, Pakistan

Tauseef Jamal
https://orcid.org/0000-0003-4965-0322
PIEAS University, Islamabad, Pakistan

Saikat Gochhait
Symbiosis Institute of Digital and Telecom Management, Constituent of Symbiosis International (Deemed University), Pune, India

ABSTRACT

The agile model is a very vast and popular model in use in the software industry currently. It changes the way software is developed. It was introduced in 2001 to overcome deficiencies of software development in a workshop arranged by researchers and practitioners who were involved with the agile concept. They introduced the complete agile manifesto. The agile model has main components that make it more viable for use in well-organized software development. One of these is scrum methodology. The reason for the agile-scrum popularity is its use for small-scale projects, making small teams and allows change requests at any stage of a project from the client. It works for client satisfaction. Instead of so much popularity and distinctive features, agile-scrum also has some limitations when used for large scale projects development that makes it less efficient for development. This article discusses the agile-scrum methodology and its limitations when using for large-scale project organization.

DOI: 10.4018/978-1-6684-3702-5.ch019

1. INTRODUCTION

The Agile model is modern and vastly in use model in the software development. It was introduced in 2001 as a complete agile manifesto. The aim of introducing was to overcome the deficiencies from the efficient software development models and make the software development easier and more efficient. The agile model develops any software in iterations and allows change request at any stage of the project and at any iteration. It always gives priority to customer satisfaction and involves the customer in software development (Balaji & Murugaiyan, 2012; Ruparelia, 2010). In the agile model, the customer is directly involved in development and requirement elicitation. Agile model completes with its components such as Scrum, this is the most known and popular agile component. The agile model works with the small teams and use for the small size project development. In the agile model, scrum has a scrum master who arranges a review meeting session on a daily basis to manage the project and gets the project's update from developers. It takes the software development at an extreme level. Due to agile distinctive features, many software industries are moved toward agile development. Instead of these features agile model also has some limitations in software development (Plonka et al., 2014; Kaisti et al., 2014; Dingsøyr & Moe, 2014). These limitations include its only use for small-scale project organizations, daily Scrum meeting sessions, Team communication, and customer involvement, less applicable for distributed development, Team Conflicts, less resourceful for complex and large systems (Dingsøyr & Moe, 2014; Sekitoleko & Evbota, 2014; Lalsing & Kishnah, 2012; Sykov et al., 2018; Tiako, 2009).

The article is designed in the following sections, section 2 explains the literature of agile model including scrum, section 3 explains the limitations of agile model while using in large software development in large organizations, section 4 explains the research methodology of paper, section 5 explains the result discussion and suggestions and section 6 explains conclusion.

2. AGILE MODEL

The agile model is now very popular and vast in use SDLC (software development life cycle model). First, the term agile was used in the 1990's for the first time in many publish papers by different researchers and practitioners. In these papers, a new idea was discussed that people (researchers and practitioners) looking for new creative, efficient and attractive approach to develop the software application in a good manner. The Jim Smith and Bob Martin were involved in the agile concept and arranged a workshop in this regard. In the workshop, they arranged ideas about the agile with others who also involved in the agile concept. In the results of that workshop, the complete agile manifesto came up in 2001. Now the agile model is very trendy in use in many software industries. The agile model design to response the particular challenges of the software industry such as no physical deliverable, short development cycle etc. An agile model is an evolutionary approach that produces high-quality software products in a cost-effective and within time (Balaji & Murugaiyan, 2012; Vijayasarathy & Turk, 2008; Moe et al., 2010; Butt, 2016). The popularity of the agile model between different software industries rather than other life cycle model is due to its unique features such it works with the small team members with 3-9 members to develop a particular software application. It gives many progressive results when using for small-scale projects in small organizations. The most owing feature of the agile model is to allow change request at any stage of the project and at any sprint/iteration. The study shows that usual times scale spends on the planning of sprints in agile software development. The agile model works in sprints as shown below in

Figure 1. The agile model provides the rapid, simple and incremental/iterative development to break down the project in smaller steps. The agile model split the project in small sprints and develops iteratively. It allows the customer to direct participation in the project development and requirement elicitation. In the agile model, the customer prioritizes the requirements. The customer can send a change request at any time and at any level of the project. The agile model gives first priority to client satisfaction. The agile model replaces the traditional software development project values such as responding to change over following a plan (Dingsøyr & Moe, 2014; Sekitoleko & Evbota, 2014; Moe et al., 2010; Doyle & Williams, 2014; Butt & Jamal, 2017).

The agile model has many components that make it more efficient and complete platform for efficient software development such as Scrum.

Figure 1. Agile Sprints (Butt & Jamal, 2017)

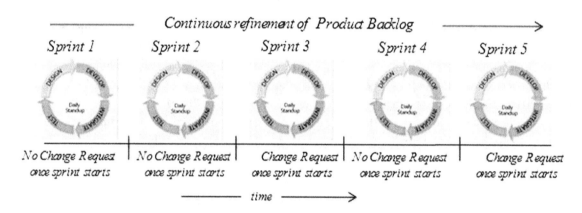

2.1. Scrum

The scrum is the most important and trendy component of the agile model. The scrum has a scrum-master who arranges a project meeting on daily basis. The scrum-master has a central role in the agile model. The duration of the meeting is less than 30 minutes. All the team members participate in the meeting to share the project updates. The scrum plays a vital role in the success of agile projects. The scrum-master and self-organized team took over the responsibilities of the project manager to detailed planning of activities. In the scrum, all team members coordinate with each other. All the developers in the team report to the scrum-master related to project. The scrum-master is also a developer who elected later. Due to his developer experience, it plays an analyst role in the agile model. The scrum master has illustrated in the Figure 2 Below. As in the diagram, the scrum master arranges a review session meeting with the team members and share updates related to tasks (Moe et al., 2010; Doyle & Williams, 2014; Butt, 2016).

Figure 2. Scrum meeting session (Moe et al., 2010)

3. AGILE LIMITATION IN LARGE SCALE ORGANIZATION

There is some difference between the large scale and small-scale project organization software development. In the large-scale organization, large projects are developed with a large number of teams. On one project many teams are working, and many teams are working on many projects in large-scale organizations. In the large organization, the project can be more complex than the small-scale organization. The numbers of team members are in a large organization more than the small one. The large projects mostly do not deliver on monthly iterations due to the size and complexity of the system. As mentioned, that agile works with the small team members and with the small-scale projects. In the large organization, project development is done distributed. In large organizations, software developer works and coordinates globally.

A study published in many papers by different researchers and practitioners that when we use agile for the small-scale project with the small team size it produces very efficient and good results (Kaisti et al., 2014; Dingsøyr & Moe, 2014; Sekitoleko & Evbota, 2014; Ktata & Lévesque, 2009; Butt, 2017). The project completes according to the client's expectations and requirement of the system, but when we use agile for large-scale development then it has many limitations (Figure 3).

3.1. Scrum Issues

The scrum is the major part of the agile software development. In the scrum the scrum master focuses more on the development team process means that how to track, optimize performance and track the project progress. For this scrum master arranges daily base meeting session less than 30 minutes to gets update from team members. This daily meeting session is also a limitation in scrum methodology. Because as mentioned that scrum plans the sprint work, effort and task etc. to team members but it is difficult to find the right person in the team for the right task (Moe et al., 2010). In the scrum mostly the team members take the task with their own plan often not discuss with the other team members. In this case when the developer does not produce the desired results and less coordinate with the team member/ scrum meeting then the scrum master decides to supervise him that ultimately create more issues. The developer then does not participate in the daily meeting session instead he was seen as an expert in current sprint (Moe et al., 2010; Hossain & Babar, 2009; Hobbs & Petit, 2017).

The scrum master also faces that team is not responding him accurately. The developers are not giving a right update of a sprint to scrum master due to this scrum master has lost trust on the team. Due to the daily meeting session the all team members become agitated and feel pressurize from the scrum master to complete their task. These daily scrum meeting issues have an awful influence on the project. The developer does not want to attend the daily meeting session and give their work update to other developers in the team.

Therefore, scrum is not applicable for the large-scale organization where the team members are greater than the agile team, projects are more complex and larger and team members are not used to daily meeting session. It is also difficult to arrange meeting session in the large-scale organization due to their geographical and distributed software development nature because it will difficult to gather all the developers at the same time (Hossain & Babar, 2009; Hobbs & Petit, 2017; Paasivaara, 2008; Butt, 2016; Butt & Jamal, 2017).

Figure 3. Agile large scale organizational

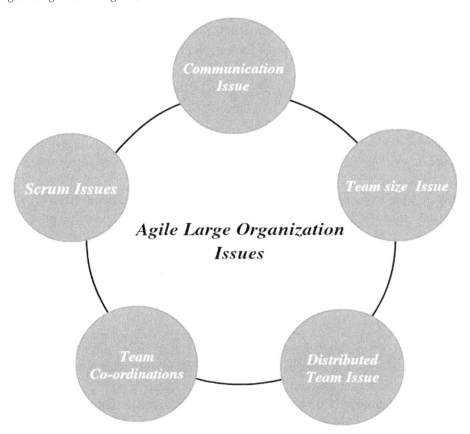

3.2. Team Co-ordinations

Team coordination explains the dependencies of teams on other teams of the project. Due to the distributed nature of development in large-scale organizations, there is a possibility that many teamwork on the same project. Large-scale software development projects are often associated with the inability for everybody to know everything. Due to distance teams face issues to coordinate with each other and share knowledge, project status and any other related information. Agile does not support the many teams to work on the same project due to its tight coordination and interconnection of team members for project success. This is a challenge in the large-scale organization (Dingsøyr & Moe, 2014; Doyle & Williams, 2014; Scheerer, 2014).

3.3. Team Size

The team size of agile for development is 3-9. When team size varies between these numbers then the agile team produces effective results. But when the team size becomes increase then it creates issues in the agile development. The agile model is designed only for the small team members and there is no mechanism in agile for an extension to support the large team size. Therefore, when the agile use in the large-scale organization where the team size and project size is greater than the small one then it creates challenges for project success and completion. As mentioned in the above scrum issues section that team members do not support and favor the daily scrum meeting session while the team size is small so when we use agile for the large team then ultimately it will create more obstacles for project completion and success. Therefore, the agile model is not suitable for the large-scale project with a large team size (Lalsing & Kishnah, 2012; Hobbs & Petit, 2017; Scheerer, 2014).

3.4. Team Communication

The project success velocity is also depending on team communication whereas in the large-scale organizations the project s developed distributed and geographically. The team size is greater than the normal team size. In a team, many persons are involved such as developers, designer, testers and leaders who have different thoughts and domain to think and do any task now these differences create many issues for successful project development. One big challenge is to combine these thoughts and domains for the single task project. These different thoughts and domain make the requirements impossible to accurately understand. It happens due to large team size and large project scale (Lalsing & Kishnah, 2012; Ktata & Lévesque, 2009; Hobbs & Petit, 2017). Due to the large team size communication between the team also becomes more complex as shown in Figure 3 below.

Figure 4. Overview of communication channel complexity (Lalsing & Kishnah, 2012)

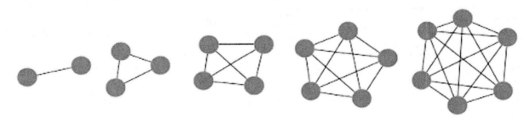

The team size in the figure 4 is explained by the grey circles. As in the figure at the start left there are only two circles that represent the two team members whereas at the last right the team size is huge and complicated. The communication between the team members is difficult. Therefore, when we use the small team as an agile model prefers and support then this issue can solve with the small team instead of the large team. But in the small agile team, there is also issues that are a daily meeting session that make the team agitate. Hence, when the agile model uses for large team size then it has no mechanism that can handle these challenges (Lalsing & Kishnah, 2012; Rolland, 2016).

3.5. Distributed Development

In the large organizations, the project size is large and team size is large, so the development mostly is done in a distributed manner. Different developers at different locations work on the same project and share their work with each other. Agile methodology for the use of distributed large-scale development is quite difficult because agile model supports the development at a single place and allow team members constantly communicate with each other so communication between the developers distributed geographically and globally is complex due to a different location, time zone, culture and way of development. The daily meeting session cannot arrange with the team. The meeting with the client becomes difficult due to distributed locations. Therefore, agile is not suitable for large-scale organizations (Rolland, 2016; Šmite, 2017; Lassenius, 2012; Razav, 2014).

Below in Table 1 lists the issues for each category, the recommendations of suggestions and an analysis of the suggestions.

Table 1. Issues and Suggestions

Contents	Issues	Recommendations	Analysis of Suggestions
Scrum	Daily meeting session	Split the meeting session into two or once on a week	• Remove issues from scrum, develop trust among team and scrum master, less pressurized developers, scrum adoption rate increase.
Team Co-ordination	Distribution development and teams	Make some mechanism for teams in ASD. Need to propose framework and processes.	• Define some project dependent parameters at the initial stage of project; assign those dependent parameters to one time. • Defined processes with new approach and concept to facilitate the team co-ordination.
Team Size	Large team challenge. Global software development.	Make Amendments in agile to support the large team size.	• Increase the team size and split them in two equal parts with their expertise.
Team Communication	Different thoughts and domain, large team complex communication	Define some standards for team communication	• Define standards for team/s communication e.g. CMMI standards for stakeholder to examine the industry.
Distributed Development	Different Locations, culture & way of development.	Make some standards to develop & elect one head as monitor/evaluator	• Implicitly/explicitly elect some one as monitor, evaluator and translator to support team/s and developer/s.

5. RESEARCH METHODOLOGY

For the research and support of our study, we find the paper in the domain related to our topic and after detailed analysis and data sets of papers and publishers explained in the below table 2. The author searched papers with keywords such as "agile methodology", "scrum large-scale organizations", "agile large-scale development", "scrum solutions for large-scale projects", "scrum global software development" and "scrum issues for large-scale projects".

Table 2. Total papers and references from publishers that contain above listed keywords

Contents	Papers	References
IEEE	6	13, 15,21,22,25, 32.
ACM	5	2, 11,18,19,33
Springer	10	3,4,5,6,10,20,28,29, 30,31
ELSEVIER	3	9,23,26, 34
Conference	4	12,16,17,27
ISI Inexed	5	1,7,8,14,24, 35,36,37

6. CONCLUSION

Agile Scrum software development done in sprints, every sprint has a specific effort and cost to complete. The Agile model now in use many software industries. It is because of its precise and distinctive features that complete with its components as scrum. But instead of these entire features agile scrum is only suitable for small-scale projects. When the agile model is used for small-scale development then it produces efficient results and complete project successfully but when used for large-scale organizations and for globally distributed software development then the project fails to complete and be successful. It is due to agile-scrum challenges in adoption of large-scale development. The agile scrum also did not make any amendments and introduced mechanism to overcome these issues from the agile large-scale development. All the other researchers just gave some suggestive models and frameworks, but these have no base point.

7. FUTURE DIRECTION

Make some amendments, new directions and introduce mechanism in agile-scrum software development to make it more suitable for the large-scale projects and globally distributed software projects. Currently it is a research domain for researchers and practitioners to introduce some new features in agile-scrum model and introduce some mechanism to overcome these challenges.

REFERENCES

Balaji, S., & Murugaiyan, M. S. (2012). Waterfall vs. V-Model vs. Agile: A comparative study on SDLC. *International Journal of Information Technology and Business Management, 2*(1), 26–30.

Ruparelia, N. B. (2010). Software development lifecycle models. *Software Engineering Notes, 35*(3), 8–13.

Plonka, L., Sharp, H., Gregory, P., & Taylor, K. (2014). UX Design in Agile: A DSDM Case Study. *Proceedings of the International Conference on Agile Software Development*. Springer. 10.1007/978-3-319-06862-6_1

Kaisti, M., Mujunen, T., Mäkilä, T., Rantala, V., & Lehtonen, T. (2014, May). Agile principles in the embedded system development. *Proceedings of the International Conference on Agile Software Development* (pp. 16-31). Springer.

Dingsøyr, T., & Moe, N. B. (2014, May). Towards principles of large-scale agile development. *Proceedings of the International Conference on Agile Software Development* (pp. 1-8). Springer.

Sekitoleko, N., Evbota, F., Knauss, E., Sandberg, A., Chaudron, M., & Olsson, H. H. (2014, May). Technical dependency challenges in large-scale agile software development. *Proceedings of the International Conference on Agile Software Development* (pp. 46-61). Springer.

Lalsing, V., & Kishnah, S. (2012). People factors in agile software development and project management. *International Journal of Software Engineering and Its Applications, 3*(1).

Vijayasarathy And Dan Turk, L. R. (2008). Agile software development: A survey of early adopters. *Journal of Information Technology Management, 19*(2).

Moe, N. B., Dingsøyr, T., & Dybå, T. (2010). A teamwork model for understanding an agile team: A case study of a Scrum project. *Information and Software Technology, 52*(5), 480–491.

Doyle, M., Williams, L., Cohn, M., & Rubin, K. S. (2014, May). Agile software development in practice. *Proceedings of the International Conference on Agile Software Development* (pp. 32-45). Springer.

Ktata, O., & Lévesque, G. (2009, May). Agile development: Issues and avenues requiring a substantial enhancement of the business perspective in large projects. Proceedings of the 2nd Canadian conference on computer science and software engineering (pp. 59-66). ACM. doi:10.1145/1557626.1557636

Rumpe, B., & Scholz, P. (2014). *Scaling The Management Of Extreme Programming Projects.*

Hossain, E., & Babar, M. A. (2009). Using Scrum in Global Software Development: A Systematic Literature Review. *Proceedings of the Fourth IEEE International Conference on Global Software Engineering*. IEEE Press. 10.1109/ICGSE.2009.25

Hobbs, B., & Petit, Y. (2017). Agile methods on large projects in large organizations. *Project Management Journal, 48*(3), 3–19.

Paasivaara, M., Durasiewicz, S., & Lassenius, C. (2008, August). Distributed agile development: Using Scrum in a large project. *Proceedings of the 2008 IEEE International Conference on Global Software Engineering* (pp. 87-95). IEEE. 10.1109/ICGSE.2008.38

Scheerer, A. (2014). Coordination in Large-Scale Agile Software Development: A Multiteam Systems Perspective. *Proceedings of the Hawaii International Conference on System Science*. Academic Press. 10.1109/HICSS.2014.587

Rolland, K. H. (2016). Problematizing Agile in the Large: Alternative Assumptions for Large-Scale Agile Development. *Proceedings of the Thirty Seventh International Conference on Information Systems*. Academic Press.

Moe, N. B., Šmite, D., Šāblis, A., Börjesson, A. L., & Andréasson, P. (2014, September). Networking in a large-scale distributed agile project. *Proceedings of the 8th ACM/IEEE International Symposium on Empirical Software Engineering and Measurement* (p. 12). ACM.

Paasivaara, M., Lassenius, C., & Heikkilä, V. T. (2012, September). Inter-team coordination in large-scale globally distributed scrum: Do scrum-of-scrums really work? *Proceedings of the ACM-IEEE international symposium on Empirical software engineering and measurement* (pp. 235-238). ACM.

Dingsøyr, T., Fægri, T. E., & Itkonen, J. (2014, December). What is large in large-scale? A taxonomy of scale for agile software development. *Proceedings of the International Conference on Product-Focused Software Process Improvement* (pp. 273-276). Springer.

Rising, L., & Janoff, N. S. (2000). The Scrum Software Development Process for Small Teams. *IEEE Software*, *17*(4), 26–32. doi:10.1109/52.854065

Razavi, A. M., & Ahmad, R. (2014, September). Agile development in large and distributed environments: A systematic literature review on organizational, managerial and cultural aspects. *Proceedings of the 2014 8th. Malaysian Software Engineering Conference (MySEC)* (pp. 216-221). IEEE.

Paasivaara, M., & Lassenius, C. (2014). Communities of practice in a large distributed agile software development organization–Case Ericsson. *Information and Software Technology*, *56*(12), 1556–1577.

Barlow, J. B., Giboney, J., Keith, M. J., Wilson, D., Schuetzler, R. M., Lowry, P. B., & Vance, A. (2011). Overview and guidance on agile development in large organizations. *Communications of the Association for Information Systems*, *29*(2), 25–44.

Lindvall, M., Muthig, D., Dagnino, A., Wallin, C., Stupperich, M., Kiefer, D., ... Kahkonen, T. (2004). Agile software development in large organizations. *Computer*, *37*(12), 26–34.

Chow, T., & Cao, D. B. (2008). A survey study of critical success factors in agile software projects. *Journal of Systems and Software*, *81*(6), 961–971.

Abdullah, E., & Abdelsatir, E. T. B. (2013, August). Extreme programming applied in a large-scale distributed system. *Proceedings of the 2013 International Conference On Computing, Electrical And Electronic Engineering (ICCEEE)* (pp. 442-446). IEEE.

Eklund, U., Olsson, H. H., & Strøm, N. J. (2014, May). Industrial challenges of scaling agile in mass-produced embedded systems. *Proceedings of the International Conference on Agile Software Development* (pp. 30-42). Springer. 10.1007/978-3-319-14358-3_4

Hossain, E., Babar, M. A., & Verner, J. (2009). How Can Agile Practices Minimize Global Software Development Co-ordination Risks? *Proceedings of the 16th European Conference EuroSPI*, Madrid, Spain, September 2-4. Springer.

Hossain, E., Bannerman, P. L., & Jeffery, D. R. (2011, June). Scrum practices in global software development: a research framework. *Proceedings of the International Conference on Product Focused Software Process Improvement* (pp. 88-102). Springer.

Trujillo, M. M., Oktaba, H., Pino, F. J., & Orozco, M. J. (2011, June). Applying agile and lean practices in a software development project into a CMMI organization. *Proceedings of the International Conference on Product Focused Software Process Improvement* (pp. 17-29). Springer.

Hayata, T., & Han, J. (2011, July). A hybrid model for IT project with Scrum. *Proceedings of 2011 IEEE International Conference on Service Operations, Logistics and Informatics* (pp. 285-290). IEEE.

Nerur, S., Mahapatra, R. K., & Mangalaraj, G. (2005, May). Challenges of Migrating to Agile Methodologies. *Communications of the ACM*, *48*(5), 72–78. doi:10.1145/1060710.1060712

Butt, S. A. (2016). Study of agile methodology with the cloud. *Pacific Science Review B Humanities and Social Sciences*, *2*(1), 22–28.

Butt, S. A., & Jamal, T. (2017). Frequent Change Request From User to Handle Cost on Project in Agile Model. *Asia Pacific Journal of Multidisciplinary Research*, *5*(2), 26–42.

Zykov, S.V., Gromoff, A., & Kazantsev, N.S. (Eds.). (2018). Software Engineering for Enterprise System Agility: Emerging Research and Opportunities: Emerging Research and Opportunities. Hershey, PA: IGI Global.

Tiako, P.F. (Ed.). (2009). Software Applications: Concepts, Methodologies, Tools, and Applications: Concepts, Methodologies, Tools, and Applications. Hershey, PA: IGI Global. doi:10.4018/978-1-60566-060-8

This research was previously published in the International Journal of Software Innovation (IJSI), 8(2); pages 85-94, copyright year 2020 by IGI Publishing (an imprint of IGI Global).

Chapter 20
Use of Software Metrics to Improve the Quality of Software Projects Using Regression Testing

Arshpreet Kaur Sidhu
Chandigarh University, India

Sumeet Kaur Sehra
GNDEC, India

ABSTRACT

Testing of software is broadly divided into three types i.e., code based, model based and specification based. To find faults at early stage, model based testing can be used in which testing can be started from design phase. Furthermore, in this chapter, to generate new test cases and to ensure the quality of changed software, regression testing is used. Early detection of faults will not only reduce the cost, time and effort of developers but also will help finding risks. We are using structural metrics to check the effect of changes made to software. Finally, the authors suggest identifying metrics and analyze the results using NDepend simulator. If results show deviation from standards then again perform regression testing to improve the quality of software.

INTRODUCTION

Testing of software is fundamental and central part of software development process. UML is the most prevailing standard language used in modeling test cases (A. K. Jena et al, 2014). Therefore, if it is pleasingly exploited it will reduce the cost and effort of testing as well as modification in code. Activity diagrams can improve the quality of the generated test cases as well as use these test cases for regression testing because it shows the overall flow of control between activities and object using activity-based relationships (Ye et al., 2011).

DOI: 10.4018/978-1-6684-3702-5.ch020

Testing of Software

Before moving to the details of work done in this chapter, we are focusing on testing first. Testing of software in a simple language is a method to find out errors and missed requirements as specified by the user. Testing can be performed by developers as unit testing and can be performed by software testing professionals to get good quality product.

Testing can be started from the early phase of software i.e. requirement phase and can be done up till deployment. Early start of testing will help in reducing the cost and time of developers because the errors and gaps can be removed as earliest possible. Testing is one process which is not confined at testing phase only. At requirement phase testing is performed in the form of analyzing and verifying the requirements. At design phase reviewing the design documents with gathered requirements is also a part of testing. At coding phase, the part of unit testing performed by developer at completion of code is also a part of testing.

Testing and Quality Assurance

Testing and Quality Assurance are interrelated terms. Testing insures the identification of errors and bugs in software whereas quality assurance focuses on accomplishment of processes and standards in the direction of verification of software. Testing is error and bug identifying technique and do not fixes bugs. To fix bugs at coding level developers can use debugging which is a part of white box and black box testing.

Types of Testing

Testing is categorized as manual and automated. In manual testing software is tested manually and end users take the role of testers to test software for bugs and unforeseen behavior. Stages at which manual testing is done are unit, integration, system and user acceptance testing. In automated testing also known as test automation the tester writes script and uses different software to test the functionality of given software. In this testing test scenarios are re-run repeatedly which were performed manually for time saving. It is assumed that automated testing improves test coverage and accuracy. GUI items, connections can be effectively tested with the help of test automation (Rathi et al., 2015; Bhullar et al., 2017).

Methods of Testing

Black Box Testing

It is a technique of testing software without knowing the internal details and working of software. Generally, in black box testing testers interact with the user interface of system by giving inputs to the system and analyzing the outputs. They hardly have details about where the inputs are working in code. This method is preferred for large segment of code but has limited coverage of test cases.

White Box Testing

In this method of testing, code and logic is tested in detailed. Also known as Open box or Glass testing. To perform this type of testing, tester must have all the knowledge of code and internal working of software. For this type of testing skilled tester is required to look into each nook and corner of code.

Grey Box Testing

In this method of testing, tester has limited knowledge of code but unlike black box testing where only user interface is tested; grey box testing has access to design documents and database. This knowledge helps tester to plan better test cases.

Levels of Testing

Different methodologies can be used for defining levels of testing. Mainly it is categorized as

Functional Testing

It is a type of black box testing in which tester tests the specifications of software. The obtained results are compared with actual functionality of software which is expected as per requirements of user.

Steps to test the functionality of software

- Find the functionality of software which is expected.
- Generation of test data according to the specification of software.
- Output based on test data and specifications.
- Execution of test cases obtained from test data.
- Comparison of expected and actual results.

These steps help in maintaining software quality and ensures that standards are been followed. Some common functional testing is unit testing, integration testing, system testing, regression testing, acceptance testing, alpha testing and beta testing (M.A. Jamil et al, 2016).

Unit Testing

This testing is performed by developers on each unit of code before handing over to professional testers. The purpose of unit testing is to check that each individual part is working correct in terms of functionality and requirements.

Integration Testing

This testing is performed when two individual parts are combined to check they are working functionally correct or not. It is carried out by two methods bottom up approach and top down approach.

System Testing

System testing is used to test the complete system as a whole after integration, to see that system is meeting the requirements and quality standards.

Regression Testing

Regression testing is the most widespread method for ensuring the quality of altered software. It examines whether altered parts of software behave as expected. The unaffected parts remain in their original behaviors. It mitigates risks and suggests selecting and executing only a set of test cases that are altered.

Acceptance Testing

Acceptance testing is most important testing to be carried out by quality assurance team to check whether software is meeting the user requirement and satisfying expected conditions. It is performed at two stages Alpha Testing and Beta Testing.

Alpha Testing

It is a first stage of testing and is performed by the team of developers and quality assurance. All the functional testing except regression testing when combined together is called as alpha testing. Latency problem, load time, spelling mistakes, broken lines, etc., are checked at low specifications in alpha testing.

Beta Testing

It is a second stage of acceptance testing after alpha testing is performed successfully. A sample group of audience tests the application at real time.

Nonfunctional Testing

Nonfunctional testing is performed on nonfunctional attributes of software which are important from the quality perspective of software. Commonly used nonfunctional testing are performance testing, load testing, stress testing, security testing.

Performance Testing

It is a method of testing which mainly focuses on performance of software such as response time, network delay. It is further classified into two types stress testing and load testing.

Load Testing

Load testing tests the behavior of software at maximum load in terms of input and at peak conditions.

Stress Testing

Stress testing tests the behavior of software in abnormal conditions like shutting down of system, network failure.

Security Testing

Security testing is used test the check points where security of software can be breached. It mainly focuses on authentication, authorization and confidentiality of software.

Probability Testing

Probability testing focuses on reusability of software and its code. The software is able to build on different platforms.

In this chapter, we are using regression testing to test the changes in behavior of software. Again to apply regression testing, identification of altered parts and to generate test cases for those altered parts of the software is difficult task. So, we can use model based generation of test cases to recount changes in test cases.

Model based approach which is used to identify the changes in the software. We generated Activity Flow graph from activity diagram. Depth first search algorithm is used traverse the graph and to generate test cases.

Metric is a quantitative gauge of degree to which a system, component or process possesses a given attribute. Using Ndepend, we can evaluate 12 metrics on application, 18 metrics on assemblies, 13 metrics on namespaces, 22 metrics on types, 19 metrics on methods, 2 metrics on fields.

Broadly we took following metrics to analyze the results using metric values.

Application Metrics

- **Number of Lines of Code (NbLOC):** This metric will compute the quantity of lines of code.
- **Number of Methods (NbMethods):** It will compute the number of methods in a class. A method can be an intangible, virtual or non-virtual method. Method can be declared in an interface, a constructor, a class constructor, a property/indexer getter or setter, an event adder or remover.
- **Number of Intermediate Language Instructions (NbILInstructions):** Computes the number of instructions inside the intermediate file which is created after compiling the source code.
- **Number of Types (NbTypes):** Computes number of types used which are defined for application, assemblies and namespaces. A type can be conceptual or an actual class, a structure, or an interface.

Dependency Metrics

- **Afferent Coupling (Ca):** The number of types outside this assembly that depend on types within this assembly. High afferent coupling indicates that the concerned assemblies have many responsibilities.

- **Efferent Coupling (Ce):** The number of types outside this assembly used by child types of this assembly. High efferent coupling indicates that the concerned assembly is dependent.

Inheritance Based Metrics

- **Depth of Inheritance (DIT):** The Depth of Inheritance Tree for a class or a structure is its number of base classes.
- **Number of Children (NOC):** The number of children for a class is the number of sub-classes. The number of children for an interface is the number of types that implement it.

Metric Showing Project Readability

- **Percentage Comment:** The amount of comments available for the code explanation.

If the percentage of comment in code is lower than 20% then it should be more commented. However, if code is commented more than 40%, is not considered a blessing as it is an insult to the intelligence of the reader.

Percentage Comment= 100*NbLinesofComment / (NbLinesofComment + NbLinesofCode)

- **Lack of Cohesion of Methods (LCOM):** The single responsibility principle states that a class should have only a single objective. Different classes should be created for implementing different scenarios and objectives. Such a class is said to be cohesive. A high LCOM value generally points to a poorly cohesive class.

LCOM= 1-(sum(MF)/M*F)

Where:
  M is the number of methods in class.
  F is the number of instance fields in the class.
  MF is the number of methods of the class accessing a particular instance field.

Further the objective to write this chapter is to select and use software metrics for improving the quality of software projects based on results of calculated metrics with the help of Ndepend simulator and regression testing.

BACKGROUND

According to American Programmer, 31.1% of computer software projects get canceled before they are completed. In other words we can say that defects in projects leads to failures. When we try to perform changes on software projects (regression testing), quality of project decreases in most of the cases due to changes in dependency metrics, inheritance based metrics, metrics stating project objectivity. Figure 1 shows the reasons due to which a project leads to failure or defects occur while testing of software.

Figure 1. Causes and Origin of Defects
Source: slideshare.net/Softwarecentral/software-metrics

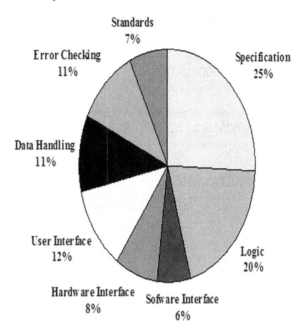

Metrics help in determining, predicting and improving the quality of software process. Few are the factors listed which motivated us to use metrics for software projects at early stages.

- It helps to estimate the cost & schedule of future projects
- It improves software quality
- It forecast future staffing needs
- It reduces future maintenance needs

PROPOSED WORK

In this section the chapter is categorized into the following steps to analyze the effect of alterations made in the project at design phase or by applying regression testing. Steps are shown in figure 2.

1. Categorization of metrics based on software into Size Based Metrics, Dependency Metrics, Inheritance Based Metrics, Project Readability Metrics.
2. Selected metrics are calculated with the help of Ndepend Simulator.
3. Assessment of calculated metrics with the Threshold values of Metrics.
4. Improve the quality of software projects based on results of computed Metrics with the help of Ndepend Simulator and by performing regression testing.

Figure 2. The proposed workflow diagram

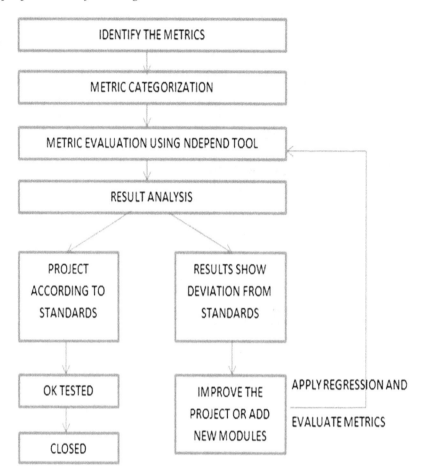

Activity Diagram

We considered a simple website of student management system in our approach. Activity diagrams are considered due to their dynamic behavior. It can construct, visualize and specify dynamic aspects of objects. Figure 3 shows the activity diagram of Student management system.

Description of Activity Diagram

1. User Login Section
    a.   User visits website by entering valid domain name.
    b.   If user is already registered, then will proceed to login section.
    c.   If user is a new user, then will go for registration section before login.
2. Registration Section
    a.   User enters his/her credentials like user ID, Name, Password, Gender, Address, etc., for registration.
    b.   All the data is send to server by clicking submit button.

c. If it is already registered with some-one else, then server generates error message.

d. Else server will proceed with the registration process by inserting user's data in the database.

e. On successful registration, server will display success message and will proceed for login section.

3. Login Section

a. User enters the ID and password for login.

b. On pressing Login button, the request is sent to the server along with user data.

c. The server retrieves user data and validate with database.

d. If the authentication is successful then server will take to the home page of website.

Figure 3. Activity diagram of online student management system

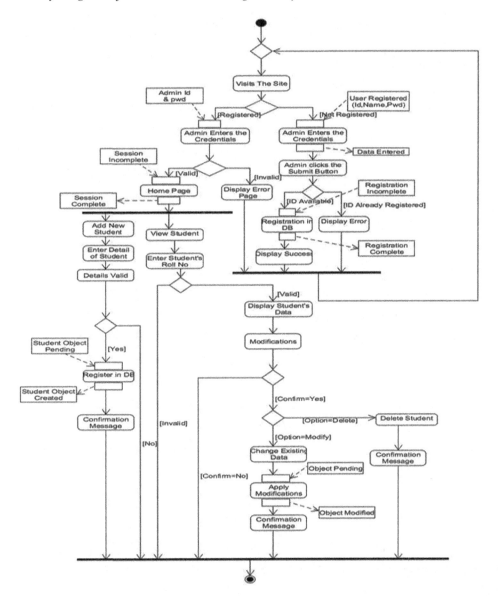

4.   **Home Page Section:** After successful login, the administrator can manage the information of students of an organization online. User is authorized to perform following tasks:
   a.   Add new student in the database.
   b.   View student of available students.
   c.   Search the data of a particular student.
   d.   Modify the details of existing students.
   e.   Delete the details of existing student

Activity Graph

Here, in this section, we construct the activity graph shown in figure 4 from activity diagram.

Figure 4. Activity Graph of online student management system

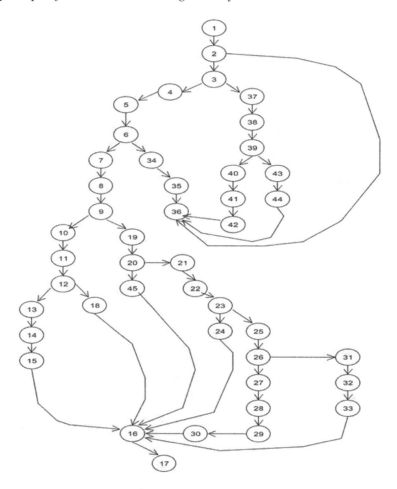

We have divided the work into three projects and evaluating metrics at each project level. At each level we are performing regression testing to check effect on metric values when we make changes to the software.

- **Project 1:** Only modules are being added without testing and validation of paths.
- **Project 2:** At Login Session validate inputs for emptiness (username and password), valid email, and length. At Regression Session validate contact number length and data type, email, emptiness. Two new modules are added.
- **Project 3:** Changes in modify and delete module. It includes the code of project 2 along with all the test sequences from regression testing and functional testing.

Test Cases (Suit1)

In our approach graph is traversed through depth first search algorithm (DFS) which visits all the nodes of graph. After traversing the graph, we will generate the possible test cases using path coverage criteria.

Possible test paths are generated after traversing graph are as follows:

- **TC1:** 1→2→3→4→5→6→7→8→9
- **TC2:** 1→2→3→4→5→6→34→35→36
- **TC3:** 1→2→3→37→38→39→40→41→42
- **TC4:** 1→2→3→37→38→39→43→44

Results

Metric values on Test Suit

Table 1. Dependency metric values on three projects

METRIC	PROJECT 1	PROJECT 2	PROJECT 3
Afferent Coupling	0	0	0
Efferent Coupling	21	23	26

Table 2. Inheritance based metric values on three projects

METRIC	PROJECT 1	PROJECT 2	PROJECT 3
Depth of Inheritance	8	28	22
Number of Children	2	7	7

Table 3. Project readability based metric values on three projects

METRIC	PROJECT 1	PROJECT 2	PROJECT 3
Comment %	24	7	7

Table 4. Project objectivity based metric values on three projects

METRIC	PROJECT 1	PROJECT 2	PROJECT 3
Lack of Cohesion Over Methods	.87	.87	.87

It can be clearly observed from metric result values from table 1 to table 4 that Ce values are increasing with changes made in projects which mean dependency is increasing. Also values of DOI (Depth of Inheritance) and NOC (Number of Children) are increasing which clearly shows that software might be hard to maintain. The values of LCOM (Lack of Cohesion over Methods) are constant that shows there is no effect of changes on cohesiveness of methods of the class.

From the results above we can improve the software quality at earliest phase with the help of metric values. With every change we can check the effect on stability and quality of software before performing those changes.

FUTURE WORK

This chapter purposes a metric based evaluation of web applications to improve the quality. By comparing metric values of different projects, with changes we found that application has become difficult to maintain. The values of coupling and inheritance become high due to regression. This gives developers a clear idea about direction of changes to be made at earliest stage. Future work involves developing a tool or mechanism to provide optional paths for changes and comparison in terms of metric values so that developers can boost the quality of software.

CONCLUSION

In this chapter we tried to calculate the effects on quality of software or web application when changes are made in accordance to the user. With the case study of simple web application of student management system, by applying regression at early stage of project results showed deviation in metrics. So, in future we can suggest use of such methods for ensuring and improving the quality of software projects. Also, this will reduce the efforts of developers in testing phase and maintenance phase.

REFERENCES

Ajay Kumar Jena., Santosh Kumar Swain, & Durga Prasad Mohapatra, A. (2014). A novel approach for test case generation from UML activity diagrams. In *Proceedings of the International Conference on Issues and Challenges in Intelligent Computing Techniques*. IEEE.

Bhullar, R. K., Pawar, L., Bajaj, R., & Manocha, A. K. (2017). Intelligent stress calculation and scheduling in segmented processor systems using buddy approach. *Journal of Intelligent & Fuzzy Systems, 32*(4), 3129–3142. doi:10.3233/JIFS-169256

Frederiksen, H. D., & Iversen, J. H. A. (2003). Implementing Software Metric Programs: A Survey of Lessons and Approaches. Hershey, PA: IGI Global.

Jamil, M. A., Arif, M., Normi, S. A. A., & Ahmad, A. A. (2016). Software Testing Techniques: A Literature Review. In *Proceedings of the 2016 6th International Conference on Information and Communication Technology for The Muslim World (ICT4M)*. IEEE.

Rathi, P., & Mehra, V. (2015). Analysis of Automation and Manual Testing Using Software Testing Tool. *International Journal of Innovations & Advancement in Computer Science, 4*.

Sapna PG, & Arunkumar, A. (2015). An approach for generating minimal test cases for regression testing. *Procedia computer science, 47*, 188-196.

Rawat, M. S., Mittal, A., & Dubey, S. K. (2012). Survey on Impact of Software Metrics on Software Quality. *International Journal of Advanced Computer Science and Applications, 3*(1).

Verma, V. & Sona Malhotra, A. (2011). Applications of Software Testing Metrics in Constructing Models of the Software Development Process. *Journal of Global Research in Computer Science, 2*(5).

Ye, N., Chen, X., Jiang, P., Ding, W., & Li, X., A. (2011). Automatic Regression Test selection based on activity diagrams. In *Proceedings of the Fifth International Conference on Secure Software Integration And Reliability Improvement.* IEEE. 10.1109/SSIRI-C.2011.31

This research was previously published in Analyzing the Role of Risk Mitigation and Monitoring in Software Development; pages 204-218, copyright year 2018 by Engineering Science Reference (an imprint of IGI Global).

Chapter 21
Trust in Open Source Software Development Communities:
A Comprehensive Analysis

Amitpal Singh Sohal

Research Scholar, IKG Punjab Technical University, Kapurthala, Punjab, India

Sunil Kumar Gupta

Department of Computer Science and Engineering, Beant College of Engineering and Technology, Gurdaspur, Punjab, India

Hardeep Singh

Department of Computer Science, Guru Nanak Dev University, Amritsar, Punjab, India

ABSTRACT

This study presents the significance of trust for the formation of an Open Source Software Development (OSSD) community. OSSD has various challenges that must be overcome for its successful operation. First is the development of a community, which requires a healthy community formation environment. Taking into consideration various factors for community formation, a strong sense of TRUST among its members has been felt. Trust development is a slow process with various methods for building and maintaining it. OSSD is teamwork but the team is of unknowns and volunteers. Trust forms a pillar for effective cooperation, which leads to a reduction in conflicts and risks, associated with quality software development. This study offers an overview of various existing trust models, which aids in the development of a trust evaluation framework for OSSD communities. Towards the end of the study, various components of the trust evaluation along with an empirical framework for the same have been proposed.

DOI: 10.4018/978-1-6684-3702-5.ch021

1. INTRODUCTION

Open source software development (OSSD) is an ideology, which has paved the way for which dedicated teams of volunteer software developers participate and contribute in various areas of software engineering. The aim of OSSD communities is to make a high quality and reliable software, no matter how complex an application may be (Asundi, 2001). The project is initiated by the core team and is made open for developers across the globe to contributing code and feature enhancements. The core team of the project analyzes the contributions from various contributors. The core team may have single or number of coordinators. Coordinators are project creators and are responsible for the evolution and growth of the community. They would take the final decision to incorporate the received code into the final build and release the next test version of the software. After rigorous testing and debugging when the required quality of software is achieved, test versions of software are promoted to be the next stable release. Further, with the passage of time new contributions in form of bug fixes and feature enhancements for the software are received. The same cycle of thorough testing and integration of code into existing software is followed. Every effort is done to attract more and more people towards the project and with the passage of time the community grows. The team members of the OSSD community provide feedback, which acts as a base for the planning of future project managing strategies. With constant efforts, gradually, the project attains high quality and upcoming issues are dealt with even better ways. The ways in which development work is coordinated and communicated amongst the developers makes it different from existing software development strategies and this is what is unique. It is intended to perform a study for improvement of the relationship among the virtual team members of an OSSD community, which in turn enhances the quality of the developed open source software. We move ahead with this work, keeping in mind the following research objectives.

1.1. Research Objectives

This study is performed to accomplish the following research objectives:

- To formulate various challenges associated with OSSD;
- To study the relevance of trust for open source systems;
- To study various methods for building and sustaining trust;
- To propose a trust evaluation framework for OSSD communities.

To achieve the aforementioned objectives of our research, a comprehensive literature analysis has been conducted. Various papers covering the nature of OSSD, existing models of software production, challenges associated with OSSD have been analyzed. Trust related aspects like trust characteristics, importance to OSSD communities, methods for building and sustaining trust in OSSD communities, existing OSSD trust models, contributions and suggestions of various researchers for trust building in virtual teams have been also analyzed.

To collect the relevant literature for this study, following search terms or keywords were used:

- Trust;
- Trust framework for open source software development communities;
- Trust in virtual teams;

- Trust in social networks;
- Trust evaluation frameworks;
- Trust enhancement mechanism.

About one hundred research papers, articles, primary studies, and few HTML pages had been downloaded. Those research papers and articles (about 60) were selected and reviewed which covered various aspects of trust, its need, importance, trust building methods, and various existing trust models. The special consideration was given to the literature related to trust building in virtual teams. It has been felt that in order to bind the virtual teams involved in OSSD, a strong need for trust amongst the team members is essential.

This research paper has been organized into eight sections each covering different aspects of OSSD movement. Section 1 provides a brief introduction to the process of OSSD including various research objectives of this study. The keywords used for searching the relevant literature are presented in the same section. Section 2 presents various challenges associated with OSSD. These challenges must be subjugated for the success of OSSD. This section ends with consequences of lack of trust amongst OSSD community members. Section 3 presents relevance of trust in OSSD including trust definitions given by various authors and methods for building and maintaining trust. Trust characteristics and contributions of various authors in this field are then analyzed along with studying of various trust models. Section 4 presents the review of various existing trust evaluation models, their evolution and feature addition with time. Section 5 presents commentary on trust after literature review. Then a set of research questions for future study has been formulated. Section 6 illustrates various components of the proposed trust evaluation along with the empirical model for the same. Section 7 presents future work directions followed by conclusions in section 8.

2. CHALLENGES OF OPEN SOURCE SOFTWARE DEVELOPMENT

Open Source Software Development is altogether a different approach of software development and hence is associated with number of challenges which must be overcome for its success. Some of the challenges of OSSD are as listed below.

1. The development team is globally distributed and may not have face to face interactions ever;
2. Team members are volunteers so cannot be forced to work and are free to quit anytime;
3. Software development is governed by formation of a community, therefore, healthy environment for community formation is required (Lewicki & Bunker, 1996);
4. Mechanism must be in place for effective communication, coordination and feedback among community members (Kasper-Fuehrer & Ashkanasy, 2001; McAllister, 1995);
5. Participant's enthusiasm (Kogut & Metiu, 2001) and positive leadership (Pavlidis, 2011) has to be maintained;
6. Trust among members in open source teams will take more time to develop due to frequent change in team composition;
7. Mechanism to overcome trust betrayal due to someone else's provocation or communication gap. System for detection of lying and ditching by the members have to developed;
8. Mechanism for conflict avoidance, handling and regaining the lost trust should be in place;

9. Mechanism for mutual support, response in newsgroup, FAQs, time needed for response, etc.;
10. Every effort must be done to increase team commitment and to reduce conflicts and associated risks;
11. Another factor to be taken into consideration is that members of community belong to different part of the world, understand different languages and belong to various cultures. Members have to understand other languages and familiarize them with each other in order to work together;
12. Third party betrayal have to be detected and handled;
13. Preserve the interaction history, dynamic trust ratings and graphical representation of trust over time.

Keeping above factors into consideration and for effective working and governance of OSSD communities, a strong bond of TRUST among community members is essential. The intend of this work is to propose a framework for development and enhancement of trust among the community members. The lack of trust among team members may cause the following effects:

1. Reduce the effectiveness of individual contribution to team (Dasgupta & Partha, 2000);
2. Concentrating on individual goals rather than team goals (Bulman, 1992);
3. Reduces trust on other team member contributions and make them feel recheck the work performed by others (Lee, 2009);
4. Insecurity (Dasgupta & Partha, 2000) and ultimately productivity and quality go to lower level (Jarvenpaa et al., 2004);
5. There is absence of any central rule enforcement authority;
6. Rule enforcement is made possible by the presence of large number of motivated people who may punish rule-breakers by 'flaming', 'kill-filing' or 'shunning'.

3. RELEVANCE OF TRUST IN OPEN SOURCE SOFTWARE DEVELOPMENT

3.1. Definitions of Trust

Trust is taken from a German word, "TROST", meaning comfort. Trust is a relationship among individuals in which one person takes risk to communicate and cooperate with the other to create a collaborative development environment (Asundi, 2001; Lane et al., 2004; Stewart & Gosain, 2006). Trust is abstract and operates at various levels. Trust among two or mode individuals can be interpersonal. Trust among groups is termed as intergroup. Organization have organizational trust whereas societal trust exists in societies. Trust is applicable in all areas and people belonging to economics, sociology, psychology, management, marketing and personality developers have explored it.

According to Mui et al. (Mui et al., 2002) trust develops with time and is based on past encounters. Such trust is also termed as "reputation-based": "Trust is a subjective expectation an agent has about another's future behavior based on the history of their encounters."

Grandison and Sloman (Grandison & Sloman, 2000) added the concept of context to trust as one cannot trust other without it. According to them "Trust is the firm belief in competence of an entity to act dependably, securely, and reliably within a specified context." It is competence to act instead of actions.

Olmedilla et al. (Olmedilla et al., 2005) defined trust in terms of actions. According to them "Trust of a party A to a party B for a service X is the measurable belief of A in that B behaves dependably for a specified period within a specified context (in relation to service X)."

3.2. Methods for Building and Maintaining Trust

Zucker (Zucker, 1986) proposed three methods in which trust can be developed in a relationship. According to the author trust can be characteristics based trust which aims for development of social culture and norms for welfare of people. It is just like member-ship of any professional organization. Second form of trust is institutions based, just like technical or professional standards which one is bound to adhere. Third type of trust is process based, in which trust is developed slowly with time. Trust develops after experience gained from social interactions, mutual adaptation and learning by doing. Virtual teams cooperate over the web and usually do not know each other. They can interact and work together effectively only if they have trust among themselves. Trust is a combination of four components (Bergquist & Ljungberg, 2001). One who trusts another is termed as Trustor. Trustor creates trust by providing some benefits to the beneficiary. Second component is, trustee, one who is trusted. Trustee holds some authority, responsibility or position due to which it is trusted and is for public benefit. Third is reason for trust and the fourth is conditions based on which one is trusted.

Trust acts as pillars for team work as it increase the extent of co-operation among members of community. Trust enhancement would help in reduction of conflicts among members, thereby, improving the software development pace and processes. Communication and cooperation help in improving the quality of software. But trust alone may not be able to improve and sustain team performance, every team member has an allocated job which it must perform. Role allocation is based on capabilities, but work done is based on intentions of the member. Trust is the measure of interdependence but has associated risks. Higher trust values existing among community members encourages new members to join the community. As membership of community increases, team performance will improve. The communities are large and open, any team member can join or quit without any obligation. This leads to a problem that long-time interactions among same members may not be there. Members may not get long time to know others and develop trust over considerable period of time (Piccoli & Ives, 2003).

Keeping in mind the changing nature of membership of open source community a quick form of trust called *Swift Trust* (Michlmayr et al., 2005) was introduced. Swift trust binds together teams that work for short interval of time, they do not meet each other and do not have any personal relationship among themselves (Kasper-Fuehrer & Ashkanasy, 2001). First type of swift trust exists in situations where the second person need first more than the first needs second. It is in interest of second person not to deceive the first one. Such type of trust is based on the self-interest of first party (Hardin, 2002). Second person must get enough incentives and should not think of deceiving the other. Such type of trust would ensure that it is in personal interest of community members to participate and contribute to the project. Second is cognitive swift trust in which the second party do not let the first party down. First party trusts the second based upon some already known characteristics. Such type of trust ensures that there are internally motivated contributors attracted towards a project (Piccoli & Ives, 2003). Both types of trust ensure a strong bond among the contributors and corresponding project.

Osterloh and Rota (Osterloh & Rota, 2004) proposed setting up of institutions or some central mechanism to ensure trust is not hampered in relationship and to keep the contributors motivated. In order for contributors to contribute to any public repository, cost of contributions must be kept low.

Costa (Costa, 2003) classified trust factors into three categories. First is team composition consisting of factors like team cohesion, technical skills of members, type of job allocated and willingness to work together in the team etc. Second is characteristics of work which covers aspects like task ambiguity, communication mechanism to work together, information requirements and dependency on others etc. Third is nature of the organization, its reputation, management principles and powers allocated to team members.

Various types of trust proposed by authors in different articles are - calculus based trust. knowledge based trust, identification (Lewicki & Bunker, 1996) based trust, cognition based and affect based trust (McAllister, 1995).

The nature of OSSD suggests that success of open source projects depend upon information exchanged among core members and other contributors of the community. The sustainability of open source software projects greatly depends upon the level of trust among its members (Sirkkala et al., 2010). Trust plays an important role in this process therefore required trust information must be renewed and updated regularly (Howison & Crowston, 2004). Non-availability of dedicated tools for communication and information exchange among members of open source communities account for decrease in trust among members of the community (Dasgupta & Partha, 2000). The success of any open source software depends upon cooperation among its community members which in trun depends upon trust among members.

Therefore, trust enhancement should start as soon as contributions from various developers are received and proper trust management system should be in place (Michlmayr et al., 2005; Bulman, 1992). Feedbacks help in trust enhancement and makes the communication more effective (Lee, 2009; Jarvenpaa et al., 2004). Every relationship has associated expectations with it which must be communicated as soon as a team is formed (Bandow, 2004). Every team member may not be quick, some may take more time to communicate. Delays and long communication times should be minimized for success of the community (Pinyol et al., 2012). Increasing trust takes long time but decrease can be sudden. Gaining lost trust may take considerable amount of time. Context of trust is very important, therefore, trust and distrust can exist together in a relationship. Certain changes are expected during the life time of a project and are usually covered by formal contracts which incorporate those changes into the project. But large number of unexpected changes also occur and are covered by trust among members which is psychological contract based on goodwill (Lewicki & Bunker, 1996; Samoladas & Stamelos, 2003). Therefore, both trust and distrust in a balanced form are required to make a healthy relationship.

Open source software development is not entirely planned but involves mutual understanding and adjustments for success of the project. When hundreds of developers coordinate then conflicts are bound to happen so a proper conflict avoidance, handling and resolution mechanism is required. Rocco (Rocco, 1998) proposed that trust would play a vital role and hence must be strengthened through meetings, social and other team formation activities. Trust develops with time and interactions but in open source environment people across the globe are part of development team. Open platforms must have mechanism to handle diverse cultures, languages and writing skills (Barbar et al., 2006). Trust cannot be built free of cost but considerable amount of effort, time and money are to be involved (Cubranic, 2001). Trust of a developer depends upon the nature and amount of contributions made to the community (de Laat, 2010).

4. EXISTING TRUST EVALUATION MODELS

In the model proposed by Yu and Liu (Yu & Liu, 2001) trust is deemed to be a non-functional requirement and should be considered at requirement gathering level phase of software development. Trust is some combination of attributes based upon which quality of the system under development could be ascertained. Approach followed was demonstrated by studying the behaviour of a Multi-Agent system under attack and examine defense mechanism needed for maintenance of trust.

According to Yan and Cofta (Yan & Cofta, 2003) trust can be described as a set of goals and statements. All the entities in a system have well defined domains. Entities are represented in form of a graph to get clear understanding of interconnections among them in the system. Representation of trust is subjective in nature and some new elements are required to bridge gaps existing in trust domains. This study was performed for Mobile Communication System. Giorgini (Giorgini et al., 2004) explained a model termed as Tropos in which a framework to evaluate trust in information systems was developed. The work aimed at securing such systems. Trust in relationships was captured at individual and social levels. Concept of trust provisioning and delegation was added. Trust owership was also proposed by the author.

Other authors like Bimrah (Bimrah, 2009) also developed trust model for information systems and included number of other relevant factors for enhancing trust computation. Concept of action based on request is proposed. Requesting others depends upon already existing trust in the relationship and knowledge about previous actions based on request acts as a guiding factor for communication. Concept of recommendation by someone known is added and it helps to locate trustworthy agent with ease. Another concept proposed by the author is trusting intention as one may trust others in specific situations only. Consequence of trust may not always be positive, and one must be prepared to deal with it. Uddin and Zulekerninr (Uddin & Zulekernine, 2008) developed a UML based trust model which takes into consideration the concept of trust from initial phases of software development and advocates trust based upon various scenarios evolving out of interactions among various agents.

The work of Avizienis et al. (Avizienis et al., 2004) proposed that systems developed have to be trustworthy and it should be assured that the system have to fulfill the expectations of its users. Research work performed was related to construction of dependable software systems. Pavlidis (Pavlidis, 2011) illustrated that most of the above said approaches are based upon some subset of trust parameters. One parameter that can further improve the trust mechanism is context dependency of trust. Another aspect stated is that the aim of developing and following software engineering principles is to design trustworthy information systems with capability of addressing stated, unstated and even unanticipated needs of customers.

Hoffman et al. (Hoffman et al., 2006) developed a trust framework and added the concept of privacy (with sub-components as anonymity, un-observability, pseudonmity and unlink-ability), security (with sub-components as integrity, confidentiality, availability, authentication and authorization), safety, availability, reliability, user expectations and usability as its components. Rohm and Milne (Rohm & Milne, 2004) presented that information systems like e-commerce, e-banking etc. collect, store and manipulate personal information like credit card numbers very easily and provide a very wider access to it. There is increase in risk that such vital data may fall into the hands of unauthorised or malicious users. This will result into decrease in trust of the information system.

Bhattacharya et al. (Bhattacharya et al., 1998) proposed another trust building model. According to this model, factors affecting trust must have some logical values and trust should be calculated based upon it. Proposed model is based upon world of two individuals that can engage in actions, which jointly determine outcomes. The actions randomly determine outcomes according to random translation functions. There is a finite set of all the possible actions and respective outcomes of persons. The outcomes have consequences on two parties. Two types of interactions are allowed in the model. Individuals interact and can either follow certain sequence of actions or simultaneous actions. Two types of situations are taken care off. First in which two parties do not know which action the other would take based upon its actions. But in second situation each party know how the other would react based upon its action. Throughout the interactions of teams involved in open source software development confusions and conflicts emerge and efforts are made to resolve them during this creative software development process.

Zacharia (Zacharia, 1999) explained SPORAS model that had proposed an open multi-agent system which takes into consideration the rating aggregation based upon regular updating of reputation after obtaining feedback from the involved parties. New user entering the system have lowest reputation. Feedback is provided by interacting parties. Reputation of new users is updated in accordance with the obtained feedback. It takes time to build reputation. Bad reputation users may leave the system and join as fresh users but would be discouraged as they have to start with lowest reputation value again. However, this may discourage new agents from entering the system even though they were most trusted in their previous societies. Most recent ratings are given higher priority while evaluating the trustworthiness.

Pinyol et al. (Pinyol et al., 2012) discussed model proposed by Jurca and Faltings with the concept of providing incentives, using a payment scheme, to agents who truthfully report about other agents when asked upon. Dishonest agents will continue to lose money whereas honest agents would gain. It introduced broker agent called as R-agents which are responsible for buying and aggregation of reputation reports from other agents in a centralised manner. They sell the reputation information to other agents whenever it is asked to do so. The main contribution of this study was to introduce a mechanism for honestly reporting. But the use of value 0 to represent cheating agents and 1 for cooperating agents would make the model unable to adapt to situation where reputation reports are represented by values like 0.1 or 0.75.

E-Bay reputation model (Hong & John, 2015) determines the trustworthiness of an agent based on its past behaviour. It is a centralised rating system which rates its partners by allocating 1, 0 or -1 as rating valves. If rating is positive then rating value 1 is assigned, 0 is assigned for neutral and in case rating is negative then -1 is assigned. Reputation value can be further supported by textual comments and past behaviour is put in public domain. Value of reputation is calculated as a single value based on summation of ratings of past six months. Centralized mechanism handles and stores all the rating values. Users need to go through textual comments for getting more information about the agent. This model keeps no check on user that may cheat after obtaining high trust value. Therefore, such mechanism may not suit well for open community-based systems.

Sabater and Sierra (Sabater & Sierra, 2002; Sabherwal, 1999) proposed a model called REGRET which is a decentralized trust evaluation reputation model. Every agent rates the performance of its partner after every interaction and record it in its local ratings database. Trust value is calculated using stored ratings and its associated weight. Recency of ratings is taken into account while allocating weights to a rating. Trust predictive power has an associated reliability value which is based upon the number of ratings taken for calculating the trust values and deviation of those ratings. Regret also have a sophisticated method to calculate witness reputation based upon witness reports which prevents dishonest reporting. Social networks are used by Regret to identify witnesses to be consulted to assess and weight witness opinions. But Regret does not specify the method to build a social network. Trust calculation in Regret is not only based upon direct trust and witness reputation but also on system and neighbourhood reputation. Regret follows a decentralised approach in which agents are empowered to evaluate trust with other agents. Efforts are done to minimise disinformation by comparing information obtained from multiple sources. Therefore, we can say that Regret follows an appropriate approach which can be used to develop a trust model for open source software development communities. Trust evaluation as per Regret model depends upon social network but it does not show the processes of building a social network.

Luketeacy et al. (Luketeacy et al., 2006) proposed a model called TRAVOS which employ probability theory to evaluate trust in a relationship. History of previous interactions is maintained and they assist in trust development. Interactions are simplified into binary ratings where value 1 is used for successful interaction and value 0 for unsuccessful rating. Further beta family of probability density function (Asundi, 2001) is used by TRAVOS to find the probability of successful interactions. Probability values hence obtained becomes that agent's trust value. Probability density function is further used to evaluate confidence level of trust values. In this model, past performance of the target agent is asked from a witness agent when computed level of confidence of target is found to be less than minimum level. Any agent which had previous interactions with target acts as witness agent and shares information in form of successful and unsuccessful interactions. To evaluate truth in trust value, received witness report is compared with own observed trust values by the evaluator. Future reliability of witness will depend upon the amount of matching of witness and own observed trust value. This process also helps to develop trust between the evaluator and witness thereby improving relationship for future interactions.

Huynh et al. (Huynh et al., 2006) proposed FIRE model which evaluates trust based upon four parameters which are Weighted direct experience, witness information, role-based trust, and third-party references. Direct experience is used to evaluate trustworthiness of the target agent and is based upon the experience of evaluator gained from their previous interactions. It is also termed as interaction trust. Witness information is gathered from other agent if they wish to share their previous experiences. This is just like asking people about the reputation of someone before personally interacting with him. This is known as witness reputation. Role-based rules are the result of certain relationships existing between target, evaluator and its domain knowledge. System may have certain rule base which will set an agent with preset trust value, e.g., there may be a parent – child relation between evaluator and target agent. Child is bound to trust his parent. There may be a trustworthy group (like some branded product) which the evaluator trusts without any question. This is termed as role-based trust. Above discussed three types of trust is calculated by the evaluator after finding the required information about trustworthiness of target agents. But there can be a situation where target agent may prove its trustworthiness to the evaluator by providing some arguments (like previously generated trust certificates from some older interactions). Before any further communication target may also want to know about reputation of the evaluator. This is termed as certified reputation and is bidirectional trust relationship between requester and provider of information. As illustrated by FIRE model, trust may originate from different sources like witness information, direct contact, some policies, regulations or rules. Taking into consideration an open community of software developers rarely have any personally association, knowledge level of peers vary greatly and certain sources of information may not always be available or adequate for evaluation of trust.

Schillo et al. (Schillo et al., 2000) proposed a trust model in which trust emerging out of interactions between two agents can be good or bad and is treated as a boolean value. Degree of satisfaction is not taken into account. The model uses probability theory to evaluate trust. Schillo evaluated the probability of an agent to be honest in coming interactions and is given by an equation $T(A, Q) = e/n$ where e is the number of times target agent was honest and n is number of situations to be observed. Every agent uses a data structure called TrustNet which is in form of a directed graph in which witnesses are represented as nodes of the graph. Parent agent would convey about the honesty of his child agent to the root node of TrustNet graph and is represented in form of information carried by edges of the graph. This model is based upon assumption that witness agents may hide positive information but would not lie at all. Information would be analysed and reported to all if found to be negative. Lying and biasing must be taken into account so as to get the exact trust values. Hiding of information is modelled in terms of probability *p* for informing about positive facts of an agent and probability *(1-p)* for hiding that information. Hidden amount of positive information is estimated using probability theory. This process can be applied from target node to the root node through all ancestoral nodes of the TrustNet. This model is used to detect deceitful agents in Artificial Societies.

Marsh (Marsh, 1994) gave one of the oldest proposed trust model. It takes into account three types of trust, i.e. basic trust, general trust and situational trust. Basic trust is calculated based upon all the experiences gathered over time by an agent. General trusting disposition is modelled using Basic trust component of this model. Good experience leads to greater trust disposition and the other way. Second component which is general trust is simply trust that an agent has over other irrespective of any situation. Situational trust is trust based upon a specific situation. Situational trust is calculated based upon general trust, its importance and utilization of the situation. Model takes into consideration optimistic, pessimistic and realistic agents. Optimistic agents take maximum value out of set of experiences, pessimistic takes minimum value whereas realistic agents takes sources of reputation into consideration. Decision of cooperation with other agents is taken based on utility of the performed action, associated risk and competence of target agent. Concept of reciprocation is introduced in which agent *x* reciprocates to agent *y* as agent *y* had helped it in the past.

Zacharia (Zacharia, 1999) elaborated on HISTOS model which deals with direct information and witness information in a very simple way. Reputation value is treated as a subjective property of the system alloted by individuals of community. It evaluates reputation based on ratings resulting out of most recent interactions. Directed graphs based TrustNet used earlier by Schillo et.al (Schillo et al., 2000) is employed for reputation evaluation. Pair wise ratings are depicted using directed graphs in which agents are represented by nodes and edges carry reputation value provided by the agent based on most recent interaction between two agents. Reputation value of an agent is recursively calculated at any level in the graph in terms of weighted mean of previous rating values that an agent received from agents below it. Model does not take context of provided reputation into consideration and there is no mechanism for detection of cheaters.

Two trust acquisition mechanisms are proposed by Esfandiari and Chandrasekharan (Esfandiari & Chandrasekharan, 2001). First mechanism is based on observation which uses Bayesian networks for representation and Bayesian learning for trust acquisition. Bayesian network structure is known and fully observable and the learning process consists only of statistical values. Second trust mechanism uses two protocols and is based on interactions among agents. First protocol is the exploratory protocol in which one agent asks the other agent for known parameters to calculate the trust degree. Trust between two interacting agents *A* and *B* is calculated by formula *T(P,Q) = (number of true replies)/(total number of such replies)*. Second is the query protocol in which agent asks for advice from already trusted agents. To take care of witness information, a directed graph is built by an agent where agents are represented by nodes of the graph and edges represent trust value between the two interacting agents. Edge between two nodes in the graph is not drawn if trust value of nodes is not known. Multiple paths between two agents in a graph may give contradictory values. This problem is solved by using the largest and smallest value among all the paths which are without cycle in graph. Further author claims that trust flows in trust graph in a similar way as data is routed in a network. Therefore, we can apply algorithms used for distributed networks successfully in this situation. Trust always have an associated context. The author proposes to represent multi-context nature of trust by using colored edges in the trust graph with one color per type of trust. One type of trust would only propagate through a particular color only. In the end author proposes to get the trust value using trust acquisition through interactions with environmental structure of the residing agents.

Yu and Singh (Yu & Singh, 2001; Yu & Singh, 2002b; Yu & Singh, 2002a) proposed the concept of quality of interactions for purpose of trust calculation based on set of values of direct interactions. The trust calculation is based upon most recent experiences with the partner agent. Upper and lower threshold values are defined by agents corresponding to QOS (Quality-of-Service) assigned to trustworthy agents, non-trustworthy agents and agents with no clear classification. Type of the service provided by fellow agent is calculated using Dempster-Shafer theory based upon historic data. If the calculated value is larger than some minimum trust value, the target agent is considered to be trustworthy agent. Target agent may not be found in the very first interaction. Witness agent can provide two kinds of information when queried about target agent. If the target agent is one whom we are interested to find, then it returns its own address otherwise referral to another agent from whom information about target can be obtained is returned. Referrals will lead to the desired agent or new referrals till the intended agent is found or depth limit is reached.The set of referral chain generated in the query process will form a graph similar to TrustNet. Information from multiple witnesses may be aggregated using Dempster's rule of combination. Direct information if available with respect to the target agent will be given preference.

The model proposed by Dasgupta (Dasgupta & Partha, 2000) is based on expectation or the belief that a party will act benignly and cooperatively. The model can be deployed for sociological problems, making and breaking of cooperative relations. Rahman and Hailes (Rahman & Hailes, 2000) in their model calculate trust based upon experiences gained from direct interactions and communications received from third party regarding the same. Agent trustworthiness is classified in form of a discrete set *{vt, t, u, vu}*. This set represents four tuples which are very trustworthy, trustworthy, untrustworthy and very untrustworthy. An agent *A* having a tuple like (0,0,3,4) for agent *B* means that during interactions *A* has experienced 3 untrustworthy and 4 very untrustworthy experiences. Therefore, final trust value is the largest value corresponding to the trust set which here is very untrustworthy. In case two values are same system returns a neutral output value. Information coming from an agent is not blindly trusted, but it is compared with earlier information received from it. If an agent communicates that a particular agent is very trustworthy but according to our own previous experience, it is untrustworthy then witness information has to be adjusted. The problem that arises is that it is not possible to detect agent who are speaking truth and provide different answers but are not lying at all. Witness information requiring least adjustment would be for agents having similar perspective for a situation which may not always be correct.

Mass and Shehory (McAllister, 1995) proposed a trust model based on concept of generation of trust certificates by an authentic neutral third party. The aim of a neutral third party was to minimize biasing. The model was validated by computing trust in open multi-agent systems. Sen and Sajja (Sen & Sajja, 2002) developed a trust model by incorporating experiences gained from direct and observed interactions. It is employed in situations where noisy observations exists which means that observed behaviour is different from actual behaviour of target agent. Fact is that direct interaction only provides the real picture. Reputation values are updated using reinforcement learning. More importance is given to updated reputation value based on interaction than the update that takes place when reputation value is updated based on observation. Reputation values lie between 0 and 1. Value larger than 0.5 is awarded as good performers and value less than 0.5 represents poor performers. One agent may ask the other about reputation of its partner. This model assumes liar agents to lie consistently about other agents. This model gives a method to evaluate the number of witnesses to be queried before a particular agent is trusted. There is only a likelihood of selection of good partner as the witnesses are randomly selected. The author has not given any mechanism to club direct experience and witness observation to compute the final reputation value.

Carbo et al. (Carbo et al., 2002) compared SPORAS with Fuzzy based reputation model in which reputation values are represented in terms of Fuzzy sets. The reputation is calculated based on some degree of satisfaction corresponding to latest interactions among partners. The new satisfaction values are aggregated with old reputation values using weighted aggregation. Weights are evaluated based on an already predicted value called remembrance or memory. The remembrance factor is based on similarities between old reputation value and satisfaction level of previous experiences. Relevance of previous experience is incremented when satisfaction level of older experience matches trust value of partner. But if satisfaction level and assigned reputation values differ then relevance value of latest interaction is incremented. Recommendations coming from a high reputation recommender are relied upon just as if they are based upon direct interactions. Recommendations of agent having bad reputation are not considered. Apart from the above discussed trust models, number of other trust models were also studied. A new evidential trust model for open communities is proposed by Wang and Sun (Wang & Sun, 2009). This model is an improvement over Yu and Singh (Yu & Singh, 2002a) model. This model used Dezert-Smarandache theory for trust acquisition. The proposed model can be used for computing trust in open communities. Gomez et al. (Gómez et al., 2006) proposed Anticipatory trust model which is based on advertisement based trust, direct trust and recommendations based trust. Another approach to ensure honest interactions among parties is to employ a trusted third party whom both the interacting parties trust. It is the duty of third party to review every aspect of communication taking place between two parties and ensure transparency.

Xiong and Liu (Xiong & Liu, 2004) proposed PeerTrust model which uses feedback obtained from peers to determine trust. Peer experience and credibility is vital as entire trust is based upon their feedback. Community members earn incentives if the provided feedback matches the real time experience. Trust is evluated and a composite trust metric if formed. This model evaluates Peer-to-Peer trust in ecommerce communities. Vercouter and Muller (Vercouter & Muller, 2010) proposed LIAR model which can be employed for Liar Identification in the community. An agent may provide higher trust rating for less rated agent or vice-versa but in both the cases an agent had given wrong trust values which is not good for any system. LIAR model ensures true value of Agent Reputation. This model ensures that social norms and other communication rules are respected. It is used for implementation of a social control of agent interaction.

Albuquerque at al. (Albuquerque et al., 2014) proposed a trust model termed as 3Gtrust which is developed for distributed systems and is based on groups of peers. This model is used to ensure that group of peers can be trusted or not. Chubin et al. (Carbo et al., 2002) discussed a trust model called CREDIT and it used fuzzy sets to evaluate trust value. It combines direct exchanges among agents together with the agent reputation. Clifford (Clifford, 2002) proposed SOLAR trust model which have a number of independent certification authorities perform the job of trust computation. Each certification authority acts as sun in solar system and other trusted parties act as planets revolving around it. Reputation value is calculated and represented using digital certificates. Chong et al. (Chong et al., 2013) proposed a multi valued trust evaluation model for cloud computing based applications. Malicious feedbacks are filtered and a trust metric to evaluate the trustworthiness of service provider is developed. This model is suitable for use in E-commerce trading partners in cloud environment. Josang et al. (Josang & Haller, 2007) developed a Bayesian Reputation System. This model is used in open dynamic environment and it calculates trust value using Dirichlet Probability Density Function. This model is binomial and multinomial rating models.

After going through different aspects of existing reputation and trust models presented by various researchers, the applicability of certain trust features to open source software development trust model are summarized in Table 1.

5. COMMENTARY ON REVIEWED WORK

Following the analysis of literature pertaining to OSSD, Trust and various Trust models, following inferences regarding the development of OSSD community trust model are drawn. The software development virtual communities have to ensure that all its members are registered. Trust helps in improving relationships and binds the virtual teams. Trust must be considered as an integral part of software development and trust requirements must be strictly incorporated into every phase of software development starting with requirement gathering stage. Otherwise, it results in conflicts with other functional and non-functional requirements of the system. Trust should be a combination of certain attributes which must be quantitatively determined and graphical represented to have a better insight into it. Trust model to be developed will calculate trust at the individual level for every contributor which in turn ensures the trustworthiness of the community. The aim of this work is to design a trustworthy system to incorporate security, authentication, reliability, usability, safety, availability and to meet all user expectation concerns.

The trust enhancement framework to be developed will have a centralized trust computation system in which every aspect of software production is finalized by a core team. Every community member must have a finite set of actions to be performed with the corresponding outcomes. Regular updating of reputation based on feedback is to be incorporated. New members enter the community with the lowest reputation which is updated with time. Trusted members of other communities must be taken care off. They should be provided with relatively higher trust values than other new community members provided they bring with them old trust certificates from their previous community. The community member may be alleviated to higher levels or may be made part of the core team if very high trust value is maintained by that member over a considerable period of time. This possible only if a mechanism for honestly trust computation is at the place. The past behavior of the community member should be in the public domain. The skill levels of the contributors differ as someone may be a good code contributor, other may be very good at debugging while someone else may be very good document writer. This leads to the conclusion that trust should be multi-valued based on different types of past contributions like contributed code, amount of code tested, help provided to other users, documentation provided etc. The correctness of the contributions has to be inspected by certain minimum numbers of community members before incorporating them into the final build of software and only then it would add to their trustworthiness. Trust development is a continuous process in which trust value is an aggregate of old and new trust values. Feedback obtained from peers will be given due importance. Framework for OSSD community will take care of all the above-stated facts.

Table 1. Key features of trust models

Author	Key Characteristics of the Proposed Trust Model	Whether Applicable to OSS Trust Model
Yu and Lin	Trust to be considered at requirement gathering level.	Yes
Yan and Cofta	Reputation in form of goals and statements with a graphical representation.	No
Giorgini et al.	Trust delegation, provisioning and ownership for developers.	Yes
Bimrah	Intention of Trust relationship among interacting parties.	Yes
Avizienis	Trust-Worthiness to be assured.	Yes
Pavlidis	Context added with trust.	Yes
Lawson and Blum	Privacy, Security, Reliability, usability, safety, availability and user expectation.	Yes
Rohm and Milne	Information systems to be highly trustworthy.	Yes
Bhatta-charya	Finite set of actions and outcomes.	Yes
Zacharia	Reputation updated after Feedback, Recency of rating.	Yes
Pinyol et al.	Incentive for Trustful agents.	Yes
E-Bay reputation model	Centralized rating system, Past behavior in public domain.	Yes
Sabater and Sierra	Decentralized trust evaluation model.	No
Luketeacy et al.	Uses probability theory.	Yes
Huynh et al.	Weighted direct experience, witness reputation, role-based trust, third party reference	No
Schillo	Trust as good or bad only.	No
Marsh	Basic trust, General trust, Situational trust, Concept of reciprocation.	No
Zacharia	Directed graph based TrustNet.	No
Esfandiary and Chandrasekharan	Multi Context nature of Trust based on observation.	Yes
Yu and Singh	Intended agent is found by chain of referrals.	No
Rahman and Hailes	Agent ranked very trustworthy, trustworthy, untrustworthy or very untrustworthy.	No
Mass and Shehory	Generation of trust certificates.	Yes
Sen and Sajja	Reinforcement learning is used where observations are noisy.	No
Carbo et al.	Fuzzy sets used, Recommendations from higher reputation agent.	No
Xiong and Liu	Feedback determines trust, Composite trust metric formed.	Yes
Vercouter and Muller	Liar identification in community.	No
Albuquerque et al.	Group of peers can be trusted or not	No
Chubin et al.	Use fuzzy sets	No
Clifford	Digital certificates used.	Yes
Josang et al.	Framework for open dynamic environment.	Yes

Finally, after going through all the aspects of OSSD methodology, the need of trust for community formation and existing trust models, the following research questions have been formulated.

RQ1: To become familiar with various processes and methodologies adopted by OSSD communities.

RQ2: To determine the challenges associated with the formation of virtual software development teams.

RQ3: To understand the importance of trust as a binding force among virtual team members.

RQ4: To identify the basic attributes based upon which trust in OSSD environments could be computed.

RQ5: To develop a relational database system (repository) for preserving the above attributes corresponding to community members.

RQ6: To develop a trust evaluation framework based on above-found trust attributes.

RQ7: To implement the proposed framework.

RQ8: To validate the proposed framework.

6. PROPOSED TRUST EVALUATION FRAMEWORK AND ITS COMPONENTS

6.1. Components of Trust Evaluation Framework

Various components of the proposed trust evaluation framework based upon which the OSSD community can evaluate the trust of its community members are:

- Code contributed by a particular OSS developer/volunteer;
- Code reviewed by a particular OSS developer/volunteer;
- Help requested by other members and relevant information provided to them by a volunteer/developer;
- Number of trustworthy members referred for joining the community;
- Amount of documentation written for the community;
- Active time spent for the betterment of the community;
- Awards/ honors received by the community members;
- Amount of monetary contributions;
- Active OSSD projects on which a particular OSS developer/volunteer is working.

The proposed trust evaluation framework also preserves the personal information of the community member and his/her login details.

6.2. The Proposed Trust Evaluation Framework

The proposed trust evaluation framework (Figure 1) starts operating as soon as a member enters into the community. The members entering into the community are always monitored by a trust calculation and update module. This module takes care of new as well as existing members of the community. Trust development is a continuous process, therefore, the trust value is updated after every interaction of member with the community. The member is marked trustworthy only if trust value is more than some minimum threshold value. The member joining the community may already be a trustworthy member of some other established community. Such member may be given higher initial trust value provided that member furnishes trust certificate from the community he is already working with. In case no such certificate is there, the member has to start afresh in the community.

As soon as the member enters the community, a decision is taken to determine whether the member is new or existing. New members are required to register themselves. Space is reserved for them in the repository, personal and professional information is taken, the user is registered, login id and password is generated and besides other things, the trust value is set to minimal. The new member now can interact with the community. Existing members can log into the system by providing a login id and password. Whenever a member logs into the system time elapsed since the last interaction is determined. If the time elapsed is less than the prescribed limit, the member is allowed further interact in the system. But if the time elapsed is more than the prescribed limit, then the member is asked about whether the member wants to retain the membership or not. If a member says yes, then control is passed to member interaction and handling interface. But if the member says no, then old trust values are preserved. Before any other operation is performed, it is ensured whether the member was trustworthy or not. If a member is trustworthy then some incentives are offered to retain him. If the incentive is accepted, control is passed to member interaction and handling interface. If the incentive is not accepted or member is found out to be non-trustworthy then trust certificate is generated and goodbye message is printed. The data of members who leave the community is stored in a different repository containing details of migrated members. This is done to ensure that only active members remain in the database. Throughout the interaction, various attributes affecting the trust value are updated which leads to the latest trust value of the member.

Figure 1. Flow of the proposed trust evaluation framework

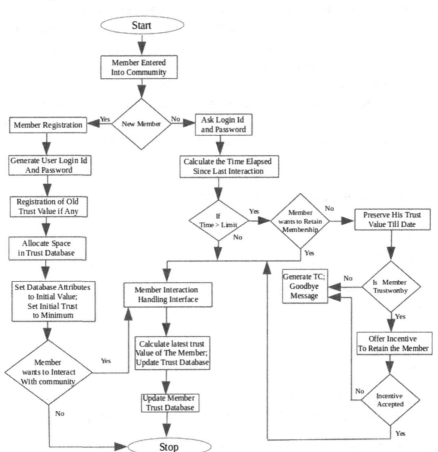

7. FUTURE WORK

The future research would aim to find answers to the research questions as illustrated above. Henceforth, one can work towards the development of a set of well-optimized databases for storage and retrieval of data corresponding to all the above-given components for trust evaluation. The process of trust computation with respect to community members can also be developed. Various algorithms to handle the process of code submission and review, documentation submission and review, member activity handling, response handling, bug tracking, and member activity analysis can be developed as a part of future work. The proposed system can then be implemented in any supporting language followed by its verification and validation by taking real-time data as an input from certain existing open source communities for analyzing trust exhibited by their members.

8. CONCLUSION

The OSSD paradigm suggests that a team of connected persons develops the intended product. It becomes very essential for a member of the development team to have trust in the other members of the team. If trust levels among team members are high, then coordination between them also raises to a higher level, which results in a higher quality of the product. Another dimension of OSSD is the geographically diverse location of its team members. It, therefore, becomes very important to install trust in such a geographically dispersed team. Ongoing through the literature, it has been found that although a large number of trust studies have been carried out in development of information systems, mobile communication, distributed systems, and various other environments, very few have been worked upon for OSSD communities. Keeping in view, the above-stated facts, it is hence proposed to develop a trust model and framework for OSSD that not only establishes trust in the OSS developers and community members but also measures and dynamically validate it as well. We will try to bridge the deficit of ontological and methodological support to model and reason about trust with its related concepts in one allied framework. Henceforth, in this work, we have proposed a trust evaluation framework along with its various components which can aid an OSSD community to evaluate the trust of its existing members.

ACKNOWLEDGMENT

Sincere thanks to Department of Research, Innovation and Consultancy, IKG Punjab Technical University, Kapurthala, Punjab, India for assistance during this study.

REFERENCES

Albuquerque, R. O., Villalba, L. J. G., & Kim, T. H. (2014). 3GTrust: Group Extension for Trust Models in Distributed Systems. *International Journal of Distributed Sensor Networks*.

Asundi, J. (2001). Software Engineering Lessons from Open Source Projects. *In: 1st Workshop on Open Source Software. ICSE.*

Avizienis, A., Laprie, J. C., & Randell, B. (2004). *Dependability and its Threats: A Taxonomy. In 18th IFIP* (pp. 91–120). Kluwer Academic Publishers.

Bandow, D. (2004). Time to Create Sound Teamwork. *Journal for Quality and Participation*, *24*(2), 41–47.

Barbar, M. A., Verner, J. M., & Nguyen, P. T. (2006). Establishing and Maintaining Trust in Software Outsourcing Relationships: An Empirical Investigation. *Journal of Systems and Software*, *80*(9), 1438–1449. doi:10.1016/j.jss.2006.10.038

Bergquist, M., & Ljungberg, J. (2001). The power of gifts: Organizing social relationships in open source communities. *Journal of Information Systems*, *1*(1), 305–320. doi:10.1046/j.1365-2575.2001.00111.x

Bhattacharya, R., Devinney, T. M., & Pillutla, M. M. (1998). A Formal Model of Trust Based on Outcomes. *Academy of Management Review*, *23*(3), 459–472. doi:10.5465/amr.1998.926621

Bimrah, K. K. (2009). A Framework for Modeling Trust during Information Systems Development [PhD Thesis]. University of East London.

Bulman, R. J. (1992). *Shattered Assumptions: Towards a new psychology of trauma*. New York: Free Press.

Carbo, J., Molina, J., & Davila, J. (2002). Comparing predictions of SPORAS vs. a Fuzzy Reputation Agent System. In *3rd International Conference on Fuzzy Sets and Fuzzy Systems* (pp. 147-153). Interlaken.

Chong, S. K., Abawajy, J., Ahmad, M., Rahmi, I., & Hamid, A. (2013). A Multilevel Trust Management Framework for Service Oriented Environment. In *International Conference on Innovation, Management and Technology Research ICIMTR 2013*, Malaysia (pp. 22 – 23).

Clifford, M. A. (2002, Dec 9-13). Networking in the Solar Trust Model: Determining Optimal Trust Paths in a Decentralized Trust Network. In *Proceedings of 18th Annual Conference on Computer Security Applications*. IEEE. doi:10.1109/CSAC.2002.1176298

Costa, A. C. (2003). Understanding the Nature and the Antecedents of Trust within Work Teams. In B. Nooteboom & F. Six (Eds.), *The Trust Process in Organizations: Empirical Studies of the Determinants and the Process of Trust Development* (pp. 105–124). Cheltenham: Edward Elgar. doi:10.4337/9781843767350.00012

Cubranic, D., & Murphy, G. C. (2001). The Ramp-Up Challenge in Open Source Software Projects. In *Workshop on Open Source Software, IEEE/ACM International Conference on Software Engineering (ICSE 01)*.

Dasgupta & Partha. (2000). Trust as a Commodity. In D. Gambetta (Ed.), *Trust: Making and Breaking Cooperative Relations. Electronic edition* (pp. 49–72). Department of Sociology, University of Oxford.

de Laat, P. B. (2010). How can Contributors to Open-Source Communities be Trusted? On the Assumption, Inference and Substitution of Trust. *Ethics and Information Technology*, *12*(4), 327–341. doi:10.100710676-010-9230-x

Esfandiari, B., & Chandrasekharan, S. (2001). On How Agents Make friends: Mechanisms for Trust Acquisition. In *Proceedings of the Fourth Workshop on Deception, Fraud and Trust in Agent Societies*, Montreal, Canada (pp. 27-34).

Giorgini, P., Massaci, F., Mylopoulos, J., & Zanone, N. (2004). Requirements Engineering for Trust Management. *International Journal of Information Security*, *5*(4), 257–274. doi:10.100710207-006-0005-7

Gómez, M., Carbó, J., & Earle, C. B. (2006). An Anticipatory Trust Model for Open Distributed Systems. In *Workshop on Anticipatory Behavior in Adaptive Learning Systems* (pp. 307-324).

Grandison, T., & Sloman, M. (2000). A Survey of Trust in Internet Applications. *IEEE Communications Surveys and Tutorials*, *4*(4), 2–16. doi:10.1109/COMST.2000.5340804

Hardin, R. (2002). *Trust and Trust-Worthiness*. New York.

Hoffman, J. L., Jenkins, K. L., & Blum, J. (2006). Trust Beyond Security: An Expanded Trust Model. *Communications of the ACM*, *49*(7), 95–101. doi:10.1145/1139922.1139924

Hong, X., & John, C. S. L. (2015, September). Modeling eBay-like reputation systems: Analysis, Characterization and Insurance Mechanism Design. *Performance Evaluation*, *91*, 132–149. doi:10.1016/j.peva.2015.06.009

Howison, J., & Crowston, K. (2004). The Perils and Pitfalls of Mining SourceForge. In *Proceedings of the International Workshop on Mining Software Repositories (MSR 2004)*, Edinburg, UK (pp. 7-11). 10.1049/ic:20040467

Huynh, T. D., Jennings, N. R., & Shadbolt, N. R. (2006). An Integrated Trust and Reputation model for open Multi-agent systems. *Journal of Autonomous Agents and Multi Agent Systems*, *13*(2), 119–154. doi:10.100710458-005-6825-4

Jarvenpaa, S. L., Shaw, T. R., & Staples, D. S. (2004). Toward Contextualized Theories of Trust: The Role of Trust in Global Virtual Teams. *Information Systems Research*, *15*(3), 250–264. doi:10.1287/isre.1040.0028

Josang, A., & Haller, J. (2007, April 10-13). Dirichlet Reputation Systems. In *ARES' 07 Proceedings of The Second International Conference on Availability, Reliability and Security* (pp. 112-119). IEEE Computer Society. 10.1109/ARES.2007.71

Kasper-Fuehrer, E. C., & Ashkanasy, N. M. (2001). Communicating Trustworthiness and Building Trust in Inter-organizational virtual organizations. *Journal of Management*, *27*(3), 235–254. doi:10.1016/S0149-2063(01)00090-3

Kogut, B., & Metiu, A. (2001). Open Source Software Development and Distributed Innovation. *Oxford Review of Economic Policy*, *17*(2), 248–264. doi:10.1093/oxrep/17.2.248

Lane, M. S., Vyver, G., Basenet, P., & Howard, S. (2004). Interpretative Insights into Interpersonal Trust and Effectiveness of Virtual Communities of Open Source Software Developers. In ACIS 2004 Proceedings.

Lee, C. (2009, May). Utilizing Open Source Tools for Online Teaching and Learning: Applying Linux Technologies. In *Strengths and Weaknesses of Open Source Software*. Hershey, PA: IGI Global.

Lewicki, R. J., & Bunker, B. B. (1996). Developing and Maintaining Trust in Work Relationships. In T. R. Tyler & R. M. Kramer (Eds.), *Trust in Organizations: Frontiers of Theory and Research* (pp. 114–139). Thousand Oaks, CA: Sage Publications. doi:10.4135/9781452243610.n7

Luketeacy, W. T., Patel, J., Jennings, N. R., & Luck, M. (2006, February 24). TRAVOS: Trust and Reputation in the Context of Inaccurate Information Sources. *Journal of Autonomous Agents and Multi-Agent Systems*, *12*(2), 183–198. doi:10.100710458-006-5952-x

Marsh, S. P. (1994). Formalising Trust as a Computational Concept [Doctoral Thesis]. University of Stirling, United Kingdom.

McAllister, D. J. (1995). Affect and Cognition Based Trust as Foundations for Interpersonal Cooperation in Organizations. *Academy of Management Journal*, *38*(1), 24–59.

Michlmayr, M., Hunt, F., & Probert, D. (2005, July 11-15). Quality Practices and Problems in Free Software Projects. In *Proceedings of the First International Conference on Open Source Systems* (pp. 24-28).

Mui, L., Mohtashemi, M., & Halberstadt, A. (2002). A Computational Model of Trust and Reputation. In: *Proceedings of the 35th International Conference on System Science* (pp. 280–287). 10.1109/HICSS.2002.994181

Olmedilla, D., Rana, O., Matthews, B., & Nejdl, W. (2005). Security and Trust Issues in Semantic Grids. In *Proceedings of the Dagsthul Seminar, Semantic Grid: The Convergence of Technologies*.

Osterloh, M., & Rota, S. (2004). Trust and Community in Open Source Software Production. *Analyse & Kritik*, 279–301.

Pavlidis, M. (2011). *Designing for Trust, CaiSE* (pp. 3–14). Doctoral Consortium.

Piccoli, G., & Ives, B. (2003). Trust and the Unintended Effects of Behavior Control in Virtual Teams. *Management Information Systems Quarterly*, *27*(3), 368–395. doi:10.2307/30036538

Pinyol, I., Sabater Mir, J., Dellunde, P., & Paolucci, M. (2012). Reputation-based Decisions for Logic based Cognitive Agents. *Autonomous Agents and Multi-Agent Systems*, *24*(1), 175–216. doi:10.100710458-010-9149-y

Rahman, A. A., & Hailes, S. (2000, January 4-7). Supporting Trust in Virtual Communities. In *Proceedings of the Hawaii's International Conference on Systems Sciences*, Maui, HI.

Rocco, E. (1998, April 18-23). Trust Breaks Down in Electronic Context but can be repaired by Some Initial face-o-face Contact. ACM. 10.1145/274644.274711

Rohm, J. A., & Milne, R. G. (2004). Just what the Doctor Ordered: The Role of Information Sensitivity and Trust in Reducing Medical Information Privacy Concern. *Journal of Business Research*, *57*(9), 1000–1011. doi:10.1016/S0148-2963(02)00345-4

Sabater, J., & Sierra, C. (2002). Reputation and Social Network Analysis in Multi-Agent Systems. In *AAMAS-2002 Proceedings of the first International Joint Conference on Autonomous agents and Multi-agent Systems* Bologna, Italy(475-482). . 10.1145/544741.544854

Sabherwal, R. (1999). The Role of Trust in Outsourced IS Development Projects. *Communications of the ACM, 42*(2), 80–86. doi:10.1145/293411.293485

Samoladas, I., & Stamelos, I. (2003). *Assessing Free/Open Source Software Quality.* Greece: Aristotle University of Informatics.

Schillo, M., Funk, P., & Rovatsos, M. (2000). Using Trust for Detecting Deceitful Agents in Artificial Societies. *Applied Artificial Intelligence.*

Sen, S., & Sajja, N. (2002). Robustness of Reputation-based Trust: Boolean Case. In *Proceedings of the first International Joint Conference on Autonomous Agents and Multi-agent Systems* (pp. 288-293). Bologna, Italy.

Sirkkala, P., Hammounda, I., & Aaltonen, T. (2010). From Proprietary to Open source: Building a Network of Trust. In *OSCOMM 2010 Proceedings of Second International Workshop on Building Sustainable Open Source Communities* (pp. 26-30).

Stewart, K. J., & Gosain, S. (2006). The Impact of Ideology on effectiveness in open source software development teams. *Management Information Systems Quarterly, 30*(2), 291–314. doi:10.2307/25148732

Uddin, M. G., & Zulekernine, M. (2008). UML-Trust: Towards Developing Trust Aware Software. In: *Proceedings of the ACM Symposium on Applied Computing,* Brazil (pp. 831-836).

Vercouter, L., & Muller, G. (2010). L.I.A.R. Achieving Social Control in Open and Decentralized Multi-agent systems. *Applied Artificial Intelligence, 24*(8), 723–768. doi:10.1080/08839514.2010.499502

Wang, J., & Sun, H. J. (2009, September 1). A New Evidential Trust Model for Open Communities. *Computer Standards & Interfaces, 31*(5), 994–1001. doi:10.1016/j.csi.2008.09.025

Xiong, L., & Liu, L. (2004, July). PeerTrust: Supporting Reputation-Based Trust for Peer-to-Peer Electronic Communities. *IEEE Transactions on Knowledge and Data Engineering, 16*(7), 843–857. doi:10.1109/TKDE.2004.1318566

Yan, Z., & Cofta, P. (2003). Methodology to Bridge Different Domains of Trust in Mobile Communications. In *Proceedings of the First International iTrust Conference* (pp. 211-224). Springer. 10.1007/3-540-44875-6_15

Yu, B., & Singh, M. P. (2001). Towards a Probabilistic Model of Distributed Reputation Management. In *Proceedings of the Fourth Workshop on Deception, Fraud and Trust in Agent Societies,* Montreal, Canada (pp. 125-137).

Yu, B., & Singh, M. P. (2002a). Distributed Reputation Management for Electronic Commerce. *Computational Intelligence, 18*(4), 535–549. doi:10.1111/1467-8640.00202

Yu, B., & Singh, M. P. (2002b). An Evidential Model of Distributed Reputation Management. In: *AAMAS-02 Proceedings of the first International Joint Conference on Autonomous Agents and Multi-agent systems,* Bologna, Italy (pp. 294-301). 10.1145/544741.544809

Yu, E., & Liu, L. (2001). Modeling Trust for System Design Using the i* Strategic Actors Framework. In *Proceedings of the International Workshop on Deception Fraud and Trust in Agent Societies* (pp. 175-194). Springer.

Zacharia, G. (1999). Collaborative Reputation Mechanisms for Online Communities.

Zucker, L. G. (1986). Production of trust: Institutional sources of economic structure. In B.W. Staw & L. L. Cummings (Eds.), Research in Organizational Behavior. Greenwich, CT: JAI Press.

This research was previously published in the International Journal of Open Source Software and Processes (IJOSSP), 9(4); pages 1-19, copyright year 2018 by IGI Publishing (an imprint of IGI Global).

Chapter 22
Triggering Specialised Knowledge in the Software Development Process:
A Case Study Analysis

Hanna Dreyer
University of Gloucestershire, UK

Martin George Wynn
https://orcid.org/0000-0001-7619-6079
University of Gloucestershire, UK

Robin Bown
https://orcid.org/0000-0001-7793-108X
University of Gloucestershire, UK

ABSTRACT

Many factors determine the success of software development projects. The exchange and harnessing of specialized knowledge amongst and between the project team members is one of these. To explore this situation, an ethnographic case study of the product-testing phase of a new human resources management system was undertaken. Extempore verbal exchanges occur through the interplay of project team members in weekly meetings, as the software was tested, analyzed, and altered in accordance with the customer's needs. Utilizing tacit knowledge from the project members as well as the group, new tacit knowledge surfaces and spirals, which allows it to build over time. Five extempore triggers surfaced during the research generated through explicit stimuli, allowing project members to share and create new knowledge. The theoretical development places these learning triggers in an interpretive framework, which could add value to other software development and project management contexts.

DOI: 10.4018/978-1-6684-3702-5.ch022

INTRODUCTION

Recent research has identified and assessed the significance of a range of issues that determine software project development outcomes (Wynn, 2018a, 2018b). These include factors concerning not only technology, but also people and process related indicators, including knowledge transfer intensity (Figure 1). In other literature, the surfacing of such knowledge in projects has been conceptualised as emanating from a combination of improvisation, project management and knowledge management activities (Leybourne & Kennedy, 2015). The issue of improvisation, however, can be seen to be at odds with established best practice project management principles. Prescriptive, probabilistic and objective based project management systems are no guarantee of success and in some cases they can create an illusion of control that is not always justified (Hodgson & Drummond, 2009). All projects have a temporal focus and the dominant logic in this field is structured planning to achieve workable projects on time. Knowledge sharing is at the core of meetings where different forms of expert knowledge are required.

Figure 1. Change factors in a software development project (at TPG DisableAids)
Source: Wynn, 2018b, p.115.

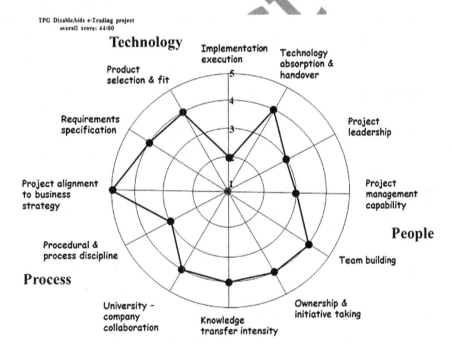

Tacit knowledge is a difficult form of knowledge to share and acquire during a project due to its intangible nature. Tacit knowledge is at the core of a knowledge based society and its exchange is still of great interest to researchers. How tacit knowledge is exchanged and used within the different project teams plays a vital role in project success. Banacu (2013) stresses the importance of tacit knowledge transfer due to companies needing it to obtain a competitive advantage. Project teams, and in particular those involved in software development, exist to provide workable solutions that incorporate and create new knowledge from the separate areas of expertise held within the team. This research analyses a project team's tacit knowledge exchange within a software development meeting environment.

White and Perry (2016) argue that there has not been enough focus on the expert knowledge of software developers and their influence on the production of information systems. This is an area where software work is highly socialized but careers were highly individualized (Benner, 2008). Their mutual standing in the work overcomes the set of partial knowledge that they each possess. Being able to manage different knowledge sources through coordination and integration is a significant challenge during such a project (de Souza et al., 2006). The focus of the research lies in exploring knowledge exchange in software development projects and sheds light on how this expert group knowledge actualises and thus contributes to theory. Embedded observation in a particular project provided the empirical material for this research.

This article discusses the findings of a research project (Dreyer, 2018) which aimed to understand how tacit knowledge surfaces within the software development process. It examines how the group knowledge generated through expert interaction can be recognised in a software development project, and used to improve project implementation (Clancy, 2006). The paper consists of five sections. After this introductory section, literature relevant to the field of study is discussed, and the following section then outlines the research methodology deployed in the study. There then follows an evaluation of the data and a discussion of research findings. In the concluding section, the main outcomes of the research are summarised and implications are discussed.

LITERATURE REVIEW

In the context of knowledge creation, the theory of tacit knowledge has been influential since the work of Nonaka and Takeuchi (1995). This created a protocol for a knowledge generating company using a Socialisation, Externalisation, Combination and Internalisation (SECI) model. In the same volume, three of the model elements are presented in a recursive pathway, as more available knowledge is created in the transfer from tacit to explicit knowledge. Internalisation is the counter flow in this model, and it occurs across and counter to the other three modalities.

The concept of tacit knowledge arises from the observation by Polanyi (1962) that "our personal knowing of a thing is unspecifiable" (p.343) to the extent that it is more than the articulated fact. Importantly, this tacit knowledge is seen as the form of knowledge that is *not* routinely articulated and embodied in human action (Scharmer, 2001; Riain, 2009). This leaves open the question of whether the knowing is not, or cannot, be articulated. Personal knowledge communication contains both these elements in ways that are difficult to separate. This will apply to knowledge from an expert who, as such, is considered to have expertise. Importantly, Nonaka and Takeuchi (1995) see the process to convert tacit knowledge to explicit knowledge as essentially context dependent, which entails physical proximity and interaction.

In this view, a shared reality and face-to-face interactions are the root of knowledge creation (Berger & Luckmann, 1967). These interactions are seen as "the key to conversion and transfer of tacit knowledge and, thus, are the triggers for the whole knowledge creation process" (Bartolacci et al., 2016, p.795). This process is holistically contained in the context, but often needs disjunctions to crystallise the knowledge available. Having several groups of experts involved moderates the flow of knowledge substantially, and hence developing a shared understanding is essential, as it is a group effort to develop software (Fischer & Ostwald, 2001). This shared reality is a form of "putting oneself into work" (Heidegger, 2001, p.160).

There have been a number of difficulties in implementing such a knowledge creation project in a timely manner, particularly in software projects (Marouf & Khalil, 2015). Project management assumes a rational approach to decision-making by project managers, but some empirical studies (Hodgson & Drummond, 2009) support the view that managerial judgment is the preferred mode of decision selection in many projects. Managerial judgment is based on situational assessment, and thus on time-constrained knowledge rather than on more prescriptive rational decision-making (Taylor, 2004).

A Husseralian approach to phenomenology is one that derives the essence of an idea. Husserl (2012) considers that a thought can emerge as a vague thought that is, in its initial stages "an inarticulate grasp" (p.255). Polanyi's (1962) use of the term "strenuous groping" and the view that "any science is grounded in a tacit ontology of its object domain" indicates the "unspoken assumption about the objects in use" (p.301). Knowledge we acquire and own is not entirely specifiable and therefore gives rise to the articulate grasping as we seek to extend our articulation of what we know. Triggers add value in a group context by enabling this process. Triggers can be seen as unique events that start a process, initiating something new. They are an initiation of a phase change in the knowledge development process that enables articulation. Accepting that there are some dynamic effects, the process of knowledge exchange will not be self-generating without interventions. These situations are not always easy to recognize, as they are not routinely articulated, and therefore the opportunity for the identification of a new understanding may be missed. Engeström, Kerosuo, and Kajamaa (2007) see these discontinuities as either mundane or directional. Directional changes can seem an anathema to the idea of continuity but continuity is not the same for all participants. These triggers, or "discontinuities" in the existing situation, can be created from outside the group, and can "trigger micro-processes of organizational learning" (Berends & Lammers, 2010, p.1060). Through the recognition of tacit knowledge triggers and the creation of an analytical framework, the group as well as the individual knowledge sources are assessed. This analysis builds upon existing theories, discussed below, which were used to understand and extract tacit knowledge.

Others have developed the idea of a shared space as the forum for knowledge development. It is possible to share knowledge through different channels; however, a shared space reinforces the relationship between colleagues allowing knowledge creation to take place (Dreyer & Wynn, 2017). These spaces are formed in different ways, such as through informal discussions during a break, emails or meetings. Developing the view of shared reality, the environment where knowledge can be exchanged and is able to build up has been called "Ba". This concept, developed by Nonaka and Teece (2001), gives a basis for knowledge to be shared and created. Nonaka and Konno (1998) see "Ba" as a mental flexibility and an ongoing dynamic process that allows new insights to be constantly generated. The space of "Ba" provides for a continuous flow of knowledge exchange, where the knowledge is able to transform and change. Knowledge is not tangible, but is able to evolve and build up tacitly through its self-transcendence. This view recognizes that this knowledge forum is a shared space where relationships can emerge (Nonaka & Teece, 2009).

Knowledge is thus not a set of facts and figures; it is not a set of statistics or applied conceits, but a "space" in which processes are constantly iterative, marked by close communication, by modelling, by mentoring, and by incessant experiential inputs that lead to outputs. Given the creation of a knowledge generating space, they recognize the need for dynamic effects. This space is not tangible, but is a fluid continuum wherein there is constant change and transformation resulting in new levels of knowledge. Knowledge is a process and never becomes finalised, which is paralleled in the software development process, where databases are built and then later updated over time with more information. However, both need knowledge or information, which is captured and put into context. It is a self-transcending and ever-spiraling evolution. Embracing the concept of "Ba" is essentially arguing for a learning culture, which has the advantage of promoting the concept of presence to each other. However, it seems that the proximity entailed in knowledge creation needs further exploration. In Heidegger's terms, this space can be seen as a "clearing" or a "shedding of light". (Heidegger, 2015, p.133).

Further work has been done on the knowledge exchange dynamic. Group tacit knowledge is the focus of Ryan and O'Connor's (2013) Theoretical Model for the acquisition and sharing of Tacit Knowledge in Teams (TMTKT). They note, "individuals draw from the team tacit knowledge and create their own tacit knowledge. This is a background process which is dynamic and reciprocal relying on constructivist situated learning" (Ryan & O'Connor, 2013, p.1618). Looking at knowledge flow, their approach allows the analysis of knowledge movement within a group. The model (Figure 2) was constructed by using a qualitative approach and the focus is to explore the flow of team tacit knowledge. The cycle of the model begins with the current state of knowledge within the team; through constructive learning, an essential part of knowledge creation and sharing which greatly develops individual knowledge. Constructive learning is, at its essence, the process of an individual assimilating new facts and experiences into a pre-existing web of knowledge and understanding (Ryan & O'Connor, 2013). The gained individual knowledge - expert knowledge - can then be shared with the team, allowing "transactive memory" to build up. In the context of this model, the "transactive memory" is defined as team tacit knowledge, where the expert knowledge from each individual in the team is stored and a common understanding is developed. Transactive memory is thus the combination of specialization, credibility and coordination of knowledge within the group (Ryan & O'Connor, 2012). Once the team has established common team tacit knowledge, which can be influenced by other human factors such as emotions or outside influences, the spiral begins anew in a continuous cycle. Team tacit knowledge and its flow allows the social analysis of the project group during the meetings. This model proposes that individual constructive learning precedes the development of transactive memory. Given the discussion above, any team tacit knowledge must be present but individualized; the transactive memory becomes focused on the project outcomes and therefore allows a team to progress in the project.

Clarke (2010) proposes a model evaluating tacit knowledge from an individual point of view (Figure 3). Incorporating the idea of triggers, knowledge input begins the process; tacit knowledge is then created through reflection; and triggers, such as group discussions and breakdowns, influence reflection on the newly gained knowledge. There are both tacit and explicit elements of this new knowledge. The tacit knowledge triggers in Clarke's model are used as a form of sensitization during this research, and are then further developed to be utilized in a group setting.

The benefit of this model (Figure 3) is the manner in which it incorporates the idea of triggers and the cycle of reflection by team members. The literature discussed above provides the theoretical basis for the analysis of tacit knowledge within teams as well as the flow of tacit knowledge and its environment. Nonaka and Teece (2009) established the "Ba" environment for tacit knowledge exchange; the SECI model allows the classification and evaluation of knowledge exchange and associated learning; Ryan and O'Connor's (2012) model provides a team view of tacit knowledge exchange, complemented by Clarke's (2010) individual perspective of tacit knowledge. Knowing more about the operation of these triggers will help develop an understanding of expert team knowledge creation.

Figure 2. Theoretical model for the acquisition and sharing of tacit knowledge in teams
Source: Ryan and O'Connor (2013)

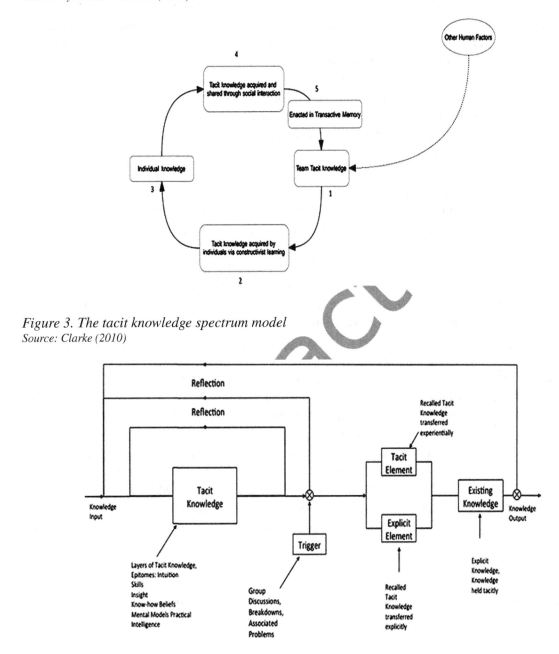

Figure 3. The tacit knowledge spectrum model
Source: Clarke (2010)

RESEARCH METHOD

The goal of the research is to show what influenced the surfacing of expert knowledge and the articulated interaction surrounding the occurrence of triggers. The aim is to provide insight into which triggers allow tacit, expert, knowledge to surface to aid teams to achieve project success. Using the theoretical ideas discussed above, a strategy of analytic generalization (Yin, 2009) was adopted to develop theory.

As noted above, an embedded case study was chosen to analyse the interactions in a potential group knowledge space. The case study is a widely used methodology within business research. Bryman and Bell (2011), for example, argue that the case study is particularly appropriate to be used in combination with a qualitative research method. A case study facilitates detailed and intensive research activity, usually in combination with an inductive approach as regards the relationship between theory and research. Saunders, Lewis and Thornhill (2009) argue that case studies are of particular value for explanatory or exploratory investigation. This research used an organization and a specific software project as a single ethnographic case study which "remains firmly grounded in the ethnographer being there" (Riain, 2009, p. 303). A case study approach allows a "detailed investigation of one or more organizations, or groups within organizations, with a view to providing an analysis of the context and processes involved in the phenomenon under study" (Hartley, 1994, p.323). They "provide the opportunity to place research into a certain context due to the selection of specific sectors, institutions, countries, etc." (Cunningham, Menter & Young, 2017, p. 923). This approach can generate a great deal of detail, and Silverman (2013) has pointed out how case studies can provide a complex and rich understanding of change projects across a period of time.

The chosen case study allowed an inside, participant, view of a software development project, where experts discussed the content needed for the development of the software product. By electing to pursue participant observation and an inductive research approach, the aim was to let the findings emerge over time. The research was conducted over a three-month period, focusing on approximately 30 hours of recorded meetings, with ten team members involved. The software environment was geared to a fast-paced project, there being a clear launch date for the new software. One of the authors was an embedded member of the software team, and an active participant in the work of that team. To develop a software product, multiple groups of experts are needed to achieve a productive knowledge flow (Fischer & Ostwald, 2001). These sessions were project meetings, which took place several times a week. Four of the team members were core, attending most of the meetings and therefore had the most influence on the project. According to Valente and Davies (1999), key actors play a central role in groups through the creation of new ideas and their understanding. The core team consisted of human resource consultants, later referred to as HR A and HR B, as well as software developers, SD A and SD B. In addition, the end user or client - CL A - was often involved in the process. Other experts from the companies joined in when their knowledge was needed, and their input is represented by the prefix HR, CL or SD depending on the company from which they come.

The focus lies within the times the meetings took place, shedding light on the expert knowledge exchanged during face-to-face formal interaction, aiming to highlight the importance of meetings. The extensive researcher involvement created a developed appreciation of the interactions at work in these meetings. The recordings of the meetings were coded through contextualization, and then systematically reviewed. First, the meetings were generally evaluated by date, which then allowed topics discussed during the meetings to surface. These transactional topics were then pulled together to find tacit knowledge, its triggers, expert and team knowledge, knowledge creation as well as the exchange over time, through the previously discussed theories. Different themes started to surface, which were previously found in the literature, such as constructive learning, individual and group tacit knowledge, as well as tacit knowledge triggers. Focusing on tacit knowledge triggers, a more in-depth analysis through a narrative, inductive approach was undertaken using the ideas of individual noemic knowledge and the interactions from being present in the discussion.

The case study and the focus on being with others allows a greater appreciation of the knowledge exchange that can develop. Using the phenomenology of Husserl (2012, pp. 86-7) which emphasizes the indutiablity of internal perception and the tenuousness of outer perceptions. The internal perceptions are noetic but they are influenced by the social environment. This interaction between what is personally known and sharing space with others should become manifest in expert project meetings. Rabanaque (2010) quotes Husserl to note that the living body is "the connecting bridge (verbindende Brucke) between subjectivity in the world and physical thinghood in the world" (p.47). Noting this standpoint has enabled the study to develop the connection between personal knowledge and contextual interaction. Thus, a cumulative picture emerged from the findings and allowed theoretical generalization in order to create new knowledge. Focusing on one project, each team member plays a crucial role in passing on tacit knowledge to his or her colleague. Knowledge elements are then passed on to other project team members through one or multiple triggers, which allows knowledge to surface. Each team member passes on his or her currently articulated knowledge. This then encourages or triggers the creation of new knowledge in the other team members. The knowledge is dragged from the tacit to the articulate in this process. This key assumption was evaluated and examined in the software development context. The triggers are related to extracts in the data where evidence of each trigger was found and established. As the research focuses on one project, knowledge passed on over time can be put into context and evaluated against knowledge that has been previously exchanged.

In the following section, the data is evaluated to highlight knowledge generating episodes. Using the knowledge exchanged in the different companies, the interplay of knowledge exchange helps further understand how the knowledge spirals within the project. Five main triggers were found, which are discussed in detail below.

RESULTS AND DISCUSSION

The knowledge within the project was spread between the different participants, and a group effort was needed to achieve success. Within each collected extract, triggers were observed which allowed tacit knowledge to surface. The goal during the analysis was first, to find evidence of tacit knowledge, and then to understand what kind of tacit knowledge was found, and lastly, to determine what made tacit knowledge surface. During this analysis phase, five main triggers were identified which are discussed below with collected extracts from the research. Clarke (2010) identified tacit knowledge triggers, but they were not identified in types. The trigger types emerged through the data as well as their impacts.

Following the transcription and analysis of the meetings, 45 extracts were selected and used to demonstrate evidence of tacit knowledge and its triggers. In this initial phase, the SECI model was used as a sensitizing approach. Within these extracts, Socialization, Internalization and Group tacit knowledge were always found; externalization was found 28 times, and combination nine. These findings were used as the basis to show tacit knowledge exchange. Then, tacit knowledge triggers were analyzed from the data. Visual triggers were found 18 times, conversational triggers 39, constructive learning triggers 19, anticipation triggers two and recall triggers seven times (Figure 4). These triggers and their operation are the focus of the following discussion.

Visual Triggers

Visual triggers allow an individual to utilize previously gained knowledge to surface by reading or seeing information. During the research, this trigger mainly surfaced when the software was looked at and edited by the team. The knowledge is gained tacitly, becomes processed, thus triggering a socialization within the group. In these scenarios, the software development company would present the developed software pages (i.e. screen design and content) to the human resource consultancy. The pages in the software were analyzed by the team and changed according to their needs when possible. This mainly focused on wording, the layout or process in which the pages were to be found and structured within the software. Visual triggers were found on numerous occasions, one example is the following:

SD A: *Multiple Pensions. Order of priority. So, when they run out of money, this one comes first, this one comes next... Say you are on 500 GBP a week and you get an attachment of earning because you failed to pay your child support. So, the attachment will have top priority. There is a level at which deductions should stop.*
HR A: *Sorry can you just go back to the pensions type.*
SD A: *Yea.*
HR A: *Just wanted to see where I can attach the file.*
SD A: *I think this needs a real thorough look; I am just skimming through it.*

In this extract, SD A explained the pensions pages. Through constructive learning, the HR consultants learned how the pensions pages functioned; during the explanations, HR A stops the discussion to refer back to a previously seen page. SD A had moved on, HR A was still processing the visually gained knowledge in the previous page and asked to go back to see if a feature was available. In another extract, one specific part of a page - the payroll ID - triggered a conversation within the group. The work reference and the ID were confused by SD A, thinking two references were used by the HR company; this triggered HR A to further explain their system of referencing employees. This visual trigger allowed conversational triggers to surface by starting socialization between the project members.

Visual triggers can also be more simplistic. In another extract, the team looks at the salary screen, and needs to rearrange the display order to fit the requirements of the HR consultants. The visual stimuli of the software triggers work and process knowledge of the HR team, which is to be combined with the software engineering environment. Similar situations were found in other extracts, where the 360 feedback is being assessed. HR A says changes within the structure of the pages will need to be done to fit the requirements of the client. HR A's tacit knowledge base of the customer as well as experience are combined with the knowledge visually gained through the software.

Throughout the data analysis there have been several extracts demonstrating how visual mediums trigger knowledge within an individual. This triggered knowledge enables the project team to further conversations, complete gaps of knowledge within the group' and thus allows group tacit knowledge to prosper. Visual triggers launch an internal process within an individual, where the tacit knowledge base is used to combine the current tacit knowledge of an individual with the new visually gained knowledge.

Conversational Triggers

Conversational triggers occur frequently during meetings. Knowledge surfaces explicitly, which is then processed by a team member. The individual will then use the newly gained knowledge, add it to their existing knowledge and create new tacit knowledge. This interaction continues within the group and allows knowledge gaps to be addressed. Due to conversations being at the center of the research, conversational triggers are one of the most frequent and are found throughout the research. The following extract demonstrates a conversational trigger:

HR A: *In an unrelated topic, we talked about sick pay, policies and rules last week. I do not have any up to date paper work from you guys. Could you send me the most recent copy?*

CL A: *I can send you the policies, because we did update them about 6 weeks ago, when we changed the sickness payroll for the organization…. So I can send that over to you. Could you copy in SD A as well? Thank you.*

SD A: *So Payroll, while you mention that…*

The analyzed extract demonstrated a conversational trigger, where HR A discusses the pay policies, this then triggers SD A's tacit knowledge, where the topic is changed to payroll. SD A listens to HR A and CL A discussing a finance related topic and this enables the recall of an unsolved issue with payroll. Later in the discussion, seen during another extract HR A furthers the topic of payroll by building on the knowledge SD A shared. Through explicit exchange within the group, knowledge spirals and builds individual knowledge within each individual. Topics of discussion are altered and enhanced by using the tacit knowledge gained from the previous group member. Their similarities trigger socialization and externalization such as in another conversation, where the discussion allows knowledge to spiral and prosper within the group. Externalized knowledge is used by several members of the project, processed and complemented by the knowledge of each individual taking part in the discussion.

Conversational triggers are one of the most frequent triggers found in the analysis of the data. Explicit communication within the group allows group tacit knowledge to build and each individual to utilize the knowledge to work to achieve project success. This trigger is often in combination with visual or constructive learning, where an external verbal medium allows an individual to take in information, process and reflect the knowledge to then externalize the new processed knowledge. This greatly supports group tacit knowledge and the core objective of a meeting - 'to get everyone on the same page'.

Constructive Learning Triggers

A constructive learning trigger occurs when a project member explains to the others a specific topic of the project. The knowledge is passed on from one person explicitly to the group as a whole, which tacitly utilizes and combines the knowledge. During the project, learning was crucial due to the software being tailored to the company. Each project group, the HR consultants, software developers as well as the customer exchanged knowledge through learning and integrating the knowledge in the software as well as its usage. This trigger also results in socialization, where questions are raised to clarify and add to the subject. An example of a constructive learning trigger can be found in the following extract:

SD A: *Is it a standard wage? You can have multiple standard wages such as London living wage. You can put pay on hold. So you know when the customer.... just going to get SD B up to speed.*

HR A: *So that is going to be the annual basic pay, sorry, the FTA (in full) isn't it? Oh no, it's going to be FTM (in full).*

SD A: *Yea.*

HR A: *Because over here you have the percentage haven't you. So will it work out?*

SD A: *I don't know, we need to ask SD B.*

HR A: *Because otherwise there is a lot of room for error.*

SD A: *The pro rata bit didn't work, the rest did. The standard hours need to be calculated to see hourly rate by default (on screen).*

When SD A explains the pay by period page to the HR consultants, constructive learning takes place. This allowed HR A to process the gained knowledge and externalize what had not yet been understood. Externalization of knowledge can also confirm newly gained knowledge. SD A explains payments, which then triggers HR A to confirm the name of annual basic pay, FTM.

Constructive learning can also be task related; another extract shows the customer as well as the HR team are trying to understand what data can be fed into the system and how it should be structured. This allows an interplay between constructive learning and conversational triggers, which can also be found in the extract above, where knowledge surfaces by teaching as well as learning and ultimately an understanding of an issue of the project is achieved.

Visual, conversational and constructive learning triggers interplay in some of the extracts. While the software pages are being shown, conversations are being triggered and furthered within the group. This also allows constructive learning to take place. Conversational triggers can also often be triggered by visual triggers. During another meeting, the recruitment page in the software triggers a conversation on how the employees are ordered, by usage or alphabetically. Here, the visually, explicitly gained knowledge triggers a thought process within each individual, which is then turned into a conversation where knowledge surfaces through discussion.

Anticipation Triggers

An anticipation trigger allows an individual to raise a topic within the group, which he or she had waited or hesitated to address. The trigger surfaces through a similar topic of discussion and allows a change of topic. In this case, the project member plans to talk about a subject during the meeting, and waits for a moment to bring it up. This is not to be put in direct comparison to a "to-do-list" or minutes, where the subjects of discussion are being listed before a meeting and discussed one after the other, but rather allows another issue to emerge through its similarity. It can surface during externalization or socialization.

During the extract shown in the conversation trigger section, SR A was anticipating discussing payroll during the meeting, but a conversational trigger allowed the finance topic to emerge. Another example of an anticipation trigger is demonstrated in an extract, which builds on a previous meeting where HR A asks to run through the 360 feedback. Here an email was sent to the group about the topic. It was not necessarily planned to discuss the topic; however, HR A specifically asks CL A to explain and run through the process. This built on the previous meeting between SD A and HR A found in the extract below:

SD A: *Now we are getting into linked records - we have done the core records. We talked about name changing, to be the item type: appraisal type; standard appraisal; 360 appraisals; and scoring appraisal. So this is something to look at with SD B tomorrow.*

HR A: *My thoughts on the whole are that we will probably have to change some of that, but I am not quite sure to what yet, until we start building the form, and then work through every stage of the process. I think it will become clearer.*

SD A: *Is there something from the old software that could make it clearer?*

HR A: *No, because they currently don't use it. I've got draft one of the questionnaire done now, which I would be happy to send to you but it hasn't even been checked by CL A yet. While we're at it, you know we talked about the summary of the feedback and SD B asked what kind of format you wanted it in? We just got some off the internet that CL A quite likes - do you want them now or should I give them to SD B?*

SD A: *To SD B -the feedback is in the process engine, so that's his / her part.*

Anticipation triggers are the least commonly found triggers within the data. The meetings were usually structured around a specific topic of the software, which was addressed. Unlike recall triggers, where knowledge pops up, anticipation triggers build around the notion of waiting to discuss a topic when the meeting allows the subject to come up.

Recall Triggers

Recall triggers surface when a topic of discussion or a visual trigger allows an individual to remember knowledge related to the subject which seemed forgotten or not shared in its entirety. This trigger can occur during any stage of the tacit knowledge process. New gained knowledge is processed through several steps, when it is initially heard or seen, and combined with existing knowledge; or when it is transformed into explicit knowledge and shared with the group, recall triggers can emerge. This can change previously shared knowledge and alter the conversation. These triggers are of significance due to the knowledge almost being forgotten and often not being able to surface, as well as the knowledge being at risk of not being shared in its entirety or differently; this could change the outcome of parts of the project.

SD A: *So they might have a monthly London weighting allowance. What do you pay by period?*

HR A: *They have a clothing allowance and a first aid allowance.*

SD A: *So those sort of things. So it has a name, pay by period name, it has a pay type, it has a period it can fall into. It has to be authorized.*

HR A: *Every period?*

SD A: *Every payment has to be authorized. Sorry yes, it is authorized on their account and then it's generated into weekly or monthly payroll as it gets signed off.*

HR A: *Would you only put in payments for that month or put in something for future months?*

SD A: *...you put it in as a go ahead, so when you set it up you select if it is set up for just once or if it runs every month.... For example, season tickets run over 10 or 12 months.*

During the above extract, SD A explains the monthly allowance page to the HR consultants and during this discussion, HR A asks how allowances are authorized. SD A first replies quickly, but then goes into more detail when recalling that the short answer was not sufficient to understand the authorization process. This internalisation process allowed SD A to clarify and further the discussion. Recall triggers can also be minimal, where an individual mistakes one thing for another. In another extract, validating recall triggers, HR A recalls a conversation from the day before and combines the current topic and processes with the previously gained bureau knowledge to fill in gaps of knowledge.

In addition, more evidence was found in an incident where HR A confuses FTA with FTM, which is a tacit process where, through knowledge recall, the initial thought is corrected. In the extract above HR A recalls previously gained work knowledge and shares it with the project members. The conversation focuses on recruitment, where HR C is the recruitment expert within the group. HR A's knowledge is triggered through HR C's uncertainties and is able to add valuable knowledge, having previously worked in the field.

Recall triggers are quite frequent throughout the meetings and they are often found in combination with conversations, constructive learning and visual stimuli. Recall triggers are an internal tacit process where knowledge 'pops up' at random. This might be related, as well as unrelated, to the discussed topic. This trigger allows an individual to communicate knowledge, which is recalled in order to further the knowledge exchange within the group, and thereby enhance group tacit knowledge. Figure 4 shows the number of triggers (left–hand 'y' axis) by category ('x' axis) found in the analysed conversational data. Conversational triggers were the most frequent, meaning that within a conversation newly gained knowledge allowed new knowledge to surface. This is followed by constructive learning triggers, visual triggers, recall triggers and anticipation triggers.

Figure 4. Tacit knowledge triggers found in the analysed data

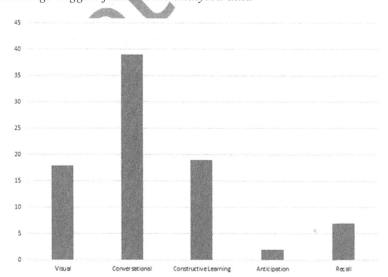

The triggers found through the research demonstrate the need to allow the creation of a knowledge-sharing place within a company as well as teams. These spaces should help teams find a safe environment which supports knowledge exchange and allows the experts within the team to share and build on each other's knowledge. Using different means throughout the meetings can also help trigger expert knowledge to surface, allowing more knowledge to spiral and build.

Figure 5. Knowledge creation and its relationship to trigger points

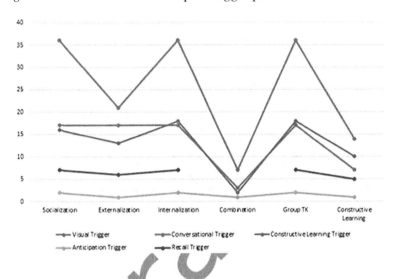

Figure 5 indicates the relationship between the creation of knowledge and the trigger points. In absolute terms, conversational triggers allow group tacit knowledge (Group TK) to surface the most. Constructive learning and visual triggers are the second and third respectively. It can also be seen that knowledge combination is the least likely to surface via these triggers, whereas socialization, internalization and group tacit knowledge were the strongest tacit knowledge exchange factors. The model helps understand the trigger points and their importance to tacit knowledge exchange.

Tacit knowledge triggers allow the exchange of expert knowledge in an organization. In the five-phase model of Nonaka and Takeuchi (1995), the process of tacit knowledge in relation to the market can be seen (Figure 6). This allows a view of the continuous cycle of sharing tacit knowledge within a company. From sharing tacit knowledge, creating concepts, justifying concepts, building an archetype and cross-levelling knowledge, the internalization process is shown. This process helps the triggers find their place in the knowledge creation process.

In summary, this research project discovered and described the development of five types of triggers that are episodic moments for tacit knowledge conversion. The different triggers that emerged through the research were:

1. **Visual Triggers:** Tacit knowledge surfacing through visual stimuli.
2. **Conversational Triggers:** Tacit knowledge surfaces through a conversation held within the team.
3. **Constructive Learning Triggers:** Tacit knowledge is enabled through a team member explaining and the others learning from them.

4. **Anticipation Triggers:** Tacit knowledge was exchanged by an individual in the group by waiting for the topic to come up or the meeting to take place.
5. **Recall Triggers:** Tacit knowledge resurfaces through discussions or visual aids, which seemed forgotten or not presented by an individual.

Figure 6. Five phase model of the organisation knowledge creation process
Source: Nonaka and Takeuchi (1995, p.84)

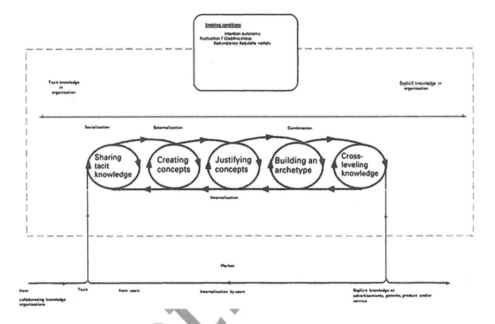

Table 1. Phenomenology of trigger types

Mode of Knowledge Generation	Trigger Type
routine-directive-productive operating	Conversational Triggers are those that become involved with productive operating towards the work
observing-discussing-revealing determination	Constructive learning Triggers are those where there is merit in further discussion about the issue.
solicitous circumspecting (circumspection)	Anticipation Triggers are those where an issue needs to be brought out in advance from the work.
authentic-seeing understanding	Visual Triggers stem from the productive observation of the material at hand.
pure beholding	Recall Triggers occur when knowledge is retained and becomes part of intelligent application.

Appreciating the role of triggers in the situated learning of software teams is a significant contribution to the understanding of how group knowledge emerges. This will also help researchers further understand the impact tacit knowledge has on project success. It is important to interpret and analyse knowledge adequately in software projects to prevent misconceptions (McAfee, 2003). Using an appreciation of a developed theory of triggers can help project teams focus on exchanging and exploring knowledge from different perspectives. Constructive learning within the group, as well as discussions to further understand the software and exploring the knowledge input from each individual are crucial for a project to succeed.

However, these moments can only be created within a dynamic environment in which an exchange of knowledge is supported by the project team. Spending time together as a team and working together is at the core of knowledge creation and transfer. Seeing the project develop over time allows strategies to surface and be applied during the software development process (Vitalari & Dickson, 1983). Bouncing ideas off one another, and subsequent mutual learning, furthers the knowledge creation process. This allows each individual to take in more knowledge and provide a better, more complete view of the subject and enables the prospect of more complete software to emerge.

In relation to categorizing these triggers, Heidegger (1992) notes that Aristotle identifies five modes bringing things into "truthful safekeeping" (p. 377). So anticipation triggers, for example, are self-reflective, in that becoming aware of them allows their incorporation into group discussion. The modes are detailed in Table 1, and it is possible to map the triggers against these modes. It should be noted that these modes are not mutually exclusive; some modes are combinations of others.

CONCLUSION

This chapter set out to further understand and progress the field of knowledge transfer and its triggers within a software development environment. This initial objective gave rise to a new theoretical idea. The conversion of tactile skills is not the crucial element in the development of group knowledge. From the empirical data conducted for this study, the process of externalisation can be considered as being with Mitsein and the joint presence of the expert group allows their presence to be a noematic bridge. The basis of expert meetings is not therefore one of discussion but the emergence of new presentations by the participants. This emergent expertise is the refinement of the phenomenological essences of what is needed to deliver the combined knowledge. This framework, based on a phenomenological approach, will aid the implementation of managerial judgement in expert group sessions. Possessing an awareness of these distinctions will facilitate knowledge capture. How they emerge opens the way to further research into what makes tacit knowledge surface within groups. Appreciating them as breaks in the flow of the project that generate knowledge is important; together with this, they are an opportunity to understand in a better way the mind of the other. Heidegger indicates that practical revealing is "a factical relationship of concern with respect to the world which is just encountered" (Heidegger, 1992, p.382). His further work resonates with this theme where the Scientist, Scholar, and Guide continue to discuss the relationship between determination, speculation, and authentic seeing (Heidegger, 2010, pp.5-6). This structure provides for valuing the unexpected, and what Berends and Antonacopoulou (2014) call "surprises", as they are not always in accord with the espoused aims of the project. This allows managers the opportunity to create environments, in which this personal knowledge can surface and be shared within the teams.

This research highlights how interaction (seen as a "noematic bridge" in terms of a shared learning conversation) with the knowledge triggers can be productive. Taylor (2004) sees triggers as risk factors, and whilst they may delay project completion, an appreciation of the operation of triggers will enable the team learning to be incorporated within an appropriate timescale. Varying the context of the project team as well as testing the triggers in day-to-day working groups can shed light on tacit knowledge triggers. This study has found that recognizing phase changes in project temporality allows managers to appreciate the knowledge gained from extempore interjections. The development of awareness of triggers in a dynamic environment helps the comprehension of expert knowledge exchange in software projects. Understating the knowledge a team has, and aiding its emergence through exchange, can ultimately lead to more productive outcomes for software development teams, and will contribute to successful and well-functioning products. The value of such an approach to the creation of knowledge is to see the concept of truth not as correctness towards the object, because in this situation it remains indeterminate. The alternative view is to see truth as non-concealment - it brings forward that which remains hidden. Using the framework to identify triggers, in the form of modes of knowing, is an approach that reveals the personal knowledge that indicates the unspoken assumptions about the objects in use discussed above. Further investigation into knowledge sharing and interaction between software project groups will help to validate the triggers.

REFERENCES

Banacu, C. S., Busu, C., & Nedelcu, A. C. (2013). Tacit Knowledge Management – Strategic Role in Disclosing the Intellectual Capital. *Proceedings of the International Management Conference, Faculty of Management, Academy of Economic Studies, Bucharest, Romania, 7*(1), 491-500.

Bartolacci, C., Cristalli, C., Isidori, D., & Niccolini, F. (2016). Ba virtual and inter-organizational evolution: A case study from an EU research project. *Journal of Knowledge Management, 20*(4), 793–811. doi:10.1108/JKM-09-2015-0342

Benner, A. (2008). *Work in the New Economy: Flexible Labor Markets in Silicon Valley.* doi:10.1002/9780470696163

Berends, H., & Antonacopoulou, E. (2014). Time and Organizational Learning: A Review and Agenda for Future Research. *International Journal of Management Reviews, 16*(4), 437–453. doi:10.1111/ijmr.12029

Berends, H., & Lammers, I. (2010). Explaining Discontinuity in Organizational Learning: A Process Analysis. *Organization Studies, 31*(8), 1045–1068. doi:10.1177/0170840610376140

Berger, P., & Luckmann, T. (1967). *The Social Construction of Reality.* New York: Anchor.

Bryman, A., & Bell, E. (2011). *Business Research Methods* (3rd ed.). Oxford, UK: Oxford University Press.

Clancy, T. (2006). *The Standish Group Report Chaos.* New York: ACM.

Clarke, T. (2010). *The development of a tacit knowledge spectrum based on the interrelationships between tacit and explicit knowledge.* Retrieved March 9 2019 from https://repository.cardiffmet.ac.uk/bitstream/handle/10369/909/T%20Clarke.pdf

Cunningham, J. A., Menter, M., & Young, C. (2017). A review of qualitative case methods trends and themes used in technology transfer research. *The Journal of Technology Transfer, 42*(4), 923–956. doi:10.100710961-016-9491-6

De Souza, K., Awazu, Y., & Baloh, P. (2006). Managing Knowledge in Global Software Development Efforts, Issues and Practices. *IEEE Software, 23*(5), 30–37. doi:10.1109/MS.2006.135

Dreyer, H. (2018). *Tacit Knowledge in a Software Development Project* (PhD Thesis). University of Gloucestershire, UK. Available at: http://eprints.glos.ac.uk/6441/1/PhD%20Thesis_Tacit%20Knowledge%20in%20a%20Software%20Development%20Project_Hanna%20Dreyer_redacted_personal_information.pdf

Dreyer, H., & Wynn, M. (2016). Tacit and Explicit Knowledge in Software Development Projects: A Combined Model for Analysis. *International Journal on Advances in Software*, 9(3&4), 154–166.

Engeström, Y., Kerosuo, H., & Kajamaa, A. (2007). Beyond discontinuity: Expansive organizational learning remembered. *Management Learning, 38*(3), 319–336. doi:10.1177/1350507607079032

Fischer, G., & Ostwald, J. (2001). Knowledge management: Problems promises realities and challenges. *IEEE Intelligent Systems, 16*(1), 60–72. doi:10.1109/5254.912386

Hartley, J. (2004). *Case Study Research*. London: Sage.

Heidegger, M. (1992). Phenomenological interpretations with respect to Aristotle: Indication of the hermeneutical situation. *Continental Philosophy Review, 25*(3–4), 355–393.

Heidegger, M. (2001). *Zollikon Seminars: Protocols - Conversations – Letters*. Evanston, IL: Northwestern University Press

Heidegger, M. (2010). *Country Path Conversations*. Bloomington, IN: Indiana University Press.

Heidegger, M. (2015). *Being and Truth*. Bloomington, IN: University Press.

Hodgson, J., & Drummond, H. (2009). Learning from fiasco: What causes decision error and how to avoid it? *Journal of General Management, 35*(2), 81–92. doi:10.1177/030630700903500206

Husserl, E. (2012). Ideas. London: Routledge. (First published in 1931)

Langford, T., & Poteat, W. (1968) Upon first sitting down to read Personal Knowledge: an introduction. Intellect and Hope: Essays in the thought of Michael Polanyi, 3-18.

Leybourne, S., & Kennedy, M. (2015). Learning to Improvise, or Improvising to Learn: Knowledge Generation and Innovative Practice. *Knowledge and Process Management, 22*(1), 1–10. doi:10.1002/kpm.1457

Marouf, L., & Khalil, O. (2015). The Influence of Individual Characteristics on Knowledge Sharing Practices Enablers and Barriers in a Project Management Context. *International Journal of Knowledge Management, 11*(1), 1–27. doi:10.4018/IJKM.2015010101

McAfee, A. (2003). When too much IT knowledge is a dangerous thing. *MIT Sloane Management Review, 44*(2), 83-89.

Nonaka, I., & Konno, N. (1998). The concept of 'Ba': Building a foundation for knowledge creation. *California Management Review, 40*(3), 40–54. doi:10.2307/41165942

Nonaka, I., & Takeuchi, H. (1995). *The Knowledge Creating Company*. Oxford, UK: Oxford University Press.

Nonaka, I., & Teece, D. (2001). *Managing Industrial Knowledge*. London: Sage.

Polanyi, M. (1962). *Personal Knowledge*. London: Routledge.

Rabanaque, L. R. (2010). The Body as Noematic Bridge Between Nature and Culture. In P. Vandevelde & S. Luft (Eds.), *Epistemology, archaeology, ethics: current investigations of Husserl's Corpus* (pp. 41–52). London: Continuum.

Riain, S. O. (2009). Extending the Ethnographic Case Study. In D. Byrne & C. C. Ragin (Eds.), *The Sage Handbook of Case Based Methods* (pp. 289–306). London: Sage. doi:10.4135/9781446249413.n17

Ryan, S., & O'Connor, R. V. (2013). Acquiring and sharing tacit knowledge in software development teams: An empirical study. *Information and Software Technology*, *55*(9), 1614–1624. doi:10.1016/j.infsof.2013.02.013

Saunders, M., Lewis, P., & Thornhill, A. (2009). *Research methods for business students* (5th ed.). Pearson Education Limited.

Scharmer, C. (2001). Self-transcending knowledge: Sensing and organizing around emerging opportunities. *Journal of Knowledge Management*, *5*(2), 137–150. doi:10.1108/13673270110393185

Silverman, D. (2013). *Doing Qualitative Research*. London: Sage.

Taylor, H. A. (2004). *Risk management and tacit knowledge in IT projects: making the implicit explicit* (PhD thesis). Queensland University of Technology. Retrieved March 8 2019 from http://eprints.qut.edu.au/15907/

Valente, T. W., & Davies, R. (1999). Accelerating the diffusion of innovations using opinion leaders. *The Annals of the American Academy of Political and Social Science*, *566*(1), 55–67. doi:10.1177/0002716299566600105

Vitalari, N., & Dickson, G. (1983). Problem solving for effective systems analysis: An experiential exploration. *Communications of the Association for Information Systems*, *26*(11), 948–956.

White, G., Parry, G., & Puckering, A. (2016). Knowledge acquisition in information system development: A case study of system developers in an international bank. *Strategic Change*, *25*(1), 81–95. doi:10.1002/jsc.2048

Wynn, M. (2018a). Technology Transfer Projects in the UK: An Analysis of University-Industry Collaboration. *International Journal of Knowledge Management, 14*(2), 52-72.

Wynn, M. (2018b). University-Industry Technology Transfer in the UK: Emerging Research and Future Opportunities. IGI-Global, Hershey, USA.

Yin, R. K. (2009). *Case Study Research Design and Methods*. London: Sage.

This research was previously published in Current Issues and Trends in Knowledge Management, Discovery, and Transfer; pages 305-329, copyright year 2020 by Information Science Reference (an imprint of IGI Global).

Chapter 23
Security Testing Framework for Web Applications

Layla Mohammed Alrawais
Prince Sultan University, Riyadh, Saudi Arabia

Mamdouh Alenezi
 https://orcid.org/0000-0001-6852-1206
Prince Sultan University, Riyadh, Saudi Arabia

Mohammad Akour
Yarmouk University, Irbid, Jordan

ABSTRACT

The growth of web-based applications has increased tremendously from last two decades. While these applications bring huge benefits to society, yet they suffer from various security threats. Although there exist various techniques to ensure the security of web applications, still a large number of applications suffer from a wide variety of attacks and result in financial loses. In this article, a security-testing framework for web applications is proposed with an argument that security of an application should be tested at every stage of software development life cycle (SDLC). Security testing is initiated from the requirement engineering phase using a keyword-analysis phase. The output of the first phase serves as input to the next phase. Different case study applications indicate that the framework assists in early detection of security threats and applying appropriate security measures. The results obtained from the implementation of the proposed framework demonstrated a high detection ratio with a less false-positive rate.

1. INTRODUCTION

The tremendous increase in the development of software applications naturally leads to thinking about the security aspects associated with these applications. To ensure security, testing is an important mechanism both to identify defects and assure that the software is working as expected (Da Mota Silveira Neto, Do Carmo MacHado, McGregor, De Almeida, & De Lemos Meira, 2011). Software testing is an important

DOI: 10.4018/978-1-6684-3702-5.ch023

and costly activity in the software development life cycle. Furthermore, inadequate software testing usually leads to major risks and consequences (Garousi & Zhi, 2013). The software testing activity continues throughout the software development life cycle (SDLC) unlike the thought that the activity of testing is performed at the end of software development. Similar to SDLC the Security Testing Life Cycle (STLC) is shown in Figure 1:

Figure 1. Security throughout the SDLC (PCI Security Standards Council, 2015)

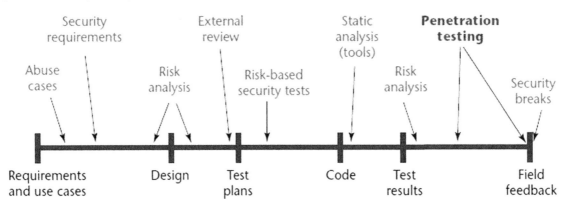

The software from the organizations often suffers from systematic faults at different levels of SDLC. The reason is the failure of following standard security practices (PCI Security Standards Council, 2015) throughout the life cycle of software. Acceptance testing and penetration testing are considered too late in the identification of bugs and at this stage, it may be possible that time and budget constraints do not allow fixing things.

Software engineering faces several challenges from several domains in order to prevent malicious attacks and adopt security measures. Testing is a widespread validation approach in the industry. Meanwhile, this approach is expensive, ad-hoc and unpredictable in effectiveness. Indeed, software testing is a broad term encompassing a variety of activities along the development cycle and beyond, aimed at different goals (Bertolino, Bertolino, & Faedo, 2007). Hence, a lot of challenges are faced by software testing (Gao, Bai, & Tsai, 2015; Harman, Jia, & Zhang, 2015). A consistent roadmap of the most relevant challenges to be addressed is required to be proposed.

Security testing is usually considered to be done at the end of software development and working software is tested using penetration testing. One major limitation of this approach is considering software testing at the end of software development activity which could be too late to tack a problem if exists (Arkin, Stender, & McGraw, 2005).

Acceptance testing and penetration testing are thought to be effective in discovering bugs/errors and issues. The issue with both of these testing types is that (1) penetration testing covers only certain bugs and a certain segment of functionality and (2) late discovery of the bugs and defects may leave the software in a state where fixing these may be prohibitively expensive in terms of time and cost.

To improve the security of software application, security models in the software development life cycle (Howard & Lipner, 2006; McGraw, 2006; Chandra, n.d.) are proposed in decades. In this research, a security-testing framework for web applications is proposed with an argument that security of an application should be tested at every stage of software development life cycle (SDLC).

Microsoft has proposed the Microsoft Security Development Lifecycle (Microsoft SDL) (Howard & Lipner, 2006) The SDL is a software development process used by Microsoft to increase reliability of software concerning software security related bugs. Microsoft SDL integrates measures in the organization processes to improve software security. BSIMM (McGraw, 2006) was proposed with the aim of developing a maturity model, which would imply to change the way organizations work in increasing the reliability and security of software applications. The Open Web Application Security Project (OWASP) proposed the OWASP Software Assurance Maturity Model (SAMM) (Chandra, n.d.) which is a usable framework to help organizations implement a strategy for application security to the specific business risks.

In this research work, we intend to provide a mechanism which ensures security testing of web applications during different phases of software development. The idea is based on the notion that early detection of security bugs could be more cost and time effective. The framework is proposed to integrate the security testing procedures so that less experienced software test engineer to able to produce better reports. Although, different security procedures are adapted during different phases of software development life cycle, yet the focus of this research work will be on risk analysis (design phase), the static analysis of the source code (implementation phase) and penetration testing (deployment phase) of applications. The objective is to assist in the security testing procedures of the software applications. The proposed framework will incorporate risk analysis, static analysis, and penetration testing procedures for the application. Only open-source web applications will be considered as case study for the thesis due to legal bindings associated with proprietary software

2. RESEARCH QUESTION

The problem tackled in this research is addressed by the following primary research question:

How do we develop a framework to identify the testing requirements of a web application for web security testing?

The main objectives of this research are:

1. To find out the challenges and the opportunities for improving the security testing in the web applications.
2. To find out the characteristics of the security requirements classification model for security testing the web applications that will help the transformation of a non-secure web application into a secure web-based applications.
3. To reduce the overall effort of security testing in web applications.
4. To investigate common characteristics and dimensions in the testing
5. To evaluate the applicability of the required tools/techniques that will be used in improving the security testing for web applications.

To provide criteria that will help tester and developer to move more effectively and efficiently towards secure web application testing

3 RESEARCH METHODOLOGY

This study is conducted in order to estimate the problems faced by developers during security vulnerabilities testing of applications. During this process, the steps taken in different phases of SDLC are evaluated. The key security testing processes are identified with their share in the overall security of the application. Following this, we propose a framework that integrates the key security processes. The implementation of the framework will be provided by considering a case study application. All the phases of the framework will be applied.

Security is the concern with the development of very first software application. Several available tools can assist in ensuring the security of applications during the software development life cycle.

3.1. The Proposed Framework

The proposed security testing framework will be elaborated considering the phases of traditional Waterfall model (Scacchi, 2001) and agile approach (extreme programming). The framework is applicable to both, traditional and agile approaches because all of these phases exist in all models, methodologies, and frameworks that are used for development of software applications. In agile approaches, the following major representatives of the Agile approach: a) *Extreme Programming (XP)* (Beck, 1999), b) *Scrum* (Rising & Janoff, 2000), c) *Feature Driven Development (FDD)* (Palmer & Felsing, 2001), d) *Adaptive Software Development (ASD)* (Stapleton, 1997). The proposed framework encompasses three important phases of SDLC i.e. Requirements analysis, Implementation, and Testing. For the rest of the research, we call this framework as RIT (Requirement, Implementation, and Testing) Framework.

The argument for the development of such framework is that the security testing should start from the very initial phase of requirement gathering and specification as it propagates till the end of software development. However, the late identification of security defects/bugs results in higher cost in terms of time and effort. The major objective of RIT framework is to identify the bug/defects at earlier stages and thus reduce overall software development time and effort. This framework guides the analysts, developer, and tester at corresponding stages and highlights the possible security vulnerabilities. The RIT framework is divided into three security testing phases where requirement analysis is the first phase, implementation is second and testing is the third phase. A description of each phase in detail is provided in subsequent sections. However, the detailed idea of the framework is explained in Figure 2:

3.2. Keyword Analysis

The first phase of any software implementation is requirement gathering, analysis, and specification. This phase is initiated by receiving basic customer requirements, which are further elaborated after defining scope, objectives, use-cases, scenarios, and sequences. The result of this phase is requirement specification document, which contains functional and non-functional requirements. Functional requirements are a list of requirements with a detailed elaboration of the functions and tasks that need to be accomplished. Non-functional requirements are user interface requirements, external user interface requirements, performance requirements and security requirements. The scope of the requirements spans to application level rather individual function level. The SRS document is passed as input to the design phase to develop the architecture and design of an application.

Figure 2. The proposed framework architecture

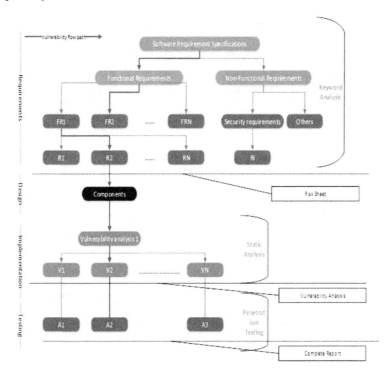

There exist different strategies for security analysis of SRS document such as risk assessment and test case generation. Risk analysis highlights the issues that could possibly be in the SRS and can affect the performance. However, it works as an indicator, does not enforce the revision of SRS for the particular requirement, and does not explicitly highlight the vulnerability that possibly exists in the functional requirement. Similarly, test-cases are generated from the point of view of clients to test the functionality on the delivery of software. These test-cases work as contracts between clients and developers to validate the user requirements, concerned with user-operations and do not test the security aspect of the software. Another implication of test-cases is the late detection of defects and bugs when the cost increases drastically for a defect or bug.

A keyword analysis mechanism is proposed to identify the possible security grey areas that require reconsideration and focus of requirement analysts. A security-keyword database is generated with all possible keywords that reflect possible vulnerabilities. The cycle of events associated with this phase is shown in Figure 3:

The keywords are searched from the text of functional and non-functional requirements. The list of keywords is passed to a database for vulnerability mapping. The mapping follows one to many relationships. There could be many vulnerabilities against one keyword. The input list can contain many entries where each entry represents one functional requirement. The format of the entry is $\{FR_i, Keyword(s)\}$ where FR is the functional requirement, i is the number of requirements. The output entry contains one additional entry, which specifies the associated vulnerabilities with the particular requirement. The SRS is updated along with the risk sheet. The process remains continuous until all risks and vulnerabilities are well understood and defined in the risk sheet. These vulnerabilities could possibly exist in the design and therefore, in the source code of the application. The format of risk sheet is given in Table 1:

Figure 3. The risk analysis procedure in requirement analysis phase

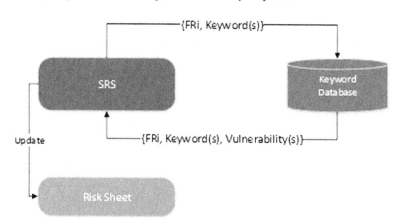

Table 1. Risk sheet template

Requirement	Revision	Vulnerabilities
FR1	3	Cross-site scripting, Buffer overflow
--	--	--

The attempt is to minimize the vulnerabilities to this level. However, certain vulnerabilities are programming specific and can only be handled in the source code.

3.2.1. Example of Keyword Analysis

Each security keyword has its corresponding vulnerability mapping. For example, Structured Query Language (SQL) statements are common to all database applications. Similarly, output messages are part of almost all applications. So the keyword "SQL" can be mapped to "SQL injection" vulnerability and "message" or "output" or "alert" can be mapped to Cross-site Scripting (XSS) vulnerability. A sample keyword to vulnerabilities mapping is shown in Table 2:

Login is a common function found in most of the applications. The description of the functional requirement of login for an application is given in Box 1:

3.2.2. Analysis

The functional requirement of login text will be searching for the keywords defined in Table 2 via a custom written script. The keywords found in the functional requirement are shown in Box 2:

Corresponding risk sheet for the functional requirement is shown in Table 3:

The risk sheet appears as the output of security testing of the requirement analysis phase for the given functional requirement. The risk sheet clearly indicates that the login module could have cross-site scripting, insecure cryptographic storage, transport layer protection and insufficient transport layer protection vulnerabilities.

Table 2. Keyword to vulnerability mapping

Keyword	Vulnerabilities
SQL	SQL Injection
Login	Insufficient Transport Layer Protection
Database	SQL Injection
Message	Cross Site Scripting
Output	Cross Site Scripting
Alert	Cross Site Scripting
Input	Cross Site Scripting
URL	Unvalidated Redirects and Forwards
Storage	Buffer overflow, Memory leak, Memory out of bound
Data	Buffer overflow, Memory leak, Memory out of bound
HTTP Authentication	CRLF Injection
HTTP	Cross-Site Request Forgery, Cross Site Scripting, Directory Traversal
Credentials, Password	Insecure Cryptographic Storage
Traffic, Communication, network	Insufficient Transport Layer Protection

Box 1

ID: FR1[1]
TITLE: Login to the application
DESC[2]: Login is the first screen that appears on application load. The user inputs username and password, which will be validated for the credentials. If the credentials are correct, the main page of the application with all controls will be loaded else the user will be prompted via error message for correct credentials at first screen.
RAT[3]: In order to provide authorized users the application access
DEP[4]: None

Box 2

ID: FR1[5]
TITLE: Login to the application
DESC[6]: Login is the first screen that appears on application load. The user inputs username and password which will be validated for the credentials. If the credentials are correct, the main page of the application with all controls will be loaded else the user will be prompted via error message for correct credentials at first screen.
RAT[7]: In order to provide authorized users the application access

Table 3. Sample risk sheet for Login function

Requirement	Revision	Vulnerabilities
FR1	0	Insufficient Transport Layer Protection, Cross Site Scripting, Insecure Cryptographic Storage
--	--	--

It is important to note that more intelligent vulnerability detection techniques from text can be used such as semantic analysis of text (Girshick, Donahue, Darrell, Berkeley, & Malik, 2012; Page, 2013; Baroni & Dinu, 2014) natural language processing (Manning, Surdeanu, Bauer et al., 2014; Cambria & White, 2014) and machine learning (Chuang & Yang, 2000). For this research, we limit our scope to keyword-based analysis only.

3.3. Targeted Static Analysis

The source code is the key artifact for any software. It contains all program logic and functions that are identified during requirement analysis phase. Security vulnerabilities always exist is the source code (Yamaguchi, Golde, Arp, & Rieck, 2014; Avgerinos, Cha, Rebert et al., 2014; Schuster, 2015). There could be many reasons for the inclusion ranging from inexperienced programmers to programming language loop holes. Static analysis of source code is technique, which identifies the security vulnerabilities that exist in the source code. However, programmer avoids doing static analysis of code due to many reasons, one of which is high false-positive detection rate (Bessey & Block, 2000) which leads to manual bug-fixing and hence, extra cost and effort. Another major reason is that the source code is analyzed thoroughly by the existing static analysis tool without any prior hint of possible security issues identification. Combining with the high false-positive rate associated with these tools, this blind security analysis leads to wastage of resources.

These weaknesses of static analysis can be covered by performing targeted static analysis. The risk sheet defined in Table 3 helps to cross-check the vulnerabilities in the code. By mapping the requirement analysis phase output (risk sheet of Table 3) as input to the targeted static analysis helps in better security testing of the code. The proposed structure of this phase to intercept security vulnerabilities is shown in Figure 4:

Figure 4. Targeted Static Analysis

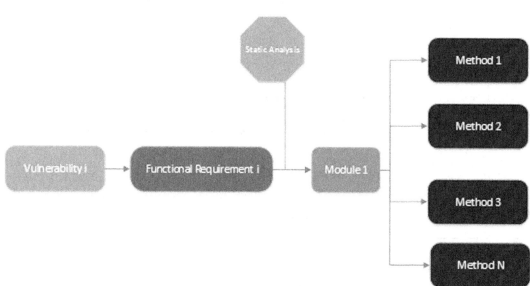

Each vulnerability identified in requirement analysis phase maps to one functional requirement. The functional requirements are implemented in the form of modules/packages or components. The module is said to be a set of related method that fulfills one functional requirement. In an object-oriented programming language, each module is composed of a set of class that further contains related methods. In procedural programming languages, such as C or JavaScript, functions or methods are the final artifacts in code instead of classes.

In static analysis tools, vulnerabilities are identified at a particular line of code which is ultimately part of a method or function. Vulnerabilities that can be corrected at this point stop further propagation of the security loop holes and their ripple effects. Once the static analysis of targeted modules is done, there should only be a list of vulnerabilities that are corrected and that remained uncorrected. This list serves as input to the testing phase (phase 3). The output of this phase is given in Table 4:

Table 4. Phase 2 output

Requirement	Module/Package	Vulnerabilities	Line of code	Description
FR1	Login	Insufficient Transport Layer Protection	20	The username and password are communicated in plain text
FR1	Login	Cross Site Scripting	80	The error message is not properly outputted in alert function.
FR1	Login	Insecure Cryptographic Storage	112	The password is stored as plain text in a file.

3.4. Targeted Penetration Testing

Testing is performed when the coding or implementation phase is completed. Three types of testing such as black box, white box, and grey box testing are done to find the defects. The major objective of these tests is to ensure that functional requirements are working perfectly. Instead, penetration testing is done on production systems to check security vulnerabilities in the code. It is important to note that the defects identified at this phase could be very costly and may require significant re-work.

Similar to the implementation phase (phase 2) which performs targeted static analysis, a targeted penetration testing for the vulnerabilities found in Section 3.3.2 are tested for possible attacks. Table 4 serves as the guideline for the ethical hacker to address the identified vulnerabilities. The strategy for penetration testing is explained as follows in Figure 5:

The steps of penetration testing are explained as follows:

1. **Performing Reconnaissance:** It denotes the work of information gathering before any real attack is planned, the idea is to collect as much interesting information a possible about the target. To achieve this, many different publicly available sources of information are used. The extracted information will often already allow detailed insight into the affected systems.
2. **Identifying Vulnerabilities:** In this step, the vulnerabilities identified in section 4.3.2 will be addressed. This is the reason for calling this phase as targeted penetration testing.

3. **Exploiting Vulnerabilities:** The penetration testers try to actively exploit the security weaknesses. Exploits are developed to, for example, to gather sensitive information or to enable pen-testers to compromise a system and manifest themselves on it.

4. **Escalating Privileges:** Once a system is successfully compromised, it is quite often possible to penetrate more systems because the pen-testers now have access to more potential targets that were not available before.

5. **Gathering Information:** The penetration testers get necessary information about the system that is required to create back doors for future use.

6. **Creating Pivot Point:** The back door is created in this phase to for future intrusion.

7. **Clean Up:** The traces of the penetration testing activity are cleaned up from the system they targeted.

8. **Reporting:** The report is a key difference between ethical hacker or penetration tester and malicious attacker. The ethical hacker is responsible to provide the report of activity to the owner of the application tested while the malicious user obviously does not report anything.

Figure 5. Penetration testing process

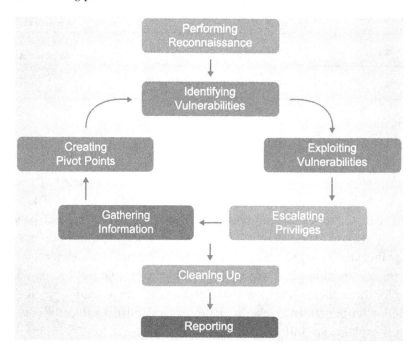

The output of any software testing activity is a report describing the tests conducted. As part of the framework, we propose a framework with each identified phase describing the vulnerabilities with their individual impact and the overall impact of all vulnerabilities in identified in this phase of overall application.

4. CASE STUDY IMPLEMENTATION

The main goal of this section is to implement the RIT framework proposed in section 3. To prove the applicability of the framework, four different case studies are considered. One case study is from academia and related to an application developed as part of the requirement engineering framework for a smart home application while other case studies are open source web application developed by the community. Complete detail of implementation for each case will be provided and results will be generated using the required metrics.

Keyword analysis is performed at first stage of requirement analysis. This task is done in order to identify matching keywords from the text of functional requirement. The keyword analysis used in this work is Sphinx8. Static analysis of code is performed to find vulnerabilities during software development process. The static analysis tools that are selected for the evaluation of case studies are open-source tools with high citations in the literature, SonarQube, RIPS (Re-enforcement PHP Software).

Penetration testing (also called ethical hacking) is a process of exploiting the security vulnerabilities of code after the deployment of the application. main tools are used for this purpose are OWASP-ZAP, Kali Linux – XSSER, Wireshark, Commix.

4.1. Case Study 1: Smart Bedroom Application

The smart bedroom application developed as part of research work for the development of requirement engineering framework for smart home applications. The application is a simulation of a bedroom and based on web technology. The phases of RIT framework are applied one by one in the following sections. Software requirement specification (SRS) document for the smart bedroom application9 to select the functional requirement and non-function requirements.

4.1.1. Phase1: Keyword Analysis

The functional requirements are mapped using Table 5. This table is at an initial stage and refined by security analysts as more and more projects come up.

Based on the vulnerability map, the identified vulnerabilities in the functional requirements are provided in Table 6:

4.1.2. Phase2: Implementation

Taking the input from requirement engineering phases, the static analysis of source code of application is done using three different tools (SonarQube10, RIPS11). The results generated from these tools can be seen in Figure 6 and 7. These results indicate a number of vulnerabilities that exist in the code. These vulnerabilities are related to cross-site scripting (XSS), directory browsing, encryption, and password autocomplete attack. It is noteworthy that these vulnerabilities are pointed out in requirement engineering phase in Table 6.

Vulnerabilities found in implementation phase corresponding to functional requirements are described in Table 7:

Table 5. Keyword to vulnerability map

Keyword	Vulnerabilities
SQL	SQL Injection
Login	Insufficient Transport Layer Protection
Database	SQL Injection
Message	Cross Site Scripting
Output	Cross Site Scripting
Alert	Cross Site Scripting
Input	Cross Site Scripting
URL	Invalid Redirects and Forwards
Storage	Buffer overflow, Memory leak, Memory out of bound
Data	Buffer overflow, Memory leak, Memory out of bound
HTTP Authentication, Authorization	CRLF Injection
HTTP	Cross-Site Request Forgery, Cross Site Scripting, Directory Traversal
Website	Cross-Site Request Forgery, Cross Site Scripting, Directory Traversal
Credentials, Password	Insecure Cryptographic Storage
Traffic, communication, network	Insufficient Transport Layer Protection

Table 6. Risk sheet of smart bedroom project

Requirement	Revision	Vulnerabilities
FR1	0	Insufficient Transport Layer Protection, Cross Site Scripting, Insecure Cryptographic Storage
FR2	0	Cross Site Scripting
FR3	0	None
FR4	0	Cross Site Scripting
FR5	0	Cross Site Scripting
FR6	0	Cross Site Scripting
FR7	0	None
FR8	0	Cross-Site Request Forgery, Cross Site Scripting, Directory Traversal
FR9	0	Insufficient Transport Layer Protection, CRLF Injection
FR10	0	Insufficient Transport Layer Protection, CRLF Injection
FR11	0	None

4.1.3. Phase3: Penetration Testing

It is important to note that Smart Home application is hosted on third party server. Launching certain attacks such as denial of service (DOS) attack may cause legal and ethical issues. Therefore, the testing attempt is made just to ensure that the attack can be launched and it would be successful.

A list of results for tests against vulnerabilities identified in Table 7 is shown in Table 8:

Figure 6. Source code analysis using SonarQube

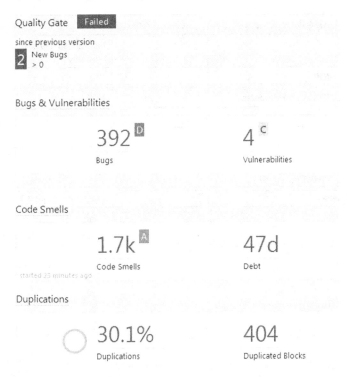

Figure 7. Source code analysis using OWASP-ZAP

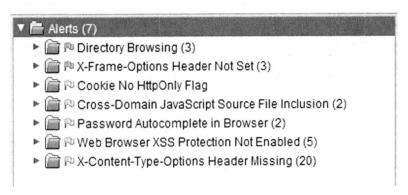

4.2. Case Study 2: PHP QR Code

QR codes are widely used for the unique identification of an object. PHP QR Code application12 is developed to generate unique QR Codes that can be utilized by any software or hardware application. QR Code generation and recognition in the context of attendance management system is discussed.

All the functional requirements are identified by the requirement engineering process proposed by the framework. These requirements are 4 main requirements.

Table 7. Static analysis output

Requirement	Module/Package	Vulnerabilities	Description
FR1	Login	7	Insufficient Transport Layer Protection, Cross Site Scripting
FR2	Power On/Off Lights	3	XSS
FR3	Power On/Off Air conditioners	3	XSS
FR4	Power On/Off LED device	3	XSS
FR5	Open/Close door		None
FR6	Open/Close window	3	XSS
FR7	Operate Monitoring Camera	0	None
FR8	Entertainment	5	Cross-Site Request Forgery, Directory Traversal
FR9	Logout	0	None
FR10	Notification	4	Web browser protection not enabled
FR11	Visualize objects	2	Header not set

Table 8. Penetration testing results

Requirement	Module/Package	Attack	Tools	Status
FR1	Login	ITLP, XSS	1- Wireshark, 2- Kali Linux -XSSER	1- Plain Username and password 2- XSS attack success
FR2	Power On/Off Lights	XSS	Kali Linux -XSSER	1- XSS attack success
FR3	Power On/Off Air conditioners	XSS	Kali Linux –XSSER	1- XSS attack success
FR4	Power On/Off LED device	XSS	Kali Linux –XSSER	1- XSS attack success
FR6	Open/Close window	XSS	Kali Linux –XSSER	1- XSS attack success
FR8	Entertainment	CSRF, Directory traversal	1- Internet Explorer 2- OWASP	1- Directory traversal successful 2- CSRF failed
FR10	Notification	Web protection	Wireshark	1- Encryption not enabled
FR11	Visualize objects	Header not set	Wireshark	1- Success

4.2.1. Phase1: Keyword Analysis

The functional requirements are mapped using Table 5. This table is at an initial stage and refined by security analysts as more and more projects come up.

Based on the vulnerability map, the identified vulnerabilities in the functional requirements are provided in Table 9:

Table 9. Risk sheet of PHP QR Code application

Requirement	Revision	Vulnerabilities
FR1	0	None
FR2	0	SQL Injection, XSS
FR3	0	SQL Injection, XSS
FR4	0	SQL Injection, XSS

4.2.2. Phase2: Implementation

Vulnerabilities found in implementation phase corresponding to functional requirements are described in Table 10:

Table 10. Static analysis output

Requirement	Module/Package	Vulnerabilities	Description
FR1	Finder pattern	XSS	3
FR2	Alignment pattern	XSS	7
FR3	Timing pattern	XSS	2
FR4	Encoded data	XSS, File Manipulation	16

Figure 8. A snapshot of PHP QR Code results

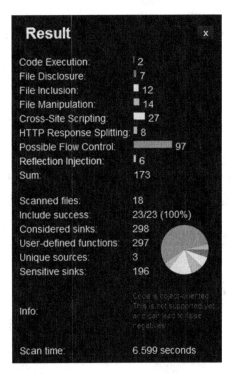

4.2.3. Phase3: Testing

The web application is hosted on a local server to verify the vulnerabilities in code. A list of results for tests against vulnerabilities identified in Table 10 is shown in Table 11:

Table 11. Penetration testing results

Requirement	Module/Package	Attack	Tools	Status
FR1	Finder pattern	XSS	Kali Linux -XSSER	1- XSS attack failed
FR2	Alignment pattern	XSS	Kali Linux -XSSER	1- XSS attack failed
FR3	Timing pattern	XSS	Kali Linux -XSSER	1- XSS attack failed
FR4	Encoded data	XSS, File Manipulation	1- XSSER 2- KeepNote	1- XSS attack failed 2- File manipulation possible

4.3. Case Study 3: Moodle

For meeting high school administrative requirements and automating the day to day operations, it is required to add various functionalities in existing Moodle13 Learning Management System (LMS). 5 main functional requirements are identified and used in this study.

4.3.1. Phase1: Keyword Analysis

The functional requirements are mapped using Table 5. This table is at an initial stage and refined by security analysts as more and more projects come up.

Based on the vulnerability map, the identified vulnerabilities in the functional requirements are provided in Table 12:

Table 12. Risk sheet of Moodle application

Requirement	Revision	Vulnerabilities
FR1	0	Insufficient Transport Layer Protection, Insecure Cryptographic Storage, SQL Injection
FR2	0	Buffer overflow, Memory leak, Memory out of bound, Insufficient Transport Layer Protection
FR3	0	Insufficient Transport Layer Protection, Buffer overflow, Memory leak
FR4	0	Insufficient Transport Layer Protection
FR5	0	Insufficient Transport Layer Protection

4.3.2. Phase2: Implementation

The vulnerabilities in the source code of the Moodle application are identified using RIPS tool. This tool is open source application developed for the security scanning of PHP based applications.

Vulnerabilities found in implementation phase corresponding to functional requirements are described in Table 13:

Table 13. Static analysis output

Requirement	Module/Package	Vulnerabilities	Count
FR1	Login	XSS, Flow Control, HTTP response splitting	138
FR2	Content Sharing (Upload Files)	XSS, Flow Control, HTTP response splitting	20
FR3	Discussion Thread	XSS, Flow Control, HTTP response splitting	241
FR4	Content Sharing	File Manipulation	23
FR5	Blog Thread	XSS, HTTP response splitting	57

Figure 9. A snapshot of Moodle results

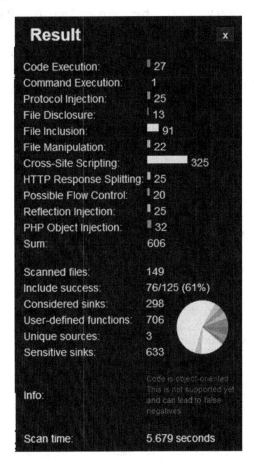

4.3.3. Phase3: Testing

A list of results for tests against vulnerabilities identified in Table 13 is shown in Table 14:

Table 14. Penetration testing results

Requirement	Module/ Package	Attack	Tools	Status
FR1	Login	XSS, HTTP response splitting	1- XSSER 2- Commix	1- XSS attack failed 2- Response splitting failed
FR2	Content Sharing (Upload Files)	XSS, HTTP response splitting	1- XSSER 2- Commix	1- XSS attack failed 2- Response splitting failed
FR3	Discussion Thread	XSS, Flow Control, HTTP response splitting	1- XSSER	XSS attack success
FR4	Content Sharing	File Manipulation	1- KeepNote	2- File manipulation possible
FR5	Blog Thread	XSS, HTTP response splitting	1- XSSER 2- Commix	1- XSS attack success, 2- Response splitting failed

4.4. Case Study 4: Social Network Visualized (SNV)

Social Networks Visualizer (SocNetV) is a flexible and user-friendly tool for the analysis and visualization of Social Networks. It lets you construct networks (mathematical graphs) with a few clicks on a virtual canvas or load networks of various formats (GraphViz, GraphML, Adjacency, Pajek, UCINET, etc) and modify them to suit your needs. SocNetV also offers a built-in web crawler, allowing you to automatically create networks from all links found in a given initial URL. The application can compute basic network properties, such as density, diameter.

6 functional requirements are identified and used in this study:

4.4.1. Phase1: Keyword Analysis

The functional requirements are mapped using Table 5. This table is at an initial stage and refined by security analysts as more and more projects come up. Based on the vulnerability map, the identified vulnerabilities in the functional requirements are provided in Table 15:

Table 15. Risk sheet of SNV application

Requirement	Revision	Vulnerabilities
FR1	0	Insufficient Transport Layer Protection, Insecure Cryptographic Storage
FR2	0	Buffer overflow, Memory leak, Memory out of bound, Insufficient Transport Layer Protection
FR3	0	Insufficient Transport Layer Protection
FR4	0	Insufficient Transport Layer Protection
FR5	0	Insufficient Transport Layer Protection
FR6	0	SQL Injection, Insufficient Transport Layer Protection

4.4.2. Phase2: Implementation

The vulnerabilities in the source code of the Moodle application are identified using CPPcheck tool. This tool is open source application developed for the security scanning of C++ based applications.

Vulnerabilities found in implementation phase corresponding to functional requirements are described in Table 16:

Table 16. Static analysis output

Requirement	Vulnerabilities	Count
FR1	Insufficient Transport Layer Protection, Insecure Cryptographic Storage	18
FR2	Buffer overflow, Memory leak, Memory out of bound, Insufficient Transport Layer Protection	138
FR3	Insufficient Transport Layer Protection	55
FR4	Insufficient Transport Layer Protection	16
FR5	Insufficient Transport Layer Protection	16
FR6	SQL Injection, Insufficient Transport Layer Protection	63

Figure 10. A snapshot of SNV results

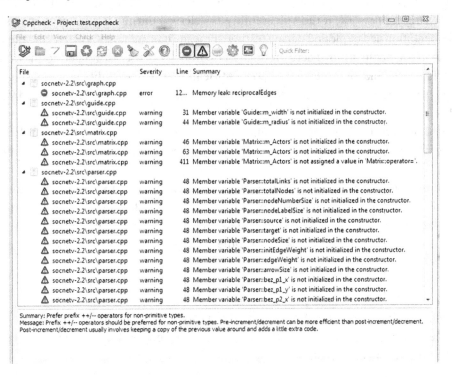

4.4.3. Phase3: Testing

A list of results for tests against vulnerabilities identified in Table 16 is shown in Table 17:

Table 17. Penetration testing results

Requirement	Attack	Tools	Status
FR1	Insufficient Transport Layer Protection, Insecure Cryptographic Storage	3- Wireshark	Un encrypted traffic
FR2	Buffer overflow, Memory leak, Memory out of bound, Insufficient Transport Layer Protection	3- KeepNote 4- Wireshark	File manipulation possible Unencrypted traffic
FR3	Insufficient Transport Layer Protection	2- Wireshark	Unencrypted traffic
FR4	Insufficient Transport Layer Protection	5- Wireshark	Unencrypted traffic
FR5	Insufficient Transport Layer Protection	3- Wireshark	Unencrypted traffic
FR6	SQL Injection, Insufficient Transport Layer Protection	4- Wireshark	Unencrypted traffic

5. RESULTS AND DISCUSSION

The focus of the analysis is security testing of a limited number of attacks. During the three phases of the security testing framework, if the vulnerability is detected during requirement analysis, identified during implementation and exploited during testing, it means it is not false-positive and the vulnerability actually exists in the application. There are many possibilities that exist related to the combination of these phases. However, the identification or no identification of vulnerability at initial stages of requirement analysis is the most important one because the bugs at this stage can be addressed without losing the schedule and cost. Identification of vulnerabilities during the second phase, implementation, can affect the schedule and cost but still the changes are manageable. However, the identification of bugs during testing phase drastically impact the schedule and cost requiring a rework on a particular section of software.

It is important to note that the vulnerability may not be detected at first stage due to missing updates in the vulnerability database. It is also possible that static analysis tools fail to detect particular vulnerability because each tool follows certain coding standard. It is also likely that correct code shows a large number of vulnerabilities due to mismatch with the coding standard. Considering this argument, the validation criteria is as follows:

- If a vulnerability is detected/exploited during all phases, there is no conflict.
- If a vulnerability is not detected/exploited during all phases, there is no conflict.
- If a vulnerability is not detected/exploited in at least two phases but one phase represents its presence then it refers to a conflict.

The evaluation will be based on the total number of vulnerabilities identified to the total number of conflicts found in the analysis.

5.1. Case Study 1: Smart Home Application

The vulnerabilities identified for the smart home application and the stage-wise description is provided in Table 18.

Table 18. Vulnerability map for smart home application

	Requirement Engineering	**Implementation**	**Testing**
XSS	Y	Y	Y
File manipulation	N	N	N
SQL injection	N	N	N
HTTP response splitting	Y	Y	N
Insufficient transport layer protection	Y	Y	Y
Directory traversal	Y	Y	Y
Flow control	N	N	N

If any vulnerability identified in a stage, it is assigned value 1 and 0.5 otherwise. The results in Figure 11 demonstrate that there is no conflict identified in the smart home application during the whole software development lifecycle.

Figure 11. Phase-wise vulnerability map (smart home app)

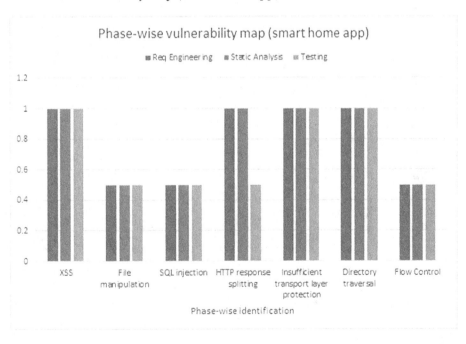

5.2. Case Study 2: PHP QR Code

The vulnerabilities identified for the PHP QR Code application and the stage-wise description is provided in Table 19.

Table 19. Vulnerability map for PHP QR Code application

	Requirement Engineering	**Implementation**	**Testing**
XSS	Y	Y	N
File manipulation	N	Y	Y
SQL injection	Y	N	N
HTTP response splitting	N	N	N
Insufficient transport layer protection	N	N	N
Directory traversal	N	N	N
Flow control	N	N	N

The results indicate that only one attack is in the conflict which is SQL injection. Cross-site scripting (XSS) and file manipulation vulnerabilities are identified in at least two phases so not fall into the category of conflict.

Figure 12. Phase-wise vulnerability map (PHP QR Code app)

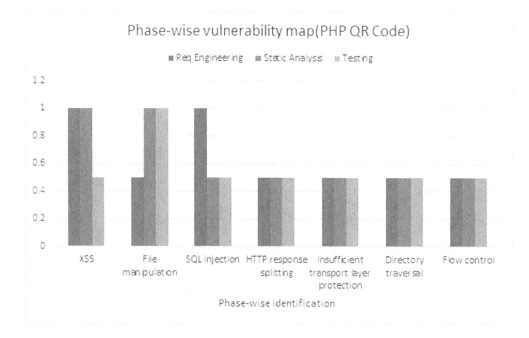

5.3. Case Study 3: Moodle

The vulnerabilities identified for Moodle application and the stage-wise description is provided in Table 20.

Table 20. Vulnerability map for Moodle application

	Requirement Engineering	**Implementation**	**Testing**
XSS	N	Y	N
File manipulation	N	Y	Y
SQL injection	Y	Y	N
HTTP response splitting	N	Y	N
Insufficient transport layer protection	N	N	N
Directory traversal	N	N	N
Flow control	Y	Y	Y

The results in Figure 13 indicate a conflict in HTTP response splitting and XSS vulnerabilities while rest of the vulnerabilities are not in conflict with each other.

Figure 13. Phase-wise vulnerability map (Moodle app)

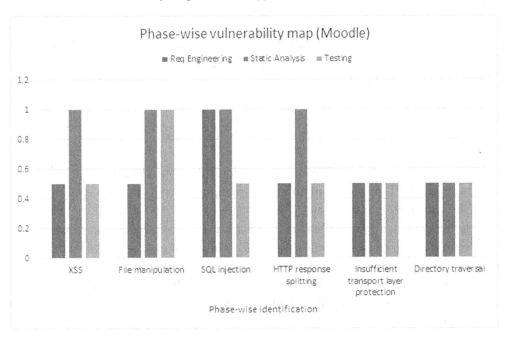

5.4. Case Study 4: Social Network Visualizer

The vulnerabilities identified for AVN application and the stage-wise description is provided in Table 21.

Table 21. Vulnerability map for SNV application

	Requirement Engineering	Implementation	Testing
XSS	N	N	N
File manipulation	N	Y	Y
SQL injection	N	N	N
HTTP response splitting	N	N	N
Insufficient transport layer protection	Y	Y	Y
Directory traversal	N	N	N
Flow control	N	N	N

The results in Figure 13 indicate no conflict in the identified vulnerabilities at every stage.

The results of applying security testing framework are summarized in Table 21. These results indicate the number of conflicts over the total number of vulnerabilities (see Table 22).

Table 22. The conflict analysis

	Total Vulnerabilities	Conflicted	Percentage Conflict
Smart Bed App	7	0	0
PHP QR Code App	7	1	14.28
Moodle App	7	2	28.56
Social Network Visualizer	6	0	0

It can be seen that there are very less number of conflicts over all detections. The appearance of conflicts is found in HTTP response splitting vulnerabilities overall. Case to case discussion of the symptoms of the vulnerability is as follows:

SQL injection appears as a vulnerability in PHP QR Code application during requirement engineering phase. However, next both phases did not observe this vulnerability. It employs that the vulnerability database needs to be updated to minimize false-positive detections.

Moodle app showed XSS and HTTP response splitting vulnerabilities during the static analysis phase. However, neither the vulnerability identified during requirement engineering phase nor in the testing phase. However, this conflict requires manual verification of code and standardizes the code to secure from any potential threat.

6. CONCLUSION AND FUTURE WORK

In this research, security testing framework (RIT) was proposed. The implementation is done in four different case studies, where first three case studies are based on traditional Waterfall model and fourth is developed using Extreme Programming approach. All the phases of the RIT framework are applied to the SRS document, source code and deployment environment of the applications and the results are generated. The evaluation of four different case-studies is performed using security testing framework. The results are promising and very less number of conflicts are indicated. The results indicate that all of the applications suffer from critical vulnerabilities and must be addressed during development phase for the robust and secure software application.

REFERENCES

Arkin, B., Stender, S., & McGraw, G. (2005). Software penetration testing. *IEEE Security and Privacy*, *3*(1), 84–87. doi:10.1109/MSP.2005.23

Avgerinos, T., Cha, S. K., Rebert, A., Schwartz, E. J., Woo, M., & Brumley, D. (2014). Automatic exploit generation. *Communications of the ACM*, *57*(2), 74–84.

Baroni, M., Dinu, G., & Kruszewski, G. (2014). Don't count, predict! A systematic comparison of context-counting vs. context-predicting semantic vectors. In Proceedings of the 52nd Annual Meeting of the Association for Computational Linguistics (Volume 1: Long Papers) (Vol. 1, pp. 238-247).

Beck, K. (1999, October). Embracing change with extreme programming. *Computer*, *32*(10), 70–77. doi:10.1109/2.796139

Bertolino, A. (2007, May). *Software testing research: Achievements, challenges, dreams. In 2007 Future of Software Engineering* (pp. 85–103). IEEE Computer Society.

Bessey, A., Block, K., Chelf, B., Chou, A., Fulton, B., Hallem, S., ... Engler, D. (2010). A few billion lines of code later: Using static analysis to find bugs in the real world. *Communications of the ACM*, *53*(2), 66–75.

Cambria, E., & White, B. (2014). Jumping NLP curves: A review of natural language processing research. *IEEE Computational Intelligence Magazine*, *9*(2), 48–57.

Chandra, P. (2009). Software assurance maturity model: A guide to building security into software development (v1.0).

Chuang, W. T., & Yang, J. (2000, July). Extracting sentence segments for text summarization: a machine learning approach. In Proceedings of the 23rd annual international ACM SIGIR conference on Research and development in information retrieval (pp. 152-159). ACM.

Da Mota Silveira Neto, P. A., Do Carmo MacHado, I., McGregor, J. D., De Almeida, E. S., & De Lemos Meira, S. R. (2011). A systematic mapping study of software product lines testing. *Information and Software Technology*, *53*(5), 407–423. doi:10.1016/j.infsof.2010.12.003

Gao, J., Bai, X., & Tsai, W. T. (2011). Cloud testing-issues, challenges, needs and practice. *Software Engineering: An International Journal*, *1*(1), 9–23.

Garousi, V., & Zhi, J. (2013). A survey of software testing practices in Canada. *Journal of Systems and Software*, *86*(5), 1354–1376. doi:10.1016/j.jss.2012.12.051

Girshick, R., Donahue, J., Darrell, T., Berkeley, U. C., & Malik, J. (2012). Rich feature hierarchies for accurate object detection and semantic segmentation. In Proceedings of the IEEE conference on computer vision and pattern recognition (pp. 580-587).

Harman, M., Jia, Y., & Zhang, Y. (2015). Achievements, open problems and challenges for search-based software testing. In 2015 IEEE 8th International Conference on Software Testing, Verification and Validation (ICST). IEEE. doi:10.1109/ICST.2015.7102580

Howard, M., & Lipner, S. (2006). *The security development lifecycle* (Vol. 8). Redmond: Microsoft Press.

Manning, C., Surdeanu, M., Bauer, J., Finkel, J., Bethard, S., & McClosky, D. (2014). The Stanford CoreNLP natural language processing toolkit. In *Proceedings of 52nd annual meeting of the association for computational linguistics: system demonstrations* (pp. 55-60)..

McGraw, G. (2006). *Software security: building security in*. Addison-Wesley Professional.

Page, H. (2013). *Connectivism : A Learning Theory for the Digital Age*.

Palmer, S. R., & Felsing, M. (2001). *A Practical Guide to Feature-Driven Development*. Pearson Education.

PCI Security Standards Council. (2015). Information Supplement : Penetration Testing Guidance. *Security*.

Rising, L., & Janoff, N. S. (2000). The Scrum Software Development Process for Small Teams. *IEEE Software*, *17*(4), 26–32. doi:10.1109/52.854065

Scacchi, W. (2001). Process models in software engineering. In Encyclopedia of software engineering.

Schuster, F., Tendyck, T., Liebchen, C., Davi, L., Sadeghi, A. R., & Holz, T. (2015). Counterfeit object-oriented programming: On the difficulty of preventing code reuse attacks in C++ applications. In *Proceedings - IEEE Symposium on Security and Privacy* (pp. 745–762). 10.1109/SP.2015.51

Stapleton, J. (1997). DSDM: Dynamic Systems Development Method: The Method in Practice.

Yamaguchi, F., Golde, N., Arp, D., & Rieck, K. (2014, May). Modeling and discovering vulnerabilities with code property graphs. In *2014 IEEE Symposium on Security and Privacy (SP)* (pp. 590-604). IEEE.

ENDNOTES

1.   Functional Requirement
2.   Description
3.   Requirement
4.   Dependency
5.   Functional Requirement

6   Description

7   Requirement

8   http://sphinxsearch.com/blog/2016/07/26/sphinx-2-2-11-release/

9   http://smarthomepsu.com/

10   Sonarqube.org

11   http://rips-scanner.sourceforge.net/

12   https://sourceforge.net/projects/phpqrcode/?source=typ_redirect

13   https://moodle.org/

This research was previously published in the International Journal of Software Innovation (IJSI), 6(3); pages 93-117, copyright year 2018 by IGI Publishing (an imprint of IGI Global).

480

Chapter 24
Threat Modeling in Agile Software Development

Martin Gilje Jaatun
 https://orcid.org/0000-0001-7127-6694
SINTEF Digital, Norway

Karin Bernsmed
SINTEF Digital, Norway

Daniela Soares Cruzes
SINTEF Digital, Norway

Inger Anne Tøndel
 https://orcid.org/0000-0001-7599-0342
SINTEF Digital, Norway

ABSTRACT

Threat modeling is a way to get an overview of possible attacks against your systems. The advantages of threat modeling include tackling security problems early, improved risk assessments, and more effective security testing. There will always be limited resources available for security, and threat modeling will allow you to focus on the most important areas first. There is no one single "correct" way of doing threat modeling, and "agile" is no excuse for not doing it. This chapter describes the authors' experiences with doing threat modeling with agile development organizations, outlining challenges to be faced and pitfalls to be avoided.

1. INTRODUCTION

Threat modeling has been identified as one of the most important activities in the Security Development Lifecycle (SDL) (Howard & Lipner, 2006). According to Jeffries (Jeffries, 2012), Microsoft SDL author Michael Howard states: "If you're only going to do one activity from the SDL, it should be threat modeling". The main idea behind threat modeling is to *think like an attacker*. A well-defined threat model

DOI: 10.4018/978-1-6684-3702-5.ch024

helps to identify threats to the different assets of a system by utilizing well-grounded assumptions on the capabilities of any attacker interested in attacking such a system. It enables the teams to identify critical areas of design, which need to be protected. Over time, various threat modeling approaches and methodologies have been developed, and are being used in the process of designing secure applications (Cruzes, Jaatun, Bernsmed, & Tøndel, 2018). The approaches vary from conceptual frameworks to practical methodologies. To speed up software delivery, many organizations have adopted an agile software development approach, in which development teams produce code in shorter iterations with frequent feedback loops. In agile software development, however, threat modeling is not widespread, and the practitioners have few sources of recommendations on how to proceed to adopt the practice in their process. In addition, in agile software development, it is often challenging in itself to adopt security practices, either because security practices are not prioritized, or because the practitioners are not able to see the relevance and importance of the activities to the improvement of the security in the project (Cruzes et al., 2018). Studies in software security usually focus on software security activities in general, and there are few empirical studies focusing on specific practices in agile software development. The threat modeling activity is particularly important in software security, since many security vulnerabilities are caused due to architectural design flaws (McGraw, 2004). Furthermore, fixing such vulnerabilities after implementation may be very costly, requiring workarounds which sometimes increase the attack surface. A well-defined threat model helps to identify threats to different assets of a system by utilizing well-grounded assumptions on the capabilities of any attacker interested in exploiting such a system. It also enables the development teams to identify critical areas of the design which need to be protected, as well as mitigation strategies. However, threat modeling can also be challenging to perform for developers, and even more so in agile software development.

This chapter is based on results from the ongoing *SoS-Agile - Science of Security for Agile Software Development* research project (https://www.sintef.no/en/digital/sos-agile/) which investigates how to meaningfully integrate software security into agile software development activities. The project started in October 2015 and will end in October 2020, and involves many software development companies in Norway. The method of choice for the project is Action Research, which is an appropriate research methodology for this investigation because of the combination of scientific and practical objectives that aligns with the basic tenet of action research, which is to merge theory and practice in a way such that real-world problems are solved by theoretically informed actions in collaboration between researchers and practitioners (Greenwood & Levin, 1998), (Davison, Martinsons, & Kock, 2004).

The remainder of this chapter is structured as follows: Section 2 outlines our approach to threat modeling in broad strokes. In Section 3 we explore some particular challenges associated with agile software development, which influence how we think about threat modeling. Section 4 offers additional recommendations on how to successfully perform threat modeling in agile software development. We conclude in Section 5.

2. FUNDAMENTAL THREAT MODELING ACTIVITIES

Threat modeling is a wide concept that encompasses a broad range of techniques that can be utilized to make a system more secure. Threat modeling usually employs two types of models; one that represents the system that is to be built and another one that represents the actual threats to the system (Shostack, 2014b). In the context of software development, what is being built can be almost anything that will use the developed software, for example a website, a mobile application or a distributed system. The threats will then represent what can go wrong with the system, which includes all the potential reasons why the software may not function as intended. Depending on the scope of the analysis, one may choose to consider not only threats that are due to malicious intervention, i.e., all the different types of attacks that may occur, but also unintentional events, which are caused by legitimate users that make mistakes. In some cases, random failures are also included as potential threats.

Our approach to threat modeling in agile software development organizations consists of a visual representation of three main elements:

- Assets that are essential or critical for the system;
- An overview over how assets are stored, processed or otherwise interact with the system, which includes systems interfaces and potential attack surfaces;
- Threats to the system, which will affect one or more of the identified assets.

These elements can be found, to a greater or lesser extent, in many threat modeling approaches (Dhillon, 2011). In the following we will briefly describe each in turn.

2.1 Asset Identification

In the organizations where we have applied threat modeling, the first step has been asset identification. An *asset* is something that needs to be protected within the system. Usually, assets are the information or services that are vital for the business operation and success, however, the concept of "assets" can also comprise other parts of the system, such as hardware, network components, domains or even people. Although Shostak (Shostack, 2014b) presents this step as optional, and Dhillon (Dhillon, 2011) does not mention the concept explicitly at all, we always perform this activity. In our experience, it creates awareness about security in the organization, it helps the developers understand which components in their systems that need to be protected, and it makes it easier to focus the discussion on relevant threats later on during the threat modeling activities. Asset identification is also included as a compulsory step in most of the existing standards for risk assessments, including ISO/IEC 27005 (ISO, 2011). Even Dhillon (Dhillon, 2011) does this implicitly, e.g., by mentioning annotations of "processes that perform critical security functions" and "encrypted or signed data flows and data stores".

Asset identification, when performed at all, is often done from the top of one's head, with the results documented in a simple list. However, we have found it useful to employ the explicit method formulated by Jaatun & Tøndel (Jaatun & Tøndel, 2008), which we have since evolved: Briefly, the developers, together with the most important stakeholders in the project, participate in a semi-structured brainstorming session, where the first step is to get all possible assets on the table. As a second step, we then engage the participants in an interactive classification session where we try to determine the assets' relative importance or value (referring to Figure 1, we don't worry about the absolute value of "sprockets", but we want to know if they are worth more or less than "sockets", etc.). Based on the developers' knowledge of the system, we finally try to determine the assets' relative ease of exploitation, and end up with a grid as exemplified in Figure 1.

In our experience, many agile teams seem to think that asset identification is a waste of time; spending too much time on documenting something that is often perceived to be obvious. However, we still believe this is a useful exercise that should be performed at least once in each project. Even if the architecture changes, it is unlikely that the assets change - and if there are fundamental changes in the system that introduce new assets, that is a natural trigger for re-doing the asset analysis.

Figure 1. Identification and classification of assets

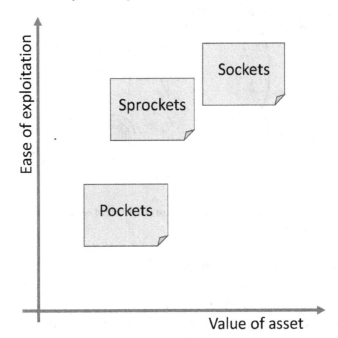

2.2 Data Flow Diagram

The second step in the threat modeling exercise is to get an overview over where the identified assets are stored, processed or otherwise interact with the system. As part of this step, it is also useful to define the interfaces of the system that is being analyzed and to identify potential attack surfaces.

As a means to get an overview of the system to be analyzed, we recommend making a Data Flow Diagram (DFD). A DFD is a graphical representation of the most important actors, processes, services, components and data stored in the system, and it highlights how information flows between each of them. An example of a DFD is shown in Figure 2, based on an OWASP threat modeling tutorial (Conklin, 2014). This example shows a simple university library system, with a web front end for access by students and staff, a login process to authenticate users, and a database system (which can be decomposed further). Users are represented by squares, and processes by circles (complex processes that can be decomposed into more detailed data flow diagrams are represented by double circles). Data flows are represented by curved arrows, and data stores are represented by two parallel lines. Finally, trust boundaries are indicated by dashed curved lines.

Drawing the DFD is usually perceived by the team to be worth it, but strictly speaking it takes too long to draw. Participating in a session where the DFD is created is good for newcomers; can be a good onboarding exercise giving new team members a useful overview of the system. The agile culture of no documentation is a detriment to gaining such an overview.

Figure 2. Example data flow diagram (redrawn from example at http://owasp.org)

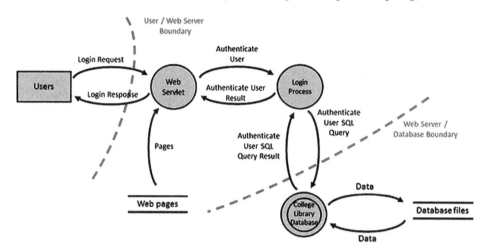

The DFD is a very suitable backdrop for performing the next step in the threat modeling exercise: threat identification and analysis.

2.3 Identification and Analysis of Threats

The last step in the threat modeling exercise is to identify and analyze all relevant threats to the system. This can be done in several ways. Here we present the approach that we have applied, using the STRIDE framework.

Back in the day, Microsoft employees Loren Kohnfelder and Praerit Garg created the STRIDE mnemonic for typical attacks (Shostack, 2014b), based on the first letter of each of the attack types:

- **Spoofing:** An attacker can pretend to be another user, component or system.
- **Tampering:** An attacker can modify data.
- **Repudiation:** An attacker (or other actor) can deny having performed an action or having sent a message if the system has insufficient mechanisms or evidence.
- **Information Disclosure:** An attacker can get read access to protected data.
- **Denial of Service (DoS):** An attacker can prevent legitimate users from using the normal functionality of the system.
- **Elevation of Privilege:** An attacker uses illegitimate means to reach an access level with other privileges than [s]he is supposed to have.

STRIDE can be used to identify threats by analyzing each of the interfaces defined in the DFD, and assess whether any of the attack types are relevant and how they could be executed. STRIDE can also be applied directly on the identified assets, to see whether they are vulnerable to spoofing, tampering, repudiation, etc. attacks.

As stated by Adam Shostak, "STRIDE is a good framework, bad taxonomy" (Shostack, 2014a). This implies that it would be dangerous to consider STRIDE an exhaustive list of threats; there could be other threat types that are relevant for the system. Privacy could be an example; even though some privacy breaks are simply information disclosure, there are more subtle issues that may need to be addressed. An obvious example is when personal data is used for other purposes than the users have consented to. Such a threat will not be identified by the sole use of STRIDE.

To drill down on selected attacks, and explore the attacker's goals and strategies, an attack tree (Schneier, 1999) can be constructed. In this way we can detail all the elements required in order to succeed with the attack, and also explore any alternatives that are available to the attacker. This will also be a good starting point for identifying security tests and possible countermeasures.

In the next section, we discuss the challenges we have experienced when applying these threat modeling activities in agile software development projects.

3. CHALLENGES IN AGILE SOFTWARE DEVELOPMENT PROJECTS

As shown by Camacho et al. (Camacho, Marczak, & Cruzes, 2016), adoption of security practices pose challenges in agile, either because security activities are not prioritized or because the developers do not see the importance of security activities in their projects. In a recent case study (Cruzes et al., 2018), in which we observed eight threat modeling sessions performed by agile software development teams, we identified a number of challenges to applying threat modeling in agile development practices. Here we report the most prominent.

Because of the lack of focus on documentation in agile teams, the teams had very little material to use as a starting point for the meetings. Further, the teams did not take the time to properly document the results from the asset identification activity, mainly because (at this point) they did not see why it would be useful. Also, even though the identification of assets naturally led to a discussion of whether they had the necessary mechanisms to protect those assets, such input was not documented during this phase and was hence not brought forward to the next phases.

Regarding the Data Flow Diagram, it was challenging both to motivate the teams to draw them, and to decide on the right level of abstraction. Some teams spent very long time on this activity. It also turned out to be challenging to map the interfaces of the system that they were modeling with the parts of the systems that other teams were responsible for. Some of the teams mentioned that they actually did not know how the system was really implemented, and the DFDs did not provide confidence that the system was actually implemented that way, especially where there was a lot of legacy code.

The study also revealed the need for better guidelines on how to organize the threat modeling activities, and the need to involve security experts in these activities. To agile teams, 1-2 hour meetings means a long time taken from the sprint hours and the teams sometimes expressed frustration when they did not manage to complete, for example, the DFD during the allocated meeting slot. It was also hard for the teams to say something about how long the models they created would be valid. In our experience, it is highly beneficial to let a security expert lead the threat modeling activities, however, most agile teams do not have such a person.

Threat modeling is a team sport (Jeffries, 2012), and this is also true for agile projects. When drawing a DFD, we like to be in a single room with all team members participating. However, when the software development division consists of distributed teams, which was the case for several of the organizations that we studied, this activity becomes quite challenging (Šmite, Moe, & Torkar, 2008). Even though the teams were used to video conferencing to replace or complement physical meetings, this turned out to be challenging when doing threat modeling. Most of the teams preferred to use the whiteboard when brainstorming around the different models that they created. However, with today's videoconferencing equipment it is generally not possible to see both the people at the other location(s) and their whiteboard at the same time, and often not even the whole whiteboard at a resolution that allows everyone to read everything. We have experimented with different configurations, but the major challenges remain unresolved. We have tried making identical drawings at each participating site, but maintaining consistency of such drawings is hard. Eventually, we expect that technological advances will iron out the kinks in such global collaboration sessions.

One thing we have found is that when threat modeling spans several sessions, it is important to share any diagrams created previously upfront. Since the diagrams may contain company sensitive information, they should be shared in a secure manner, e.g., not sent in regular email.

4. KEY FACTORS FOR SUCCESSFUL THREAT MODELING

The challenges identified in our study (Cruzes et al., 2018), together with challenges previously identified by Tuma et al. (Tuma, Calikli, & Scandariato, 2018), Dhillon (Dhillon, 2011), Assal and Chiasson (Assal & Chiasson, 2018), and Jaatun et al. (Jaatun, Jensen, Meland, & Tøndel, 2011), enabled us to identify a set of key factors for successful threat modeling in agile software development organizations.

4.1 Motivate the Team

Motivating the team is a prerequisite for a successful result! Make sure to explain the purpose of the threat modeling activities up-front and inform the team what they can expect as output of the activity. In particular they need to understand how the outputs can be used in the software development process. Once the purpose has been explained, hopefully the team is already motivated. Further motivation may be provided through educational activities such as short courses, preferably built around previous incidents that were caused by security bugs or flaws in the software of the system that is being developed.

4.2 Invite a Security Expert

Make sure that a security expert participates in all the threat modeling activities. This will help to focus the discussions, leverage relevant results and speed up the work. The security experts should both facilitate the discussions and document the results. He or she does not have to be a member of the development team, in fact, as already stated, most agile teams do not even have a security expert. Engaging someone external to the team has been shown to be a successful approach (Cruzes et al., 2018). However, in the long run it is unrealistic to expect that the software development organization will fund such an external resource. In order to make the security work self-sustainable, the role of the security expert should be eventually assumed by the security champion in the team. What security expertise is needed? Jeffries (Jeffries, 2012) refers to required security training in the SDL guideline (Microsoft, 2012), and states that it is "ideal that team members have an interest in security". The basic concepts in the SDL training include Secure Design, Threat Modeling, Secure Coding, Security Testing, and Privacy. Intriguingly, among the recommended resources are the Bell-LaPadula model and the Biba model – not something we would have thought the average developer would try to tackle!

We have found that teams that had a good architect from the beginning usually have many things covered, so that when threat modeling is performed on an existing system, few new unmitigated threats emerge. In general, this rhymes with results from Oyetoyan et al. (Oyetoyan, Jaatun, & Cruzes, 2017), who found that years of experience correlate with level of software security expertise.

Threat modeling may not be perceived as worthwhile for old systems, particularly for components which are slated for being phased out. Management support for security work is clearly vital (Assal & Chiasson, 2018); lack of such support is detrimental to software security morale, as exemplified by this skeptical quote from a team member at the end of a session: "Will there be hours for implementing security?"

4.3 Manage System Complexity

If threat modeling is performed for the first time with a team, then a good strategy is to limit the scope by zooming in on a selected part of the system. You should also spend some time on understanding the organization's mission and business goals. This will ensure that the asset identification activity includes information and services that are vital to the organization's interest and hence critical to protect. Draw a DFD upfront and decide which part of the system has priority to be analyzed first.

4.4 Short and Efficient Meetings

To agile teams, a 1-2 hour meeting means a long time taken from the sprint hours. Therefore, a thorough preparation of the meetings is crucial for success. The security expert facilitating the meeting needs to make sure that all preparations that could speed up the meeting are done on beforehand. In cases where a team has one or two very strong personalities, the facilitator may have to be active in ensuring that all voices are heard and that the meetings do not exceed the allocated time slot.

4.5 Involve the Remote Team(s)

Whenever the threat modeling activities involve two or more teams connected via videoconferencing, pick one location to be the "main" location, and provide a whiteboard with the data flow diagram here, visible on video to the other locations. Usually, the main location will be the site with the most developers participating. The current technological limitations require that some extra preparations are required for a successful remote session. All groups of remote participants should produce a large printout of

- Asset diagram (placed in value/ease of exploitation grid)
- Data flow diagrams
- STRIDE definition

If the remote participants have access to more display units in addition to those used for the videoconferencing solution, these may be used instead of the printouts; the important thing is to have these items easily available for reference during the discussion. The STRIDE definition may seem superfluous, but we have found that it is a useful reminder for the teams, and even when the definition is well known by the participants it serves as a minimal checklist for guiding the discussion.

4.6 Pick the Best Tool to Solve the Task

Most of the existing tools for threat modeling activities either lack maturity, or they are targeted for security experts (Tuma et al., 2018). These tools may therefore be too complicated for the average developer, and it will be counter-productive to try to force developers to learn a new tool for doing something they already fear is a waste of time. Tools should be chosen carefully, preferably involving security experts, security champions, and representatives from the average developers. It is normally better to err on the side of choosing too few or too simple tools.

4.7 Know the "Definition of Done"

When an organization is just starting out doing threat modeling, knowing when "enough is enough" will be hard. However, instead of letting this cramp the threat modeling initiative into indecision, it is better to simply make some broad requirements that every team can follow, e.g.: "Each team must perform at least one threat modeling session per major system component per quarter." The work will then be "done" (for now) when this session has been completed.

One problem we have experienced is that when a team really gets into the spirit of threat modeling, they sometimes "go wild". How to focus on valid threats? In this case it is particularly useful to have a facilitator (or experienced security champion) to steer the discussion in the right direction.

4.8 Document the Results

All identified assets need to be recorded in central repository, such as the team's issue tracking system (Jira, TFS, or similar). The DFDs should similarly be stored in a central repository. The issue tracking system should also be used to ensure that identified threats are handled in the code (see below).

4.9 Ensure Results Are Propagated to the Code

We have found that the best way of ensuring that threat modeling results end up in the code, is to create a "risk" ticket for each security issue that arises during the modeling sessions. This allows the issue to be handled in a manner that will be familiar to the developers, without introducing any new process elements. Broadly speaking, such tickets will fall into two categories: Either something that needs to be added by the developers, or something that needs to be discussed by other parts of the team. The second type of ticket will then either be closed after discussion (nothing needs to be done), or be transformed into the first type.

5. CONCLUSION

We have studied how threat modeling can be performed in modern software development, and have outlined here a recipe that should work in most agile organizations.

In his keynote at the XP conference in Porto, Portugal on May 23rd 2018, Kent Beck responded to a prioritization question: "If I had to choose, I'd drop security". This reinforces the impression that agile developers are still prone to falling into the trap of "we'll fix security later; we just need to make this work first". It is clear that in some cases, temporarily deprecating security requirements is the right thing to do, but the problem is that most security requirements treated this way end up being simply forgotten. In a previous discussion with another agile developer (Hellesøy, 2017), the point was raised that developers need to start treating technical debt (and thus, security debt) just like financial debt – you may be able to live with some security issues for a limited time, but if you cannot keep up with the down payments, you will eventually be facing bankruptcy.

An important side-effect of involving a development team in threat modeling is a general improvement in security awareness, to the point where the developers potentially become enthusiastic about security (Jeffries, 2012).

Finally, it's not enough to identify threats, management must also prioritize mitigating them!

ACKNOWLEDGMENT

This work was supported by the SoS-Agile project: Science of Security in Agile Software Development, funded by the Research Council of Norway (grant number 247678).

REFERENCES

Assal, H., & Chiasson, S. (2018). Security in the software development lifecycle. In *Fourteenth symposium on usable privacy and security (SOUPS 2018)* (pp. 281-296). Academic Press.

Camacho, C. R., Marczak, S., & Cruzes, D. S. (2016, Aug). Agile team members perceptions on non-functional testing: Influencing factors from an empirical study. In *2016 11th international conference on availability, reliability and security (ARES)* (p. 582-589). Academic Press. doi: 10.1109/ARES.2016.98

Conklin, L. (2014). *CRV2 AppThreatModeling*. Retrieved from https://www.owasp.org/index.php/CRV2AppThreatModeling

Cruzes, D. S., Jaatun, M. G., Bernsmed, K., & Tøndel, I. A. (2018). Challenges and Experiences with Applying Microsoft Threat Modeling in Agile Development Projects. *Proceedings of the 25th Australasian Software Engineering Conference (ASWEC)*.

Davison, R., Martinsons, M. G., & Kock, N. (2004). Principles of canonical action research. *Information Systems Journal*, *14*(1), 65–86. doi:10.1111/j.1365-2575.2004.00162.x

Dhillon, D. (2011, July). Developer-driven threat modeling: Lessons learned in the trenches. *IEEE Security and Privacy*, *9*(4), 41–47. doi:10.1109/MSP.2011.47

Greenwood, D., & Levin, M. (1998). *Introduction to action research: Social research for social change*. SAGE Publications. Retrieved from https://books.google.no/books?id=nipHAAAAMAAJ

Howard, M., & Lipner, S. (2006). *The security development lifecycle*. Microsoft Press.

ISO/IEC 27005:2011 Information technology - Security techniques - Information security risk management. (2011). Retrieved from https://www.iso.org/standard/56742.html

Jaatun, M. G., Jensen, J., Meland, P. H., & Tøndel, I. A. (2011). A Lightweight Approach to Secure Software Engineering. In *A Multidisciplinary Introduction to Information Security* (pp. 183–216). CRC Press.

Jaatun, M. G., & Tøndel, I. A. (2008). Covering your assets in software engineering. In *The third international conference on availability, reliability and security (ARES 2008)* (pp. 1172-1179). Barcelona, Spain: ARES. 10.1109/ARES.2008.8

Jeffries, C. (2012). *Threat modeling and agile development practices.* Retrieved from https://technet. microsoft.com/en-us/security/hh855044.aspx

McGraw, G. (2004). Software security. *Security & Privacy, IEEE, 2*(2), 80–83. doi:10.1109/MSECP.2004.1281254

Microsoft. (2012). *Pre-SDL Requirements: Security Training.* Retrieved from https://msdn.microsoft. com/en-us/library/windows/desktop/cc307407.aspx

Oyetoyan, T. D., Jaatun, M. G., & Cruzes, D. S. (2017). A lightweight measurement of software security skills, usage and training needs in agile teams. *International Journal of Secure Software Engineering, 8*(1), 1–27. doi:10.4018/IJSSE.2017010101

Schneier, B. (1999). Attack trees. *Dr. Dobb's Journal, 24*(12), 21–29.

Shostack, A. (2014a). Elevation of privilege: Drawing developers into threat modeling. *2014 USENIX summit on gaming, games, and gamification in security education (3GSE 14).*

Shostack, A. (2014b). *Threat modeling: Designing for security.* Wiley.

Smite, D., Moe, N. B., & Torkar, R. (2008). Pitfalls in remote team coordination: Lessons learned from a case study. In A. Jedlitschka & O. Salo (Eds.), *Product-focused software process improvement* (pp. 345–359). Berlin: Springer Berlin Heidelberg. doi:10.1007/978-3-540-69566-0_28

Tuma, K., Calikli, G., & Scandariato, R. (2018). Threat analysis of software systems: A systematic literature review. *Journal of Systems and Software, 144.*

This research was previously published in Exploring Security in Software Architecture and Design; pages 1-14, copyright year 2019 by Information Science Reference (an imprint of IGI Global).

Chapter 25
Cloud Enhances Agile Software Development

Saikat Gochhait

https://orcid.org/0000-0003-4583-9208

Symbiosis Institute of Digital and Telecom Management, Symbiosis International University, India

Shariq Aziz Butt

https://orcid.org/0000-0002-5820-4028

University of Lahore, Pakistan

Tauseef Jamal

https://orcid.org/0000-0003-4965-0322

PIEAS University, Pakistan

Arshad Ali

University of Lahore, Pakistan

ABSTRACT

The software industries follow some patterns (i.e., process model to develop any software product). Agile methodology is the most famous and used process model. It is a trend to develop efficient software products with high client satisfaction. In this chapter, the authors discuss agile methodology and its components, benefits, and drawbacks while using the cloud computing in agile software development, existing frameworks for agile-cloud combination, and some security measures.

CLOUD COMPUTING

Introduction

The cloud computing is the most trendy domain for e-Business due to its services that facilitate the customers. These customers include large scale organizations, IT experts, Data Storage, and handling industries and e-commerce businesses. Now cloud computing is emerging with many fields like smart

DOI: 10.4018/978-1-6684-3702-5.ch025

health, mobile e-commerce, online education systems, and social business interactions. Cloud computing is playing an enormous role in software development due to its inimitable features that make the software development efficient. These features include data storage, use of servers, network infrastructures, data security, pay as per use, the data controller and use of hardware and software tools. The pay as per use is the most owing feature that enhances cloud adoption in industries. The second reason is, the user only needs to pay for services that use not for the entire package and it is the main reason for the organization's shift on the cloud (Qureshi, 2015 ; Pandey, 2009). For accessing these services the cloud computing has different infrastructures that include the three types of clouds and three types of services platforms. These three clouds types are public cloud, private cloud, and hybrid cloud and three types of services are IaaS (Infrastructure as a Service), PaaS (Platform as a Service) and SaaS (Software as a Service). The combination of these services and cloud types has a great impact on cloud adoption (Buyya, 2011).

Cloud Services

Figure 1 is explaining the cloud's services with facilities that the cloud provides to organizations. Every service of the cloud has different facility and support for single user and organizations. The **SaaS** provides the user different types of services as like incorporates enterprise services (ERP), digital signature, CRM applications, the board applications (explicit to coordinated associations financial support, increase sales, seek instruments and so on. This service is used when the information is confidential for the organizations. The **PaaS** supports the consumer for development applications, testing applications, and database integrations. The **IaaS** is a model that gives customers the likelihood to store data, data backup & recovery, services management, capacity, organize resources (which might be utilized to run any software product, including working frameworks) and platform hosting (Leaf, 2011).

The approach these services the cloud has 3 types of infrastructure, **Public Cloud**: this infrastructure is publically available and owned by the cloud service provider, **Private Cloud**: this infrastructure is owned for a single organization and managed by organization internal or external. The **Hybrid Cloud**: is the combination of these cloud infrastructures. The infrastructure is formed by at least two public networks or on another hand private cloud interconnected to guarantee the transportability of information and applications as shown in Figure 2 (Leaf, 2011 ; Xu, 2012).

PROS AND CONS OF CLOUD

Benefits of The Cloud for e-Commerce Industries

The cloud computing provides different types of benefits that engage the users to use cloud's resources. Some of these benefits are as follows:

1. It's providing the cost and scale benefit to e-commerce and global business industries. The cost benefits directly influence the scale benefit i;e means that when the organization increases the resource scale than the cost increase. But it still facilitates the industries in term of money saving (Zhang, 2014 ; Uscatu, 2014).

Figure 1. Cloud Services to Consumers (Leaf, 2011)

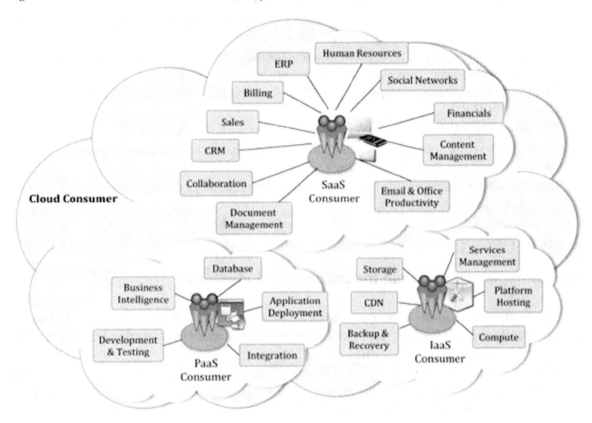

Figure 2. Types of cloud networks (Petznick, 2018)

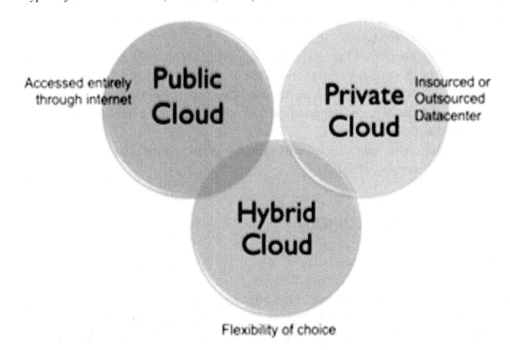

2.	Cloud also provides a platform for industries to share there processes, application and organizational integration. It supports within the organization and with other different organizations to integrate the processes that they wish to collaborate (Zhang, 2014).

3.	Currently, cloud computing is providing next-generation architectures for storing data, new software to use, network-centric, server-centric, computing speed and virtualization space (Abbadi, 2011).

4.	Cloud computing provides different types of service providers with choices for users with agility

5.	(Petznick, 2018).

6.	The most owing benefit of cloud computing for industries is the adaptation to the market need. It means that when an organization needs to compete with the market competition then the cloud can support to meet these requirements (Jin.Y, 2017).

7.	Cloud computing facilitates the business to consolidation i;e helps the organization to do business in a precise way (Johson, 2015).

8.	Cloud computing facilitates the e-Commerce business such as Amazon to target the new clients and get knowledge about the client's current requirements (Johson, 2015).

Disadvantages of The Cloud for Ecommerce Industries

1.	The security of data is the most important factor for any e-Business and it is still a big challenge in cloud computing. In the cloud the security issues include data loss and the threat to the organization's data and software (Sood, 2012).

2.	Costing in the cloud is the second issue for organizations and for individual users. However, the cloud reduces the cost of infrastructure but on the other hand, increase the cost of the data communication. It means the cost of data transmission from a public cloud to community cloud (Buyya, 2017).

3.	The cloud service provider is a resource pool i;e virtualization and multi-tenancy. The provider makes the costing of resources complex than the regular data centers (Tsukishima, 2009).

4.	Another issue with the service provider is the high-security risk. The service provider can reveal information for personal benefits (Pathak, D, 2016).

5.	The issue for organizations is the service level agreement. The cloud users do not have control on the resources; the users do not need to ensure the quality, availability, reliability, and performance of these resources when consumers have migrated their core business functions onto their entrusted cloud. In other words, it is vital for consumers to obtain guarantees from providers on service delivery (Lucredio, D, 2012).

6.	The organizations have reliability issue as well, the cloud computing services suffered from few hours' outages (Lucredio, D, 2012).

AGILE SOFTWARE DEVELOPMENT

Introduction

There is a major consensus that the nature of the software process has a great impact either positive or negative on the quality of the software applications. Henceforth, enhancing process's quality helps in developing efficient software applications on time and within the cost with less imperfection. The numerous software industries are directing software process enhancement activities to upgrade their development in creating software. Currently, the agile methodology is using globally in software industries to develop software applications. It is due to agile's unique features like product development within quality, cost, deadline, meet user requirements, client satisfaction and trust in the team(s). The agile methodology is complete with its widely followed components such as Scrum methodology, Extreme Programming (XP) and Test-driven development (TDD) (Butt, S. A, 2016). The agile was introduced to overcome the challenges from the efficient software development. All previous software development life cycles have some issues to meet the client's requirements and to develop qualitative products. However, the agile main features are client satisfaction, meet user requirements and promote the client-developer interaction, frequent delivery of sprints to get feedback from the client and team coordination to produce the qualitative products (Darwish, 2015).

Agile Components

Scrum Methodology

The scrum methodology is the most useful component of agile methodology to manage and develop projects. It delivers the product in different small sprints. The main objective of the project splitting into small iterations is to get feedback from the client frequently, allow change request and promote client-developer communication. The scrum methodology improves the requirement gathering mechanism in agile software development. The elicited requirements by the product owner (stakeholder) are stored in product backlog as user stories. The developers select the user stories from the product backlog and start the sprint planning as shown in Figure 3. The scrum also supports testing during the sprint phase (Jaiswal, 2015; Butt, S. A, 2016).

Issues and solutions [19]

- Un-stability is an issue in distributed and large scale software development for industries. The cloud makes the development stable for the organization by providing a single platform as a service.
- The distributed scrum project development issue is the lack of documentation sharing among teams but the cloud computing facilitates them to share and store a document at single place private cloud.
- The scrum methodology faces communication and coordination issue between teams in distributed project development. Cloud computing facilitates the scrum methodology to overcome this issue with social-cloud services.
- Anytime the developers can get feedback from the client. Additionally, the developers can also get feedback from other developers and teams.

Extreme Programming (XP)

Extreme programming supports the four major values in agile methodology like communications, simplicity, feedback, and courage. The XP performs four basic activities coding, testing, listening and debugging. These all values and factors lead to 12 core practices of agile methodology such as planning

Figure 3. Scrum methodology

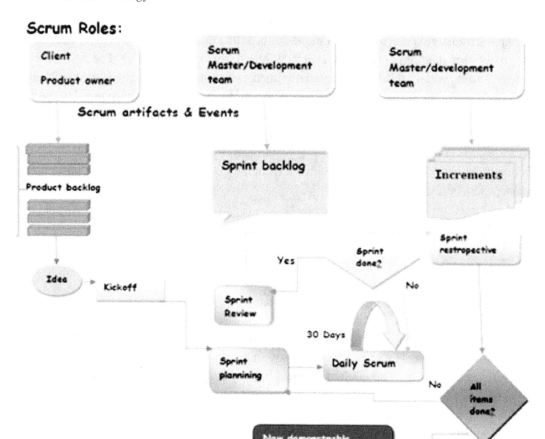

game, small sprint releases, metaphors, product design, testing, refactoring, pair programming, collective ownership, continuous integration, 40-hour weeks, on-site customers, and coding standards. The XP allows developing products in a timely manner (Guha, 2010; Qureshi, 2015).

Issues and Solution

- Cloud computing facilitates Extreme Programming in product designing to make it reusable.
- Cloud computing helps the XP for product planning and development.

Test Driven Development (TDD)

This component of the agile methodology ensures the product quality and makes the final product free from errors and faults. In the TDD short test cases are developed simultaneously with the sprint development according to the user stories in that sprint. These short test cases ensure the completion of user stories in a sprint and make sure that the product is developed according to user requirements. The TDD helps to remove all bugs from the product during iterations delivery to client (Alagarsamy, 2012; Juristo, 2016).

Issues and Solutions

- In the distributed development the testing and integration of sprints is an issue. The cloud computing resolves this issue by facilitating users to store code, test code, and merge sprints at single place.
- Cloud computing also facilitates TDD with different testing tools offered by service providers. The organizations can rent any testing tool according to the application.
- The use of the cloud can reduce software testing cost.

AGLIE-CLOUD BASED DEVELOPMENT

Impact of Cloud on Agile Development

The software development needs efficient processes to develop quality products with less use of resources i.e., tool and hardware. The software industries are interested to get more profit from business with less expenditure. The agile methodology has a great combination with cloud computing to enhance software development at less cost. The main purpose of merging is to remove some issues present in agile software development. The cloud is improving the agile development processes such as testing, run time feedback, data storage, coordination, and communication. As agile always allows the client to give change request and can also give new requirement at any stage of the project therefore over the cloud services it becomes easy to manage the project. The agile-cloud combination is shown in Figure 4 (Butt, S. A, 2016).

Figure 4. Agile-Cloud Combination (Butt, S. A, 2016)

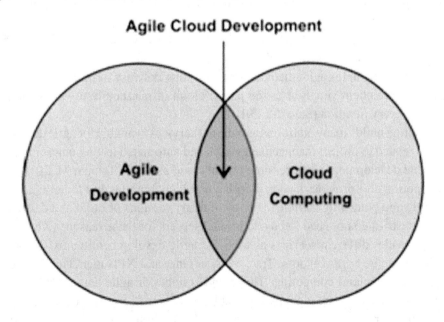

Benefits and Challenges of Agile-Cloud

Agile-Cloud Benefits

The Agile-Cloud Combination has some benefits that increase the adoption of cloud in agile software industries which are as follows (Colmeiro, 2012):

1. The major benefit of cloud computing to software industries is the cost control of software development. As this cost includes the hardware cost, installation cost, effort cost, licensed tool's cost, and product support tool's cost. Cloud computing facilitates agile development to overcome these costs by renting these tools and services. Now the software industries only have to pay as per use of services and tools and not need to buy till the project completion (Colmeiro, 2012).
2. Cloud computing facilitates agile industries in distributed software development. In the distributed development the major issue faced by the teams is communication that cloud computing assists with the cloud-based social technologies. These cloud social technologies include video conference, knowledge management, and web portals. This cloud service facilitates the scrum methodology in daily basis communication between the developers and teams located in distributed environments (Alagarsamy, 2012).
3. The cloud computing supports the agile software industries to store data on the cloud as much they need to store. The storing capacity can easily be increased on the cloud by only pay extra but still, the storing cost on cloud is less as compared to their own storage cost (Dhar, S, 2012).
4. Cloud computing supports the agile methodology in the iteration's testing. In agile methodology, the iterations are tested with the use of the TDD concept. In the TDD the tests are made according to user stories simultaneously in each iteration. Cloud computing facilitates agile testing with the TaaS (Testing as Service). The TaaS provides different kinds of testing tools as per the need of a product. Hence the organizations do not need to buy a licensed new testing tool for each project; simply the organizations can pay TaaS for testing each project according to test requirement. TaaS improves product quality before product deployment (Khan, M. M, 2016).
5. Cloud computing makes agile development a parallel activity where the tasks can be completed efficiently and effectively (Siau, K, (2005).
6. The cloud computing helps agile methodology in instant delivery of iteration to the client for getting feedback. The client simply uses the public cloud infrastructure to verify the requirement's completion in every iteration (Sato, M, 2010).
7. Cloud computing builds many platforms as external services available for agile development. These services are related to project management issues and automated testing environments. These services for agile development are accessible on the cloud as SaaS (Tanner, M, 2016).
8. Cloud computing also provides a code merging and branching facility to agile development. The code merging and branching include the copy of many versions of build and development stages. The agile industries do not need to buy additional servers for these reasons (Khan, M. F, 2013).
9. The cloud provides different services as tools for agile development teams. These tools include JIRA, Mingle, Rally, Scrum Works, Trac, Version One, and XPlanner. The SaaS provides these tools as services in cloud computing. This cloud service for agile teams facilitates them with 4 benefits; First, these tools are globally accessible by all teams. Second, using the tool team members can easily share information across all teams. Third, these tools are not required to install and

deploy internally. Fourth, these tools are scalable i;e agile teams can increase the scale and add new members without degrading the performance of the tool. It also removes team collaboration issue from the Extreme Programming.

10. The cloud-agile combination is improving customer experience in agile development (Krasteva, 2013).

11. Cloud computing provides new infrastructures for agile development (Krasteva, 2013).

12. The cloud helps the agile software industries to target market and find new customers (Butt, S. A, 2017).

13. Cloud computing assists the agile development for productive team utilization with a stable workload (Krasteva, 2013).

14. Time of decision making and to see its consequence is reduced using the cloud-agile combination (Butt, S. A, 2016).

15. The refactoring of an existing application becomes easy with the services of cloud infrastructures in cost-effective ways (Butt, S. A, 2019).

Agile-Cloud Issues

The Agile-Cloud Combination has some drawbacks that influence the less adoption of cloud in agile software industries which are stated below ((Butt, S. A, 2019):

1. The major issue with the agile-cloud combination is the data security of software applications. As some software applications have precious information about the users i.e., banking applications. The banking software application has valuable information of users like credit card, bank account detail and balance information. These applications can't be developed and tested easily with the assistance of cloud services due to security risks that include data loss, threats to data and organization's software (Butt, S. A, 2017).

2. The second major limitation in agile-cloud combination is interoperability during the migration of organizations to cloud computing. It is due to the change in the development environment when migrating to cloud computing. The interoperability issue affects SaaS with other activities. These SaaS activities identify interoperability problems and implement interoperability components. Cloud computing has to provide different services to all organizations to make services compatible for use when they migrate. The migration for the software industries is costly (Cito, 2015).

3. The cloud-agile combination has risk associated with the cloud service provider called a third entity in the cloud computing environment. Cloud computing has many different service providers such as Amazon, Microsoft Azure, and IBM cloud. The service provider can reveal the information for their personal benefits (Hashmi, 2011).

4. The software organizations need 24/7 availability of services, especially when the organizations working are distributed. But they are sometimes not able to provide services due to severe damage. This may lead to a high potential loss for the software industry (Patidar, 2011).

5. The project safety on cloud is difficult because during the development of the team(s) use tools to support project on public cloud, this may lead to disclosing the project code, documentation and configuration data (Singh,S, 2016).

6. The software testing has some issues with cloud computing as different software applications need suitable tools for requirements testing, therefore provide all types of testing tools to organizations

is difficult for the cloud. There are some standards for developing any software application. When software organizations merge with the cloud for efficient software development then the cloud does not provide and maintain these standards (Mohagheghi, 2011).

7.   While using the cloud the developers face Data Lock-In issue. The data lock-in means that when the developers shift from one cloud to another cloud then the developer face platform flexibility issue. This issue mostly arises when the developer is using the PaaS service of the cloud. The developers face this issue due to service providers in the cloud because every service provider has a different platform, elasticity, flexibility, and type of services to users (Guha, 2010).

FRAMEWORKLS FOR AGILE-CLOUD

In this section, we are explaining the existing frameworks for agile-cloud development. The main objective of these frameworks is to promote the cloud computing adoption in software industries in terms of secure development, reduced development cost, better utilization of the cloud's services and migration to the cloud.

3.3.1 For global distributed agile development, a framework is proposed by authors in (Younas, 2016). The main objective of the framework is to provide developers the software and hardware infrastructure like IDEs to code. The existing framework has four steps to explain the working of the current framework as shown in Figure 5. In the first step, the cloud can facilitate the agile development team by providing different kinds of services and tools such as Axosoft, PlanBox, and Jira. In the second step, the framework guides the organizations to select the platform for development according to the size, business need, and type of application. The third phase of the framework guides the organizations to select the cloud repository. Because in the distributed development a number of developers work on the same project modules, therefore, they need a central tool to merge the code such as GitHub. The fourth phase of the framework guides the organizations for selection of cloud's platform for efficient developer's communication and collaboration.

2.2.2. In [29], the authors provide a framework with 5 layers to support agile software testing. The framework's first layer includes the testing on a tenant with service contributor layer. The second layer facilitates agile testing to provide test task management support. A tester describes a test scenario. It means that the cloud provides a guest operating system with setting up the facility to test the code. The third layer is a tested resource management layer, which manages the resources for tester from start to end. The fourth layer of the framework provides the test layer with components such as testing service composition, testing service pool, and testing task reduce. The last and fifth layer supports the agile organizations to test the databases as shown in Figure 6.

There are different tools that enhance agile software development with the combination of cloud computing as shown in Table 1.

Security Measures

There are different existing security models to enhance the security of data on the cloud. The objectives of the proposed models are prevention from vulnerable attacks, control data leakage, and modifications, and improving client's and organization's contentment (Sood, 2012).

Figure 5. Distributed agile development framework (Younas, 2016)

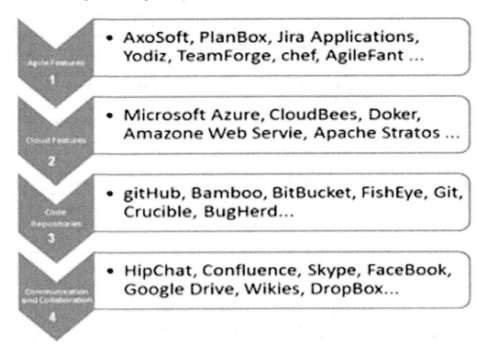

Figure 6. Five Layers Framework for agile cloud (Banzai, 2010)

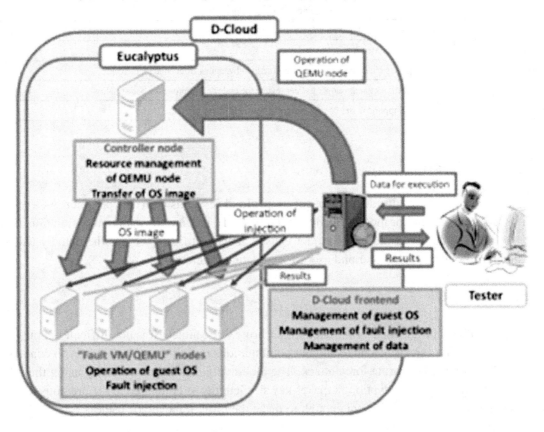

Table 1. Tools for Agile Cloud Development

Tool	Description
Jira software	Project management and issue tracking
Zapier	Connect Axosoft with many other services and tools.
Jenkins	Open source automation server, plug-in to support building, testing, deploying and automation for virtually any project.
Apache Stratos	Provides an environment for developing, test, and run cloud-based applications. PaaS framework to run PHP, MySql, and tomcat.
Salesforce.Com	Enhances the customer and developer relation in agile development by customer relationship management (CRM). It is a platform to control all interactions of client and developer.
Puppet Enterprise	It manages infrastructures patching and configuration of operating systems and devices for agile.
Google App, Engine, Compute Engine	Building scalable web applications, virtual machines, and scalable cloud resources.
Microsoft azure	The integrated tools, pre-built templates, and managed PaaS services.
Amazon Web Service	It facilitates the agile in terms of reliable, scalable, and inexpensive cloud computing services, storage, database, and analytics, application, and deployment services.
Coordination and Communication tools	
HipChat	Provides a private chat infrastructure plus it uses for sharing files.
Confluence	Promotes the teamwork by collaboration, team organizing and discuss work in a team and between teams.
Merge and sharing code tools	
BitBucket	Code collaboration using pull requests and comments. It is used to build and deploy software.
Bamboo	Code Merging.
FishEye	Helps in code finding and tracking of subversions from code repositories.
Crucible	Allows the developer to Peer review the code and improve the code quality.
BugHerd	Supports in the Bug tracking

Un-Authorized Server

In this security endanger an intruder can get access to cloud server as a service provider. As a result of this, an intruder can destroy or modify the data of the user. To prevent the data in this situation, Secure Socket Layer (SSL) certification in this model is used. This certificate secures the data by using the digital signature concept of provider and user to send data on the cloud.

Brute Force Attack

Data on the cloud can be attacked by intruders like a brute force attack. It is not difficult to crack using current computers that can crunch huge number combinations rapidly so as to decide each conceivable key in an effort known as a brute force attack. The cloud data can be prevented by using the 128-bit Secure Socket Layer (SSL) encryption; it makes key size lengthy as compared to the previous size of 40 bits. This lengthy key size is sufficient enough to make the brute force attack useless.

Threat From the Service Provider

The service provider can also reveal the information for personal benefits. To secure the information from the service provider the best solution is the encryption of data stored on the cloud. Secure Socket Layer (SSL) can secure the communication of data.

Tampering of Data

In cloud computing un-authorized users can temper data, therefore to secure the data Message Authentication code (MAC) approach can be used. A MAC code is generated by the data owner before sending on a cloud. The receiver verifies the code if the code is same only then the user can integrate data.

CASE STUDY

Netsol Technologies is a Multinational software organization located in Pakistan. The number of employee in the Netsol is more than 1800. Netsol mostly develops smart software technologies for all kinds of industries. It has national as well as international clients ((Butt, S. A, 2017).

Due to economic and technological requirements, the Netsol is also using cloud computing services; in this regard, Netsol has introduced the LeasePak Solution by using the Microsoft Azure cloud. The LeasePak is an end to end portfolio management solution for the US-based finance industry. The LeasePak is used by the Blue Chip auto and equipment finance companies. The LeasePak solution is robust, scalable and highly functional for the automobile leasing industry. The basic objective of the LeasePak solution is to satisfy the client, get new business, meet the client's requirements and make communication easy with the client. The Azure provides a very flexible environment of the cloud for Netsol. The IT persons develop the LeasePak in VB.Net 7.0 and introduce the mAccount solution in LeasePak. The mAccount facilitates the customers to track their project details, contract, payment details, and new project update status. The MAzure facilitates the Netsol clients in terms of scalability, the security of data and a stable environment. The cloud supports Netsol clients to use the technology in a flexible manner. The cloud increases the business value of Netsol in terms of getting new clients. The MAzure reduces the cost of Netsol through this LeasePak solution 90% as stated by the chief founder of the company.

As mentioned in the Table.2 that some benefits and limitations face by the industry while using the cloud-agile combination for development. The major benefits of the software industry is reduction in the cost of development. The cloud has no limitations for the industry related to cost. The cloud also provide support to the team/s to involve the client in the project development. It controls the change of request from the client side and develop project according to client's requirements. The cloud facilitate industry related to bandwidth issue and has no limitation. The major issue that the industry face is the trust on cloud service providers. The cloud do not provide any authentic support to the customers related to security of data. The cloud-agile combination also facilitate the developers to tract project progress, inputs and outputs. The major support of cloud to industry by providing the different tools are in terms of cost, easiness to develop project's contents, easily availability of services, software testing tools and splitting of project in different small iterations. Using the tools on cloud the industry can get run-time feedback from client, which save developers time to complete the project and understand the client requirements.

Table 2. Industrial case study of project with agile-cloud combination

Key Attributes	Benefits	Limitation
Customer involvement	√	x
Bandwidth limitations	√	x
Lack of trust	x	√
Project tracking	√	x
Management of change requests from client	√	x
Tools support	√	√
Client Run-time feedback	√	x
Data security	x	x
Cost	√	x

FUTURE WORK

Cloud-Agile is a great combination to enhance software development. This combination makes software development efficient and facilitates the software industries to make more business. As the agile-cloud has some benefits for development, on the other hand, it also has some challenges that affect cloud adoption in agile industries. Existing work has some frameworks that try to overcome these challenges but still, it is a research domain to introduce new frameworks. The agile-cloud combination has a data security issue that needs to address in new frameworks.

CONCLUSION

The agile software development is getting benefits from cloud services. The major benefit is reduction in cost during the software development and testing. Cloud computing is providing different kind of testing tools to test the software product according to its functionality by TaaS service of cloud. On the other hand the major issue with the cloud adoption in the agile industries is data security. The cloud has less secured environment to protect the customer's data. Existing work include many security frameworks and approaches to secure the data on cloud but have some limitations due to new threats launched by intruders. Therefore there is need to introduce new security approaches to secure the data on cloud.

REFERENCES

Agrawal, D., Das, S., & El Abbadi, A. (2011, March). Big data and cloud computing: current state and future opportunities. In *Proceedings of the 14th International Conference on Extending Database Technology* (pp. 530-533). ACM. 10.1145/1951365.1951432

Almudarra, F., & Qureshi, B. (2015). Issues in adopting agile development principles for mobile cloud computing applications. *Procedia Computer Science, 52*, 1133–1140. doi:10.1016/j.procs.2015.05.131

Banzai, T., Koizumi, H., Kanbayashi, R., Imada, T., Hanawa, T., & Sato, M. (2010, May). D-cloud: Design of a software testing environment for reliable distributed systems using cloud computing technology. In *2010 10th IEEE/ACM International Conference on Cluster, Cloud and Grid Computing* (pp. 631-636). IEEE.

Butt, S. A., Abbas, S. A., & Ahsan, M. (2016). Software development life cycle & software quality measuring types. *Asian Journal of Mathematics and Computer Research*, 112-122.

Butt, S. A. (2016). Study of agile methodology with the cloud. *Pacific Science Review B. Humanities and Social Sciences*, 2(1), 22–28.

Butt, S. A. (2016). Analysis of unfair means cases in computer-based examination systems. *Pacific Science Review B. Humanities and Social Sciences*, 2(2), 75–79.

Butt, S. A., & Jamal, T. (2017). Frequent change request from user to handle cost on project in agile model. *Proc. of Asia Pacific Journal of Multidisciplinary Research*, 5(2), 26–42.

Butt, S. A., Tariq, M. I., Jamal, T., Ali, A., Martinez, J. L. D., & De-La-Hoz-Franco, E. (2019). Predictive Variables for Agile Development Merging Cloud Computing Services. *IEEE Access: Practical Innovations, Open Solutions*, 7, 99273–99282. doi:10.1109/ACCESS.2019.2929169

Buyya, R., Garg, S. K., & Calheiros, R. N. (2011, December). *SLA-oriented resource provisioning for cloud computing: Challenges, architecture, and solutions. In 2011 international conference on cloud and service computing* (pp. 1–10). IEEE.

Cito, J., Leitner, P., Fritz, T., & Gall, H. C. (2015, August). The making of cloud applications: An empirical study on software development for the cloud. In *Proceedings of the 2015 10th Joint Meeting on Foundations of Software Engineering* (pp. 393-403). ACM. 10.1145/2786805.2786826

da Silva, E. A. N., & Lucredio, D. (2012, September). Software engineering for the cloud: A research roadmap. In *2012 26th Brazilian Symposium on Software Engineering* (pp. 71-80). IEEE. 10.1109/SBES.2012.12

Dhar, S. (2012). From outsourcing to Cloud computing: Evolution of IT services. *Management Research Review*, 35(8), 664–675. doi:10.1108/01409171211247677

Erickson, J., Lyytinen, K., & Siau, K. (2005). Agile modeling, agile software development, and extreme programming: The state of research. *Journal of Database Management*, 16(4), 88–100. doi:10.4018/jdm.2005100105

Fucci, D., Erdogmus, H., Turhan, B., Oivo, M., & Juristo, N. (2016). A dissection of the test-driven development process: Does it really matter to test-first or to test-last? *IEEE Transactions on Software Engineering*, 43(7), 597–614. doi:10.1109/TSE.2016.2616877

Ghilic-Micu, B., Stoica, M., & Uscatu, C. R. (2014). Cloud Computing and Agile Organization Development. *Informatica Economica, 18*(4).

Guha, R., & Al-Dabass, D. (2010, December). Impact of web 2.0 and cloud computing platform on software engineering. In *2010 International Symposium on Electronic System Design* (pp. 213-218). IEEE. 10.1109/ISED.2010.48

Gupta, G., & Pathak, D. (2016). *Cloud Computing:"Secured Service Provider for data mining. International Journal Of Engineering And Computer Science.*

Haig-Smith, T., & Tanner, M. (2016). Cloud Computing as an Enabler of Agile Global Software Development. *Issues in Informing Science & Information Technology, 13.*

Hashmi, S. I., Clerc, V., Razavian, M., Manteli, C., Tamburri, D. A., Lago, P., ... Richardson, I. (2011, August). Using the cloud to facilitate global software development challenges. In *2011 IEEE Sixth International Conference on Global Software Engineering Workshop* (pp. 70-77). IEEE. 10.1109/ICGSE-W.2011.19

Hentschel, R., Leyh, C., & Petznick, A. (2018). Current cloud challenges in Germany: The perspective of cloud service providers. *Journal of Cloud Computing, 7*(1), 5. doi:10.118613677-018-0107-6

Ibrahim, M. H., & Darwish, N. R. (2015). Investigation of Adherence Degree of Agile Requirements Engineering Practices in Non-Agile Software Development Organizations. *International Journal of Advanced Computer Science and Applications, 6*(1).

Jin, Y., & Wen, Y. (2017). When cloud media meets network function virtualization: Challenges and applications. *IEEE MultiMedia.*

Jinno, M., & Tsukishima, Y. (2009, March). Virtualized optical network (VON) for agile cloud computing environment. In *2009 Conference on Optical Fiber Communication-incudes post-deadline papers* (pp. 1-3). IEEE. 10.1364/OFC.2009.OMG1

Katherine, A. V., & Alagarsamy, K. (2012). Software testing in cloud platform: A survey. *International Journal of Computers and Applications, 46*(6), 21–25.

Krasteva, I., Stavros, S., & Ilieva, S. (2013). Agile model-driven modernization to the service cloud. *The Eighth International Conference on Internet and Web Applications and Services (ICIW 2013).*

Liu, F., Tong, J., Mao, J., Bohn, R., Messina, J., Badger, L., & Leaf, D. (2011). NIST cloud computing reference architecture. *NIST special publication, 500*(2011), 1-28.

Maciá Pérez, F., Berna-Martinez, J. V., Marcos-Jorquera, D., Lorenzo Fonseca, I., & Ferrándiz Colmeiro, A. (2012). *Cloud agile manufacturing.* Academic Press.

Mansouri, Y., Toosi, A. N., & Buyya, R. (2017). *Cost optimization for dynamic replication and migration of data in cloud data centers. IEEE Transactions on Cloud Computing.*

Mohagheghi, P., & Sæther, T. (2011, July). Software engineering challenges for migration to the service cloud paradigm: Ongoing work in the remics project. In *2011 IEEE World Congress on Services* (pp. 507-514). IEEE. 10.1109/SERVICES.2011.26

Nazir, A., Raana, A., & Khan, M. F. (2013). Cloud Computing ensembles Agile Development Methodologies for Successful Project Development. *International Journal of Modern Education and Computer Science, 5*(11), 28–35. doi:10.5815/ijmecs.2013.11.04

Padilla, R. S., Milton, S. K., & Johnson, L. W. (2015). Components of service value in business-to-business Cloud Computing. *Journal of Cloud Computing, 4*(1), 15. doi:10.118613677-015-0040-x

Patidar, S., Rane, D., & Jain, P. (2011, December). Challenges of software development on cloud platform. In *2011 World Congress on Information and Communication Technologies*(pp. 1009-1013). IEEE. 10.1109/WICT.2011.6141386

Raj, G., Yadav, K., & Jaiswal, A. (2015, February). Emphasis on testing assimilation using cloud computing for improvised agile SCRUM framework. In *2015 International Conference on Futuristic Trends on Computational Analysis and Knowledge Management (ABLAZE)* (pp. 219-225). IEEE. 10.1109/ABLAZE.2015.7154995

Singh, S., & Chana, I. (2016). A survey on resource scheduling in cloud computing: Issues and challenges. *Journal of Grid Computing*, *14*(2), 217–264. doi:10.100710723-015-9359-2

Sood, S. K. (2012). A combined approach to ensure data security in cloud computing. *Journal of Network and Computer Applications*, *35*(6), 1831–1838. doi:10.1016/j.jnca.2012.07.007

Vecchiola, C., Pandey, S., & Buyya, R. (2009, December). High-performance cloud computing: A view of scientific applications. In *2009 10th International Symposium on Pervasive Systems, Algorithms, and Networks* (pp. 4-16). IEEE. 10.1109/I-SPAN.2009.150

Xu, X. (2012). From cloud computing to cloud manufacturing. *Robotics and Computer-integrated Manufacturing*, *28*(1), 75–86. doi:10.1016/j.rcim.2011.07.002

Younas, M., Ghani, I., Jawawi, D. N., & Khan, M. M. (2016). A Framework for agile development in cloud computing environment. *Journal of Internet Computing and Services 2016*.

Zhang, L., Luo, Y., Tao, F., Li, B. H., Ren, L., Zhang, X., ... Liu, Y. (2014). Cloud manufacturing: A new manufacturing paradigm. *Enterprise Information Systems*, *8*(2), 167–187. doi:10.1080/17517575.2012.683812

This research was previously published in Cloud Computing Applications and Techniques for E-Commerce; pages 28-49, copyright year 2020 by Engineering Science Reference (an imprint of IGI Global).

Index

A

F

G

H

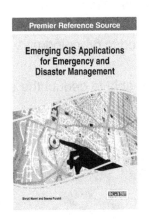
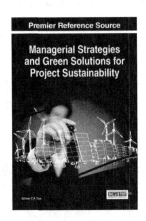

IGI Global Author Services

Providing a high-quality, affordable, and expeditious service, IGI Global's Author Services enable authors to streamline their publishing process, increase chance of acceptance, and adhere to IGI Global's publication standards.

Benefits of Author Services:

- **Professional Service:** All our editors, designers, and translators are experts in their field with years of experience and professional certifications.

- **Quality Guarantee & Certificate:** Each order is returned with a quality guarantee and certificate of professional completion.

- **Timeliness:** All editorial orders have a guaranteed return timeframe of 3-5 business days and translation orders are guaranteed in 7-10 business days.

- **Affordable Pricing:** IGI Global Author Services are competitively priced compared to other industry service providers.

- **APC Reimbursement:** IGI Global authors publishing Open Access (OA) will be able to deduct the cost of editing and other IGI Global author services from their OA APC publishing fee.

Author Services Offered:

 English Language Copy Editing
Professional, native English language copy editors improve your manuscript's grammar, spelling, punctuation, terminology, semantics, consistency, flow, formatting, and more.

 Scientific & Scholarly Editing
A Ph.D. level review for qualities such as originality and significance, interest to researchers, level of methodology and analysis, coverage of literature, organization, quality of writing, and strengths and weaknesses.

 Figure, Table, Chart & Equation Conversions
Work with IGI Global's graphic designers before submission to enhance and design all figures and charts to IGI Global's specific standards for clarity.

 Translation
Providing 70 language options, including Simplified and Traditional Chinese, Spanish, Arabic, German, French, and more.

Hear What the Experts Are Saying About IGI Global's Author Services

"Publishing with IGI Global has been *an amazing experience* for me for sharing my research. The *strong academic production* support ensures quality and timely completion." **– Prof. Margaret Niess, Oregon State University, USA**

"The service was *very fast, very thorough, and very helpful* in ensuring our chapter meets the criteria and requirements of the book's editors. I was *quite impressed and happy* with your service." **– Prof. Tom Brinthaupt, Middle Tennessee State University, USA**